AF767470

EU CIVIL SERVICE LAW: A PRACTITIONER'S GUIDE

This practical commentary interprets EU Staff Regulations on the basis of a rich set of judgments handed down by the EU courts over more than 70 years, complemented by insightful case studies on recent landmark decisions.

In addition to presenting key aspects of employment law applicable to officials and other agents of the EU institutions, the book considers future legal developments. Several important areas of Union law meet in the practice of civil service matters: fundamental rights; general principles of EU law; social and labour law; family and tax law; and procedural, administrative, institutional and constitutional law. Mader explores this intersection across chapters covering civil service law context, its legal framework and interpretative principles; it covers procedural and substantial EU civil service law and closes with a chapter on collective EU civil service law.

The result is an invaluable English-language commentary by one of the field's leading figures, written for all staff employed by EU institutions (and similar bodies) and for all organisations that apply and interpret EU civil service law, as well as for colleagues working across EU law, civil service and public sector law.

EU Civil Service Law

A Practitioner's Guide

Oliver Mader

•HART•

OXFORD • LONDON • NEW YORK • NEW DELHI • SYDNEY

HART PUBLISHING

Bloomsbury Publishing Plc

Kemp House, Chawley Park, Cumnor Hill, Oxford, OX2 9PH, UK

1385 Broadway, New York, NY 10018, USA

29 Earlsfort Terrace, Dublin 2, Ireland

HART PUBLISHING, the Hart/Stag logo, BLOOMSBURY and the Diana logo are trademarks of Bloomsbury Publishing Plc

First published in Great Britain 2024

Copyright © Oliver Mader, 2024

Oliver Mader has asserted his right under the Copyright, Designs and Patents Act 1988 to be identified as Author of this work.

All rights reserved. No part of this publication may be reproduced or transmitted in any form or by any means, electronic or mechanical, including photocopying, recording, or any information storage or retrieval system, without prior permission in writing from the publishers.

While every care has been taken to ensure the accuracy of this work, no responsibility for loss or damage occasioned to any person acting or refraining from action as a result of any statement in it can be accepted by the authors, editors or publishers.

All UK Government legislation and other public sector information used in the work is Crown Copyright ©. All House of Lords and House of Commons information used in the work is Parliamentary Copyright ©. This information is reused under the terms of the Open Government Licence v3.0 (http://www.nationalarchives.gov.uk/doc/open-government-licence/version/3) except where otherwise stated.

All Eur-lex material used in the work is © European Union, http://eur-lex.europa.eu/, 1998–2024.

A catalogue record for this book is available from the British Library.

A catalogue record for this book is available from the Library of Congress.

ISBN: HB: 978-1-50997-792-5
ePDF: 978-1-50997-790-1
ePub: 978-1-50997-791-8

Typeset by Compuscript Ltd, Shannon
Printed and bound in Great Britain by CPI Group (UK) Ltd, Croydon CR0 4YY

MIX
Paper | Supporting responsible forestry
FSC® C013604

To find out more about our authors and books visit www.hartpublishing.co.uk. Here you will find extracts, author information, details of forthcoming events and the option to sign up for our newsletters.

FOREWORD

I am honoured to have been asked to write a foreword to Oliver Mader's book on EU Civil Service Law.

Since reading the manuscript of the book, I have been enthusiastic and impressed by it.

In my position,[1] I am called upon to deal with questions of EU Civil Service Law on an almost daily basis. In my view and experience, Oliver Mader's book gives a complete, up-to-date and systematised overview of all relevant issues in EU Civil Service Law. Divided into four well-defined chapters respectively dealing with general legal framework, procedural law, individual employment relations and collective employment relations, the book analyses these issues in-depth and in a structured way, giving the reader theoretical as well as practical guidance on all these issues.

References to case-law and publications are abundant and very useful. Methodologically, the book follows very closely the rich case-law of the EU Courts on EU Civil Service Law, which allows the reader to understand how legal questions in EU Civil Service Law have been dealt with in the past, whilst at the same time discovering where there may be room for further developments in this area of EU law.

There are not many books on EU Civil Service Law on the market, and only a small number of these are in English, notwithstanding the factual importance of that language in the EU. Whilst the number of practitioners in the area of EU Civil Service Law is rather limited, this may be due to the fact that there are very few publications on the subject matter. This book will undoubtedly be of great use to all staff employed by the EU institutions and agencies interested in knowing their rights and obligations in EU Civil Service Law, as well as to interested practitioners for finding their way into this thrilling area of EU law. I am convinced the book will also give continuous guidance to experienced practitioners, including those who deal with EU Civil Service Law on a regular basis in the EU institutions, in private practice and within the trade unions and staff associations.

In addition, whereas EU Civil Service Law only applies to a defined set of persons (EU staff and agents), it is often seen as a 'laboratory' for other areas of EU law, because of the importance of general principles and fundamental rights in interpreting and applying EU Civil Service Law (such as the rights of the defence, the right to good administration, non-discrimination, access to the file, and legitimate expectations). For that reason, Oliver Mader's book should also attract the attention of practitioners and/or researchers in areas other than EU Civil Service Law.

[1] Evidently, this foreword expresses my personal views and not those of the institution for which I work.

The book is definitely a recommended read for anyone even remotely interested in the area of EU Civil Service Law and an important contribution towards the understanding of Union law in general.

Jan Inghelram
Director
Legal Adviser on Administrative Matters
of the Court of Justice of the European Union

PREFACE

This book is meant to provide an up-to-date thematic guidance, reference and practical commentary on EU Civil Service Law, specifically in those areas having the most relevance to the staff employed, the employing institutions (functionally represented by the appointing authorities), and those advising or deciding on EU staff matters. It comes therefore as a 'Practitioner's Guide'.

A vibrant set of judgments handed down by the EU courts in the course of 70 years has shaped the subject matter, and continues to do so at high speed. The book comments on the most significant aspects of EU employment law, tries to reveal the enduring threads that run through it, and attempts to predict future legal developments deriving from the Staff Regulations, other applicable statutory law and EU case-law. The case-law consists of the decisions handed down by the General Court, the Court of Justice of the European Union, and the EU Civil Service Tribunal during its existence from 2006 to 2016. The book's intention is to focus on the most important issues and to depict how legal questions are typically resolved. A number of areas of Union law meet in the practice of civil service matters: general principles of law; fundamental rights; labour law; family law; tax and social law; procedural, administrative, institutional and constitutional law. Also for that reason, EU Civil Service Law has the potential to function as a 'precursor' area of law that can pave the way, for example, for shaping a general administrative law of the Union.

The book applies two modes of presentation with differing perspectives. The first is an abstract commentary on the central terms and provisions of the Staff Regulations, describing the line of jurisprudence developed by the courts. The second approach uses specific case studies to present and discuss specific examples of recent landmark decisions, followed by practical observations. Each of the selected case studies contains a brief summary, explains the background of the central legal question of the case, describes the facts and main arguments, and elucidates the reasoning of the courts when deciding the case. Each case study concludes with some comments that place the case in context, draw conclusions about its practical handling, and attempt to provide recommendations for action. At the same time, the cases illustrate how EU jurisprudence has been forging the development of EU Civil Service Law.

As a practical guide, the heuristic method applied in this book is to align with the case-law developed over the years; therefore, it often uses the precise or paraphrased wording shaped by the courts. The subject indexes and table of contents should assist the reader in finding the answers to a given legal problem. The book is structured as four chapters. Chapter 1 describes the context in which EU Civil Service Law is embedded, its legal framework, and the general principles that guide its interpretation. The next two chapters cover procedural aspects (ie, the administrative procedures and court proceedings), plus the substance of EU Civil Service Law. For litigation, this broadly means the difference between the admissibility (chapter 2) and the merits of an application (chapter 3). For reasons of presentation and illustration, admissibility and merits are not strictly allocated to chapter 2 and chapter 3 respectively: some parts under chapter 2 (section VII) refer to the merits and some parts at the beginning of chapter 3 are matters that touch upon the admissibility. The book closes with a chapter 4 on collective EU Civil Service Law.

I would like to express my gratitude to Dr Jan Inghelram for his invaluable comments; to Dr Ulrich Reithmann, Dr Niels Bracke and Erik Kowal as well as to Sinéad Moloney at Hart Publishing. I will be very grateful for any comments, hints or criticisms that might be included in any future edition to maximise the book's practical usefulness in a complex and dynamic field of law.

OM

CONTENTS

ABBREVIATIONS

AECE	Authority Empowered to Conclude Contracts of Employment
AG	Advocate General
AHCC	Autorité habilitée à conclure des contrats d'engagement
AIPN	Autorité investie du pouvoir de nomination
Art/Arts	Article/Articles
BVerfG	Bundesverfassungsgericht (Germany)
CCP	Congé de/pour convenance personnelle
CCP	*French* for Central Staff Committee
CdT	Translation Centre for the Bodies of the EU
CEDEFOP	European Centre for the Develpopment of Vocational Training
CEEP	European Centre of Employers and Enterprises providing Public Service
CEOS	Conditions of Employment of Other Servants
CFSP	Common Foreign and Security Policy
CHAFEA	Consumers, Health, Agriculture and Food Executive Agency)
CIR	Common Insurance Rules
CJEU	Court of Justice of the European Union (as institution)
CLP	*French* for Local Staff Committee
CoR	European Committee of the Regions
CPAP	Continuous positive airway pressure
CST	Civil Service Tribunal
DG	Directorate General
DRV	Deutsche Rentenversicherung Bund
EACEA	European Education and Culture Executive Agency
EASA	European Union Aviation Safety Agency
ECA	European Court of Auditors
ECB	European Central Bank

ECDC	European Centre for Disease Prevention and Control
ECHR	European Convention on Human Rights
ECJ	Court of Justice of the European Union (as the Court)
EDA	European Defence Agency
EEA	European Environment Agency
EEAS	European External Action Service
EESC	European Economic and Social Committee
EFCA	European Fisheries Control Agency
EFSA	European Food Safety Authority
EIB	European Investment Bank
EIGE	European Institute for Gender Equality
EIOPA	European Insurance and Occupational Pensions Authority
EISMEA	European Innovation Council and SMEs Executive Agency
EIT	European Institute of Innovation and Technology
EMA/EMEA	European Medicines Agency
EMCDDA	European Monitoring Centre for Drugs and Drug Addiction
EMSA	European Maritime Safety Agency
ENISA	European Union Agency for Cybersecurity
EP	European Parliament
EPPO	European Public Prosecutor's Office
EPSO	European Personnel Selection Office
ERA	European Union Agency for Railways
ERC	European Research Council
ESA	European School of Administration
ESC	European Social Charter
ESCB	European System of Central Banks
ETF	European Training Foundation
ETUC	European Trade Union Confederation
EU	European Union
EUI	European University Institute
EUIPO	European Union Intellectual Property Office (OHIM)

eu-LISA	European Union Agency for the operational management of large-Scale IT systems in the area of freedom, security and justice
Eurojust	EU Agency for Criminal Justice Cooperation
FRA	Fundamental Rights Agency
FRC	Fundamental Rights Charter
Frontex	European Border and Coast Guard Agency
GC	General Court of the Court of Justice of the European Union
GIP	General Implementing Provisions
GSA	European GNSS Agency
IDOC	Investigation and Disciplinary Office
ILO	International Labour Organization
ITER	International Thermonuclear Experimental Reactor
Jd	Joined
JSIS	Joint Sickness Insurance Scheme
MEP	Member of Parliament
OIB	Office for Infrastructure and Logistics in Brussels
OIL	Office for Infrastructure and Logistics in Luxembourg
OJ	Official Journal of the EU
OLAF	European Anti-Fraud Office
Para/paras	Paragraph/paragraphs
PMO	Office for the Administration and Payment of Individual Entitlements
REA	European Research Executive Agency
RoP	Rules of Procedure
SFIE	Syndicat des Fonctionnaires Internationaux et Européens
SR	Staff Regulations
SRB	Single Resolution Board
TEU	Treaty on European Union
TFEU	Treaty on the Functioning of the European Union
TPSR	Transitional Pension Scheme of the EIB
UNCRPD	UN Convention on the Rights of Persons with Disabilities
UNICE	Union of Industrial and Employers" Confederation of Europe
v vs	versus/against

INDEX OF CASES (SELECTION FOR CASE STUDIES)

C European Court of Justice: ECJ

T General Court: GC

F Civil Service Tribunal (2006–16): CST

Case C-114/19 P, Commission v Di Bernardo of 11 June 2020
Case C-116/21 P, Commission v VW of 14 July 2022 (Joined Cases C-116/21 P, VW; C-117/21 P, BT; C-118/21 P, RN; C-138/21 P, BT; C-139/21 P, VW)
Case C-119/19 P and C-126/19 P, Commission v Carreras Sequeros and Others
Case C-132/18 P, Commission v Tuerck of 15 May 2019
Case C-139/18 P, CJ v ECDC of 3 April 2019
Case C-162/20 P, WV v EEAS of 3 March 2022
Case C-249/20 P, Commission v UG of 25 November 2021
Case C-366/21 P, Picard v Commission of 15 December 2022
Case C-377/16, Spain v European Parliament of 26 March 2019
Case C-43/17 P, Jenkinson v Council, Commission, EEAS, Eulex of 5 July 2018
Case C-460/18 P, HK v Commission of 19 December 2019
Case C-621/16 P, Commission v Italy of 26 March 2019
Case C-68/22 P, EIB v KL of 22 December 2022
Case C-680/16 P, Wolff and Remedia v Commission of 27 March 2019
Case C-728/17 P, Commission v Brouillard of 7 March 2019
Case C-831/18 P, Commission v RQ of 18 June 2020
Case C-894/19 P, Parliament v UZ of 21 October 2021
Case C-93/19 P, EEAS v Hebberecht of 19 November 2020
Case F-111/12, Nardone v Commission of 2 October 2013
Case F-4/13, Cwik v Commission of 8 December 2014
Case F-46/11, Tzirani v Commission of 11 July 2013
Case F-65/11, Schönberger v Parliament of 20 March 2012
Case T-12/21 R, PJ v EIT of 13 April 2021
Case T-121/20, IP v Commission of 6 October 2021
Case T-128/17, Isabel Torné v Commission of 14 December 2018
Case T-170/17 R, RW v Commission of 17 May 2017
Case T-170/17, RW v Commission of 8 May 2019
Case T-181/00, Carmelo Morello v Commission of 12 December 2002
Case T-213/19, AW v Parliament of 28 May 2020
Case T-220/20, Kerstens v Commission of 20 October 2021
Case T-274/04, Rounis v Commission of 8 December 2005

Case T-275/17, Curto v Parliament of 13 July 2018
Case T-298/20, KD v EUIPO of 26 October 2022
Case T-310/18, EPSU and Goudriaan v Commission of 24 October 2019
Case T-315/17, Hebberecht v EEAS of 27 November 2018
Case T-370/20, KL v EIB of 24 November 2021
Case T-377/17, SQ v EIB of 13 July 2018
Case T-4/17, Coedo Suarez v Council of 13 December 2017
Case T-402/18, R Aquino and Others v EP of 29 January 2020
Case T-462/17, TO v EEA of 11 June 2019
Case T-47/18, UZ v Parliament of 20 September 2019
Case T-471/18, WV v EEAS of 29 January 2020
Case T-511/18, XH v Commission of 25 June 2020
Case T-518/16, Carreras Sequeros v Commission of 4 December 2018
Case T-566/16, Josefsson v European Parliament of 17 May 2018
Case T-567/16, McCoy v Committee of the Regions of 23 October 2018
Case T-571/17 RENV, UG v Commission of 21 June 2023
Case T-571/17, UG v Commission of 2 April 2020 and order of 13 November 2020
Case T-572/16, Brouillard v Commission of 13 October 2017
Case T-574/16, HK v Commission of 3 May 2018
Case T-728/16, Tuerck v Commission of 5 December 2017
Case T-736/19, HA v Commission of 16 December 2020
Case T-769/16, Picard v Commission of 24 March 2021
Case T-790/21, PL v Commission of 15 November 2023
Case T-808/17, Pethke v EUIPO of 3 December 2019
Case T-811/16, Di Bernardo v Commission of 29 November 2018
Case T-9/17, RI v Council of 12 July 2018

LIST OF CASE STUDIES

1

EU Civil Service Law as Legal Subject-Matter

I. Purpose and Scope

1. EU Civil Service and Case-Law

Civil service law is – after intellectual property law – the area of Union law that represents the second largest number of cases brought before the courts of the European Union (EU). Since 1952, a total of over 5,000 cases relating to civil service law and the Staff Regulations (SR) have been decided and settled out of a total of over 40,000 cases.[1] This case-law has not only developed employment law in the narrow sense, but over time it has significantly spurred advances in EU administrative law, institutional law, procedural law and individual legal positions such as the EU's stance on fundamental rights, long before a fundamental rights charter was drafted. For that reason, EU civil service law also functions – in the field of research on EU integration – as a test bed for the horizontal application of (for instance) EU procedural administrative law.[2]

2. Autonomous Character of EU Civil Service Law

Similarly to national labour law, EU civil service law is deeply intertwined with human resource management, as well as with the fundamental ability of the employing Union institutions to be operational and to fulfil their institutional tasks within the EU constitutional architecture. The rights and obligations of individual officials and the various categories of agent have evolved into a complex and dynamic field of law closely shaped by the jurisprudence of the EU courts. It features aspects both of individual and of collective labour law which have shaped a *sui generis* system of employment. The organisation of EU administration may appear similar to certain national systems of civil service, such as the French design of job descriptions, hierarchical and procedural customs. However, historically, it was clear from an early stage of the foundation of the European Communities that a proper civil service must be a self-contained regime, independent from national systems and particularly independent from national influence or even predominance, may it be on the political, judicial or the normative level. It is fair to say that the autonomy of the EU civil service from national law of the EU Member States (and their national civil services) is one of the expressions of the autonomous *sui generis* character of the Union's

[1] The number of such judgments amounts to over 13,000, *cf* on the total number of judgments, CJEU Annual Reports 2020, 190; 2021, 263; and 2022, 22. The total number of *settled legal cases* also includes procedures conducted in different instances, though strictly speaking pertaining to the same case.

[2] *cf* Mader, *Verteidigungsrechte* (2006) 197 ff.

constitutional setting itself.[3] Through the decades, an explicit objective of an autonomous EU civil service is to recruit and maintain highly qualified, capable, independent and loyal servants who have been selected on the basis of their merits and serve only the interests of the European institutions, rather than personal or national interests.[4] A side effect of a self-contained regime of EU civil service combined with the competition-based recruitment method (and on this point comparable with national civil service systems) is the relatively high level of protection of current staff, especially of officials *stricto sensu*, from the pressure of an open labour market.[5]

3. On the Role of the Judiciary and Remedies

The procedural aspects of civil service law, both on the administrative level and before the courts, exhibit some distinctive features due to the degree of specialisation of the subject matter. Unlike in other areas of Union law, in civil service law the courts have unlimited jurisdiction in 'disputes of a financial character'[6] (Art 91(1) SR). This gives them a wide scope for adjudicating all aspects of employment matters, including the compensation of damages for material and non-material harm suffered by a given member of staff. Some specialities – such as the goals of accelerating the pre-litigation and court procedures and achieving an amicable settlement – may be ascribed to the large number of complaints lodged, and of the staff cases brought in front of the courts.[7] At the same time, both procedural acceleration and amicable settlements are desirable for protecting the trust and integrity of the labour relationship that in many cases is still ongoing and/or is supposed to continue. As a positive element in general labour law, the advantage of – and need for – a constructive, predictable working environment in EU institutions has been recognised by the courts. In that sense, at various instances, the courts have emphasised the importance of legal certainty for the situation of a civil servant, and have acknowledged the stress and anxiety that may be caused by a (sustained) uncertain professional situation during the career of an official.[8] The procedural specificities and autonomous character of the legal matter as being separate from the rules of national law have strongly encouraged a relatively coherent evolution in terms of the

[3] EU law as an 'independent source of law', *cf* ECJ, 6/64, ECLI:EU:C:1964:66, 594 – *Flaminio Costa v ENEL*; ECJ, 26/62, ECLI:EU:C:1963:1, 12 – *van Gend & Loos v Netherlands Inland Revenue Administration*; ECJ, Opinion 1/91, ECLI:EU:C:1991:490, paras 30, 35, 47; ECJ, Opinion 2/13, ECLI:EU:C:2014:2454, paras 166 ff; ECJ, Opinion 1/92, ECLI:EU:C:1992:189, paras 17/18, 22, 24, 29, 36.

[4] *cf* Art 27(1) SR: 'highest standard of ability, efficiency and integrity, recruited on the broadest possible geographical basis'.

[5] This is of strategic relevance for the employment relationship of the individual staff member, but also for collective representation of staff interests, see chapter 4.

[6] See chapter 2, II.1.

[7] Van Raepenbusch, 'L'apport jurisprudentiel du Tribunal de la fonction publique de l'Union européenne' in Govaere/Vandersanden (eds), *La fonction publique communautaire* (2008) 152. Sceptical about labour law conciliation, Joris, 'L'administration face au contentieux de la fonction publique communautaire' in Govaere/Vandersanden (eds), *La fonction publique communautaire* (2008) 78 ('an administrative court'). Regarding amicable settlements, see also Vandersanden, 'La procédure et les voies de recours' in Govaere/Vandersanden (eds), *La fonction publique communautaire* (2008) 116 ff; CJEU Annual Report 2007, 217. On the major role of civil service law for the development of legal principles, see Gervasoni (2010) 46 *Cahiers de droit européen* 775 ff; Kraemer, 'The European Union Civil Service Tribunal: A New Community Court Examined After Four Years of Operation' (2009) 46 *CMLR* 1873, eg, to compensate for a lack of equality of arms Gervasoni (2010) 46 *Cahiers de droit européen* 742. On the social role model and pacification function of civil service case law, see Van Raepenbusch, 'L'apport jurisprudentiel du Tribunal de la fonction publique de l'Union européenne' in Govaere/Vandersanden(eds), *La fonction publique communautaire* (2008) 152; Levi, 'Droits fondamentaux et principes généraux de droit de la fonction publique communautaire' in Govaere/Vandersanden (eds), *La fonction publique communautaire* (2008) 110.

[8] See, eg, chapter 3, II.12.

legal subject matter being addressed. However, 'coherence' should not be understood to mean that the level of judicial protection afforded, or judicial control executed, is the same across all areas of EU civil service law. Instead, the sheer quantity of employment law cases brought before the courts, as well as the robust case-driven and exclusive jurisdiction of the EU courts, free from interference by national jurisprudence, has widely promoted the autonomous shaping of the many detailed facets of the EU civil service employment relationship that today makes it possible to speak about a well-established jurisprudence which covers a broad range of legal issues.

The four key elements determining the review system are:

- The organisation of the court proceedings (including their timing and aspects of amicable settlements)
- The decision-making regarding the admissibility of applications
- The decision on the merits of claims
- The decision on the cost of the proceedings

Always within the applicable statutory framework of, for example, rules of procedure or material law, each of these areas may have an effect on the attractiveness of the review system for prospective applicants who decide to concern the judiciary with a certain claim. On one side, the flexibility and space for manoeuvre for an administration in managing its human resources may be reduced, while on the other side a staff member seeking review may be deterred by the hurdles they perceive when pursuing their claim. Judicial self-restraint is only one piece of the jigsaw. As is the case in other fields of law, the fine-tuning of the admissibility requirements may sometimes have more relevance for the institution of the Court of Justice of the European Union (ECJ) itself than the merits of the substantive legal issue in question. The task of the courts in that regard is to oversee and manage the consequences of applying all four of the above-mentioned key areas of the review system in full awareness of their interdependence in order to develop the legal subject-matter in a manner that will continue to create a consistent, effective, fair and predictable employment regime within the overall framework of Union law. At the same time, it will be in the interests of an orderly administration of justice to deter unnecessary legal disputes and – as is often in the interests of the parties to litigation – to resolve disputes at an early stage and/or via amicable settlements.[9] Knowledge, predictability, clarity of the law and a reasonable degree of legal certainty will contribute towards this goal, as well as balance the case-load of the courts at an acceptable level.

4. EU Civil Service in Figures and Institutional Setting

EU civil service law sets out the employment and working conditions of the approximately 65,000 officials and other staff who work in the seven main institutions (Art 13 Treaty on European Union), the institutions as determined in (Art 1b SR, and other agencies and institutions possessing a legal personality at various places of employment in the EU and third countries.[10] Around

[9] 'At all stages of the procedure, including the time when the application is filed, the General Court may examine the possibilities of an amicable settlement of the dispute and may try to facilitate such settlement', Art 50a(2) Statute CJEU; see chapter 2, VI.

[10] According to the budget for 2021 ([2021] OJ L93/29), the number of posts (permanent and temporary) is 39,327 in the institutions and 8,140 in other EU bodies having a legal personality. The remaining employees are made up of contract staff from the European institutions, around 1,900 parliamentary assistants, and local staff in third countries

50 per cent of the total EU staff are employed in the Commission, which has over 32,000 employees, and around 17 per cent (11,000 employees) in the 48 EU agencies currently in existence.[11] In 2023, around 14,000 senior civil servants (AD),[12] 8,200 assistant/secretarial staff (AST/SC) and over 7,500 contract staff were employed in the Commission alone. In terms of nationality distribution in the Commission, Belgians rank first with 13.9 per cent (about 4,500 staff), followed by Italian and French nationals.[13]

The SR and Conditions of Employment of Other Servants (CEOS) apply to the seven Union institutions themselves (Art 13 TEU), to equivalent European services defined as 'institutions' such as the Economic and Social Committee, the Committee of the Regions, the EU Ombudsman and the Data Protection Supervisor,[14] and to the agencies and other bodies.[15] They largely apply to the staff of the European External Action Service (EEAS), Article 27(3) TEU.[16] The regime of EU civil service law (including the jurisdiction of the courts of the Court of Justice of the European Union (CJEU) under Article 270 of the Treaty on the Functioning of the European Union – TFEU)[17] is also of importance for the staff of bodies enjoying more independence within the family of European institutions, such as the European Investment Bank (EIB)[18] and the European Central Bank (ECB).[19]

(possibly under local conditions). Another larger group of legal addressees of service law in the broader sense are retired former employees and surviving dependants, for whom around 27,800 pensions are in force. In addition, certain provisions of the service law apply to the approximately 500,000 job applicants through the selection process, and to the family members of employees who receive social benefits. For details, see working document Com(2020) 300 for the financial year 2021, part II.

[11] European Commission HR key figures as of 1 January 2023; ECA Annual Report on EU agencies 2017 ([2018] OJ C434/01/11); also ECA Special Report 08/2021 on Frontex, 12, according to which the staff under the SR will be increased to 3,000 people by 2027, and will include short-term and long-term secondments involving 10,000 people.

[12] Abbreviations *cf* Art 5 SR.

[13] European Commission HR key figures (by year), available at: ec.europa.eu/info/about-european-commission/organisational-structure/commission-staff_en.

[14] Art 1b SR.

[15] See, eg, for EIOPA: Art 68 Regulation (EU) No 1094/2010 establishing a European Supervisory Authority (European Insurance and Occupational Pensions Authority) [2010] OJ L331. A new category has been introduced for the temporary staff of agencies, Art 2 lit f SR.

[16] Council Decision 2010/427/EU on the organisation and functioning of the European External Action Service [2010] OJ L201/30–40. Special regulations were added to the SR by Regulation (EC) No 1080/2010 [2010] OJ L311/1–8. On the EEAS in general, Kaltenborn/Holzhauer (2012) *EuR* 100; Sichel (2011) *EuR* 447; ECA Special Report [2014] OJ C203/4 on national seconded experts.

[17] CST, F-130/07, ECLI:EU:F:2009:114, para 52 – *Vinci v ECB*, on differences at the ECB in the preliminary proceedings compared with the SR; CST, F-84/08, ECLI:EU:F:2010:134, paras 47, 50 – *Cerafogli v ECB* on the analogous application of the SR in the case of claims for damages against the ECB. On ETF's status as employer: CST, F-87/08, ECLI:EU:F:2010:159, para 5 – *Schuerings v ETF*; for special features at the EIB, *cf* CST, F-59/09, ECLI:EU:F:2014:248, para 153 – *De Nicola v EIB* (preliminary proceedings), appeal GC, T-264/11 P, paras 70/71; CST, F-49/10, paras 64 ff – *De Nicola v EIB*, the judgment was partially set aside on another legal issue. *cf* on the Council of Europe, Freudenschuss, 'The European official: The example of the official of the Council of Europe' in FS Wimmer, *Recht Politik Wirtschaft Dynamische Perspektiven: Festschrift für Norbert Wimmer* (2008) 111–21.

[18] *cf* jurisdiction of the CJEU for EIB civil service disputes, Art 41a(1) EIB Staff Regulations (last amended 1 August 2023).

[19] Art 36 of the Protocol on the Statute of the ESCB and of the ECB [1992] OJ C191/78. Since the ECB is an EU institution in the sense of Art 13 TEU, the ECB staff could have been integrated into the framework of the EU Staff Regulations. However, this has not been done, reflecting the independence of the ECB in accordance with Art 282(3) TFEU. On applicable rules for the ECB: Conditions of Employment for Staff of the European Central Bank, latest amendment of 1 January 2023, and ECB Staff Rules of 1 November 2018. Remy in Perillo/Giacobbo-Peyronnel (eds), *Statut de la fonction publique de l'Union européenne: Commentaire article par article* (2017) 445–58.

The following section sets out the main normative framework within which EU civil service law is implemented, followed by an overview of the general principles governing EU civil service law.

II. Normative Framework

1. Staff Regulations

The central legislative document for EU civil service law is the Staff Regulations (SR). In its 235 pages, Regulation No 31, which dates from 1962, determines the provisions 'laying down the Staff Regulations of Officials and the Conditions of Employment of Other Servants of the European Economic Community and the European Atomic Energy Community'.[20] The SR and the CEOS have been amended more than 135 times in the course of the 60 plus years since their entry into force; the last time was in 2013/2014.[21] The SR laid down the rights and obligations, application and scope of the EU's civil service law. The status of officials is statutory, while the other servants have a mixed status which is partially statutory and partially contractual.[22] There are 15 Annexes containing complementary and procedural provisions attached to the SR, while the Conditions of Employment of Other Servants are followed by one single Annex containing transitional provisions. There is no formal hierarchy between the fundamental rules as contained in the text of the SR and the Annexes thereto. Both categories of rules were adopted by the Council. However, depending on the case, there may be a substantive hierarchy between them, so that the Annexes must be interpreted by reference to the basic rules and the system of the EU civil service, as laid down in the SR properly so-called.[23]

The SR contain rules binding on the institutions, officials and other servants, plus rules that are binding on the EU Member States wherever they have a role to play in their implementation. The latter aspect is particularly visible in the area of social protection.[24] The entire system of EU civil service law is a legal regime independent from national law; it takes precedence over national law where the latter would hinder its full implementation.[25] On the other hand, it is possible for there to be litigation which falls outside the scope of the SR that involves EU civil servants, namely regarding criminal charges or liability claims levied against them under national – mostly Member States' – law. In these cases, the EU institutions would involve the national judicial systems and law enforcement mechanisms; typically, the EU institution will conduct supplementary disciplinary proceedings under the SR.

[20] Regulation of 14 June 1962 [1962] OJ P45/1385, last amended by Regulation (EU) No 423/2014 of 16 April 2014 [2014] OJ L129/12. Website with consolidated SR available at: www.staff-regulations.eu.

[21] The reform was adopted in 2013 and entered into force in 2014, Regulation (EU, Euratom) No 1023/2013 of the European Parliament and of the Council of 22 October 2013 amending the Staff Regulations of Officials of the European Union and the Conditions of Employment of Other Servants of the European Union [2013] OJ L287/15–62. It is hereafter referred to as the 'reform of 2014'.

[22] See chapter 3, I.1.

[23] CST, F-110/11, ECLI:EU:F:2012:174, para 69 – *Lebedef and Others v Commission.*

[24] ECJ, C-92/02, ECLI:EU:C:2003:652, para 35 – *Nina Kristiansen.*

[25] CST, F-24/06, ECLI:EU:F:2007:121, para 83 – *Abarca Montiel v Commission* with further references. For the relationship to national labour law, see Potvin-Solis/Lelièvre (2012) *RUE* 284 on ECJ, 232/84, ECLI:EU:C:1985:392 – *Commission v Tordeur*, emphasising the special characteristics of the European public service GC, T-184/00, ECLI:EU:T:2003:39, para 56 – *Drouvis*, confirmed by ECJ, C-187/03 P, ECLI:EU:C:2004:280.

Article 110 SR refers to a number of other normative instruments that are important for the employment relationship. These are norms that give effect to the SR, including general implementing provisions and rules adopted by agreement between the appointing authorities of the institutions.

2. General Implementing Provisions

The first type of normative instruments are 'General Implementing Provisions' (GIP) that 'shall be adopted by the appointing authority of each institution after consulting the Staff Committee and the Staff Regulations Committee' (Art 110(1) SR).[26] Other internal rules[27] may complement the SR and CEOS, for example the provisions on community tax[28] or on privileges and exemptions.[29] Internal administrative instructions cannot overrule[30] higher-ranking provisions, and their application is subject to judicial control. Implementing regulations must be brought to the attention of the staff in a suitable form.[31] The Commission is empowered to adopt delegated acts concerning certain aspects of the working conditions; of the implementation of the remuneration rules; and of the social security scheme.[32] The involvement of the Staff Regulations Committee ensures that the implementing measures of the Staff Regulations taken by the different institutions are consistent and respect the principle of the integrity of the Staff Regulations.[33] The degree of an institution's obligation to adopt GIP was a matter of dispute in jurisprudence. In *Alba Aguilera*, the General Court (GC) had argued that prior adoption of GIP is a mandatory requirement for decisions to be legally adopted, and that the EEAS had breached its obligation to adopt GIP that are laid down in Articles 10 and 1(3) Annex X SR.[34] In appeal, the ECJ did not embrace such a broad interpretation of an alleged necessity to adopt GIP, but found that Article 1(3) Annex X SR 'is merely a procedural reference intended to specify the method according to which

[26] On the scope of Art 110 SR: CST, F-47/07, ECLI:EU:F:2009:103, para 48 – *Behmer v EP*.

[27] On liability, *cf* CST, F-59/09, ECLI:EU:F:2014:248, paras 185, 190 – *De Nicola v EIB*; on equal treatment CST, F-25/07, ECLI:EU:F:2010:163, para 145 – *Bleser v ECJ*.

[28] On taxation, see Regulation (EEC/Euratom/ECSC) No 260/68 of the Council of 29 February 1968 laying down the conditions and procedure for applying the tax for the benefit of the European Communities [1968] OJ L56/8, last amended [2002] OJ L264/15. The supplementary special levy at 5.5% expired at the end of 2012 and was reintroduced with the 2014 reform as a solidarity levy with tiered, slightly increased rates.

[29] Art 23 SR; [1967] OJ 152/13, last amended by Art 1 (7) lit d, para 8, para 14 Protocol No 1 to the Treaty of Lisbon [2007] OJ C306.

[30] CST, Jd Cases F-138/06 and F-37/08, ECLI:EU:F:2009:48, para 140 – *Meister v OHIM*; CST, F-98/07, ECLI:EU:F:2009:7, para 55 – *Petrilli v Commission*; CST, F-126/07, ECLI:EU:F:2008:136, paras 33, 68 – *Van Beers v Commission*. Eg, the administration cannot exempt itself by way of internal instructions from observing the duty of care, CST, F-62/10, ECLI:EU:F:2011:141, para 82 – *Esders v Commission*. Further to the general rules of interpretation of the hierarchy of norms, internal instructions are not applicable in the event of a violation of higher-ranking law, see CJEU Annual Report 2012, 217, CST, F-11/11, ECLI:EU:F:2012:8, paras 40, 42, 51 – *Bouillez v Council*. If an institution has imposed such a code of conduct on itself, it cannot deviate from it without giving reasons, CST, F-46/09, ECLI:EU:F:2011:101, para 76 – *V v EP*. Legal certainty does not require the administration to restrict its leeway in the implementation provisions, but rather that the rights and obligations of those involved are regulated clearly and recognisable, CST, F-121/10, ECLI:EU:F:2011:174, para 88 – *Heath v ECB*.

[31] Art 25(3) SR and GC, T-33/99, ECLI:EU:T:2000:94 – *Mendez Pinedo v ECB* (posting notice, staff notifications); CST, F-80/08, ECLI:EU:F:2009:160, paras 88, 86 – *Wenig v Commission* (transfer of responsibility from the College to the individual Commissioner); meanwhile it is perceived to be sufficient to announce internal service instructions by e-mail, combined with the possibility of consulting the institution's website, CST, F-66/09, ECLI:EU:F:2010:168, para 54 – *Saracco v ECB*.

[32] Art 111 ff SR.

[33] GC, T-119/17, ECLI:EU:T:2018:183, para 37 – *Alba Aguilera v EEAS*.

[34] Ibid, paras 33–44, referring to GC, T-792/14 P, EU:T:2016:156, para 33 – *Vanhalewyn v EEAS*.

general implementing provisions are to be adopted'.[35] An important characteristic of GIP is that they cannot restrict or reduce the scope of those regulations through explaining more fully a clear term of the SR.[36] More broadly, there may also be agreement among different administrative services about how to interpret certain provisions of the SR. But the administration does not have powers to derogate from an explicit provision of the SR via internal rules for implementing the SR, for example by rules adopted by agreement (see section 3 below), or by internal instructions, administrative notices or informational documents.

A variety of GIP have been adopted, for example those relating to Article 43 SR (annual report and reporting procedure); Article 45 SR (promotion), transfer of pension rights; Article 42a SR (parental leave); Article 45a(5) SR (certification procedure), the conduct of administrative enquiries and disciplinary procedures,[37] the rules for officials serving in third countries, and regarding the engagement of temporary staff and contract staff.[38] The GIP also have significance for the EU agencies: in the interests of the uniformity of civil service law and the comparability of employment relationships further to Article 110(2) SR, the implementing rules adopted by the Commission (to give effect to the SR) and the general implementing provisions apply by analogy to the agencies, except where an agency has opted for a derogation within a nine-month period.

3. Rules Adopted by Agreement

Article 110(4) SR addresses another category of implementing norms, namely 'rules adopted by agreement between the appointing authorities of the institutions'. Such interinstitutional agreements apply in all institutions and agencies under the SR, whereas the agencies are not counted as institutions for the adoption of implementing rules, but must be consulted before adopting the rules. For instance, there is a common agreement regarding insurance against the risk of occupational disease or accidents, Article 73(1) SR.[39] Article 110(5) SR speaks about regular consultations between administrative departments of the institutions and the agencies 'concerning the application of these Staff Regulations'; this could result in a uniform practice of the institutions as to the application of certain provisions of the SR. A conclusion adopted by the Committee of Heads of Administration as part of this process does not have the effect of binding the appointing authority when it adopts individual measures implementing a provision of the SR.[40] The institutions are not empowered to derogate from the explicit rules of the SR by way of, for example, internal directive, administrative communication or note for information.[41]

[35] ECJ, C-427/18 P, ECLI:EU:C:2020:109, para 72 – *EEAS v Alba Aguilera*; still, there is a residual obligation to adopt GIP where the relevant provision of the SR is so unclear and imprecise that any application of it must be arbitrary (*cf* paras 57 ff).

[36] GC, T-75/89, ECLI:EU:T:1990:88 – *Brems v Council*; confirmed by ECJ, C-70/91 P, ECLI:EU:C:1992:201, para 16 – *Council v Brems*.

[37] Art 2(3) Annex IX SR, see chapter 3, II.20.

[38] Overview of the various GIP in the Report from the Commission on GIP in the Institutions of 28 May 2021 COM(2021) 258 final. For the period from 2017 to 2019, the Commission counted 100 *Rules adopted by agreement*; 162 *General implementing provisions*; and 378 *Other implementing rules*.

[39] See chapter 3, V.

[40] GC, T-48/89, ECLI:EU:T:1990:50, para 17 – *Beltrante and Others v Council*; GC, T-302/01, ECLI:EU:T:2003:276, para 42 – *Birkhoff v Commission*.

[41] Levi/Rodrigues et al, *Fonction publique de l'Union européenne* (2020) 13.

4. Transparency and Register at the CJEU

Rules giving effect to the SR, including GIP and rules adopted by agreement between the appointing authorities of the institutions, shall be brought to the attention of the staff, Article 110(4) SR. Also, the CJEU shall administer a register of the rules adopted by the appointing authority of each institution to give effect to the SR.

5. Internal Instructions

An institution may draw up rules by means of an internal decision of general effect to govern the exercise of the discretion conferred on it by the SR. Such general instruction typically creates a self-binding effect. For example, an internal directive concerning the determination of grade and step on recruitment must be regarded as a rule of practice which the administration imposes on itself and from which it may not depart without specifying the reasons which have led it to do so, since otherwise the principle of equal treatment would be infringed.[42]

6. International Agreements

So far, international agreements are having no measurable impact on EU civil service law. However, since Article 216(2) TFEU stipulates that 'Agreements concluded by the Union are binding upon the institutions of the Union and on its Member States', it is conceivable that law stemming from public international law may influence the employment relationship too where the EU expresses its intention to be bound in its institutions. For instance, this could apply where the EU has acceded to international treaties such as the Istanbul Convention,[43] the UN Convention on the Rights of Persons with Disabilities (UNCRPD),[44] or (in the future) the European Convention on Human Rights (ECHR).[45] The hierarchical level of such law derived from international agreements would be below primary law but above secondary law, thus needing to be taken into account in legislative activities of the EU relating to (in this case) civil service law. Whether an individual can derive rights from international agreements is a matter to be assessed in line with the *Kupferberg* principles[46] and will be dependent on whether such a stipulation is unconditional and sufficiently precise to have direct effect (ie, whether it is 'self-executing'), and must be considered in the context of the Agreement of which it forms part.

7. Towards the Public: Code of Good Administrative Behaviour

Regarding the ethical standards by which EU institutions wish to be measured in their dealings with the public (ie, in an 'external' dimension), the development by the Ombudsman of a

[42] GC, T-2/90, ECLI:EU:T:1991:11, paras 61 ff – *Ferreira de Freitas*; GC, T-328/01, ECLI:EU:T:2004:13, para 50 – *Robinson v EP*.

[43] Council of Europe Convention on preventing and combating violence against women and domestic violence (CETS No 210) of 11 May 2011, signed by the EU on 13 June 2017, ratified 1 June 2023.

[44] The UN Convention on the Rights of Persons with Disabilities has been in force for the EU since 22 January 2011.

[45] Art 6(2) TEU; on the ramifications of a general accession of the EU to the Council of Europe, Mader (2011) 49(4) *AVR* 435–68.

[46] ECJ, 104/81, ECLI:EU:C:1982:362, para 23 – *Kupferberg*.

'European Code of Good Administrative Behaviour'[47] (the Code) of EU services was a major milestone. In their relations with the public, the Code applies to all officials and other servants covered by the SR and the CEOS. In accordance with Articles 2 and 3 of the Code, it contains the general principles of good administrative behaviour which apply to all relations of the institutions and their administrations with the public, unless they are governed by specific provisions. However, the principles *do not* apply to the relations between the institution and its officials: these are governed by the Staff Regulations.[48] The Code may nevertheless have an indirect *soft-law* effect on the internal dimension of the employment relationship, or play a procedural role in certain constellations. Finally, the rules governing a potential future EU 'ethics body' may further influence the normative framework relating to behavioural and disciplinary rules, for example regarding the acceptance of gifts, entertainment, conflicts of interest, revolving doors, asset declarations, lobbying, whistleblowing and anti-harassment.[49] Yet formally, the draft interinstitutional agreement for setting up an ethics body limits the scope of its application to the *members* of the participating institutions (ie, Commissioners, MEPs, etc).[50]

III. General Principles of EU Civil Service Law

1. Legislative Competence for Civil Service Law and Procedures

a. *Article 336 TFEU as Legal Basis*

The legal basis for the establishment of an independent EU civil service is enshrined in Article 336 TFEU. The Treaty of Lisbon determined that the method to legislate on SR and the CEOS should be the ordinary legislative procedure by means of an EU regulation; this strengthens the powers of the Parliament compared with previously, where only its consultation was required.[51] The SR and CEOS are central components of the strengthened administrative dimension in the Lisbon Treaty.[52] Article 336, in conjunction with Article 298 TFEU, commits the European administration to the goals of *openness, efficiency* and *independence*. Independence is required above all in relation to the Member States and their administrations.[53] It is only with sufficient autonomy that

[47] Originally developed by the European Ombudsman on 28 July 1999, adopted by the Commission on 13 September 2000 [2000] OJ L308, by Parliament on 6 September 2001, and available at: ommun.eu/!rNf4xr and by the other respective bodies.

[48] CST, F-96/09, ECLI:EU:F:2012:129, para 90 – *Cuallado Martorell v Commission*; CST, F-116/07 ECLI:EU:F:2010:77, paras 86, 196 – *Tomas v EP*; Potvin-Solis/Lelièvre (2012) *RUE* 272, is critical of this, because, for example, the administration's prescribed reference to deadlines and legal remedies would improve the effective legal protection of employees.

[49] Proposal for an interinstitutional ethics body, COM(2023) 311 final of 8 June 2023; EP Resolution of 16 September 2021 'Strengthening transparency and integrity in the EU institutions by setting up an independent EU ethics body', P9 TA(2021)0396; Alemanno, *Towards an EU Ethics Body* (2020); ECA Special Report No 13/2019 'The ethical frameworks of the audited EU institutions: scope for improvement'.

[50] Art 1(1) and Art 2 of Annex 1 draft agreement; on the members see also, chapter 2, I.4.

[51] Council Decision of 23 June 1981 establishing a tripartite consultation procedure for relations with staff, Council document 6073/03, in the event of changes to the Staff Regulations, the CEOS and their rules on salaries and pensions must be interpreted accordingly.

[52] Gärditz (2010) *DÖV* 453.

[53] This attribute has its roots in the very early raison d'être of the EU, mentioned in the Schuman declaration of 9 May 1950, when it speaks about the '*solidarité de fait*' among countries that relinquish their say in areas entrusted to the supranational level. Any conferral would be ineffective if it was undermined by civil services dependent on the Member States; Krijtenburg, 'Schmuan's timeless frame of reference for the EU today and tomorrow' in Waechter/Becker/Neubauer (eds), *Robert Schuman* (2022) 118 ff.

a European administration can retain its ability to assess and act, and be able to resist political, economic and administrative influence on the part of the Member States.[54] A cornerstone of the EU administration's independence is successful human resource management,[55] for which the autonomy of its personnel is an indispensable core component.[56] Criticism in regard to matters of independence is therefore primarily directed at external appointments to top positions, which are subject to the influence of the Member States' governments.[57]

The legal relationships of the members of the institutions (Commissioners, etc) do not fall under Article 336 TFEU, but under separate legal bases for the employment relationships of these political actors.[58]

b. Staff Regulations Committee and Trilogue

The Staff Regulations Committee is involved in the ordinary legislative procedure, which entails a number of procedural specialties. The Staff Regulations Committee consists of equal numbers of representatives of the institutions and representatives of their staff committees. The Committee is consulted by the Commission on any proposal to amend the Staff Regulations.[59] The periods for delivering the opinions requested by the Staff Committee, the Joint Committee and the Staff Regulations Committee are prescribed by the institution and may not be less than 15 working days.[60] Such an opinion is not binding. The Staff Regulations Committee must be consulted again[61] in the event of significant changes to proposals in the legislative process, which is interpreted to mean when *the Commission itself* submits a new, significantly modified proposal. Whether the changes are significant is not to be judged by the individual effects they have on those concerned, but by the purpose the changes serve and what position they have in the overall structure of the legislative proposal.[62]

[54] Sebastiani, 'L'évaluation de la réforme' in Govaere/Vandersanden (eds), *La fonction publique communautaire* (2008) 29; it is critical for addressing independence in the 2004 reform.

[55] See COM (2011) 890 Recital No 3, and 2, 3 and Recital No 7 of Regulation (EU/Euratom) No 1023/2013 [2013] OJ L287.

[56] Dalle-Crode, *Le fonctionnaire communautaire* (2008) 12. Special rules for staffing the EEAS.

[57] Sebastiani, 'L'évaluation de la réforme' in Govaere/Vandersanden (eds), *La communau publique ommunautaire* (2008) 41, argues that the SR reform's lowering of entry grades (a) endangers the capacity of the services to fill their top positions from within their own ranks, and (b) hinders a 'renationalisation' of these functions.

[58] MEPs: Art 223(2) TFEU, Decision 2005/684/EC, Euratom of the EP of 28 September 2005 adopting the Statute for Members of the European Parliament [2005] OJ L262/1–10; Ombudsman: Art 228(4) TFEU, *cf* EP resolution of 12 February 2019 [2020] OJ C449; salaries of the members of the Commission, the members of the Court of Justice, etc, Art 243 TFEU, in addition to Regulation (EU) No 2016/300 of the Council of 29 February 2016 on the official salaries for high-ranking officials in the EU [2016] OJ L58. On the level of legal protection afforded to Advocates General, see GC, T-180/20, ECLI:EU:T:2020:473 – *Sharpston v Council and Conference of Representatives of the Governments of the Member States*; GC, T-184/20, ECLI:EU:T:2020:474 – *Sharpston v ECJ*; GC, T-550/20, ECLI:EU:T:2020:475 – *Sharpston v Council and Heads of State or Government*; ECJ, C-423/20 P(R), ECLI:EU:C:2020:700 – *Council v Sharpston*; ECJ, C-424/20 P(R), ECLI:EU:C:2020:705 – *Council v Sharpston*; ECJ, C-684/20 P, ECLI:EU:C:2021:486 – *Sharpston v Council and Conference of Representatives of the Governments of the Member States*; ECJ, C-685/20 P, ECLI:EU:C:2021:485 – *Sharpston v Council and Representatives of the Governments of the Member States.* In consequence, acts adopted by representatives of the governments of the Member States, acting not in their capacity as members of the Council of the European Union or of the European Council but as representatives of their own governments, and thus collectively exercising the powers of the Member States, are not subject to judicial review by the EU courts.

[59] Art 10 SR.

[60] Art 10a SR.

[61] GC, T-58/05, ECLI:EU:T:2007:218, paras 35 ff – *Centeno Mediavilla and Others v Commission*; confirmed by ECJ, C-443/07 P, ECLI:EU:C:2008:767, paras 29, 49 – *Centeno Mediavilla and Others v Commission.*

[62] GC, T-58/05, ECLI:EU:T:2007:218, paras 35 ff – *Centeno Mediavilla and Others v Commission.*

Before the judicial review of this aspect of the 2014 reform, it was unclear whether the Staff Regulations Committee had to be consulted again if, in the course of the 'trilogue procedure' involving the Commission, Parliament and Council, significant changes to the draft legislative act were not formally introduced by the Commission, but by the Parliament or the Council. The courts answered this question in the negative with an interpretation close to the wording of Article 10 SR.[63] This consequent narrow understanding of the right of the Committee to be consulted appears justifiable, but has been met with criticism. In practice, a reconsultation of the Staff Regulations Committee, which would relate not only to amendments tabled by the Commission but also to those tabled by the Council or Parliament, would lead to a change in the process and cause delays in the legislative process; it also would constrain the interplay between the Council and Parliament.[64] The provision for the consultation of the Committee and the corresponding deadline specification were already in force before the introduction of the co-decision procedure and the ordinary legislative procedure.[65] It can be argued that the complexity of the ordinary legislative procedure was not taken into account when the provision was introduced. Ultimately, the question of whether a renewed hearing of the Staff Regulations Committee is required in the event of a significant change to the proposal (even beyond the case of a formal new contribution) needs to be assessed in accordance with the purpose of Article 10 SR and the degree of collective codetermination expressed therein. A broad interpretation may delay the proceedings. The risk of an overly narrow interpretation is that it can lead to 'top-heavy' legislative procedures in which particularly contentious issues are deliberately introduced late, so that no further hearing can take place. However, this would also mean that the Commission was not granted an opportunity to exercise its right of initiative in relation to these amendments, which could amount to a breach of its monopoly to initiate legislation under Article 17(2) TEU.[66] So at least a legislative clarification of the wording of Article 10 or 10a SR – which has the potential to increase the acceptance and legitimacy of the procedure – could be helpful, by taking into account the complexity of the ordinary legislative procedure in the trilogue and ensuring an appropriate degree of transparent collective codetermination.

c. *Staff Committee and Trade Unions*

It is the common practice of the Commission to give an opportunity to comment within the course of the legislative procedure under Article 336 TFEU not only to the Staff Regulations Committee, but also to the Staff Committee.[67] In addition, a so-called 'concertation' is practised, during which the trade unions are consulted.[68] The role of the staff committees is described in chapter 4.I.

According to the wording of Article 336 TFEU, the 'other institutions concerned' are to be consulted before the regulation is passed. This refers to the main institutions under Article 13 TEU and the institutions determined under Article 1b SR. However, the ECB has its own SR and is therefore not included in the category of 'institutions concerned'; hence consulting it would not be mandatory. The European Council (although formally not active in legislation itself,

[63] GC, T-17/14, ECLI:EU:T:2016:489, paras 135, 137 ff – *U4U and Others v EP and Council.*

[64] Narrow interpretation: Eggers/Linder, 'Art 336 TFEU' in Grabitz/Hilf, *Das Recht der EU*, 60th edn (2016) para 24a.

[65] Art 10(2) sentence 2 SR was introduced in 1968, the deadline of Art 10a SR in 1972.

[66] On the importance of this right, *cf* ECJ, C-24/20, ECLI:EU:C:2022:911 – *Commission v Council.*

[67] Art 9 para 3 SR; there is no legal obligation to do so: ECJ, 1253/79, ECLI:EU:C:1982:38, para 28 – *Battaglia v Commission.*

[68] Chapter 4; Art 10c, 24b SR, Art 11, 81, 127 CEOS.

cf Art 15(1) sentence 2 TEU) is also involved in the legislative process via the Council, so that there is no obligation to consult it either.[69] On the other hand, the Court of Auditors and the Court of Justice are affected, and can issue opinions before the regulation is adopted.

2. *Other* Staff Regulations? The Scope of Article 336 and the Core Tasks Doctrine

According to the wording of Article 336 TFEU, the legislator lays down the SR of officials of the European Union and the CEOS of the Union. Thus, as introduced above, Article 336 TFEU is the legal basis for the SR (and CEOS) 'of the Union'. Now, the question that arises and that is of importance for the institutional structures, human resource management and employment situation of EU bodies is whether the legislator is free to also introduce *other* staff regulations on the basis of Article 336 TFEU that deviate from the existing SR, and the question particularly is: whether the legislator is free to introduce personnel provisions for the institutions created by it and endowed with their own legal personality (such as EU agencies).

As a preliminary remark on this, firstly it should be borne in mind that numerous administrative bodies of the Union have been formed over time which, because of their founding act or their name, appear to be independent bodies, but are in fact attached to the Commission. For example, the EPSO Personnel Selection Office[70] and the Publications Office are staffed by Commission staff and the SR apply to them. There are also institutions whose names suggest independence, but which are ultimately Commission departments: OLAF,[71] the PMO,[72] OIB,[73] OIL.[74] Secondly, the legislator has created other bodies and given legal personality to them, which are to be distinguished from the first category above; these are executive agencies, regulatory agencies (ie, decentralised agencies), joint undertakings and technology initiatives. The SR do not automatically apply to their staff because they are not officials 'of the Union'. With regard to these institutions, the question arises as to the legislative freedom for the application of the SR or any other arrangement for the employment relationship.

According to one view[75] (here called the 'other opinion'), which relies on the cases *Mulfinger*[76] and *Sanders*,[77] the SR are always to be applied to the staff of a body if that body performs tasks which had been assigned to an institution of the Union by the Treaties (TEU/TFEU). If, on the other hand, the body performs tasks that the Treaties do not reserve for an institution, the legislator is free to choose the SR or other arrangement. While the SR (or the CEOS) must be applied to the staff of the executive agencies, the legislator is free in the case of decentralised agencies to

[69] Eggers/Linder, 'Art 336 TFEU' in Grabitz/Hilf, *Das Recht der EU*, 60th edn (2016) para 28.

[70] Decision 2002/620/EC of the European Parliament, the Council, the Commission, the Court of Justice, the Court of Auditors, the Economic and Social Committee, the Committee of the Regions and the European Ombudsman of 25 July 2002 establishing the Personnel Selection Office of the European Communities [2002] OJ L197.

[71] However, with the power to issue its own rules of procedure: Commission Decision 1999/352 (EC, ECCS, Euratom) of 28 April 1999 establishing the European Anti-Fraud Office [1999] OJ L136.

[72] Commission Decision 2003/522/EC of 6 November 2002 establishing the Office for the Administration and Payment of Individual Entitlements [2003] OJ L183.

[73] Commission Decision 2003/523/EC of 6 November 2002 establishing the Office for Infrastructure and Logistics in Brussels [2003] OJ L183/35.

[74] Commission Decision 2003/524/EC of 6 November 2002 establishing the Office for Infrastructure and Logistics in Luxembourg [2003] OJ L183/40.

[75] Eggers/Linder, 'Art 336 TFEU' in Grabitz/Hilf, *Das Recht der EU*, 60th edn (2016) paras 18 ff.

[76] ECJ, 249/87, ECLI:EU:C:1989:614, paras 10/11 – *Mulfinger and Others v Commission.*

[77] GC, T-45/01, ECLI:EU:T:2004:289, para 115 – *Sanders v Commission.*

regulate the employment relationships under private law. This view makes a distinction according to the Treaties' assignment of tasks to an institution, but fails to take into account that even where such assignment is given, there are certain employment situations which need not be governed by the SR because they do not relate to the core of the task. Concretely, in *Mulfinger*, the applicants sought employment under the SR as language teachers at the Commission.[78] Although the ECJ recognised in *Mulfinger* that the language training of the staff is important, it is not one of the tasks assigned to the institutions by the Treaties. Therefore, the ECJ rightly rejects their entitlement to be employed under the SR.

Solution

Instead, it is submitted here that Article 336 TFEU and the above case-law are to be understood in the following way: according to the opinion of the ECJ it can be assumed that the SR and the CEOS enacted under Article 336 do not represent exhaustive regulations, but that the Union is, in principle, free to enter into private law contractual relationships.

At the same time, a circumvention of the norm must be prevented, which would occur if contractual conditions were not determined as a function of service requirements, but in order to circumvent the SR.[79] Article 336 has to serve as legal basis and the regulations of the SR issued according to Article 336 are to be applied to staff, if the respective body performs tasks that have been assigned to it by the Treaties or on the basis of the subsidiary powers under Article 352 TFEU in the context of a policy defined by the Treaties, but only insofar as *core* tasks of that Union body are concerned.[80] If that is the case, the legislator may not resort to an 'escape' from the SR (or CEOS), neither via a different design nor by applying a different procedure than provided for in Article 336. Nevertheless, there still remains a wide range of legislative leeway, especially in the context of the CEOS and flexibilisation, for example for parliamentary assistants. A good example is provided by the executive agencies, which the Commission uses under its control and responsibility to entrust them with specific management tasks of Union programmes: the bodies role to execute *core* tasks brings about a narrowing of leeway in the employment relationships. So if, for example, Article 18 of Regulation No 58/2003[81] stipulates that executive agencies can employ temporary and contract staff in addition to Commission staff and that the contracts can be set up under public or private law, this must be interpreted in such a way that private law employment contracts are only permitted in exceptional cases, namely as far as ancillary functions are concerned.

If an institution delegates its own powers to other bodies, it may anyway not circumvent the applicable provisions and must assign delegated tasks explicitly (*Meroni* principles).[82] It is therefore not decisive whether the tasks are assigned by the Treaties/primary law or by secondary law. The tasks of regulatory agencies (decentralised agencies) are typically not assigned to a body *in the Treaties*, but in a founding regulation. In any case, there is an allocation of tasks under Union law. The other opinion (on the basis of *Mulfinger*) is too much concerned about whether the tasks of the new body are reserved for an institution under primary law. What is decisive,

[78] Similarly, the applicants in the case *Sanders* were project staff in the JET Joint Undertaking.

[79] What this circumvention can consist of must be clarified in each case on the basis of the limits of the assessment authority. In the case of *Mulfinger*, for example, there was no circumvention, although open-ended contracts were awarded, which indicate that the tasks performed are not based on just a temporary need (para 12).

[80] Translators, language trainers, canteen staff, building security, cleaning and driving services, and possibly other administrative tasks are not typically active in the core area of a facility.

[81] Council Regulation (EC) No 58/2003 of December 19, 2002 laying down the statute for executive agencies to be entrusted with certain tasks in the management of Community programmes [2003] OJ L11.

[82] On the *Meroni* principles, see chapter 3, I.1.a.

however, is the question whether the specific job responsibility belongs to the *core tasks* of the respective Union institution or if it involves only a supporting (ancillary) function. With this approach, the concrete case constellation of *Mulfinger* can be easily solved in line with the findings of the ECJ, because the applicants (as language teachers) did not perform any core function of the Commission.

The legislative practice of referring to the SR and the CEOS in the founding legal bases of EU bodies whose act of creation also endowed them with their own legal personality promotes the uniformity of EU staff employment, the independence of the EU civil service, and the general protection of its staff. In that sense, for example, the Commission's translation and interpreting services are carried out largely under the SR; in another example, the European Parliament (EP) reincluded building security staff under the SR.

The legislator is free to design, adapt and differentiate the terms of employment with regard to those staff who do not perform a core function (to be determined according to the area of responsibility of the institution), outside the scope of Article 336 TFEU. This can be done, for example, by drafting special staff regulations,[83] or by referring to national labour law. It is also possible to refer to the SR and the CEOS, but introducing modifications where necessary.[84]

As a consequence of the opinion proposed here, the scope of application of private labour law is smaller than in the view of the other opinion mentioned above. However, it should be borne in mind that the CEOS already offer extensive organisational freedom that is being applied in the practice of the agencies. It can therefore be stated that in accordance with Article 336 TFEU, the application of SR and CEOS is mandatory where the staff are performing tasks connected with the core functions of the body they are working for (regardless of whether these core functions were assigned by primary legislation or secondary legislation). The legislator enjoys discretion when regulating functions whose character is merely a supporting (ancillary) one, and has the option of employing tailor-made solutions, including those that invoke private law.

3. Historical Development and Civil Service Reforms

In 2004, the SR – which had remained essentially unchanged for a long time – were extensively modernised,[85] supplemented by special rules for EEAS[86] staff and parliamentary assistants,[87] and further developed in the reform of 2014.[88] The 2004 reform strengthened the legal position of civil servants, for example, by the further development of non-discrimination policy,[89] by an

[83] eg, for CEDEFOP in the old Art 13 of Council Regulation (EEC) No 337/75 [1975] OJ L39; since a change in 1995, Art 13 of the Regulation refers to the SR and the CEOS.

[84] The legislator is free to create or maintain status differences across various categories of staff employed (CST, F-53/05, ECLI:EU:F:2007:183 para 83 – *Tunon*); however, the method of applying modified SR and/or CEOS makes the existence of differences and classifications within the workforce very visible and is thus an HR policy that can lead to frustration among staff.

[85] Regulation (EC) No 723/2004 of 22 March 2004 [2004] OJ L184/1–118; Commission, *An administration serving half a billion European citizens, European Commission staff reform* (2004). *cf* on the 2004 reform, eg, Rogalla (2003) 38 *EuR* 670.

[86] Cassagnabere in Perillo/Giacobbo-Peyronnel (eds), *Statut de la fonction publique de l'Union euro péenne: Commentaire article par article* (2017) 411–26.

[87] For the parliamentary assistants, Art 2 lit e and Art 125 ff SR, and Regulation (EC) No 160/2009 [2009] OJ L55. Michon, 'Assistant parlementaire au Parlement eu ropéen: un tremplin pour une carrière européenne' (2008) *Sociologie du travail* 169–83. See also, chapter 3, II.1.

[88] Ponzano, 'La fonction publique euro péenne: une évaluation d'ensemble' (2019) *Revue du droit de l'Union européenne* 51–57.

[89] Art 1d SR.

improved legal framework for dealing with sexual harassment and bullying,[90] and by guaranteeing freedom of expression.[91] Efforts to improve employment conditions for women required the introduction of more flexible working conditions and various family-related and partnership-related benefits, such as new types of leave[92] or allowances[93] for children of preschool age. The reform of 2014 continued this development. For example, it improved protection[94] against dismissal for certain staff in the event of pregnancy; parental and family leave; family allowances; a doubling of dependant allowances in the case of disability or long-term illness;[95] and established a single parent's entitlement to work part-time.[96] The overall aim of the SR was thus to improve the compatibility of work and family life.[97]

The reforms of 2004 and 2014 sharpened the focus on service performance, for example in the appraisal and promotion system, the new career structure, and the procedures connected with inadequate professional performance. For appraisals, and especially for promotions to grade AD 13 or AST 10 upwards, the reforms emphasised the importance of the responsibility assumed as well as the work achieved, plus the behaviour of employees during their probationary period.[98] Numerous changes simplified the regulations in the context of a desire to make financial savings,[99] such as by reducing basic starting salaries, introducing a new function group for secretarial services with lower salaries, streamlining the probationary period procedures, introducing restrictions on the advancement of officials without special management positions, repeatedly raising the retirement age, and discontinuing early retirement without deductions, etc. In addition, the 2014 reform suspended the salary adjustment for two calendar years, while the so-called 'solidarity levy'[100] was (re)introduced. Some groups of staff were affected by changes in compensation for travel expenses, relocation costs, home leave/travelling time, the number of annual leave days, and special allowances or rest leave on account of particularly difficult living conditions. Another modification under the 2014 reform was the option of early retirement (Art 50 SR) for senior temporary staff of political groups in Parliament.[101] In addition, the reform introduced a new method for automatically determining salary adjustments on the basis of statistical data, thus effectively making redundant a separate political decision-making process.[102] The transitional rules for introducing both reforms were designed to avoid making abrupt cuts in salary, and sought as far as possible to preserve the status quo for those staff who were already employed at the moment that they entered into force.

The 2004 reform was complemented by the creation of EPSO as the selection office, and by improvements in determining personnel requirements, greater transparency in the selection processes, reduced waiting times in the recruitment process,[103] as well as measures in strategic

[90] Art 12a SR.

[91] Art 17 and 17a SR.

[92] Art 42a SR.

[93] Art 3(2) Annex VII SR.

[94] eg, Art 47, 139 CEOS.

[95] Arts 42a, 58, 67 SR, Art 6 Annex V SR.

[96] Art 55a SR.

[97] Art 1e(1) SR.

[98] *cf* Art 34(1) SR; Henneberger/Sudjana, 'Performance incentives for civil servants in the European Communities and in Germany: a legal comparison' (2007) *Journal of Civil Service Law* 181.

[99] The long-term savings of the 2014 reform over the period from 2014 to 2064 are calculated by the European Court of Auditors at €19.2 billion; according to the Commission, the 2004 reform delivered savings of €5 billion by 2020, see Commission press release, IP/11/799 BC of 29 June 2011.

[100] Art 66a SR. It did not affect allowances or pensions.

[101] Art 48 a CEOS.

[102] Art 65 SR, Annex XIII. See chapter 3, III.1.d.

[103] Gauer (2007) 137. See also Special Report No 10/2012 of the European Court of Auditors: *Effectiveness of staff development in the European Commission.*

planning and programming, financial management, etc.[104] With a view to enhancing the equality of the Union's citizens, the 2014 reform introduced the possibility for each institution to adopt separate recruitment measures where a significant nationality imbalance in the staff composition was identified. General selection procedures could remain restricted to nationals of certain Member States, as was previously the case when they joined the EU. However, according to Article 27(2) SR and Article 12(1) CEOS, these measures must be appropriate and justified, and must never involve the adoption of recruitment criteria that are not based on merit. The 2014 reform was preceded by a lively discussion in which the changes of 2004 were criticised as insufficient. For example, the Parliament called for the SR to be modernised and adapted to a changing labour world.[105] Savings were sought in training and publications, travel and office expenses,[106] and remuneration.[107]

The two reforms gave rise to a significant number of legal disputes,[108] while practically all of the changes introduced by the reforms were upheld by the courts.[109] Overall, the desired cost savings (without taking into account the cost of outsourced services and increased risks) were able to be realised, but also resulted in less favourable employment conditions, making the EU less attractive as an employer.[110]

4. Principles of Interpretation

Provisions of civil service law are to be interpreted in line with the common rules of interpretation: according to the letter and the historical, systematic and teleological method,[111] as an

[104] See Fitch, 'The General Framework of the Administrative Reform' in Govaere/Vandersanden (eds) *La fonction publique communautaire* (2008) 5 ff.

[105] eg, a reduction in the number of travel leave days, the abolition of time off in lieu at management level, a reduction in the number of office closure days (which, together with public holidays, are now restricted to a maximum of 14 working days per annum), the abolition of age-related seniority levels, the establishment of a transparent and comprehensible promotion system, the performance of management tasks as a prerequisite for promotion to AD12, etc. See European Parliament, Budgetary Control Committee, 'Working Document on the Reform of the Staff Regulations of Officials of the European Communities and Conditions of Employment for Other Servants', 14 February 2012, PE480.777v 02-00).

[106] Commission press release IP/11/499 of 20 April 2011.

[107] See Commission IP/11/816, MEMO/11/473, MEMO/11/907 and Communication from the Commission, 'A budget for Europe 2020', COM (2011) 500, 26, 94 ff.

[108] On the 2004 reform, see Joris, 'L'administration face au contentieux de la fonction publique communautaire' in Govaere/Vandersanden (eds), *La fonction publique communautaire* (2008) 65, Sebastiani, 'L'évaluation de la réforme' in Govaere/Vandersanden (eds), *La fonction publique communautaire* (2008) 41. Regarding transitional arrangements in general, CST, F-22/07, ECLI:EU:F:2008:104 – *Lafili v Commission*; GC, T-135/05, ECLI:EU:T:2006:366, paras 85/86 – *Campoli v Commission*; and ECJ, C-127/80, ECLI:EU:C:1982:86 – *Grogan v Commission*. Principles such as the principle of acquired rights can restrict changes in law (GC, T-123/89, ECLI:EU:T:1990:24, para 34 – *Chomel v Commission*; ECJ, 159/82, ECLI:EU:C:1983:242, para 8 – *Verli-Wallace v Commission*); proportionality (GC, T-439/09, ECLI:EU:T:2011:600, paras 83, 90 ff – *Purvis v EP*); equal treatment (ECJ, C-496/08, ECLI:EU:C:2010:116, para 100 – *Angé Serrano and Others v EP*).

[109] As an example, the reduction of annual leave entitlement: reduction decision annulled by GC, T-518/16, ECLI:EU:T:2018:873 – *Carreras Sequeros and Others v Commission*; GC judgment set aside in the appeal: ECJ, Jd Cases C-119/19 P and C-126/19 P, ECLI:EU:C:2020:676 – *Commission v Carreras Sequeros and Others*.

[110] European Court of Auditors Special Report No 15/2019: 'Implementation of the 2014 staff reform package at the Commission – large savings but not without consequences for staff'.

[111] Such as Epiney in Bieber/Epiney/Haag, *Europarecht und Politik*, 9th edn (2011) § 9, paras 14 ff, and Hobe, (2023) *Europarecht* 117/118. On the interpretation of provisions according to goal and systematic, see CST, F-27/10, ECLI:EU:F:2011:20, paras 40, 49 – *Begue and Others v Commission*. If there are several exclusion criteria, it may not be possible to consider them individually, but only to look at them as a whole, see CST, F-23/10, ECLI:EU:F:2011:162, para 79 – *Allen v Commission*. The interpretation must not deprive the provision of (almost) all effectiveness, CST, F-98/07, ECLI:EU:F:2009:7, para 49 – *Petrilli v Commission*; CST, F-6/08, ECLI:EU:F:2008:160, para 73 – *Blais v ECB*. Exceptional

autonomous legal matter[112] of Union[113] law in accordance with the Treaties and general principles of Union law.[114] Interpretation other than by wording presupposes that the legislative intent is not clear without doubt from the legal text itself.[115] Other principles are the need for a narrow interpretation of provisions giving rise to a claim,[116] as well as the strict (ie, narrow) interpretation of exceptions.[117] Recourse to national law only occurs if there is an express reference to such law.[118] A general principle of interpretation is that a measure must be interpreted, as far as possible, in such a way as not to affect its validity and in conformity with primary law as a whole and, in particular, with the provisions of the EU Fundamental Rights Charter (FRC).[119]

5. Directives and Civil Service Law

An interesting question is how far the content of EU directives can influence the development of civil service law. Directives are addressed to the Member States, Article 288 TFEU. Hence – and in line with the autonomy of EU civil service law – the provisions of directives are not directly applicable to it, either when legislating civil service law under Article 336 TFEU or when implementing the SR or CEOS.[120] On the other hand, there are good reasons in principle why the institutions of the EU should not fall short of the minimum standards that the Member States set for themselves in the legislative instruments that the directives represent. In addition, directives typically contain reasonings which may point to labour law principles and the underlying

provisions are to be interpreted strictly, such as enumerated powers, see CST, F-22/05 RENV, ECLI:EU:F:2009:120, para 95 – *Neophytou v Commission*; this is different in the case of transitional provisions if there would otherwise be a regulatory gap, CST, F-29/05, ECLI:EU:F:2010:114, paras 67 ff, 71 – *Vivier v Commission*. See also, Potacs, 'Effet utile as a principle of interpretation' (2009) *EuR* 465. On the interpretation taking into account the ECHR in CST, F-1/05, ECLI:EU:F:2006:112, paras 66/67 – *Landgren v ETF*, *cf* Gervasoni (2010) 46 *Cahiers de droit européen* 776; on the interpretation according to guidelines, social law and higher-ranking legal principles, Gervasoni (2010) 46 *Cahiers de droit européen* 738; and on the interpretation of implementing regulations in accordance with the basic regulation CST, F-81/10, ECLI:EU:F:2011:120, para 51 – *Praskevicius v EP*. CST, F-85/10, ECLI:EU:F:2012:97, 133 – *AI v CJEU*. The administration has a special duty of care when interpreting officials' requests, CST, F-87/11, ECLI:EU:F:2013:10, paras 29, 23 – *Wallström v Frontex*.

112 CST, F-95/09, ECLI:EU:F:2011:9, para 57 – *Skareby v Commission*; CST, F-45/07, ECLI:EU:F:2010:72, paras 62 ff – *Mandt v EP*; CST, F-144/07, ECLI:EU:F:2008:163, para 37 *Efstatopoulos v Commission* (from an equality point of view); CST, F-145/06, ECLI:EU:F:2008:65, para 64 – *Pascual-García v Commission* (term professional experience); CST, F-68/06, ECLI:EU:F:2008:39, para 42 *Bakema v Commission* (diploma); CST, F-122/06, ECLI:EU:F:2007:208, para 35 – *Roodhuijzen v Commission*, CST, ECLI:EU:F:2007:208, para 35 – *Roodhuijzen v Commission* (cohabitation); status-specific reference concept without family-related reference components, CST, F-24/06, ECLI:EU:F:2007:121, paras 81, 100 – *Abarca Montiel v Commission*. Gervasoni (2010) 46 *Cahiers de droit européen* 737.

113 CST, F-65/07, ECLI:EU:F:2009:43, para 121 – *Aayhan and Others v Commission*.

114 CST, F-6/08, ECLI:EU:F:2008:160, para 74 – *Blais v ECB* (observance of higher-ranking law); CST, F-10/06, ECLI:EU:F:2006:139, para 24 – *André v Commission* (objective of the provision); CST, Jd Cases F-69/07 and F-60/08, ECLI:EU:F:2009:128 – *O v Commission* (freedom of movement); narrow interpretation of the wording.

115 CST, F-11/08, ECLI:EU:F:2009:53, para 69 – *Mölling v Europol*.

116 CST, F-10/06, ECLI:EU:F:2006:139, para 40 – *André v Commission*; CST, F-24/06, ECLI:EU:F:2007:121, para 83 – *Abarca Montiel v Commission*; CST, F-131/07, ECLI:EU:F:2008:159, para 32 – *Baniel-Kubinova and Others v Commission*; CST, F-12/08, ECLI:EU:F:2009:57, para 36 – *Nardin v EP*; CST, F-32/08, ECLI:EU:F:2009:3, para 32 – *Klein v Commission*; CST, F-109/10, ECLI:EU:F:2012:66, para 24 – *AU v Commission*.

117 GC, T-128/17, ECLI:EU:T:2018:969, para 80 – *Torné v Commission*; ECJ, C-360/11, EU:C:2013:17, para 18 – *Commission v Spain*; as long as such interpretation does not run counter to the objectives pursued by the EU legislature or to the system established by the SR and the CEOS.

118 GC, T-92/91, ECLI:EU:T:1993:50 – *Henrichs v Commission* (offset of pension emoluments with national salaries); CST, F-32/08, ECLI:EU:F:2009:3, para 35 – *Klein v Commission* (dependent child); Reithmann (2011) 1 *EuR* 125.

119 ECJ, C-579/12 RX-II, ECLI:EU:C:2013:570, para 40 – *Réexamen Commission v Strack*; ECJ, C-12/11, ECLI:EU:C:2013:43, para 44 – *McDonagh*.

120 ECJ, C-25/02, ECLI:EU:C:2003:435, para 24 – *Rinke v Ärztekammer Hamburg*; CST, F-134/07, ECLI:EU:F:2009:51, para 86 – *Adjemian*; GC, T-495/04, ECLI:EU:T:2008:160, para 43 – *Belfass*.

concepts that motivated the legislation. Regarding how far such considerations can and should influence EU civil service law, a consistent line has not yet emerged and would have to be drawn very carefully, taking into account the special legal character and particular circumstances of the application of EU civil service law.[121] Altogether, there are four areas in which it appears that directives can have an impact on civil service law: (1) in cases of an explicit reference in civil service law to the provision of a directive; (2) in order to fill a gap in the SR; (3) where a directive expresses a general principle of law; and (4) as a rule of interpretation in line with the duty to cooperate in good faith.

Explicit reference

A provision may expressly refer to an article of a directive or to a directive as a whole. Article 1e(2) SR[122] contains a dynamic reference to directives, which the ECJ[123] interprets so widely that all directives relating to health protection (including the organisation of working time) are included. There is reason to criticise this as going too far,[124] partly because the SR already contain provisions on the organisation of working time, and partly because a softening of the conclusive normative character of the SR would lead to legal uncertainty. In another case too the ECJ[125] applies the reference under Article 1e(2) SR extensively to the provision[126] of a directive which is thereby extended into a specification of the fundamental right to paid annual leave based on Article 31(2) FRC. This also raises doubts because, given the existing (SR) rules on annual leave, there is no scope for applying the directive provision by reference, which would otherwise lead to a low (minimum) standard in the protection of fundamental rights.

Filling a gap in the SR

In its judgment on the *Landgren* case, the Civil Service Tribunal (CST) considered that a recourse to directives and international conventions was possible where, in its opinion, civil service law was incomplete, such as in regard to the scope of the obligation to motivate a decision that terminated the employment of a temporary agent.[127] The provision in the Directive would make it possible to complement the incomplete regulation under the SR. In the appeal, the GC[128] no longer applied this reference.

[121] Mader, 'Art 336 TFEU' in von der Groeben/Schwarze/Hatje/Terhechte (eds), *Europäisches Unionsrecht*, 8th edn (2024) para 9; Eggers/Linder, 'Art 336 TFEU' in Grabitz/Hilf/Nettesheim (eds), *Das Recht der EU* (2016) para 100; Kraemer, 'The European Union Civil Service Tribunal: A New Community Court Examined After Four Years of Operation' (2009) 46 *CMLR* 1909 ff; Petrlík, 'Invocabilité variable des directives dans le domaine de la fonction publique de l'Union européenne' (2013) *Law & European affairs* 803–11.

[122] 'Officials in active employment shall be accorded working conditions complying with appropriate health and safety standards at least equivalent to the minimum requirements applicable under measures adopted in these areas pursuant to the Treaties', and accordingly for contract staff and temporary agents under Art 10(1) and Art 80(4) CEOS. Reithmann, 'The duty of care in the case law of the European Union Civil Service Tribunal' (2019) 186.

[123] ECJ, C-579/12 RX-II, ECLI:EU:C:2013:570, para 42 f – *Réexamen Commission v Strack.*

[124] Eggers/Linder, 'Art 336 TFEU' in Grabitz/Hilf/Nettesheim (eds), *Das Recht der EU* (2016) para 96.

[125] ECJ, Jd Cases C-119/19 P and C-126/19 P, ECLI:EU:C:2020:676, paras 115–27 – *Commission v Carreras Sequeros and Others.*

[126] Art 7(1) Directive 2003/88/EC of the European Parliament and of the Council of 4 November 2003 on certain aspects of the organisation of working time [2003] OJ L299/9–19.

[127] CST, F-1/05, ECLI:EU:F:2006:112, paras 66/67 – *Landgren v ETF*; see, in the same judgment, para 69 on Convention 158 of the International Labour Organization adopted on 22 June 1982 and on the European Social Charter of the Council of Europe (No 163); with reference to ECJ, C-212/04, ECLI:EU:C:2006:443, para 54 – *Adeneler*. In another case on the question of a temporary interruption of parental leave, the CST, Jd Cases F-51/05 and F-18/06, ECLI:EU:F:2007:221, para 164 – *Duyster v Commission*, considered Directive No 96/34/EC of the Council of 3 June 1996 on the framework agreement on parental leave concluded by UNICE, CEEP and ETUC to be applicable.

[128] GC, T-404/06 P, ECLI:EU:T:2009:313, paras 169, 172 – *ETF v Landgren.*

General principles of law contained in directives

Provisions contained in a directive may bind an EU institution indirectly if they express a general principle of Union law which is thus applicable to the institution.[129] A general principle of law (not 'only' a principle) could, for example, be derived from the considerations contained in the preamble (recitals) of a directive. In such a case it is not the directive itself that becomes the basis, but the general principle derived from it. In *Carreras Sequeros*, a case in which the extent of annual leave entitlement under Article 31(2) FRC had to be determined, the GC[130] derived a principle of non-regression concerning standards of social protection from the text of the preamble of Directive 2003/88,[131] and asserted the existence of a desired continuous improvement of working conditions over time. On appeal, the ECJ[132] set the judgment aside. The ideas and reasoning on which a legislative act (directive) relies may contain or be built on a general principle of law that will transpire in the recitals of a directive.

In other instances where case-law refers to directives, it is not even expressly a 'general principle' that is invoked, but rather the concept of a certain *level of protection* afforded to persons under directives within the Member States, which according to the courts the EU institutions in their respective areas of competence shall not fall short of. For these cases, it is submitted that *this is* the *principle* that the courts actually refer to: maintaining the level of legal protection within the institutions, as it is established under the directives for the jurisdiction of the Member States. For example, according to Article 7 of Directive 2002/14[133] the Member States shall ensure that employees' representatives, when carrying out their functions, enjoy adequate protection and guarantees to enable them to perform properly the duties which have been assigned to them. The courts[134] refer to this provision to argue that the dismissal of an employee's representative on the ground of his or her status or the functions which he or she performs in his or her capacity as a representative is incompatible with the protection required by Article 7 of that Directive, and apply this to EU civil service.

It should be noted that if general principles determined from directives ultimately lead to an interpretation of fundamental rights under the Charter, there is a risk that secondary law may be used as a standard for fundamental rights. This would be contrary to the hierarchy of norms that demands the opposite: that fundamental rights and other primary law provisions should be used to interpret the content of secondary law. However, the directive itself remains an instrument of secondary law and for that reason cannot alter, let alone overrule, either a provision under the SR or a provision contained in the FRC. It cannot overrule the SR due to the specialised legal nature of the SR, and it cannot overrule the FRC because of the hierarchical structure: the Charter is on the level of primary law (Art 6(1) TEU), and is not subject to a modifying interpretation derived from secondary law.

[129] CST, F-65/07, ECLI:EU:F:2009:43, para 113 – *Aayhan and Others v EP*.

[130] GC, T-518/16, ECLI:EU:T:2018:873, para 87 – *Carreras Sequeros and Others v Commission*. See case study at the end of this section.

[131] Directive 2003/88/EG of the European Parliament and of the Council of 4 November 2003 on certain aspects of the organisation of working time [2003] OJ L299/9–19.

[132] ECJ, Jd Cases C-119/19 P and C-126/19 P, ECLI:EU:C:2020:676 – *Commission v Carreras Sequeros and Others*.

[133] Directive 2002/14/EC of the European Parliament and of the Council of 11 March 2002 establishing a general framework for informing and consulting employees in the European Community – Joint declaration of the European Parliament, the Council and the Commission on employee representation [2002] OJ L80/29–34.

[134] GC, T-571/17, ECLI:EU:T:2020:141, paras 158 ff – *UG v Commission*; ECJ, C-405/08, ECLI:EU:C:2010:69, paras 58/59 – *Ingeniørforeningen i Danmark*.

Duty to cooperate in good faith
In its judgment on *Aayhan*, the CST had to decide whether a directive may be relied on as regards relations between institutions and their staff. It found that an obligation to interpret the SR in the light of directives can be derived from the principle of sincere cooperation (which at the time was termed 'duty to cooperate in good faith').[135] The Member States have a duty to act in good faith, as do the institutions in relation to the Member States and the institutions among themselves.[136] The CST concluded that the directive does not in itself comprise the basis for a plea of illegality against a provision of the SR, but it may be relied on for interpreting the rules of the SR. For instance, the directive's provisions can make explicit the EU legislature's intention to make stable employment a prime objective in terms of the EU's labour relations.

Consequently, the brief overview of the four areas mentioned above confirms that care should be exercised when resorting to directives (or principles derived from directives) to develop civil service law. In practice, taking into account the comprehensive and autonomous character of the specialised labour law regime as set out in the SR and CEOS, there hardly seems to be any room left for gap-filling or an interpretation in conformity with directives that could not also be filled from within the SR or by recourse to fundamental rights. Such an approach would further curb judicial 'creativity' when deducing general principles from secondary legislation, and would therefore increase legal certainty. Conversely, fundamental rights and general principles of law do have an impact on the interpretation of civil service law, as the subsequent section will illustrate.

Case Study on Article 31(2) FRC, Directives and Reduction of Annual Leave

Reduction of the annual leave of staff working in Delegations

Case T-518/16, *Carreras Sequeros and Others v Commission* of 4 December 2018
Case C-119/19 P and C-126/19 P, *Commission v Carreras Sequeros and Others*

In Brief

At first instance, the General Court had quashed a central element of the most recent reform of staff regulations (2014) – a reduction in the number of annual leave days – that was of significance for colleagues working in Delegations. However, the decision was set aside in appeal by the Court of Justice (ECJ), and the action was dismissed.

Facts of the Case

The applicants were officials and contract agents working in EU Delegations when the most recent staff regulations reform (Regulation No 1023/2013) entered into force no later

[135] At the time based on Art 10 EC, later: Art 4(3) TEU; CST, F-65/07, ECLI:EU:F:2009:43, paras 111–21 – *Aayhan and Others v EP*.

[136] CST, F-65/07, ECLI:EU:F:2009:43, para 118 – *Aayhan and Others v EP*, with further references; CST, F-134/07, ECLI:EU:F:2009:51, para 93 – *Adjemian*; appeal: GC, T-325/09 P, ECLI:EU:T:2011:506 – *Adjemian and Others v Commission*.

than the start of 2014. In its new clause (Art 6 Annex X SR), the reform gradually reduced the basic annual leave entitlement from 42 days to 24 days during a three-year transition period.

Decisions of the General Court and of the Court of Justice

The General Court (GC) annulled the Commission's decisions that attributed a reduced number of annual leave days to the applicants, on the grounds that the legal basis for these decisions (the new Article 6 Annex X SR) was not correctly adopted in the legislative process. The Court stated that the second paragraph of Article 31 FRC ('fair and just working conditions') had to be read in conjunction with the text of Directive No 2003/88 on working time (before August 2004: Directive No 93/104) and the explanation given to Article 31(2) FRA (the right to an annual period of paid leave) by the Convention Presidency, as well as Articles 151 and 153 TFEU and Article 52(1) FRC on the limitation of Charter rights. In particular, the GC read the following words of the Directive's preamble

> (4) the improvement of workers' safety, hygiene and health at work is an objective which should not be subordinated to purely economic considerations

in the sense that although the Directive does not explicitly prohibit a reduction of standards, *in principle, it favours the improvement* of living and working conditions. A reduction of annual leave as such does not infringe Article 31(2) FRC, but – argued the GC – the significant reduction of annual leave over a period of 3 years from 42 days to 24 days is not compatible with the above-stated principle that *favours the improvement* of living and working conditions, and thus interferes with the right to annual leave.

Restrictions of fundamental rights have to meet objectives of general interest, and must not be disproportionate or affect the essence of the protected right. The legislator had brought forward the goals of modernisation, cost-efficiency and savings. Here, the GC stated that in view of the objective of the Directive ('the improvement of workers' safety, hygiene and health at work is an objective which should not be subordinated to purely economic considerations'), the above-stated reasons for the legislation do not constitute a legitimate objective because they invoke purely economic considerations in order to justify the reduction of annual leave.

As to the *proportionality* of the new Article 6 Annex X SR, the GC stated that the legislator had failed to examine the consequences of its legislation on the health and safety of the staff in third countries, and of other modalities of reduction, bearing in mind that annual leave directly contributes to improving the protection of the health and safety of workers. In addition, the legislator had not taken into account that staff serving *within* the EU are entitled to up to 30 days of annual leave. Finally, the legislator had not examined whether *rest leave* guarantees sufficient protection of health and safety, particularly since it is only granted on an exceptional basis.

Consequently, the GC concluded that when it adopted the new Article 6 Annex X, the legislator had not verified whether this provision was effectively justified by an objective of general interest and disproportionate to the objective being pursued.

The ECJ, in appeal, found that the annual leave entitlement of the applicants in any case exceeded the minimum requirements laid down in Article 7(1) of Directive 2003/88, namely 20 days of leave. Therefore the entitlement under the legislation 'cannot be regarded as being contrary to the nature and purpose of the fundamental right to paid annual leave' set out in Article 31(2) FRC. Despite leading to a reduction in the number of days of paid annual leave to which the persons concerned were entitled under an earlier provision, the new provision still maintained a period of leave that exceeded the minimum requirements laid down.

Comments

1. The central point of the GC judgment amounted to a reading of Article 31(2) FRC as being *in opposition to a setback of social standards*, at least to the extent that the reduction of the number of annual leave days was motivated exclusively by economic grounds and without a proper proportionality test having been applied. It invoked the Charter right (read in conjunction with the other provisions) as an *objective standard* and measure of the legislative act. This interpretation confirmed the significance of a Charter principle as a benchmark both for legislation and for the social protection of staff.
2. The motivation given for the legislative reform was thin and concentrated on three areas: modernisation, transparency and cost-saving. The GC held that a justification of the interference solely based on economic grounds (cost-saving) was insufficient in view of the rights protected by Article 31 FRC, and that a legislative proportionality test[137] could have led to other results. It was not the reduction of annual leave as such that was declared illegal by the GC, but the way the reduction was handled in the legislative process: it lacked the indication of an objective of general interest beyond purely economic reasons, and lacked a test of proportionality. The legislature was not prevented from reintroducing a reduction of annual leave, but when doing so it would have to (1) indicate objectives of general interest beyond those of a purely economic nature, and (2) conduct a proportionality test.
3. The GC adopted a high level of protection derived from the Charter and the Directive, which is also remarkable because the judgment explicitly concedes that Directive No 2003/88 requires a minimum annual paid leave of (only) 20 days, and that Article 23 of the Directive cannot be read as prohibiting a reduction of standards because it applies only when the Directive is being *implemented* (which was not the case here). Meanwhile, the GC derived an interpretation from indent 4 of the Directive's preamble (despite its inapplicability) and used it as a central motivation for its decision. The GC took an implicit stance regarding whether Article 31(2) FRC, Articles 151 and 153 TFEU constituted minimum standards or (higher) adequate standards of social protection: it did not adduce the minimum annual leave of 20 days explicitly stipulated in the Directive, but used the purpose of the Directive to argue that in principle it favours the improvement of living and working conditions. If this reading is maintained, any (substantial) deterioration of standards introduced by legislation would interfere with the right laid down in Article 31(2) FRC, and would require a qualified justification. That was the point that the ECJ in appeal did not want to uphold, and it therefore set aside the decision of the GC.

[137] Art 52(1), Art 51(1) FRC.

6. Impact of Fundamental Rights and General Principles of Law

Fundamental rights are applicable in the context of EU civil service law,[138] and influence the exercise of administrative decision-making.[139] Historically, civil service law is an area that has substantively contributed to the development of a fundamental rights system in Union law. Originally based on general principles of law and later positively codified and anchored in primary law as the EU Fundamental Rights Charter (FRC), fundamental rights have progressively gained in importance. It can be observed that case law is increasingly applying fundamental rights as a standard of legality, including its use to justify liability for damages in cases of violations of fundamental rights.[140] Since the time the FRC obtained binding legal nature in primary law and therefore the same hierarchical level as the Treaties[141] (ie, since the entry into force of the Treaty of Lisbon on 1 December 2009) the dynamic has further increased and hence improved the level of legal protection of staff. The circle of fundamental rights of the FRC applicable in civil service law is not a priori limited to certain areas, however it is clear that *ratione materiae* or *ratione personae* some rights will have typically more relevance in employment circumstances than others, such as the respect for private and family life,[142] protection of personal data,[143] freedom of thought, conscience and religion,[144] freedom of expression and information,[145] freedom of assembly and of association,[146] equality before the law and non-discrimination,[147] equality between women and men,[148] Integration of persons with disabilities,[149] right of collective bargaining and action,[150] fair and just working conditions,[151] family and professional life,[152] social security and social assistance, health care,[153] right to an effective remedy and to a fair trial,[154] presumption of innocence and rights of the defence,[155] etc.

The following baselines developed by the case-law can be retained when applying fundamental rights of the FRC in staff matters:

- According to Article 51(1) FRC, the Charter provisions are addressed, inter alia, to the institutions of the Union, which are, therefore, required to respect the rights enshrined in it.[156]

[138] Art 6(1) TEU, Art 51(1) sentence 1 FRC; ECJ, C-447/09, ECLI:EU:C:2011:573, para 47 – *Prigge and Others v Deutsche Lufthansa*; on the relationship to free movement (migrant workers) ECJ, C-293/03, ECLI:EU:C:2004:821, para 36 – *My*, and CST, F-54/06, ECLI:EU:F:2007:103 – *Davis v Commission*. For interpretation in compliance with the ECHR: CST, F-1/05, ECLI:EU:F:2006:112 – *Landgren v ETF*, *cf* Gervasoni (2010) 46 *Cahiers de droit européen* 776.

[139] Reithmann (2009) *EuR* 816; (2012) *EuR* 720.

[140] Violation of data confidentiality by the use of health-related data stemming from a medical assessment – damages €2,500, violation of Arts 7 and 8 FRC: GC, T-528/18, ECLI:EU:T:2019:594 – *XI v Commission*.

[141] Art 6(1) TEU; ECJ, C-447/09, ECLI:EU:C:2011:573, para 38 – *Prigge and Others v Deutsche Lufthansa*.

[142] Art 7 FRC.

[143] Art 8 FRC.

[144] Art 10 FRC.

[145] Art 11 FRC, chapter 3, II.9.

[146] Art 12 FRC.

[147] Arts 20 and 21 FRC.

[148] Art 23 FRC.

[149] Art 26 FRC.

[150] Art 28 FRC; on collective bargaining and the right of association, see chapter 4 II.

[151] Art 31 FRC.

[152] Art 33 FRC.

[153] Arts 34 and 35 FRC.

[154] Art 47 FRC. The right to a fair trial, also expressed in the term *audi et alteram partem*, forms part of the rights of the defence. As such it is both a principle of substantial law, eg, in disciplinary proceedings, and of procedural law to be complied with in litigation; on the latter aspect see chapter 2, IX.

[155] Art 48 FRC.

[156] ECJ, C-579/12 RX-II, ECLI:EU:C:2013:570, para 39 – *Réexamen Commission v Strack*.

- Limitations on the exercise of the rights recognised by the FRC in relation to matters of the EU civil service – even where these are in the interests of the service and promote the common good – must not result in a disproportionate encroachment on a fundamental right, and must respect the essence of that right (see below).[157]
- An act by EU institutions in the field of civil service law must be interpreted, as far as possible, in such a way as not to affect its validity and in conformity with primary law as a whole and, in particular, consistency with the provisions of the FRC.[158]
- In line with general interpretative rules (Art 52(1) FRC), an infringement of the *essence* of a fundamental right cannot be justified under any circumstances.
- Conversely, no staff employed may invoke his or her rights under the SR of the FRC in an abusive manner or with fraudulent intent.[159] A breach of the law by a staff employee must not benefit him or her.[160]

General principles of law

There is a significant impact of general principles of law in civil service matters beyond their systematic and historical function in the process of carving EU fundamental rights as described above. The most important general principles of law in this context are the principles of good administration,[161] equal treatment, the rights of the defence, and the right to effective judicial protection. These are expressed in individual rights, such as the right to an impartial,[162] fair decision made within a reasonable period of time, or the right to be heard, transparency and disclosure requirements, legal certainty[163] and the duty of care.[164,165] The right to be heard entails other rights, such as access to the case file and the right to obtain a properly motivated decision.[166] Similarly, the right to equal treatment is specifically reflected in various civil service constellations, such as in the right to career advancement or the requirement for stability of a selection board.[167] For example, if it can be shown that the Selection Board's unstable composition affected the equal treatment of the candidates of a competition, this would constitute a breach of essential procedural requirements without it being necessary to evidence that the result

[157] CST, F-40/05, ECLI:EU:F:2007:189, para 233 – *Andreasen v Commission* (on Art 17a SR).

[158] ECJ, C-579/12 RX-II, ECLI:EU:C:2013:570, para 40 – *Réexamen Commission v Strack*; ECJ, C-12/11, ECLI:EU:C:2013:43, para 44 – *McDonagh*.

[159] *cf* CST, F-92/09, ECLI:EU:F:2010:140, para 74 – *U v EP*.

[160] CST, F-40/10, ECLI:EU:F:2011:67, para 30 – *Lebedef v Commission*.

[161] Galetta, 'The General Principles of EU Administrative Procedural Law, In-depth Analysis for the JURI Committee of the EP', PE 519.224 (2015); Grzeszick, 'Das Grundrecht auf eine gute Verwaltung' (2006) *EuR* 161–81; Levi, 'Droits fondamentaux et principes généraux de droit de la fonction publique communautaire' in Govaere/Vandersanden (eds), *La fonction publique communautaire* (2008) 89 ff; Masson, 'L'apport du contentieux de la fonction publique au principe naissant en droit de l'Union européenne d'intelligibilite des normes' (2011) *Revue universelle des droits de l'homme* 96–103.

[162] On impartiality: GC, T-808/17, ECLI:EU:T:2019:832, paras 42 ff – *Pethke v EUIPO*; ECJ, C-139/18 P, ECLI:EU:C:2019:281, para 44 – *CJ v ECDC*; GC, T-47/18, ECLI:EU:T:2019:650, paras 45 ff – *UZ v EP*; CJEU Annual Report 2012, 216 with reference to CST, F-58/10, ECLI:EU:F:2012:130 – *Allgeier v FRA*; CST, F-131/15, ECLI:EU:F:2016:154 – *Stips v Commission*.

[163] Guarantee of legal certainty may appear in various facets: administratively, contractually or normatively, where it means that a legal basis must be sufficiently clear, precise and predictable as regards its effects, especially where they may have negative consequences on individuals and undertakings, see case study in chapter 4, IV.

[164] See chapter 3, II.9.d.

[165] Gervasoni (2010) 46 *Cahiers de droit européen* 780.

[166] Mader, *Verteidigungsrechte* (2006) 197 ff, 227 ff; ECJ, 69/83, ECLI:EU:C:1984:225, para 36 – *Lux v ECA*; CST, F-99/06, ECLI:EU:F:2007:87, para 92 – *Lópes Teruel v OHIM*. See section 6.c.

[167] GC, T-610/18 ECLI:EU:T:2021:5, para 118 – *ZR v EUIPO*; GC,T-165/03, EU:T:2004:331, para 39 – *Vonier v Commission*; CST, F-5/08, ECLI:EU:F:2010:111, paras 39 ff, 48ff, 52 ff – *Brune v Commission*.

of the competition might have been different if the essential procedural requirements in question had been complied with.[168]

It is noteworthy that the principle of *equal treatment* has a different content depending on whether it addresses measures taken by the appointing authority or whether it applies to the EU legislature.[169] Further, also principles of European labour and social law addressed to the Member States can be of importance in conjunction with Article 1e SR and the labour law duty of loyalty towards civil servants.[170] *Loyalty* is a Janus-faced principle that addresses the institutions as employers in their relations towards the servants and at the same time obliges the servants towards their institution.[171]

The *principle of proportionality* (an expression of the rule of law) is widely being used in Union law including in EU civil service law, as a method of choice among various appropriate measures, and also in order to balance or reconcile competing interests or values of comparable nature. It is expressly mentioned in Article 1d(6) SR next to non-discrimination and acknowledged as a general principle of Union law.[172] In a very general expression, the 'content and form of Union action shall not exceed what is necessary to achieve the objectives of the Treaties' (Art 5(4) TEU). Restricting measures must be suitable to reach the objective of general interest pursued, the measures adopted should not exceed the limits of what is appropriate and necessary in order to attain the objectives legitimately pursued by the legislation in question and, where there is a choice between several appropriate measures, recourse must be had to the least onerous, and the disadvantages caused must not be disproportionate to the aims pursued.[173] This last element of proportionality is not always applied, sometimes it is conceived as a ban to impose a burden on the individual that is excessive in relation to the objective sought to be achieved (proportionality in the narrow sense).

Of lesser importance are principles relating to the objectives of administrative organisation, such as filling a permanent position with a civil servant,[174] the overall structure of remuneration within an institution,[175] or programmatic principles such as the unity of European administration[176] or the uniformity[177] of civil service law.

[168] GC, T-535/22, ECLI:EU:T:2023:653, paras 77 ff, 82 – *NZ v Commission* (incomplete selection board at deliberation, compensation for non-material damage suffered €4,000).

[169] See here below, section b. and in chapter 2, VII.2.

[170] CST, F-105/09, ECLI:EU:F:2011:41, para 54 – *Scheefer v EP* on Art 1e SR and Council Directive 1999/70/EC of 28 June 1999 concerning the framework agreement on fixed-term work concluded by ETUC, UNICE and CEEP [1999] OJ L175/43; CST, F-65/07, ECLI:EU:F:2009:43, paras 118 ff – *Aayhan and Others v Commission*; GC, T-325/09 P, ECLI:EU:T:2011:506, paras 96, 103 – *Adjemian and Others v Commission*; CST, F-134/07, ECLI:EU:F:2009:51, para 86 – *Adjemian*. On minimum requirements for improving the living and working conditions of workers in the Member States by aligning national provisions and practices, see CST, F-65/07, ECLI:EU:F:2009:43, paras 113 ff– *Aayhan and Others v Commission*; GC, T-268/11 P, ECLI:EU:T:2012:588, paras 33–55 – *Commission v Strack*, set aside in appeal: ECJ, C-579/12 RX-II, ECLI:EU:C:2013:570. On Directive 92/85/EEC: CST, F-54/11, ECLI:EU:F:2012:114, paras 133 ff, 138 – *BG v Ombudsman*. See chapter 3, II.17.c.

[171] See chapter 3, II.7. and 9, and case study at the end of chapter 4, IV.3.

[172] *cf* Art 52(1) FRC; TFEU Protocol No 2 on the application of the principles of subsidiarity and proportionality [2016] OJ C202/206–09; also Art 14 Annex IX SR.

[173] *cf* ECJ, C-173/22 P, ECLI:EU:C:2023:932, paras 52/53 – *MG v EIB*; ECJ, C-55/94, ECLI:EU:C:1995:411, para 37 – *Gebhard*; Kadelbach, 'Art 5 TEU' in von der Groeben/Schwarze/Hatje/Terhechte (eds), *Europäisches Unionsrecht*, 8th edn (2022) paras 49–54; Jarass, 'Art 28 FRC' *Charta der Grundrechte der EU*, paras 15/16.

[174] CST, F-8/10, ECLI:EU:F:2010:151, paras 78, 81 – *Gheysens v Council*; CST, F-59/11, ECLI:EU:F:2012:164 – *Sipos v OHIM*.

[175] CST, F-31/09, ECLI:EU:F:2010:139, paras 17 ff – *Noël v Council*.

[176] CST, F-83/05, ECLI:EU:F:2010:158, paras 49, 55, 58 – *Ezerniece Liljeberg and Others v Commission*.

[177] Uniformity among institutions is a concept rather weakly rooted in staff management: instead, within the framework of their discretionary powers, the institutions enjoy a 'principle of autonomy'. However, this is not the case where the principle of equal treatment is violated: GC, T-453/20, ECLI:EU:T:2021:339, para 52 – *KZ v Commission*; GC, T-580/16, ECLI:EU:T:2017:291, para 57, *Azoulay and Others v EP*.

a. Good Administration

The principle of good administration (also expressed in Art 41 FRC) is a wide-ranging principle which contains aspects of relevance for the employment relationship, as it requires that the interests of employees must also be taken into account when deciding on the situation of an official.[178] 'Good administration' is a collective term that embraces other principles in which it crystallises.[179] For that reason, in earlier literature, good administration has been described as a *programmatic statement*: it does not confer a right on the individual whose violation would lead to the annulment of acts.[180] Nor does it serve as a benchmark of legality for legislation duly adopted by the Council.[181] What is of higher importance for the benefit of the staff are the individual and specific rights that can be invoked under the principle of good administration. Such individual and specific rights include an impartial[182] (ie, both subjectively impartial and objectively impartial)[183] procedure, the right to have matters that affect oneself handled fairly and within a reasonable time, reasonable deadlines, the right to be heard, access to files (in particular, personnel files),[184] the right to have all relevant aspects of a case carefully and diligently examined,[185] and the obligation of the administration to state reasons for its decisions.[186]

Compliance with diligence requirements can play a role in cases of Union liability. For instance, the institution has to diligently collect the factual information necessary for the exercise of its broad discretion. This is even more important where the exercise of that discretion is only subject to a limited judicial review that is confined to examining whether a manifest error has been committed. So the competent institution's obligation to examine carefully and impartially all the relevant elements of an individual case is a necessary prerequisite for enabling the courts to ascertain whether the elements of fact and law on which the exercise of that broad discretion depends were present. There is no discretion concerning the respect for the principle of diligence. Consequently, a simple breach of the principle of diligence is sufficient to establish the existence of a sufficiently serious breach in terms of the liability preconditions.[187]

Where an institution takes its administrative decisions[188] too hesitantly, this can constitute a violation, as can the failure to comply with the rules of jurisdiction.[189] In special cases, the principle of good administration can create an obligation on the side of the administration to provide a more extensive statement of reasons for an act.[190]

[178] CST, F-126/07, ECLI:EU:F:2008:136, para 174 – *Van Beers v Commission*; CST, T-11/03, ECLI:EU:T:2004:77 – *Afari v ECB*. On the inviolability of the home, see Gervasoni (2010) 46 *Cahiers de droit européen* 776 on CST, F-56/09, ECLI:EU:F:2010:48, paras 58 ff – *Marcuccio v Commission*.

[179] *cf* the term 'good governance' or, most prominently, the values under Art 2 TEU as the highest constitutional level from which general principles of law are being derived.

[180] Gervasoni (2010) 46 Cahiers *de droit européen* 779; Levi/Rodrigues et al, *Fonction publique de l'Union européenne* (2020) 23.

[181] CST, F-29/09, ECLI:EU:F:2010:120, para 71 – *Lebedef and Jones v Commission*.

[182] Impartiality in appeal proceedings against an assessment: GC, T-808/17, ECLI:EU:T:2019:832, paras 42 ff – *Pethke v EUIPO*; ECJ, C-139/18 P, ECLI:EU:C:2019:281, para 44 – *CJ v ECDC*; on impartiality in disciplinary proceedings: GC, T-47/18, ECLI:EU:T:2019:650, paras 45 ff – *UZ v EP*, confirmed in ECJ, C-894/19 P, ECLI:EU:C:2021:863 – *EP v UZ*.

[183] Subjectively impartial: no member of the body concerned shall display bias or personal prejudice; objectively impartial: the institution must offer sufficient structural guarantees to eliminate any reasonable doubt as to any prejudice, GC, T-808/17, ECLI:EU:T:2019:832, para 46 – *Pethke v EUIPO*.

[184] CST, F-102/15, EU:F:2016:117 – *FS v EESC*.

[185] ECJ, C-269/90, ECLI:EU:C:1991:438, para 22 – *Technische Universität München*.

[186] CST, F-99/06, ECLI:EU:F:2007:87, para 92 – *Lópes Teruel v OHIM*.

[187] GC, T-351/03, ECLI:EU:T:2007:212, paras 117/118 – *Schneider Electric v Commission*; GC, T-217/11, ECLI:EU:T:205:238, paras 84–86 – *Staelen v Ombudsman*.

[188] GC, T-394/03, ECLI:EU:T:2006:111, para 162 – *Angeletti v Commission*, see chapter 3, V.1.

[189] CST, F-45/08 and F-99/07, ECLI:EU:F:2009:84, paras 87/88 – *Bernard v Europol*, a violation which may be acknowledged ex officio.

[190] This will however not be checked ex officio by the court, meaning that a failure of the administration to provide an extended justification would already need to have been raised at the stage of the complaint, see CST, F-9/11,

At the end of this chapter, three of the general principles of law with the highest importance in EU civil service law will be highlighted, namely: equal treatment, the right to be heard, and legitimate expectations.

b. Equal Treatment

In accordance with Article 1d(1) SR (and similarly under Art 21 FRC), 'any discrimination based on any ground such as sex, race, colour, ethnic or social origin, genetic features, language, religion or belief, political or any other opinion, membership of a national minority, property, birth, disability, age, or sexual orientation shall be prohibited'. The principle of equal treatment must not prevent the institutions from maintaining or adopting measures providing for specific advantages in order to make it easier for the under-represented sex to pursue a vocational activity, or to prevent or compensate for disadvantages in professional careers.[191] Similarly, positive measures for maintaining or making adaptations for persons with disabilities are allowed.[192] The protection of the rights and interests of officials with disabilities must always have its limit in compliance with the applicable rules – an institution's duty to have regard for the welfare of its staff can never induce it to infringe the law.[193]

A legislative and administrative principle

The principle of equal treatment is addressed both to the legislature when adopting norms and to the appointing authority when adopting administrative decisions (though the content of the principle is not identical in both cases). The principle requires 'that comparable situations must not be treated differently, and different situations must not be treated in the same way, unless such treatment is objectively justified'.[194] Specifically for the area of the SR, the objective justification must take into account the purpose of the provision and the group of persons concerned.[195]

No 'equality in injustice'

Staff members may not rely on equal treatment in breaches of the law: there is no such thing as 'equality in injustice'.[196] Thus, the obligation to treat staff in similar situations equally finds its limitation in the principle of legality – the need to comply with the law.[197]

ECLI:EU:F:2011:196, para 32 – *Sabbag Afota v Council*; CST, F-74/10, ECLI:EU:F:2011:171, paras 44/45, 49 – *Kimman v Commission* on the separate justification in appraisals, appeal decision GC, T-644/11 P, ECLI:EU:T:2014:613 – *Kimman v Commission*.

[191] Art 1d(2) SR; on positive measures, see GC, T-181/01, ECLI:EU:T:2005:33 – *Hectors*.

[192] Art 1d(4) SR.

[193] CST, F-62/10, ECLI:EU:F:2011:141, paras 71, 80–82 – *Esders v Commission* (on the official's refusal of a change of the place of his service from Berlin to Brussels).

[194] ECJ, C-236/09, ECLI:EU:C:2011:100, para 28 – *Test-Achats*; ECJ, C-127/07, ECLI:EU:C:2008:728, para 23 – *Arcelor Atlantique et Lorraine and Others*.

[195] ECJ, Jd Cases C-75/82 and 117/82, ECLI:EU:C:1984:116, para 17 – *Razzouk and Beydoun*; ECJ, C-443/07, ECLI:EU:C:2008:67 – *Centeno Mediavilla*. On unequal treatment due to a change in the law, see CST, F-115/05, ECLI:EU:F:2007:10, para 59 – *Vienne and Others v EP*; CST, F-47/07, ECLI:EU:F:2009:103, para 53 – *Behmer v EP*. A disciplinary sanction against or dismissal of a pregnant woman does not yet indicate discrimination, see CST, F-54/11, ECLI:EU:F:2012:114, paras 135 ff – *BG v Ombudsman*, appeal dismissed. For substantial law on non-discrimination and equal treatment, see chapter 3, II.9.a., with a case study on equal treatment (*Hebberecht v EEAS*).

[196] CST, F-80/09, ECLI:EU:F:2010:165, para 45 – *Lenz v Commission*; CST, F-4/07, ECLI:EU:F:2008:22, paras 34, 81 – *Skoulidi v Commission*; GC, T-329/03, ECLI:EU:T:2005:103 – *Ricci v Commission*, but the result is different in CST, F-115/07, ECLI:EU:F:2009:41 – *Balieu-Steinmetz and Noworyta v EP*, because the institution could not prove that there was in fact no legal basis for the requested payments, CJEU Annual Report 2009, 202.

[197] GC, T-621/22, ECLI:EU:T:2023:805, paras 109/110 – *SB v EEAS*.

Various fields of application of equal treatment

Strengthening the ban on discrimination in the SR was a central part of the reforms of 2004 and 2014.[198] The principle of equal treatment of men and women – Article 1d(2) SR – is intended in the abstract,[199] ie, it is to be taken into account at recruitment or promotion even where there is no choice between different applicants.[200] Article 1d(2) SR permits specific preferential[201] measures and obliges the appointing authorities to take reasonable precautions.[202] As a corollary of equal treatment, the 2014 reform revised the definition of disability and expressly included the possibility of benefits (Art 1d(4) SR). Also, non-marital partnerships are treated like marriages within the framework of Article 1(2) lit c Annex VII SR.[203] The SR explicitly state that any limitation of the principle of non-discrimination and the principle of proportionality must be justified on objective and reasonable grounds, and must be aimed at legitimate objectives in the general interest in the framework of staff policy.[204] These objectives may in particular justify stipulating a mandatory retirement age and a minimum age for drawing a retirement pension.[205]

Reverse burden of proof

In order to increase the probability of enforcement in the area of equal treatment (Art 1d SR), the *onus* is reversed (whereas this reversal does not apply in disciplinary proceedings): where persons covered by the SR who consider themselves wronged establish facts from which it may be presumed that there has been direct or indirect discrimination, the *onus* will be on the institution to prove that there has been no breach of the principle of equal treatment.[206] The question as to how far facts have to be established in order to give rise to the presumption of a discrimination, has frequently been answered by the courts with a plausibility yardstick, adjusted to the various fields of labour law application, also accepting statistical argumentation. For example, when a measure distinguishing between employees on the basis of their hours of work has in practice an adverse impact on substantially more members of one or other sex, it would be up to the employer to show that it is based on objectively justified factors unrelated to any discrimination on grounds of sex. Or, in respect to remuneration, where a system of pay is wholly lacking in transparency, it is for the employer to prove that his practice in the matter of wages is not discriminatory, if a female worker establishes, in relation to a relatively large number of employees, that the average pay for women is less than that for men.[207] The facts from which it may be presumed that there has been direct or indirect discrimination in assessing the merits of staff could stem from a comparison of the merits which does not take account of reduced performance placing one of the compared officials in an objectively different situation from the others.[208]

[198] *cf* Levi, 'Droits fondamentaux et principes généraux de droit de la fonction publique communautaire' in Govaere/Vandersanden (eds), *La fonction publique communautaire* (2008) 82. On discrimination CST, F-80/09, ECLI:EU:F:2010:165, paras 41 ff – *Lenz v Commission*. On compensatory measures in the event of a disability under Art 1d SR, Art 80(4) CEOS.

[199] GC, T-45/90, ECLI:EU:T:1992:7 – *Speybrouck v EP*.

[200] Art 1d (2) SR – a directly applicable right of the individual: ECJ, C-93/19 P, ECLI:EU:C:2020:946, para 38 – *EEAS v Hebberecht*.

[201] A non-legally binding, programmatic phrase in the sense that the individual cannot directly rely on Art 1d(3) for positive discrimination, but only on the provisions implementing the norm: ECJ, C-93/19 P, ECLI:EU:C:2020:946, paras 38 ff – *EEAS v Hebberecht*; CST, F-46/07, ECLI:EU:F:2008:129, paras 181 ff – *Tzirani v Commission*.

[202] Art 1d(4), Art 28 lit e SR for the disabled.

[203] CST, F-122/06, ECLI:EU:F:2007:208, paras 36, 52 – *Roodhuijzen v Commission*.

[204] Art 1d(6) SR.

[205] *cf* Art 1d(6); ECJ, C-411/05, ECLI:EU:C:2007:604 – *Palacios de la Villa*.

[206] Art 1d(5) SR.

[207] ECJ, 109/88, ECLI:EU:C:1989:383, para 16 – *Danfoss*; ECJ, C-127/92, ECLI:EU:C:1993:859, para 14 – *Enderby*.

[208] CST, F-50/11, ECLI:EU:F:2012:51, para 65 – *Buxton v EP*.

Regarding the establishment of facts which allow a presumption of discrimination, jurisprudence has opined that previous circumstances must to be taken into account. In that sense, a discrimination (which in the case decided, was based on sex) cannot be presumed with regard to an act which has previously been found not to be otherwise vitiated by an error of law or a manifest error of assessment.[209] Also, the GC found that discrimination 'may not be presumed to exist merely because a candidate is pregnant'.[210]

Scope of application ratione personae
The provisions on equal treatment and non-discrimination under Article 1d SR apply to officials, and 'by analogy' also to temporary agents and to contract staff,[211] as well as to special advisers,[212] and to accredited parliamentary assistants,[213] but not to local staff.[214]

c. Right to be Heard/Rights of the Defence

Fundamental procedural right
The right to be heard – as an important element of the *rights of the defence* – is widely recognised in case-law as a general legal principle of EU law and a fundamental procedural right. There are individual areas under statutory law in which it is laid down explicitly,[215] but it applies even beyond such areas as it has a horizontal scope of application in EU administrative law.[216] It is of great practical and legal importance. The right of a person to be heard before any individual measure is taken which would affect him or her adversely is enshrined in Article 41(2) lit a FRC.[217] It is supplemented by the right of access to the file[218] and to other relevant documents.[219] Access to the file is to be granted even where there is no express stipulation of the right.[220] In terms of scope, in general the right to be heard includes the right to be informed before a decision is made, to comment on the information presented, and therefore to be able to influence the decision-making process.[221] In addition, the person concerned is entitled to be informed in sufficient detail, at the stage of submitting his or her observations, what action may be taken on the basis of that information.[222]

The right to be heard does not become superfluous merely because the person concerned has the opportunity to lodge a complaint,[223] or because there are internal (administrative) difficulties

[209] GC, Jd Cases T-112/96 and T-115/96, ECLI:EU:T:1999:134, para 116 – *Séché v Commission*; GC, T-706/16 P, ECLI:EU:T:2017:758, para 57 – *HB v Commission.*
[210] GC, T-181/01, ECLI:EU:T:2003:13, para 124 – *Hectors v EP.*
[211] Art 10(1) CEOS and Art 80(4) CEOS respectively. The term 'by analogy' does not mean that it has exactly the same meaning as in the SR, but is applied in a way that is 'similar where the circumstances are comparable'.
[212] Art 124 CEOS.
[213] Art 128(1) CEOS, yet taking into account the relationship of mutual trust between the MEP and his accredited parliamentary assistant. Currall in Perillo/Giacobbo-Peyronnel (eds), *Statut de la fonction publique de l'Union européenne: Commentaire article par article* (2017) 67/68.
[214] *contra*, Arts 120–22 CEOS.
[215] Art 26 SR (right to personal file); Art 38 SR (secondment); Art 43(3) SR (appraisal/annual report); Art 49 SR (compulsory resignation); Arts 3, 22 and 23 Annex IX (disciplinary proceedings).
[216] Mader, *Verteidigungsrechte* (2006) 44, 229 ff, 387 ff; Gattinara, *ERA-Forum* (2019) 19(4) 571–83, available at: link.springer.com/article/10.1007/s12027-018-0543-.
[217] *cf* complementary rights in Art 47 and Art 48 FRC.
[218] ECJ, 115/80, ECLI:EU:C:1981:308, para 12 – *Demont.*
[219] CST, F-27/09, ECLI:EU:F:2014:212, para 54 – *Hanschmann v Europol.*
[220] ECJ, C-316/97, ECLI:EU:C:1998:558, para 33 – *EP v Gaspari.*
[221] GC, T-566/16, ECLI:EU:T:2018:278, para 30 – *Josefsson v EP*; Mader, *Verteidigungsrechte* (2006) 198.
[222] GC, T-650/20, ECLI:EU:T:2023:305, para 65 – *KD v EUIPO.*
[223] GC, T-237/00, ECLI:EU:T:2005:437, para 94 – *Reynolds v EP.*

in the decision-making process,[224] or because it is argued that the 'same decision would be taken anyway'.[225] The right to be heard is also an expression of mutual trust in the employment relationship,[226] and survives a unilateral or bilateral erosion: even where the relationship of trust is already destroyed, the right to be heard must not be dispensed with.[227] If a person concerned does not attend a hearing in disciplinary proceedings for personal health reasons, the decision to impose sanctions nevertheless violates his or her rights of the defence unless the administration can prove that the person concerned is responsible for his or her non-attendance.[228]

Dynamic intensity

In terms of intensity, the scope of the right to be heard varies dynamically:[229] whereas on matters in which the appointing authority's decision-making power is characterised by wide discretion, the respect for procedural rights as a balancing counterweight is of particular importance.[230] The extent of the right to be heard differs with the intensity with which the staff member is affected.[231] A staff member does not necessarily have to be consulted before organisational measures are taken (eg, internal reorganisation of services),[232] nor is there a mandatory hearing of senior (ie, political) officials[233] in cases of dismissal.[234] Hearings are not required to communicate with the staff member in their mother tongue.[235]

Healing of the infringement

Where the rights of the defence have been infringed, a healing of the administrative procedure, for example through a subsequent (later) hearing, is not ruled out a priori, but may become impossible due to time constraints.[236]

[224] ECJ, C-297/08, ECLI:EU:C:2010:115, para 83 – *Commission v Italy*; CST, F-137/14, ECLI:EU:F:2016:14, para 77 – *GV v EEAS*.

[225] CST, F-55/14, ECLI:EU:F:2015:66, para 40 – *EE v Commission*; CST, F-137/14, ECLI:EU:F:2016:14, paras 78/79 – *GV v EEAS*.

[226] ECJ, 125/8, ECLI:EU:C:1981:248 – *Arning v Commission*; GC, T-52/90, ECLI:EU:T:1992:12 – *Volger v EP*. On the observance of the rights of defence and the right to be heard, Gervasoni (2010) 46 *Cahiers de droit européen* 776; CJEU Annual Report 2012, 216 with further references, CST, F-26/10, ECLI:EU:F:2011:163, paras 49, 53 – *AZ v Commission*, not applicable, for example, in the procedure for determining disability, CST, F-41/06 RENV, ECLI:EU:F:2012:149, para 79 – *Marcuccio v Commission*, see chapter 3, V.7.b; or against an internal reassignment of post, CST, Jd Cases F-88/09 and 48/10, ECLI:EU:F:2012:171, para 144 – *Z v ECJ*, GC, T-88/13P, ECLI:EU:T:2015:393 – *Z v ECJ*. On the relationship between the right to be informed and the confidentiality of internal investigations, eg, CST, F-63/09, ECLI:EU:F:2012:193 – *Donati v ECB*; CST, Jd Cases F-7/11 and 60/11, ECLI:EU:F:2012:195, paras 100 ff – *AX v ECB*, also in view of Art 41 FRC (due to the efficiency of such investigations, only access to the content, not to the document itself); CST, Jd Cases F-88/09 and 48/10, ECLI:EU:F:2012:171, paras 95, 222, 78 – *Z v ECJ* (here only inspection by the counsel in the court's premises); the confidentiality of testimonies in front of an investigative panel can also be in the interests of the staff employed and may be relevant for the decision making, see CST, F-58/10, ECLI:EU:F:2012:130, paras 73, 76/77 – *Allgeier v FRA*. On the admission of legal counsel, see CST, F-63/09, ECLI:EU:F:2012:193, paras 137 ff – *Donati v ECB*; CST, Jd Cases F-88/09 and 48/10, ECLI:EU:F:2012:171, para 60 – *Z v ECJ*.

[227] GC, T-160/17, ECLI:EU:T:2019:1, para 40 – *RY v Commission*; GC, T-59/17, ECLI:EU:T:2019:140 – *L v EP*; disputed: Gervasoni (2010) 46 *Cahiers de droit européen* 785 with reference to CST, F-89/08, ECLI:EU:F:2010:11 – *P v EP*.

[228] GC, T-743/16 RENV, ECLI:EU:T:2018:937, para 148 – *CX v Commission*.

[229] Mader, *Verteidigungsrechte* (2006) 198 ff, 235 ff.

[230] ECJ, 19/70, ECLI:EU:C:1971:74, paras 8 ff – *Almini*; Mader, *Verteidigungsrechte* (2006) 201.

[231] CST, F-43/10, ECLI:EU:F:2012:184, para 91 – *Cerafogli v ECB*.

[232] GC, T-597/16, ECLI:EU:T:2018:338, para 80 – *OW v EASA*.

[233] ECJ, C-111/02 P, ECLI:EU:C:2004:265, paras 57 ff – *EP v Reynolds*.

[234] ECJ, 19/87, ECLI:EU:C:1988:165 – *Hecq v Commission*; ECJ, C-149/86, ECLI:EU:C:1988:179 – *Santarelli*; GC, T-33/90, ECLI:EU:T:1991:59 – *Von Bonkewitz-Lindner v EP*; CST, F-4/09, ECLI:EU:F:2010:24, paras 58, 61 – *De Britto Patrício-Dias v Commission*.

[235] CST, Jd Cases F-51/05 and F-18/06, ECLI:EU:F:2007:221, paras 57, 59 – *Duyster v Commission*; CST, F-134/06, ECLI:EU:F:2008:40, para 101 – *Bordini v Commission*.

[236] Mader, *Verteidigungsrechte* (2006) 369 ff, 368 on the question of healing of violated rights of the defence in court proceedings: according to the correct opinion, healing at that stage is to be rejected; in the administrative procedure GC, T-225/18, ECLI:EU:T:2019:595, para 44 – *Manéa v CdT*.

Condition of decisiveness
The legal consequences of violating the right to be heard – and in the same context, the principle of fair trial (*audi et alteram partem/principe du contradictoire*) – depend on the decisiveness of the infringement: an omitted or incorrect hearing only leads to the annulment of the decision made in violation of the procedure if the procedure could have led to a different result without the irregularity;[237] or, in another formulation specific for civil service law, if a different result cannot be completely ruled out.[238] Practically, this means that only in the exceptional case where the appointing authority could not possibly have taken any other decision, the infringement of the rights of the defence does not lead to the annulment of the decision (because it would inevitably lead to the adoption of a decision identical, in substance, to the annulled decision).[239] For that assessment, the objective circumstances at the time of the administrative decision have to be taken into account.[240] See the case study at the end of this chapter.

d. Legitimate Expectations

Preconditions
The fundamental principle of the protection of legitimate expectations[241] comes into play when a person acting within his or her competences has created legitimate expectations by means of precise, unconditional and consistent assurances, the non-fulfilment of which would be contrary to good faith.[242] The principle of legitimate expectations is asserted by staff in cases across a wide

[237] CST, F-50/10, ECLI:EU:F:2012:51, para 89 – *Buxton v EP*; GC, Jd Cases T-246/04 and T-71/05, ECLI:EU:T:2007:34, para 149 – *Wunenburger v Commission*; CST, F -51/07, ECLI:EU:F:2008:112, para 81 – *Bui Van v Commission*; ECJ, C-173/22 P, ECLI:EU:C:2023:932, paras 36–41 – *MG v EIB* (whereas the administration has to exercise their own discretion and cannot, for doing this, refer to national authorities). However not, if procedural errors were only of minor importance: CST, F-113/10, ECLI:EU:F:2012:20, para 75 – *AT v EACEA*. On the error when exercising discretion Reithmann (2008) *EuR* 294; (2009) *EuR* 816; (2011) 1 *EuR* 142; Schiano/Potvin-Solis (2012) *RUE* 613, 615: the error does not have to be serious; Gervasoni (2010) 46 *Cahiers de droit européen* 761, 781 ff in cases with a particularly large discretion, CST, F-10/07, ECLI:EU:F:2007:161, paras 66–71 – *Botos v Commission*. Critical as to an individual assessment of the errors in addition to the overall picture: Potvin-Solis/Lelièvre (2012) *RUE* 271. On the assessment by examination boards see Gervasoni (2010) 46 *Cahiers de droit européen* 742. Overview of errors and consequences Reithmann (2014) *EuR* 125. Basically, the objective circumstances at the time of the administrative decision are decisive.

[238] ECJ, C-831/18 P, ECLI:EU:2020:481, para 106 – *Commission v RQ*; ECJ, C-141/08 P, ECLI:EU:C:2009:598, para 94 – *Foshan Shunde Yongjian Housewares & Hardware v Council*; this also applies in litigation: ECJ, C-831/18 P, ECLI:EU:C:2020:481, para 106 – *Commission v RQ*, and chapter 2, IX. On the rights of the defence and potential different outcome of the proceedings Mader, *Verteidigungsrechte* (2006) 377 ff, 387 ff.

[239] ECJ, C-173/22 P, ECLI:EU:C:2023:932, para 37 – *MG v EIB*.

[240] Where the administration does not have full knowledge of the circumstances when taking the decision: CST, F-97/12, ECLI:EU:F:2013:142, para 60 – *Thomé v Commission*.

[241] *cf* Levi, 'Droits fondamentaux et principes généraux de droit de la fonction publique communautaire' in Govaere/Van dersanden (eds), *La fonction publique communautaire* (2008) 89; GC, T-235/94, EU:T:1996:22, paras 63 and 65 – *Galtieri v EP*; GC, T-329/03, ECLI:EU:T:2005:103, para 79 – *Ricci v Commission*; CST, F-4/07 ECLI:EU:F:2008:22 – *Skoulidi v Commission*; CST, F-126/07, ECLI:EU:F:2008:136, para 70 – *Van Beers v Commission*; CST, F-46/07, ECLI:EU:F:2008:129, para 159 – *Tzirani v Commission*. The protection of legitimate expectations must not lead to a practice that would be incompatible with the SR: CST, F-81/10, ECLI:EU:F:2011:120, para 67 – *Praskevicius v EP*; CST, F-14/11, ECLI:EU:F:2012:74, para 61 – *AW v Commission*.

[242] On assurances: CST, F-28/10, ECLI:EU:F:2011:23, para 41 – *Mioni v Commission*: not just by having paid out amounts of money (even over years); and CST, F-82/08, ECLI:EU:F:2011:45, para 100 – *Clarke and Others v OHIM* (withdrawal of a decision does not imply any assurance that the decision will not be issued in the same way again); GC, T-3/92, ECLI:EU:T:1994:15, para 58 – *Latham v Commission*.

range of subject matters.[243] In order to be able to claim entitlement to it, four[244] conditions have to be satisfied:

- The first consists of the mentioned three sub-conditions of the *precise, unconditional* and *consistent* assurance given.
- The second is that the assurance must originate from authorised and reliable sources, given to the person concerned by the EU authorities.
- The third condition is that an assurance must be such as to give rise to a legitimate expectation on the part of the person to whom they are addressed.
- The fourth condition is that the assurance must comply with the law.[245]

The fourth condition raises the question of how far an official can rely on the lawfulness of an act of the administration where an error is committed which is or is not realised by the administration itself. Here, the case-law states that the expectations of a staff member cannot be regarded as legitimate, where the official exercising due care could not fail to be aware of the unlawful nature of the act. Officials cannot rely on legitimate expectations in the continuation of manifestly unlawful acts, even if the administration itself failed on a number of occasions to realise its error.[246] Organisational measures of transitional and provisional character cannot amount to an assurance, either;[247] similarly, those acts that are, by their nature, undergoing constant change according to changes in the economic climate, such as that of the fixing of weightings affecting officials' pensions or correction factors are not assurances as such.[248] Also, the fact that a candidate who has passed a competition procedure is inscribed on a reserve list does not amount to an assurance.[249] In the same way (violation of the third condition of the principle), it cannot give rise to a legitimate expectation on the part of a nominated candidate to a post, if the nomination was challenged at the court by a competitor within the time limits for bringing an action.[250] The fourth (and third) condition would not be satisfied, if an appointment procedure of the person relying on legitimate expectations was vitiated by an infringment of the recruitment procedure stipulated in the vacancy notice.[251]

Legitimate expectations vs changes

A recurring question is whether this principle can be claimed in order to prevent disadvantageous consequences of legal or legislative changes. Yet, legitimate expectations cannot hamper

[243] CST, F-50/06, ECLI:EU:F:2007:70, para 43 – *Lebedef-Caponi v Commission* (assessment); CST, F-25/05, ECLI:EU:F:2006:47, para 54 – *McSweeney and Armstrong v Commission* (no retrospective tightening of the recruitment criteria); CST, F-88/05, ECLI:EU:F:2006:136, para 90 – *Kubanski v Commission* (recruitment criteria according to the notice).

[244] Case-law also mentions these as a list of 'three' conditions, by combining condition one and two: GC, T-696/14 P, ECLI:EU:T:2016:30, para 43 – *Bernat Montagut Viladot*; GC, Jd Cases T-66/96 and T-221/97, ECLI:EU:T:1998:187, paras 104–07 – *Mellett v ECJ*; GC, T-3/92, ECLI:EU:T:1994:15, para 58 – *Latham v Commission*; GC, T-329/03, ECLI:EU:T:2005:103, para 79 – *Ricci v Commission*; CST, F-4/07, ECLI:EU:F:2008:22, para 38 – *Skoulidi v Commission*.

[245] GC, T-205/01, ECLI:EU:T:2002:269, para 54 – *Ronsse v Commission*.

[246] GC, T-491/08, ECLI:EU:T:2010:191, paras 44–51– *Bui Van v Commission*.

[247] GC, T-93/96, ECLI:EU:T:1998:171, paras 71/72 – *Presle v CEDEFOP*.

[248] GC, Jd Cases T-238/95, T-239/95, T-240/95, T-241/95 and T-242/95, ECLI:EU:T:1998:151, paras 52–54 – *Mongelli and Others v Commission*.

[249] GC, T-329/03, ECLI:EU:T:2005:103, paras 79 ff – *Ricci v Commission*.

[250] GC, T-250/16 P, ECLI:EU:T:2017:866, para 112 – *Spadafora*.

[251] GC, T-561/16, ECLI:EU:T:2018:29, para 68 – *Galocha v European Joint Undertaking for ITER and the Development of Fusion Energy*; confirmed in appeal ECJ, C-243/18 P, ECLI:EU:C:2019:378, paras 65 ff – *Fusion for Energy v Galocha*. Similarly, a statement the execution of which would not be in line with the applicable law can only be understood as a 'political statement' or gesture: GC, T-177/22, ECLI:EU:T:2023:256, para 61 – *Chambers v Commission* (on Brexit consequences).

legal changes (particularly of the SR) which were adopted in the interests of the service as long as an identical treatment of those affected is guaranteed, and as long as well-acquired rights[252] are assured.[253] One argument for this is that the basic legal relationship between civil servants (officials *stricto sensu*) and the Union is of a statutory nature, not a contractual one.[254] It is not possible to rely on the principle of legal certainty or legitimate expectations to challenge the lawfulness of legislative changes or of a new regulatory provision, because the staff employed do not have a right to continue their work under the same SR as existed at the time of recruitment.[255] However, new rules must be introduced with a sufficiently long transitional period, and they must apply only to new situations and to the future effects of situations which arose under the previous rules.[256]

Case Study on the Right to be Heard

Infringement of the *right to be heard*: Annulment of the decision to terminate a contract

Case T-566/16, *Josefsson v European Parliament* of 17 May 2018

In Brief

The *rights of the defence* are fundamental principles of EU law. Persons concerned must be given the opportunity, before the drawing up of a decision adversely affecting them, to make their views effectively known as to the truth and relevance of the facts and circumstances on which that decision was based. The right to be heard implies that the person concerned must have the possibility of influencing the decision-making process at issue.

Facts

The applicant was engaged by a political Group of the European Parliament as a member of temporary staff for an indefinite period. Following the elections of 2014, the Secretariat

[252] Admittedly, the recourse to *well-acquired rights* can easily turn circular, where the acquired rights are tested according to the standards of protection of legitimate expectations and legal certainty: *cf* CST, F-31/10, ECLI:EU:F:2012:80, para 48 – *Guittet v Commission*; CST, F-63/10, ECLI:EU:F:2012:81, paras 105, 42, 57, 60 – *BL v Commission*; Reithmann (2014) *EuR* 111.

[253] See CST, F-47/07, ECLI:EU:F:2009:103, paras 53/54 – *Behmer v EP*. There is no protection of legitimate expectations, for example, to continue at the salary level as before the 2004 reform, CST, F-59/05, ECLI:EU:F:2006:105, para 73 – *De Smedt v Commission*, and generally not in areas of law that are subject to continuous adjustments to the economic situation, CST, F-105/05, ECLI:EU:F:2007:128, paras 138 ff – *Wils v EP*. On the immediate effectiveness and retroactive effect of general legal changes, CST, F-25/07, ECLI:EU:F:2010:163, paras 127 ff – *Bleser v ECJ*, CST, F-31/10, ECLI:EU:F:2012:80, paras 47, 63 ff – *Guittet v Commission*; and on the relationship between the protection of legitimate expectations and legislative freedom to change the law Gervasoni (2010) 46 *Cahiers de droit européen* 754, 778; ECJ, C-496/08, ECLI:EU:C:2010:116, paras 82, 91 – *Angé Serrano and Others v EP*; CST, F-105/05, ECLI:EU:F:2007:128, paras 138 ff, 153 – *Wils v EP*, but also on the legislative leeway in GC, T-184/00, ECLI:EU:T:2003:39, para 57 – *Drouvis*; ECJ, C-187/03 P, ECLI:EU:C:2004:280 – *Drouvis*.

[254] ECJ, Jd Cases C-119/19 P and C-126/19 P, ECLI:EU:C:2020:676, para 143 – *Commission v Carreras Sequeros and Others*.

[255] GC, T-516/16, T -536/16, ECLI:EU:T:2019:267, para 96 – *Alvarez y Bejarano and Others v Commission*; GC, T-538/16, ECLI:EU:T:2022:365, para 58 – *Schaffrin v Commission*.

[256] *cf* chapter 3, I.5.

of the Group was reorganised and the Group terminated the applicant's contract, claiming that the dismissal was due to the reorganisation of the Group's Secretariat, which was necessary as a result of the parliamentary elections, and because of a new division of tasks and new competences of staff.

Court Decision

The General Court (GC) annulled the decision to terminate the applicant's contract. The infringement of the right to be heard must be decisive for the outcome of the administrative decision: ie, had it not been for that irregularity, the outcome of the decision would have been different. The GC applied this concept widely: it could not be ruled out that if the applicant had been properly heard he would indeed have been able to influence the decision-making process in question.

Comments

1. The present case is in line with the standing case-law on the infringement of the right to be heard and other *rights of the defence*. In *Meyrl* the dismissal was motivated not only by a reorganisation of a Parliamentary Group, but also on the basis of behavioural reasons. The GC in *EP v Meyrl*[257] considered a proper hearing on only one of the two reasons to be sufficient during the dismissal procedure. Originally, the Civil Service Tribunal had decided differently at first instance of that case (F-147/15, *Meyrl*):[258] it had ruled that a proper hearing on both motivations brought forward by the employing authority was required.
2. Practically, it is important to know that an appointing authority might introduce other reasons for dismissal after a hearing on one reason for dismissal had taken place. However, a hearing will only fulfil its purpose if it relates to a specific motivation for the decision which is to be taken. In other words, a reason for dismissal cannot be taken into account legally if a hearing specifically relating to that reason has not taken place.
3. One counter-argument of the Parliament in *Josefsson* was that the applicant had allegedly been heard, because he was invited to the presentation of the new organigram before being confronted with the termination of his employment. However, this presentation was not considered by the GC to be an appropriate hearing of the individual, taking into account also that his dismissal was at stake. Furthermore, even if he had guessed that the meeting concerned the possibility of his dismissal, the period available to him to prepare for a pre-dismissal interview was insufficient to be able to conclude that the conditions had been created which would have enabled him to effectively make known his views during that meeting. It can thus be noted that the GC considers one day of preparation time to be insufficient for a pre-dismissal interview.

[257] GC, T-699/16 P, ECLI:EU:T:2017:524 – *EP v Meyrl*.
[258] CST, F-147/15, ECLI:EU:F:2016:157 – *Meyrl v EP*.

4. The employing authority may not plead internal difficulties in its decision-making processes, including difficulties relating to opposition on the part of individuals, in order to justify its failure to comply with legal obligations.[259]
5. Case-law does not accept the argument that if the applicant had been properly heard, the employing authority would have taken the same decision anyway. Such approach would nullify the principle of the *right to be heard* and take away its essential content. It cannot be ruled out that if the applicant had been properly heard he would have been able to influence the decision-making process.[260]
6. The dispute in *Josefsson* started with a reorganisation of the applicant's workplace. There is, in principle, no need to hear a staff member in cases of a mere reassignment or internal reorganisation of services.[261]

[259] *cf* ECJ, C-297/08, ECLI:EU:C:2010:115, para 83 – *Commission v Italy*; CST, F-137/14, ECLI:EU:F:2016:14, para 77 – *GV v EEAS*.
[260] CST, F-55/14, ECLI:EU:F:2015:66, para 40 – *EE v Commission*; CST, F-137/14, ECLI:EU:F:2016:14, paras 78/79 – *GV v EEAS*.
[261] GC, T-597/16, ECLI:EU:T:2018:338, paras 51, 80 – *OW v EASA*.

2

Review System: Admissibility of Applications and Procedural Matters in EU Civil Service Law

The review system pertaining to civil service law is structured as two phases: a staff member who wishes to challenge an act adversely affecting him or her, or who wishes that a certain act is adopted towards him or her, cannot (apart from exceptions) refer the matter directly to the court, but has to follow a specific pre-litigation complaint procedure foreseen under Article 90 of the Staff Regulations (SR). In the first phase, the staff member makes a request to the administration, thereby giving it the opportunity to decide whether to adopt a decision or repeal an act, or to refuse to do so. Only after this initial complaint procedure has been completed can the contentious phase (Art 91 SR) commence before the General Court (GC).

This chapter explores the preconditions for these procedures, first by outlining the institutional aspects of European Union (EU) civil service jurisdiction and the nature of the remedies available, then by examining the admissibility of an application at the GC. Finally, the chapter outlines in more detail the procedural steps of remedies in staff matters and the scope of judicial review. It concludes with a description of the judges' options for decision-making and enforcement, and the possibilities for appealing against the GC's findings to the Court of Justice of the European Union (ECJ).

I. Jurisdiction for Staff Matters

The Court of Justice has exclusive jurisdiction under Article 270 of the Treaty on the Functioning of the European Union (TFEU) to decide in disputes under civil service law between the Union and its servants, to the exclusion of national remedies. Recourse to the national courts of the place of employment is open to local employees under Article 124 of the Conditions of Employment of Other Servants (CEOS) and, if it is agreed so, under arbitral jurisdiction according to Article 122 CEOS.[1]

[1] ECJ, C-249/87, ECLI:EU:C:1989:614 – *Mulfiger v Commission*, except where local staff are affected in their own rights under the SR or CEOS, *cf* CST, F-57/08, ECLI:EU:F:2009:152 – *Palazzo v Commission* (pension rights); ECJ, Jd Cases 87 and 130/77, 22/83, 9 and 10/84, ECLI:EU:C:1985:318, para 24 – *Salerno v Commission and Council*; Gauer (2007) 66. CST, F-88/07, ECLI:EU:F:2008:141 – *Domíngues González v Commission*; Gervasoni (2010) 46 *Cahiers de droit européen* 743; Potvin-Solis/Lelièvre (2011) *RUE* 611, (2012) *RUE* 266; and Schiano/Potvin-Solis (2012) *RUE* 609; Henrichs (1980) *EuR* 134; (1982) *EuR* 231; (1985) *EuR* 171; (1988) *EuR* 302; Reithmann (2008) *EuR* 270–95; (2009) *EuR* 801–19; (2011) 1 *EuR* 121–44; (2011) 6 *EuR* 871–95; 2012 *EuR* 696–724; (2014) *EuR* 100; (2014) 6 *EuR*. On arbitral jurisdiction under Art 272 TFEU and the combination with national/local jurisdiction, see ECJ, C-43/17 P, ECLI:EU:C:2018:531 – *Jenkinson v Council, Commission, EEAS, Eulex*.

1. General Court and Court of Justice, Civil Service Tribunal

Within the structures of the Court of Justice of the European Union (CJEU) as the institution, originally, staff cases were dealt with by the Court of Justice (ECJ) directly. In 1989, the European Court of First Instance (today the General Court) took over jurisdiction as the entry court of first instance. Between 2006 and 2016, the Civil Service Tribunal of the Union (CST) was functionally responsible as the specialised[2] court of first instance. Since 2016, the General Court once again has jurisdiction at first instance according to Article 256(1), Article 270 TFEU.[3] The jurisdiction on staff matters at first instance was transferred from the CST[4] to the GC at about the same time as a reform of the GC and the doubling of the number of judges to two persons per Member State.[5] Nowadays, a typical EU civil service court case therefore commences at the GC. However, since the SR are binding in their entirety and directly applicable in all Member States,[6] a national case constellation – though on rare occasions – can be the starting point for court proceedings at a Member State's court with a referral under Article 267 TFEU to the ECJ for preliminary ruling.[7] For the same reason, it is possible that infringement proceedings launched by the Commission against a Member State may contain subject matters of relevance for EU civil service law;[8] or even the action of a Member State against the European Parliament.[9]

2. Chambers

Further to a decision[10] on the assignment of judges to chambers, cases stemming from the employment relationship (staff matters) are at present assigned to the fourth, fifth, ninth and tenth chambers of the General Court in turn according to the order (ie, the date) in which the cases are registered at the Registry.[11] The President of the General Court may derogate from the rota, in order to take account of any connection between cases or with a view to ensuring an even spread of the workload.[12] The Court sits in chambers consisting of three or five judges.[13]

[2] Art 257 TFEU, Art 62c of the Statute of the CJEU (hereinafter Statute CJEU). After closure of the CST into the GC, the discussion about having specialised courts within the ECJ structure has practically ceased; Butler (2020) 17(3) *International Organizations Law Review* 586–632.

[3] Art 50a of the Protocol on the Statute CJEU; ECJ, C-903/19, ECLI:EU:C:2021:95 – *DQ*; ECJ, C-494/14, ECLI:EU:C:2015:692 – *EU v Axa Belgium SA*; ECJ, C-166/12, ECLI:EU:C:2013:792 – *Radek Časta v Česká správa sociálního zabezpečení*.

[4] Regulation (EU) No 2016/1192 of 6 July 2016 [2016] OJ L200; Gattinara, 'Les rôles de la Cour de justice et du Tribunal de l'Union après la dissolution du Tribunal de la fonction publique européenne' (2017) *RUE* 157–70. On the consequences of a procedural irregularity in appointing a judge: C-542/18 RX-II and C-543/18 RX-II, ECLI:EU:C:2020:232 – *Simpson v Council* and *HG v Commission*; Bocquillon, 'Les conséquences de la réforme de l'architecture juridictionnelle de l'Union européenne sur le contentieux de la fonction publique' (2017) 6 *Journal de droit européen* 218–24; Bradley, 'Création et suppression du Tribunal de la fonction publique de la fonction publique' in Cartier Bresson/Dero-Bugny (eds), *Les réformes de la Cour de justice de l'Union européenne* (2020) 103–12.

[5] Two members of the GC per Member State since 1 September 2019 in accordance with Art 48 lit c Statute CJEU.

[6] Art 288(2) TFEU.

[7] eg, on the interpretation of provisions relating to social security, ECJ, C-903/19, ECLI:EU:C:2021:95 – *DQ* on the transfer of pension rights of EU staff returning to national administration; or on the interpretation of the Protocol on Privileges and Immunities in relation to national taxes, ECJ, C-333/88, ECLI:EU:C:1990:131, para 18 – *Tither*.

[8] ECJ, C-260/86, ECLI:EU:C:1988:91 – *Commission v Belgium*.

[9] *cf* ECJ, C-377/16, ECLI:EU:C:2019:249 – *Spain v EP*, see Art 51 Statute CJEU.

[10] For the period between September 2022 and August 2025 [2022] OJ C398/3–7.

[11] Criteria for the assignment of cases to Chambers [2023] OJ C286/2.

[12] Whereas in applying a derogation from the rota the case would still be assigned to one of the other three specialised chambers.

[13] Art 50(1) Statute CJEU.

3. Language

The language of the proceedings may be chosen by the applicant in accordance with Article 45 Rules of Procedure (RoP)[14] of the GC from among the 24 languages specified in Article 44 RoP, whereas in practice the majority of litigation is in French. The judgments are always published in French and in the language of the case, and sometimes also in other languages; rarely, they are published in most or all of the official languages of the EU.[15] The working language of the Court is French.

4. Lawsuits against and by Members of Institutions

Complaints and actions against members of the EU institutions (ie, members of the College of Commissioners and similar posts) do not fall within the scope of civil service law under Article 270 TFEU.[16] Likewise, an application by a member for annulment of a measure of the institution cannot be introduced under Article 270 TFEU, but only under Article 263 TFEU.[17] As a consequence, a potential entitlement rooted in a person's membership of that body (or in civil service law) cannot be asserted by way of a counterclaim either. This is due to the systematic differences of both the proceedings initiated against members of the institutions and of proceedings of members against the institutions.[18]

II. Remedies

The admissible type of action under Articles 90/91 SR to adjudicate in disputes of civil service law further to Article 270 TFEU is an application for annulment *sui generis*. As its object, it seeks the annulment of an act adversely affecting the applicant and, where necessary, compensation for damages[19] or payment of remuneration.[20]

1. Annulment of the Act

The admissible remedy that provides legal protection in cases of civil service law is substantially a negative one: the application to *annul* the aggrieving act. It therefore consists in a claim for

[14] Rules of Procedure (RoP) of the GC 2015, last amended November 2022.

[15] The choice of the language of the proceedings must not have an effect on the cost that an applicant might incur when ordered to bear the administration's legal fees, CST, F-55/08 DEP, ECLI:EU:F:2011:155, para 35 – *De Nicola v EIB*.

[16] *cf* the special provisions in Art 245(2) TFEU, Art 286(6) TFEU; ECJ, C-432/04, ECLI:EU:C:2006:455 – *Commission v Cresson*; ECJ, C-130/19, ECLI:EU:C:2021:782 – *ECA v Pinxten*.

[17] ECJ, C-221/14 P, ECLI:EU:C:2015:126, paras 38/39 – *H v CJEU*; consequently, for these constellations, also the complaint procedure of Art 90 SR does not apply.

[18] ECJ, C-130/19, ECLI:EU:C:2021:782, para 911 – *ECA v Pinxten*.

[19] Reithmann (2008) *EuR* 277; (2009) *EuR* 805; (2011) 1 *EuR* 127; (2011) 6 *EuR* 876; (2012) *EuR* 703; on the independence of this civil service legal institution, CST, F-50/09, ECLI:EU:F:2011:55, paras 209 ff – *Missir Mamachi de Lusignano v Commission*, and GC, T-143/09, ECLI:EU:T:2010:531, para 46 – *Commission v Petrilli*. Requirements for damages and their amounts: Mader, 'Der Anspruch auf Entschädigung ex aequo et bono im EU-Dienstrecht – Schadenersatz für EU-Bedienstete nach billigem Ermessen' (2012) *EuR* 358 ff; CST, Jd Cases F-124/05 and F-96/06, ECLI:EU:F:2010:2, para 166 – *A and G v Commission*.

[20] ECJ, C-135/06 P, ECLI:EU:C:2007:812, para 65 – *Weißenfels v EP*; CST, Jd Cases F-45/08 and F-99/07, ECLI:EU:F:2009:84, para 58 – *Bernard v Europol* (salary increase).

annulment of the contested act and (in the case of a separable content with additional grievance) also of the decision rejecting the complaint. On the other hand, declaratory motions[21] – ie, applications aimed at determining the existence or nonexistence of a legal relationship or other forms of order sought that would impose explicit obligations on the defendant – are inadmissible, since they would amount to an instruction given to the institutions on how to implement the law.[22] Such instructions may occur in the framework of the *urgent procedure*, namely in suspension of operation or other interim measures,[23] but not in direct action, except in disputes of a *financial character* (see below).

An action may deal with the denial of an applicant's request to execute an act or to take a decision. It may therefore indirectly bring into play elements of an action for performance. Thus, occasionally, judgments can have the effect of directly shaping the legal relationship, for example when temporary employment contracts are reclassified as permanent ones.[24] An application for annulment may be addressed against decisions taken in favour of others, for example competitors who are on a reserve list or on a promotion list, while the applicant is not.[25]

Unlimited jurisdiction in disputes of a financial character

As a specialty in civil service litigation, the courts have unlimited jurisdiction in disputes of a *financial character*, Article 91(1) SR. This functions to conclusively decide on a matter in its legal and factual bearing on the employment relationship, including all its financial ramifications, for example on the payment of a pension, allowance, remuneration, invalidity pension, default interest, or compensation for material and non-material harm suffered by the staff employed. Disputes of a financial character are not only actions brought by staff members seeking to have an institution held liable, but also all those claims that seek payment by an institution to a staff member of a sum which the latter considers to be due to him or her under the SR or other measure governing their working relations.[26]

Where, for example, the applicant is asking the court to rule on the legality of the decision not to recognise his status as an 'invalid' person and to order the institution to pay him a sum of money, it must be understood that that action is a dispute of a financial character. This is because the decision to regard the applicant as 'not invalid' has direct consequences for the continuation of the party's situation as a member of staff, and therefore on his remuneration and financial rights.[27]

[21] CST, Jd Cases F-20/08, F-34/08 and F-75/08, ECLI:EU:F:2009:132, paras 23 ff – *Aparício and Others v Commission* (determination of alleged illegality of implementing provisions).

[22] GC, T-571/17, ECLI:EU:T:2020:141, para 108 – *UG v Commission*; GC, T-561/16, ECLI:EU:T:2018:29, para 74 – *Galocha v European Joint Undertaking for ITER and the Development of Fusion Energy*; CST, F-56/09, ECLI:EU:F:2010:48, para 78 – *Marcuccio v Commission*; CST, F-58/10, ECLI:EU:F:2012:130, para 49 – *Allgeier v FRA*; if necessary, reinterpretation takes place, see CST, F-104/10, ECLI:EU:F:2013:64, paras 33, 71 – *de Pretis Cagnodo and Others v Commission*; on the relationship between the action for payment and the action for annulment, see CST, F-76/11, ECLI:EU:F:2012:173, para 22 – *Grazyte v Commission*, confirmed by GC, T-86/13 P, ECLI: EU:T:2014:815; Reithmann (2011) 1 *EuR* 126. For orders *cf* CST, F-105/09, ECLI:EU:F:2011:41, para 24 – *Scheefer v EP*; CST, F-105/11, ECLI:EU:F:2012:84, para 56 – *Davids* (conversion of successive fixed-term contracts into a contract of unlimited duration).

[23] See section VI.5. below.

[24] *cf* Potvin-Solis/Lelièvre (2012) *RUE* 284.

[25] CST, F-44/05 RENV, ECLI:EU:F:2012:144, paras 105, 126 – *Strack v Commission*; CST, F-1/11, ECLI:EU:F:2012:157, paras 52 ff – *Soukup v Commission*; CST, F-53/08, ECLI:EU:F:2010:37, para 80 – *Bouillez and Others v Council*; CST, F-39/07, ECLI:EU:F:2009:45, para 42 – *Campos Valls v Council*. The applicant's own rejection and the appointment of the competitor must be challenged separately, CST, F-55/10, ECLI:EU:F:2011:94, para 31 – *AS v Commission*, in appeal: GC, T-476/11 P, ECLI:EU:T:2013:557, paras 31 ff – *Commission v Moschonaki*; Reithmann (2011) 6 *EuR* 886.

[26] ECJ, C-135/06 P, ECLI:EU:C:2007:812, para 65 – *Weißenfels v EP*; GC, T-369/22, ECLI:EU:T:2023:855, para 99 – *Heßler v Commission*; GC, T-529/20, ECLI:EU:T:2022:523, para 67 – *LR v EIB*.

[27] GC, T-370/20, ECLI:EU:T:2021:822, para 118 – *KL v EIB*; ECJ, C-583/08 P, ECLI:EU:C:2010:287, para 47 – *Gogos*; CST, F-124/11, ECLI:EU:F:2013:137, para 73 – *Possanzini v Frontex*.

An unlimited jurisdiction in disputes of a financial character does not mean that an action for compensation can 'stand alone' where this claim is closely linked to a claim for annulment: in that case, the claim for annulment has to be successful itself. Where, on the other hand, a claim for compensation for material or non-material damage is closely associated with a claim for annulment that has to be dismissed as inadmissible or unfounded, this financial claim must be rejected, too.[28]

Plea of illegality

An admissible action under Article 270 TFEU can pave the way for an incidental judicial review of a measure of general application under a plea of illegality (Art 277 TFEU),[29] provided the usual preconditions[30] for a plea of illegality are fulfilled.

2. Compensation for Damages

A successful claim for compensation of harm or damages[31] on the basis of Article 270 TFEU first requires a violation of legal provisions. As a specialty in the area of civil service law, the non-contractual liability of the institutions of the Union is aggravated[32] and serves to compensate its employees for the damage they have suffered as a result of every illegality of the Union committed in its function as employer. Liability for damages presupposes unlawful conduct by the institution resulting in actual and certain harm to the staff member;[33] further, there must be a causal (direct and certain)[34] link between the act and the harm.[35] It is not a prerequisite of a claim under non-contractual liability to prove that the norm violated by the institution has the purpose of protecting the interests of the individual.[36] As a corollary of the unlimited jurisdiction in disputes of a financial character, the courts can also decide on the award of damages ex officio.[37] The

[28] GC, T-517/16, ECLI:EU:T:2017:283, para 69 – *HF v EP*; GC, T-369/22, ECLI:EU:T:2023:855, para 102 – *Heßler v Commission*.

[29] CST, F-123/10, ECLI:EU:F:2012:6, para 34 – *Bancale and Buccheri v Commission*; CST, F-121/10, ECLI:EU:F:2011:174, para 64 – *Heath v ECB*.

[30] *cf* TWD case law: ECJ, C-188/92, ECLI:EU:C:1994:90, para 17 – *Textilwerke Deggendorf*; ECJ, C-239/99, ECLI:EU:C:2001:101, para 37 – *Nachi Europe*; ECJ, C-441/05, ECLI:EU:C:2007:150, para 40 – *Roquette Frères*.

[31] Overview on damage claims in civil service law: Mader, 'Le droit à l'indemnisation ex aequo et bono dans la fonction publique européenne' (2013) 96(2) *KritV/CritQ/Rcrit* 154–64; Mader, 'Der Anspruch auf Entschädigung ex aequo et bono im EU-Dienstrecht – Schadenersatz für EU-Bedienstete nach billigem Ermessen' (2012) *EuR* 355.

[32] GC, T-571/17, ECLI:EU:T:2020:141, para 83 – *UG v Commission* ('responsabilité accrue').

[33] Burden of proof on the applicant: CST, F-63/10, ECLI:EU:F:2012:81, para 98 – *BL v Commission*.

[34] CST, F-91/10, ECLI:EU:F:2013:34, para 76 – *AK v Commission*.

[35] GC, T-881/16, ECLI:EU:T:2019:5, para 47 – *HJ v EMA*; GC, T-603/16, ECLI:EU:T:2018:820, paras 245, 254 – *Brahma v ECJ*.

[36] CST, F-30/08, ECLI:EU:F:2010:43, para 131 – *Nanopoulos v Commission*; GC, T-143/09 P, ECLI:EU:T:2010:531 – *Commission v Petrilli*. On the aim of achieving stricter liability of the organs as employers and on the abandonment of earlier, stricter case-law, Potvin-Solis/Lelièvre (2012) *RUE* 270. *cf* also, GC, T-80/09 P, ECLI:EU:T:2011:347, para 43 – *Commission v Q* and generally also CST, F-50/09 ECLI:EU:F:2011:55 – *Missir Mamachi de Lusignano v Commission* with example cases of liability. On liability causality, see Potvin-Solis/Lelièvre (2011) *RUE* 612. Due to the duty of care in civil service law, the compensation follows different rules to those under Arts 268 and 340 TFEU, CST, F-89/11, ECLI:EU:F:2013:83, para 98 – *Goetz v CoR* with further references; Mader, 'Der Anspruch auf Entschädigung ex aequo et bono im EU-Dienstrecht – Schadenersatz für EU-Bedienstete nach billigem Ermessen' (2012) *EuR* 355.

[37] CST, F-53/08, ECLI:EU:F:2010:37, para 90 – *Bouillez and Others v Council*; while the principles of the adversarial procedure must still be observed, GC, T-491/08, ECLI:EU:T:2010:191, paras 83 ff – *Bui Van v Commission*, compensation for non-material harm may not be awarded instead of compensation for material harm, GC, T-80/09 P, ECLI:EU:T:2011:347, para 73 – *Commission v Q*; Potvin-Solis/Lelièvre (2012) *RUE* 281.

claim for compensation for harm suffered under the non-contractual liability of the institutions embraces both the material[38] damage and the non-material damage.

Material damage

The amount to be compensated for material damage corresponds to the pecuniary damage suffered by the person concerned. Both the reliance interest (damage caused by relying on compliant conduct) and the lost profit (*lucrum cessans*) must be reimbursed. This concept envisages restitution and shall put the person who suffered the damage in the same situation as if the act adversely affecting him or her had never taken place or if a legal decision had been taken from the outset in favour of the person who suffered the harm.[39]

Non-material damage

As to the compensation of *non*-material damage, the annulment of an unlawful act will in itself constitute appropriate and, in principle, sufficient reparation for any non-material damage which that act may have caused, unless the applicant demonstrates that he or she has suffered non-material damage which cannot be compensated in full by that annulment.[40] That is the case where the applicant demonstrates that he or she has suffered non-material damage which is separable from the unlawfulness giving rise to the annulment and which cannot be fully compensated for by that annulment.[41] In particular this constellation may be given, for example, where the unlawful act contains an explicitly negative assessment of the abilities or conduct of the person concerned which is liable to cause him or her harm,[42] or where feelings of injustice, incomprehension or frustration were caused to the applicant as a result of the appointing authority's conduct during the pre-litigation stage (the court takes into account the applicant's state of insecurity, uncertainty and distress, as well as the length of time that has elapsed).[43] By way of example for another category of non-material damage, the following case study reflects on preconditions for the compensation of non-material damage caused by excessive delay before taking decisions.

[38] eg, in the event of unlawful contract termination, it consists of the difference between the lost income and the income actually received, unemployment or similar benefits, CST, F-6/10, ECLI:EU:F:2011:139, para 126 – *Munch v OHIM*; Reithmann (2014) *EuR* 106.

[39] Also the amount of non-material damages is often determined by the court at its discretion and on a flat-rate basis, *cf* CST, F-101/09, ECLI:EU:F:2011:133 point 106 – *AA v Commission* (€120,000 for hypothetical employment with average career progression).

[40] GC, T-116/03, ECLI:EU:T:2004:325, para 127 – *Montalto v Council*; ECJ, C-558/17 P, ECLI:EU:C:2019:289, para 80 – *OZ v EIB*; ECJ, Jd Cases 44/85, 77/85, 294/85 and 295/85, ECLI:EU:C:1987:348, para 2 – *Hochbaum and Rawes v Commission*; GC, T-365/21, ECLI:EU:T:2023:25, para 70 – *TJ v EEAS*; CST, F-7/09, ECLI:EU:F:2010:9, para 65 – *Faria v OHIM*; CST, F-32/06, ECLI:EU:F:2007:169, paras 76 ff – *De la Cruz and Others v European Agency for Safety and Health at Work*; CST, F-6/07, ECLI:EU:F:2008:55, para 147 – *Suvikas v Council*; CST, F-50/09, ECLI:EU:F:2011:55, paras 209 ff – *Missir Mamachi de Lusignano v Commission.*

[41] GC, T-352/17, ECLI:EU:T:2018:319, para 78 – *Korwin-Mikke v EP*; GC, T-370/20, ECLI:EU:T:2021:822, para 131 – *KL v EIB.*

[42] GC, T-571/16, ECLI:EU:T:2019:301, para 233 – *PT v EIB.*

[43] GC, T-601/16, ECLI:EU:T:2017:757, para 84 – *Paraskevaidis v Cedefop*; GC, T-365/21, ECLI:EU:T:2023:25, paras 65, 66 – *TJ v EEAS*; GC, T-483/16 RENV, ECLI:EU:T:2020:225, para 448 – *Cerafogli v ECB*; GC, T-164/20, ECLI:EU:T:2023:35, para 66 – *BG v EP*; ECJ, C-343/87, ECLI:EU:C:1990:49, para 27 – *Culin v Commission*; CST, F-55/10, ECLI:EU:F:2011:94, paras 79 ff – *AS v Commission.*

Case Study on Damages

Excessive time for taking a decision: On delays and compensation for non-material damages

Case T-275/17, *Curto v Parliament* of 13 July 2018
Case F-65/11, *Schönberger v Parliament* of 20 March 2012
Case T-274/04, *Rounis v Commission* of 8 December 2005
Case T-181/00, *Carmelo Morello v Commission* of 12 December 2002
Case F-4/13, *Cwik v Commission* of 8 December 2014
Case F-46/11, *Tzirani v Commission* of 11 July 2013
Case F-111/12, *Nardone v Commission* of 2 October 2013
Case T-790/21, *PL v Commission* of 15 November 2023

In Brief

The appointing authority has to take an adequate decision within a reasonable time, for example relating to a promotion, an evaluation, a disciplinary procedure or the attribution of merit points. This is even more important when the uncertainty and insecurity has lasted for a long time and has heavily affected the official. Cases of maladministration on the side of the appointing authority can lead to considerable compensation for material and non-material damage.

Facts and Court Decisions

The applicant questioned the allocation of merit points. He also turned to the Ombudsman to complain about the alleged personnel administration's unfair attribution of points. The Ombudsman decided in favour of the applicant, but it took 16 months until the reasoning of the decision on the attribution of points was communicated. The applicant only learned that a new decision had been taken because he had launched a petition in the meantime. In total, it took six years to revise the original decision of the administration (Case F-65/11, *Schönberger v EP*).[44]

Another group of cases relates to the unjustified initiation of disciplinary proceedings against officials, particularly if the proceedings are not immediately terminated once it turns out that they are not justified. In Joined Cases F-124/05 and F-96/06, *A and G v Commission*[45] the period between the time when allegations were brought against the official and the termination of the disciplinary procedure was 10 years. Where reproaches in a disciplinary procedure are unjustified, the procedure shall be immediately stopped and – in view of the publicity of the procedure – a public apology may have to be made to the wrongly accused official. In the above-mentioned case in which this was not correctly handled, the appointing authority had to pay damages of €25,000 for breaching its duty to act within a reasonable time.

Where a staff report was compiled too late or was not compiled at all, case-law allows for compensation for the non-material damages suffered (*cf* Case T-274/04, *Rounis v*

[44] CST, F-65/11, ECLI:EU:F:2012:34 – *Schönberger v EP*.
[45] CST, Jd Cases F-124/05 and F-96/06, ECLI:EU:F:2010:2 – *A and G v Commission*.

Commission[46] and Case T-181/00, *Carmelo Morello v Commission*).[47] A period of five and a half months was considered to be an over-long delay for drawing up a revised staff report (Case F-4/13, *Cwik v Commission*).[48] In this case, the delays that were caused by the employing authority (in total over four years) prompted the CST to annul the decision establishing the staff report. When assessing the delay, the court will look at the appropriate length of the individual steps within the procedure as well as at the procedure's overall duration. In Cwik, the CST further granted a compensation for non-material damage of €15,000 to the applicant for having suffered uncertainty and frustration due to the delays.

In Case F-46/11, *Tzirani v Commission*,[49] the administrative investigation further to a request for assistance lasted for 32 months, 11 months of which elapsed without any action. Here, the CST awarded compensation of €6,000 to the applicant for the non-material damage linked to the excessive duration of the procedure and the breach of the duty to have regard for the welfare of officials. In Case T-790/21, *PL v Commission*,[50] the decision-making process for a change of duties lasted for eight years, a compensation of €3,000 was awarded.

The necessity to observe an appropriate duration of the procedure also applies to medical assessments. It is of significance that the court considers the speed of the work of the Medical Committee to be within the sphere of responsibility of the administration, *cf* Case F-111/12, *Nardone v Commission*.[51] In that case, an amount of €4,000 for damages was attributed for an overlong delay to establish the medical report.

Comments

1. Unjustified delays in administrative decision-making are not only a nuisance, but can amount to maladministration. Not taking a decision, or delaying it, has consequences. Refusal of managerial responsibility forces others to take their decisions regarding the allocation of resources, and causes suffering which arises from uncertainty and insecurity.
2. The legal consequence of an action for annulment is that the act (decision) is annulled *ex tunc*. Although in staff cases the court has broader scope to interfere, here too the usual decision is (only) to annul the decision that was being contested. The appointing authority then has to draw its conclusions from the judgment and take administrative decisions that are in line with the law as decided in the judgment and its reasoning. Regularly, the annulment of the contested decision is considered a sufficient remedy for the infringement of the law.
3. The damage caused to the official may not be completely offset by the mere annulment of an illegal decision by the appointing authority. In that case, the court additionally grants compensation for damages that remain as a separate consequence even after the decision is annulled. The calculation of material damages caused by maladministration may sometimes be difficult, but the court exercises considerable discretion (*ex aequo et bono*) as to the determination of the non-material damages that remain once a wrongful decision has been annulled.

[46] GC, T-274/04, ECLI:EU:T:2005:442 – *Rounis v Commission.*
[47] GC, T-181/00, ECLI:EU:T:2002:313 – *Carmelo Morello v Commission.*
[48] CST, F-4/13, ECLI:EU:F:2014:263 – *Cwik v Commission.*
[49] CST, F-46/11, ECLI:EU:F:2013:115 – *Tzirani v Commission.*
[50] GC, T-790/21, ECLI:EU:T:2023:724, paras 235, 239 – *PL v Commission.*
[51] CST, F-111/12, ECLI:EU:F:2013:140 – *Nardone v Commission.*

III. Right to Bring an Action

Civil servants

According to the wording of Article 270 TFEU, the Court of Justice decides 'in any dispute between the Union and its servants'. Servants means that *ratione personae* – as an initial approximation – all persons to whom the SR and CEOS apply are entitled to bring an action.[52] It has been clarified by case-law that candidates, former staff members and surviving dependants of former staff members are also recognised as having the right to bring an action, insofar as the SR or the CEOS grant rights to them: persons who have the status neither of officials nor of employees, but who claim that status, are also examined within that framework.[53]

The conditions and procedures leading to appointment

Not all provisions of the SR or CEOS are applicable or have to be applicable to a person per se; in some contexts, it may be only the pay and employment conditions that fall within the scope of the SR or CEOS and the competence of the respective Authority Empowered to Conclude Contracts of Employment (AECE).[54] Therefore, the right of a candidate to bring an action against the decision not to appoint her or him does not depend on whether the conditions of employment apply, but on the applicable *conditions and procedures leading to her or his appointment*. For example, in the case of the European Public Prosecutor's Office (EPPO), Article 96 of the EPPO Regulation[55] states that the SR or CEOS shall apply to the EPPO 'unless otherwise provided for in this Regulation'. However, first, the appointment of prosecutors is effected by an implementing decision of the Council, based on the mentioned Regulation. The procedure *leading* to such appointment is outside the SR or CEOS. Hence, legal review against this decision is only possible within the framework of an action for annulment under Article 263 TFEU, while an action under Article 270 TFEU would be manifestly inadmissible.[56] Secondly, the disciplinary regime applying to the EPPO is governed by the EPPO Regulation;[57] Article 86 SR and Annex IX of the SR do not apply to the EPPO.

Staff of the European Investment Bank

Further to Article 41 EIB Staff Regulations, any member of staff may submit to the European Investment Bank (EIB) President a request for review of an act adversely affecting him or her. The request must be lodged within two months from the written notification of this act to the member of staff concerned. The CJEU shall have jurisdiction in all disputes between the Bank and the members of staff regarding the legality of an act adversely affecting the person concerned after internal redress procedures (including a request for review) have been exhausted. Disputes shall be brought within three months.[58]

[52] Officials under Art 1 SR in conjunction with Arts 90, 91 SR, other staff: Arts 46, 117 and 124 CEOS.

[53] GC, T-502/16, EU:T:2019:795, paras 48–64 – *Stefano Missir Mamachi di Lusignano and Others v Commission*; confirmed in the appeal: ECJ, C-54/20 P, ECLI:EU:C:2022:349, para 54 – *Commission v Stefano Missir Mamachi di Lusignano and Others*; ECJ, Jd Cases 81-88/74, ECLI:EU:C:1975:139, paras 5/7 – *Marenco and Others v Commission*; on local staff: see chapter 2, I; trade unions and staff associations, see chapter 4, II.

[54] In French AIPN autorité investie du pouvoir de nomination.

[55] Regulation (EU) 2017/1939 [2017] OJ L283.

[56] GC, T-334/21, ECLI:EU:T:2022:375 – *Mendes de Almeida v Council*.

[57] *cf* there Art 14(5) and Art 16(5), which refer to the ability of the European Chief Prosecutor or a European Prosecutor respectively to perform his or her duties or that he or she is guilty of serious misconduct.

[58] Art 41a EIB Staff Regulations. ECJ, C-110/75, ECLI:EU:C:1976:88 – *Mills v EIB*; other rules apply by analogy to the SR, *cf* GC, T-140/97, ECLI:EU:T:1999:176, para 77 – *Hautem v EIB*.

Staff of the European Cental Bank

Similarly, Article 36.2 of the Protocol on the European Cental Bank (ECB) statute[59] refers disputes to the jurisdiction of the CJEU 'within the limits and under the conditions laid down in the conditions of employment', meaning that all the internal means of review under the conditions of employment[60] first have to be exhausted before it is possible to file an action with the CJEU.[61]

Professional associations and trade unions

Since the status of trade unions and staff associations is recognised by the SR,[62] they can bring an action as an addressee of an act under Union law,[63] or otherwise where they defend their own rights. They may not represent civil servants as applicants, but can join individual actions filed by their members as interveners, provided that the legal dispute affects their collective interests.[64]

Staff Committee

The Staff Committee has no capacity to bring legal proceedings, because the manifestations of the will of the Committee, as the ECJ held,[65] are intended to be operative only within the institution.

Common Foreign and Security Policy

The CJEU does not have jurisdiction in the area of the Common Foreign and Security Policy (CFSP) and the legal acts enacted on its basis.[66] Nevertheless, the EU courts do have jurisdiction both for EU staff members and for officials seconded by the Member States regarding acts relating to personnel management under the CFSP, because as far as the *performance of their duties* is concerned, both are subject to the same rules. Yet, the avenues of review and legal basis for filing an action are different (Art 270 TFEU for EU servants vs Art 263 TFEU for seconded staff).[67]

[59] Statute of the European System of Central Banks and of the European Central Bank [1992] OJ C191/78.

[60] Arts 41 and 42 of the Conditions of Employment for Staff of the European Central Bank of 9 June 1998, last amended on 1 January 2023.

[61] GC, T-20/01, ECLI:EU:T:2001:287, paras 80 ff – *Cerafogli v ECB.*

[62] Art 24b SR, Art 10b and 10c SR, see chapter 4, II. Casado García-Hirschfeld, 'Le rôle des syndicats des fonctionnaires européens dans le contentieux de la fonction publique communautaire' (2010) *Revue du marché commun et de l'Union européenne* 426–30.

[63] ECJ, Jd Cases C-193/87 and C-194/87, ECLI:EU:C:1989:185, paras 45/46 – *Maurissen and Others v ECA*; GC, T-78/91, ECLI:EU:T:1991:67 – *Moat v Commission.*

[64] ECJ, 72/74, ECLI:EU:C:1975:43 – *Union Syndicale and Others v Council*; GC, T-84/91, ECLI:EU:T:1992:103 – *Meskens v EP*; GC, T-42/90, ECLI:EU:T:1992:19 – *Bertelli v Commission*; CST, F-87/13, ECLI:EU:F:2014:53 – *Colart and Others v EP.*

[65] ECJ, 15/63, ECLI:EU:C:1963:47, 51 – *Lasalle v EP.*

[66] Art 24(1)(2) final sentence TEU and Art 275(1) TFEU.

[67] *cf* EUPM in Bosnia and Herzegovina: ECJ, C-455/14 P, ECLI:EU:C:2016:569, paras 42–59 – *H v Council, Commission and EUPM*, while officials seconded by Member States rely on Art 263 TFEU to file an action for annulment (not on Art 270 TFEU). It is different in the case of a disciplinary measure against an official seconded by a Member State, where the measure was solely attributable to the Member State: GC, T-383/13, ECLI:EU:T:2015:246, para 40 – *Chatzianagnostou v Council.* Eulex measures: GC, T-410/13, ECLI:EU:T:2014:871 – *Bitiqi and Others v Commission, EEAS and Eulex* (in the absence of an arbitration clause, no jurisdiction of the GC, but national court jurisdiction, *cf* Art 274 TFEU). *cf* chapter 3, II.1. ECJ, C-730/18 P, ECLI:EU:C:2020:505 – *SC v Eulex Kosovo*; ECJ, C-785/22 P, ECLI:EU:C:2024:52 – *Eulex Kosovo v SC*, confirming GC, T-242/17 RENV, ECLI:EU:T:2022:637 – *SC v Eulex Kosovo.*

Case Study on Jurisdiction: Arbitration

A 'direct connection' of obligations in various employment contracts can establish the jurisdiction of the General Court under the arbitration clause

Case C-43/17 P, *Jenkinson v Council, Commission, EEAS, Eulex* of 5 July 2018

In Brief

In an application for the recategorisation of a series of fixed-term contracts, the effects of the previous employment contracts also need to be taken into account, despite the fact that only the final fixed-term employment contract contained the arbitration clause that establishes the jurisdiction of the General Court.

Facts and Court Decisions

The applicant was employed under a series of fixed-term contracts in various international missions of the EU. His final fixed-term contract was not renewed. The applicant requested – among other things – a recategorisation of all the contractual relationships as an 'employment of an indefinite duration'. This was denied. The last of his fixed-term contracts contained a clause that stipulated the jurisdiction of the CJEU over any dispute relating to the contract, on the basis of Article 272 TFEU (arbitration), while his previous contracts referred to Belgian state courts as the litigation venue.

Central Legal Question

Does the General Court have jurisdiction under the arbitration procedure (Art 272 TFEU) to hear claims based on contracts prior to the final fixed-term contract, even though these did not contain such arbitration clauses?

Findings of the General Court (First Instance)

The GC found that since the action was brought under Article 272 TFEU (arbitration procedure) it 'manifestly lacks jurisdiction' to decide over claims arising from contracts prior to the final fixed-term contract, because the former contracts expressly gave jurisdiction to the Belgian courts.

Decision of the Court of Justice (in Appeal)

The Court of Justice first states that its jurisdiction is to be determined only by Article 272 TFEU and the terms of the contractual arbitration clause, not by provisions of national law. Then the ECJ finds that the GC has jurisdiction to hear and determine claims arising from the final fixed-term contract and prior contracts which are directly connected with that final contract. In the view of the applicant the claims are linked to the existence of a single, continuous employment relationship based on a series of consecutive fixed-term contracts. The ECJ decided to refer the case back to the GC to verify whether and to what extent it was entitled to take account of the previous employment contracts in assessing the applicant's claims.

Comments

1. Although the judgment is not yet on the recategorisation of a specific series of fixed-term contracts in international missions, it is an important step on admissibility matters relating to the recategorisation where a series of individual employment contracts specified different jurisdictions.
2. In this case, the ECJ clarifies in its appeal decision the scope of the arbitration jurisdiction of the GC (Art 272 TFEU), and at the same time extends the legal protection for staff who request recategorisation of their employment contracts. The GC had refused jurisdiction, on the basis of the perspective that each contract contains a separate clause regarding jurisdiction, and thus separated those former contracts which referred to the Belgian state courts. In the appeal, the ECJ allows for a more global perspective when it states that jurisdiction is given where the claims arise from the final fixed-term contract or from prior contracts which are directly connected with that final contract. The recategorisation claim is linked to the existence of a single, continuous employment relationship. This, in the view of the ECJ (and Advocate General), justifies the required 'direct connection' of the claims with obligations stemming from the final contract that contains the arbitration clause which establishes the jurisdiction of the GC. The last contract thus functions as a 'door' through which directly connected claims can also be heard at the Court. In the view of the GC, the scope of the material entitlement would have followed the literal contractual limitations of jurisdiction to hear the case, whereas in the view of the ECJ the jurisdiction follows the scope of the 'directly connected' material obligations.
3. The recategorisation of a series of fixed-term contracts entails considering the direct connection of the obligations of these contracts. For such a claim, the effects of the previous employment contracts have to be taken into account.[68]
4. Had the ECJ not introduced the concept of a 'direct connection' of obligations linked to the final fixed-term contract, it would have meant that the appointing authority could block a recategorisation of a series of employment contracts relatively simply, by intentionally stipulating different (alternating) jurisdiction clauses in the contracts with its staff. This is because any recategorisation of a series of contracts has to start by referring to a specific jurisdiction – typically the jurisdiction of the last employment contract. If the GC was restricted to looking solely at the last contract, any such recategorisation would become impossible.

IV. Defendant

The defendant of an action under EU civil service law is always[69] an EU institution, despite the fact that Article 91 SR speaks about a dispute between the 'Union' and any person to whom the SR apply. An action may be addressed against the EU institutions and those bodies that are defined as *Institutions* under Article 1b SR, as defendants.

[68] The GC had to decide on this again: GC, T-602/15 RENV, ECLI:EU:T:2021:764 – *Jenkinson v Council and Others*.

[69] Assuming the standard case of a direct application under Art 270 TFEU; this is obviously different in the rare cases of requests for preliminary rulings, Art 267 TFEU.

Where powers are delegated under Article 2 SR, actions must be brought against the body to which the appointing authority is accountable.[70] Part of the powers can be transferred by one or more institutions to one of the institutions or to a joint body. Likewise, an action for compensation of damages for non-contractual liability, based on the allegation of a Commissioner's illegal conduct, must be brought against the Commission itself, since it stems from the employment relationship.[71]

Participation of interveners

The Member States may join proceedings (only) as interveners. Also, other institutions, other members of staff, trade unions and professional associations may join as interveners. The preconditions for intervention are stipulated in Article 40 Statute CJEU and Article 142 ff RoP GC: Member States and the institutions[72] of the Union may intervene as privileged interveners. Conversely, the other bodies, offices and agencies of the Union and any other person will have to establish an interest in the result of the case submitted to the court, in order to be granted application to intervene. The intervener must accept the case as she or he finds it at the time of her or his intervention, and an application to intervene shall be limited to supporting the form of order sought by one of the parties.

V. Subject Matter and Reviewable Act

1. *Ratione Materiae*

As to the subject matter of an application, all disputes arising from the employment relationship of the parties can be brought before the court.[73] Any act adversely affecting the applicant – whether oral, written or implied – can be contested, including an omission.[74] The subject of the dispute is the *initial* measure affecting the applicant.[75]

Specialty: Recruitment procedure and 'complex administrative operation doctrine'

In the staff selection process, the subject of the dispute is the decision of the administration rejecting the applicant's request for review,[76] except in cases where such a review is not required.[77] In the context of a recruitment procedure, which is a 'complex administrative operation' consisting

[70] Art 91a SR; Art 335 TFEU on the legal personality of the Union and the power to be a party to legal proceedings, as well as of each institution in matters relating to their respective operation. On delegated powers of the AECE, GC, T-248/10, ECLI:EU:T:2013:534 – *Italy v Commission*; GC, T-17/17, ECLI:EU:T:2018:645, *Constantinescu v EP*.

[71] ECJ, C-758/19, ECLI:EU:C:2021:603, para 33 – *OH v ID*.

[72] Art 13(1) TEU.

[73] CST, F-105/09, ECLI:EU:F:2011:41, para 21 – *Scheefer v EP*.

[74] GC, T-46/90, ECLI:EU:T:1993:54, para 14 – *Devillez v EP*; GC, T-6/91, ECLI:EU:T:1990:26, para 22 – *Pfloeschner v Commission*.

[75] On this principle and its exceptions, see ECJ, Case 293/87, ECLI:EU:C:1989:8, para 7 – *Vainker v EP*; CST, F-86/08, ECLI:EU:F:2009:161, paras 27/28 – *Voslamber v Commission*; GC, T-205/04, ECLI:EU:T:2007:346, para 27 – *Ianiello*; CST, F-93/08, ECLI:EU:F:2009:151, para 42 – *N v EP*; GC, T-309/03, ECLI:EU:T:2006:110, para 43 – *Camós Grau*; CST, F-25/07, ECLI:EU:F:2010:163, para 46 – *Bleser v Commission* (initial decision in the form of the decision rejecting the complaint); in individual cases, it does not harm if only the decision rejecting the complaint is challenged, CST, F-76/11, ECLI:EU:F:2012:173, paras 22/23 – *Grazyte v Commission*, confirmed by GC, T-86/13 P, ECLI:EU:T:2014:815.

[76] GC, T-243/99, ECLI:EU:T:2001:167 – *Buisson v Commission*; CST, F-5/08, ECLI:EU:F:2010:111, para 18 – *Brune*.

[77] GC, T-133/89, ECLI:EU:T:1990:36, paras 17/18 – *Burban v EP*, *contra*: a complaint procedure seems pointless because the institution concerned does not have the power to annul or amend the decisions of a selection board; GC, T-243/99, ECLI:EU:T:2001:167, para 35 – *Buisson v Commission*. See section VI.1.g. below.

of a series of closely linked decisions, irregularities which have arisen during the conduct of the selection procedure or during the organisation of the selection procedure can be the subject of a dispute against a subsequent individual decision, for example a decision not to admit a candidate to the tests. In accordance with the *complex administrative operation doctrine*, there must be a 'close connection' or 'close link' between the statement of reasons for the individual decision at issue and the plea of illegality raised against the notice of competition. Thus, exceptionally, a candidate may await the individual decision and then invoke a plea of illegality (Art 277 TFEU) against the notice of competition, provided that the earlier alleged irregularity is *closely linked* to the reasoning of the decision that is subsequently contested.[78]

The decision rejecting the complaint

A *decision rejecting the complaint* (Art 91(2) SR) that is only of confirmatory character without independent content does not add to the subject matter of the action. In any case, a claim for annulment addressed against such a decision does no harm either: it has the effect of bringing the original act before the court. An express decision rejecting a pre-litigation complaint may, however, in view of its content, not be confirmatory of the measure challenged. That is the case where the decision rejecting the complaint contains a re-examination of the situation of the person concerned in the light of new elements of law or of fact, or where it changes or adds to the original decision. In such circumstances, the rejection of the complaint constitutes a measure subject to review by the judicature, which will take it into consideration when assessing the legality of the contested measure or will even regard it as an act adversely affecting the applicant replacing the contested measure.[79] Hence, a decision rejecting the complaint may be the subject of an action insofar as it contains legal or factual circumstances which have arisen after the initial decision was taken, or if it changes the initial decision.[80] Because of procedural precaution, many applications include in the subject and form of order sought the decision rejecting the complaint, because that decision may have brought additional reasons that provide clarification and adjudication on the complaints raised by the applicant, which could on their side add independent content to the subject of litigation.[81]

2. Reviewable Act

As an important definition of the EU judicial review system provides, only measures which come from the competent authority and include a definitive position adopted by the administration which produces binding legal effects[82] 'capable of directly and

[78] On details of the doctrine and the term 'close link' or 'close connection', see ECJ, C-448/93 P, ECLI:EU:C:1995:264, paras 17, 19 – *Commission v Noonan*; ECJ, C-511/21 P, ECLI:EU:C:2023:208, para 54 – *Commission v Ana Calhau Correia de Paiva*; NB: This amounts to an extension of the admissibility requirements under Art 277 TFEU; see opinion of AG Medina – C-511/21 P, ECLI:EU:C:2022:902, paras 47–64 – *Commission v Ana Calhau Correia de Paiva*.

[79] GC, T-584/16, ECLI:EU:T:2017:282, para 71 – *HF v EP*; GC, T-529/22, ECLI:EU:T:2023:618, para 14 – *QT v EIB*.

[80] CST, F-94/11, ECLI:EU:F:2013:41, para 41 – *Brune v Commission*; GC, T-347/12 P, ECLI:EU:2014:268, paras 31–33 – *Mocová v Commission*; GC, T-21/22, ECLI:EU:T:2023:153, paras 16–19 – *NY v Commission*. Separate errors of law contained only in the decision rejecting the complaint are generally not relevant for an action against the initial measure, CST, F-2/09, ECLI:EU:F:2010:12, paras 38, 45/46 – *Menghi v ENISA*.

[81] GC, T-529/22, ECLI:EU:T:2023:618, para 16 – *QT v EIB*.

[82] CST, F-74/06, ECLI:EU:F:2008:48, para 172 – *Longinidis v Cedefop*; CST, F-104/05, ECLI:EU:F:2008:13, para 84 – *Valero Jordana v Commission*; CST, Jd Cases F-124/05 and F-96/06, ECLI:EU:F:2010:2, para 229 – *A and G v Commission*. On legal advice changing the legal situation and on waiver of immunity, see Potvin-Solis/ Lelièvre (2011) *RUE* 614 and (2012) *RUE* 268; Gervasoni (2010) 46 *Cahiers de droit européen* 753, 769 and GC, T-261/09 P, ECLI:EU:T:2010:215, paras

immediately[83] affecting the applicant's interests by bringing about a distinct change in his legal position constitute acts adversely affecting him'[84] are *reviewable acts*.

A reviewable act may also be a decision against another person or a general provision,[85] provided it is not a regulation of general application but contains a bundle of individual decisions in which the implementing measure is already laid out, ie, where the number and the identity of those who could be affected by it have been definitively determined.[86] A person is not adversely affected by an act if the legal consequence already results directly from other legal bases, such as the SR or an employment contract.[87] An agreement between the institution(s) and the trade unions, associations or other similar organisations cannot as such be a reviewable act for an individual staff member.[88]

Also acts introduced gradually by way of transitional measures when introducing a new regulation can constitute an act capable of *directly and immediately* affecting the applicant's interest; these are considered in their entirety, because the transitional measures are directly connected with the new regulation.[89] It would be unnatural to challenge transitional measures separately.

Whether the contested act is legally binding has to be assessed by its nature and effect. A consequence of this is that even an explicitly 'non-binding' email response to an enquiry about the staff member's pension entitlements can amount to a reviewable act.[90] Whether the reply is meant to be binding is to be assessed not by regarding solely its form, but by an assessment of its content and context, as well as of the powers of the institution providing the reply.[91] As a corollary of this case-law, staff members can request binding information about their entitlements (long) before their retirement commences and, if necessary, can seek a review of the reply. On this, see the case study on *Picard* on reviewable acts discussed below.

Purely informational references to a legal opinion,[92] internal notes,[93] etc, either do not produce binding legal effects or do not bring about a distinct change in a staff member's legal position,

46 ff – *Commission v Violetti and Others*; Mader (2018) *EuR* 339, 351 relating to an act of disclosure of information by OLAF to national authorities.

[83] Another, very common line of case-law applies the term 'individually' instead of 'immediately': CJEU, C-379/03 P, ECLI:EU:C:2004:580, para 15 – *Pérez Escolar v Commission*.

[84] GC, T-334/16 P, ECLI:EU:T:2018:723, para 50 – *FN and Others*; GC, T -311/09 P, EU:T:2011:734, para 74 – *Marcuccio*; CST, F-82/08, ECLI:EU:F:2011:45, paras 74/75 – *Clarke and Others v OHIM*; acts adversely affecting include, eg, the termination of the contract and the definitive (negative) appraisal report: GC, T-571/17, ECLI:EU:T:2020:141, paras 33–36 – *UG v Commission*.

[85] GC, Jd Cases T-66/96 and T-221/97, ECLI:EU:T:1998:187 – *Mellett v ECJ*.

[86] ECJ, Jd Cases 87 and 130/77, 22/83, 9 and 10/84, ECLI:EU:C:1985:318, paras 26 ff – *Salerno v Commission and Council*; ECJ, 80/79, ECLI:EU:C:1989:314 – *Ooms v Commission*. This can be a decision on a general salary increase, whereby the CST assumes that this increase is implemented by individual decisions, which are, on their side, communicated in the salary statement as reviewable acts, see CST, F-114/10, ECLI:EU:F:2011:173, paras 42, 48/49 – *Bowles and Others v ECB*; CST, F-121/10, ECLI:EU:F:2011:174, para 64 – *Heath v ECB*.

[87] Non-renewal of a fixed-term contract see CJEU Annual Report 2010, 209; CST, F-8/10, ECLI:EU:F:2010:151, para 64 – *Gheysens v Council*.

[88] For details, see chapter 4, I.4.

[89] GC, T-518/16, ECLI:EU:T:2018:873, paras 33–39 – *Carreras Sequeros and Others*; confirmed by ECJ, Jd Cases C-119/19 P and C-126/19 P, ECLI:EU:C:2020:676, para 75 – *Commission v Carreras Sequeros and Others*.

[90] ECJ, C-366/21 P, ECLI:EU:2022:C:984, paras 95–114 – *Picard v Commission*.

[91] ibid.

[92] CST, F-82/09, ECLI:EU:F:2010:154, paras 31, 12 – *Nolin v Commission*; but *cf* CST, F-73/09, ECLI:EU:F:2011:40, paras 42, 44 – *Sukup v Commission*.

[93] The decisive factor is the existence of an impairment of the legal status in the individual case, *cf* Mader (2018) *EuR* 339, 340 ff; CST, F-98/05, ECLI:EU:F:2008:11, paras 30, 98 – *Di Bucci v Commission* with further references; CST, Jd Cases F-27/06 and F-75/06, ECLI:EU:F:2007:89 – *Lofaro v Commission* (probationary report not independently reviewable); also ECJ, T-156/08 P, ECLI:EU:T:2009:69, para 56 – *R v Commission*; GC, T-511/18, ECLI:EU:T:2020:291, para 135 – *XH v Commission*.

and are therefore not reviewable. Likewise, the mere confirmation[94] of an earlier act that does not contain any new circumstances and is not based on a re-examination of the legal situation of the person concerned is not reviewable. On the other hand, a decision taken after a reassessment of the earlier act which was necessary due to the appearance of substantially new facts *is* reviewable, and not merely confirmatory.[95]

Organisational measures

As to the nature of organisational changes or transfers of staff into other services or other positions, there is not yet a common line.[96] In line with the approach found by the CST in *Kerstens*, the following is suggested: in principle, an organisational change or transfer falls within the category of the internal administrative self-organisation of an institution, and thus is not an act that can be contested by a staff member. However, *insofar as it modifies the conditions of the exercise and nature of the functions of an official*, a reassignment or change of duties – even one which does not affect their rank – can harm the 'moral interests and the future prospects' of the applicant, and can therefore adversely affect the applicant. For instance, the Court argued that even given positions of equal rank, certain functions would be better than others at leading to a promotion because of the nature of the responsibilities exercised.[97] It is suggested that if this can be shown, particularly for circumstances in which a staff member appears to be personally targeted by a measure, the organisational change or transfer should be reviewable. Likewise, where the reassignment to another post occurs further to a request for assistance under Article 24 SR (ie, as a measure to protect the staff member), the reassignment process has to respect the right to be heard, failing which it is perceived as a decision adversely affecting the staff member.[98]

Reviewable or not reviewable? Other examples

Salary statements are not decisions in themselves, but a way in which a decision can be made known to the staff member, which means that the factual availability of a salary statement is capable of initiating limitation periods (Art 90 SR, etc).[99]

As a rule, a preparatory statement is not of a binding nature and hence does not adversely affect the applicant;[100] but it can turn into a reviewable act if it also determines the subsequent final decision, such as when a promotion list is drawn up.[101] Implicit decisions are relevant in

[94] ECJ, 24/69, ECLI:EU:C:1970:22 – *Nebe v Commission*; ECJ, 23/80, ECLI:EU:C:1980:284 – *Grasselli v Commission*, ECR 1980, 3709, 3720. On a repeated complaint CST, F-60/08 and F-69/07, ECLI:EU: F:2008:181, paras 48/49 – *O v Commission*; CST, F-83/15, EU:F:2016:22 – *Pujante Cuadrupani*; it is different if the confirmation is preceded by a further legal examination: *cf* GC, Jd Cases T-568/16 and T-599/16, ECLI:EU:T:2018:347, para 57 – *Spagnolli*.

[95] GC, T-175/15, ECLI:EU:T:2017:694, para 154 – *Mabrouk v Council*: a fact is new if it did not exist at the time the action was performed or was not taken into account when it was performed; it will be essential if it significantly changes the applicant's legal situation as it was at the time the earlier act came into being, so that it is fair to raise doubts as to the merits of the act. An act is also not *purely confirmatory* if it has a different subject matter: ECJ, C-202/20 P, ECLI:EU:C:2021:385, para 21 – *Necci v Commission*.

[96] CST, F-52/08, ECLI:EU:F:2009:54, para 35 – *Plasa v Commission* (transfer); CST, F-119/06, ECLI:EU:F:2008:54, paras 42 ff, 45 – *Kerstens v Commission*; but CST, F-4/09, ECLI:EU:F:2010:24, para 53 – *De Britto Patricio-Dias v Commission*.

[97] GC, Jd Cases T-78/96 and T-170/96, ECLI:EU:T:1998:112, para 47 – *W v Commission*; CST, F-119/06, ECLI:EU:F:2008:54, paras 42–46 – *Kerstens v Commission*.

[98] GC, T-61/22, ECLI:EU:T:2023:201, para 56 – *OD v Eurojust*, even though the applicant never actually carried out the tasks under her reassignment.

[99] CJEU Annual Report 2008, 207; the first salary statement from which the decision is visible is to be contested, CST, F-103/05, ECLI:EU:F:2008:45, paras 175 ff – *Pickering v Commission*. Sceptical: CST, F-101/05, ECLI:EU:F:2006:58, para 55 – *Grünheid v Commission*, where this concerns the classification of the official.

[100] Nor can they be reviewed incidentally: GC, T-571/17, ECLI:EU:T:2020:141, para 31 – *UG v Commission*.

[101] Reithmann (2009) *EuR* 804; CST, F-86/08, ECLI:EU:F:2009:161, para 36 – *Voslamber v Commission*.

competitor disputes, for example where in addition to the competitor's promotion, the applicant's own non-promotion can also be contested.[102]

The fact that a staff member was personally involved in concluding his or her own contract does not prevent an individual contractual provision[103] or a time limitation from adversely affecting them.[104]

Case Study on Reviewable Acts

Increase in pension of 5.56%, even where staff cannot prove 'functional continuity'

Case C-366/21 P, *Picard v Commission* of 15 December 2022
Case T-769/16, *Picard v Commission* of 24 March 2021

In Brief

The courts specify the pension rights of contract staff and rule on effective judicial protection. This case is of general relevance in its part on the admissibility and the definition of a reviewable act; further, on its substance, it is of relevance for the pension rights of contract staff. The ECJ decided that the benefits of the transitional regime for staff *other than officials*[105] who already had contracts before 2014 also apply to the many colleagues who cannot show they have worked in 'functional continuity' of their service (due to performing varied functions on the basis of a variety of contracts), but who have nevertheless contributed continuously to the pension scheme. In the specific case, the applicant asked about the implications of the 2014 reform for his pension rights. The ECJ decided that the administration's reply concerning this was binding and was thus challengeable at the Court. The ECJ found that the applicant had continued to contribute to the pension scheme, and hence is entitled to the benefits of the (more favourable) transitional scheme.

Background

Under Articles 21 and 22 Annex XIII SR, officials who entered the service between 1 May 2004 and 31 December 2013 shall be entitled to 1.9 % of their salary for every year of pensionable service. Officials aged 35 or more on 1 May 2014 and who entered the service before 1 January 2014 shall become entitled to a retirement pension at a certain age indicated there. Under Article 1(1) of the Annex to the CEOS, Articles 21 and 22 Annex XIII SR shall apply by analogy to other servants employed on 31 December 2013.

[102] CST, F-39/07, ECLI:EU:F:2009:45, para 42 – *Campos Valls v Council*; CST, F-53/08, ECLI:EU:F:2010:37, paras 21, 80, 93 – *Bouillez and Others v Council*; CST, F-15/08, ECLI:EU:F:2010:7, para 27 – *Wiame v Commission*; GC, T-476/11 P, ECLI:EU:T:2013:557, paras 31 ff – *Commission v Moshonaki*.

[103] CST, F-19/08, ECLI:EU:F:2009:75, paras 96 ff – *Bennett v OHIM*; CST, F-105/09, ECLI:EU:F:2011:41, para 48 – *Scheefer v Parlament*; Sebastiani, 'L'évaluation de la réforme' in Govaere/Vandersanden (eds), *La fonction publique communautaire* (2008) 39.

[104] CJEU Annual Report 2010, 209.

[105] The judgment in this case is not relevant for officials, nor for staff who entered the service on 1 January 2014 or later.

Facts of the Case

The applicant was recruited by the Commission in 2008 as contract staff, and received several renewals and an indefinite contract in the first function group. In 2014, he received a new indefinite contract in the second function group. The 2014 reform defines a new annual rate of acquisition of pension rights of 1.8%, which is less favourable than the previous rate of 1.9%. In addition, Article 77(5) of the SR sets the retirement age at 66 years, compared with 63 years previously. A transitional regime (Arts 21 and 22 of Annex XIII SR) stipulated that an official who entered the service between May 2004 and 31 December 2013 – despite the changes under the reform – continues to benefit from the annual accrual rate of pension rights of 1.9%. In addition, a civil servant who was aged 35 on 1 May 2014 and entered the service before 1 January 2014 is entitled to a retirement pension at the age of 64 years and 8 months. As cited above, Article 1(1) of the Annex to CEOS provides that those transitional provisions are to apply 'by analogy' to other staff employed on 31 December 2013.

The applicant, who was unclear about the implications of the 2014 reform for his situation, requested an explanation from the manager of the Pensions Sector of the Office for the Administration and Payment of Individual Entitlements (PMO). The manager informed the applicant in an email that his pension rights had been modified as a result of the change of contract, and that the applicant's standard retirement age and annual rate of acquisition of pension rights had therefore changed to 66 years and 1.8% respectively as from 1 June 2014 (the date on which his second contract took effect). The applicant lodged a complaint and filed an action against the PMO's reply.

Decisions of the General Court and the Court of Justice

The GC dismissed the action by deciding that it was in any case unfounded, without ruling on the admissibility. On the substance, it interpreted the phrase 'by analogy' in Article 1(1) Annex CEOS (which refers to the benefits of the transitional clauses) to mean that the employment relationship of contract staff is comparable to that of officials under the SR only insofar as no new contract has been concluded. Hence, the GC asked whether or not the applicant had started a new employment relationship. In this sense, it examined the contracts concluded between the applicant and the Commission and the characteristics of the posts on which he was engaged, and found that the change of function group had called into question the 'functional continuity' of the applicant's employment relationship with the administration of the EU. Accordingly, the GC decided that the second contract of the applicant had given rise to a new entry into service, which did not allow the applicant to benefit – for that new contract – from the application of the transitional provisions laid down in Annex XIII SR concerning the annual rate of accrual of pension rights and the retirement age.

In its decision on the appeal, the ECJ sets aside the GC's judgment at first instance and annuls the decision of the PMO on the applicant's pension rights.

The Ground of Appeal

The ECJ finds that the GC erred in law when applying Article 1(1) Annex CEOS: the words 'by analogy' must not be interpreted in the sense that this required that a new contract should not make a substantial change in the duties of that member of staff such as to call into question the functional continuity of his employment relationship. Instead, a contextual interpretation of Article 1(1) Annex CEOS demands that a staff member who had contributed to the financing of the pension scheme should benefit from transitional provisions – by analogy with what applies to officials in that same situation. Officials who entered the service before the date of the 2014 reform and whose duties would be substantially altered after this date would not, by that fact alone, lose the benefit of those transitional provisions. These officials too would continue to pay contributions to the pension scheme during the period of service. What counts for applying the transitional provisions relating to the pension scheme is to assess whether, as a member of the contract staff, the applicant is in a situation similar to that of an official. The similarity of both situations is in the change to the employment relationship after 31 December 2013 without any interruption in the payment of contributions to the EU pension scheme. Both groups shall benefit from the transitional provisions, because they both have not stopped contributing to the pension scheme. After having stated this error in law committed by the GC, the ECJ decides itself on the case.

Admissibility

(a) The GC had not dealt with admissibility questions, assuming that the applicant's pleas were without merits. The ECJ considered the action for annulment to be admissible. The central admissibility question was whether the reply of the PMO on the applicant's enquiry about his pension rights constituted an act adversely affecting an official within the meaning of Article 90(2) SR. According to the case-law, only acts or measures which produce binding legal effects capable of directly and immediately affecting the person's interests by bringing about a distinct change in his legal position are acts adversely affecting him within the meaning of Article 90(2) SR.

(b) The Commission had argued that the email reply of the PMO was not a legally binding act, because it contained the caveat 'please note that this message is sent by way of information and does not constitute a decision of the appointing authority/AECE that may be challenged pursuant to Article 90 of the Staff Regulations.' The ECJ emphasises that it is required to examine the content and context of the act as well as the powers of the institution that adopted it, instead of solely referring to the form, which would amount to giving precedence to the form of the act over its actual substance. The PMO had conveyed that the applicant's 'pension rights [had] been modified as a result of the change of contract' and indicated the applicant's retirement age and the annual rate of pension rights. The PMO manager thus stated that the applicant could not benefit from the transitional measures under Article 1(1) Annex to CEOS. The ECJ followed the opinion of Advocate General Pikamäe and deduced from this reply by the PMO that it was not meant for information purposes only, but as a precise assurance that, in the view of the administration, the specified provisions applied to the applicant's situation. The department responsible for the management and payment of pension at PMO has provided the answer to the applicant.

(c) In regard to the argument brought forward by the Commission that the final decision on pension rights will be only taken upon the beginning of the retirement, the ECJ holds that the information about future rights affects the legal position of an applicant immediately and directly, otherwise the applicant would be able to ascertain his rights only at the time of retirement and would, until that time, be placed in a state of uncertainty as regards not only his financial situation, but also the age at which he may apply for retirement, which does not allow him to make immediate appropriate personal arrangements.

(d) The Commission argued that the information about future pension rights was only an intermediate measure, but not the challengeable final decision. To this, the ECJ replies that an intermediate measure which has independent legal effects may be the subject matter of an action for annulment where the illegality attaching to that measure cannot be remedied in an action brought against the final decision for which it represents a preparatory step. Where a challenge to the legality of an intermediate act in a later action against the final decision is not capable of ensuring effective judicial protection for the applicant against the effects of that act, it must be capable of being the subject matter of an action for annulment. That – in the opinion of the ECJ – is the case here: since the bringing of an action for annulment against the final decision adopted by the Commission at the time of retirement would not be liable to afford effective judicial protection to the staff member, the reply of the PMO constitutes an act adversely affecting him and must be capable of forming the subject matter of an action for annulment.

Substance

On the merits of the case, the ECJ applied a contextual interpretation of the Article 1(1) Annex CEOS and the transitional provisions. The applicant was employed under a contract on 31 December 2013 and had continuously contributed to the pension scheme. The ECJ thus concludes that the applicant – although his contract had been substantially amended after that date – shall benefit from the transitional scheme at the higher rate of pension rights, namely 1.9%, and the right to a retirement pension at the age of (here) 64 years and 8 months. The decision of the PMO had to be annulled as being contrary to Article 1(1) of the Annex to SR.

Comments

1. While, on the merits, the GC put the emphasis on the functional continuity of the applicant's employment relationship with the administration of the EU, the ECJ instead focuses on the question of whether the applicant had continued to contribute to the pension scheme (which he did). This is indeed the right aspect of comparison between the situation of a contract staff member and that of an official, for the purpose of applying the transitional provisions under Article 1(1) Annex to CEOS and the pension rights under Articles 21 and 22 Annex XIII SR.
2. The judgment of the ECJ in *Picard* is an important decision on the pension rights of staff other than officials, the benefits of which can now be claimed by all staff who were under contract on 31 December 2013 and experienced substantial alterations in their contracts afterwards. So far, such staff with substantial alterations in their contracts had not benefited from the transitional regime. As the 2014 reform defines a new annual rate of acquisition of pension rights of 1.8% for every year of pensionable service, which is less favourable than the previous rate of 1.9% under the transitional regime, the difference in payment equals to 5.56% of the pension amount (0.1% points out of 1.8%) for these periods.
3. As a consequence of the judgment, it is up to the administration to provide clarity about pension rights. Pending such clarification, staff will actively seek to be informed

about their rights and, when doing so, will accurately choose the responsible department for these questions. Whether the reply is meant to be binding is to be assessed not by regarding solely its form, but by assessing its content and context, as well as the powers of the institution providing the reply.

4. This line of case-law is very beneficial for staff: it increases effective judicial protection and produces a higher level of legal certainty. While the effects of actions for annulment only extend between the parties, in the specific constellation decided in this case, it is a matter that can now be claimed by all staff concerned, in accordance with the procedures foreseen (see comment 3 above).
5. What is of interest to staff in general is the possibility of obtaining reliable advice about future pension rights. The administration's answer may have an informal appearance, but still – due to its content and context – can amount to a legally binding and therefore challengeable act, ie, an 'act affecting the applicant adversely' in the sense of Article 90(2) SR.
6. The concept of clarifying uncertainties about the legal situation of staff should also apply to other rights beside pension entitlements. The case at hand made clear that replies by the administration may have a binding effect immediately (with the consequence of it being possible to challenge the decision in the courts), even though a conclusive entitlement will be determined only years in the future.
7. Without stating its method explicitly, the ECJ relied on the arguments developed to establish legitimate expectations under Union law. The emergence of legitimate expectations requires 'precise, unconditional and consistent information coming from authorised and reliable sources'.[106] In the present case, the ECJ does not examine every single precondition set up by the cited case-law for the existence of legitimate expectations, but has applied selected arguments in order to establish the important admissibility precondition of a measure which produces 'binding legal effects capable of directly and immediately affecting the applicant's interests by bringing about a distinct change in his or her legal position', for example that the manager in the PMO is the one responsible for providing the requested information. The method applied by the ECJ in this case is in line with its emerging jurisprudence whereby it uses general principles of law and fundamental rights as a means to determine reviewable acts in actions for annulment.[107]
8. Where the CEOS speaks about the application of a certain clause contained in the SR 'by analogy' (and it does so many times), this regularly does not mean that the provision applies in exactly the same way as in the SR, but instead in a way that is 'similar where the circumstances are comparable'.[108] The analogy requires a certain adjustment to the working conditions of the other servants.[109]

[106] See GC, Jd Cases T-66/96 and T-221/97, ECLI:EU:T:1998:187, paras 104–07 – *Mellett v ECJ*; GC, T-3/92, ECLI:EU:T:1994:15, para 58 – *Latham*; GC, T-329/03, ECLI:EU:T:2005:103, para 79 – *Ricci v Commission*; CST, F-4/07, ECLI:EU:F:2008:22, para 38 – *Skoulidi v Commission*. See chapter 1, III.6.d.

[107] Mader (2018) *EuR* 339–60.

[108] eg, Arts 6, 10, 11, 13, 15, 16, 20, 21, 27–30, etc CEOS and in the Annex of the CEOS.

[109] Currall in Perillo/Giacobbo-Peyronnel (eds), *Statut de la fonction publique de l'Union européenne: Commentaire article par article* (2017) 67/68.

VI. The Procedure in Staff Matters

General principles

Court proceedings in civil service matters are characterised by the principle of party disposition[110] as well as by the principle of an adversarial process, according to which the court shall 'take into consideration only those procedural documents and items which have been made available to the representatives of the parties and on which they have been given an opportunity of expressing their views'.[111] In order to grant effective legal protection, the court must have available in the file all required information, including confidential data, in order to be able to make a decision in full knowledge of the circumstances.[112] Importantly, litigation at the court is preceded by a preliminary complaint procedure that shall be treated in more detail below, followed by the description of other characteristic formal preconditions that must be fulfilled by an application in staff matters to be admissible.

Single judge, parties in the hearing

It is specific to civil service matters that a case may be transferred to a single judge,[113] except where a plea of illegality (Art 277 TFEU) is expressly raised against an act of general application.[114] Another specific feature is that in the course of the oral hearing the judges and Advocate General (AG) may invite the parties themselves to express their views on certain aspects of the case.[115]

Amicable settlement

In general, employment law is a thankful area for amicable settlements, because it typically affects the long-term relations of the parties, with manifold aspects of persisting human interaction. In EU civil service matters, amicable settlements may play an important role, both in out-of-court settlements (Art 124 RoP),[116] and in settlements reached at the initiative of the court (Art 125a–125d RoP). So far, it remains an open empirical question why and in which circumstances settlements in practice prove to be successful, or fail. One hypothesis is that the

[110] CST, F-64/10, ECLI:EU:F:2011:72, para 16 – *Mantzouratos v EP*. The court may not decide *ultra petita*, but award damages in the area of unlimited jurisdiction (disputes of a financial character) without the party's request, CST, F-53/08, ECLI:EU:F:2010:37, para 90 – *Bouillez and Others v Council*, provided that the defendant was able to comment on this, *cf* GC, T-491/08 P, ECLI:EU:T:2010:191, paras 83 ff – *Bui Van v Commission*.

[111] Art 64 RoP; Reithmann (2012) *EuR* 724; Potvin-Solis/Lelièvre (2011) *RUE* 613; ECJ, C-197/09 RX-II ECLI:EU:C:2009:391 – *M v EMEA*; CST, F-50/09, ECLI:EU:F:2011:55, paras 125 ff, *Missir Mamachi de Lusignano v Commission*, the judgment was overturned on another point of law; however, it is not necessary to subject a request to adversarial dispute if in any case it does not significantly change the legal position of the parties, CST, F-132/07, ECLI:EU:F:2011:4, para 31 – *Strack v Commission* (extension of deadline). It also does not violate the adversarial principle if the court ignores applications for evidence that it does not consider relevant to the dispute, see CST, F-52/09, ECLI:EU:F:2010:98, para 50 – *Da Silva Pinto Branco v ECJ*. On procedural measures to obtain information Gervasoni (2010) 46 *Cahiers de droit européen* 752 and GC, T-560/08 P, ECLI:EU:T:2010:192, para 62 – *Commission v Meierhofer*, according to which the court may not draw any conclusions from the lack of information in the file as long as it has not used the means provided for in its RoP to obtain the submission of the information by the party concerned; it may have to issue an order to take evidence. On the limits of evidence in adversarial proceedings, see CST, F-82/09, ECLI:EU:F:2010:154, para 96 – *Nolin v Commission*.

[112] CST, F-50/09, ECLI:EU:F:2011:55, para 115 – *Missir Mamachi de Lusignano v Commission*; CST, F-45/07, ECLI:EU:F:2010:72, para 116 – *Mandt v EP*.

[113] Art 29(1) lit b RoP.

[114] Art 29(2) lit b RoP.

[115] Art 110(4) RoP.

[116] Van Raepenbusch (2013) *Revue des Affaires Européennes* (*Law & European Affairs*) 291–98.

persistance of the same working environment for the staff member after settlement (or judgment, respectively) is important. Other opinions claim the opposite: settlement attempts could be more successful where the employment relationship in the institution has ended or is about to end.[117]

The RoP require the GC to examine, at all stages of the procedure, the possibilities of an amicable settlement of all or part of the dispute between the parties. The GC may instruct the Judge-Rapporteur, assisted by the Registrar, to seek the amicable settlement of a dispute, by proposing solutions, adopting appropriate measures, requesting the parties to produce documents, or also by inviting them to (separate) meetings. The success of the amicable settlement depends to a high degree on the capacities and case knowledge of the individual judge acting as 'facilitator'.[118] In accordance with Article 125a RoP, it is always the one instructed judge (Judge-Rapporteur) who conducts the settlement process, not the entire chamber.

The interests of the parties in their efforts to find an amicable settlement are protected in the sense that no opinion, suggestion, proposal, concession or document drawn up for this purpose may be relied upon as evidence by the court or the main parties in the judicial proceedings.[119] Material produced in the context of the amicable settlement procedure shall be entered in a specific register; an intervener may not have access to material in the separate file.[120] Also, the documents contained in the specific register are not to be passed on to the appeal instance, because they have no meaning in the case of an appeal where the attempts to settle have failed by definition.[121] There is no specific timing prescribed for the settlement process. If it turns out to require more time, the chamber may decide to stay proceedings of the case.[122]

Where the main parties come to an agreement before the Judge-Rapporteur on a solution which brings the dispute to an end, they may request that the terms of that Agreement be recorded in a document signed by the Judge-Rapporteur and by the Registrar; the case shall be removed from the register by reasoned order of the President.[123] The content of the settlement may be inserted in the order to remove the case from the register, if one party so requests and the other does not oppose.[124] The President shall give a decision as to costs in accordance with the Agreement between the parties or, failing that, at his discretion. Also a decision as to the costs of an intervener shall be taken, where applicable.

The effect of an amicable settlement is that it brings the dispute to an end insofar as stipulated between the parties in their Agreement. The subject matter of the dispute thus brought to an end is not amenable to judicial review any more, whereas the exact extent of the settlement is subject to interpretation.[125]

[117] Or where the defendant is an agency: Perillo/Giacobbo-Peyronnel in Perillo/Giacobbo-Peyronnel (eds), *Statut de la fonction publique de l'Union européenne: Commentaire article par article* (2017) 597.

[118] ibid, 593, who emphasise the importance of a specialisation of judges to conduct settlement attempts (598).

[119] Art 125d RoP.

[120] Art 125c RoP.

[121] Perillo/Giacobbo-Peyronnel in Perillo/Giacobbo-Peyronnel (eds), *Statut de la fonction publique de l'Union européenne: Commentaire article par article* (2017) 597.

[122] Art 69 lit c or d RoP; Perillo/Giacobbo-Peyronnel in Perillo/Giacobbo-Peyronnel (eds), *Statut de la fonction publique de l'Union européenne: Commentaire article par article* (2017) 598.

[123] Art 125b(1, 2) RoP; CST, F-22/14, ECLI:EU:F:2016:135 – *Gyarmathy v EMCDDA*.

[124] CST, F-47/12, ECLI:EU:F:2013:28 – *M v EMA*.

[125] GC, T-129/21, ECLI:EU:T:2022:424, para 43 – *Colombani v EEAS*; confirmed in appeal ECJ, C-595/22 P, ECLI:EU:C:2023:884, paras 20–26 – *Colombani v EEAS*.

1. Pre-Contentious Procedure: The Complaint – Article 90 SR

Purpose of the pre-contentious procedure

Preliminary (also pre-litigation or pre-contentious) procedures are intended both to encourage an amicable resolution of a dispute and to delimit its subject matter.[126] Preliminary procedures provide an opportunity – on the initiative of the official – for the administration to rectify a situation where the law permits or even obliges a correction to be made. When deciding on these Article 90 SR requests – which in practice are predominantly *complaints* against a decision adversely affecting the staff member (see section b below) – the institution exercises an administrative function, not a judicial one.[127]

Criticism and reflections de lege ferenda

Experience has shown that the quoted primary goal of a complaint procedure – namely to provide the parties with an opportunity to find an amicable solution – is rarely achieved. This circumstance has attracted some criticism[128] regarding the usefulness of the complaint procedure, particularly when taking into account the SR's own stipulation that the appointing authority is under no obligation to reply to a complaint at all, or to make a decision concerning the staff member's request. The institution may choose instead to implicitly refuse the complaint or request by means of a default decision after a silence of four months (see the subsequent sections). Critics have submitted that the internal administrative follow-up of a complaint procedure is not formally regulated; that the Legal Service, or the service which is the subject matter of the complaint, is not necessarily represented; that no minutes are made of relevant meetings; and that the meeting's result is not communicated to the complainant. This criticism implies that the existing preliminary procedure should be changed to allow the immediate filing of an action at the GC after the matter in question has been submitted to the administration (with a specific deadline that allows for the time needed to make a decision). This would motivate the parties to find an amicable solution at the Court. The sometimes considerable duration of the preliminary procedure may deprive an applicant of the object of (or interest in) a court action. It has also been proposed to establish a system of mediators, or else an external conciliation committee.[129] It is noteworthy that examples of such external intermediate appeal bodies already exist, *cf* the system of judicial review of the 58 international organisations that currently recognise the jurisdiction of the Administrative Tribunal of the International Labour Organization. It is therefore suggested that, before one system is replaced by another, to compare the experience gained with each of them and thoroughly evaluate the advantages of an EU review system that has developed over decades and is thus to a large extent able to provide legal certainty. A less radical change, but one that would still have a favourable impact, could be to shorten the deadline periods for deciding on complaints, and to abolish the option of implicit decision-making on the side of the appointing authority.

a. Article 90(1) and 90(2) SR: Trigger and Complaint

The preliminary procedure starts with the idea that any active intervention by the appointing authority has to be triggered by the person who takes an interest in it: he must first request that

[126] GC, T-53/92, ECLI:EU:T:1993:6, para 16 – *Piette de Stachelski v Commission*; ECJ, 168/83, ECLI:EU:C:1985:5 [1985] ECR 83, 97 – *Pasqualdi-Gherardi v EP*; ECJ, 142/85, ECLI:EU:C:1986:405 – *Schwiering v ECA*.

[127] GC, T-86/98, ECLI:EU:T:2000:15, para 61 – *Gouloussis v Commission*.

[128] Levi/Rodrigues et al, *Fonction publique de l'Union européenne* (2020) para 347.

[129] ibid.

the administration take a decision relating to him (Art 90(1) SR) and, if rejected, file a complaint against an act that affects the person adversely.[130] The response period for the authority is four months. If at the end of that period no reply to the request has been received, this shall be deemed to constitute an implied decision rejecting it, against which a complaint may be lodged.[131] There is no specific time-limit for the request to take a decision, but case-law requires that the request be made *within a reasonable period*. The 'reasonableness' of the period must be appraised in the light of all the circumstances specific to each case and, in particular, the importance of the case for the person concerned, its complexity and the conduct of the parties to the case.[132]

b. Article 90(2) SR Complaint

If the act affecting the person adversely already exists (Art 90(2) SR),[133] the request to take a decision is superfluous, ie, the procedure begins with the complaint. The complaint must be lodged within three months as of the dates enumerated in Article 90(2) SR. Here too, a four-month period applies from the date on which the complaint was lodged regarding the reasoned decision of the authority.[134] If at the end of that period no reply to the complaint has been received, this shall be deemed to constitute an implied decision rejecting it, against which an appeal may be lodged under Article 91 SR. The complaint procedure must also be followed if the staff member wants to contest the recovery of a financial benefit, even if the recovery was preceded by the withdrawal decision.[135]

When deciding on the complaint, the authority is not bound solely by the reasons for the decision, but can supplement its reasoning. The structure of Article 90(2) SR implies that the administration may amend the statement of reasons provided in the original decision at the stage of its decision rejecting the complaint; respectively, in the case of an implied decision, it may provide a reasoning for the first time in its decision rejecting the complaint.[136]

c. Effect of the Administration Exceeding the Article 90 SR Time-Limits

If the appointing authority fails to comply with the time limits laid down in Article 90 SR, the adopted decisions are neverthelss valid. The failure may, however, render the institution concerned liable for any damage caused to those involved, provided that in order to obtain compensation for the alleged damage they have followed the stages of the pre-litigation procedure.[137]

[130] Critical: Vandersanden, 'La procedure et les voies de recours' in Govaere/Vandersanden (eds), *La fonction publique communautaire* (2008) 115, who instead considers Art 25 SR to be sufficient. A mere request for information is not enough: Van Raepenbusch, 'L'apport jurisprudentiel du Tribunal de la fonction publique de l'Union européenne' in Gova ere/Vandersanden (eds), *La fonction publique communautaire* (2008) 176.

[131] Art 90(1)3 SR.

[132] ECJ, C-334/12 RX-II, ECLI:EU:C:2013:134, para 28 – *Arango Jaramillo and Others v EIB*; ECJ, Jd Cases C-238/99 P, C-244/99 P, C-245/99 P, C-247/99 P, C-250/99 P to C-252/99 P and C-254/99 P, ECLI:EU:C:2002:582, para 187 – *Limburgse Vinyl Maatschappij and Others v Commission.*

[133] Similar procedure foreseen in separate staff regulations, eg, Art 41 EIB Staff Regulations, with intermediate conciliation procedure.

[134] Art 90(2) sentence 4 and sentence 5 SR.

[135] See CST, F-3/09, ECLI:EU:F:2009:162, paras 79/80 – *Ridolfi v Commission* to weigh up the procedural economy.

[136] GC, T-283/08 P, ECLI:EU:T:2011:338, para 72 – *Longinidis v Cedefop*; GC, T-347/12 P, ECLI:EU:2014:268, para 35 – *Mocová v Commission.*

[137] GC, T-267/03, ECLI:EU:T:2005:23, para 84 – *Roccato v Commission*; CST, F-72/06, ECLI:EU:F:2009:40, para 60 – *Verheyden v Commission*; CST, Jd Cases F-138/06 and F-37/08, ECLI:EU:F:2009:48, para 212 – *Meister v OHIM.*

d. Addressee of the Complaint

Regularly, the request to take a decision and the complaint have to be addressed to the appointing authority of the applicant. In connection with investigations by the European Anti-Fraud Office (OLAF), the request to take a decision relating to himself within the meaning of Article 90(1) SR may be submitted to the Director of OLAF.[138] Similarly, within his sphere of competence of the European Data Protection Supervisor, the request or complaint has to be submitted to the Supervisor.[139]

e. Stay of Execution and Interim Measures

According to Article 91(4) SR, by way of derogation from the above complaint procedure, the person concerned may file the action *immediately* after submitting a complaint, provided that the applicant immediately requests either a stay of execution of the contested act or the adoption of interim measures. The proceedings in the principal action before the GC shall then be suspended until such time as an express or implied decision rejecting the complaint is taken.[140]

f. Damages and Preliminary Procedure

Damages must be claimed within a reasonable period of time[141] or, if based on an act capable of being reviewed, the damage claim must be part of the complaint procedure, hence it must be introduced during the preliminary procedure.[142] Case-law has seen exceptions in legally difficult individual cases[143] or where the lawsuit changes from an application for annulment to an application for damages.[144] The general line of admissibility of damage claims is that following the rejection of a complaint against an act adversely affecting the staff employed, both pleas are admissible: the annulment of the act adversely affecting the applicant, and the damage claim. However, once an action has been brought concerning the lawfulness of an act, the court may grant compensation *only* if that compensation is to remedy damage suffered by the person as a result of the unlawfulness of the act adversely affecting him or her which is the subject matter of the action or, at the very least, damage resulting from unlawfulness which is closely linked to that same act.[145]

[138] Art 90a SR.

[139] Art 90b SR.

[140] See section VI.7.b. below.

[141] CST, F-125/05, ECLI:EU:F:2007:18, para 81 – *Tsarnavas v Commission*. On the independence of the compensation for damages under civil service law vis-à-vis other liability under Union law: CST, F-50/09, ECLI:EU:F:2011:55, para 209 – *Missir Mamachi de Lusignano v Commission*; CST, F-89/11, ECLI:EU:F:2013:83, para 98 – *Goetz v CoR*; Mader, 'Le droit à l'indemnisation ex aequo et bono dans la fonction publique européenne' (2013) 96(2) *KritV/CritQ/Rcrit* 154–64.

[142] Reithmann (2008) *EuR* 277; (2009) *EuR* 805; Mader, 'Der Anspruch auf Entschädigung ex aequo et bono im EU-Dienstrecht – Schadenersatz für EU-Bedienstete nach billigem Ermessen' (2012) *EuR* 355, 365 f. Dispensable in the case of a direct connection between an action for annulment and an action for damages, CST, F-82/08, ECLI:EU:F:2011:45, para 211 – *Clarke and Others v OHIM*, and against excessively high requirements for parallel claims, the appeal decision, GC, T-101/11, ECLI:EU:T:2012:223, para 68 – *Mizuno KK v OHIM*.

[143] CST, F-19/08, ECLI:EU:F:2009:75, paras 167 ff – *Bennett v OHIM*; CST, F-6/07, ECLI:EU:F:2008:55, para 127 – *Suvikas v Council*; CST, Jd Cases F-44/06 and F-94/06, ECLI:EU:F:2007:66 – *C and F v Commission*.

[144] CST, F-4/07, ECLI:EU:F:2008:22, para 59 – *Skoulidi v Commission*; but CST, F-42/05, ECLI:EU:T:2008:71, paras 16, 60 – *Rossi Ferreiras v Commission*. On the relationship between the application for annulment and the application for damages, see also CST, F-104/09, ECLI:EU:F:2011:29, para 103 – *Canga Fano v Council*.

[145] GC, T-80/09 P, ECLI:EU:T:2011:347, paras 60 and 63 – *Commission v Q*; GC, T-365/21, ECLI:EU:T:2023:25, paras 65, 66 – *TJ v EEAS*.

Compensation for damages can also be awarded by the court ex officio without a request (and thus without a preliminary procedure).[146]

g. Competition and Preliminary Procedure

In principle, errors in the examination of the admission criteria of a competition procedure must first be challenged by a complaint.[147] Requests for review of unlawful conduct of European Personnel Selection Office (EPSO) and for breach of any of the provisions of the competition or its publication notice may be lodged with EPSO. A complaint against acts of the Selection Board would have to be lodged against EPSO. Yet, exceptionally, a complaint is not mandatory here, as is described below.

h. Exceptions from the Mandatory Character of the Complaint Procedure

Case-law has developed two exceptions to the mandatory character of the complaint procedure, namely (1) where the decisions are rooted in the assessments of the Selection Board and (2) in appraisals of the reporting officer. The reason is that it seems superfluous to insist on the mandatory completion of a complaint procedure as a precondition of admissibility of the court action where the administration itself does not have the powers to change the contested decision. A preliminary procedure under such conditions would lack effectiveness and amount to a pure formality. Therefore, exceptionally, a direct action can be filed immediately. This is pertinent for decisions of the Selection Board either where an action can be filed before EPSO has decided on the complaint, or without going through the complaint procedure at all.[148] However, the limitation periods for a complaint procedure (if any) and subsequent action have to be observed.

In the same way, actions against appraisal reports[149] can be directly filed to the GC as soon as they are final.[150] Here again, the reasoning for a complaint procedure not being mandatory is that the report expresses the opinion freely drawn up by the reporting officer, not by the appointing

[146] CST, F-53/08, ECLI:EU:F:2010:37, para 90 – *Bouillez and Others v Council*, but not applicable for reimbursement of medical expenses under Art 72 SR, CST, F -23/10, ECLI:EU:F:2011:162, paras 114 ff – *Allen v Commission*, and only in disputes of a financial character, CST, F-96/09, ECLI:EU:F:2012:129, para 73 – *Cuallado Martorell v Commission*. Groups of claims for compensation CST, F-63/13, ECLI:EU:F:2014:177, paras 54 ff, 63 – *Psarras v ENISA* (non-implementation of a judgment) and Mader, 'Le droit à l'indemnisation ex aequo et bono dans la fonction publique européenne' (2013) 96(2) *KritV/CritQ/Rcrit* 154–64.

[147] EPSO Guide for Open Competitions [2012] OJ C270 A; CST, F-77/08, ECLI:EU:F:2010:133, para 35 – *Vicente Carbajosa and Others v Commission* provides an overview of the judicial and extrajudicial legal remedies.

[148] EPSO Guide [2010] OJ C184 A, 12. On direct actions, see CJEU Annual Report 2012, 204; CST, F-66/11, ECLI:EU:F:2012:88, para 37 – *Cristina v Commission*; CST, F-93/11, ECLI:EU:F:2013:40, para 46 – *Taghani*; ECJ, 7/77, ECLI:EU:C:1978:68, para 6/9 – *von Wüllerstorff v Commission*; ECJ, 44/71, ECLI:EU:C:1972:53, *Marcato v Commission*; ECJ, 52/85, ECLI:EU:C:1986:199 – *Rihoux and Others v Commission*. Where EPSO has refused additional information, see CST, F-96/09, ECLI:EU:F:2012:129, para 55 – *Cuallado Martorell v Commission*. The vast majority of proceedings are initiated as complaints, not as direct complaints, Schiano/ Potvin-Solis/ (2012) *RUE* 612. If both paths are followed, it is not necessary to wait for the conclusion of the complaint proceedings before filing a complaint, CST, F-66/11 and F-83/11, ECLI:EU:F:2012:88/90 – *Cristina v Commission*; on the suspension until the appeal decision is made CST, F-51/11, ECLI:EU:F:2013:26, para 25 – *Pachtitis v Commission*. On challenging the notice of a selection procedure, see CST, F-29/11, ECLI:EU:F:2012:172, para 42 with further references – *BA v Commission*.

[149] Art 43 SR.

[150] ECJ, Jd Cases 6/79 and 97/79, ECLI:EU:C:1980:178, para 15 – *Grassi v Council*; GC, T-298/20, ECLI:EU:T:2022:671, para 22 – *KD v EUIPO*; GC, T-54/92, ECLI:EU:T:1994:283, para 22 – *Schneider v Commission*; CST, F-538/06 and F-37/08, ECLI:EU:F:2009:48, paras 138–40 – *Meister v OHIM*; GC, T-573/16, ECLI:EU:T:2019:481, para 135 – *PT v EIB*; GC, T-401/11 P, ECLI:EU:T:2014:625, para 72 – *Missir Mamachi di Lusignano v Commission*; ECJ, 6/79 and 97/79, ECLI:EU:C:1980:178, para 15 – *Grassi v Council*; ECJ, 140/87, ECLI:EU:C:1988:540 – *Bevan v Commission*.

authority as such. According to the *KD v EUIPO*[151] case-law, it is neither necessary to go through the complaint procedure nor – a fortiori – to go through the *appeal procedure* foreseen in the general implementing provisions (GIP)[152] before filing a complaint and/or an action. As a result of this, going through an *appeal procedure* as set out in the GIP is possible and may be 'desirable', but is not a prerequisite for the admissibility of a court application. The *appeal procedure* will therefore retain its significance mainly for the first phase of the appraisal procedure, in which the appraisal report is not yet final. This is further discussed in the case study on appraisal reports in chapter 3, II.13.e.

Other exceptions?

So far, exceptions from mandatory complaint procedures are only recognised for these two groups (acts of selection boards and appraisal reports). It remains to be seen whether the courts either narrow these exceptions or even treat in a similar way the assessments of other internal bodies such as those listed in Article 9 SR and in Annex II SR (most prominently, the Invalidity Committee), so that remedies against their acts adversely affecting the applicant would also be exempted from the mandatory character of the complaint procedure.

An argument in favour of such development would be that – while the assessment of a selection board or the reporting officer, which are both human resource matters within the realm of administration – the character of medical assessments of an invalidity committee is, rather, not administrative; their conclusions seem therefore even less susceptible to verification by an administrative service than the two groups of acts which case-law has exempted from the mandatory complaint procedure.

As to disciplinary boards, it can be well argued that the conclusions (adversely affecting the applicant) of a disciplinary board themselves should be reviewable, if the appointing authority adopts the conclusions for its own decision-making.[153] It is argued here that also in this case a preliminary complaint procedure against the Board's conclusions would be superfluous for the reasons mentioned above.

Calculation of periods, dates and time limits

Periods, dates and time limits are calculated in line with Regulation No 1182/71.[154] The complaint period of three months starts with the notification[155] of the decision or the rejection of the request; in the event of the administration's inaction it starts upon the implied rejection.[156]

[151] GC, T-298/20, ECLI:EU:T:2022:671, para 22 – *KD v EUIPO*; appeal: ECJ, C-5/23 P – *EUIPO v KD*.

[152] *cf* Commission decision of 16 December 2013 with general implementing provisions for Art 43 and Art 44(1) SR, C(2013) 8985 final; see there Art 7.

[153] In this sense GC, T-693/16 P-RENV-RX, ECLI:EU:T:2021:895, para 170 – *HG v Commission*.

[154] Council Regulation (EEC, Euratom) of 3 June 1971 [1971] OJ L124/1; CST, F-62/08, ECLI:EU:F:2009:88 – *Senevier v Commission* and CST, F-27/11, ECLI:EU:F:2013: 2, para 47 – *BO v Commission*. On the question of proof of receipt, see CST, F-3/05, ECLI:EU:F:2006:31, para 28 – *Schmit v Commission*. On a Saturday, see CST, F-76/09, ECLI: EU:F:2011:12, para 43 – *AH v Commission*.

[155] This may be an electronic notification in the human resource management system, eg, Sysper, *cf* CST, F-59/06, ECLI:EU:F:2007:71 – *Kerstens v Commission*; the authority cannot invoke a delay if it cannot prove that the decision was received via Sysper, GC, T-526/16, ECLI:EU:T:2018:963, para 35 – *FC v Commission*. The complaint period may also start at the time the notification of the decision (here, not to extend the validity of a reserve list) is published on the internet: GC, T-727/21, ECLI:EU:T:2023:136, para 42 – *TO v AUEA*.

[156] However, Art 91(3) SR does not apply by analogy to the complaint procedure, CST, F-62/08, ECLI:EU:F:2009:88 – *Senevier v Commission*; on the fiction of notification if a registered letter is not picked up CST, F-25/10, ECLI:EU:F:2010:171, paras 38 ff, 44 – *AG v EP*; Schiano/Potvin-Solis (2012) *RUE* 616; Gervasoni (2010) 46 *Cahiers de droit européen* 781; CST, F-87/11, ECLI:EU:F:2013:10, paras 34 ff – *Wahlström v Frontex* (case of wrong postal code, paras 27, 44).

The requested re-examination of an act *for new facts* is subject to qualified preconditions;[157] such re-examination can cause the deadline periods to reset, particularly (but not exclusively) where re-examination is undertaken upon the administration's own initiative.[158] It is not considered to be a *new fact* if the court finds that an administrative decision of general scope which was the basis of the measure affecting the applicant adversely, infringes the SR.[159] However, the adoption of a new regulatory act can imply such a new fact.[160]

2. The Correspondence Rule

The rule of correspondence (also *principle of consistency* or *principle of the identity of the subject matter of the dispute*)[161] is an important specialty in EU civil service law. It requires 'correspondence' or identity between the subject matter of the complaint and that of the action. Thus, pleas that are *closely related* to the complaint are admissible;[162] also a *substantiation*[163] and the *amplification* of a plea brought forward in the complaint are allowed,[164] as well as other grounds based on legal or factual circumstances that only became known in the course of the proceedings.[165] The effect of the correspondence rule is that the parties (especially the complainant) limit the scope of court proceedings to that of the pre-contentious dispute at the complaint stage.[166] New legal pleas and new lines of argumentation relating to facts that have already been introduced are barred if they had not been raised in the complaint.[167] The correspondence rule is violated if the court application changes the subject matter or the ground of the complaint (ie, contesting the substantive or procedural legality of the act). The action does not have to be directed against the same decision as was the complaint, but against the same content.[168] However, a plea of

[157] Reithmann (2009) *EuR* 804; CST, F-111/06, ECLI:EU:F:2007:163, para 26 – *Giannopoulos v Council* (new and substantial facts).

[158] CST, F-111/06, ECLI:EU:F:2007:163, para 26 – *Giannopoulos v Council.*

[159] CST, F-81/08, ECLI:EU:F:2009:59, para 48 – *Ketselidou v Commission.*

[160] CST, F-92/05, ECLI:EU:F:2007:9, para 69 – *Genette v Commission.*

[161] *Règle de concordance*, in five judgments also called the 'rule of harmony', GC, T-4/96, ECLI:EU:T:1997:103, para 98 – *S v ECJ*; GC, T-154/05, CLI:EU:T:2007:322, para 122 – *Lo Giudice v Commission*; CST, F-25/07, ECLI:EU:F:2010:163, para 42 – *Bleser v Commission*; CST, F-45/07, ECLI:EU:F:2010:72, paras 115 ff – *Mandt v EP*; CST, Jd Cases F-124/05 and F-96/06, ECLI:EU:F:2010:2, para 245 – *A and G v Commission*; CST, F-15/07, ECLI:EU:F:2008:158, para 31 – *K v EP*; CST, F-138/06, ECLI:EU:F:2009:48, para 145 – *Meister v OHIM*; CST, F-148/06, ECLI:EU:F:2008:169, para 50 – *Collée v EP*; CST, F-144/07, ECLI:EU:F:2008:163, para 43 – *Efstathopoulos v EP*; further: GC, T-476/11 P, ECLI:EU:T:2013:557, paras 71 ff – *Commission v Moschonaki*; Gervasoni (2010) 46 *Cahiers de droit européen* 752; Wegener, 'Art 270 TFEU' in Calliess/Ruffert, *EUV/AEUV*, 6th edn (2022) para 7.

[162] ECJ, 306/81, ECLI:EU:C:1983:143, para 9 – *Verros v EP*. The plea of illegality may coincide with an implicit objection of wrong interpretation, CST, F-97/08, ECLI:EU:F:2010:73, paras 55 ff – *Füller-Tomlinson v EP.*

[163] ECJ, 58/75, ECLI:EU:C:1976:102, [1976] ECR, 1139, 1153 *Sergy v Commission*; ECJ, Jd Cases 75 and 117/82, ECLI:EU:C:1984:116 – *Razzouk and Beydoun v Commission*; ECJ, 13/86, ECLI:EU:C:1987:144 – *von Bonkewitz-Lindner v EP*; CST, F-14/09, ECLI:EU:F:2010:167, para 27 – *Almeida Campos and Others v Council*; on damages: CST, F-50/09, ECLI:EU: F:2011:55, para 84, *Missir Mamachi de Lusignano v Commission*, appeal decision GC, T-401/11 P, ECLI:EU:T:2014:625.

[164] CST, Jd Cases F-124/05 and F-96/06, ECLI:EU:F:2010:2, para 245 – *A and G v Commission.*

[165] ECJ, 306/81, ECLI:EU:C:1983:143, para 9 – *Verros v EP*; GC, T-160 and 161/89, ECLI:EU:T:1990:86, para 20 – *Kalavros.*

[166] CST, F-65/07, ECLI:EU:F:2009:43, para 137 – *Aayhan and Others v EP*; CST, F-43/10, ECLI:EU:F:2012:184, para 69 – *Cerafogli v ECB*; Vandersanden, 'La procedure et les voies de recours' in Govaere/Vandersanden (eds), *La fonction publique communautaire* (2008) 113.

[167] Germelmann, *Die Rechtskraft von Gerichtsentscheidungen in der Europäischen Union* (2009) 364; Sachs, *Die ex-officio-Prüfung durch die Gemeinschaftsgericht* (2008) 57, 106.

[168] CST, F-100/08, ECLI:EU:F:2010:35, para 32 – *Petrilli v Commission.*

illegality (Art 277 TFEU) can be raised for the first time at the court, and does not fall under the correspondence rule.[169]

Rule of correspondence and legal representation

As opposed to the filing of an application at the court, a complaint in the pre-contentious procedure does not have to be filed by an attorney. Further, the costs of the complaint procedure (ie, legal advice at that stage) are regularly irrecoverable. Hence, frequently, a staff member is not yet being advised by an attorney during the complaint phase. Under the correspondence rule, a lack of instruction leads to a limitation of the scope of arguments in litigation and thus reduces the staff member's chances of successful outcome. Viewed from a different angle, the correspondence rule makes it advisable (despite the irrecoverable cost) to consult a lawyer, because of the preclusion of arguments that were not introduced in the complaint stage. In addition, the professional legal assessment of a matter by a lawyer in the early phase before or during the complaint procedure (including potential negotiations in connection with amicable settlements, where applicable) can help to reduce the case load of the courts.

Scope of the rule of correspondence

The exact scope of the correspondence rule is in transition. While case-law of the 1970s saw the need for the rule with the purpose of facilitating the extrajudicial resolution of disputes, this justification has become less convincing in recent years. The complaint procedure still serves as an effective filter for disputes and gives the administration the opportunity to either correct any irregularities or defend the legality of its decisions before any legal proceedings are brought. As such, there is clearly a need to demarcate the subject matter of a dispute at an early stage. Whether this is justifiable by an analogy[170] to the GC RoP[171] is more than doubtful, bearing in mind the differences in the types of procedure. Even so, the *principle of effective judicial protection* demands that the guarantee of an effective remedy should not be narrowed by provisions preceding the judicial stage to the point of excessively undermining the principle. The goal of (desirable) extrajudicial resolution of disputes 'is not a fundamental right and cannot therefore justify the radical restriction of the possibilities of access to judicial proceedings available to officials'.[172] As a result, the correspondence rule should be understood as barring arguments at litigation stage that alter the relief sought in the complaint or its 'cause of action'. As the CST has opined in *Mandt*, the concept of 'cause of action' must be given a broad interpretation. The 'cause of action of the dispute' would be the applicant's challenge to the substantive legality of the contested decision or, in the alternative, the challenge to its procedural legality. The rule of correspondence would not be complied with where the applicant, who criticises in her or his administrative complaint solely the formal validity of the act adversely affecting her or him, raises substantive pleas in the originating application; or in the opposite case where the applicant, after having disputed in her or his complaint only the substantive legality of the act adversely affecting her or him, submits an application containing pleas relating to the formal validity of that act, including its procedural aspects.[173]

The conclusion is the following: should this line of *Mandt* case-law continue to be consolidated, it will be of key importance in order for a prospective applicant to maintain full scope of

[169] GC, T-787/14 P, ECLI:EU:T:2016:633, para 78 – *ECB v Cerafogli.*

[170] In this sense, CST, Jd Cases F-124/05 and F-96/06, ECLI:EU:F:2010:2, para 245 – *A and G v Commission.*

[171] Art 84(2) RoP GC stipulates that 'no new plea in law may be introduced in the course of proceedings unless it is based on matters of law or of fact which come to light in the course of the procedure'.

[172] CST, F-45/07, ECLI:EU:F:2010:72, para 118 – *Mandt v EP.*

[173] ibid, paras 119/120.

her or his cause of action to construe the arguments of a complaint in a way that they challenge *both* the substantive *and* the procedural legality of the contested act. As long as the general line of case-law does not side with the CST in *Mandt*, the complaint will still need to set out the subject of all legal arguments ('set the tone') relied on in the action, next to introducing relevant facts. The court application will then be free to further elaborate on the arguments, substantiate them in more detail, and amplify the pleas.

3. Time Limit for Bringing an Action

The time limit for filing the application to the GC is three months,[174] extended by the period on account of distance of 10 days,[175] and begins to run either once the complaint has not been remedied within four months (in the case of implied rejection), or once it is expressly rejected. The first official notification of the decision is decisive, but not, for example, previous actual knowledge of its content.[176] In the case of several complaints against an act, the last complaint decision is only decisive if it contains new aspects.[177] If a complaint is rejected by express decision after being rejected by implied decision but before the period for lodging an action has expired, the period for lodging the court action runs afresh.[178] This reset of the period only applies to the time limit for filing an action after complaint, but not to the time limit for lodging a complaint after a request under Article 90(1) SR has been rejected by implied decision.[179] Deadlines for filing an action and deadlines for complaints are mandatory law; neither the parties nor the court may modify or dispense with them.[180] However, other time limits for bringing an action may apply that are based on special provisions.[181] Compliance with legal deadlines is checked by the court ex officio,[182] for which – in the interests of legal certainty – strict standards apply.[183] Deadlines are not extended if the institution states that it is still examining the case[184] or while negotiations for an amicable settlement are ongoing.[185]

4. Form and Language of Application

The application and all other documents in the litigation phase are filed electronically via *e-curia*.[186] The complaint decision may be notified by the institution to the representing lawyer

[174] Art 91(3) SR, there called 'appeal'.

[175] Art 60 RoP GC.

[176] ECJ, 31/76, ECLI:EU:C:1977:79 – *Macevicius v EP*; CST, F-114/05, ECLI:EU:F:2006:106, paras 35 ff – *Combescot v Commission*; Reithmann, EuR 2008, 276 ; ECJ, C-334/12 RX-II, ECLI:EU:C:2013:134, paras 28 ff, 46 – *Arango Jaramillo and Others v EIB*.

[177] CST, F-58/07, ECLI:EU:F:2008:170 – *Collote v Commission*.

[178] Art 91(3), final sentence SR.

[179] GC, T-55/92, ECLI:EU:T:1993:65, para 34 – *Knijff v ERH*.

[180] GC, T-272/19, ECLI:EU:2020:361, para 22 – *TO v EEAS*.

[181] *cf* Art 41a EIB Staff Regulations, taking into account the possibility of a conciliation procedure.

[182] ECJ, Jd Cases 75 and 117/82, EU:C:1984:116, ECR 1984, 1509, 1529 – *Razzouk and Beydoun v Commission*; CST, F-114/05, ECLI:EU:F:2006:106, paras 37, 39 – *Combescot v Commission*.

[183] ECJ, 24/69, ECLI:EU:C:1970:22 – *Nebe v Commission*; CST, F-111/06, ECLI:EU:F:2007:163, paras 26, 28 – *Giannopoulos v Council*; CST, F-130/05, ECLI:EU:F:2007:227, paras 50, 59 – *Soares v Commission*.

[184] ECJ, 40/71, ECLI:EU:C:1972:9 – *Richez-Praise v Commission*. But CST, F-102/07, ECLI:EU:F:2009:129, para 47 – *Kerstens v Commission*.

[185] ECJ, Jd Cases 75 and 117/82, ECLI:EU:C:1984:116, [1984] ECR 1509, 1529 – *Razzouk and Beydoun v Commission*; but CST, F-104/07, ECLI:EU:F:2009:93, paras 49/50 – *Hoppenbrouwers v Commission*.

[186] Art 56a RoP, with the exceptions mentioned therein.

who submitted the complaint.[187] The complaint decision is drafted in a language that is deemed appropriate; the authority can prove the ability of the addressee to take note of the decision.[188] In order to effect notification, the administration is not limited to the employee's mother tongue; the language chosen for the complaint is also suitable if the complainant does not understand it himself.[189]

5. Legal Interest in Bringing an Action

In order to be able to seek the annulment of an act which adversely affects the applicant, an interest in legal protection is required, meaning that at the time[190] he brings the action, the person must have a personal and direct interest, or in the words of the GC: 'a vested and present interest, which is sufficiently established to have that act annulled, such an interest assuming that the claim is likely, if successful, to benefit him'.[191] An action seeking the annulment of the (entire) reserve list in a recruitment procedure is not necessarily inadmissible for being 'excessive';[192] the interests of an unsuccessful candidate in bringing an action in such cases has to be assessed in the individual case and it may embrace the interests to annul the (entire) result of the procedure.[193]

On the other hand, there is no interest if the applicant's concern cannot be possibly satisfied by the application or does not benefit him. Moreover, there may be no personal and direct interest in granting legal protection even in the case of measures adversely affecting the applicant if there were mere procedural errors without consequence or the applicant's legal position remained unchanged without the error.[194]

Asserting the application of a general principle of law does not confer a subjective right to the applicant as such. The principle of sound administration, for example, does not confer any right on individuals, except where it constitutes the expression of a specific right. In practice, there is a tendency to uphold interest in legal protection, thus not making inadmissible such a plea in law;[195] because it is only when those arguments are considered in detail that it can be determined whether the administration may have infringed a specific right alleged to be the expression of the principle of sound administration. However, the required interest presupposes that the legal remedy will entail a benefit.[196] Thus, an applicant cannot claim the illegality of exam questions

[187] CST, F-137/07, ECLI:EU:F:2009:46 – *Sergio and Others v Commission.*

[188] GC, T-118/99, ECLI:EU:T:2001:44 – *Bonaiti Brighina v Commission*; Reithmann (2011) 1 *EuR* 124.

[189] CST, F-31/11, ECLI:EU:F:2012:28, paras 17–25, 27 – *BI v Cedefop*: if the administration announces a later translation of the document, the time period does not start only when the translation is communicated.

[190] ECJ, C-202/20 P, ECLI:EU:C:2021:385, para 26 – *Necci v Commission.*

[191] GC, T-80/09, ECLI:EU:T:2011:347, paras 156 ff – *Commission v Q*; GC, Jd Cases T-35/05, T-61/05, T-107/05, T-108/05 and T-139/05, ECLI:EU:T:2006:365, para 35 – *Agne-Dapper and Others v Commission.*

[192] First labelled as excessive by GC, T-488/18, ECLI:EU:T:2021:76, para 180 – *XC v Commission*, then repealed by the ECJ.

[193] ECJ, C-527/21 P, ECLI:EU:C:2023:850, para 68 – *XC v Commission.* See also ECJ, C-243/18 P, ECLI:EU:C:2019:378, paras 46/47 – *Fusion for Energy v Galocha* and chapter 3, II.4.c.

[194] CST, F-42/10, ECLI:EU:F:2012:64, paras 27 ff – *Skareby v Commission*; CST, F-83/07, ECLI:EU:F:2009:158, para 66 – *Zangerl-Posselt v Commission*; CST, F-15/08, ECLI:EU:F:2010:7, para 27 – *Wiame v Commission.*

[195] CST, F-87/08, ECLI:EU:F:2010:159, para 39 – *Schuerings v ETF* (duty of care), set aside on another legal issue; CST, F-88/08, ECLI:EU:F:2010:160, para 39 – *Vandeuren v ETF* (good administration), set aside on another legal issue.

[196] This was denied in CST, F-23/09, ECLI:EU:F:2010:138, paras 39, 42, 50 – *Cerafogli v ECB* where the appointment of a competitor was challenged by an invalid staff member; more open: CST, F-55/10, ECLI:EU:F:2011:94, para 29 – *AS v Commission* for considering invalidity as a potentially reversible condition, and the appeal decision GC, T-476/11 P, ECLI:EU:T:2013:557, para 53 – *Commission v Moschonaki.* The spouse of a civil servant can also have an interest in legal protection insofar as the SR grant own entitlements, eg, Art 72 SR, CST, F-104/10, ECLI:EU:F:2013:64, paras 40, 51 – *de Pretis Cagnodo and Others v Commission.*

that he answered correctly.[197] There is no interest in legal protection if the act adversely affecting the applicant is eliminated before the action is brought and it has no after-effects.[198] The interest in legal protection can result from the risk of a possible future recovery claim about whose unfoundedness the applicant is seeking certainty.[199] The mere interest in a subsequent claim for damages is not sufficient without further specification.[200]

6. Proper Filing of Action and Forms of Order Sought

The court procedure for filing a direct action under Article 270 TFEU is stipulated in Article 50 ff RoP. The application must contain the subject matter of the proceedings, the pleas in law, the arguments relied on and a summary of those pleas in law, the form of order sought, and any evidence.[201] The file must be sufficiently clear and concise as to enable the defendant to prepare the defence and to permit the court – possibly without further information – to take the decision.[202] It is not sufficient for the applicant to raise general and abstract complaints from which it does not become clear how his personal situation is affected.[203]

The pleas in law, plus the factual and legal justification, must result from the text of the application itself;[204] it is not sufficient to merely list the pleas in the Annexes or to introduce them only in the oral hearing.[205] The application has to adequately present the facts, the legal opinion and its relevance for the case.[206] A reference to the text of an application in another case is not sufficient.[207]

Inadmissible are: forms of order sought that the court should determine the illegality of a provision of Union law (although an incidental test and subsequent declaration under a plea of illegality is possible with regard to norms that form the legal basis of the contested decision or if it is essentially based on them);[208] forms of order sought that instruct the enforcement of

[197] CST, F-2/07, ECLI:EU:F:2010:22, paras 183, 186 – *Matos Martins v Commission*.

[198] GC, T-49/91, ECLI:EU:T:1992:72, paras 24, 26 – *Turner v Commission*; ECJ, C-198/07 P, ECLI:EU:C:2008:761, paras 44, 45 – *Gordon v Commission*; CST, F-71/08, ECLI:EU:F:2009:150, para 31 – *N v EP*; CST, F-93/08, ECLI:EU:F:2009:151, para 46 – *N v EP*; CST, F-80/08 R, ECLI:EU:F:2008:175, para 34 – *Wenig v Commission* (review of dismissal after retirement). CST, F-107/11, ECLI:EU:F:2012:182 – *Ntouvas v ECDC* (review of a post-resignation appraisal), appeal dismissed; CST, F-55/10, ECLI:EU:F:2011:94, para 29 – *AS v Commission* (legal protection despite invalidity), Potvin-Solis/Lelièvre (2011) *RUE* 614.

[199] GC, T-170/17, ECLI:EU:T:2019:309, paras 41 ff – *RW v Commission*.

[200] GC, T-467/17, ECLI:EU:T:2019:646, para 56 – *Barata v EP*.

[201] Art 76 lit d–f RoP; *cf* Art 21(1) Statute CJEU, Art 120 lit c RoP ECJ.

[202] CST, F-29/11, ECLI:EU:F:2012:172, para 73 – *BA v Commission*; CST, F-76/09, ECLI:EU:F:2011:12, para 29 – *AH v Commission*; CST, F-16/09, ECLI:EU:F:2009:164, para 42 – *de Britto Patrício-Dias v Commission*; CST, F-95/06, ECLI:EU:F:2008:62, paras 121–25 – *Taruffi v Commission*; CST, F-18/09, ECLI:EU:F:2011:180, paras 43 ff – *Merhzaoui v Commission*; this also applies to damage claims, *cf* CST, F-1/11, ECLI:EU:F:2012:157– para 67 – *Soukoup v Commission*. Too strict, however, in CST, F-87/05, ECLI:EU:F:2006:65, paras 38, 39 – *Ott and Others v Commission*, qualifying the submissions as mere abstract considerations; on this point repealed in GC, T-250/06 P, ECLI:EU:T:2008:164, paras 94–101.

[203] CST, F-2/07, ECLI:EU:F:2010:22, para 162 – *Matos Martins v Commission*.

[204] CST, F-2/09, ECLI:EU:F:2010:12, paras 111, 114 – *Menghi v ENISA*; CST, F-31/06, ECLI:EU:F:2011:151, para 57 – *Pino v Commission*; CST, F-12/10, ECLI:EU:F:2012:29, para 15 – *Kerstens v Commission*.

[205] CST, F-31/06, ECLI:EU:F:2011:151, para 57 – *Pino v Commission*.

[206] CST, F-124/07, ECLI:EU:C:2008:196, paras 67/68, 116, 149 – *Beheer v Commission*. It is not the task of the court to develop arguments itself, CST, F-98/09, ECLI:EU:F:2011:156, paras 75, 84 – *Whitehead v ECB*; CST, F-20/09, ECLI:EU:F:2011:181, para 24 – *Juvyns v Council*. Essential details can be concise, but must be coherent and comprehensible directly from the application, CST, F-6/10, ECLI:EU:F:2011:139, para 92 – *Munch v OHIM*.

[207] CST, Jd Cases F-124/05 and F-96/06, ECLI:EU:F:2010:2, para 312 – *A and G v Commission*.

[208] CST, F-38/10, ECLI:EU:F:2011:43, para 23 – *Vakalis v Commission*, appeal dismissed; CST, F-64/10, ECLI:EU:F:2011:72, paras 23/24 – *Mantzouratos v EP*; CST, F-74/08, ECLI:EU:F:2009:142, para 37 – *Ramaekers-Jørgensen*;

the judgment;[209] forms of order sought that determine how a judgment annulling a decision is to be implemented, or other requests aimed at determining the obligation on the part of the administration.[210]

7. Urgent Procedures: Expedited Procedure and Interim Relief

The two types of urgent procedures at the GC are the expedited procedure and interim relief (ie, the application for suspension or other interim measures).

a. *Expedited Procedure*

The special provisions for the expedited procedure are stipulated in Articles 151–55 RoP. The GC may, at the request of the applicant or the defendant, after hearing the other main party, decide, having regard to the particular urgency and the circumstances of the case, to adjudicate under an expedited procedure. The request is to be made by a separate document lodged at the same time as the application initiating the proceedings, specifying the particular urgency of the case.[211] The court may also decide so of its own motion on a proposal from the Judge-Rapporteur in exceptional circumstances and after hearing the main parties. The GC may prescribe conditions as to the volume and presentation of the pleadings of the main parties, as to the subsequent conduct of the proceedings, or as to the pleas in law and arguments. Depending on the compliance of the parties with the conditions, the decision to adjudicate under an expedited procedure may be revoked; the proceedings shall then continue in accordance with the ordinary procedure. In practice, cases of granted expedited procedure in civil service law are rare.[212]

b. *Interim Relief: Suspension of Enforcement and Other Interim Measures*

In line with the fundamental *presumption of legality*[213] of acts of EU institutions, under Article 278 sentence 1 TFEU, actions brought before the court do not have suspensory effect. However, the court may, exceptionally, if it considers that circumstances so require,[214] order that application of the contested act be suspended, Article 278, sentence 2 TFEU. Articles 156–61 RoP deal with the suspension of enforcement or other interim measures. An application to suspend the operation is admissible only if the applicant has challenged that measure in an action before the

CST, F-29/09, ECLI:EU:F:2010:120, paras 29 ff – *Lebedef and Jones*; CST, F-43/09, ECLI:EU:F:2010:121, para 81 – *Van Heuckelom v Europol*; close connection, CST, F-56/11, ECLI:EU:F:2013:49, para 33 – *Lebedef v Commission*; CST, F-29/11, ECLI:EU:F:2012:172, para 39 – *BA v Commission*; CST, F- 42/11, ECLI:EU:F:2012:196, paras 34 ff – *Honnefelder v Commission.*

[209] CST, F-56/09, ECLI:EU:F:2010:48, paras 81, 82 – *Marcuccio v Commission.*

[210] CST, F-102/08, ECLI:EU:F:2010:21, para 26 – *Marcuccio v Commission*, the appeal was dismissed. CST, F-80/09, ECLI:EU:F:2010:165, para 21 – *Lenz v Commission*; CST, F-105/09, ECLI:EU:F:2011:41, para 24 – *Scheefer v EP*; CST, F-11/10, ECLI:EU:F:2010:69, paras 29/30 – *Palou Martinez v Commission*. There is no need for legal protection for the determination of an alleged illegality as a basis for a later claim for damages, CST, F-44/05 RENV, ECLI:EU:F:2012:144, para 64 – *Strack v Commission*. Gervasoni (2010) 46 *Cahiers de droit européen* 782 on ECJ, C-135/06 P, ECLI:EU:C:2007:812, para 65 – *Weißenfels v EP*; Reithmann (2011) 1 *EuR* 143, 144 and (2009) *EuR* 803.

[211] Art 152(1) RoP; GC, T-833/16, ECLI:EU:T:2017:766, para 16 – *Karp v EP*.

[212] So far, two cases: GC, T-131/20, ECLI:EU:T:2020:381, paras 18, 25 – *IR v Commission*; GC, T-572/08 P, ECLI:EU:T:2009:209, para 14 – *Commission v Traore*.

[213] GC, T-12/21 R, ECLI:EU:T:2021:184, para 35 – *PJ v EIT*.

[214] GC, T-131/16 R, ECLI:EU:T:2016:427, para 12– *Belgium v Commission*.

GC. An application for the adoption of one of the other interim measures referred to in Article 279 TFEU is admissible only if it is made by a main party to a case before the GC and relates to that case. As a specialty in civil service matters, an application to suspend the operation of an act or to adopt other interim measures may be presented as soon as the complaint under Article 90(2) SR has been submitted. Article 91(4) SR stipulates for this case that after submitting a complaint to the appointing authority pursuant to Article 90(2) SR, the court action (there called 'appeal') can be filed *immediately* with the GC, 'provided that such action is accompanied by an application either for a stay of execution of the contested act or for the adoption of interim measures'. The proceedings in the principal action shall then be suspended until such time as an express or implied decision rejecting the complaint is taken. The application to suspend the operation of an act or to adopt other interim measures shall be made in a separate document that states the subject matter of the proceedings, the circumstances giving rise to urgency, and the pleas of fact and law establishing a prima facie case for the interim measure applied for, together with all the evidence and offers of evidence available to justify the grant of interim measures.

As opposed to an application's form of order sought, which intends to set aside the contested act, interim measures can exceptionally have a regulatory character in order to ensure the effectiveness of the interim relief. Interim measures can occur cumulatively with the suspension of enforcement.[215] However, interim measures must remain provisional in nature and may neither anticipate nor prejudice the decision on the main issue.[216] The purpose of proceedings for interim relief is to safeguard the full effectiveness of the definitive future decision, in order to ensure that there is no lacuna in the legal protection provided by the Court of Justice.[217]

The requirements for provisional legal protection are high. At the level of admissibility, it should be noted that the request to suspend enforcement (Article 278 TFEU) cannot in principle be directed against the rejection of a (refused) beneficial decision. This is because the suspension of the enforcement of an administrative refusal does not change the official's legal situation.[218] It is a prerequisite for the admissibility of an interim measure (Art 279 TFEU) that there is a sufficiently close link between the interim measure sought and the subject matter of the main action.[219] At the level of merits, the following three cumulative conditions must be fulfilled in both types of request for interim relief (ie, suspension of execution and adoption of interim measures):

(1) *Sufficient prospects of success* in the main proceedings, ie, a *fumus boni iuris*[220] or (in the terms of Art 156(4) RoP) a prima facie case. This is satisfied if, 'at the stage of the proceedings for interim relief, there is a major legal or factual disagreement whose resolution is not immediately obvious, so that the action is not *prima facie* without reasonable substance'.[221]
(2) *Urgency* of the order for interim relief. The urgency of interim relief must be assessed in light of the need for an interim relief to avoid causing serious and irreparable harm to the party

[215] GC, T-12/21 R, ECLI:EU:T:2021:184 – *PJ v EIT*.
[216] See case study in chapter 3, II.9.d.
[217] GC, T-78/04 R, ECLI:EU:T:2004:204, para 44 – *Sumitomo Chemical*; ECJ, C-393/96 P(R) ECLI:EU:C:1997:42, para 36 – *Antonissen*.
[218] ECJ, 206/89 R, ECLI:EU:C:1997:226, para 14 – *S v Commission*; GC, T-12/21 R, ECLI:EU:T:2021:184, para 39 – *PJ v EIT*; ECJ, C-486/01 PR and C-488/01 PR, ECLI:EU:C:2002:116, para 73 – *Front National and Martinez v EP*.
[219] GC, T-78/04 R, ECLI:EU:T:2004:204, para 43 – *Sumitomo Chemical*.
[220] GC, T-13/91 R, ECLI:EU:T:1991:19, para 18 – *Harrison v Commission*. See case study in chapter 3, II.9.d.
[221] ECJ, C-431/14 PR, ECLI:EU:C:2014:2418, para 20 – *Greece v Commission*; ECJ, C-56/89 R, ECLI:EU:C:1989:238, para 31 – *Publishers Association v Commission*.

requesting the measure.[222] The necessity of the order must be made credible in fact and in law. Many requests for interim relief fail on the lack of urgency.

(3) The court carries out a risk assessment: do the interests of the applicant in suspending the enforcement of the act prevail over the interests of the defendant in upholding the enforcement? In this assessment, it must be determined whether the possible annulment of an act by a subsequent judgment in the main action would still allow the situation created by the interim measure to be reversed and, conversely, whether a suspension of enforcement would have the effect that the goals pursued with the contested act could no longer be achieved in the event of a negative judgment in the main proceedings.[223]

The judge enjoys a large degree of discretion when determining the method of verification of these conditions.[224] Mere financial damage is usually not enough, because it can be repaired later according to the above principles.[225] Also a threat to the applicant's basic needs as a result of a dismissal must also be specifically and precisely explained.[226] There is little prospect of interim relief for alleged mistakes in the context of a selection procedure, because the Selection Board and the appointing authority can review their decisions and, if necessary, seek equitable solutions, so that there is no risk of irreparable damage.[227]

8. Legal Aid

A person who, because of his or her financial situation, is wholly or partly unable to meet the costs of the proceedings shall be entitled to legal aid.[228] The economic situation of the applicant is assessed taking into account objective factors such as income, assets and family situation, which must be demonstrated by means of supporting documents and certificates issued by national authorities.[229] As Article 147(7) RoP states, the introduction of an application for legal aid shall, for the person who made it, suspend the time limit prescribed for the bringing of an action until the date of service of the order making a decision. An order granting legal aid may specify the amount to be paid to the lawyer instructed to represent the person concerned or fix a limit for the lawyer's disbursements and fees. Depending on the outcome of the main proceedings,[230] where, by virtue of the decision closing the proceedings, the recipient of legal aid has to bear his own costs, these are covered by the court cashier, as determined by the President of the General Court. Where another party has to pay the costs of the recipient of legal aid, that other party shall be required to refund to the court cashier any sums advanced by way of aid (or shared cost, if equity so requires).

[222] GC, T-103/10 P(R), ECLI:EU:T:2010:164, paras 34 ff – *EP v U*; CST, F-104/10 (R), ECLI:EU:F:2011:15 – *de Pretis Cagnodo v Commission*; CST, F-80/08 R, ECLI:EU:F:2008:175 – *Wenig v Commission.*

[223] ECJ, C-512/16 P(R), ECLI:EU:C:2017:149, para 127 – *EMA v MSD*; GC, T-12/21 R, ECLI:EU:T:2021:184, para 83 – *PJ v EIT.*

[224] CST, F-41/10 RENV, ECLI:EU:F:2010:89, para 22 – *Bermejo Garde v EESC.*

[225] CST, F-1/07 R, ECLI:EU:F:2007:34 – *Chassagne v Commission*; CST, F-98/07 R, ECLI:EU:F:2007:203 – *Petrilli v Commission.*

[226] GC, T-103/10 P(R), ECLI:EU:T:2010:164, paras 35 ff, 56 – *EP v U*; ECJ, 92/78 R, ECLI:EU:C:1978:106, paras 8/9 – *Simmenthal.*

[227] CST, F-142/06 R, ECLI:EU:F:2007:20 – *Bligny v Commission*; CST, F-83/07 R, ECLI:EU:F:2007:154 – *Zangerl-Posselt v Commission.*

[228] Art 146 ff RoP, *cf* a mandatory application form in the practical instructions for parties.

[229] CST, F-142/07, ECLI:EU:F:2009:52 – *Kaminska v CoR.*

[230] Art 149 RoP.

VII. Scope of the Assessment on the Merits and Extent of Review

This section treats some questions on the relationship between admissibility or procedural matters on the one hand, and the merits or matters of substantial law on the other.

1. Procedural Economy: When to Decide on Admissibility

There is no statutory rule prescribing expressly a need to examine and decide on the admissibility of an action before proceeding to the examination of the case's merits. It therefore happens in practice that parts of the admissibility check are skipped by the court, relying on arguments of procedural economy or the orderly administration of justice.[231] It is submitted that although a thorough admissibility check may turn out to be complex, it is risky to skip it. First, this is because skipping the assessment of admissibility means that the court will take its (negative) decision on the merits without deciding on matters that are regularly much more important for the *functioning* of the EU judicial system and the jurisdiction of the CJEU itself than a decision on a question of substantial law may be. Secondly, as a rule, the examination of admissibility requirements take *logical* precedence over considerations on the merits. Finally, in cases involving a protracted assessment of admissibility requirements for the sake of alleged 'procedural economy', it is not unknown for the conclusive solution and settlement of legal disputes to be considerably *delayed* in an unfruitful ping-pong between instances.

2. The Extent of the Review of Legality

The review of legality of an act within the meaning of Article 90(2), Article 91(1) sentence 1 SR initially focuses on the verification of *procedural errors* and a *manifest error of assessment*. Procedural errors while adopting an act can only lead to the annulment of the act if a different result would have been possible had the correct procedure been followed – or at least, if this does not appear to be impossible.[232] The tendency developed on this by case-law is the following: the greater the discretion available when taking a decision, the more closely the authority must follow the applicable procedure. In other words, procedural mistakes in a decision-making context with large discretion preponderate.[233] On the other hand, where procedural mistakes were committed by an institution having reduced discretion, the errors are less relevant because they have a less decisive impact on the procedure's outcome. Obviously, the mere assertion by the administration

[231] See CST, F-14/12, ECLI:EU:F:2013:167, paras 37, 50 – *Schönberger v ERH.*

[232] CST, F-50/10, ECLI:EU:F:2012:51, para 89 – *Buxton v EP*; GC, T -246/04 and T -71/05, ECLI:EU:T:2007:34, para 149 – *Wunenburger v Commission*; CST, F-83/07, ECLI:EU:F:2009:158, para 66 – *Zangerl-Posselt v Commission*; CST, F-51/07, ECLI:EU:F:2008:112, para 81 – *Bui Van v Commission*. CST, F-113/10, ECLI:EU:F:2012:20, para 75 – *AT v EACEA*; Reithmann (2009) *EuR* 816; (2011) 1 *EuR* 142, (2011) 6 *EuR* 871; Schiano/Potvin-Solis (2012) *RUE* 613, 615; differentiating Gervasoni (2010) 46 *Cahiers de droit européen* 761, 781 ff, pleading for a particularly large scope, CST, F-10/07, ECLI:EU:F:2007:161, paras 66–71 – *Botos v Commission*; Potvin-Solis/Lelièvre (2012) *RUE* 271; on the assessment by selection boards, Gervasoni (2010) 46 *Cahiers de droit européen* 742. Overview Reithmann (2014) *EuR* 125/126. Basically, what counts are the objective circumstances at the time of the administrative decision; where the administration did not have full knowledge of the circumstances when taking the decision: CST, F-97/12, ECLI:EU:F:2013:142, paras 60/61 – *Thomé v Commission.*

[233] On the doctrine of the consequences of procedural errors and their relevance for the decision, see Mader, *Verteidigungsrechte* (2006) 387 ff.

that hypothetically, without procedural error, the same (adversely affecting) decision would have been taken, is not sufficient. Example (1): the right to be heard may not be dispensed with in many processes of civil service law characterised by wide discretion, such as a dismissal or the adoption of disciplinary measures. Example (2): temporal irregularities in a procedure rarely lead to the success of an application for annulment,[234] especially since an annulment would prolong the procedure even further.[235] See the case study on the right to be heard at the end of chapter 1.

The SR, CEOS or Article 270 TFEU do not list a closed catalogue of grounds for annulment of acts under civil service law (as opposed to Art 263 TFEU). The traditional grounds accepted under Article 270 TFEU are construed in parallel with Article 263 TFEU:

- Infringement of the SR or the CEOS or of any rule of law relating to their application
- Lack of competence
- Infringement of an essential procedural requirement
- Misuse of powers

In addition, case-law has developed grounds for annulment stemming from the violation of *general principles of law*, *fundamental rights*,[236] and *manifest errors of assessment*. The ECJ (confirming the GC)[237] in *Righini* enumerates the following grounds: violation of essential procedural requirements; basing the decision on an incorrect or incomplete factual basis; misuse of powers; error of law; lack of reasoning; and manifest errors of assessment.[238] As to the first ground for annulment under Article 270 TFEU enumerated above, where it is alleged by an applicant that there has been an *infringement of the SR or the CEOS or of any rule of law relating to their application*, an assessment of the compliance with or the infringement of material EU civil service law as illustrated in chapter 3 has to be carried out.

The degree of judicial self-restraint in reviewing errors (especially when applying the yardstick of *manifest* errors of assessment) correlates with the respective scope of the discretion granted to the administration when taking their decisions.[239] A successful legality review of a discretionary administrative act would have to find that the level of a minor procedural error was exceeded, and instead amounted to a *manifest* error. An error of assessment when taking an administrative decision is *manifest* if it is easily recognisable and can be detected with certainty on the basis of the criteria that the legislature has established for these decisions.[240] Misuse of powers

[234] CST, F-55/08 RENV, ECLI:EU:F:2011:159, para 123 – *De Nicola v EIB*; GC, T-37/10 P, ECLI: EU:T:2012:205, para 102 – *De Nicola v EIB*.

[235] CST, F-33/08, ECLI:EU:F:2009:141, para 211 – *V v Commission*; however under certain conditions accepted in disciplinary proceedings, CST, F-12/10, ECLI:EU:F:2012:29, para 124 – *Kerstens v Commission*; CST, F-77/09, ECLI:EU:F:2011:2, para 146 – *Nijs v ECA*, see chapter 3, II.20.

[236] Here, eg, Arts 41, 42 or 31 FRC. The method of using provisions contained in directives (in particular their preamble) for deriving principles applicable in law due to a lack of express fundamental rights (GC, T-518/16, ECLI:EU:T:2018:873, para 87 – *Carreras Sequeros and Others*; repealed by ECJ, Jd Cases C-119/19 P and C-126/19 P, ECLI:EU:C:2020:676 – *Commission v Carreras Sequeros and Others*) is to be seen critically in light of the hierarchy of norms, see chapter 1, III.5.

[237] GC, T-145/04, ECLI:EU:T:2005:395, para 53 – *Righini v Commission*; GC, T-6/02, ECLI:EU:T:2002:239, para 36 – *Platte v Commission*.

[238] ECJ, C-57/06 P, ECLI:EU:C:2007:65, para 14 – *Righini v Commission*. There are lines of jurisprudence that appear to adjust the exact yardstick for review depending on the area of administrative decision-making: eg a decision not to renew the contract of a member of the temporary staff is limited to ascertaining whether there has been no error of law, no manifest error in the assessment of the interests of the service which may have provided grounds for that decision and no misuse of powers, and that there has been no breach of the duty to have regard for the welfare of staff, and that the administration has not committed material inaccuracies: GC, T-563/22, ECLI:EU:T:2024:72, para 27 – VP – Cedefop; GC, T-591/16, ECLI:EU:T:2018:938, para 47 – *Wahlström v Frontex*; GC, T-296/21, ECLI:EU:T:2022:808, para 50 – *SU v EIOPA*.

[239] GC, T-571/17, ECLI:EU:T:2020:141, para 59 – *UG v Commission*.

[240] CST, F -104/09, ECLI:EU:F:2011:29, para 35 – *Canga Fano v Council*.

occurs when the administrative authority exercises its powers for an entirely different purpose than that for which they were conferred.[241] The evidence brought forward must be sufficient to invalidate the plausibility of the assessment made by the administration. Thus, a plea of manifest error of assessment must be dismissed if, despite the evidence, the assessment in question can be regarded as correct or justifiable.[242] The argumentation is based on the idea that administrative leeway to take decisions must retain its practical effectiveness,[243] and, secondly, that the court may not replace the assessment of the administration with its own.[244] Nevertheless, the GC has availed itself on occasion of a broader scope of review when it emphasised the need to carry out a comprehensive review of all essential factual and legal circumstances, in order to guarantee effective legal protection when determining proportionality between legal breach and sanction in disciplinary matters.[245]

Incidental review of a legislative provision: The sole test is that of arbitrariness

The discretion granted to the *legislature* is even larger. Therefore, in the case of an incidental review[246] of a legislative provision (especially of the SR) in the context of an Article 270 TFEU action, case-law overall draws a narrow line for judicial review, justifying this restraint by the wide discretion granted to the legislature when adopting norms. It merely amounts to a test of arbitrariness committed by the legislature. As confirmed by the ECJ, judicial review of a provision contained in the SR or CEOS (eg, related to the principles of proportionality, non-discrimination, or equal treatment) only embraces the question of whether the legislative provision differentiates arbitrarily or whether it differentiates in a way that is manifestly 'unsuitable' or 'inappropriate' in the light of its objective, or whether it is manifestly inappropriate with regard to the objective of public interest pursued.[247] An earlier line of case-law developed by the GC,[248] which imposed less judicial self-restraint on the court with regard to legislative provisions (by allowing the court to go as far as asking itself whether the disputed legislative provision went manifestly beyond what was necessary to achieve its goal), was therefore abandoned.

Lack of competence

The starting point is the idea that a decision has to be taken by the competent authority, and that failing to do so renders the decision illegal. Decisions determining the distribution of powers

[241] CST, F-104/09, ECLI:EU:F:2011:29, para 95 – *Canga Fano v Council*; CST, F-124/05 and F-96/06, ECLI:EU:F:2010:2, para 363 – *A and G v Commission*; GC, T-571/17, ECLI:EU:T:2020:141, para 59 – *UG v Commission*; GC, T-606/22, ECLI:EU:T:2023:654, para 61 – *RN v EUIPO* ('on the basis of objective, relevant and consistent evidence').

[242] CJEU Annual Report 2011, 228; CST, F-80/10, ECLI:EU:F:2011:172, para 34 – *AJ v Commission*; CST, F-2/11, ECLI:EU:F:2012:194, para 53 – *BW v Commission*, CST, F-1/11, ECLI:EU:F:2012:157, para 34 – *Soukoup v Commission*.

[243] CST, F-113/10, ECLI:EU:F:2012:20, paras 73 ff – *AT v EACEA*; leeway may sometimes be justified by the limited resources of the administration, *cf* CST, F-42/10, ECLI:EU:F:2012:64, para 38 – *Scareby v Commission*. Critical: Vandersanden, 'La procedure et les voies de recours' in Govaere/Vandersanden (eds), *La fonction publique communautaire* (2008) 127 and partly also Gervasoni (2010) 46 *Cahiers de droit européen* 750 ff, 781 ff. On the leeway of review enjoyed by medical committees CST, F-47/10, ECLI:EU:F:2011:137, para 110 – *Hecq v Commission*; CST, F-46/09, ECLI:EU:F:2011:101, para 72 – *V v EP*; on those of experts, see CST, F-121/10, ECLI:EU:F:2011:174, para 90 – *Heath v ECB*.

[244] GC, T-175/09 P, ECLI:EU:T:2010:534, paras 46 ff – *Council v Stols*.

[245] GC, T-184/11 P, ECLI:EU:T:2012:236, paras 85, 89 – *Bart Nijs v ECA* ('organe judiciaire de pleine juridiction'); Schiano/Potvin-Solis (2012) *RUE* 610.

[246] Plea of illegality, Art 277 TFEU.

[247] On the test of arbitrariness: ECJ, Jd Cases C-116/21 P to C-118/21 P, C-138/21 P and C-139/21 P, ECLI:EU:C:2022:557, paras 117, 127 ff, 152 ff – *VW, BT, RN*.

[248] GC, T-243/18, ECLI:EU:T:2020:619, para 66 – *VW v Commission*; GC, T-315/19, ECLI:EU:T:2020:622, para 67 – *BT v Commission*. On procedural irregularities, non-transparency and manifest error of assessment in the procedure leading to the appointment of a competitor: ECJ, C-613/21 P, ECLI:EU:C:2023:51 – *EP v Carbajo Ferrero*.

devolved to the appointing authority constitute rules of internal organisation of the institution.[249] Decisions taken by an incompetent authority due to non-compliance with such rules on the distribution of powers can only be annulled if non-compliance with the rules risks undermining the guarantees granted to officials by the SR or by the rules of good administration in matters of personnel management.[250]

3. Disputes of a Financial Character

A very important exception to the limited scope of legal review in civil service matters is adjudication in *disputes of a financial character*. According to Article 91(1) sentence 2 SR, in disputes of a financial character the Court of Justice shall have unlimited jurisdiction. This implies the judicial review of discretionary administrative decisions up to and including cancellation or modification of the measures taken.[251] Many questions arising from within the framework of the employment relationship involve not only single, separable administrative decisions, but a cluster of related or consequential rights, where an unlimited jurisdiction shall ensure that the court is in a position to provide a 'complete solution' to the dispute. For example, the decision of the appointing authority on the classification of officials does not only have an impact on the career of the persons concerned and their personal position within the hierarchy of the authority, but also has direct effects on their pecuniary rights, in particular the level of their remuneration under the SR. Likewise, the decision not to renew a contract has a direct effect on the continuity of the persons as members of staff, and therefore on their remuneration and pecuniary rights.[252] This serves to guarantee the effectiveness of the judgments that annul decisions in staff cases, so that 'if the annulment of a decision of the appointing authority which contains errors of law is not sufficient to assist the official concerned in enforcing his rights or to protect his interests effectively, the Courts of the European Union may award compensation of their own motion'.[253] In civil service law, it is acknowledged that the court can award damages[254] of its own motion both in liability litigation and in disputes about other matters,[255] at least where these are of a financial character.[256]

[249] GC, Jd Cases T-118/04 and T-134/04, ECLI:EU:T:2007:37, para 67 – *Caló v Commission*.

[250] ibid, para 68; ECJ, 49/72, ECLI:EU:C:1973:58, para 13, *Drescig v Commission*; GC, T-266/21, ECLI:EU:T:2022:566, paras 75/76 – *Casanova v Commission*. On the lack of competence, see chapter 3, I.1.a.

[251] Reithmann (2011) 1 *EuR* 144; Sachs, *Die ex-officio-Prüfung durch die Gemeinschaftsgericht* (2008) 38; Germelmann, *Die Rechtskraft von Gerichtsentscheidungen in der Europäischen Union* (2009) 56, 59. Regarding liability claims for damages, the payment claims based on the SR or CEOS are also subject to unlimited jurisdiction, CST, F-89/10, ECLI:EU:F:2011:129, para 35 – *Bovagnet v Commission*; CST, F-6/10, ECLI:EU:F:2011:139, para 125 – *Munch v OHIM*. But here too, the CST saw itself as not being in a position to determine the adjustment rate for a requested salary increase – CST, F-114/10, ECLI:EU:F:2011:173, para 78 – *Bowles and Others v ECB*.

[252] ECJ, C-583/08 P, ECLI:EU:C:2010:287, paras 44 ff – *Gogos*; CST, F-124/11, ECLI:EU:F:2013:137, paras 70 ff – *Possanzini v Frontex*.

[253] CST, F-124/11, ECLI:EU:F:2013:137, para 75 – *Possanzini v Frontex*; ECJ, C-583/08 P, ECLI:EU:C:2010:287, para 50 – *Gogos*; CST, F-53/08, ECLI:EU:F:2010:37, para 90 – *Bouillez and Others v Council*; CST, F-96/09, ECLI:EU:F:2012:129, para 73 – *Cuallado Martorell v Commission*.

[254] Overview on damages and compensation for pain and suffering: Mader, 'Der Anspruch auf Entschädigung ex aequo et bono im EU-Dienstrecht – Schadenersatz für EU-Bedienstete nach billigem Ermessen' (2012) *EuR* 355; Mader, 'Le droit à l'indemnisation ex aequo et bono dans la fonction publique européenne' (2013) 96(2) *KritV/CritQ/Rcrit* 154–64.

[255] Distinguishing liability from other disputes of financial character: CST, F-105/09, ECLI:EU:F:2011:41, para 68 – *Scheefer v EP*; CST, F-83/09, ECLI:EU:F:2011:66, paras 88 ff – *Kalmár v Europol*. No damages may be awarded for the payment of salaries if another decision still has to be taken about them, since that examination must not be anticipated: CST, F-63/11, ECLI:EU:F:2012:83, paras 66/67 – *Macchia v Commission*.

[256] Reithmann (2008) *EuR* 277; (2009) *EuR* 805; (2011) 1 *EuR* 127, 144; Sachs, *Die ex-officio-Prüfung durch die Gemeinschaftsgericht* (2008) 56, 59; CST, F-49/08, ECLI:EU:F:2009:76, para 39 – *Giannini v Commission*. With regard to

Otherwise, the court may take into account aspects of its own motion only to a very limited extent,[257] such as the fulfilment of admissibility requirements for bringing the action,[258] the conditions for a case being *lis pendens* or the force of *res judicata*,[259] rules of jurisdiction,[260] essential procedural rules[261] (in particular the obligation to state reasons under Art 25 SR),[262] and the rights of the defence.[263]

Some lines of case-law point in the direction also that public policy pleas relating to substantive legality[264] and, in general, higher-ranking law[265] are areas where the court may take into account aspects of its own motion.[266]

4. Impact of General Principles of Law

When the courts carry out a legality review based on substantive civil service law the argumentation is often based on general principles of Union law as well as civil service-specific principles of law,[267] particularly the principle of equality, the protection of legitimate expectations, the duty to state reasons,[268] the duty of care, the fundamental rights of the procedure and the rights of the

an application beyond claims for monetary benefits, claims for damages and arrears of remuneration to all other claims with only pecuniary effects, ie, for 'almost all legal disputes' Brückner, (1972) *ZBR* 44–47, 44 with the result of concerns about legal competence. With regard to a claim for damages in addition to the claim for additional payment including interest, CST, F-114/10, ECLI:EU:F:2011:173, para 44 – *Bowles and Others v ECB*.

[257] CST, F-60/08 and F-69/07, ECLI:EU:F:2008:181, para 143 – *O v Commission*. Because of the *ne ultra petita* principle, the court may not reinterpret the main subject of the complaint; however, it must not be obliged to consider only the arguments on which the parties have based their submissions, because otherwise it would have to base its decision on incorrect legal considerations, GC, T-58/08 P, ECLI:EU:T:2009:385, para 34 – *Commission v Roodhuijzen*; on the use of underlying legal provisions by the court's own motion CST, F-50/09, ECLI:EU:F:2011:55, para 140 – *Missir Mamachi de Lusignano v Commission*; see also CST, F-55/10, ECLI:EU:F:2011:94, para 50 – *AS v Commission*.

[258] CST, Jd Cases F-124/05 and F-96/06, ECLI:EU:F:2010:2, para 143 – *A and G v Commission*.

[259] CST, F-38/10, ECLI:EU:F:2011:43, paras 37 ff – *Vakalis v Commission*; the appeal was dismissed. On the admissibility of the complaint to the CST when the same subject matter is pending before the ECJ, see CST, F-13/10, ECLI:EU:F:2011:161, para 102 – *De Nicola v EIB*, partial annulment in the appeal GC, T-618/11P, ECLI:EU:T:2013:479. On the legal force of court orders CST, F-104/10, ECLI:EU:F:2013:64, para 66 – *de Pretis Cagnodo and Others v Commission*. On the legal force of a decision that there is no longer any need to adjudicate, CST, F-52/05 RENV, ECLI:EU:F:2008:161, paras 19/20 – *Q v Commission*. No *res judicata* if the decision related to another damage, CST, F-91/10, ECLI:EU:F:2013:34, para 61 – *AK v Commission* (distinguishes damage caused by an incorrect decision from damage caused by a delayed appraisal).

[260] CST, Jd Cases F-45/08 and F-99/07, ECLI:EU:F:2009:84, paras 84, 86 – *Bernard v Europol*; CST, F-80/08 R, ECLI:EU:F:2008:175, paras 83, 87 – *Wenig v Commission*; CST, F-49/09, ECLI:EU:F:2010:123, para 39 – *Wendler v Commission*. *cf* GC, T-160/08 P, ECLI:EU:T:2010:294, para 61 – *Putterie-De Beukelaer* v Commission: dropping additional requirements as still set up by GC, Jd Cases T-118/04 and T-134/04, ECLI:EU:T:2007:37, paras 67/68 – *Calò v Commission*, according to Gervasoni (2010) 46 *Cahiers de droit européen* 780.

[261] CST, F-64/10, ECLI:EU:F:2011:72, para 37 – *Mantzouratos v EP*.

[262] CST, F-47/07, ECLI:EU:F:2009:103, para 93 – *Behmer v EP*; Levi, 'Droits fondamentaux et principes généraux de droit de la fonction publique communautaire' in Govaere/Vandersanden (eds), *La fonction publique communautaire* (2008) 103; CST, F-60/08 and F-69/07, ECLI:EU:F:2008:181, paras 71, 80 – *O v Commission*.

[263] CST, F-27/09, ECLI:EU:F:2010:58 – *Hanschmann v Europol*; CST, F-99/06, ECLI:EU:F:2007:87, para 93 – *López Teruel v Commission*. See Levi, 'Droits fondamentaux et principes généraux de droit de la fonction publique communautaire' in Govaere/Vandersanden (eds), *La fonction publique communautaire* (2008) 95.

[264] CST, F-31/07, ECLI:EU:F:2008:23 – *Putterie-De-Beukelaer v Commission*, but left open in the appeal decision GC, T-160/08 P, ECLI:EU:T:2010:294 – *Putterie-De Beukelaer v Commission*, according to Gervasoni (2010) 46 *Cahiers de droit européen* 748; CST, F-49/09, ECLI:EU:F:2010:123, para 39 – *Wendler v Commission*; CST, F-38/10, ECLI:EU:F:2011:43, paras 37 ff – *Vakalis v Commission*; CST, F-22/05 RENV, ECLI:EU:F:2009:120, paras 56, 58 – *Neophytou v Commission*. Gervasoni (2010) 46 *Cahiers de droit européen* 749. The examination of a provision by the court of its own motion only extends to the material scope of the provision, not to its possible illegality.

[265] CST, F-60/08 and F-69/07, ECLI:EU:F:2008:181, paras 144, 146 – *O v Commission*.

[266] But see for the opposite: ECJ, C-358/15 P, ECLI:EU:C:2016:338, para 89 – *Bank of Industry and Mine v Council*.

[267] see chapter 3 and chapter 1, II. and III.5. and 6; Levi, 'Droits fondamentaux et principes généraux de droit de la fonction publique communautaire' in Govaere/Vandersanden (eds), *La fonction publique communautaire* (2008) 81 ff; Reithmann (2012) *EuR* 720 ff.

[268] Art 25(2) sentence 2 SR, Art 296(2) TFEU, Art 41(2)(c) FRC.

defence, as well as the right to good administration.[269] Some principles – in the event of their breach – cannot justify the annulment of the contested act, but can only set out the grounds for liability.[270]

Secondary Union law addressed to the Member States can indirectly oblige the appointing authorities if it expresses a general principle of law; or if the SR[271] refer to this; or if the duty of loyalty requires that the Union does not apply a lower standard to itself than it prescribes for the Member States.[272] The Commission, as guardian[273] of the Treaties, has a particular duty as an employer to interpret strictly the obligations imposed on the Member States, and to exercise restrictive discretion on the use of safety regulations.[274]

5. *Reformatio in Peius*

At least outside the field of criminal law, it is recognised that an applicant who has brought an action against an act adversely affecting her or him should not be exposed to the risk that such an action would place them in a less favourable position than they would have been in had they not brought that action. A *reformatio in peius* would be contrary to the three principles which underlie this concept: respect for the rights of the defence, legal certainty, and the protection of legitimate expectations.[275] This is intended to apply in a procedural sense in connection with a remedy initiated by the party, as an expression of the principle of party disposition, not as an individual right under substantial law to preserve a given legislative situation of benefit to the applicant.[276] Therefore, a prohibition of *reformatio in peius* may not be used as an argument to prevent legislative changes to the SR, or to prevent the administration making arrangements regarding the grading classification of civil servants.[277]

VIII. Decisions of the Court and Enforceability

1. Judgment or Order

The GC concludes the proceedings[278] either by judgment; or by an order if the action is inadmissible as apparent from the file and no new aspects are expected from an oral hearing;[279] or if the

[269] Reithmann (2008) *EuR* 272; (2009) *EuR* 802 and 818; (2011) 1 *EuR* 142; (2012) *EuR* 696, 720; Reithmann, *Fürsorgepflicht* (2019); On the right to an impartial trial, reasonable time limits, a fair hearing, access to personal files, reasoning: CST, F-99/06, ECLI:EU:F:2007:87, para 92 – *López Teruel v OHIM*; to clear rules on responsibilities CST, F-89/07, ECLI:EU:F:2008:97 – *Kuchta v ECB*.

[270] On the principle of good faith in actions for damages: CST, F- 8/10, ECLI:EU:F:2010:151, para 87 – *Gheysens v Council.*

[271] Art 1e(2) SR.

[272] CJEU Annual Report 2009 199; CST, F-65/07, ECLI:EU:F:2009:43 – *Aayhan and Others v Commission* and CST, Joined Cases F-134/07 and F-8/08, ECLI:EU:F:2009:51 – *Adjemian and Others v Commission.*

[273] Art 17(1) TEU.

[274] CST, F-50/09, ECLI:EU:F:2011:55, para 126 – *Missir Mamachi de Lusignano v Commission* on the protection of employees in accordance with Directive 89/391 in conjunction with Art 1e SR.

[275] ECJ, C-455/06, ECLI:EU:C:2008:650, para 47 – *Heemskerk and Schaap.*

[276] On *reformatio in peius* in other areas of EU administrative law: Mader, *Verteidigungsrechte* (2006) 261.

[277] CST, F-25/07, ECLI:EU:F:2010:163, paras 132 ff – *Bleser v Commission.*

[278] Art 116 ff RoP.

[279] CST, F-87/06, ECLI:EU:F:2007:52 (on the old Art 111 RoP) – *Manté v Council*; GoD, F-13/07, ECLI:EU:F:2007:68 – *L v EMEA*, and CST, F-51/06, ECLI:EU:F:2007:108 – *Tesoka v FEACVT.*

action must obviously fail for substantive reasons.[280] It decides of its own motion where the case is devoid of purpose and there is no longer any need to adjudicate on it.[281] Apart from this, the RoP establish a number of other situations where the GC decides by order.[282] Further to Article 266 TFEU, the unsuccessful institution is required to take the necessary measures to comply with the judgment itself, without delay.[283] Under the principle of legality, the institutions are obliged to act in an objectively legally compliant way from the outset (and even more so after having clarified the matter in the course of litigation, under Art 266 TFEU); for instance, they must not intentionally create a situation that requires correction of their rules by their addressees for those rules to become legal. Hence, institutions cannot rely on a so-called partial retention, meaning the speculation that the court will uphold a practice despite its illegal aspects and only reduce the content to the legally permitted provisions.

Effects

A judgment only has legal force *inter partes*. Third parties cannot claim the effect of an annulment for themselves. However, the party that is successful in the application for annulment can invoke the retrospective nullity of the act against all. The annulment has the effect of retroactively eliminating that measure from the legal system. Where the measure annulled has already been carried out, the abolition of its effects means that the applicant must be restored to the legal position he was in before it was adopted.[284] An alternative equitable compensation may only suffice in the case of major obstacles to the implementation of the annulling judgment, however not where the restoration merely encounters 'practical difficulties'.[285] The substance that is to be implemented by the institution is the operative part of the judgment and the grounds which led to it, and which constitute its essential basis.[286]

In terms of the Union institution's objective compliance obligation, the follow-up action to be taken by the unsuccessful body under Article 266 TFEU may have an effect on other persons when generally reinstating lawful conditions, or when seeking to prevent violations of the principle of equal treatment. However, other affected parties cannot invoke the new judgment as such for themselves, but can only benefit from it insofar as they have filed an action within the time limits prescribed. For them, a judgment usually does not represent a new matter of fact that would cause the limitation periods to start afresh.[287]

2. Decision as to Costs

A decision as to costs shall be given in the judgment or order which closes the proceedings.

[280] Art 126 RoP; CST, F-129/06, ECLI:EU:F:2007:166 – *Salvador Roldán v Commission.*

[281] Art 131 RoP; CST, F-11/05 RENV, ECLI:EU:F:2009:154, para 28 – *Chassange v Commission.*

[282] Art 55(2), Art 103(3), Art 105(6), Art 125b(2), Arts 127–29, Art 132, Art 149(2), Art 158 and Art 176 RoP.

[283] CST, F-9/08, ECLI:EU:F:2009:106, para 21 – *Rosenbaum v Commission*; CST, F-35/08, ECLI:EU:F:2010:51, para 73 – *Pachtitis v Commission*; on the leeway of the institution concerning how to apply the measures for implementing a judgment, CST, F-104/08, ECLI:EU:F:2010:23, para 41 – *Angelidis v EP*; CST, F-15/05, ECLI:EU:F:2008:81 – *Andrés and Others v ECB*; more narrow: Germelmann, *Die Rechtskraft von Gerichtsentscheidungen in der Europäischen Union* (2009) 426, 428. Sceptical: Vandersanden, 'La procedure et les voies de recours' in Govaere/Vandersanden (eds), *La fonction publique communautaire* (2008) 136/137.

[284] *Ex tunc* effect of an annulment: CST, F-105/09, ECLI:EU:F:2011:41, para 69 – *Scheefer v EP.*

[285] CST, F-94/11, ECLI:EU:F:2013:41, para 58 – *Brune v Commission.*

[286] ECJ, C-8/99 P, ECLI:EU:C:2000:404, paras 19/20 – *Gómez de Enterría y Sanchez v EP.*

[287] GC, T-175/15, ECLI:EU:T:2017:694, paras 154/155 – *Mabrouk v Council*; ECJ, C-310/97, ECLI:EU:C:1999:407, para 56 – *Assi Domain*; ECJ, 52/64, ECLI:EU:C:1965:123 – *Pfloeschner*; but: GC, T-86/98, ECLI:EU:T:2001:42, para 45 – *Inpesca v Commission.*

Cost risk after abolition of former privilege

Until 2006, when the CST was created,[288] officials did not have to bear the cost of the opponent party (or interveners) even if the proceedings were unsuccessful. This previous 'civil servants' privilege' was abandoned. As in other areas of litigation in the EU courts, the unsuccessful party in civil service matters shall nowadays be ordered to pay the costs (proportionately in partial victory/loss) if they have been applied for in the successful party's pleadings, Article 134(1) RoP. If equity so requires, a different proportion of the cost share can be decided.[289] Article 135 RoP distinguishes between a reduced cost for reasons of equity and a (partial) cost share where a party – even a successful one – has made the opposing party incur costs which the court holds to be unreasonable or vexatious. The reimbursable costs of an institution – which typically acts as a defendant at first instance – normally only encompass the mission costs of the internal staff working on the case who would have to travel to Luxembourg for the hearing. Yet it may also include the costs of external lawyers advising the institution on the matter in litigation. Since it is unclear whether and to what extent the institution will make use of external lawyers in addition to the resources of its own services (in practice, meaning how far it can be shown that the involvement of external lawyers was necessary despite the existence of an internal legal service), there remains a cost risk on the applicant's side that is difficult to determine quantitatively. This is perceived as putting a strain of uncertainty on the applicant which may occasionally amount to a strategic advantage for the defendant institution.

Necessarily incurred costs

The only costs eligible for reimbursement are: (1) sums payable to witnesses and experts; and (2) expenses necessarily incurred by the parties for the proceedings, in particular travel and subsistence expenses and the remuneration of agents, advisers or lawyers.[290]

In the absence of relevant statutory provisions laying down standards for the reimbursement of expenses or fee-scales, case-law has developed five criteria for determining the scope of what are *necessarily* incurred expenses:[291] the court has to assess the facts of the case to determine:

a. The purpose and nature of the proceedings[292]
b. The significance of the case from the point of view of EU law[293]
c. The difficulties presented by the case[294]
d. The amount of work generated by the proceedings for the agents and advisers involved[295]
e. The financial interests[296] which the parties had in the proceedings

[288] ie, entry into force of Council Decision 2004/752/EC, Euratom of 2 November 2004 establishing the European Union Civil Service Tribunal [2004] OJ L333/7, Art 7(5) of Annex I.

[289] On equitable share see in particular, CST, F-6/08, ECLI:EU:F:2008:160 – *Blais v ECB*; cost share in case of legal aid: Art 146 ff [149] RoP, CST, F-53/07, ECLI:EU:F:2008:148 – *Iordanova v Commission*; CST, F-117/10, ECLI:EU:F:2011:148, para 30 – *Van Soest v Commission*; CST, F-50/09, ECLI:EU:F:2011:55, para 230 – *Missir Mamachi de Lusignano v Commission*: for delay of the proceedings by the defendant (Commission).

[290] Art 140 RoP. CST, F-7/08 DEP, ECLI:EU:F:2010:32, paras 23 ff – *Schönberger v EP*.

[291] Jürschick/Dörrfuss (2023) *EuZW* 253–57; GC, T-342/99 DEP, ECLI:EU:T:2004:192, para 18 – *Airtours v Commission*.

[292] GC, T-310/00 DEP, ECLI:EU:T:2008:32 – *Verizon v Commission*.

[293] GC, T-2/93 DEPE, ECLI:EU:T:1998:255 – *Air France v Commission*; GC, T-310/00 DEP, ECLI:EU:T:2008:32 – *Verizon v Commission*.

[294] GC, T-163/05 DEP, ECLI:EU:T:2011:638 – *Bundesverband deutscher Banken v Commission*; GC, T-414/08 DEP, ECLI:EU:T:2015:726 – *Latvijas autoru apvienība and Others v Commission*.

[295] Which is the number of working hours that were objectively required for the procedure, GC, T-233/99 DEP ECLI:EU:T:2006:406, para 29 – *Land Nordrhein-Westfalen v Commission*; ECJ, Jd Cases C-325/13 P-DEP and C-326/13 P-DEP, ECLI:EU:C:2017:556, para 28 – *Peek & Cloppenburg*, reduced workload due to high competence of the representatives.

[296] GC, T-310/00 DEP, ECLI:EU:T:2008:32, paras 13, 32, 54 – *Verizon v Commission*; GC, T-54/02 OP-DEP, ECLI:EU:T:2009:464, para 51 – *Bayerische Hypo- und Vereinsbank*.

The circumstances for the existence and extent of these benchmarks are to be presented by the party claiming reimbursement of expenses in detail and with due reasoning. Costs incurred for coordinating a multitude of parties on the same side among themselves, as well as for coordinating among interveners[297] on the same side, are not eligible for reimbursement.

Costs of court proceedings

According to Article 139 RoP, *court* proceedings are generally free of charge, but avoidable costs can be charged to the party that caused them.

Costs of complaint procedure

Costs incurred by the staff member before lodging the application are regarded as irrecoverable.[298] Only costs incurred during the contentious proceedings proper, ie, the proceedings which commence with the institution of the action are recoverable. The legislature's specific intention in making that distinction is to discourage the official from instructing a lawyer during the pre-contentious procedure.[299]

Form of order sought on costs

An explicit form of order sought on costs is required. Without the respective form of order sought, the winning party too must bear its costs itself.[300] A form of order sought on costs is also required in order to defend against costs arising from the intervention or attempted intervention of an intervener.[301] Procedural errors committed by the administration may lead to the applicant being partially successful in the recovery of costs, even if they are not sufficient to win on the principal matter of the case.[302] As to the legal interest on late payment, the central bank rate shall apply, up to a maximum of the rate requested.[303]

Combined plea for compensation of damages and costs

In practice, the costs of a party which has been unsuccessful only in its plea on compensation for damages, but has otherwise been successful in its plea for annulment (connected with the same matter) are often fully charged on the defendant institution for being, on its side, unsuccessful in the principal matter of the annulment of the contested decision.

[297] GC, T-414/08 DEP, ECLI:EU:T:2015:726, para 45 – *Latvijas autoru apvienība and Others v Commission.*

[298] GC, T-80/97 DEP, ECLI:EU:T:2002:1, para 25 – *Starway SA v Council*; GC, T-251/00 DEP, ECLI:EU:T:2004:353, paras 21/22 – *Lagardère and Canal+ v Commission.*

[299] On the recovery of cost incurred in the course of special procedures of civil service law, see Art 51(8) SR where the proceedings for dismissal for incompetence end without any decision being taken to dismiss or downgrade; also Art 21(2) Annex IX SR (discretionary decision on cost at the end of disciplinary procedures).

[300] See Art 136(4) RoP; CST, F-91/07, ECLI:EU:F:2009:92, para 100 – *Torijano Montero v Council*; CST, Jd Cases F-116/07, F-13/08 and F-31/08, ECLI:EU:F:2010:77, paras 224, 228 – *Tomas v EP*, but more strictly the appeal decision T-317/08, ECLI:EU:C:2010:146, para 105; CST, F-23/09, ECLI:EU:F:2010:138, para 66 – *Cerafogli v ECB.* Effect on the cost of breaches of law by the administration that did not lead to a victory in the principal matter, see Reithmann (2012) *EuR* 720.

[301] Art 138 RoP therefore only regulates the fate of the costs of the intervener himself, not the costs that the intervener causes at other parties involved.

[302] On the application, see CST, F-81/10, ECLI:EU:F:2011:120, para 93 – *Praskevicius v EP*; CST, F-139/07, ECLI:EU:F:2009:105, paras 146, 148 – *van Arum v EP*; CST, F-141/07, ECLI:EU:F:2008:99 – *Maniscalco v Commission.* Partial success with costs due to procedural errors, eg, CST, F-74/10, ECLI:EU:F:2011:171, paras 76, 122 – *Kimman v Commission*; CST, F-68/10, ECLI:EU:F:2011:135, paras 41, 102 – *Behnke v Commission*; CST, F-41/11, ECLI:EU:F:2012:82, paras 53, 57 – *Mocová v Commission.* Reithmann (2014) *EuR*) 125/126.

[303] CST, F-14/08 DEP, ECLI:EU:F:2009:149 – *X v EP.*

3. Enforcement

Judgments in disputes of a financial character can be enforced according to Articles 280, 299 TFEU. Usually, the appointing authorities offset claims against employees against their entitlements, for example to remuneration.[304] Other types of judgment, by their very nature, are not capable of being enforced; Article 266 TFEU applies to them by analogy.

IX. Remedy: Appeal

According to Article 256(1) 2 TFEU in conjunction with Article 56 ff Statute CJEU, an appeal can be lodged with the ECJ against final decisions of the GC and decisions of the GC disposing of the substantive issues in part only, or disposing of a procedural issue concerning a plea of lack of competence or inadmissibility. An appeal may be brought by any party which has been unsuccessful, in whole or in part, in its submissions. Interveners (other than the Member States and the institutions of the Union) may bring such an appeal only where the decision of the GC directly affects them. In disputes between the Union and its servants, an appeal may not be brought by Member States and institutions of the Union which did not intervene in the proceedings before the GC.[305] In line with Article 278(1) TFEU an appeal brought before the ECJ shall not have suspensory effect; the ECJ may, however, if it considers that circumstances so require, order that application of the contested act be suspended, or prescribe any necessary interim measures.[306]

If the appeal is well founded, the ECJ shall quash the decision of the GC. It may itself give final judgment in the matter, where the state of the proceedings so permits, or refer the case back to the GC for judgment. The ECJ cannot itself give final judgment in the matter, as long as aspects of the case require examination of complex questions of fact which had not been assessed in first instance.[307] Where a case is referred back, the GC shall be bound by the decision of the ECJ on points of law.[308] A case decided upon by the GC after it had been referred back by the ECJ to the GC, can be subject to another appeal to the ECJ.[309]

Appeal limited to points of law

Importantly, the appeal to the ECJ is *limited to points of law*: the appellant can only base it on

1. a lack of competence of the GC, or
2. a breach of procedure before it which adversely affects the interests of the appellant, or
3. an infringement of Union law by the GC.[310]

No appeal shall lie regarding only the amount of the costs or the party ordered to pay them. For example, relating to the ground for appeal based on a breach of procedure, the fundamental

[304] CST, F-56/09, ECLI:EU:F:2010:48, para 59 – *Marcuccio v Commission*; CST, F-49/08, ECLI:EU:F:2009:76, para 23 – *Giannini v Commission*; against the offsetting of claims with remuneration *cf* GC, T-214/00, ECLI:EU:T:2001:172 – *X v Commission*. Seyr, 'La Jurisprudence du TFP, questions de fond' (2011) *Revue universale des Droits de l'Homme* 44 ff.

[305] Art 56 (2, 3) Statute CJEU.

[306] Arts 278, 279 TFEU, section VI.7.b. above.

[307] ECJ, C-408/04 P, ECLI:EU:C:2008:236, para 111 – *Commission v Salzgitter*.

[308] Art 61 Statute CJEU, Art 170 RoP CJEU, which stipulates that the subject matter of the proceedings before the GC may not be changed in the appeal, *cf* ECJ, C-283/90 P, ECLI:EU:C:1991:361, paras 9/10 – *Vidrányi v Commission*.

[309] ECJ, C-415/15 P, ECLI:EU:C:2017:216 – *Stichting Woonpunt v Commission*, GC, T-203/10 RENV II.

[310] Art 58 Statute CJEU. On the scope of examination in the appeal proceedings ECJ, C-301/02 P, ECLI:EU:C:2005:306, para 78 – *Tralli v ECB*; Lelièvre/Potvin-Solis (2011) *RUE* 612, and Gervasoni (2010) 46 *Cahiers de droit européen* 790.

principle of the rights of the defence can come into play, thus in a similar way as in the appointing authority's adoption of decisions on the administrative level (*cf*, eg, in disciplinary proceedings). In order to satisfy the requirements of the right to a fair trial (Art 47 of the Fundamental Rights Charter, FRC), the EU courts must ensure that the principle of *audi et alteram partem* is respected in proceedings before them and that the courts themselves respect that principle, which applies to any procedure which may result in a decision by an EU institution perceptibly affecting a person's interests,[311] including matters of civil service law.[312] It confers on each party to proceedings the right to be apprised of the documents produced and observations made by the other party as well as of the matters raised by the courts of their own motion on which they intend to found their decision and to discuss all these issues; and it confers on each party the right to be able to debate and be heard on, the matters of fact and of law which will determine the outcome of the proceedings.[313] An infringement of the principle of fair trial (*audi et alteram partem*) only entails the annulment of the decision if the procedure could have led to a different outcome in the absence of that infringement, or at least that a different outcome cannot be totally ruled out.[314] In the practice of EU civil service law, this means that only in an exceptional case that the court (or likewise in administrative proceedings: the authority) could not possibly have taken any other decision, the infringement of the rights of the defence does not lead to the annulment of the decision.

Next to the three appeal categories mentioned in Article 58 Statute CJEU (lack of competence of the GC, breach of procedure before it, infringement of Union law by the GC), the appeal to the ECJ may also embrace other categories of review on points of law, as developed by case-law:[315]

- The substantive inaccuracy of those findings as apparent from the documents in the file,
- the distortion of the evidence by the GC,[316]
- the legal characterisation of that evidence and
- the question whether the rules relating to the burden of proof and the taking of evidence have been observed,
- the inadequate or contradictory reasoning of the grounds of the GC's decision.[317]

Form and procedure

The appeal may be brought at the Registry of the Court of Justice or of the General Court.[318] The time limit is two months, extended by the period on account of distance, Article 51 RoP ECJ. An appeal must identify precisely the contested points of the judgment under appeal, the pleas in law and the legal arguments specifically advanced in support of the appeal, as well as the form of

[311] ECJ, C-530/12 P, EU:C:2014:186, para 53 – *OHIM v National Lottery Commission*; ECJ, C-58/12 P, EU:C:2013:770, para 32 – *Groupe Gascogne v Commission*; ECJ, C-40/12 P, ECLI:EU:C:2013:768, para 28 – *Gascogne Sack Deutschland v Commission*.

[312] ECJ, Jd Cases C-584/20 P and C-621/20 P, ECLI:EU:C:2021:601, paras 56 ff – *Commission v Landesbank Baden-Württemberg and SRB*.

[313] ibid, para 59.

[314] ECJ, C-831/18 P, ECLI:EU:C:2020:481, para 106 – *Commission v RQ*. On the rights of the defence and potential different outcome of the proceedings Mader, *Verteidigungsrechte* (2006) 377 ff, 387 ff on the specialties in civil service law.

[315] ECJ, C-413/06 P, ECLI:EU:C:2008:392, para 29 – *Bertelsmann and Sony Corporation of America v Impala*; ECJ, Jd Cases C-403/04 P and C-405/04 P, ECLI:EU:C:2007:52, para 39; GC, T-347/12 P, ECLI:EU:2014:268, para 62 – *Mocová v Commission*.

[316] Whereas the distortion has to be manifestly apparent from the file, without having to carry out another assessment of facts or evidence: ECJ, C-57/06 P, ECLI:EU:2007:65, para 33 – *Righini v Commission*; ECJ, C-8/95 P, ECLI:EU:C:1998:257, point 72 – *New Holland Ford v Commission*.

[317] ECJ, C-401/96 P, ECLI:EU:C:1998:208, para 53 – *Somaco SARL v Commission*.

[318] Art 167 ff RoP ECJ.

order sought by the appellant, failing which the appeal or the ground of appeal concerned may be inadmissible.[319] A ground of appeal supported by an argument that is not sufficiently clear and precise to enable the ECJ to exercise its powers of judicial review, in particular because essential elements on which the ground of appeal is based are not indicated sufficiently coherently and intelligibly in the text of the appeal, which is worded in a vague and ambiguous manner in that regard, does not satisfy those requirements and must be dismissed as inadmissible. An appeal lacking coherent structure which simply makes general statements and contains no specific indications as to the points of the decision under appeal which may be vitiated by an error of law will be dismissed as 'clearly inadmissible'.[320] The appeal procedure consists of a written part and an oral part, whereas the ECJ, having heard the Advocate General and the parties, may dispense with the oral procedure.

Repetition of pleas and new plea in law

Repetition or reproduction of the pleas in law and arguments previously submitted at first instance amounts to a request for re-examination of the application submitted, which the ECJ does not have jurisdiction to undertake.[321] On the other hand, a party is not allowed for the first time in appeal to submit a plea in law which it has not raised in first instance. The appeal is confined to a review of the findings of law on the pleas argued before.[322]

Appeal manifestly inadmissible or manifestly unfounded

Article 181 RoP ECJ stipulates that, where the appeal (or cross-appeal) is, in whole or in part, manifestly inadmissible or manifestly unfounded, the Court may at any time, acting on a proposal from the Judge-Rapporteur and after hearing the Advocate General, decide by reasoned order to dismiss that appeal (or cross-appeal) in whole or in part. As a specialty in civil service law,[323] the statement of reasons for the decision may be prepared by the Advocate General. This reasoning is then fully incorporated into the decision issued by the competent chamber of the Court, which simply states that 'for the reasons stated by the Advocate General, the appeal must be dismissed'.

X. Complaint to the Ombudsman

Before concluding this chapter on the review system, which focused on litigation, it shall be mentioned rather by way of excursion, that civil servants are free to turn to the European Ombudsman. Further to Article 228 TFEU, the Ombudsman is empowered to receive complaints from any citizen of the Union or any natural or legal person residing or having its registered office in a Member State concerning instances of maladministration in the activities of the Union institutions, bodies, offices or agencies, with the exception of the ECJ acting in its judicial role.[324] A complaint with the Ombudsman provides for officials and other servants an alternative remedy

[319] Art 256(1) 2nd sub-para TFEU, Art 58(1) Statute CJEU, Art 168(1)(d)(e) and Art 169(2) RoP ECJ; ECJ, C-833/19 P, ECLI:EU:C:2021:950, para 50 – *Council v Hamas*; ECJ, C-366/21 P, ECLI:EU:2022:C:984, para 52 – *Picard v Commission*. In addition, a summary of the pleas in law has to be added.

[320] ECJ, C-366/21 P, ECLI:EU:2022:C:984, para 52 – *Picard v Commission* para 53; ECJ, C-295/12 P, ECLI:EU:C:2014:2062, para 30 – *Telefónica v Commission*.

[321] ECJ, C-466/19 P, ECLI:EU:C:2021:76, para 45 – *Qualcomm and Qualcomm Europe v Commission*; ECJ, C-68/22 P, ECLI:EU:C:2022:1029, para 72 – *EIB v KL*; ECJ, C-244/92 P, ECLI:EU:C:1993:152, para 10 – *Kupka-Floridi v EESC*.

[322] ECJ, C-136/92 P, ECLI:EU:C:1994:211, para 59 – *Commission v Brazzelli Lualdi and Others*.

[323] This practice is at present limited to civil service law, public procurement and access to documents.

[324] Mader (2013) *EuR* 348 ff.

to that of an action before the GC in order to protect their interests. Yet, the objective of such a complaint is different, as the outcome will be a legally non-binding recommendation by the Ombudsman on the subject matter, and (in case) the setting out of a finding of maladministration. Further, the two remedies cannot be pursued at the same time. Although complaints submitted to the Ombudsman do not affect time limits for litigation, the Ombudsman must nonetheless terminate consideration of a complaint and declare it inadmissible if the citizen simultaneously brings an appeal before the GC based on the same facts that are or have been the subject of legal proceedings.[325]

Complaint procedure for civil servants

A complaint shall be lodged within two years of the date on which the facts on which it is based came to the attention of the complainant, *cf* Article 2(3) Statute[326] of the European Ombudsman. Complaints concerning employment relations between the Union institutions, bodies, offices or agencies and their staff shall be admissible only if the person concerned has exhausted all internal administrative procedures, in particular the pre-contentious complaint procedure of Article 90 SR, and the competent authority of the Union institution, body, office or agency concerned has taken a decision or the time limits for its reply have expired.[327] The Ombudsman shall also be entitled to verify the measures adopted by the competent authority of the Union institution, body, office or agency concerned to ensure the protection of alleged victims of harassment and to restore a healthy and safe working environment respecting the dignity of the persons concerned while an administrative enquiry is ongoing, provided that the persons concerned have exhausted the internal administrative procedures in relation to these measures. The Ombudsman shall inform the Union institution, body, office or agency concerned of a registered complaint, as soon as that complaint has been declared admissible and the decision has been taken to open an enquiry.[328]

Scope of protection

The right of a complaint with the Ombudsman consists of the following elements:[329] (1) a right to lodge the complaint; (2) a right that the complaint is received by the institution; (3) a right that the Ombudsman examines its content; (4) a right that the Ombudsman decides on the advisability of further enquiry; and (5) a right of the complainant to be informed about the treatment. The Ombudsman enjoys very wide discretion as regards the merits of complaints and the way in which it deals with them, and that in so doing it is under no obligation as to the result to be achieved. An aspect that might be of importance when considering the treatment of a matter by this remedy is the right of the Ombudsman to conduct enquiries, be provided with information and have access to the file which in its scope – depending on the case – will reach beyond the scope of the right of access to the file provided for an official under the SR.[330]

Pros and cons

A complaint of an official with the Ombudsman may bring about an improvement of administrative practice and structures, since the Ombudsman's remit is to investigate and opine on instances

[325] Art 228(1) TFEU; GC, T-209/00, ECLI:EU:T:2002:94, paras 65–67 – *Lamberts v Ombudsman.*

[326] Regulation (EU, Euratom) 2021/1163 of the European Parliament of 24 June 2021 laying down the regulations and general conditions governing the performance of the Ombudsman's duties [2021] OJ L253/1–10.

[327] Art 2(6) and (7) Statute of the European Ombudsman.

[328] Art 2(7) Statute of the European Ombudsman.

[329] Mader (2013) *EuR* 368.

[330] *cf* Arts 3, 4, 5 and 8 Statute of the European Ombudsman.

of maladministration in the activities of the Union institutions. It has to be carefully assessed if this objective coincides with the goals of a staff member who seeks to protect individual interests. The treatment of the matter by the Ombudsman will regularly be faster than in litigation, but may also take longer if it involves lengthy enquiries and several phases. The advantages of a complaint to the Ombudsman is that the access hurdles are low and formal preconditions marginal, no attorney is required to represent the complainant.[331] Finally, there is no risk for the complainant to bear the cost of a defendant institution (including the Ombudsman itself) or intervener. The risk is rather connected with not having a legally enforceable decision in hand once the procedure is completed. There is no remedy against the recommendation (draft or final) provided by the Ombudsman, neither against its report. A matter of civil service decided on the merits by the Ombudsman cannot be brought to the courts any further.[332]

Non-contractual liability

It is conceivable that the Ombudsman may become liable for damages. Case-law has accepted that only 'in very exceptional circumstances' would it be possible to demonstrate that the Ombudsman has committed a sufficiently serious breach of Union law in the performance of its duties likely to cause damage to the citizen concerned, and would thus engage the Union's non-contractual liability.[333]

Complaint and reviewable act

Including, but not only in matters of civil service law, a complaint with the Ombudsman under specific circumstances may indirectly help overcome a situation in which an act is not reviewable any further (eg, it is time-barred) and where an application to annul the act would therefore be inadmissible. This could be the case where the recommendation of the Ombudsman subsequent to a complaint on the matter causes the institution that has adopted the earlier act to undertake a new assessment of the legal situation. A decision taken after a reassessment of the earlier act is reviewable, and not merely confirmatory.[334] In that sense, a complaint could reopen the door towards an admissible application.

[331] Pilorge-Vrancken, *Le droit de la fonction publique de l'Union européenne* (2017) 314/315; Vandersanden, (2010) 46 *CDE* 569 ff, on the difference between maladministration and the adoption of an illegal act.

[332] *contra*: Art 2(6) Statute of the European Ombudsman in conjunction with Art 90 SR.

[333] ECJ, C-234/02 P, ECLI:EU:C:2004:174, paras 49 ff 60 – *Ombudsman v Lamberts* (only 'where the Ombudsman manifestly and gravely disregarded the limits on its discretion').

[334] *cf* section V.2. above; GC, Jd Cases T-568/16 and T-599/16, ECLI:EU:T:2018:347, para 57 – *Spagnolli*; ECJ, C-202/20 P, ECLI:EU:C:2021:385, para 21 – *Necci v Commission*.

3

On the Substance: Material EU Civil Service Law

Chapter 3 is dedicated to substantial European Union (EU) Civil Service law. For the purpose of illustration, it starts by considering the framework of administrative decision-making, whereas some aspects of this belong to the realm of procedure (or in terms of litigation – admissibility) treated in the former chapter: the specific nature and circumstances of the acts of appointing authorities and of decisions taken on staff matters, as well as the potential grievances stemming from them. The following sections analyse the legal status of staff employed, starting with the various types of staff, along the chronological pathway of the official's career, from selection up to termination of service, with a final part on disciplinary measures. The final sections deal with remuneration, insurance and pensions as well as the important subjects of invalidity, occupational disease, accident and incapcity to work.

I. The Framework of Administrative Decision-Making

Further to considering how acts of the appointing authorities come into being, this following section treats the key obligation to state the reasons for decisions and looks at the scope of this reasoning; then it discusses the rules that apply to the changing and withdrawal of decisions, as well as to their retroactivity; finally, it comments on the recovery of overpayments and the financial liability of the official.

1. The Appointing Authority and its Legal Acts

According to Article 2 of the Staff Regulations (SR), each institution shall determine who within it shall exercise the powers conferred by the SR on the appointing authority.[1] As a variation of this, one or more institutions may entrust to any one of them or to an interinstitutional body the exercise of some or all of the powers conferred on the appointing authority other than decisions relating to appointments, promotions or transfers of officials.[2] Thus, the powers on appointments, promotions and transfers remain within the institution itself.

[1] In French: AIPN, autorité investie du pouvoir de nomination.
[2] Art 2(2) SR; examples for this are the organisational set up of EPSO and ESA; Sant'Anna in Perillo/Giacobbo-Peyronnel (eds), *Statut de la fonction publique de l'Union européenne: Commentaire article par article* (2017) 27 ff.

It is thus to be decided in every institution who is to assume the authority to adopt the acts relating to the management of staff under the SR, as part of the internal organisational management of the institutions.[3] Even if a publication of the decision on the appointing authority is not foreseen in the SR, the principles of legal certainty, clarity and good administration warrant that rules are clearly established and made known to those who have to apply them and to whom they apply. In this sense, the determination of powers has to be made known *adequately* in each institution.[4]

The link between the institutions and their staff can be of a statutory and/or contractual nature. The statutory link is established by unilateral decision of the 'appointing authority' on the appointment of the official and other tenure-related acts in accordance with the SR. The links established in other categories of staff (beyond officials *stricto sensu*) contain elements of a contractual nature, which leads to a mixture in the application of statutory law and components of a contract under public law, by the Conditions of Employment of Other Servants (CEOS). These contracts can be of fixed-term duration or of indefinite duration, with the option of termination. The two main categories of links established by contract are temporary agents and contract agents. The contract is signed between the agent and the authority that acts in the function of the Authority Empowered to Conclude Contracts of Employment (AECE).[5] Thus, the terminology is *appointing authority* for officials appointed and *AECE* for staff employed by contract.

By its legal acts, the appointing authority (AECE respectively) determines the status of staff employed: it states, grants, changes or denies entitlements, exercising the powers conferred upon it by the SR. The acts can be formal (in writing), but also verbal/oral or tacit/implicit.[6] The decisive factor is whether they have the *effect* of individually and directly changing the legal status of those affected. They are subject to administrative review for complaints and judicial control in accordance with Articles 90 and 91 SR and Article 270 of the Treaty on the Functioning of the European Union (TFEU), see chapter 2.

a. Competence, Sub-Delegation and Principles of Sound Administration

An orderly administration presupposes that the person taking a decision or otherwise adopting an act is empowered to do so: the author of the act needs to have the competence required for taking the decision. Administrative competence within an institution is typically allocated by delegation or sub-delegation. According to settled case-law, a delegation of powers cannot be presumed and – even when entitled to delegate its powers – the delegating authority must take an express decision transferring them and the delegation can relate only to clearly defined

[3] On delegation and sub-delegation, see subsequent section a.

[4] CST, F-80/08, ECLI:EU:F:2009:160, paras 90, 96 – *Wenig v Commission*; GC, Jd Cases T-118/04 and T-134/04, ECLI:EU:T:2007:37, para 70 – *Caló v Commission*; Sant'Anna in Perillo/Giacobbo-Peyronnel (eds), *Statut de la fonction publique de l'Union européenne: Commentaire article par article* (2017) 27/28.

[5] In French: AHCC, autorité habilitée à conclure des contrats d'engagement. For the different categories of staff, see section II.1. below.

[6] Implicitly, for example, listing of the total points or of the list of promoted officials: these can be contested by those officials who are not enlisted, eg, CST, F-83/06, ECLI:EU:F:2008:165, para 43 – *Schell v Commission*; CST, F-113/06, ECLI:EU:F:2008:166, para 31 – *Bouis and Others v Commission*. On the preclusive effect of a salary statement with regard to a payment that is not mentioned therein, see CST, F-56/12, ECLI:EU:F:2013:96, para 22 – *Buschak v Commission*. On special formal requirements, eg, in the case of appointment, see Annual Report 2012, 217 with reference to CST, F-57/11, ECLI:EU:F:2014:254, paras 30, 66 – *Eklund v Commission*.

executive powers.[7] More precisely, the Court of Justice of the European Union (ECJ) in its *Meroni* case-law has laid down four basic requirements for a delegation to be lawful:

(1) A delegating authority cannot confer upon the authority receiving the delegation powers different from those which it has itself received under the Treaty (*nemo plus iuris transferre potest quam ipse habet*).[8]
(2) The delegation of discretionary powers is not permitted. The ECJ considers the balance of powers to be 'characteristic of the institutional structure of the [Union]' and a 'fundamental guarantee'. Delegating a discretionary power would 'render that guarantee ineffective'.
(3) A delegation of powers can only involve clearly defined executive powers, the use of which must be entirely subject to supervision.
(4) The transfer of authority by the delegating authority must take place in an express decision.

Although these principles were developed for the relationship between various authorities/institutions, the substance of it also applies to the internal – hierarchical – organisation within an appointing authority.

The consequences of the *Meroni* case-law for the decisions adopted in civil service law are that in cases where a sub-delegation of powers is not established (eg, not transferred by express decision), it must be concluded that the act towards the staff member was adopted by an authority without the competence to do so. An act adopted without competence may be annulled only if the failure to comply with the competence rules adversely affects either (1) one of the guarantees given to officials by the SR *or* (2) the principles of good administration in matters of staff administration.[9]

A line of case-law[10] interprets the second of these alternatives in the sense that the rules of sound administration in the management of staff require that the allocation of powers within the institutions be clearly defined and published. A decision taken without competence has to be annulled where the lack of competence stems from an allocation of powers that is not clearly defined or published. Thus, in such a constellation it would not be required to further examine whether – additionally – the failure to comply with the competence rules adversely affects one of the guarantees given to officials by the SR. Already the non-existence of a clearly defined and published delegation is sufficient to justify the annulment of the decision taken without competence.

b. Judicial Review vs Administrative Leeway

The scope of judicial review inversely correlates with the level of discretion afforded to the administration.[11] As a rule of thumb, the broader the leeway the institution enjoys in

[7] ECJ, 9/56 and 10/56, ECLI:EU:C:1958:7/8, 43 ff, 149–52, 153 and 154 – *Meroni*; ECJ, C-301/02 P, ECLI:EU:C:2005:306, para 43 – *Tralli v ECB*. For details, Mader, 'Art 298 TFEU' in von der Groeben/Schwarze/Hatje/Terhechte (eds), *Europäisches Unionsrecht*, 8th edn (2024) para 22.

[8] *cf* Ulpian, *Digest* 50.17.54.

[9] ECJ, 49/72, ECLI:EU:C:1973:58, para 13 – *Drescig v Commission*; GC, Jd Cases T-118/04 and T-134/04, ECLI:EU:T:2007:37, paras 66–68 – *Caló v Commission*; GC, T-555/16, ECLI:EU:T:2017:817, para 52 – *Teeäär v ECB*; GC, T-529/22, ECLI:EU:T:2023:618, para 29 – *QT v EIB* (recovery decision not signed by competent director-general but by head of unit).

[10] ibid, *QT v EIB*, para 30.

[11] On the scope and level of judicial assessment, Vandersanden, 'La procédure et les voies de recours' in Govaere/Vandersanden (eds), *La fonction publique communautaire* (2008) 126 ff; Reithmann (2014) *EuR* 108. Critical, eg, Levi, 'Droits fondamentaux et principes généraux de droit de la fonction publique communautaire' in Govaere/Vandersanden (eds), *La fonction publique communautaire* (2008) 81.

a given decision-making process, the less any judicial control will intervene. Any exercise of judicial review will seek to uphold the practical effectiveness of administrative discretion in decision-making.[12] In general, judicial control is limited to compliance with a rule-based administrative procedure, the recognition of an appropriate factual basis, and the detection of manifest errors of assessment and misuse of powers.[13] What is typically not subject to review is, for example, the assessment of the technical knowledge of a candidate or of evaluated staff on the basis of complex appraisals.[14] In the area of personnel policy, with regard to equal treatment, judicial review is limited to testing arbitrariness or manifestly inappropriate measures with regard to the objective pursued.[15] In view of the presumption of legality of the measures taken by the administration, the evidence must be sufficient to render the plausibility of the assessment made by it irrelevant, and it must be proven that the administration has exceeded the limits of its discretion,[16] whereas the court will not replace the assessment of the administration with its own.[17] Judicial review is largely limited in respect to medical findings, and it differs according to whether they stem from the institution's medical staff or from a joint medical committee.[18]

2. Acts Adversely Affecting an Official

Every act adversely affecting the staff employed requires an express, clear and precise legal basis.[19] The decisive factor is whether a measure affects the person directly and individually with legal consequences for his or her legal status.[20] As illustrated above[21] on admissibility questions, for example the legal information in which the appointing authority commits itself towards the official is reviewable,[22] but declaratory communications without own content, repeated acts, preparatory internal files or mere abstract general regulations are not reviewable.[23]

In accordance with Article 25(2) sentence 1 SR, each individual decision must be notified to the person concerned in writing, without delay, in a suitable language.[24] Problems in proving the

[12] CST, F-113/10, ECLI:EU:F:2012:20, paras 73 ff – *AT v EACEA*; on the relationship between leeway and legal certainty, CST, F-121/10, ECLI:EU:F:2011:174, para 88 – *Heath v ECB*.

[13] See chapter 2, VII.2. – 'Reviewable Act'.

[14] CST, F-74/10, ECLI:EU:F:2011:171, para 89 – *Kimman v Commission* (career appraisal). This case law is also applied by analogy for decisions taken by experts (here: actuary), CST, F-121/10, ECLI:EU:F:2011:174, para 90 – *Heath v ECB*.

[15] CST, F-38/10, ECLI:EU:F:2011:43, para 71 – *Vakalis v Commission*.

[16] CST, F-9/10, ECLI:EU:F:2011:160, paras 22 ff – *AC v Council*.

[17] CST, F-51/08 RENV, ECLI:EU:F:2011:193, para 37 – *Stols v Council*.

[18] CST, F-104/10, ECLI:EU:F:2013:64, para 85 – *de Pretis Cagnodo and Others v Commission*.

[19] CST, F-82/09, ECLI:EU:F:2010:154, paras 50/51 – *Nolin v Commission*. Where the administration bases its decision on several reasons, an annulment is only possible where all reasons fail: it is not sufficient for an annulment if only some are erroneous, but others can still support the decision.

[20] CST, Jd Cases F-124/05 and F-96/06, ECLI:EU:F:2010:2, para 233 – *A and G v Commission* (cancellation of exemption from jurisdiction); on the results of selection procedures, see CST, F-48/09, ECLI:EU:F:2010:38, para 44 – *Schopphoven v Commission*; on rotation: CST, F-110/10, ECLI:EU:F:2011:182, paras 23, 30 – *Couyoufa v Commission*.

[21] Chapter 2, V.2.

[22] CST, F-86/08, ECLI:EU:F:2009:161, para 36 – *Voslamber v Commission*. Salary notifications: CST, F-101/05, ECLI:EU:F:2006:58, para 55 – *Grünheid v Commission*; Gervasoni (2010) 46 *Cahiers de droit européen* 752, CST, F-103/05, ECLI:EU:F:2008:45, paras 75 ff – *Pickering v Commission* (contesting a salary statement in which the salary change is reflected for the first time) and CST, F-110/11, ECLI: EU:F:2012:174, para 34 – *Lebedef and Others v Commission*.

[23] GC, T-192/99, ECLI:EU:T:2001:72 – *Dunnett v EIB*. Measures of a general nature such as the 'general promotion policy' are not reviewable, CST, Jd Cases F-138/06 and F-37/08, ECLI:EU:F:2009:48, para 203 – *Meister v OHIM*.

[24] The decision must be drafted in a language the person concerned is familiar with, CST, Jd Cases F-138/06 and F-37/08, ECLI:EU:F:2009:48, paras 31/32 – *Meister v OHIM*; Reithmann (2011) 1 *EuR* 124. There is no right under Art 41

notification[25] can be reduced by using registered mail with fictitious delivery.[26] Article 25(3) SR stipulates that decisions regarding the appointment, establishment, promotion, transfer, determination of administrative status, and termination of service of an official shall be published in the institution to which the official belongs.

3. The Obligation to Motivate a Decision (Statement of Reasons)

Basis and effect

Article 25(2) sentence 2 SR and Article 296 TFEU oblige the administration to formally include a reasoning for a decision adversely affecting an official.[27] In principle, the violation of the obligation to motivate – being an essential defect of form – makes a decision liable to annulment.[28] The examination of the existence and the scope of the reasons forms part of the review of essential procedural requirements and of the formal legality of the respective decision.[29] The obligation to state reasons is, due to its importance as a matter of public policy, not subject to the discretion of the parties at any stage of the proceedings. A lack of reasoning can therefore also be determined ex officio by the Union judge.[30] Yet, the court is required to raise such a plea of its own motion only where a statement of reasons is clearly absent or inadequate, but not where there is ('only') a breach of a specific obligation to state reasons.[31]

The level of judicial scrutiny of the obligation to motivate a decision is the corollary of the absence of judicial control over matters of wide discretion (eg, medical assessments).[32] A contradictory or incomprehensible motivation is equivalent to a lack of reasoning.[33] One of the grounds brought forward by the courts for the importance of reasoning was that an administration dispensing with sufficient reasons to motivate its decision calls into question the system of separation of functions and the institutional balance between the administration and the judge, as the reasoning is also meant to avoid the dispute being brought before the judge.[34]

FRC or Regulation (EEC) No 1/1958 to receive replies in mother tongue or the language in which the proceedings have started, CST, F-9/10, ECLI:EU:F:2011:160, paras 119 ff – *AC v Council*; CST, F-57/11, ECLI:EU:F:2014:254, para 101 – *Eklund v Commission*.

[25] See CST, F-13/09, ECLI:EU:F:2010:45, paras 23 ff – *Peláez Jimeno v EP*; CST, F-56/09, ECLI:EU:F:2010:48, paras 35ff – *Marcuccio v Commission*; Reithmann (2008) *EuR* 276, 279, 295; (2011) 1 *EuR* 130; and (2011) 6 *EuR* 894.

[26] CST, F-25/10, ECLI:EU:F:2010:171, para 44 – *AG v EP* (fictitious delivery for registered mail, but may be rebutted by proof to the contrary); CST, F-87/11, ECLI:EU:F:2013:10, paras 36 ff – *Wallström v Frontex*.

[27] The term 'legal acts' in Art 296 TFEU is interpreted widely. On the soundness of motivation: CST, F-1/09, ECLI:EU:F:2009:155, para 41 – *Putterie-De-Beukelaer v Commission*; CST, F-80/09, ECLI:EU:F:2010:165, para 29 – *Lenz v Commission*; CST, F-4/10, ECLI:EU:F:2011:134, para 71 – *Nastvogel v Council*.

[28] GC, T-880/19, ECLI:EU:T:2021:325, paras 45/45 – *Lianopoulou v Commission*; GC, T-156/89 ECLI:EU:T:1991:33 – *Valverde Mordt v ECJ*; GC, T-117/01, ECLI:EU:T:2002:35 – *Parra v Commission*; on the requirement of a hypothetical different outcome of a decision had a proper reasoning been attached: Levi, 'Droits fondamentaux et principes généraux de droit de la fonction publique communautaire' in Govaere/Vandersanden (eds), *La fonction publique communautaire* (2008) 103; CST, F-4/10, ECLI:EU:F:2011:134, paras 33, 42/43 – *Nastvogel v Council*; CST, F-86/11, ECLI:EU:F:2013:56, paras 96 ff, 110 – *McCoy v CoR*.

[29] CST, F-74/11, ECLI:EU:F:2013:22, para 31 – *Bojc Golob v Commission*.

[30] CST, F-149/15, ECLI:EU:F:2016:155, para 93 – *HG v Commission* (set aside on a different point by GC, T-693/16 P-RENV-RX, ECLI:EU:T:2021:895 – *HG v Commission*).

[31] CST, F-74/10, ECLI:EU:F:2011:171, paras 44 ff – *Kimman v Commission*.

[32] GC, T-880/19, ECLI:EU:T:2021:325, para 45 – *Lianopoulou v Commission*.

[33] ECJ, C-114/19 P, ECLI:EU:C:2020:457, para 55 – *Commission v Di Bernardo*.

[34] GC, T-237/00, ECLI:EU:T:2005:437, para 106 – *Reynolds v EP*.

Scope of the statement of reasons

The motivation must be complete[35] and, in principle, individualised.[36] It must state precisely the facts that have an unfavourable effect on the addressee,[37] as well as the considerations that led the administration to the decision,[38] so that the addressee can obtain information about the content and scope of the measure and the chances of success of a remedy.[39] The concrete scope of the obligation to state reasons depends on the nature of the act in question and the context in which it was adopted. The statement of reasons must be appropriate to the measure at issue and must disclose clearly and unequivocally the reasoning followed by the institution which adopted that measure in such a way as to enable the persons concerned to ascertain the reasons for it and to enable the competent court to review its legality. Thus, the level of detail of a statement of reasons depends on the circumstances of each case, in particular the content of the measure in question, the nature of the reasons given and the interest which the addressees of the measure, or other parties to whom it is of direct and individual concern, may have in obtaining explanations. It is not necessary for the reasoning to go into all the relevant facts and points of law.[40] The scope of a statement of reasons may be reduced if the facts are already known to the addressee from the context.[41]

Timing

In principle, the grounds for a decision must be given at the same time as the decision itself,[42] but it is legally sufficient that the addressee can recognise the scope of the contested decision based on the circumstances of the individual case or based on the decision rejecting the complaint.[43] Thus, a reasoning can be given or amended in the decision rejecting the complaint.[44] In terms of content, the decision must indicate who it stems from and what the

[35] But the assessment in an appraisal report does not have to address all the questions raised by the person assessed, CST, F-74/10, ECLI:EU:F:2011:171, paras 95, 115 – *Kimman v Commission*, appeal decision GC, T-644/11 P, ECLI:EU:T:2014:613, para 125. On incompleteness: CST, F-50/ 07, ECLI:EU:F:2008:147, paras 6, 24/25, 28 – *Hristova v Commission*.

[36] The justification must not be stereotypical or fail to take into account the individual circumstances: CST, F-18/09, ECLI:EU:F:2011:180, paras 73/74 – *Merhzaoui v Council*; CST, F-7/11 and 60/11, ECLI:EU: F:2012:195, para 131 – *AX v ECB*, different for promotion lists, eg, CST, F-83/06, ECLI:EU:F:2008:165, para 89 – *Schell v Commission*.

[37] On the other hand, no grounds for denial of promotion have to be provided as to what the higher merits of the other applicants were: CST, F-125/15, ECLI:EU:F:2016:164, paras 29, 30, 33 – *HB v Commission*; GC, T-668/16 P, ECLI:EU:T:2017:802, paras 41–44 – *HL v Commission*.

[38] CST, F-40/05, ECLI:EU:F:2007:189, para 260 – *Andreasen v Commission*. The scope of reasoning depends on the decision's legal basis and is not increased as a result of a previous annulment or due to Art 266 TFEU: CST, F-77/11, ECLI:EU:F:2012:187, para 22 – *Van Neyghem v Council*.

[39] CST, F-102/07, ECLI:EU:F:2009:129, para 162 – *Kerstens v Commission*.

[40] On all these criteria cited: ECJ, C-114/19 P, ECLI:EU:C:2020:457, para 29 – *Commission v Di Bernardo*. See case study at the end of this section.

[41] GC, T-100/00, ECLI:EU:T:2001:75, para 53 – *Campoli v Commission*.

[42] See ECJ, 195/80, ECLI:EU:F:2013:201, para 22 – *Michel v EP*; ECJ, C-17/07 P, ECLI:EU:C:2008:134, para 50 – *Neirinck v Commission*; CST, F-26/10, ECLI:EU:F:2011:163, paras 37 ff – *AZ v Commission* (amendment and change of reasoning). A later specification of the reasoning is possible: CST, F-9/11, ECLI:EU:F:2011:196, paras 62–65 – *Sabbag Afota v Council*; CST, F-44/14, ECLI:EU:T:2016:465, paras 79–83 – *Pohjanmäki v Council*; Levi, 'Droits fondamentaux et principes généraux de droit de la fonction publique communautaire' in Govaere/Vandersanden (eds), *La fonction publique communautaire* (2008) 103.

[43] CST, F-136/06, ECLI:EU:F:2008:168, para 104 – *Reali v Commission*; CST, F-43/08, ECLI:EU:F:2009:70, paras 12, 41 – *Spee v Europol*.

[44] GC, T-20/09 P, ECLI:EU:T:2011:257, paras 65 ff – *Marcuccio v Commission*.

signatory's power to act results from, but it does not have to contain information on the legal basis or even its wording.[45] A motivation provided in the course of the pre-litigation procedure may be amended by complementary specifications during the proceedings;[46] however, an incorrect statement of reasons initially set out in the act being challenged must not be substituted by a completely new set of reasons in front of the court.[47]

Cases of limited duty to state reasons

In exceptional cases (eg, because of the large number of addressees in an open competition) it is permitted to initially only give a summary statement of reasons and to submit the specific reasons later, but only insofar as this subsequent submission does not lead to a violation of the rights of defence.[48]

The duty to state reasons in the selection process of competitions can only prevail over confidentiality requirements in certain individual cases.[49] In principle, within the framework of the computer-aided admission tests, applicants cannot insist on seeing the multiple-choice questions or the (correct) answers, but only the total of the correctly ticked answers. In assessment centre tests, the overall grades for the evaluated individual skills are communicated, and also on request a copy of the answers to the written questions, whereas the factors relating to individual or comparative assessments of candidates and the corrected work itself are subject to a secrecy[50] that is upheld by the courts.[51] There were grounds to believe that the requirements for the scope of the obligation to state reasons could increase, for example, in the case of unsuccessful selection processes[52] or in the case of dismissals.[53] However, this has not yet materialised:[54] in both areas, knowledge of the reasons from the context is still considered sufficient.[55]

[45] CST, F-41/06 RENV, ECLI:EU:F:2012:149, para 74 – *Marcuccio v Commission.*

[46] GC, T-338/00 and T-376/00, EU:T:2002:314, para 55 – *Morello v Commission.*

[47] GC, T-601/16, ECLI:EU:T:2017:757, para 43 – *Paraskevaidis v Cedefop*; GC, T-218/02, EU:T:2005:343, para 63 – *Napoli Buzzanca v Commission*; CST, Jd Cases F-7/11 and 60/11, ECLI:EU:F:2012:195, para 160 – *AX v ECB*; CST, F-81/07, ECLI:EU:F:2008:125, paras 29, 37 – *Barbin v EP*; CST, F-23/10, ECLI:EU:F:2011:162, paras 98 ff – *Allen v Commission.* The institution is not entitled to substitute an entirely new statement of reasons for the initial erroneous statement: GC, T-71/96, ECLI:EU:T:1997:170, para 79 – *Berlingieri Vinzek*; GC, T-317/22, ECLI:EU:T:2023:620, para 26 – *PF v EP.*

[48] ECJ, C-114/19 P, ECLI:EU:C:2020:457, para 59 – *Commission v Di Bernardo.*

[49] See the judgment of the CST, F-74/07, ECLI:EU:F:2008:127, paras 40, 46 – *Meierhofer v Commission*, whereby it was decisive that the additional information was requested there by the Court; CST, F-96/09, ECLI:EU:F:2012:129, para 102 – *Cuallado Martorell v Commission*; CST, F-6/07, ECLI:EU:F:2008:55, paras 57, 61 – *Suvikas v Council.*

[50] On secrecy, see the following case study.

[51] See EPSO Guide to Open Competitions [2010] OJ C184 A, 11; CST, F-96/09, ECLI:EU:F:2012:129, paras 84 ff – *Cuallado Martorell v Commission.* On *reasoning vs secrecy* regarding statements on the assessment of character, see CST, F-112/10, ECLI:EU:F:2012:179, para 90 – *Trentea v FRA* (appeal dismissed, GC, T-107/13 P, ECLI:EU:T:2015:20).

[52] CST, F-74/07, ECLI:EU:F:2008:127, para 40 – *Meierhofer v Commission.*

[53] CST, F-1/05, ECLI:EU:F:2006:112, para 65 – *Landgren v ETF.* The appeal decision, GC, T-404/06 P, ECLI:EU:T:2009:313, confirmed the initial judgment, but with less emphasis on social law aspects, Gervasoni (2010) 46 *Cahiers de droit européen* 735.

[54] Vandersanden, 'La procédure et les voies de recours' in Govaere/Vandersanden (eds), *La fonction publique communautaire* (2008) 130; Van Raepenbusch, 'L'apport jurisprudentiel du Tribunal de la fonction publique de l'Union européenne' in Govaere/Vandersanden (eds), *La fonction publique communautaire* (2008) 155; Levi, 'Droits fondamentaux et principes généraux de droit de la fonction publique communautaire' in Govaere/Vandersanden (eds), *La fonction publique communautaire* (2008) 101.

[55] CST, F-89/08, ECLI:EU:F:2010:11, para 79 – *P v EP.*

Case Study on the Obligation to State Reasons[56]

On the importance of the statement of reasons

Case C-114/19 P, *Commission v D Di Bernardo* of 11 June 2020
Case T-811/16, *Di Bernardo v Commission* of 29 November 2018

In Brief

Article 296 TFEU stipulates 'Legal acts shall state the reasons on which they are based'. The Court of Justice confirmed and redefined the right of a candidate in an open competition to obtain a statement of reasons for the decision not to admit him to the list of successful candidates. Together with a rejection decision, the Selection Board has to provide reasons for its decision and has to indicate the selection criteria, even if the candidate had not requested the communication of reasons or criteria. Where the reasoning of a decision is inadequate, the administration may only in exceptional circumstances supplement the statement of reasons during the proceedings.

Facts of the Case and Procedure

The applicant participated in an open competition for the establishment of 'Secretaries/Clerks'. After he had taken part in the assessment test, the Selection Board asked him to provide further information on his professional experience. The Board wished to obtain detailed job descriptions signed by his previous employers and copies of the contracts of employment. The applicant sent a detailed job description and explained why he did not possess such descriptions for other sections: the Italian company which had employed him had been dissolved and he was not in a position to provide these documents. He instead submitted other documents, including Italian national collective labour agreements, with a description of the duties linked to various employment contracts. The Selection Board decided not to place him on the list of successful candidates in the open competition because he did not satisfy the requirement of a minimum duration of three years of professional experience in the field related to the nature of the duties. The Board informed the applicant that it had established selection criteria to assess whether the qualifications and professional experience of candidates matched the competencies required for the positions to be filled.

The Court's Decision and the Arguments of the Parties

The ECJ confirms the judgment of the General Court (GC) of November 2018 which had annulled the decision of the Selection Board for infringement of the obligation to state reasons. The Commission appealed against this judgment and lost the case at the ECJ.

The Commission pleaded that the GC had failed to take sufficient account of the legal and factual context of the disputed decision, while the adequacy of a statement of reasons must be assessed in the light of the context of the decision concerned and not merely of

[56] See also the case study in section II.13.e, below.

its wording. On this plea, the ECJ recalls that the statement of reasons required under Article 296 TFEU for measures adopted by EU institutions

> must be appropriate to the measure at issue and must disclose clearly and unequivocally the reasoning followed by the institution which adopted that measure in such a way as to enable the persons concerned to ascertain the reasons for it and to enable the competent court to review its legality. The requirements to be satisfied by the statement of reasons depend on all the circumstances of each case, in particular the content of the measure in question, the nature of the reasons given and the interest which the addressees of the measure, or other parties to whom it is of direct and individual concern, may have in obtaining explanations. It is not necessary for the reasoning to go into all the relevant facts and points of law, since the question whether the statement of reasons meets the requirements of Article 296 TFEU must be assessed with regard not only to its wording but also to its context and to all the legal rules governing the matter in question.[57]

The ECJ differentiates the argument brought forward by the Commission that in competitions with a large number of participants, the Selection Board is authorised to give summary reasons for a refusal to select a candidate. In a competition involving a large number of candidates, the Selection Board may initially inform the candidates only of the criteria and the result of the selection. Then it may subsequently provide individual explanations to those candidates who expressly so request. The GC had already pointed out that in the case in hand the Selection Board took its decision after all the candidates had already taken part in the admission tests and the other tests. The Selection Board therefore only had to deal with the smaller number of candidates on the shortlist. So, the workload relating to an open competition cannot serve here as an argument for failing to motivate the decision to reject the applicant.

Also the Commission's argument that the applicant had never tried to ascertain the selection criteria was rejected by the ECJ, because even where the Selection Board is initially obliged to provide only summary reasons, as in a competition involving a large number of participants, those reasons must include an indication of the selection criteria. The selection criteria constitute a minimum of information which must in any event be provided to candidates, at the latest at the same time as the results of the competition concerned. Finally, the ECJ stated that the secrecy of the proceedings of the Selection Board (Art 6 Annex III SR) cannot be used to hide the criteria applied for the selection.

On the question of whether the statement of reasons can be supplemented later

As to the timing of the statement of reasons, the ECJ recalls that it must, in principle, be communicated to the person concerned at the same time as the act adversely affecting him. A failure to state reasons cannot be remedied during the court proceedings. However, where there is not an absence of reasoning but an inadequacy of reasoning, explanations given in the course of the procedure may, in exceptional cases, remedy that inadequacy. In a competition involving a large number of candidates, the institution may be unable,

[57] ECJ, C-114/19 P, ECLI:EU:C:2020:457, para 29 – *Commission v Di Bernardo*; GC, T-451/20, ECLI:EU:T:2023:276, para 37 – *Meta*; GC, T-272/21, ECLI:EU:T:2023:373, para 50 – *Puigdemont i Casamajó and Others.*

from a practical point of view, to provide each candidate with an adequate statement of reasons in good time. In these circumstances it is exceptionally permitted to produce evidence before the courts, such as the minutes of selection boards.

Comments

1. The central purpose of a reasoning is that it *enables the persons concerned to ascertain the reasons for a decision and to enable the competent court to review its legality*. Absence or lack of reasoning may make an administrative decision liable to annulment, and may lead to the award of damages.[58] The lack of reasoning can be raised by the court ex officio.[59]
2. Normatively, the obligation to state reasons does not only stem from Article 296 TFEU, but also from Article 41(2)c of the Fundamental Rights Charter (FRC). In the context of decisions specifically against officials, Article 25(2) SR stipulates this obligation as 'Any decision adversely affecting an official shall state the grounds on which it is based'. The scope of this obligation differs depending on content and context. Specifically in the case of recruitment processes, the duty to give reasons has to be reconciled with confidentiality requirements.
3. The present judgment follows the line of case-law on the necessity of the statement of reasons. In principle, the reasoning has to be provided together with the decision itself; it cannot be supplemented later during the court proceedings.[60] However, to a certain extent the inadequacy of an existing statement of reasons can be healed later during the court proceedings. This balanced approach is necessary in order to avoid the administration abstaining from providing reasoning altogether (knowing that it can be still delivered anyway), but is otherwise free to reduce a reasoning to match the content and context.
4. The ECJ accepts that the specific situation of mass procedures involving large numbers of candidates, like an open competition, can justify the exceptional reduction of a reasoning (summary reasons).
5. The ECJ clarifies that a 'contradictory or unintelligible statement of reasons' also amounts to a failure to state reasons.
6. The healing of an insufficient reasoning during court proceedings is 'not automatic', as the ECJ emphasises. If reasons are supplemented at the court stage, the judges must still ascertain whether the additional statement of reasons is liable to infringe the *rights of the defence*.
7. As the ECJ confirms, 'secrecy' cannot be used as an argument to preclude communication of the objective factors and criteria for assessment.[61]
8. This judgment is important for EU selection boards (and other services), as it confirms that the statement of reasons in the rejection of a candidate has to be provided without it having to be asked for; likewise, the selection criteria have to be provided without being asked for.

[58] CST, F-116/11, ECLI:EU:F:2013:92 – *Vacca v Commission*.
[59] CST, F-149/15, ECLI:EU:F:2016:155, para 93 – *HG v Commission*.
[60] ECJ, C-521/09 P, ECLI:EU:C:2011:620, para 149 – *Elf Aquitaine v Commission*.
[61] ECJ, C-254/95 P, ECLI:EU:C:1995:288, paras 26–28 – *EP v Innamorati*.

4. Changes and Withdrawals of Decisions

Both favourable and adverse decisions can be modified and withdrawn, especially in the event of a change in the legal situation or where the measure is tainted by illegality. Changes and withdrawals must be expressed clearly, are subject to limitations of legitimate expectations and acquired rights,[62] and are allowed only within a reasonable period.[63] Individual decisions conferring a right cannot be unilaterally reversed if they are lawful.[64]

5. Retroactive Decisions

In exceptional cases, decisions by the appointing authority can also be issued retroactively, mostly in order to correct an illegal situation.[65] However, in the interest of legal certainty[66] this is only permissible if the situation requires it, if legitimate expectations are sufficiently taken into account,[67] and if the retroactive decision is taken within a reasonable period of time.[68] This also applies to a retroactive change in the law as well as to an interpretation specifying a normative content.[69] Otherwise, in the absence of a positive system of horizontal administrative EU law, general principles for assessing the admissibility of measures with retroactive effect have to be applied: where a measure affects a situation that has started and ended in the past, retroactivity would only be permissible in exceptional cases under mandatory requirements, as it could adversely affect acquired rights,[70] while in the case of a measure affecting a situation that has started in the past and still continues, case-law allows for legislative and administrative flexibility but requires the adoption of transitional measures in order to comply with the principle of proportionality.[71]

[62] GC, T-416/04, ECLI:EU:T:2006:281, para 161 – *Kontouli v Council*; CST, F-51/07, ECLI:EU:F:2008:112, paras 55 ff – *Bui Van v Commission*; CST, F-57/11, ECLI:EU:F:2014:254, para 69 – *Eklund v Commission*; CST, F-25/07, ECLI:EU:F:2010:163, para 128 – *Bleser v ECJ*.

[63] GC, T-491/08, ECLI:EU:T:2010:191, paras 58 and 60–62 – *Bui Van v Commission*. When assessing the appropriate period, the period of three months cannot have a general basis, but the circumstances of the individual case must be taken into account, see also Gervasoni (2010) 46 *Cahiers de droit européen* 786.

[64] *cf* ECJ, 7/56, 3/57 to 7/57, ECLI:EU:C:1957:7 – *Algera*; CST, F-92/05, ECLI:EU:F:2007:9 – *Genette v Commission*. Differentiating: CST, F-122/10, ECLI:EU:F:2012:180, paras 58, 60, 74 – *Cocchi and Falcione v Commission*; an offer of civil servant status is a mere declaration of intent which can be withdrawn, already due to the strict form of appointment under civil service law, *cf* CJEU Annual Report 2012, 217, with reference to CST, F-57/11, ECLI:EU:F:2014:254, paras 30, 76 – *Eklund v Commission*.

[65] ECJ, C-90/95 P, ECLI:EU:C:1997:198 – *De Compte v EP*; restrictive ECJ, 54/77, ECLI:EU:C:1978:45 – *Herpels v Commission*; CST, F-135/07, ECLI:EU:F:2008:114 – *Smadja v Commission*.

[66] See ECJ, C-238/99 P, C-244/99 P, C-245/99 P, C-247/99 P, C-250/99 P to C-252/99 P on balancing legal certainty and legality; ECJ, C-254/99 P, ECLI:EU:C:2002:582, para 187 – *Limburgse Vinyl Maatschappij and Others v Commission*; CST, F-4/10, ECLI:EU:F:2011:134, para 44 – *Nastvogel v Council*. It is important whether individual rights are created by the legal act in question, as is the balancing of interests, in this sense ECJ, 42/59 and 49/59, ECLI:EU:C:1961:5 – *SNUPAT v High Authority*, and ECJ, 14/61, ECLI:EU:C:1962:28 – *Koninklijke Nederlandsche Hoogovens en Staalfabrieken v High Authority*; CST, F-51/07, ECLI:EU:F:2008:112, paras 67 and 70 – *Bui Van v Commission*.

[67] GC, T-177/95, ECLI:EU:T:1996:187 – *Barraux and Others v Commission*; GC, T-23/96, ECLI:EU:T:1998:203 – *De Persio v Commission*; GC, T-175/97, ECLI:EU:T:2000:259 – *Bareyt and Others v Commission*.

[68] See GC, T-491/08, ECLI:EU:T:2010:191 – *Bui Van v Commission* repealing CST, F-51/07, ECLI:EU:F:2008:112 – *Bui Van v Commission*.

[69] See CST, F-31/10, ECLI:EU:F:2012:80, paras 47, 63 ff – *Guittet v Commission* and Potvin-Solis (2011) *RUE* 616 (change in law); CST, F-27/08, ECLI:EU:F:2009:44, paras 86, 89, 111 – *Simões Dos Santos v OHIM* (interpretation).

[70] ECJ, C-258/80, ECLI:EU:C:1982:56, paras 11/12 – *Metallurgica Rumi v Commission*; GC, T-220/00, ECLI:EU:T:2003:193, para 44 – *Cheil Jedang*.

[71] ECJ, 96/77, ECLI:EU:C:1978:26, paras 49 ff – *Ancienne Maison Marcel Bauche*; Mader, *Verteidigungsrechte* (2006) 261.

A retroactive application for benefits is possible in principle, but may also be subject to strict limitations, mostly focusing on the errors committed by the administration and whether these were recognisable by the person concerned.[72]

6. Recovery of Overpayments

Under Article 85(1) SR, 'any sum overpaid shall be recovered if the recipient was aware that there was no due reason for the payment or if the fact of the overpayment was patently such that he could not have been unaware of it'.

a. *Character and Scope of Recovery*

As case-law has clarified, there is no discretion on the appointing authority's side whether or not to recover the overpayment.[73] Once the conditions for the recovery of undue payments are met, the institution must recover the amounts that the staff member had unduly received. Article 85 SR 'relates only to the financial relationship between an official who has received overpayments and the employer institution'. Moreover, that provision does not take into account the possible consequences of the recovery for the staff member with regard to other persons who may have benefited directly or indirectly from the overpayments subject to recovery by the institution, these being matters of private law.[74]

b. *Statutory Limitation Period*

The AECE's request for recovery must be made no later than five years from the date on which the sum was paid (limitation period).[75] Where the appointing authority is able to establish that the recipient deliberately misled the administration with a view to obtaining the sum concerned, the request for recovery shall not be invalidated even if this five-year period has elapsed. The opening of an investigation by the European Anti-Fraud Office (OLAF) on the facts giving rise to a recovery do not cause an interruption or suspension of the five-year limitation period for recovery; this is due to the principle of legal certainty, which demands that a limitation period must be defined in advance and prevents the administration 'from indefinitely delaying the exercise of its powers'. Limitation is to be interpreted strictly, but subject to certain – though changeable – legislative choices: it depends on 'the historical and social circumstances prevailing in a society at a given time'.[76]

[72] CST, F-73/09, ECLI:EU:F:2011:40, paras 57 ff – *Sukup v Commission*; on benefits claimed retroactively that were retained due to administrative errors: GC, T-338/16 P, ECLI:EU:T:2018:98 – *Zink v Commission* (no application by analogy of time limitation under the Financial Regulation); also GC, T-529/22, ECLI:EU:T:2023:618, paras 56 – *QT v EIB* on the relationship towards the limitation period under the Financial Regulation (Art 105 Financial Regulation, under which interruptions of the limitation period may occur). A potential case of application of a retroactive benefit could be, eg, the higher pension payment under the *Picard* case-law for retired staff who entered service on 31 December 2013 or earlier. See chapter 2, V.2. and chapter 3, IV.6.

[73] GC, T-782/14 P, ECLI:EU:T:2016:29, para 43 – *DF v Commission*.

[74] ibid, para 54; thus the applicant could not hold the fact against the recovery that he had paid maintenance allowance to the former spouse, impossible for him to recover.

[75] Art 85(2) SR, likewise in Art 16.3 EIB Staff Regulations.

[76] GC, T-529/22, ECLI:EU:T:2023:618, paras 42–46 – *QT v EIB*.

It can be assumed also that other kinds of procedures that are carried out to check the correctness of expenditures, for example an internal or external audit, do not cause an interruption or suspension of the five-year limitation period for recovery under Article 85 SR. As a result of this case-law on the uninterrupted running of limitation periods, recovery decisions may be issued before investigations by the recovering institution, investigations by OLAF, audits etc, are completed.

c. *Preconditions for Recovery*

Both preconditions have to be satisfied for a recovery:

(1) The payment was done with no due reason and
(2a) the recipient was aware of this, or, in the alternative
(2b) the overpayment was patently such that he could not have been unaware of it.

In the first of those two alternatives (2a), it is for the administration to prove that the recipient was actually aware that the payment was undue. In the second alternative (2b), the administration would have to prove that the undue nature of the payment would not escape the notice of an official exercising ordinary care, for which account must be taken, in each case, of the ability of the official concerned to carry out the necessary checks.[77]

Patently such and objectivised standard

This above test, suggested by the Civil Service Tribunal (CST) in *Achab*, is thus is a little irritating in that it attempts to combine an objective standard ('an official exercising ordinary care') with a subjective perspective of the 'ability of the official concerned' 'in each case'. In order to make this applicable in practice, the line will have to rely on a objectivised standard. Concerning the test if an irregularity underlying the overpayment was 'patently such that he could not have been unaware', it is important to know that the assessment of the 'patently such' is not the one of the administration but of the staff member.[78] Recovery is due where the error is one which *would not escape the notice of an official exercising ordinary care, who is deemed to know the rules governing his salary*, taking into account the degree of clarity of the applicable provisions.[79] The level of care expected depends, inter alia, on the official's level of responsibility, his grade and seniority, and the degree of clarity of the provisions. There is an expectation that an official with a high grade and long service is better capable of recognising an overpayment.[80] It is not necessary for the official concerned, in the exercise of his duty of diligence, to be able to determine the precise extent of the error made by the administration. The fact that he has doubts about the validity of the payments in question is sufficient for him to be obliged to contact the administration so that it can carry out the necessary checks.[81]

[77] CST, F-21/12, ECLI:EU:F:2013:95, para 44 – *Achab v EESC.*

[78] GC, Jd Cases T-568/16 and T-599/16, ECLI:EU:T:2018:347, paras 165, 168 – *Spagnolli*; CST, F-136/15, ECLI:EU:F:2016:169, para 57 – *HD v EP*: 'the fact that the administration did not cease to pay the education allowance does not affect the conclusion that the official concerned knew or could have known of that failure, and the official cannot, on the basis of good faith, escape the obligation to repay an allowance paid without justification'. The existence of conflicting legal opinions regarding the matter of irregularity may point to the conclusion that the official could not have ascertained an overpayment: GC, T-111/89, ECLI:EU:T:1990:46, para 49 – *Schreiber v Council.*

[79] GC, Jd Cases T-568/16 and T-599/16, ECLI:EU:T:2018:347, para 152 – *Spagnolli*: an 'error which a normally diligent official who is supposed to be familiar with the rules governing his remuneration ought to have detected'.

[80] GC, T-430/13 P, ECLI:EU:T:2015:122, paras 29–32 – *EESC v Achab*; ECJ, C-420/04 P, ECLI:EU:C:2005:482, para 59 – *Gouvras v Commission.*

[81] GC, T-782/14 P, ECLI:EU:T:2016:29, para 27 – *DF v Commission*; CST, F-72/12, ECLI:EU:F:2013:184, para 50 – *Roulet v Commission*; GC, T-604/16, ECLI:EU:T:2018:562, paras 119/120 – *HD v EP.*

7. Financial Liability of the Official

While Article 85 SR applies to the recovery of sums unduly paid to the staff member, Article 22 SR deals with the financial *liability* of staff: an official 'may be required to make good, in whole or in part, any damage suffered by the Union as a result of serious misconduct on his part in the course of or in connection with the performance of his duties'. As provided for in Article 22 SR, the appointing authority has to give a reasoned decision in accordance with the procedure laid down in regard to disciplinary matters.[82] When deciding on the substance of such a case the court exercises unlimited jurisdiction, including the possibility to take into account efforts of the official to reduce damage and an overall assessment of the situation giving rise or contributing to the damage. Contrary to the recovery of undue sums under Article 85 SR (five-year limitation period), there is no legal limitation period for the adoption of a decision under Article 22 SR; however, the institution is required by virtue of legal certainty to adopt the decision 'within a reasonable time'.[83]

II. The Legal Status of Staff Employed

The following part in its 20 sections explores the main characteristics of the legal status of staff employed: starting with the types of staff and function groups, the career paths and competition procedures, followed by a core section on the mutual rights and obligations of the civil servant, including the central term of the *duty of care* and the protection against harassment, the present rules governing whistleblowing, then the appraisal and promotion exercises, the conditions for transfer, change of function group and change of duties, up to the termination of service and the handling of disciplinary procedures.

1. Types of Staff and Classification in Function Groups

The staff of the European institutions is made up of officials under the SR, plus temporary staff, contract staff, contract staff for auxiliary tasks and special advisers contracted under the CEOS,[84] as well as local staff working on the basis of employment and service contracts under national law. Special regulations apply in part to staff in the European External Action Service (EEAS) and to accredited parliamentary assistants or other specified categories of staff.[85] The SR and CEOS do not apply to seconded national experts.[86]

[82] See section II.20. below.

[83] GC, T-693/16 P-RENV-RX, ECLI:EU:T:2021:895, para 308 – *HG v Commission*.

[84] On the applicability of Regulation (EEC) No 1408/71 to civil servants, see ECJ, C-293/03, ECLI:EU:C:2004:821, para 36 – *My*. On the principle of good faith in performance of the contract, see CST, F-19/08, ECLI:EU:F:2009:75, paras 96, 98 – *Bennett and Others v OHIM*; Gervasoni (2010) 46 *Cahiers de droit européen* 778. Commission report on the use of contract agents in 2011, COM(2013) 87; Murdoch/Trondal, 'Contracted government: unveiling the European Commission's contracted staff' *West European Politics* (2013) 1, 1. Purchase of external services is not a circumvention of labour protections if the choice of national law reflects a legitimate interest and national legal protection is available, Gervasoni (2010) 46 *Cahiers de droit européen* 743 with reference to CST, F-88/07, ECLI:EU:F:2008:141 – *Gonzalez v Commission*.

[85] *cf* Art 14 EIB Staff Regulations, last amended 1 September 2020, which defines four categories of staff at the EIB.

[86] CST, F-53/06, ECLI:EU:F:2006:100, para 22 – *Gualtieri v Commission*. But see chapter 2, III.

Further to Article 5(1) SR, the posts under the SR are classified according to the nature and importance of the duties to which they relate: there is an administrators' function group (AD), an assistants' function group (AST), and a secretaries' and clerks' function group (AST/SC). As to the grading within the function groups, group AD comprises 12 grades corresponding to managerial, conceptual and analytical, linguistic and scientific duties; the AST function group comprises 11 grades corresponding to executive and technical duties; and the AST/SC function group comprises six grades corresponding to clerical and secretarial duties.[87] The term 'category' in this context is used to refer to the former function groups A*, B*, C* and D*, ie, those that existed before the reform of 2004. Each function group is also divided into the different types of posts listed in Annex I SR.[88] Differences in status between the different categories of staff, and the types, classifications into function groups, and grades that enable some to enjoy advantages that are not granted to others, are allowed and intended; they are a consequence of the legitimate requirements of the service and the tasks assigned.[89] However, identical conditions of recruitment and career shall apply to all officials belonging to the same function group.[90] Staff who are objectively placed in identical conditions or situations must be subject to the same rules.[91]

The classification as set out by Article 5 SR (AD, AST, function groups) also applies to temporary[92] agents 'by analogy',[93] however not to contract staff.[94] The provision of Article 5(5) SR under which identical conditions of recruitment and service career shall apply to all officials belonging to the same function group applies neither to temporary nor to contract staff.[95]

a. *Officials*

Civil servants are appointed for life by a unilateral act, either via assignment or by transfer to an established post.[96] The appointment takes effect on the date specified in the appointing instrument, Article 3 SR.[97] The instrument appointing an official shall state the date on which the appointment takes effect. The unilateral character of the appointment by the administration prohibits the transfer of considerations stemming from contract law for the purpose of interpreting the status of the official.[98] Pursuant to Articles 27 and 28 SR, the prerequisites for appointment are professional qualifications, the highest standard of ability, efficiency, integrity, adequate health, citizenship of one of the Member States,[99] certain language skills and other listed preconditions.

[87] Art 5(2) SR.

[88] Art 5(4) SR.

[89] CST, F-65/07, ECLI:EU:F:2009:43, para 104 – *Aayhan and Others v Commission*; ECJ, Jd Cases 118/82 to 123/82, ECLI:EU:C:1983:270, para 22 – *Celant and Others v Commission.*

[90] Art 5(5) SR.

[91] GC, T-325/09 P, ECLI:EU:T:2011:506, para 86 – *Adjemian and Others v Commission.*

[92] Art 10(1) CEOS.

[93] On the meaning of 'by analogy', see chapter 2, V.2. at the end.

[94] *cf* the different scheme provided in Art 80 CEOS, and Art 80(4) and (5) CEOS.

[95] Art 10(1) CEOS, Art 80 CEOS.

[96] Art 1a(1) SR, Art 7 SR.

[97] Not constitutive, *cf* Gauer (2007) 67, but on the formal requirement: CST, F-1/06, ECLI:EU:F:2007:25, paras 41, 44, 50 ff – *Fernández Ortiz v Commission*; CST, F-41/05, ECLI:EU:F:2010:116, para 43 – *Jacobs v Commission.*

[98] ECJ, 102/75, ECLI:EU:C:1976:172, para 16 – *Petersen v Commission.*

[99] On Brexit issues: pursuant to Art 28(a) SR, the nationality of a Member State is a prerequisite for *appointment* as a civil servant, but the appointing authority may waive the nationality requirement; however, this exemption is not applicable for service in a third country: Art 1 Appendix X SR. For *temporary* agents, the CEOS contains a similar provision in Art 12 (2) lit a CEOS, but further to Art 47 CEOS both for staff with limited and unlimited contracts, as soon as the conditions of Art 12 (2) lit a CEOS are no longer fulfilled (here: nationality of an EU Member State), the appointing authority can either terminate the contract (respecting the notice periods) or grant an exception. At the beginning of 2021, the Commission still employed over 600 British nationals. Bray/Rodrigues, 'L'impact du Brexit sur le fonctionnement des institutions de l'UE: aspects relatifs à la fonction publique européenne, Lexisnexis Dossier' (February 2018).

b. Temporary Staff

Temporary staff are employed for a limited or unlimited period in a temporary post (Art 2 lit a CEOS) or temporarily in a permanent post (Art 2 lit b CEOS) in order to cover temporary staffing needs. In both cases, the posts are included in the list of posts appended to the section of the budget relating to each institution. They essentially perform activities that are also assigned to officials. Temporary staff according to Article 2 lit c CEOS are staff other than officials who assist mandated officials and elected representatives as listed in that provision for an unlimited period on the basis of a special position of trust, whereas the employment can be terminated if the latter no longer exists.[100] In 2009, a special regulation was created for parliamentary assistants, who previously also held this status.[101] The (continued) existence of the basis of trust is established as the essence of a stable employment relationship as regards these assistants, which raises the question of legal protection in the event of contract termination. The 2014 reform provides for a conciliation procedure;[102] suspension of the period of notice in the event of pregnancy; installation allowance and resettlement allowance.[103]

The provisions for temporary research staff under Article 2 lit d CEOS were aligned with the general rules.[104] The officials seconded by Member States' diplomatic services within the framework of the EEAS who are deployed on a temporary basis in a permanent post enjoy a special status under Article 2 lit e, Article 50b and Article 50c CEOS.[105]

The 2014 reform[106] created the new status of temporary agent of an EU agency, while this status had already been conferred previously by analogy. Staff are recruited by means of a competitive selection process, although as a rule only lower positions are filled via external selection. As a specialty, in the event of unpaid leave the position occupied does not have to be kept vacant in the meantime; this is because of the smaller number of staff allocated to these bodies. In the interests of comparable employment relationships, the principles governing promotions were regulated separately,[107] which the agencies supplement with their own implementing regulations. The members of the temporary staff keep the grade and step they have attained when starting a new or subsequent employment relationship (ie, one that immediately follows on from a preceding contract), whether this is in the same agency further to an internal vacancy or in a different agency.[108]

c. Contract Staff

Contract staff under Article 3a CEOS[109] perform subordinate but *long-term* tasks with limited initiative and autonomy, in particular to perform manual or administrative support service tasks

[100] CST, F-89/08, ECLI:EU:F:2010:11, para 113 – *P v EP*; Reithmann (2012) *EuR* 713. This does not apply to staff employed under Art 2 lit a and 2 lit b CEOS; Potvin-Solis/Lelièvre (2011) *RUE* 285 with reference to GC, T-406/04, ECLI:EU:T:2006:322, para 50 – *Bonnet v ECJ*. In general on the terminability of contracts and the appropriate justification, Cortese, 'Reasonableness of legislative choices and protection against (discriminatory) dismissal of temporary staff: does the approach of the Court of Justice of the European Union to judicial review and judicial control meet high rule of law standards?' (2012) 12(4) *ERA Forum* 641–52.

[101] Regulation (EC) No 160/2009 [2009] OJ L55/1–8; Arts 5a and 125 ff CEOS.

[102] Art 139(3a) CEOS.

[103] Art 132a CEOS, Art 139(1d) CEOS.

[104] Gauer (2007) 80/81.

[105] And Art 3 ff of Regulation (EU/Euratom) No 1080/2010.

[106] Art 2 lit f and Arts 51–56 CEOS.

[107] Art 54 CEOS.

[108] Art 55 CEOS.

[109] In conjunction with Art 79 ff and Art 85 ff CEOS.

in an institution, in the agencies and in EU Delegations.[110] *Contract staff for auxiliary tasks* under Article 3b CEOS[111] are hired for temporary tasks or as a temporary replacement and are therefore *time-limited.* The 2014 reform doubled the maximum period of employment to six years.[112] Nowadays, contract staff are eligible to apply for internal positions under the condition of minimum periods of prior service, or else their engagement is only possible to a certain extent. It is characteristic for both types of contract staff (3a and 3b) that they do not occupy posts included in the establishment plan appended to the section of the budget relating to the institution.

Recourse to successive fixed-term contracts of engagement is permitted, provided that the tasks do not increase continuously; for example auxiliary staff engaged on a fixed-term contract during periods of massive staffing needs during the sessions of Parliament.

In the context of the application of the CEOS and the question of successive fixed-term contracts of engagement, there is no such thing as a right[113] to enjoy a stable employment relationship.[114] However, according to settled case-law[115] it is not permitted to apply the CEOS for several consecutive fixed-term employment contracts in order to procure services in response to a continuous demand for the performing of permanent tasks. In the event of abuse by the appointing authority, the fixed-term employment contract can be reinterpreted as being an engagement for an indefinite period under Article 8 CEOS if it falls under an employment status that does not only allow fixed-term engagements.[116] Under certain conditions established by the *Adjemian* case-law, fixed-term employment contracts can be converted into contracts of indefinite duration.[117]

d. Local Staff

Local staff under Article 4, 120–22 CEOS cover the demand for additional local personnel in places outside the EU according to local practice for manual or service duties, or for other activities for which an official or other servant within the meaning of Article 1 CEOS cannot be used.

[110] For details, see Jansen, 'Les modifications apportées au statut' in Govaere/Vandersanden (eds), *La fonction publique communautaire* (2008) 19; Van Raepenbusch, 'L'apport jurisprudentiel du Tribunal de la fonction publique de l`Union européenne' in Govaere/Vandersanden (eds), *La fonction publique communautaire* (2008) 170. On conference interpreters under Art 90 CEOS, see CST, F-71/10, ECLI:EU:F:2012:71, paras 59 ff – *Cantisani v Commission.* Jacob, 'Les agents contractuels de l'Union européenne: les nouvelles dispositions générales d'exécution de la Commission européenne: des modifications au régime actuel ou l'amorce d'une politique nouvelle?' (2018) *Revue du droit de l'Union européenne* 51–90; Jacob, 'Les agents contractuels de l'Union européenne: la jurisprudence de la Cour de justice de l'Union européenne (2019) *Revue du droit de l'Union européenne* 121–39.

[111] In conjunction with Art 79 ff and Art 88 ff CEOS.

[112] Art 88(1b) CEOS.

[113] Gervasoni (2010) 46 *Cahiers de droit européen* 767 with further references.

[114] In contrast to the status afforded to officials *stricto sensu*: due to the long term perspective, stability is a recognised principle for them under the SR, *cf* GC, T-484/22, ECLI:EU:T:2023:741, para 70 – *QN v eu-LISA.*

[115] GC, T-325/09 P, ECLI:EU:T:2011:506, para 67 – *Adjemian and Others v Commission* and the original case CST, Jd Cases F-134/07 and F -8/08, ECLI:EU:F:2009:51, paras 131/132 – *Adjemian.*

[116] CST, F-65/07, ECLI:EU:F:2009:43, paras 84/85, 103, 135 – *Aayhan and Others v Commission* (for the contracts with the European Parliament limited to session periods), Gervasoni (2010) 46 *Cahiers de droit européen* 739, and Jansen, 'Les modifications apportées au statut' in Govaere/Vandersanden (eds), *La fonction publique communautaire* (2008) 19 and CJEU Annual Report 2009, 204. On the discretion when determining the maximum periods for contracts, GC, T-143/09 P, ECLI:EU:T:2010:531, paras 34/35 – *Commission v Petrilli.* On the duty of care when exercising the discretion, CST, F-135/11, F-110/12 and F-51/13, ECLI:EU:F:2013:93, paras 59 ff – *BU v EMA.* Stricter: GC, T-107/11 P, ECLI:EU:T:2013:624, paras 102/103 – *ETF v Schuerings* and GC, T-108/11 P, ECLI:EU:T:2013:625, paras 94, 103 – *ETF v Michel,* and GC, T-368/12 P, ECLI:EU:T:2014:266, paras 56/57 – *Macchia v Commission*: no mandatory test of potential continued employment in other posts. For the requirements for an effective hearing, see, eg, CST, F-124/11, ECLI:EU:F:2013:137 paras 60/61 – *Possanzini v Frontex.*

[117] GC, T-325/09 P, ECLI:EU:T:2011:506, paras 66/67 – *Adjemian and Others v Commission*; see section II.19.d. below.

They are assigned to a post not included in the list of posts appended to the section of the budget relating to each institution. Their employment relationship is based on the labour law applicable at the place of work,[118] and the authority assumes the employer's share of the social security costs in accordance with the law of the place where they perform their duties. Depending on the (free) contractual arrangement, disputes are to be brought before the courts of the Member States, and in third countries also before arbitration courts.[119] The aim of the 2004 reform was to phase out these positions in Commission representations and EU Delegations and to replace them with contract staff.[120]

e. *Special Advisers*

A special adviser is a person who, by reason of his or her special qualifications and notwithstanding their gainful employment in some other capacity, is engaged to assist one of the institutions either regularly or for a specified period and who is paid from the total appropriations for the purpose under the section of the budget relating to the institution.[121] It is not a post listed in the establishment plan appended to the budget. The contract, which is a direct agreement between the adviser concerned and the authority, may last a maximum of two years, but shall be renewable.

f. *Seconded National Civil Servants*

Civil servants belonging to national administrations (so-called *experts nationaux détachés*, END, or *national experts*) may work in the institutions of the Union on a temporary basis, but are not civil servants within the meaning of the SR.[122] In return, EU officials are increasingly being seconded to national administrations or other institutions while retaining their official position and remuneration, *cf* Articles 37–39 SR.[123]

g. *Other Servants*

There is a certain tendency (at times also in the other direction) to reintroduce contract staff in order to have less recourse to external experts or assistants by means of a service or employment contract under national law, or to external provider companies. This is a matter of flexible human resource management.[124] As long as there are legitimate interests for doing so, it is not a procedural abuse to agree on national law, including the jurisdiction of national courts for such contracts.[125] A different question – to be answered on a more detailed level – is in how far this can be aligned with consistent human resource management and an effective organisation of workforce.

[118] Art 120 CEOS.

[119] See chapter 2, III. with case study on arbitration.

[120] Gauer (2007) 77 with additional references. On taxation, ECJ, C-288/04, ECLI:EU:C:2005:526 – *AB*: the status decision under Union law is binding on the national (tax) authorities.

[121] Art 5 in conjunction with Arts 123–24 CEOS.

[122] CST, F-53/06, ECLI:EU:F:2006:100, paras 23, 24 – *Gualtieri v Commission.*

[123] CST, F-55/09, ECLI:EU:F:2010:44, paras 52, 71 – *Maxwell v Commission.* Gauer, *Die Reform des Europäischen öffentlichen Dienstrechts* (2007) 79; Dalle-Crode (2008) 35.

[124] Gauer, *Die Reform des Europäischen öffentlichen Dienstrechts* (2007) 79.

[125] CST, F-88/07, ECLI:EU:F:2008:141 – *Gonzalez v Commission.*

2. Career Paths

Since the 2004 reform, the two function groups for administrators (AD) and assistants (AST) have replaced all previous horizontal career paths as well as the special career path LA (Language Service)[126] and have allowed further advancement through promotion and the changing of one's function group. There is now less emphasis on entry qualification, to the benefit of performance. The 2014 reform restricted progression along the normal career path and generally required special managerial responsibilities for positions in grades from AD 13 or AST 11 and higher. Additionally, a lower-paid career path for secretarial assistants (AST/SC) has been introduced. This resulted in a new career track for the existing AST staff, because they were assigned to separate function groups during the transitional period,[127] with promotions only being possible along the respective career tracks.

3. Staffing

Officials are appointed, transferred and promoted by being assigned to a post at a level previously determined by the appointing authority.[128] As Article 4(1) SR specifies, no appointment or promotion shall be made for any purpose other than that of filling a vacant post as provided in the SR. First, the vacant post to be filled has to be advertised, Article 4(2) SR, ie, notified to the staff of that institution once the appointing authority decides that the vacancy is to be filled. The associated job description defines the criteria used for selecting the most suitable candidate.[129] Recruitment should be of the highest standard in terms of the successful candidate's ability, merit and integrity, and should have the broadest possible geographical basis in terms of the nationals of the Member States. The 2014 reform establishes the possibility for the institutions to take appropriate action in the event of a significant imbalance in the composition of the service by nationality.[130] Before filling a vacant post in an institution, the appointing authority shall first consider whether the post can be filled by transfer or by AST to AD appointment,[131] or by promotion within the institution from a list of suitable candidates,[132] or through internal competition.[133] In addition, the selection process may be based on competition based on qualifications and/or examinations, with a view to creating a reserve list for possible later use. This serves to develop career paths in line with the principle of a right to career advancement,[134] which is in itself an

[126] Gauer (2007) 93.

[127] Annex XIII, Art 31(2) SR.

[128] Change in the assessment for replacements, CST, F-91/07, ECLI:EU:F:2009:92, para 86 – *Torijano Montero v Council.*

[129] CST, F-25/05, ECLI:EU:F:2006:47, para 40 – *McSweeney and Armstrong v Commission*; CST, F-88/05, ECLI:EU:F:2006:136, para 80 – *Kubanski v Commission.*

[130] The appointment criterion of suitability based on merit remains the priority, *cf* Art 27(2) sentence 2 SR.

[131] Art 45a SR.

[132] Art 30 SR.

[133] Art 29(1) SR in conjunction with Art 4(3) SR.

[134] Levi, 'Droits fondamentaux et principes généraux de droit de la fonction publique communautaire' in Govaere/Vandersanden (eds), *La fonction publique communautaire* (2008) 92; CST, F-82/08, ECLI:EU:F:2011:45, para 165 – *Clarke and Others v OHIM*; GC, T-330/00 and T-114/01, ECLI:EU:T:2002:250 – *Cocchi and Hainz.* An internal competition must not solely aim to appoint a previously selected person, ECJ, 142/85, ECLI:EU:C:1986:405 – *Schwiering v ECA*; ECJ, 105/75, ECLI:EU:C:1976:128 – *Giuffrida v Council*; but requires a proper performance comparison of the candidates, CST, F-59/09, ECLI:EU:F:2014:248, para 200 – *De Nicola v EIB*, partly repealed because of another legal issue. A competition for staff of the Commission's 'services rattachés' is not open to those of executive agencies, CST, F-10/11, ECLI:EU:F:2012:158, para 44 – *Ghiba v Commission.*

expression of the principle of equality.[135] The revised (2014) version of Article 29(1) SR expressly foresees the possibility of immediately launching a competition for selection. As a further consequence of the 2014 reform, contract staff may participate in an internal competition.

The secondment of established officials to cabinets of members of the Commission or of other institutions mentioned in Article 37(1) lit a, second indent SR, must not be conducted in way that could jeopardise the transparency either of the hierarchy or of the given structure of the services.[136] In addition, the exercise of functions in the cabinet of the respective members can induce staff to exercise powers that go beyond their formal function, while enjoying the assurance of political backing. In this constellation of proximity to political decision-makers, some lines of conflict have arisen in the past, as well as – especially towards the end of a political mandate – cases of 'parachutage',[137] ie, the filling of higher positions in the line management of general directorates 'from above'.[138] Particularly under these circumstances, compliance with conflict-of-interest rules can come into play.[139]

Within narrow limits,[140] a procedure outside competition may be applied for the recruitment of senior officials,[141] and, in exceptional cases, also recruitment to posts which require special qualifications. Similarly, a general vacancy notice for AD 15 and 16 posts involving external applicants is only published on a case-by-case basis.[142] It has not yet been clarified to what extent these positions should from the outset be filled only for a limited period of time, in accordance with the political mandate inherent to the positions (*cf* Art 2 lit b CEOS). There may be separate competitions for cabinet staff under Article 2 lit c CEOS and for the services of the European Parliament (EP).[143]

The appointing authority may enlarge the circle of possible candidates in the search for the best-qualified person before making its decision.[144] It must remain[145] within the scope of the original job advertisement and cannot lower the requirements for external applicants.[146] In principle, the appointing authority is not obliged to complete a recruitment procedure by appointing one of the applicants, but can close it as unsuccessful and readvertise the position.[147]

[135] See CST, F-33/07, ECLI:EU:F:2008:25, para 88 – *Toronjo Benitez v Commission*. CST, F-112/10, ECLI:EU:F:2012:179, paras 45 ff – *Trentea v Fundamental Rights Agency* (confirmed in appeal GC, T-107/13 P, ECLI:EU:T:2015:20): a procedure for recruiting external staff is not only possible once it becomes clear that no internal staff member is available; despite the prior test of potential internal recruitment, a simultaneous publication of a vacancy notice is allowed.

[136] CST, F-128/07, ECLI:EU:F:2009:30 – *Menidiatis v Commission*; Annual Report 2009, 202.

[137] Stevens/Stevens, *Brussels Bureaucrats?* (2000) 84 ff.

[138] Nugent/Rhinard, *The European Commission* (2015) 216; Mehde, 'Europäisches Dienstrecht' in Terhechte (ed), *Verwaltungsrecht der Europäischen Union* (2022) § 39, para 14.

[139] *cf* Art 4 SR for the purpose of appointment or promotion, conflicts of interest are to be avoided, and independence must be maintained, *cf* Art 11(3) SR. On the criticism of the practical handling (maladministration) and the procedure for appointing Secretaries-General of the Commission: European Ombudsman, decision in the Jd Cases Nos 488/2018/KR and 514/2018/KR – *Selmayr*.

[140] GC, T-586/93, ECLI:EU:T:1995:54 – *Kotzonis v EESC*.

[141] Art 29(2) SR: directors-general or their equivalent in grade AD 16 or AD 15 and directors or their equivalent in grade AD 15 or AD 14.

[142] Gauer (2007) 174.

[143] Art 29(3), (4) SR.

[144] GC, T-586/93, ECLI:EU:T:1995:54, paras 43 ff – *Kotzonis v EESC*; GC, T-97/99 and T-99/99, ECLI:EU:T:2001:8, para 56 with reference – *Chamier and O'Hannrachain v EP*.

[145] ibid; GC, T-237/95, ECLI:EU:C:1999:152 – *Carbajo Ferrero v EP*; CST, F-88/05, ECLI:EU:F:2006:136, paras 80, 90 – *Kubanski v Commission*.

[146] GC, T-586/93, ECLI:EU:T:1995:54, para 45 – *Kotzonis v EESC*.

[147] GC, T-562/93, ECLI:EU:T:1995:181 – *Obst v Commission*; especially if the recruitment procedure was flawed, GC, T-166/00, ECLI:EU:T:2001:51 – *Hirschfeldt v EUA*; CST, F-104/08, ECLI:EU:F:2010:23, paras 40, 58, 92 – *Angelidis v EP*; also CST, F-8/10, ECLI:EU:F:2010:151, paras 89 ff – *Gheysens v Council*. This also applies to a general recruitment procedure, even if an action has led to the annulment of the applicant's rejection and the judgment must be implemented under Art 266 TFEU, CST, F-79/11, ECLI:EU:F:2012:89, para 37 – *Menidiatis v Commission*. However, the appointing

The appointing authority does not have to follow an order of priority determined by the Selection Board of a competition, within the list of suitable candidates. However, if the applicants are divided into several groups of varying merit, appointments from the second or subsequent group may only be made once all the applicants from the next higher group have been hired.[148]

4. Selection Procedures, Competitions

a. Overview

The purpose of conducting competitions, which are based on the French *concours* system, is to select the best candidates.[149] The selection procedure varies according to the number of vacancies to be filled, and in the case of external competitions, according to the size of the reserve list to be drawn up.[150]

The size of the reserve list will be determined in accordance with the interests of the service. In individual cases, the interests of staff may have to be taken into account if, for example, their contracts of employment contain a termination clause that is conditional on the successful completion of a general competition. Different procedures are carried out for generalists, specialists, linguists and assistants. The focus of competition tests has shifted from knowledge-based to competency-based tests. EU knowledge is tested during a test of professional knowledge.[151]

The pre-selection test[152] is carried out as a computer-based test involving multiple-choice questions.[153] The tests may focus on linguistic and abstract-logical reasoning, numeracy skills and knowledge of the relevant subject matter. Situational judgment may also be tested. If successful, an assessment centre test follows. The procedure at the assessment centre includes various possible tests, such as case studies, structured interviews, practical language tests, etc.

In external competition procedures, first the eligibility requirements are determined by the institutions.[154] The required formal initial education and training should ensure that the applicants have mastered their profession and can be employed in the European context without further major training. Often advertisements are published only for certain professional fields. Unlike in earlier years, external competitions are now held annually, also in order to increase the certainty of planning for interested university graduates.[155] Further to the call for applications,

authority may be limited in its decision to discontinue the recruitment procedure – especially if it is already in an advanced stage – insofar as there must be objective and sufficient reasons for the discontinuation of the procedure that were unknown at the time the proceedings were initiated, CST, F-44/05 RENV, ECLI:EU:F:2012:144, para 122 – *Strack v Commission*; CST, F-113/07, ECLI:EU:F:2011:44, para 90 – *Šimonis*. The resumption of the proceedings can be a way of equitably implementing an annulment decision, but there is no right of the successful applicant to have a 'dialogue' about this, CST, F-94/11, ECLI:EU:F:2013:41, paras 58, 69 ff – *Brune v Commission*.

[148] Gauer (2007) 32; Decision 2002/621/EG of 25 July 2002 on the organisation and operation of EPSO [2002] OJ L197.

[149] CST, F-35/08, ECLI:EU:F:2010:51, para 62 – *Pachtitis v Commission*. The participants in the competition are to be treated equally; it would be inadmissible to set different conditions for the applicants in the same competition via internal administrative regulations, CST, F-85/05, ECLI:EU:F:2010:131, para 98 – *Sørensen v Commission*; however, the institutions are authorised to classify graduates of the same competition at different levels, CST, F-83/05, ECLI:EU:F:2010:158, paras 49 ff, 58, 79 – *Ezerniece Liljeberg and Others v Commission*.

[150] CST, F-19/08, ECLI:EU:F:2009:75, para 116 – *Bennett and Others v OHIM*. Inclusion in the reserve list does not establish legitimate expectations; the administration retains the right to reject an applicant, CST, F-57/11, ECLI:EU:F:2014:254, para 76 – *Eklund v Commission*.

[151] EPSO Guide to Open Competitions [2010] OJ C184 A.

[152] The legal requirements for the selection process also apply here: CST, F-35/08, ECLI:EU:F:2010:51, para 57 – *Pachtitis v Commission*.

[153] CST, F-48/09, ECLI:EU:F:2010:38, para 37 – *Schopphoven v Commission*.

[154] CST, F-99/08, ECLI:EU:F:2009:153, para 27 ff – *Di Prospero v Commission*.

[155] Commission press release IP/11/462 of 12 April 2011.

a candidate registers on the European Personnel Selection Office (EPSO) website, where the process is handled online.[156]

Since 2003, the appointing authorities have been using the EPSO selection office[157] to organise the competitions.[158] For each procedure, it appoints a chairperson (designated by the appointing authority) and the members of an independent selection board, which assesses the performance and suitability of the applicants.[159] The appointing authority and the Staff Committee each designate the same number of members.

As an independent entity, the Selection Board does not take instructions from the appointing authority.[160] This includes preparing the examination texts, marking the exam papers, holding the oral exam and thence compiling the list of suitable candidates. The work of the Selection Board shall be secret.[161] The courts restrain themselves when exercising their judicial control of the assessments made by the Selection Board on the knowledge and suitability of candidates.[162] However, the formal setting of the work prescribed for a selection board must be respected: a lack of stability on the part of the Selection Board that amounts to an infringement of the principle of equal treatment is reviewable by the court.[163]

b. *Language in Selection Procedures*

Similar to the *internal vs external* differentiation of the language regime applicable to the communication of staff within the institutions (working languages) vis-à-vis the communication of servants with the citizens or Member States (laid down in Regulation 1/58),[164] the language regime of selection procedures differentiates whether the selection is of internal or of external nature: internal selection procedures may freely stipulate language knowledge as is necessitated for the functionality of service, also going beyond the minimum requirements under Article 28 lit f SR.[165]

[156] CST, F-121/05, ECLI:EU:F:2007:102, para 87 – *De Meerleer v Commission.*

[157] Decision 2002/621/EC [2002] OJ L197/53. See also, European Court of Auditors: Efficiency and effectiveness of the personnel selection activities of the European Personnel Selection Office: ECA Special Report No 9/2009 and ECA Special Report No 23/2020: European Personnel Selection Office (EPSO): *Time to adapt the selection process to changing recruitment needs*; Kramer, *The Reform of the European Personnel Selection Office (EPSO) Selection Procedures: The First Lessons Learned* (2011) *EIPAscope* 33–36.

[158] Art 2(2) in conjunction with Art 30(2) SR, Annex III SR. Andreone, 'La sélection, le recrutement et l'engagement des fonctionnaires de l'Union européenne' (2019) *Revue de l'Union européenne* 626; Singer, 'Les concours EPSO: faut-il en rire ou en pleurer?' (2015) *JurisNews: Fonction publique européenne* 37 ff.

[159] Art 3(1) Annex III SR; on a gender quota when staffing the committee, CST, F-50/08, ECLI:EU:F:2010:148, para 43 – *Bartha v Commission*; CST, F-35/08, ECLI:EU:F:2010:51, paras 50 ff, 68 – *Pachtitis v Commission*; CST, Jd Cases F-20/08, F-34/08 and F-75/08, ECLI:EU:F:2009:132, para 78 – *Aparício and Others v Commission*; CST, F-65/10, ECLI:EU:F:2012:178, para 55 – *Mata Blanco v Commission.*

[160] CST, F-35/08, ECLI:EU:F:2010:51, paras 57 ff – *Pachtitis v Commission* (selection and assessment of the examination questions of the pre-selection tests not conducted by the Selection Committee, but by EPSO). Conversely, the appointing authority is not bound by any mistakes made by the Selection Committee and it must close the individual application file even if, eg, the absence of some recruitment conditions appears only later, CST, F-117/10, ECLI:EU:F:2011:148, para 24 – *Van Soest v Commission.*

[161] Art 6 Annex III SR; GC, T-203/98, ECLI:EU:T:2000:130 – *Tzikis v Commission*; CST, F-16/07, ECLI:EU:F:2008:51, para 63 – *Dragoman v Commission*; CST, F-6/07, ECLI:EU:F:2008:55, paras 57/58 – *Suvikas v Council*; strict handling in CST, F-19/07, ECLI:EU:F:2007:212, paras 32 ff – *Kerelov v Commission.*

[162] Correspondence of the number of points expressed as a grade with the narrative part of the assessment is subject to review at court for an obvious contradiction, CST, F-127/07, ECLI:EU:F:2008:113, para 34 – *Coto Moreno v Commission.*

[163] This is indicated if the Selection Board as a whole has never met in order to perform a collective appraisal and to adopt its decisions on the basis of an overview of all test results: GC, T-20/21, ECLI:EU:T:2022:427, para 72 – *VI v Commission.*

[164] Regulation No 1 determining the languages to be used by the European Economic Community 1958/17, 385/386, as last amended by act of 23 September 2003 [2003] OJ L236/33.

[165] GC, T-376/03, ECLI:EU:T:2005:116, paras 37–39 – *Hendrickx v Council.*

The language requirements for the external selection procedures are as follows: EPSO typically publishes the call for expressions of interest in all 24 official languages. Under certain conditions,[166] the call may be restricted to those languages that are required as a second language according to the respective profile; the exams themselves may also be confined to individual languages.[167] Unequal treatment resulting from a restriction of the language regime to a limited number of official languages is only permissible if the restriction is objectively justified; is based on the actual needs of the service; and is proportionate to those needs. Where specific language skills are required, this requirement must be based on clear, objective and foreseeable criteria that enable candidates to understand why they need to meet it, and that allow the EU courts to verify that the requirement is lawful.[168] An unjustified restriction in the choice of the language of the competition notice and the language for correspondence during the selection procedure can lead to the illegality of the procedure;[169] likewise, a modification (restriction or extension) of the selection criteria mentioned in the notice can lead to the illegality of the procedure, or to illegal exclusions from the procedure.[170]

Case Study on Selection Procedures

Discrimination based on language in staff selection procedures: In principle, not allowed

Case C-377/16, *Spain v EP* of 26 March 2019
Case C-621/16 P, *Commission v Italy* of 26 March 2019

In Brief

Discrimination based on language: a differentiation in treatment based on language is in principle not allowed in the procedures for selecting staff for the EU institutions. However, such a differentiation is permissible provided that it meets the actual needs of the service, is proportionate to those needs, and is motivated by clear, objective and foreseeable criteria.

[166] ECJ, C-377/16, ECLI:EU:C:2019:249 – *Spain v EP*; ECJ, C-621/16 P, ECLI:EU:C:2019:251 – *Commission v Italy*: discrimination based on language must be related to the actual needs of the service, and must be proportionate and based on clear, objective and foreseeable criteria. This was confirmed in a similar case where the ECJ opined that it is not a given that the specific second language will actually be used in daily work, thus the limitation of second languages in the competition to three specific languages was considered to be an infringement of Art 1d SR: ECJ, C-623/20 P, ECLI:EU:C:2023:97 – *Commission v Italy*; GC, T-631/20, ECLI:EU:T:2022:426 – *MZ v Commission*; GC, T-713/20, ECLI:EU:T:2022:513, paras 47–49 – *OQ v Commission*. See case study below.

[167] GC, T-205/07, ECLI:EU:T:2011:25, paras 49 ff – *Italy v Commission*; CST, F-7/07, ECLI:EU:F:2011:97, paras 91, 106 – *Angioi v Commission*; CST, F-82/08, ECLI:EU:F:2011:45, para 172 – *Clarke and Others v OHIM*. See also, CJEU Annual Report 2012, 218 with reference to CST, F-29/11, ECLI:EU:F:2012:172 – *BA v Commission*. Even if this is aimed at a specific nationality, this applies even to persons whose mother tongue is not recognised as an official language in the Member State, *cf* CST, F-29/11, ECLI:EU:F:2012:172, para 82 – *BA v Commission*.

[168] ECJ, C-621/16 P, ECLI:EU:C:2019:251, para 103 – *Commission v Italy*; ECJ, C-377/16, ECLI:EU:C:2019:249, para 69 – *Spain v EP*.

[169] ECJ, C-621/16 P, ECLI:EU:C:2019:251, para 124 – *Commission v Italy*; ECJ, C-566/10 P, ECLI:EU:C:2012:752 – *Italy v Commission*; *cf* notice in [2013] OJ C200 A, 3 and in [2014] OJ C74 A, 3. Commission press release MEMO/11/161; GC, T-185/05, ECLI:EU:T: 2008:519 – *Italy v Commission*, and Potvin-Solis (2011) *RUE* 616. GC, Jd Cases T-401/16 and T-443/16, ECLI:EU:T:2020:409 – *Spain and Italy v Commission*, confirmed by ECJ, C-635/20 P, ECLI:EU:C:2023:98 – *Commission v Spain and Italy*.

[170] GC, T-430/20, ECLI:EU:T:2021:791, paras 41/42 – *KV v Commission*.

Facts and Decision in Case C-377/16

The European Parliament had launched a call for expressions of interest for the establishment of a database of candidates to work as drivers. The application form was available only in English, French and German. In addition to a thorough knowledge of one of the 24 official EU languages as 'language 1' of the selection procedure, candidates were required to have a satisfactory knowledge of English, French or German as 'language 2'. The Parliament justified that restriction on the choice of 'language 2' by 'the interests of the service, which require newly recruited staff to be immediately operational and able to communicate effectively in their daily work' and by the fact that those three languages are the most widely used within the institution. Spain brought an action against the Parliament. The Court of Justice has jurisdiction to decide on this action further to Article 51 of the Statute of the CJEU (being an action of a Member State against an act of the European Parliament).

In its judgment, the ECJ (Grand Chamber) annuls the call for expressions of interest and declares the database established under that call void. The Staff Regulations prohibit any discrimination, *including discrimination on grounds of language*. Differences of treatment on grounds of language *may be authorised if they are justified by a legitimate objective of general interest*, such as the interests of the service or even the actual needs relating to the duties that the persons recruited will be required to carry out. In a selection procedure, the institutions enjoy broad discretion when assessing the qualifications and merits of the candidates that are to be taken into consideration. However, they are required not only to ensure that any difference in treatment based on language is one that meets the interests of the service and is *proportionate* to them, but also to *justify such a difference by clear, objective and foreseeable criteria* that enable candidates to understand the grounds for that difference in treatment and the courts of the European Union to review its lawfulness.

First, the application form was available only in English, French and German. Because there was no indication that it was possible to complete the application form in any other of the official EU languages, it was reasonable for the candidates to assume that it was mandatory to complete the form in one of those three languages. This resulted in a difference of treatment based on language, which is in principle prohibited. The Parliament did not show that there was a *legitimate objective of general interest* justifying such a difference in treatment.

Secondly, the restriction of the choice of 'language 2' to English, French and German constituted another difference of treatment based on language. The call for applications did not justify that restriction in relation to the specific language needs relating to the functions that the recruited drivers would have to perform. The ECJ observes that neither the fact that drivers must perform their duties in French-speaking or German-speaking cities, nor the fact that the persons conveyed most often use the English language, are such as to justify restricting the choice of 'language 2' to the three languages mentioned above. The Parliament did not establish how each of those languages would be particularly useful for the performance of the duties in question and why that choice could not include other official languages which might be relevant to those duties. Moreover, insofar as the Parliament has not adopted internal rules governing its language regime, it cannot be affirmed that those three languages are necessarily the most useful languages for all duties in that institution.

Facts and Decision in Case C-621/16 P

Italy had brought two actions against the Commission to the General Court (GC). As a result, two notices of open competition of the European Personnel Selection Office (EPSO) were annulled on the grounds that it was unlawful to restrict the choice of 'language 2' of the competition to English, French and German, and to restrict to those three languages the choice of language of communication between the candidates and the EPSO.

The ECJ confirmed the decision of the GC which correctly held that a candidate's highest standards of ability, efficiency and integrity are independent of language knowledge. Consequently, the GC did not err in holding that the objective of recruiting officials of the highest standard of ability, efficiency and integrity does not justify a difference in treatment based on language. There must be 'concrete indications' making it possible to establish, objectively, that there was an interests of the service justifying the restriction regarding the choice of 'language 2' of the competition.

While competition notices must be published in full in the *Official Journal* in all the official EU languages, the EPSO is not obliged to communicate with a candidate in a language freely chosen by the latter. However, the restriction on the choice of language of communication between candidates and the EPSO to a limited number of official languages must be justified. The EPSO had not provided such justification.

Comments

1. Both judgments continue the protective line of jurisprudence on discrimination based on language. Rules limiting the choice of language must provide for clear, objective and foreseeable criteria. The administration has to provide a statement of reasons regarding such rules. In earlier case-law the GC had given less emphasis to the language requirements and was already corrected by the ECJ.[171]
2. The requirement to possess a knowledge of specific languages may be objectively justified in the interests of the service, and the required level of knowledge of the languages must be proportionate to the genuine needs of the service.[172]
3. In view of the difficulty the administration has in justifying the exclusive use of specific languages for duty purposes and the required motivation for why a particular selection cannot include other official languages relevant to those duties, it can be assumed that a future practice will be inclined to open up the language choice and include more or all official languages in similar selection procedures.
4. Since the database in the first case discussed above was declared void, the judgment had a negative side effect for those candidates who were included in the database but had not yet been recruited. The ECJ considered that the mere inclusion of candidates in the database cannot create a *legitimate expectation*.[173] Those candidates could not rely on a voided call for expressions of interest. On the other hand, the candidates who had already been recruited on the basis of their inclusion in the database could trust that their signed contracts would be upheld. So the voiding of the database had no impact on the recruitment already performed.

[171] ECJ, C-566/10 P, ECLI:EU:C:2012:752 – *Italy v Commission.*
[172] ECJ, Jd Cases 79/74 and 22/75, ECLI:EU:C:1975:85 – *Küster v EP.*
[173] See chapter 1, III.6.d.

A consequence of the above-mentioned differentiation of the applicable language regime depending on whether the selection process is of internal or of external nature is that the external selection procedures may render results that make it difficult for the institutions to ensure availability of staff with specific language knowledge that are immediately operational after recruitment under an external selection procedure.[174]

c. *Remedies*

On the general preconditions for review see chapter 2, III. Rejected or unsuccessful candidates often object to decisions regarding the formal entry requirements such as diplomas,[175] the type and duration of required professional experience,[176] and alleged procedural errors or disruptions during the examination.[177] In addition, the examination results or questions may be challenged.[178] Apart from staff employed, also candidates who aspire to the respective legal status are entitled to bring an action. The guarantee of effective judicial protection prohibits reserving the right to challenge a vacancy notice to those candidates who already possess the grade allocated to the position that is to be filled.[179] Conditions in the vacancy notice that exclude the application of officials who are eligible for transfer or promotion adversely affect such officials.[180] The appointing authority is generally not allowed to ban parallel applications involving several competitions that are being conducted at the same time.[181]

The rejected candidate is limited to requesting the annulment of an illegal act,[182] to the effect that the suitability and performance of the person concerned must be tested again.[183] Inclusion in the reserve list or (re)admission to the examinations may not be sought, because the court cannot itself assess a candidate's suitability and exam performance in comparison to others or issue instructions to that effect.[184] In the event of errors, the entire procedure is not automatically called into question, nor would it have to be repeated.[185] Case-law instead requires a balancing exercise that takes into account the consequences arising from the annulment of a measure relating to the selection procedures. A judgment will reconcile the interests of candidates disadvantaged by an irregularity which occurred during that procedure with the interests of other candidates, ie, the

[174] Currall in Perillo/Giacobbo-Peyronnel (eds), *Statut de la fonction publique de l'Union européenne* (2017) 56/57.

[175] CST, F-83/07, ECLI:EU:F:2009:158, paras 51 ff – *Zangerl-Posselt v Commission*; CST, F-97/12, ECLI:EU:F:2013:142, para 51 – *Thomé v Commission*.

[176] CST, F-12/05, ECLI:EU:F:2006:68, para 38 – *Tas v Commission*.

[177] CST, Jd Cases F-20/08, F-34/08 and F-75/08, ECLI:EU:F:2009:132, paras 77/78 – *Aparício and Others v Commission*.

[178] CST, F-2/07, ECLI:EU:F:2010:22, paras 167, 171, 83 – *Matos Martins v Commission*.

[179] CST, F-91/07, ECLI:EU:F:2009:92, paras 27, 31 – *Torijano Montero v Council*; ECJ – 79/74, ECLI:EU:C:1975:85, paras 5/6 – *Küster v EP*; ECJ, 25/77, ECLI:EU:C:1978:100, paras 7, 8 – *De Roubaix v Commission*.

[180] CST, F-91/07, ECLI:EU:F:2009:92, para 27 – *Torijano Montero v Council*; CST, F-23/09, ECLI:EU:F:2010:138, para 47 – *Cerafogli v ECB*; CST, F-51/10, ECLI:EU:F:2012:136, para 36 – *Bermejo Garde v EESC* (appeal dismissed).

[181] Arg: Art 27(1) SR; CST, F-99/08, ECLI:EU:F:2009:153, paras 27 ff – *Di Prospero v Commission*; CJEU Annual Report 2009, 201, Gervasoni (2010) 46 *Cahiers de droit européen* 787; CST, F-24/11, ECLI:EU:F:2013:4, paras 54 ff – *Katrakasas v Commission*.

[182] Irrespective of whether or not the result of the competition changes, GC, T-95/98, ECLI:EU:T:2000:85 – *Gogos v Commission*.

[183] GC, T-243/99, ECLI:EU:T:2001:167, para 37 – *Buisson v Commission*.

[184] The administration can apply an equitable solution when implementing the judgment under Art 266 TFEU, which may be the repetition of an examination, CST, F-42/11, ECLI:EU:F:2012:196, paras 40, 50 – *Honnefelder v Commission*, but not inclusion in the reserve list without examination, CST, F-51/11, ECLI:EU:F:2013:26, para 49 – *Pachtitis v Commission*.

[185] CST, Jd Cases F-20/08, F-34/08 and F-75/08, ECLI:EU:F:2009:132, para 77 – *Aparício and Others v Commission*. (proportionality and good administration); CST, F-53/08, ECLI:EU:F:2010:37, para 89 – *Bouillez and Others v Council*. ECJ Annual Report 2012, 218 on CST, F-42/11, ECLI:EU:F:2012:196, paras 49 ff – *Honnefelder v Commission* (appeal dismissed) on the possibility of reopening the competition.

legitimate expectations of the candidates already selected.[186] This involves a weighing of the nature and effects of the irregularity in question and the various possible measures to reconcile the need to restore the rights of the injured applicant with the situation of third parties and the interests of the service; also the number of persons affected by the irregularity of the selection procedure and the number of successful candidates may be relevant factors in such an assessment.[187]

Applications for interim relief, for provisional admission, or for suspension until a decision has been made on the eligibility to participate are consistently rejected, often with the argument of the high number of other candidates who are unaffected.[188]

The courts allow for wide discretion on the part of the appointing authority when formulating the recruitment conditions, and on the part of the Selection Board when setting the requirements, evaluating test performances and designing the procedure. The courts only assess whether the limits have been observed,[189] such as whether the conditions for the job advertisement were correctly applied, whether the content and procedure of the examinations could have favoured or disadvantaged individual candidates, and whether manifest errors in assessing the performance of individuals may have occurred.[190] Judicial review serves to ensure equal treatment and objectivity in the procedure.[191]

The obligation to motivate decisions during the competition selection process is limited, on the basis of the argument that the work of the Selection Board is subject to secrecy. In individual cases, the duty to provide grounds may outweigh the secrecy requirement.[192] Submission of the test paper together with the evaluation forms and an explanatory letter may suffice.[193]

[186] ECJ, C-242/90 P, ECLI:EU:C:1993:284, para 14 – *Commission v Albani and Others*; ECJ, C-377/16, ECLI:EU:C:2019:249, para 83 – *Spain v EP*.

[187] ECJ, C-243/18 P, ECLI:EU:C:2019:378, paras 46/47 – *Fusion for Energy v Galocha*.

[188] GC, T-167/99 R, ECLI:EU:T:1999:151 – *Giulietti v Commission*; GC, T-173/99 R, ECLI:EU:T:1999:168 – *Elkaim and Others v Commission*; GC, T-101/00 R, ECLI:EU:T:2000:126 – *Martín de Pablos v Commission*.

[189] CST, F-127/07, ECLI:EU:F:2008:113, paras 32 ff, 38 – *Coto Moreno v Commission*; CST, F-48/09, ECLI:EU:F:2010:38, para 26 – *Schopphoven v Commission* (assessing the legality of the process). On criteria, conditions and modalities of competitions, CST, F-37/05, ECLI:EU:F:2009:121, paras 55, 57 – *Brown v Commission*; CST, Jd Cases F-124/05 and F-96/06, ECLI:EU:F:2010:2, paras 173, 188 – *A and G v Commission*; required qualifications may not be interpreted independently of job description, CST, F-39/07, ECLI:EU:F:2009:45 – *Campos Valls v Council*. The Board may determine and weight the criteria as part of the notice of the competition, CST, F-65/10, ECLI:EU:F:2012:178, para 55 – *Mata Blanco v Commission*. The evaluation of a candidate's test performance falls within the wide discretion of the Selection Board and is subject to a review by the judge only as to a breach of the rules applicable to the work of the Selection Board, para 93; an oral examination may include aspects such as coherence, structuring, clarity and presentation, para 66. What exclusively counts is performance in the exam itself; previous performance is irrelevant, CST, F-17/11, ECLI:EU:F:2013:14, paras 168 – *BB v Commission*.

[190] It is not permitted to lower the required number of points in the course of the procedure in order to obtain additional successful candidates for the following test phases, *cf* GC, T-24/01, ECLI:EU:T:2003:52, paras 52, 56–61 – *Staelen v EP*. Preferential conditions for candidates with more knowledge in certain areas are allowed, CST, F-2/07, ECLI:EU:F:2010:22, para 181 – *Matos Martins v Commission* (here mathematicians and lawyers); on composition of the Board, CST, F-22/05, ECLI:EU:F:2006:133, paras 45, 56 – *Neophytou v Commission* and mostly CST, F-22/05 RENV, ECLI:EU:F:2009:120, paras 197 ff, 112 ff – *Neophytou v Commission*. An assigned mark and the verbal description must be coherent, CST, F-85/10, ECLI:EU:F:2012:97, para 108 – *AI v CJEU*. CST, F- 97/12, ECLI:EU:F:2013:142, para 51 – *Thomé v Commission*. Examiners are not lacking in impartiality if they know candidates or have had disagreements with them, CST, F-85/10, ECLI:EU:F:2012:97, paras 47, 81, 110 – *AI v CJEU*; CST, F-2/11, ECLI:EU:F:2012:194, para 114 – *BW v Commission*; CST, F-1/11, ECLI:EU:F:2012:157, para 38 – *Soukup v Commission*. It is not an indication of errors in the own evaluation if other candidates were successful in challenging their evaluations, CST, F-24/11, ECLI:EU:F:2013:4, para 195 – *Katrakasas v Commission*.

[191] CST, F-1/11, ECLI:EU:F:2012:157, para 32 – *Soukup v Commission*.

[192] A request for information based on the notice of the competition can be based on Arts 41, 42 and 47 FRC, *cf.* CJEU Annual Report 2012, 218 with reference to CST, F-96/09, ECLI:EU:F:2012:129 – *Cuallado Martorell v Commission*. For individual cases, see CST, F-74/07, ECLI:EU:F:2008:127, paras 40 ff – *Meierhofer v Commission* (non-transparent overall assessment, changing explanations by the administration, lack of motivation of the decision – the candidate was able to submit a precise protocol about the course of the examination); CST, 74/07 RENV, ECLI:EU:F:2011:63,

Case Study on the Recognition of Qualifications in Open Competitions

What is a 'full legal education'?

Case C-728/17 P, *Commission v Brouillard* of 7 March 2019
Case T-572/16, *Brouillard v Commission* of 13 October 2017

In Brief

The judgment clarifies a criterion of technical capacity in an open EPSO competition, namely whether a French diploma fulfils the condition of 'full legal education'. That diploma had been acquired by a procedure in which French authorities declared the experience of the applicant to be equivalent to a diploma in law. The Court of Justice (ECJ) in *Brouillard* confirmed the decision of the General Court (GC) in which it had to interpret the term 'full legal education' within the meaning of an EPSO competition notice. The EPSO had erred in law when setting aside the applicant's Master's degree in law as allegedly not fulfilling the technical capacity requirements of the competition. In the absence of specific Union law rules, it is the national provisions that guide the interpretation whether a diploma fulfils the conditions of the competition notice.

Facts and Arguments

The applicant had participated in an open competition for lawyer-linguists (AD 7) at the Court of Justice of the European Union. The EPSO publication notice of this competition required a diploma at a level of education corresponding to a full legal education obtained in a Belgian, French or Luxembourg higher education establishment where courses are taught in French and attested by a diploma corresponding to at least the level of a Master's degree in French law (four years of study) or the degree in Belgian law (five years of study) and, for diplomas obtained after the entry into force of the 2004 reform harmonising educational degrees, at Master's 2 level (five years of study).

The applicant stated that he had obtained the Master's 2 degree in law at the University of Poitiers following the procedure of a 'validation of experience' foreseen by the French Education Act, according to which validation has the same effects as success in the test or in the tests of the knowledge and skills it replaces.

The EPSO Selection Board decided not to admit the applicant to the next phase of the competition procedure on the ground that it was not justified by 'a level of education corresponding to a full legal education followed in a Belgian, French or Luxembourg higher education establishment'. The applicant objected that the decision of the national

paras 44 ff – *Meierhofer v Commission* and Interpretation in CST, F-96/09, ECLI:EU:F:2012:129, para 102 – *Cuallado Martorell v Commission*. More restrictive CST, F-6/07, ECLI:EU:F:2008:55, paras 57, 61 – *Suvikas v Council*. However, the GC may not draw any conclusions from the absence of certain information in the file due to secrecy, as long as it has not exhausted the means provided for in its RoP to enforce disclosure from the party concerned, GC, T-560/08 P, ECLI:EU:T:2010:192, paras 61/62 – *Commission v Meierhofer*. Regarding the start of time limitation periods (here, in the promotion procedure): a candidate may have knowledge of the total number of points and their composition only from the moment of access to the personal promotion file, GC, T-311/04, ECLI:EU:T:2006:329, paras 112 ff – *Buendia Sierra v Commission*.

[193] CST, F-127/07, ECLI:EU:F:2008:113, para 57 – *Coto Moreno v Commission*; on the statement of reasons *cf* section I.3. above.

examination jury to award a diploma can only be questioned by an administrative body with corresponding competences granted by the French state.

Court Decision

The Selection Board of the EPSO has to respect the terms of the competition notice. The judgments confirm that the EPSO was not entitled to interpret the criterion of a 'full legal education' (*formation juridique complète*) within the meaning of the notice of the EPSO competition as a wide requirement in the sense that it covers a full legal studies course or a general law degree course, ie, a full legal education covering several legal disciplines. Where the candidate has a diploma attesting that he has passed the required tests and attains 'a level of education corresponding to a complete cycle of university studies' within the meaning of Article 5(1) 3(c)(i) SR, that diploma must be regarded as being sufficient to justify admission. The courts applied this conclusion to the applicant's situation and stated that he had completed at least four years of study and therefore possessed the requisite skills and knowledge.

Such an interpretation is based on the principle that the holding of the diploma required comprises sufficient proof in itself that the candidate has fulfilled all the requirements referred to in those provisions, including that of possessing a 'full legal education'.

The courts held that by applying its extensive interpretation, the EPSO also disregarded the scope of the relevant provisions of the French Code of Education, which the Selection Board was required to take into consideration when interpreting the competition notice. The courts decided that in the absence of specific Union law rules to the contrary, the requirement of possession of the diploma and the question of whether the diploma fulfils the conditions of the competition notice must be interpreted in the light of the relevant national provisions.

Contrary to the Commission's opinion, the applicant was not required to provide EPSO with an act recognising the equivalence of his various diplomas to a Belgian licence, a French Master's degree, or a Maste'rs degree 2 proving five years of study and awarded by a competent authority.

Comments

1. The applicant could base his argument on the national procedure of a 'validation of experience' that declared his experience equivalent to a diploma.
2. He was not required to provide the EPSO with any other act evidencing the equivalence of his various diplomas to a Belgian licence, a French Master's degree, or a Master's degree 2 with five years of study.
3. The Selection Board had to take into consideration the relevant provisions of the French Code of Education when interpreting the scope of the text of the competition notice. This conclusion of the judgment could bring the EPSO into a difficult situation because on the one hand, the Selection Board is required to accept declarations of equivalence by national authorities without being able to challenge them; on the other hand, it might find itself in a situation where it has to interpret its own terms in the light of national provisions.

5. Physical Fitness

Only applicants with the required physical fitness to perform the duties required may be appointed.[194] The applicant must be medically examined[195] by the institution's medical officer and answer questions about previous illnesses truthfully and completely, but applicants cannot be expected to reveal full details of the state of their health to the prospective employer.[196] A negative result may be reviewed by a medical committee. The committee's medical findings are binding as long as they were made correctly in terms of the procedure, and insofar as the medical justification supports the rejection of an applicant.[197] The alleged abusive submission of new medical certificates for the same illness when determining occupational disability does not justify the rejection of an applicant, because this is to be treated as a matter of disciplinary law.[198] Forecasts of the development of the state of health can be taken into account.[199] In view of the personal rights of the individuals affected, any medical tests to which they are subjected require their consent.[200]

Disabilities

An applicant with a handicap satisfies the health requirements of Article 28 lit e SR if the person can perform the essential functions of the job when reasonable accommodation is made; the appointing authority must take appropriate measures that will enable their access to and their exercise of employment, career advancement and participation in training, unless such measures would impose a disproportionate burden on the employer.[201] The distribution of the burden of proof stipulated in Article 1d(5) SR applies.[202]

If the pre-appointment medical examination reveals illness or frailty, it is possible to grant social security protection in the event of invalidity or death only under certain conditions.[203] However, account must be taken of whether the person was forced to change his or her type of contract and had to undergo the examination again for that reason.[204]

6. Grading

Candidates selected shall be appointed to the grade of the function group set out in the notice of the competition they have passed.[205] Likewise, grade and step must be specified in the contract

[194] Art 28 lit e, Art 33 SR, Art 12(2) lit d, Art 13 CEOS; GC, T-10/93, ECLI:EU:T:1994:39 – *A v Commission* (compatible with ECHR).

[195] On the applicant's medical officer, CST, F-95/05, ECLI:EU:F:2007:226, paras 70, 72 – *N v Commission*.

[196] GC, T-197/98, ECLI:EU:T:2000:86 – *Rudolph v Commission*; CST, F-46/09, ECLI:EU:F:2011:101, paras 163 ff – *V v EP*.

[197] CST, F-39/05, ECLI:EU:F:2006:57, paras 74/75 – *Beau v Commission* (no obligation to apply a benchmark of best medical practice).

[198] CST, F-97/09, ECLI:EU:F:2010:153, para 59 – *Taillard v EP*, on new certificates (para 53).

[199] ECJ, 155/78, ECLI:EU:C:1980:150, paras 10/11 – *M v Commission*.

[200] GC, T-121/89 and 13/90, ECLI:EU:T:1992:96 – *X v Commission*. On tests at recruitment, see Levi, 'Droits fondamentaux et principes généraux de droit de la fonction publique communautaire' in Govaere/Vandersanden (eds), *La fonction publique communautaire* (2008) 109 (not against the will of the applicant, but if he does not take a required test, the administration cannot be obliged to employ him). Results of an earlier medical exam may not be passed on to another body for a separate recruitment process, CST, F-46/09, ECLI:EU:F:2011:101, para 143 – *V v EP*.

[201] Art 1d(4) SR.

[202] For details on reverse burden of proof, see chapter 1, III.6.b.

[203] *cf* Art 32, 100 CEOS.

[204] CST, Joined Cases F-60/08 and F-69/07, ECLI:EU:F:2009:128, paras 120, 136 – *O v Commission*; ECJ, C-293/03, ECLI:EU:C:2004:821, para 36 – *My*. Even if the applicant conceals health risks, the administration may only draw conclusions from this on the basis of medical advice, CST, F-4/11, ECLI:EU:F:2012:96, para 37 – *AV v Commission*.

[205] Art 31(1) SR.

of a temporary agent,[206] on the basis of grading criteria to be decided beforehand.[207] For some functions, such as that of a head of unit, a bandwidth (separation of grade and function) is provided for; the institutions do not specify the grade precisely in the job advertisement, so that the administration has leeway to classify it within the framework of the publication of the job advertisement.[208] The labour market situation may be taken into account for this purpose.[209] Assurances that go beyond the applicable provisions of classification and recruitment procedure are irrelevant.[210] Grading and classification led to numerous disputes after the 2004 reform, such as appointments to lower grades than previously announced in competitions, as well as the reclassification of former local staff as contract staff.[211]

The Directive on the recognition of professional qualifications[212] does not limit the discretion of an institution when it compares the respective value of diplomas in its recruitment policy.[213] Unless this is contrary to specific provisions of Union law, the question of whether a diploma meets the criteria of the vacancy notice must be determined in the light of relevant national provisions.[214] When assessing the equivalence of diplomas as part of the competition, professional experience may have to be taken into account in order to assess the posession of certain required qualifications. The refusal to recognise the equivalence of a diploma can amount to a violation of the free movement of workers under Article 45 TFEU.[215]

The selected official shall be recruited at the first step in his grade,[216] but the appointing authority may allow additional seniority up to a maximum of 24 months, to take account of the training and professional experience of the person.[217] This also applies to temporary staff.[218] Members of the temporary staff shall retain the seniority in the step acquired in that capacity if they are appointed as officials having the same grade immediately following the period of temporary service.[219] The same applies in the case of a transfer to a new temporary engagement,[220] as well as for agency temporary staff.[221] An appointment that qualifies as a promotion, but entails remaining in the same grade as before, must not involve assignment to a lower step – and hence receiving lower remuneration.[222]

[206] Art 10(2) CEOS.

[207] Art 15(1) sub 1 sentence 2 CEOS.

[208] The administration tended to classify according to the previous salary group of the successful applicant, Gervasoni (2010) 46 *Cahiers de droit européen* 761. The legal solution of the CST to apply a prior objective classification was not accepted by the GC, see GC, T-56/07 P, ECLI:EU:T:2008:260, paras 80–82 – *Economidis v Commission*; on this, Joris, 'L'administration face au contentieux de la fonction publique communautaire' in Govaere/Vandersanden (eds), *La fonction publique communautaire* (2008) 74; and Van Raepenbusch, 'Lapport jurisprudentiel du Tribunal de la fonction publique de l`Union européenne' in Govaere/Vandersanden (eds), *La fonction publique communautaire* (2008) 163; GC, T-572/08 P, ECLI:EU:T:2009:209, paras 38, 41 – *Commission v Traore.*

[209] CST, F-111/06, ECLI:EU:F:2007:163, paras 71/72 – *Giannopoulos v Council.*

[210] GC, T-18/90, ECLI:EU:T:1991:21, para 5 – *Jongen v Commission.*

[211] ECJ, C-443/07 P, ECLI:EU:C:2008:767 – *Centeno Mediavilla*, Gervasoni (2010) 46 *Cahiers de droit européen* 758. CST, F-32/06, ECLI:EU:F:2007:169 – *De la Cruz v European Agency for Safety and Health at Work* (local agents, successful).

[212] Directive 2005/36/EC [2005] OJ L255/22–142.

[213] CST, F-136/06, ECLI:EU:F:2008:168, para 85 – *Reali v Commission.*

[214] GC, T-572/16, ECLI:EU:T:2017:720 – *Brouillard v Commission*, confirmed by ECJ, C-728/17 P, ECLI:EU:C:2019:178 – *Commission v Brouillard.*

[215] GC, T-713/20, ECLI:EU:T:2022:513, paras 47–49 – *OQ v Commission.*

[216] Art 32(1) SR; on exceptions Art 32(2) SR; ECJ, 33/67, ECLI:EU:C:1968:16 – *Kurrer v Council*; ECJ, 102/75, ECLI:EU:C:1976:172, para 16 – *Petersen v Commission.*

[217] Criteria: GC, T-100/96, ECLI:EU:T:1998:245 – *Vicente Nuñez v Commission.*

[218] Art 15 CEOS.

[219] Art 32(3) SR.

[220] Art 15(1) sub 1 sentence 2 CEOS.

[221] Art 55 CEOS. For a different grade, see GC, T-146/96, ECLI:EU:T:1998:50 – *De Abreu v ECJ.*

[222] CST, F-21/06, ECLI:EU:F:2007:116 – *Da Silva v Commission.*

7. Field of Activity

A position is associated with the assignment of corresponding tasks. The appointing authority has wide discretion to organise the work and adapt it to changing needs.[223] This may only be exercised in the interests of the service, but it does not require the consent of the officials concerned.[224] For their part, an official is bound by the obligation to work,[225] and by loyalty duties,[226] to 'assist and tender advice to his superiors; he shall be responsible for the performance of the duties assigned to him',[227] to accept any assignment consistent with his office, in accordance with the needs of the service, at the place of employment of the institution where he performs his duties.[228] This requires the subordination of every civil servant to the instructions of his superiors;[229] he may also be subordinated to the instructions of civil servants of the same rank.[230] The officer is entitled to an activity appropriate to his rank in the function group and grade[231] – a right that limits the organisational discretion of the institution.[232] Tasks must be assigned which broadly correspond to those of a post in the respective grade and function group,[233] but there is no entitlement to a specific function.[234] The lack of a (sufficiently explicit) definition of tasks is a violation of Article 7 SR[235] and of the duty of care.[236]

8. Probationary Period

A probationary period must be completed before an official may be established.[237] It serves to determine the suitability of the official for his job. If the official's work or conduct during the probationary period has proven inadequate to justify a lifetime appointment to the civil service, he shall be dismissed.[238] There are equivalent provisions for other servants.[239] A dismissal under this provision entails a compensation payment equal to one-third of basic salary for each month

[223] GC, T-49/91, ECLI:EU:T:1992:72 – *Turner v Commission*; CST, F-4/09, ECLI:EU:F:2010:24, paras 58, 61, paras 36, 38 and 52 – *De Britto Patrício-Dias v Commission*.

[224] CST, F-55/06, ECLI:EU:F:2007:15, paras 55 ff – *De Albuquerque v Commission* or CST, F-41/10 RENV, ECLI:EU:F:2012:135, paras 148 ff, 159 – *Bermejo Garde v EESC*, set aside in the appeal GC, T-530/12 P, ECLI:EU:T:2014:860, paras 106–10, and newly decided in CST, F-41/10 RENV, ECLI:EU:F:2016:123; CST, F-88/09 and 48/10, ECLI:EU:F:2012:171, para 126 ff – *Z v ECJ*; GC, T-88/13P, ECLI:EU:T:2015:393 – *Z v ECJ* or CST, F-23/05, ECLI:EU:F:2007:75, paras 135, 140, 169 – *Giraudy v Commission* (allegations in the press).

[225] GC, T-146/89, ECLI:EU:T:1991:61 – *Williams v ECA* (duty of loyalty applies comprehensively).

[226] Dalle-Crode (2008) 457 ff.

[227] Art 21 SR.

[228] ECJ, 161/80 and 162/80, ECLI:EU:C:1981:51 – *Carbognani and Zabetta v Commission*; ECJ, 23-24/87, ECLI:EU:C:1988:406 – *Aldinger and Others v EP*; GC, T-93/96, ECLI:EU:T:1998:171 – *Presle v Cedefop*.

[229] ECJ, 338/82, ECLI:EU:C:1984:181 – *Albertini and Montagnani v Commission*.

[230] AD officer may be instructed by AST officers, CST, F-49/08, ECLI:EU:F:2009:76, para 72 – *Giannini v Commission*.

[231] Art 7(1) SR; GC, T-59/91 and 79/91, ECLI:EU:T:1992:87 – *Eppe v Commission*.

[232] CST, F-119/06, ECLI:EU:F:2008:54, paras 832 ff, 96 ff – *Kerstens v Commission*.

[233] On change of duties and temporary occupation, see section II.16. below.

[234] Reorganisation can be justified by previous changes in personnel or the desired increase in efficiency, CST, F-119/06, ECLI:EU:F:2008:54, paras 86, 98 – *Kerstens v Commission*.

[235] ECJ, C-299/21 P, ECLI:EU:C:2022:429, para 128 – *EM v EP*.

[236] CST, Jd Cases F-138/06 and F-37/08, ECLI:EU:F:2009:48, paras 93, 99, 123, 216 – *Meister v OHIM*.

[237] Art 34 SR.

[238] Art 34(3) sub 3 SR.

[239] Art 14(3) sub 3, Art 84 CEOS. On another probationary period after several contracts for temporary service, see CST, F-63/07, ECLI:EU:F:2009:18, paras 66 ff – *Patsarika v Cedefop*.

of probation completed.[240] The purpose of the probationary period is to enable the administration to assess[241] the applicant's suitability for a particular post, the mental attitude with which he performs his duties, and his efficiency in service. The appointing authority must deploy the person concerned accordingly, give him a real opportunity within this framework to demonstrate his abilities, and give him guidance.[242] If the civil servant is to be reassigned to another post for the probationary period, this can only be done up to the end of the probationary period; the civil servant has no right to continue the probationary period elsewhere.[243] The administration may decide to alter the conditions under which a probationary period is served. Where such an alteration is made as a *result of the conduct of the person* concerned, that person cannot rely on it in support of a claim that he was not put in a position to carry out the duties entrusted to him and seek to justify, on that basis, the fact that he did not achieve the objectives set for him. More general, a staff member may not rely on his own act in order to escape his professional obligations.[244]

The appointing authority enjoys wide discretion with limited judicial control when deciding about the passing or failure of the probationary period, and its extension.[245] The report under Article 34(3) SR on the ability of the probationer to perform the duties pertaining to his post and also on his efficiency and conduct in the service is intended to ensure that his suitability or unsuitability can be determined objectively and comprehensively, and that the person concerned is in a position to protect his interests.[246] It shall therefore be created in good time, but delays do not necessarily invalidate it.[247] The interpretation of the contract that is required to take a decision on an extension represents an assessment of the facts that cannot be separated from the contract.[248] However, if there were doubts about suitability, the probationary period used to be extended in order to be able to test the probationer's suitability for a different deployment. Here, the 2014 reform limits the duration of the probationary period to – uniformly – nine months, which can only be extended in the event of an interruption due to illness, maternity leave or an accident, but not if there are doubts about suitability. It cannot be extended beyond a total period of 15 months. A dismissal must now occur if the probationer's work or overall conduct, within the meaning of Title II of the SR (Rights and Obligations), prohibit a lifetime appointment. The time limit for the probationer to submit comments on the probationary report has been greatly reduced, namely to eight working days. In addition, it was made clear that not only at the end of the probationary period, but also at any time before it, a report can be drawn up and the probationer dismissed. The same applies to temporary and contract staff.[249]

[240] Art 84(4) CEOS; this may be combined with other compensations and set off against other allowances, like under Art 48b CEOS: GC, T-462/17, ECLI:EU:T:2019:397, para 121 – *TO v EEA*, see case study in section II.19.d. below.

[241] GC, T-26/91, ECLI:EU:T:1992:53 – *Kupka-Floridi v EESC* (definition of probationary period).

[242] If an official realises there are problems, he must point them out himself, CST, F-2/11, ECLI:EU:F:2012:194, para 107 – *BW v Commission*. The suitability of the probationary post is a question of organisational discretion, CST, F-73/07, ECLI:EU:F:2008:42, paras 31, 39 – *Doktor v Council*.

[243] CST, F-112/06, ECLI:EU:F:2007:178, para 77 – *Krcova v ECJ*.

[244] Wording of CST, F-5/12, ECLI:EU:F:2013:75, para 57 – *Bogusz v Frontex*.

[245] CST, F-85/08, ECLI:EU:F:2009:94, para 72 – *Notarnicola v ECA*; CST, F-2/09, ECLI:EU:F:2010:12, para 74 – *Menghi v ENISA*. Comprehensive: CST, F-5/12, ECLI:EU:F:2014:179, paras 72 ff, 59 – *Bogusz v Frontex*.

[246] General: CST, F-112/06, ECLI:EU:F:2007:178, para 33 – *Krcova v ECJ*. Once the probationary period has expired, it can no longer be extended retrospectively due to legal certainty and the protection of legitimate expectations, CST, F-78/11, ECLI:EU:F:2013:90, para 63 – *BM v ECB*.

[247] CST, F-73/07, ECLI:EU:F:2008:42, paras 53 ff – *Doktor v Council*.

[248] ECJ, C-730/18 P, ECLI:EU:C:2020:505, para 55 – *SC v Eulex Kosovo*.

[249] Art 34(2) SR, Art 14(2) and Art 84(2) CEOS.

9. Mutual Rights and Obligations

The civil servant status establishes a relationship of mutual trust between the appointing authority and the staff it employs, which on the one hand obliges the staff to cooperate and obey,[250] and on the other, imposes special duties of assistance and care on the administration in accordance with the SR. Central behavioural obligations of officials are prescribed in Articles 11–26a SR, including, for example, impartiality,[251] loyalty[252] and independence from the instructions of third parties, the duty to report and mitigate conflicts of interest,[253] the obligation to disclose the spouse's professional activity,[254] and the requirement to refrain from any action or behaviour which might reflect adversely on the position: Article 12 SR.

Loyalty, dignity

The duty of loyalty has a wide scope. It implies, for example, that officials must facilitate the task of the administration in determining the extent of their pecuniary entitlements under the SR.[255] Loyalty is binding on every official not only towards his superiors but also towards the institution to which they belong. Thus, for example, the dissemination of insults in regard to members of an institution are considered to also harm the reputation of the Union.[256] As an obligation on the official, the official's duty of loyalty includes to refrain from conduct likely to prejudice the dignity and respect due to the EU.[257] A failure to cooperate or demonstrate appropriate dignity is not subject to the condition that the official must have benefited from that failure or that the failure in question must have harmed the institution.[258] Obviously, activities falling within the realm of corruption unquestionably constitute a failure to comply with the duty of loyalty.[259] The staff member must refrain from conduct that could be detrimental to the dignity and respect that is due to the institution and its authorities. At the same time, the loyalty and dignity obligation on the side of civil servants can be perceived as an objective reflex of the citizens' fundamental right to good administration[260] under Article 41 FRC that binds the EU institutions and other bodies.[261] The duty of loyalty extends beyond the performance of specific tasks, to the whole

[250] Dalle-Crode (2008) 469; *cf* also, Rémy Hernu, 'Le devoir de loyauté du fonctionnaire des Communautés Européennes' (2002) 38(4) *Revue trimestrielle de droit européen* 686–724, 686. Instructions to the staff are sufficient, there is no requirement to issue individual instructions to each employee, CST, F-74/10, ECLI:EU:F:2011:171, para 100 – *Kimman v Commission*, set aside on another point.

[251] Whereas impartiality also appears as an individual right of the staff member, derived from the principle of sound administration, see at the end of this section II.9. and the case study below.

[252] Arts 11, 17a SR. On avoidance of conflicts of interest and on a broad interpretation of the obligations under Art 11a SR, see CJEU Annual Report 2012, 220 with reference to CST, F-36/11, ECLI:EU:F:2012:49 – *BD v Commission*. On the requirements for the dissemination of information, see, eg, CST, F-41/10 RENV, ECLI:EU:F:2012:135, para 148 ff – *Bermejo Garde v EESC*, set aside and referred back on appeal GC, T-530/12 P, ECLI:EU:T:2014:860, paras 106–10, damages €25,000: CST, F-41/10 RENV, ECLI: EU:F:2016:123.

[253] Art 11, Art 11a SR.

[254] Art 13 SR.

[255] CST, F-42/14, ECLI:EU:F:2014:250, paras 108, 123 – *EH v Commission* (here: to clearly notify changes in the family situation).

[256] GC, T-259/97, ECLI:EU:T:2000:208, para 44 – *Teixera Neves v CJEU*; this can be all the more so if the member of staff is in a high grade: GC, T-273/94, ECLI:EU:T:1997:71, para 129 – *N v Commission*.

[257] CST, F-133/15, ECLI:EU:F:2016:127, para 187 – *HI v Commission*.

[258] GC, Jd Cases T-24/98 and T-241/99, ECLI:EU:T:2001:175, para 76 – *E v Commission*; CST, F-80/11, ECLI:EU:2013:159, para 66 – *Gomes Moreira v ECDC*.

[259] GC, T-197/00, ECLI:EU:T:2002:135, para 73 – *Onidi v Commission*.

[260] See chapter 1, III.6.a.

[261] CST, F-80/11, ECLI:EU:2013:159, para 61 – *Gomes Moreira v ECDC*; Livolsi/Schiano in Perillo/Giacobbo-Peyronnel (eds), *Statut de la fonction publique de l'Union européenne: Commentaire article par article* (2017) 170.

relationship between the official and the institution. For example, remarks during an electoral campaign concerning the Staff Committee fall within the sphere of relations between an official and her or his institution.[262] This wide concept of loyalty has to be reconciled with the fundamental right of freedom of expression.

Freedom of expression

The right to freedom of expression and to publish is a fundamental right,[263] also guaranteed by the FRC.[264] The freedom of expression comprises the right to articulate orally or in writing dissenting opinions or minority opinions by comparison to the institution's line. This may be done so in circumstances of the normal course of work or, for example, during the appraisal exercise under Article 43 SR in observations relating to the Annual Report. Case-law has stated on this that Articles 12 and 21 SR do not constitute a bar to the freedom of expression of officials, but rather place reasonable limits on the exercise of that fundamental right, in the interests of the service. The right to freedom of expression and to publish shall be exercised with due respect to the principles of loyalty and impartiality;[265] it cannot be exercised by means of defamatory or insulting statements.[266] For example, comments considered relevant for the Annual Report have to be exercised in a manner compatible with Articles 12 and 21 SR. The scope of this freedom is wide and finds its limits in 'grossly insulting language', an 'extreme and aggressive choice of words', in 'tone and expressions which cannot be reconciled with the obligations relating to the dignity of the post and respect for the authorities of the institution' and in an 'unseemly conduct'.[267]

The fundamental right of free expression does not constitute an unfettered prerogative but may be subject to restrictions, provided that the restrictions in fact correspond to objectives of general public interest pursued by the Union and do not amount to, with regard to the objectives pursued, a disproportionate and intolerable interference which infringes upon the very substance of the rights protected.[268] Case-law has acknowledged *objectives of general public interest* that may justify such limitations of the freedom of expression, for example derived from Article 10(2) ECHR, that freedom 'carries with it duties and responsibilities', and may

> be subject to such formalities, conditions, restrictions or penalties as are prescribed by law and are necessary in a democratic society, in the interests of national security, territorial integrity or public safety, for the prevention of disorder or crime, for the protection of health or morals, for the protection of the reputation or rights of others, for preventing the disclosure of information received in confidence, or for maintaining the authority and impartiality of the judiciary.[269]

[262] GC, T-146/94, ECLI:EU:T:1996:34, para 98 – *Williams v ECA.*

[263] GC, T-82/99, ECLI:EU:T:2000:193, para 129 – *Cwik v Commission*, and C-340/00 P, ECLI:EU:C:2001:701 – *Commission v Cwik*; GC, Jd Cases T-34/96 and T-163/96, ECLI:EU:T:1999:102, paras 57/58 – *Connolly v Commission*, and ECJ, C-274/99 P, ECLI:EU:C:2001:127 – *Connolly v Commission*; ECJ, C-100/88, ECLI:EU:C:1989:638, para 16 – *Oyowe and Traore v Commission.*

[264] Art 11 FRC.

[265] Arts 12, 17, 17a SR; GC, T-608/18, ECLI:EU:T:2020:249 – *Sammut v EP*. Rémy Hernu, 'Le devoir de loyauté du fonctionnaire des Communautés européennes' (2002) 38(4) *Revue trimestrielle de droit européen* 686–724.

[266] GC, T-146/94, ECLI:EU:T:1996:34, para 101 – *Williams v ECA.*

[267] ECJ, C-150/98 P, ECLI:EU:C:1999:616, para 59 – *ESC v E.*

[268] ECJ, C-274/99 P, ECLI:EU:C:2001:127, para 148 – *Connolly v Commission*; ECJ, 265/87, ECLI:EU:C:1989:303, para 15 – *Schräder v Hauptzollamt Gronau*; ECJ, C-404/92 P, ECLI:EU:C:1994:361, para 18 – *X v Commission*; GC, T-176/94, ECLI:EU:T:1995:139, para 33 – *K v Commission.*

[269] ECJ, C-274/99 P, ECLI:EU:C:2001:127, para 40 – *Connolly v Commission.*

The interests of the Union and conflict of interests

An official shall carry out his duties and conduct himself solely with the interests of the Union in mind, Article 11(1) SR.[270] The official's independence[271] serves the purpose of protecting the public interest, the interests of the EU institutions in their mission, and the trust between the institutions and their staff employed.[272] In order to implement this practically, an official shall not deal with a matter in which, directly or indirectly, he has any personal interest such as to impair his independence, and, in particular, family and financial interests and is under an obligation to immediately inform the appointing authority (Art 11a SR). Again, this duty has a wide scope: any circumstance which, in the light of the servant's position and of the specific circumstances of the matter, must reasonably be understood by the person concerned as being likely to be seen by third parties as a possible source of impairment of his independence.[273] Independence in relation to third parties must not be assessed solely from a subjective point of view. In particular in the management of public funding, it embraces any conduct that is likely to impair the image of the institutions, on an objective view, and to undermine the confidence which the institutions should inspire in the public.[274] Case-law has linked the obligation to act in the interests of the Union and to refrain from conflict of interests with the obligations of loyalty and cooperation.[275]

The fact of professional or family relationships between an official and a third party cannot, in principle, *automatically* mean that the independence of that official is impaired, or appears to be impaired, wherever it falls to the official to decide a matter in which the third party is involved.[276] The reality of any conflict of interest is for the appointing authority to assess. In other words, Article 11a SR does not permit officials and other members of staff themselves to make the assessment. The obligations to avoid conflicts of interests and to declare potential situations point towards the person inside the institution. As an important practical example, where a person inside an institution is a family member of a person external to the institution the person external to the institution is not prevented from carrying out a professional activity within a company which is subject to the authority of the institution in question. Similarly, it does not prevent a family member of an official from applying for admission to a competition or a for a post where the selection process involves a competition selection board or selection panel.[277] The obligation to behave with integrity and discretion as regards the acceptance of certain appointments or benefits persist also after leaving the service, Article 16 SR, which also provides for cooling off periods.

Other behavioural obligations

Other important behavioural obligations of civil servants are the ban on psychological and sexual harassment;[278] the ban on engaging in an outside activity without permission, whether paid or unpaid;[279] the residence obligation;[280] the obligation to protest to his immediate

[270] *cf* also the duties set out in Arts 11a, 12b, 13, 15, 16 SR; which constitute the 'pillars of deontology of EU civil service law': CST, F-80/11, ECLI:EU:2013:159, para 61 – *Gomes Moreira v ECDC.*

[271] *cf* Art 11(3), Art 11a (1), Art 11a(3) SR.

[272] CST, F-80/11, ECLI:EU:2013:159, para 62 – *Gomes Moreira v ECDC*; Livolsi/Schiano in Perillo/Giacobbo-Peyronnel (eds), *Statut de la fonction publique de l'Union européenne: Commentaire article par article* (2017) 171.

[273] CST, F-36/11, ECLI:EU:F:2012:49, para 68 – *BD v Commission.*

[274] ibid, para 68.

[275] CST, F-80/11, ECLI:EU:2013:159, para 61 – *Gomes Moreira v ECDC.*

[276] CST, F-133/15, ECLI:EU:F:2016:127, paras 193 ff – *HI v Commission.*

[277] Subject to the declaratory obligation: CST, F-133/15, ECLI:EU:F:2016:127, para 196 – *HI v Commission.*

[278] Art 12a SR.

[279] Art 12b SR; CJEU Annual Report 2003, 190 with further reference; Rogalla (2005) 40 *EuR* 542.

[280] Art 20 SR; Dalle-Crode (2008) 457.

superior when receiving orders which the official considers to be irregular or likely to give rise to serious difficulties ('duty of remonstration');[281] the obligation to report possible unlawful acts ('whistleblowing');[282] and others. The official's duties include reserve and moderation, objectivity and impartiality, and respect for the dignity of the function, the reputation of other persons, and the presumption of innocence.[283] The official's duty of loyalty and cooperation includes, for example, participation in medical examinations in the procedure for determining invalidity: 'to exercise all due care to respond to the invitations to appear before the invalidity committee'.[284]

The 2014 reform in particular further restricted lobbying and the flexibility of former senior executives to engage in external consultancy.[285] Other parts of the SR also give rise to obligations on the part of the official, such as the obligation to provide one's personal address or other information belonging to the private sphere.[286] Violations of the duties imposed by the SR may be liable to disciplinary measures.[287]

A number of areas of mutual rights and obligations that are central for the EU civil service status shall be highlighted below: equal treatment and non-discrimination; social protection; protection against harassment; and the principle of the duty of care, followed by sections on the staff members' request for assistance and the institutions' duty to provide assistance, as well as an overview on privileges and immunities. Before that, a case study will illustrate the principle of impartiality as both a central obligation and a right enjoyed by every civil servant.

Case Study on the Principle of Impartiality

Impartiality in EU civil service law

Case C-894/19 P, *Parliament v UZ* of 21 October 2021
Case T-47/18, *UZ v Parliament* of 20 September 2019
Case T-220/20, *Kerstens v Commission* of 20 October 2021
Case T-808/17, *Pethke v EUIPO* of 3 December 2019
Case C-139/18 P, *CJ v ECDC* of 3 April 2019
Case C-680/16 P, *Wolff and Remedia v Commission* of 27 March 2019
Case C-831/18 P, *Commission v RQ* of 18 June 2020
Case T-567/16, *McCoy v Committee of the Regions* of 23 October 2018

[281] Art 21a SR; below case study on the *duty of care*, at the end of section II.9.
[282] Section II.10. below.
[283] CST, F-88/09 and F-48/10, ECLI:EU: F:2012:171, para 251 – *Z v ECJ*, on appeal GC, T-88/13 P, ECLI:EU:T:2015:393.
[284] CST, F-41/06 RENV, ECLI:EU:F:2012:149, para 98 – *Marcuccio v Commission*.
[285] *cf* Arts 16 and 40 SR, Art 17 CEOS. On attempts to address 'revolving doors' and conflicts of interest issues, see EP Resolution of 16 September 2021, 'Strengthening transparency and integrity in the EU institutions by setting up an independent EU ethics body', P9_TA(2021)0396; and, including on the splitting of the current disciplinary system into disciplinary and ethical violations: Alemanno, 'Towards an EU Ethics Body' (2020); ECA Special Report No 13/2019, 'The ethical frameworks of the audited EU institutions: scope for improvement'.
[286] Art 55 SR; Dalle-Crode,(2008) 458; Levi, 'Droits fondamentaux et principes généraux de droit de la fonction publique communautaire' in Govaere/Vandersanden (eds), *La fonction publique communautaire* (2008) 108.
[287] Art 86 SR, see section II.20. below.

In Brief

The principle of impartiality is one of the central obligations of EU civil servants, and at the same time a right enjoyed by every civil servant. The institutions have to comply with both manifestations of the principle: subjective impartiality and objective impartiality.

Impartiality and Staff Regulations

Artcle 11 SR stipulates: 'An official shall carry out his duties and conduct himself solely with the interests of the Union in mind. He shall neither seek nor take instructions from any government, authority, organisation or person outside his institution. He shall carry out the duties assigned to him objectively, impartially and in keeping with his duty of loyalty to the Union.'

Impartiality and Charter of Fundamental Rights

At the same time, every civil servant can rely on the right stipulated in Article 41 FRC, because the institutions, bodies, offices and agencies of the Union are also required to respect the right to good administration towards their employed staff. According to Article 41(1) FRC, 'each person has the right to have his or her affairs handled impartially … by the institutions, bodies, offices and agencies of the Union', including in matters relating to the management of the civil service, such as the appointment, assessment, promotion and disciplining of staff.

What is Impartiality of the Institutions?

Impartiality is a principle of general application in all administrative procedures. An infringement of the principle of impartiality is treated as an infringement of the fundamental rights of the defence and can lead to annulment of the administrative decision taken when breaching the right. Impartiality extends to all areas of activity of the EU administration, including the management of the civil service. The ECJ describes the content of impartiality in two manifestations: on the one hand a subjective impartiality, according to which no member of the institution concerned may show bias or personal prejudice and, on the other hand, an objective impartiality in the sense that the institution must provide sufficient guarantees to rule out any legitimate doubt as to any prejudice. As the ECJ stated in *Wolff* and Remedia *v Commission*[288] the institutions have to comply with both components of the requirement of impartiality: subjective and objective. Whereas the ECJ applies a rather general concept of impartiality which is open to interpretation in its case-law, the Code of Good Administrative Behaviour of the European Ombudsman highlights specific and particularly serious examples of the lack of impartiality, such as conflicts of interest for personal, family, political or financial reasons.

The requirement of impartiality imposed on the institutions, bodies, offices and agencies in the exercise of their functions seeks to ensure equal treatment. That requirement is intended, in particular, to avoid any conflict of interests of officials and other servants acting on behalf of the institutions, bodies, offices and agencies. Given the fundamental

[288] ECJ, C-680/16 P, ECLI:EU:C:2019:257 – *Wolff and Remedia v Commission.*

importance of ensuring independence and integrity, both for the internal functioning and the outward appearance of the institutions, the requirement of impartiality covers all circumstances in which an official or servant must reasonably see that, in the eyes of third parties, they may appear to be capable of impairing his or her independence in that area.

A single breach of impartiality may 'infect' a chain of cooperative decision-making, even when it involves several different institutions: where a number of EU institutions, bodies, offices or agencies are given separate responsibilities of their own in the context of a procedure that is liable to result in a decision adversely affecting an individual, each of those entities is required, in respect of its own activities, to comply with the requirement of objective impartiality. Consequently, even where only one of them has breached that requirement, such a breach is liable to render the decision adopted by the other entity at the end of the procedure at issue unlawful.

The general lines of this concept shall be illustrated by examples of impartiality in disciplinary proceedings, in proceedings of the Invalidity Committee, and in the appeal procedure against an appraisal report.

Impartiality in Disciplinary Proceedings

The applicant in *UZ v Parliament*,[289] a head of unit, filed an application against the disciplinary decision to downgrade her and to reset her promotion points to zero, for the reason of alleged harassment. Several of her colleagues had filed complaints against her. She challenged the disciplinary decision on the basis of an infringement of her right of impartiality. A disciplinary procedure is divided into two distinct stages. The first stage consists of an impartial administrative investigation followed by the drafting of an investigation report, and is closed, after the person concerned has been heard on the facts alleged against him or her, by conclusions drawn from that report. The second stage consists of the disciplinary proceedings proper, which are initiated by the appointing authority on the basis of that investigation report. These consist either in the initiation of disciplinary proceedings without consultation of the Disciplinary Board, or in the matter being referred to that Board, on the basis of a report drawn up by the appointing authority in the light of the conclusions of the investigation and of the comments submitted by the person concerned in relation to that investigation.

The GC found in that case that at the time of his appointment, an investigator had already met one of the complainants and could already have held a negative opinion of the applicant. This called into question the objective impartiality of the investigator. Lack of impartiality is a procedural irregularity that can justify the annulment of a measure only if, had it not been for such an irregularity, the outcome of the procedure might have been different. However, no strict evidence is required here: case-law applies this criterion in the sense that it cannot be ruled out that if the administrative investigation had been conducted with care and impartiality, the investigation might have resulted in a different initial assessment of the facts and hence led to different consequences.

In particular, an infringement of objective impartiality cannot be easily remedied, as it is likely to undermine the legality of the administrative procedure as a whole. *Wolff and Remedia v Commission* was about the role of a rapporteur in an assessment committee.

[289] GC, T-47/18, ECLI:EU:T:2019:650 – *UZ v EP*, confirmed in ECJ, C-894/19 P, ECLI:EU:C:2021:863 – *EP v UZ*.

In its judgment, the ECJ refrained from examining whether or not the participation of a certain expert had influenced the decision adopted, and instead confined itself to finding that there was a legitimate doubt which could not be dispelled as to objective impartiality.

Similarly, in *Kerstens v Commission*,[290] an investigation leading to the disciplinary sanction of a reprimand was organised by a person who already had knowledge about the facts underlying the investigation before the procedure commenced. This raised legitimate doubts as to the objective impartiality of the investigation.

Impartiality in Proceedings of an Invalidity Committee

The Case of *McCoy*[291] related to the decision-making of an invalidity committee. The applicant had doubts about the impartiality of the doctor appointed by the institution. These doubts were based on the fact that this doctor had already expressed an opinion unfavourable to him at a meeting of the Invalidity Committee at a time when no medical examination – much less the 'in-depth' medical examination – could have been carried out. In addition, in this case, the institution did not consult the summary medical report and the opinions of the three doctors on the Invalidity Committee in order to gain a fuller picture of the file. The institution's decision (based on the conclusions of the Invalidity Committee), which refused to recognise the occupational origin of the applicant's disease, had to be annulled by the GC.

Impartiality in the Appeal Procedure against an Appraisal Report

In *Pethke v EUIPO*[292] the GC treated the question of whether a superior was an impartial appeal body for the review of the appraisal report of a staff member, where the same superior had previously played an important role in setting up the respective appraisal report, in the capacity of reporting officer. Prior knowledge of facts alone does not make a person partial. For example, reporting officers cannot be regarded as being biased and non-objective solely because they are involved as superiors in the professional activities of their staff. Quite the opposite; rather, it is that involvement which enables them to provide the most appropriate assessment of the activities of the staff member. Here, however, the applicant's former superior, who was in charge during three-quarters of the period in question, was instrumental in drawing up the assessment in question. The fact that he again decided in the internal appeal procedure raised doubts as to his impartiality as appeal assessor. Here, the GC decided that the obligation of impartiality constitutes a fundamental guarantee which must be respected, since otherwise the staff member would be deprived of his effective right to a genuine review. This is also important regarding the functionality of an institution: an internal appraisal review procedure can contribute to the objectivity of the assessment and thus prevent litigation.

In more general terms, the ECJ held in *CJ v ECDC*[293] that an appeal assessment must not be entrusted to a hierarchical subordinate of the reporting officer. Staff members

[290] GC, T-220/20, ECLI:EU:T:2021:716 – *Kerstens v Commission.*
[291] GC, T-567/16, ECLI:EU:T:2018:708 – *McCoy v Committee of the Regions.*
[292] GC, T-808/17, ECLI:EU:T:2019:832 – *Pethke v EUIPO.*
[293] ECJ, C-139/18 P, ECLI:EU:C:2019:281 – *CJ v ECDC.*

who challenge their appraisal reports must be sure that a genuine review will be carried out. That presupposes that the appeal assessor is able to assess freely the merits of the staff member's complaint and, where appropriate, uphold it by calling into question the reporting officer's appraisal. It is doubtful whether that would be the case where an appeal assessor who is hierarchically subordinate to the reporting officer conducts the appeal, and is therefore himself assessed by the reporting officer.

Impartiality as a Charter Right

Case-law bases the right to an impartial procedure both on the obligation of officials to act impartially (Art 11(1) SR) and on the fundamental right to Good Administration stipulated in Article 41 of the EU Charter of Fundamental Rights (FRC). That combination is noteworthy because it connects the obligation of the superior towards his collaborator with the fundamental right of the latter. Acting on behalf of the institution, the superior is bound by – and the staff member can rely on – the right guaranteed by the Charter, irrespective of the internal administrative nature of the dispute. Still, in terms of the addressee of the fundamental right, it needs to be emphasised that the obligation to act in compliance with the right falls on the institution, for whom the superior acts, not on them personally.

Procedural Guarantees and the Margin of Discretion

Impartiality in procedure touches on the fundamental rights of the defence. The wide margin of discretion enjoyed by the employing institutions in many areas of civil service law must be counterbalanced by a particular focus on the course of the procedure for that purpose.[294] Case-law stipulates that where an EU institution has wide discretionary powers, compliance with the procedural safeguards provided for in the EU legal order is even more important.[295] Those guarantees include, in particular, the duty of the institution to examine carefully and impartially all the relevant aspects of the case. In other words, any infringement of procedural rules (including impartiality) in administrative areas that grant wide discretion to decision-makers is given particular scrutiny by the Union's judges.

a. Non-Discrimination and Equal Treatment

The 2004 reform sought to strengthen the protection of fundamental rights, such as by emphasising the right to freedom of expression,[296] by regulating the handling of an official's publication

[294] GC, T-92/01, ECLI:EU:T:2002:220, para 24 – *Girardot v Commission*; GC, T-336/02, ECLI:EU:T:2005:115, para 38 – *Christensen v Commission*.

[295] ECJ, C-269/90, ECLI:EU:C:1991:438, para 14 – *Technische Universität München*.

[296] Levi, 'Droits fondamentaux et principes généraux de droit de la fonction publique communautaire' in Govaere/Vandersanden (eds), *La fonction publique communautaire* (2008) 104; GC, T-183/96, ECLI:EU:T:1998:37 – *E v EESC*; ECJ, C-150/98 P, ECLI:EU:C:1999:616 – *EESC v E* (comments on assessment by supervisors); CST, Jd Cases F-138/06 and F-37/08, ECLI:EU:F:2009:48, para 130 – *Meister v OHIM* (insulting criticism of restructuring measures); CST, F-49/06, ECLI:EU:F:2008:126, para 60 ff – *Nijs v ECA* (no right to disparage colleagues or superiors in their professional qualities without proof). The special circumstances of the individual case must always be taken into account, *cf* GC, T-259/97, ECLI:EU:T:2000:208 – *Teixera Neves v CJEU* (freedom of opinion of staff representatives in staff meetings); *cf* on the new regulation as a codification of previous case law Dalle-Crode (2005) 43.

of any matter dealing with the work of the Union,[297] and – most prominently – the prohibition of discrimination[298] based on any ground such as sex, race,[299] colour, ethnic or social origin, genetic features, language,[300] religion[301] or belief, political or any other opinion, membership of a national minority,[302] property, birth, disability,[303] age,[304] or sexual orientation.[305]

Discrimination based on nationality is not mentioned in Article 1d SR explicitly but is comprised as well by the ban on discrimination (the provision bans 'discrimination based on any ground such as', and is open to other areas of discrimination beyond the examples given). Article 7 SR states that the assignment of an official to a post is without regard to nationality. In case of a significant imbalance between nationalities among officials in an institution which is not justified by objective criteria, each institution shall adopt appropriate measures to balance nationalities (which in other places is addressed as 'geographical balance'), always based on merit.[306] In recruitment, a post must not be reserved to a specific nationality without this being justified by objective reasons of service. But nationality can be a preferential factor in order to maintain or to re-establish a geographical balance, where otherwise the merits of the different candidates are equivalent.[307]

When facts are established from which it may be presumed that there has been direct or indirect discrimination, the burden of proof shifts to the institution.[308] The content of legal terms regarding the concept of discrimination stipulated under Article 1d SR – where not otherwise defined in the SR – may be determined in line with the definitions applied by Directive 2000/43[309] and Directive 2000/78.[310]

[297] Including the option of approval by default, Art 17a SR.

[298] Art 1d(1) SR.

[299] Pleas based on racial discrimination were raised several times in case-law on staff matters, but have so far not been successful: GC, T-11/03, ECLI:EU:T:2004:77, paras 134, 147, 153–75, 206 – *Afari v ECB*; CST, F-90/07, ECLI:EU:F:2008:142, paras 102/103 – *Traore v Commission*, confirmed by GC, T-572/08 P, ECLI:EU:T:2009:209; CST, F-43/05, ECLI:EU:F:2007:14, paras 100/101– *Chassagne v Commission*; CST, F-39/06, ECLI:EU:F:2007:63, para 32 – *Chassagne v Commission*; CST, F-61/06, ECLI:EU:F:2008:98, paras 107/108, 162, 169 – *Sapara v Eurojust*; CST, Jd Cases F-106/13 and F-25/14, ECLI:EU:F:2015:118, para 27 – *DD v FRA*; GC, T-632/19, ECLI:EU:T:2021:434, paras 132, 149 ff – *DD v FRA* (ECJ, C-587/21 P).

[300] *cf* section II.4.b. below.

[301] ECJ, C-157/15, ECLI:EU:C:2017:203 – *Achbita v G4S*; ECJ, C-188/15, ECLI:EU:C:2017:204 – *Bougnaoui v Micropole (Islamic headscarf)*; ECJ, 130/75, ECLI:EU:C:1976:142 – *Prais v Council* (date of competition impossible for religious reasons).

[302] As long as a language is not declared to be an official language under Regulation 1/58, it may not be relied upon to justify discrimination of a 'minority' in a competition, CST, F-29/11, ECLI:EU:F:2012:172, paras 62, 82 – *BA v Commission*.

[303] CST, F-62/10, ECLI:EU:F:2011:141, paras 71, 80–82 – *Esders v Commission*; chapter 1, III.6.b.

[304] ECJ, C-144/04, ECLI:EU:C:2005:709, paras 53/54, 60–65, 75 – *Mangold*; CST, F-36/14, ECLI:EU:F:2015:48, paras 36, 53 – *Bischoff*; CST, F-52/15, ECLI:EU:F:2015:127, paras 33–35, 50 – *Xenakis*; CST, F-36/05, ECLI:EU:F:2010:115, paras 60–65 – *Schulze v Commission*.

[305] ECJ, Jd Cases C-122/99 P and C-125/99, ECLI:EU:C:2001:304 P – *D and Sweden v Council*; CST, F-79/14, ECLI:EU:F:2015:63, paras 82/83 – *EG v EP* (on access to legal marriage of a same-sex couple); GC, Jd Cases T-124/01 and T-320/01, ECLI:EU:T:2003:153, para 80 – *Del Vaglio v Commission* (disclosure of information relating to sexual orientation cannot be avoided when requesting certain financial benefits).

[306] Art 27 SR, Art 12(1) CEOS.

[307] GC, Jd Cases T-112/96 and T-115/96, ECLI:EU:T:1999:134, paras 190–92 – *Séché v Commission*; GC, T-361/03, ECLI:EU:T:2005:433, paras 52–54 – *Vanlangendonck v Commission*.

[308] Art 1d(5) SR, not applying in disciplinary proceedings; Dalle-Crode (2008) 52 ff.

[309] Council Directive 2000/43/EC of 29 June 2000 implementing the principle of equal treatment between persons irrespective of racial or ethnic origin [2000] OJ L180/22–26.

[310] Council Directive 2000/78/EC of 27 November 2000 establishing a general framework for equal treatment in employment and occupation [2000] OJ L303/16–22.

Men and women

Full equality in practice between men and women in working life is an essential element to be considered in the implementation of all aspects of the SR.[311] This corresponds to the fundamental right to equality expressed in Articles 21 and 23 FRC. Case-law infers from this provision that the administration is under an obligation to take into account gender-specific considerations regarding equality between men and women as one of the various factors in its decisions. This obligation applies regardless of whether, in an individual case, several persons are actually to be compared in a type of competitive situation, for example when applying for a vacancy.[312] Equality allows for specific advantages that would make it easier for the under-represented sex[313] to pursue a vocational activity, or to prevent or compensate for disadvantages in professional careers. The 2014 reform included an obligation for the institutions to determine[314] measures and actions to promote equal opportunities for men and women, and to redress such de facto inequalities as might hamper opportunities for women in these areas. It is important to note that, in terms of legal protection, an individual cannot directly rely on a right to positive discrimination; instead, the enforcement of the right presupposes general implementation measures. The practical concept of equality between women and men as shaped by case-law shall be further considered in the following case study.

Case Study on Equal Treatment

Absence of equality considerations can justify the annulment of a decision, even if there is no one to compare with

Case C-93/19 P, *EEAS v Hebberecht* of 19 November 2020
Case T-315/17, *Hebberecht v EEAS* of 27 November 2018

In Brief

Equality between men and women must be taken into account as one factor when deciding on the possible extension of a posting in a managerial position. An intriguing feature in this case-law is that equality has to be considered even where there is no choice to be made between several candidates. This strict line of applying the principle of equality between men and women – as an individual right derived directly from Article. 1d SR – is also of relevance in other circumstances. However, positive discrimination that favours the under-represented sex requires a set of general implementing measures in order to be applicable to the individual.

[311] Art 1d(2) SR.
[312] ECJ, C-93/19 P, ECLI:EU:C:2020:946, paras 48, 53 – *EEAS v Hebberecht*, on appeal GC, T-315/17, ECLI:EU:T:2018:842, *Hebberecht v EEAS*; see case study on equal treatment below.
[313] Likewise for persons with disabilities, Art 1d(4) SR; ECJ, C-93/19 P, ECLI:EU:C:2020:946, para 38 – *EEAS v Hebberecht*; CST, F-46/07, ECLI:EU:F:2008:129, paras 181 ff – *Tzirani v Commission*.
[314] Art 1d(3) SR: by agreement, after consulting the Staff Regulations Committee.

Legal Background

Article 1d of the SR provides:

'(1) … any discrimination based on any ground … shall be prohibited'.

(2) 'With a view to ensuring full equality in practice between men and women in working life, which shall be an essential element to be considered in the implementation of all aspects of these Staff Regulations, the principle of equal treatment shall not prevent the institutions … from maintaining or adopting measures providing for specific advantages in order to make it easier for the under-represented sex to pursue a vocational activity or to prevent or compensate for disadvantages in professional careers'.

(3) The appointing authorities of the institutions shall determine … measures and actions to promote equal opportunities for men and women in the areas covered by these Staff Regulations, and shall adopt the appropriate provisions notably to redress such de facto inequalities as hamper opportunities for women in these areas'.

Facts of the Case and Procedure

The applicant was appointed as Head of Delegation in Ethiopia for a four-year term. The rules of a rotation exercise offered the officials of Delegations the possibility to request an early rotation or an extension of posting. Such requests would be granted only in exceptional, duly substantiated cases in the light of the interests of the service. The applicant requested that her posting be extended for a fifth year. The EEAS refused that request, stating, inter alia, that 'in the interests of ensuring regular rotation of Heads of Delegations, a clear policy of rotation after a maximum of four years in the post has generally been implemented'. The applicant challenged this decision at the General Court (GC), which decided in her favour; this was confirmed by the ECJ.

The Arguments of the Parties and the Decisions of the Courts

In front of the GC, the applicant raised three pleas in law: an infringement of the interests and continuity of the service; of the obligation of transparency; and of the principle of equal treatment. The GC rejected the first two pleas as unfounded, likewise an allegation of a discrimination on grounds of race. However, it upheld the plea concerning the measures to be taken in respect of women. The GC pointed out that Article 1d(2) SR not only provides for the adoption of measures by the EU institutions but it states, without prescribing any conditions, that equality between men and women is an 'essential' element to be considered in the implementation of 'all' aspects of the SR. It concluded that, by excluding equality between men and women from the considerations underlying the adoption of the contested decision, the EEAS had infringed Article 1d(2) and (3) SR. The GC found that the contested EEAS decision could have been different if equality between men and women had not, as a matter of principle, been excluded from the assessment of the candidates at the outset.

In its appeal in front of the ECJ, the EEAS argued that the policy of equal opportunities for men and women must be applied at the time of the annual rotation of staff between the EEAS headquarters and the Union Delegations, or between the Union Delegations, when vacancy notices for the positions concerned are published. However, such a policy could 'hardly be applied to decisions extending a term of office, which are by their nature individual decisions for which there is no competition between several candidates'. The EEAS would then be obliged, so it argued, to favour requests from women, irrespective of whether that is in the interests of the service; furthermore, this would amount – in the opinion of the EEAS – to an individual right of the under-represented sex to have her term of office extended.

The ECJ differentiates the two parts of Article 1d(2) SR in the sense that as an individual right, the principle of equality between men and women does not require any implementing measure for its application. However, that is not the case with specific advantages referred to in the second part of Article 1d(2) SR that are intended to make it easier for the under-represented sex to pursue a vocational activity: individual decisions granting specific advantages to make it easier for the under-represented sex to pursue a vocational activity cannot be adopted in the absence of general measures implementing the second part of Article 1d(2) SR. When adopting implementing measures, due regard must be had to the principle of proportionality, which requires that derogations must remain within the limits of what is appropriate and necessary in order to achieve the aim, and that the principle of equal treatment should as far as possible be reconciled with the requirements of the aim thus pursued.[315]

In the absence of measures implementing the second part of Article 1d(2) SR, an institution is not relieved of the obligation to take account of the principle of equality between men and women when adopting an individual decision. This is because – so confirms the ECJ – equality between men and women is an 'essential' element to be considered in the implementation of 'all' aspects of the SR, without that declaration being accompanied by any time limit or condition, and without it being subject to the adoption of measures. The principle of equality, which excludes all discrimination on grounds of sex, is not limited to competitive situations between candidates, but also requires an examination of whether the treatment accorded, in this case to a woman, would have been accorded equally to a man in a comparable situation. When they adopt decisions relating to the organisation of their departments, institutions have to weigh up the various interests at stake, taking into account, inter alia, the principle of equal treatment and the interests of the service.

The ECJ confirms the assessment of the GC, insofar as it cannot be ruled out that considerations relating to equality between men and women might militate in favour of granting the request for extension, with the result that the EEAS was required to take into account, as one factor, the need to ensure equality between men and women. This principle has to be taken into account when adopting an individual decision, even if this decision does not entail a choice between several persons.

Comments

1. It is important to note the two parts of Article 1d(2) SR: (a) the individual right derived from the principle of equality between men and women; and (b) the actions of positive discrimination for the under-represented sex. Actions of positive discrimination

[315] *cf* ECJ, C-173/22 P, ECLI:EU:C:2023:932, paras 52/53 – *MG v EIB*.

presuppose implementing measures for translating them into individual decisions. By contrast, an individual can directly rely upon the principle of equality between men and women, as expressed in the first part of Article 1d (2) SR. The absence of implementing measures does not relieve the institution from having to observe the principle of equality.

2. As Advocate General Kokott has correctly noted, Article 1d SR codifies and reflects Articles 21 and 23 of the Charter of Fundamental Rights (FRC) for the decision-making practice of the appointing authorities. Case-law recognised equal treatment of men and women as an actionable fundamental right very early on.[316]
3. When adopting implementing measures for positive discrimination in favour of the under-represented sex and applying them to the individual case, the principle of proportionality has to be respected.
4. Institutions have broad discretion regarding the adoption of their self-organisational rules. To counterbalance this, the institutions have to follow the procedural safeguards in place for weighing various interests against each other. The judgment shows that an internal organisational rule which calls for administrative decisions to be taken solely on the basis of the interests of the service falls short of the indispensable considerations prescribed by the principle of equality. The weighing process for a decision concerning a woman would thus have to contain an assessment of whether a man would have been treated the same in a comparable situation, and vice versa. It was the a priori exclusion of this weighing process on equality considerations that was sanctioned by the courts.
5. The case at hand only treats the situation of a decision taken in the framework of a rotation exercise, and on the specific question regarding the extension of an assignment in the mobility scheme of the usual four-year posting duration. However, the provision of Article 1d(2) SR in respect of equality between men and women, and in respect of actions of positive discrimination in favour of the under-represented sex, has a much broader scope of application. The ECJ interprets the wording of Article 1d(2) SR in a way that supports this broad scope, and calls for equality to be considered as an 'essential element' in 'all' aspects of the SR. The obligation to consider equality between men and women affects many areas, such as the filling of vacancies, the decision-making process for the extension of contracts of limited duration, and decisions on promotions.
6. It can be deduced that where an institution refuses from the outset to take considerations of equality (gender-specific elements) into account in such situations, the decisions adopted in these circumstances can be liable to annulment in the same way as if other important procedural elements (eg, the reasoning of the decision) were missing.
7. Once annulled, the institution would have to take the decision afresh, this time with the appropriate weighing of the gender-specific elements. This does not mean that the institution must take a different decision regarding the substantive issue (in this instance, the request to extend an assignment).

[316] See chapter 1, III.6.b.

Non-marital partnerships

Non-marital partnerships shall be treated as marriage for the purpose of applying the SR, provided certain conditions[317] are met, Article 1d(1) sentence 2 SR.[318]

b. Social Protection

Another element in the picture of the general rights and duties that are typical for civil servant status is the system of social protection anchored in Article 1e SR, namely the right to measures of a social nature, including specific measures to enable working life to be reconciled with family life, and to services provided by the social welfare bodies of Article 9 SR, ie, the Staff Committee, joint committees, disciplinary boards, joint advisory committees on professional incompetence, the Reports Committee, and the Invalidity Committee. In addition, Article 10 SR provides that a Staff Regulations Committee shall be set up consisting of representatives of the institutions of the Union and an equal number of their Staff Committee representatives. The status of trade unions and staff associations is also recognised by the SR.[319] Former officials may have access to limited specific measures of a social nature. Article 1e SR applies 'by analogy' to temporary agents and contract agents,[320] whereas 'by analogy' means that it is not exactly the same for these types of staff, but 'similar where the circumstances are comparable'.[321] It does not apply to special advisers, nor to accredited parliamentary assistants or local staff.[322]

In terms of content, Article 1e(2) SR guarantees working conditions with appropriate health and safety standards that are at least equivalent to the minimum requirements applicable under the measures adopted in these areas pursuant to the Treaties.[323]

c. Protection against Harassment

Questions relating to harassment and to the protection of staff against harassment are of high practical importance. All staff shall work in an environment free of psychological and sexual harassment.[324] Every staff member is obliged to refrain from harassment. Also parliamentarians (MEPs) are under the obligation to abstain from harassment, as is explicitly stipulated in Article 10(6) of the Parliament's Rules of Procedure.[325] Point 5 of Annex II of the Parliament's Rules of Procedure (Code of Appropriate Behaviour) stipulates that

> Members will cooperate promptly and fully with the procedures in place for managing situations of conflict or harassment (psychological or sexual), including responding promptly to any allegations of harassment. Members should take part in specialised training organised for them on preventing conflict and harassment in the workplace and on good office management.

[317] Art 1(2)(c) Annex VII SR.

[318] Levi, 'Droits fondamentaux et principes généraux de droit de la fonction publique communautaire' in Govaere/Vandersanden (eds), *La fonction publique communautaire* (2008) 83.

[319] Art 24b SR, Art 10b and 10c SR, see chapter 4, II.

[320] Art 10(1) CEOS and Art 80(4) CEOS respectively.

[321] See chapter 2, V.2. at the end.

[322] Currall in Perillo/Giacobbo-Peyronnel (eds), *Statut de la fonction publique de l'Union européenne: Commentaire article par article* (2017) 75.

[323] CST, F-91/08, ECLI:EU:F:2010:13, para 43 – *Pleijte v Commission*; case-law concedes that there is, however, no absolute duty on the institutions to guarantee safety and health of their staff: CST, F-157/12, ECLI:EU:F:2014:164, para 110 – *BN v EP*.

[324] *cf* Art 12a SR; Commission decision of 26 April 2006, C (2006) 1624; CJEU Annual Report 2012, 221 with further references.

[325] RoP in the version of the 9th parliamentary term, November 2023.

The ban on harassing behaviour is also based on the values and principles laid down in the Treaties and Article 31 FRC, which provides that 'every worker has the right to working conditions which respect his or her health, safety and dignity'.[326] The SR (and the other applicable rules) differentiate between two different appearances of harassment: *psychological* and *sexual*.

No retaliation against victim and witness

The SR further state explicitly that the victim of psychological or sexual harassment shall not suffer any prejudicial effects on the part of the institution. Likewise, any member of staff who has given evidence on psychological or sexual harassment shall not suffer any prejudicial effects on the part of the institution, provided the person has acted honestly. The proviso of the witness acting 'honestly' in the last part of the sentence was normatively not considered to be necessary for the victim, because this precondition is already comprised in the status and definition of 'victim'.

Sexual harassment definition

Sexual harassment is defined as 'conduct relating to sex which is unwanted by the person to whom it is directed and which has the purpose or effect of offending that person or creating an intimidating, hostile, offensive or disturbing environment'.[327]

Sexual harassment as discrimination based on gender

The additional sentence in Article 12a(4) SR – but not contained in Article 12a(3) SR on psychological harassment – that '[s]exual harassment shall be treated as discrimination based on gender' is of benefit to the victims of sexual harassment. It honours the insight that identifying sexual harassment and harassment relating to sex as a dignity issue, or labelling them as a health and safety problem, provides insufficient justice: instead, it places the focus on the individual instead of pointing to the systemic discrimination aspect of this form of harassment. Framing sexual harassment instead as *discrimination based on gender* offers the victim procedural and substantive protection, and harmonises with the legal protection standards developed for the Member States under Directive 2006/54,[328] ie, by providing judicial remedies even after the employment relationship has ended; shifting the burden of proof; prohibiting victimisation; establishing the standing of trade unions, NGOs and other legal entities; establishing specialised equality bodies; and most importantly, the no-fault requirement is relevant for the defence against sexual harassment,[329] and is important for enforcing its prohibition The finding of sexual harassment is not subject to the requirement of evidencing any kind of fault or any malicious intent (see below).[330] As is the case in discrimination scenarios, the burden of proof is shifted away from the person harassed; in other words, once the person has established facts from which it may be presumed that there has been sexual harassment, the onus is on the alleged harasser to prove the opposite.

[326] *cf* GC, T-275/17, ECLI:EU:T:2018:479, paras 80/81 – *Curto v EP* and the case study at the end of this section.

[327] Art 12a(3), 12a(4) SR.

[328] *cf* Art 9 and Art 19 of Directive 2006/54/EC of the European Parliament and of the Council of 5 July 2006 on the implementation of the principle of equal opportunities and equal treatment of men and women in matters of employment and occupation (recast) [2006] OJ L204/23–36. Also Council Directive 97/80/EC of 15 December 1997 on the burden of proof in cases of discrimination based on sex [1998] OJ L14/6.

[329] Commission, European equality law review Issue 2/2019, 28/29.

[330] In discrimination cases, the no-fault requirement is also reflected in the use of the terms 'with the purpose or effect' in the relevant definitions of gender equality directives.

Psychological harassment

Psychological harassment is defined as, first, 'any improper conduct that takes place over a period, is repetitive or systematic and involves physical behaviour, spoken or written language, gestures or other acts that are intentional and that may undermine the personality, dignity or physical or psychological integrity of any person'. Psychological harassment must be understood as a process that occurs over time and presupposes the existence of repetitive or continual behaviour which is 'intentional', as opposed to 'accidental'. Secondly, in order to fall under that definition, such physical behaviour, spoken or written language, gestures or other acts must have the effect of undermining the personality, dignity or physical or psychological integrity of a person. A conduct is 'improper' if an impartial and reasonable observer, of normal sensitivity and in the same situation, would consider the behaviour or act in question to be excessive and open to criticism.[331] Judicial review of an alleged harassment is exercised broadly as a *comprehensive* check of the facts in the light of the above-mentioned conditions,[332] instead of a *manifest error of assessment* control only.

Not required: malicious intent

A key feature of the definition of harassment arising from case-law is that its subjective element only requires wilful intent as to the intentional commission of the acts in question, while the *effect of the harassment no longer has to be intended*.[333] The dispute about whether Article 12a(3) SR requires the victim to prove wilful (malicious) intent on the part of the accused person has been decided by the courts, also having recourse to the equal treatment Directive.[334] Malicious intent on the part of the alleged harasser would not be reconcilable with the definition of 'harassment' provided by the Directive.[335]

It is not necessary to establish that the physical behaviour, spoken or written language, gestures or other acts in question were committed with the intention of undermining the personality, dignity or physical or psychological integrity of a person. There can be psychological harassment without it being established that the harasser had any intention to discredit the victim or deliberately impair the latter's working conditions through his conduct. It is sufficient that such conduct, provided that it was intentional, objectively led to such consequences.[336] Evidence that an alleged harasser intended to discredit the victim with his actions or intentionally worsen their working conditions is not required; the mere objective occurrence of such consequences is sufficient. However, despite this facilitation as to the subjective element of harassment, it still remains difficult[337] to prove the existence of psychological harassment, mostly because the improper

[331] GC, T-275/17, ECLI:EU:T:2018:479, para 78 – *Curto v EP*.

[332] 'improper conduct … with the effect of undermining', see case study on harassment below.

[333] GC, T-218/17, ECLI:EU:T:2018:393, para 120 – *HF v EP*; CST, F-71/10, ECLI:EU:F:2012:71, para 89 – *Cantisani v Commission*; CST, F-12/13, ECLI:EU:F:2014:214, para 77 – *CQ v EP*; CST, F-26/09, ECLI:EU:F:2010:17, para 72 – *N v EP*; CST, Jd Cases F-138/06 and F-37/08, ECLI:EU:F:2009:48, para 103 – *Meister v OHIM*. See, however, Gervasoni (2010) 46 *Cahiers de droit européen* 736 with reference to GC, T-154/05, ECLI:EU:T:2007:322 – *Lo Giudice v Commission*. Diamandouros, 'The Perspective of the European Ombudsman' in Govaere/Vandersanden (eds), *La fonction publique communautaire* (2008) 54 emphasises the right of the individual not to be subject to harassment. On harassment as discrimination, see Levi, 'Droits fondamentaux et principes généraux de droit de la function publique communautaire' in Govaere/Vandersanden (eds), *La fonction publique communautaire* (2008) 87. On the obligation of the administration to protect the health of the alleged victim, by thorough enquiry, CST, F-95/09, ECLI:EU:F:2011:9, paras 24 ff – *Scareby v Commission*.

[334] Council Directive 2000/78/EC of 27 November 2000 establishing a general framework for equal treatment in employment and occupation [2000] OJ L303/16.

[335] CST, F-52/05, ECLI:EU:F:2008:161, para 137 – *Q v Commission*.

[336] GC, T-218/17, ECLI:EU:T:2018:393, para 120 – *HF v EP*.

[337] GC, T-592/16, ECLI:EU:T:2017:897 – *HQ v CPVO*.

conduct must have taken place over a certain period of time, repeatedly or systematically, and must have involved physical behaviour,[338] whereas 'repeatedly' does not mean that the harassing conduct is repeated in the same way, but may acknowledge the cumulative effect of various forms of conduct.[339] Case-law may take into account whether the victim of psychological harassment has contributed to the escalation of a dispute.[340]

Procedural aspects

In practical terms, it is of high importance for a victim of harassment (whether psychological or sexual) to preserve any evidence and to seek the institution's assistance by lodging a *formal request for assistance under Article 24 SR* in a timely manner.[341] Structurally and strategically of great significance, the request for assistance is the way to involve the appointing authority and thus invoke the obligations of the institution towards the staff employed, in order to be able to draw on and enforce these rights.

Investigations

The request can lead into preliminary investigations that would take place before a decision on disciplinary proceedings is taken.[342] Most EU institutions have informal anti-harassment procedures in place to determine if formal investigation and disciplinary proceedings shall be started. An important aspect in this context is the protection both of an appropriate level of confidentiality and of the rights of the defence of the alleged harasser.[343] Although an investigation panel entrusted with such a task cannot be equated with a 'tribunal' in the sense of Article 47 FRC (with the consequence that complainants cannot rely on the fair trial provision in order to be heard),[344] the alleged victim of harassment is able to rely on the right to be heard during the investigation as derived from the principle of good administration.[345]

[338] CST, F-41/10 RENV, ECLI:EU:F:2012:135, para 188 – *Bermejo Garde v EESC*. A single measure (dismissal) is not sufficient to qualify as harassment, CST, F-2/09, ECLI:EU:F:2010:12, paras 67 ff, 70 ff – *Menghi v ENISA* (discreditation in front of others), CST, F-26/09, ECLI:EU:F:2010:17, paras 72 ff – *N v EP*, nor do supposed 'jokes' alone qualify, as long as they are stopped on request, CST, F-61/06, ECLI:EU:F:2008:98, para 106 – *Sapara v Eurojust*. Further not qualifying as harassment: the appointing authority expresses objective criticism (also if expressed towards third parties), CST, F-15/07, ECLI:EU:F:2008:158, para 38 – *K v EP*), critical assessment (CST, F-49/08, ECLI:EU:F:2009:76, para 136 – *Giannini v Commission*, or other unfavourable statements as long as they are based on precise factual findings in content and tone and do not reveal personal animosity or manifestly excessive or inappropriate value judgements (CST, F-1/09, ECLI:EU:F:2009:155, para 84 – *Putterie-De-Beukelaer v Commission*). Other aspects in CST, F-2/09, ECLI:EU:F:2010:12, paras 79, 87, 89, 94, 97 – *Menghi v ENISA* and in CST, F-26/09, ECLI:EU:F:2010:17, paras 77, 80 – *N v EP*. On invoking harassment in the event of dismissal due to insufficient performance, see CJEU Annual Report 2012, 221 with reference to CST, F-113/10, ECLI:EU:F:2012:20, para 73 ff – *AT v EACEA*; CST, F-124/10, ECLI:EU:F:2013:21, para 75 – *Vassiliki Labiri v EESC*. On the refusal of an institution to move an official temporarily to another post, in the context of a request for assistance based on an allegation of psychological harassment, the harmful consequences for the presumed victim and compensation for the non-material damage (€10,000) suffered, CST, F-52/05 RENV, ECLI:EU:F:2012:139, para 27 – *Q v Commission*. Reithmann (2014) *EuR* 116.

[339] GC, T-377/17, ECLI:EU:T:2018:478 – *SQ v EIB*; see case study on harassment below.

[340] CST, Jd Cases F-138/06 and F-37/08, ECLI:EU:F:2009:48, para 130 – *Meister v OHIM* (insulting criticism on the occasion of institutional reorganisation measures).

[341] See the following case study and sections II.9.d., 9.e. below.

[342] See section II.20. below.

[343] On personal data protection in harassment procedures, see the 'Guidelines concerning the processing of personal data during the selection of confidential counsellors and the informal procedures for cases of harassment in European institutions and bodies' by the European Data Protection Supervisor of 2011, available at: edps.europa.eu/sites/default/files/publication/11-02-18_harassment_guidelines_en.pdf.

[344] ECJ, C-558/17 P, ECLI:EU:C:2019:289, paras 47–49 – *OZ v EIB*, referring to ECJ, C-64/16, ECLI:EU:C:2018:117, para 38 – *Associação Sindical dos Juízes Portugueses*.

[345] ibid, *OZ v EIB*, para 50.

For contesting an act adopted by the appointing authority after having lodged a request for assistance, the alleged victim will need to evidence that he or she is adversely affected, which could be the case, for instance:

- By the administration's refusal to investigate the alleged harassment.
- By concluding the investigation to the dissatisfaction of the alleged victim.[346]
- By not disclosing the non-confidential parts of the investigation report to the alleged victim of harassment.[347]
- By not respecting the right to be heard of the alleged victim in the course of the investigation against an alleged harasser.[348]

Whether the claimed harassment actually exists is to be determined by its objective reality, along the mentioned characterisation of the behaviour in question as 'improper': whether an impartial and reasonable observer, endowed with normal sensitivity and placed in the same conditions, would consider the behaviour excessive and open to criticism.[349] The investigation report must not leave open the question of whether harassment objectively took place.[350]

Retaliation

When staff members who consider themselves to be the victims of harassment and challenge an act adopted by the administration in an action for annulment of that act, by claiming an alleged measure of *retaliation*, the persons concerned must adduce at least prima facie evidence that the contested decision constitutes, entirely or in part, a retaliatory measure against them.[351]

Case Study on Psychological Harassment

When psychological harassment occurs and the person concerned requests assistance, the employing authority has to act appropriately within reasonable time. Otherwise, the staff member may be entitled to damages

Case T-275/17, *Curto v Parliament* of 13 July 2018
Case T-377/17, *SQ v EIB* of 13 July 2018

[346] CST, F-124/10, ECLI:EU:F:2013:21, para 57 – *Vassiliki Labiri v EESC.*

[347] GC, T-65/19, ECLI:EU:T:2021:454, para 169 – *AI v ECDC.*

[348] This presupposes that the statements made by the person accused of harassment and the various witnesses heard is disclosed to this person, who is thus put in a position effectively to submit observations before the investigation is completed, or at least before a decision is taken, ECJ, C-558/17 P, ECLI:EU:C:2019:289, paras 59/60 – *OZ v EIB* (breach of Art 41 FRC); this was differently decided at first instance by the GC, T-607/16, ECLI:EU:T:2017:495, paras 53/54 – *OZ v EIB* which held that the administrative authority has to undertake a balancing exercise between the right of the person who is the subject of the complaint to exercise his/her rights of defence and the right of the complainant to have the complaint examined properly. The GC found that authority's duty of confidentiality allowed to refuse the hearing of the alleged victim and the disclosure of statements of witnesses.

[349] CST, F-124/10, ECLI:EU:F:2013:21, para 67 – *Vassiliki Labiri v EESC.*

[350] ibid, paras 73/74.

[351] CST, F-157/12, ECLI:EU:F:2014:164, para 67 – *BN v EP*; GC, T-613/21, ECLI:EU:T:2023:739, paras 126–28, 149 – *XH v Commission.*

In Brief

The duty of the employing authority to provide assistance to a staff member implies that a request for assistance will be handled reasonably fast. In the two cases above, the General Court (GC) ordered the European Parliament (EP) and the European Investment Bank (EIB) to pay €10,000 each to staff members who had suffered psychological harassment. The GC confirms its jurisprudence on what constitutes 'psychological harassment' and clarifies the scope of its powers of judicial review and of the duties of institutions to initiate disciplinary proceedings in cases of psychological harassment.

Facts

In Case T-275/17,[352] *Curto, a* Member of Parliament (MEP) requested the appointing authority to terminate the contract of her assistant (the applicant of the case) by stating that without seeking permission, the assistant had not come to work for one week. The assistant submitted a request for assistance by the EP (Art 24 SR) and reported that the MEP had insulted her with humiliating and scornful language, threats and insults.

In Case T-377/17,[353] *SQ v EIB*, the applicant claimed that a director had removed her from a position of responsibility without due cause, that he had belittled her, had spoken to her inappropriately, aggressively, disdainfully and accusingly, had withheld certain information, had failed to provide her with feedback on her performance at work, and had treated her unfavourably compared with other individuals. The EIB requested the Director to apologise to the staff member and stated that if a new complaint against him was made during the following three years, the appointing authority would initiate a disciplinary procedure against him. The EIB informed the staff member that the procedure had to 'remain strictly confidential', including within the institution itself.

The General Court's Decisions

The GC confirmed the definition of 'psychological harassment':

Article 12a(3) SR defines psychological harassment as 'improper conduct' with the following two cumulative qualifications:

1. The term covers improper conduct in the form of physical behaviour, spoken or written language, gestures or other acts, which take place over a period and are repetitive or systematic, suggesting that psychological harassment must be understood as a process that occurs over time and presupposes the existence of repetitive or continual behaviour which is intentional, as opposed to accidental.
2. Such physical behaviour, spoken or written language, gestures or other acts must have the effect of undermining the personality, dignity or physical or psychological integrity of a person.

The GC *comprehensively reviews* the facts concerning the two above-mentioned conditions. In *Curto*, the Court decided that an MEP is required to have due regard for the dignity and health of the assistants. The nature and, in particular, the singular vulgarity

[352] GC, T-275/17, ECLI:EU:T:2018:479 – *Curto v EP*.
[353] GC, T-377/17, ECLI:EU:T:2018:478 – *SQ v EIB*.

of the language that the MEP used with her assistant constitute belittlement, both of the assistant herself and of her work. The GC accepted neither the closeness of the MEP's relationship with her assistant nor the tense atmosphere as justifications for the MEP's behaviour. The request for assistance (including the administrative enquiry) was not handled appropriately by the EP, because it took too long to be acted on. The GC therefore awarded €10,000 in damages to the assistant.

In *SQ v EIB*, the GC considered that the definition of 'psychological harassment' does not require that the harassing conduct is repeated in the same way. The *cumulative effect* of the other kinds of conduct that could undermine the self-esteem and self-confidence of the person affected by that conduct also has to be taken into account. In *SQ v EIB*, the EIB had failed to examine whether each of the Director's alleged acts could, in conjunction with the other alleged acts, have objectively resulted in undermining the administrator's self-esteem and confidence.

The GC found that the EIB had adopted an insufficient measure when it stated that disciplinary proceedings would be initated against the Director only if there was further inappropriate conduct within a three-year period. If action needs to be taken, it has to be immediate. The EIB was also incorrect in making the statement about repeated reprehensible conduct dependent on whether the harassed staff member decided to file a complaint. Finally, the GC decided that the EIB had no right to impose a condition of confidentiality on its decision, which amounted to prohibiting the disclosure of the existence and nature of the events to third parties. It awarded damages of €10,000 against the EIB for having unjustifiably imposed an obligation of silence on the harassed person.

Comments

1. The institution has to take its duty to provide assistance seriously. A practical prerequisite for this is that the harassed staff member is actually and in a timely fashion turning to the appointing authority in order to request assistance (Art 24 SR). On receiving the request, the administration is not supposed to make light of the improper behaviour or delay countermeasures.
2. The second case (*SQ v EIB*) illustrates that the authority must not issue gagging orders (ie, unjustifiably impose silence on the victim). Otherwise, the harassed person could not even make use of the information or documents to claim damages against the harasser in a national court. It would run counter to the goal of preventing and penalising all instances of psychological harassment within the institutions.
3. The following four counter-arguments or strategies on the part of the administration when its attention is drawn to alleged psychological harassment are not valid defences:
   a. The harassing behaviour towards the other colleague (and subsequent inaction by the employing authority) cannot be justified by the claim that the two persons are 'close to each other' or that there is a 'tense atmosphere' at work.
   b. It is not permissible to split harassing behaviour and only have regard to each single act. The acts that form harassment do not need to be repeated in the same way, but can consist in various *different* acts which, taken together, constitute psychological harassment.

   c. If there is harassment, not taking action or deferring action to future repetitions, is not an option.
   d. The employing authority must not impose an obligation of confidentiality on the victim.
4. The failure to handle an occurrence of psychological harassment in a timely way not only hampers the ability of an institution to fulfil its mandate, but can lead to serious health problems for staff, even to the point of causing invalidity of the staff member and the emergence of occupational diseases. Medical conditions generated by psychological harassment can be equivalent in severity to other illnesses, such as those caused by accidents.[354]

d. *The Duty of Care*

The duty of care is a central concept in EU civil service law.[355] The employer is obliged to have regard for the welfare of the officials.[356] The duty of care reflects, but does not modify, the balance of reciprocal rights and duties[357] that the SR have established in the relationship between the institution (represented by the appointing authority) and its officials.[358] It is not possible to derive a right from it that would conflict with the SR; more exactly, an official cannot rely on the duty to have regard for his welfare to obtain advantages which he cannot be granted under the SR.[359] It is possible that a breach of the duty of care may be healed in the course of the procedure.[360]

The duty of care can affect every aspect of the civil service employment relationship.[361] In particular, the appointing authority must, when taking decisions concerning the official, take into account not only the interests of the service, but also that of the official concerned.[362]

[354] On invalidity, occupational diseases and accidents, see section V. below.

[355] Overview: Reithmann, *Die dienstrechtliche Fürsorgepflicht in der Rechtsprechung des Gerichts für den öffentlichen Dienst der Europäischen Union* (2019); Livolsi, 'Le devoir de sollicitude dans le contentieux récent de la fonction publique de l'Union européenne' (2014) *Revue des affaires européennes* (*Law & European Affairs*) 369–82.

[356] General: Potvin-Solis/Lelièvre (2011) *RUE* 270 with reference to CST, F-25/07, ECLI:EU:F:2010:163, para 119 – *Bleser v ECJ*; CST, F-50/09 ECLI:EU:F:2011:55, para 220 – *Missir Mamachi de Lusignano v Commission*, and appeal decision GC, T-401/11 P, ECLI:EU:T:2014:625, para 53; CST, F-8/10, ECLI:EU:F:2010:151, para 76 – *Gheysens v Council*; CST, F-92/09, ECLI:EU:F:2010:140, para 64 – *U v EP*.

[357] CST, F-35/07, ECLI:EU:F:2008:150, para 67 – *Klug v EMEA*; CST, F-63/07, ECLI:EU:F:2009:18, para 39 – *Patsarika v Cedefop*.

[358] CST, F-73/07, ECLI:EU:F:2008:42, paras 41, 80 – *Doktor v Council*; GC, T-81/96, ECLI:EU:T:1997:111, para 91 – *Apostolidis and Others v Commission*.

[359] GC, T-67/99, ECLI:EU:T:2000:169, paras 68/69 – *K v Commission*; CST, F-73/07, ECLI:EU:F:2008:42, paras 43, 80 – *Doktor v Council*; CST, F-76/06, ECLI:EU:F:2007:193, para 48 – *Tsirimokos v EP*.

[360] CST, F-83/06, ECLI:EU:F:2008:165, paras 107/108 – *Schell v Commission*.

[361] Levi, 'Droits fondamentaux et principes généraux de droit de la fonction publique communautaire' in Govaere/Vandersanden (eds), *La fonction publique communautaire* (2008) 90 ff, 96; Mader, *Verteidigungsrechte* (2006) 197 ff, on adversarial proceedings, equality of arms (*cf* in competition law: GC, T-36/91, ECLI:EU:T:1995:118 – *ICI v Commission*), right to have legal counsel, presumption of innocence, access to personal files; see also, Gervasoni (2010) 46 *Cahiers de droit européen* 776. Reithmann (2008) *EuR* 294; (2009) *EuR* 818; (2011) *EuR* 122 and 137; CST, F-23/05, ECLI:EU:F:2007:75, paras 149, 180 – *Giraudy v Commission* (failed to reply after violent attacks by the press), on this Van Raepenbusch, 'L'apport jurisprudentiel du Tribunal de la fonction publique de l'Union européenne' in Govaere/Vandersanden (eds), *La fonction publique communautaire* (2008) 159; CST, F-21/06, ECLI:EU:F:2007:116, para 80 – *Da Silva v Commission*; CST, F-92/09, ECLI:EU:F:2010:140, paras 83, 85 – *U v EP* (dismissal of a civil servant based on Art 51 SR without clarifying the state of mental health).

[362] GC, T-709/19, ECLI:EU:T:2021:389, para 91 – *GW v ECA*; ECJ, C-591/19 P, ECLI:EU:C:2021:468, para 61 – *Commission v De Esteban Alonso*; GC, T-432/18, ECLI:EU:T:2019:749, para 60 – *Palo v Commission*; CST, F-67/15,

The obligations arising for the administration from the duty of care are substantially enhanced where it may appear that an official's physical or mental health is shown to be affected.[363] The medical service of an institution, especially where its attention is drawn to the allegedly harmful consequences that an administrative decision might have for the health of the person, has to ascertain the reality and the extent of the risks referred to and inform the appointing authority of the result of its examination. Known or stated health problems must be taken into account in the decision.[364] The protection of the rights and interests of officials is bounded by compliance with the applicable rules (SR), and reliance on an institution's duty to have regard for the welfare of its staff can therefore never lead to the infringement of a legislative rule. Likewise, an internal decision of general application that places strict limits on the institution's exercise of its discretion when applying the SR may not lead to a disrespect of the duty of care.[365]

If the official is adversely affected by the behaviour of other officials or third parties, the appointing authority must take appropriate measures to remedy an unlawful situation with sufficient solicitude[366] and speed.[367] For example, decisions about a promotion, an appraisal,[368] a medical assessment,[369] disciplinary proceedings[370] or the award of merit points[371] must be made within a reasonable time.[372]

The appointing authority's duty of care towards its employees does not prevent it from cooperating with the criminal prosecution authorities of the Member States, provided that the interests of the service are not violated and constitutional guarantees are not circumvented. Where OLAF passes on intelligence stemming from its investigation to national prosecution authorities, such disclosure cannot be challenged by the official concerned, because it is not considered to be an act adversely affecting the person.[373]

The Covid-19 pandemic called for a special application of the duty of care for the physical, mental and social health of all employees (see subsequent case study). Social segregation was one of the primary non-pharmacological interventions for combating the pandemic. Whether a right to telework or to work in a home office during the pandemic can be derived from the duty of care has not yet been fully clarified. This will be mostly answered in the affirmative, considering the exceptional situation during the pandemic; the weighing of interests in individual cases should take personal and family circumstances into account.[374]

ECLI:EU:F:2016:153 – *Opreana v Commission*; CST, F-26/09, ECLI:EU:F:2010:17, para 91 – *N v EP*; CST, F-47/09, ECLI:EU:F:2010:36, para 65 – *Fries Guggenheim v Cedefop*.

[363] CST, F-62/10, ECLI:EU:F:2011:141, para 80 – *Esders v Commission*.

[364] GC, T-298/20, ECLI:EU:T:2022:671, para 121 – *KD v EUIPO*; GC, T-431/18, EU:T:2019:781, para 106 – *WN v EP*.

[365] CST, F-62/10, ECLI:EU:F:2011:141, para 81 – *Esders v Commission*.

[366] CST, F-43/06, ECLI:EU:F:2007:162, para 111 – *Talvela v Commission*.

[367] CST, F-52/05 RENV, ECLI:EU:F:2012:139, para 31 – *Q v Commission*; CST, F-52/05, ECLI:EU:F:2007:165, para 205 – *Q v Commission*; CST, Jd Cases F-138/06 and F-37/08, ECLI:EU:F:2009:48, paras 73/74 – *Meister v OHIM*.

[368] GC, T-274/04, ECLI:EU:T:2005:442 – *Rounis v Commission*; GC, T-181/00, ECLI:EU:T:2002:313, para 130 – *Carmelo Morello v Commission*; CST, F-4/13, ECLI:EU:F:2014:263 – *Cwik v Commission*.

[369] CST, F-111/12, ECLI:EU:F:2013:140 – *Nardone v Commission*.

[370] CST, Jd Cases F-124/05 and F-96/06, ECLI:EU:F:2010:2, para 233 – *A and G v Commission*; CST, F-46/11, ECLI:EU:F:2013:115 – *Tzirani v Commission*.

[371] CST, F-65/11, ECLI:EU:F:2012:34 – *Schönberger v EP*.

[372] Mader (2013) *CritV/CritQ/RCrit* 154, 160/161.

[373] GC, T-261/09 P, ECLI:EU:T:2010:215, paras 46 ff, 73 – *Commission v Violetti and Others*, repealing CST, F-5/05 and F-7/05, ECLI:EU:F:2009:39, para 78 – *Violetti and Others v Commission*; Mader (2018) *EuR* 339, 351/352; ECJ, C-615/19 P, ECLI:EU:C:2021:133 – *Dalli*.

[374] Interim order GC, T-12/21 R, ECLI:EU:T:2021:184 – *PJ v EIT* (here, however, the special case of ordering telework from the place of origin of the employees, where the family is located, ie, contrary to the rule of Art 20 SR).

Case Study on the Duty of Care

Covid-19 pandemic: Telework at place of origin

Case T-12/21 R, *PJ v EIT* of 13 April 2021

In Brief

The interim measure handed down by the General Court (GC) ordered that the European Institute of Innovation and Technology (EIT) in Budapest has to allow the applicant to perform telework from her place of origin in Germany until the restrictions linked to the health crisis imposed by the authorities in Germany and Hungary are lifted. She remained obliged to visit her duty station ad hoc for reasons relating to the interests of the service. The GC explicitly orders the interim measure to be applied, namely to allow telework from Germany. This is substantially justified by the EIT's duty of care for the applicant, also taking into account her personal and family situation. This order of interim measures was of relevance for staff who sought to work from their places of origin during the pandemic, and who could justify this by their personal/family situation.

Facts of the Case and Procedure

The applicant was a temporary agent of the EIT, where she was Head of Unit and part of the EIT Management Team. Her place of employment and usual residence was in Budapest, but at weekends she has regularly travelled to Cologne, which is her place of origin and where her children of minor age and her spouse permanently reside. Since the beginning of the Covid-19 pandemic, the EIT has adopted a number of measures in accordance with the policy of the European Commission. The instructions included, in particular, the implementation of general teleworking. After a number of changes to the rules, including permanent telework and a weekly rotation system, staff were ordered to do their teleworking *at the duty station*, namely Budapest. The EIT laid down that telework from abroad can only be authorised exceptionally, for example in the case of a separated family. The application of this exception allows a staff member whose spouse, partner or children permanently reside in another Member State to telecommute from abroad to be with their family. Line managers had to ensure that there were no negative consequences on staff performance. The applicant requested to work from abroad and relied in particular on the existence of travel restrictions, closure of schools and quarantine requirements in Germany, which did not allow her to be in contact with her family on her return, as well as on the high risks relating to travel. This request was refused with the arguments that permanent telework was not possible, that several tasks required the physical presence of the applicant, and that her absence could be prejudicial to the management of her team. The applicant brought an action for annulment against the decision in which the Director of the EIT refused her request for teleworking from her place of origin; she also filed an application for interim relief.

The Decision of the Court

With its order of 13 April 2021, the President of the General Court first decided to suspend the decision of the Director of the EIT who refused the applicant permission to telework from her place of origin (Cologne). Secondly, the President of the General Court ordered that the EIT will authorise the applicant to telework from the place of residence of her children (Cologne) for as long as the situation relating to the Covid-19 pandemic warrants it, and without prejudice to her obligation to visit her duty station (Budapest) for reasons relating to the interests of the service.

The Arguments of the Parties and the Reasoning of the Court

The GC describes the preconditions for suspending the application of a contested act (Art 278 TFEU), and for interim measures (Art 279 TFEU). First, if a decision only denies the desired act (a negative administrative measure), the suspension of its application is in principle inadmissible, because it cannot have the effect of modifying the applicant's situation. Secondly, interim measures are ancillary to the main proceedings, and they must not fall outside the framework of the final decision likely to be taken by the GC in the main proceedings. The GC states that in exceptional circumstances, and in order to ensure effective judicial protection, interim measures may anticipate the possible consequences that the administration would have to draw from an annulment judgment.

As to the merits of the request for interim measures, the GC tests the precondition of a '*fumus boni juris*', which means that at least one of the pleas relied on appears, at first glance, to have a substantive foundation. This is the case when one of these pleas reveals the existence of an important legal or factual dispute whose resolution is not immediately clear and therefore merits a detailed examination (which must be the subject of the main proceedings on the merits). The applicant claimed a failure to comply with the obligation to balance the interests of the service against her interests in accordance with the duty of care. She stated that the Director of the EIT had not taken into account the circumstances which she had invoked, and never explained to her the real, concrete and legitimate reasons which would prevent her from teleworking from abroad. She expressed her willingness to travel and work at the EIT premises if she was informed in advance of an important meeting justifying her presence there. The applicant alleged that the contested decision constituted an infringement of her right to private and family life provided for in Article 7 FRC, taking into account the rights of the child under Article 24 FRC, as well as her right to fair working conditions, Article 31 FRC.

In the opinion of the GC it was acceptable for the applicant to base her arguments relating to health measures during the Covid-19 pandemic on the assumption that Commission rules apply by analogy to the EIT, instead of referring to rules adopted by the EIT. The GC notes that the main dispute raises a novel and delicate question relating to the interpretation of the obligation of residence at the place of employment arising from Article 20 SR in the particular circumstances imposed by the Covid-19 pandemic. The GC states a reminder that the institutions have wide discretion in the organisation of their services and the organisation of the working conditions of their staff in accordance with the constraints imposed by the health situation, but that the exercise of this power must be carried out in accordance with the duty of care. This principle reflects the balance of rights and reciprocal obligations that the SR have created in the relations between the public authority and public service officials. The balance implies the authority also taking into account the interests of the agent concerned. Interim measures require not only a '*fumus boni juris*' but also urgency. Urgency means a need for a provisional ruling in order to avoid serious and irreparable damage being caused to the party requesting the claim.

The EIT argued that the applicant had not demonstrated damage attributable to the application of the contested decision. She had signed an employment contract by which she accepted that her place of employment is in Budapest and in this regard notably benefits from a expatriation allowance. The constraints concerning the applicant's possible trips were closely linked to her personal choice to work in Budapest without her family, the consequences of which were temporarily exacerbated by the pandemic. The GC refuses the argumentation of the EIT that the situation was due to a 'personal choice' of the applicant, stating that the EIT had put in place rules to adapt to the pandemic situation using a case-by-case assessment. When these rules are applied to the applicant's particular situation, her ability to maintain regular contact with her children is at risk of being compromised – a contact she had managed to maintain before the pandemic despite the distance between her place of employment and the place of residence of her family.

Finally, the GC balances the risks associated with each of the possible solutions of the interim proceedings: whether or not the interests of the party seeking interim measures in obtaining the suspension of the execution of the contested act prevails over the interests of its immediate application. The balance of interests tilts in favour of the applicant.

The EIT – so states the GC – did not put forward any argument of an administrative or pecuniary nature, based in particular on the expatriation or other allowance, that was aimed at demonstrating the negative impact that the granting of a possible interim measure could have on the proper functioning and organisation of the service. However, it cannot be excluded that the applicant's presence at her place of employment for important meetings on site may be necessary and justified in the interests of the service.

Comments

1. In its order on interim measures of *PJ v EIT*,[375] the GC took a decision in favour of the applicant's request to telework from her place of origin (Germany), where she can be with her partner and children. This is, in essence, based on the *duty of care* of the EIT towards the applicant and her obligations vis-à-vis her family.
2. It does not become fully clear from the order to what extent these conclusions are all drawn from the *duty of care* or also from Article 7 FRC (right to family life), or from the other Charter rights quoted (Arts 24, 31 FRC). An institution has to protect the health and security of its staff.[376] The Covid-19 pandemic provides an evident scenario for the need of health protection measures in favour of all staff. In the case at hand, the GC balanced the interests of the service and the interests of the agent in the context of the Covid-19 pandemic, and concluded that the *duty of care* embraces measures of greater care and support measures to respond to personal situations that entail special difficulties for the staff. Presumably, it will be hard to separate a personal situation from the family situation of that same person. Therefore, the concept of the *duty of care* might include protective measures relating to the family situation of an applicant.[377] An argument in its favour would be that a complete separation of the personal situation (physical, mental and social health) of a staff member from his

[375] GC, T-12/21 R, ECLI:EU:T:2021:184, para 35 – *PJ v EIT*.

[376] CST, F-157/12, ECLI:EU:F:2014:164, para 107 – *BN v EP*; ECJ, C-84/94, ECLI:EU:C:1996:431, para 15 – *UK v Council*.

[377] The GC has not elaborated on this (neither on Art 20 SR regarding the obligation of residence of an official at the place of employment), because the case was amicably settled: GC, T-12/21, ECLI:EU:T:2021:563 – *PJ v EIT*.

family situation would be unnatural: on the contrary, the family situation has a major impact on all these health aspects.

3. The order not only suspends the application of the contested decision of the EIT, but specifically prescribes the interim measures for the EIT to adopt: namely to allow the applicant to telework from her place of origin. Although this is rare, one has to bear in mind that – fully in line with earlier case-law – the judge hearing an application for interim relief (Art 279 TFEU) has powers whose impact vis-à-vis the institutions of the European Union goes beyond the effects of a judgment annulling a measure, provided that those interim measures apply only for the duration of the main proceedings, do not prejudge the decision on the main application, and do not undermine the practical effect of that decision.[378]
4. The interim measure somehow produced the final result whereby it ordered that the telework shall be practically allowed up to the end of the pandemic situation. Effective judicial protection warrants the GC providing for an explicit order that the applicant is allowed to telework from her place of origin.
5. Subsequent case-law clarified that the administrative measure to suspend payment of the expatriation allowance (Art 4 Annex VII SR) for staff working from home during the pandemic was illegal. Article 20 SR on the obligation of residence of an official has to be read in conjunction with Article 55 SR, according to which officials in active employment shall at all times be at the disposal of their institution. The GC argued that the need to maintain residence and thus the need to receive the expatriation allowance serving to entertain the residence persists also in times of obligatory home office working; furthermore, the SR do not foresee a legal basis for suspending payment of the expatriation allowance.[379]

e. *Request for Assistance – Duty to Provide Assistance*

Assistance and compensation for damage

Article 24 SR obliges the institution to provide assistance to officials and protect them – ex officio[380] – against 'threats, insulting or defamatory acts or utterances, or any attack to person or property to which he or a member of his family is subjected by reason of his position or duties'.[381] It shall compensate for the damage suffered as a result.[382] The compensation comes with two caveats: (1) the damage suffered by the official must not have been caused intentionally or through gross negligence of the official; and (2) the official has been unable to obtain compensation from the person who caused that damage under national law. The admissibility of an action for compensation brought by an official under Article 24(2) SR against the institution is thus

[378] GC, T-198/12 R, ECLI:EU:T:2013:245, para 33 – *Germany v Commission.*

[379] GC, T-39/21, ECLI:EU:T:2023:204, paras 100–08 – *PP and Others v EP.*

[380] ECJ, 229/84, ECLI:EU:C:1986:241 – *Sommerlatte v Commission* (preservation of pension rights vis-à-vis Member States); ECJ, 128/75, ECLI:EU:C:1976:139 – *N v Commission.*

[381] Not against attacks that are attributable to the private sphere of those affected, such as a community crèche, GC, T-67/99, ECLI:EU:T:2000:169 – *K v Commission.*

[382] Art 24(2) SR.

subject to the exhaustion of domestic legal remedies insofar as these provide effective protection for the individuals concerned and can result in reparation of the damage alleged.[383]

Multilateral constellations

Though the duty to provide assistance (also duty to assist) to its staff is an obligation of the appointing authority, it does not primarily exist as a bilateral relationship between the appointing authority[384] and the individual civil servant, but rather as a triangular relationship aimed at protection against attacks committed by third parties, as well as by other staff, superiors and colleagues.[385] The duty to assist does not merely apply in cases of the delayed processing of requests[386] or unreasonable internal organisational measures[387] by the appointing authority. But it does apply where the assistance of the appointing authority is indispensable for the enforcement of rights under the SR against third parties.[388] It is not a prerequisite that the conduct of the third party has already been found to be unlawful by a court, but it must reasonably be seen as an attack on the rights of officials.[389] In particular, in the event of an incident which is incompatible with the good order and smooth running of the service, the administration must intervene with all necessary vigour and respond with the rapidity and solicitude required by the circumstances of the case so as to ascertain the facts and, having done so, to take the appropriate action with full knowledge of the matter.[390] Such action could, for example, be to initiate investigations,[391] or to keep the individuals involved away from each other.[392] If the official seeks assistance against criminal accusations in the press, the institution's failure to provide assistance does not violate the presumption of innocence.[393]

European Parliament and involvement of Members

A specific and frequent constellation concerns the EP (though this can, *mutatis mutandis*, apply to other institutions, too): where the person against whom allegations have been made is an MEP, the EP's administration does not have the power to initiate disciplinary proceedings against him or her. That is why, in its internal rules, the EP conferred on the President of the European Parliament the powers held by the AECE as regards disciplinary measures against Members. The President has to hear the Member if he intends to discipline him or her.[394] However, the

[383] CST, F-71/10, ECLI:EU:F:2012:71, paras 130 ff – *Cantisani v Commission*; CST, F-58/10, ECLI:EU:F:2012:130, para 82 – *Allgeier v FRA*.

[384] GC, T-61/18, ECLI:EU:T:2019:217 – *Rodriguez v Commission*.

[385] GC, T-154/05, ECLI:EU:T:2007:322, para 135 – *Lo Giudice v Commission*; CST, F-35/07, ECLI:EU:F:2008:150, para 73 – *Klug v EMEA*; CST, F-2/09, ECLI:EU:F:2010:12, para 128 – *Menghi v ENISA*. General on the obligation to provide assistance, CST, F-50/09 ECLI:EU:F:2011:55, paras 221 ff – *Missir Mamachi de Lusignano v Commission*, judgment set aside on another point of law; Van Raepenbusch, 'L'apport jurisprudentiel du Tribunal de la fonction publique de l'Union européenne' (2008) 168, and Levi, 'Droits fondamentaux et principes généraux de droit de la fonction publique communautaire' in Govaere/Vandersanden (eds), *La fonction publique communautaire* (2008) 88, criticise an alleged lack of will on the part of the administration to provide quick and effective assistance.

[386] ECJ, 115/76, ECLI:EU:C:1978:67 – *Leonardini v Commission*.

[387] ECJ, 124/78, ECLI:EU:C:1979:192 – *List v Commission*; ECJ, 111/86, ECLI:EU:C:1987:562– *Delauche v Commission*.

[388] ECJ, C-137/88, ECLI:EU:C:1990:69 – *Schneemann and Others v Commission*, and Opinion GA Tesauro, C-137/88, ECLI:EU:C:1989:586 – *Schneemann and Others v Commission*.

[389] CST, F-115/05, ECLI:EU:F:2007:10 – *Vienne and Others v EP*; CST, F-3/06, ECLI:EU:F:2007:13 – *Frankin and Others v Commission*.

[390] GC, T-275/17, ECLI:EU:T:2018:479, para 97 – *Curto v EP*; see also, GC, T-377/17, ECLI:EU:T:2018:478 – *SQ v EIB*.

[391] CST, Jd Cases F-138/06 and F-37/08, ECLI:EU:F:2009:48, paras 73/74 – *Meister v OHIM*.

[392] See CST, F-52/05 RENV, ECLI:EU:F:2012:139, para 31 – *Q v Commission*, issued according to GC, T-80/09 P, ECLI:EU:T:2011:347, para 100 – *Commission v Q*. Distance can, eg, be achieved by assigning other tasks.

[393] See Art 6(2) ECHR; CST, F-75/09, ECLI:EU:F:2010:150, paras 60–63 – *Wenig v Commission*.

[394] Art 12(1) of the Decision of the Bureau of the Parliament of 14 April 2014, later decision of 2 July 2018.

administration still has the power to adopt any measure directly concerning the staff member requesting assistance.[395] As the Court held, the delegation of that power regarding disciplinary measures to the President *cannot result in the AECE being deprived of its discretion* in adopting the measures that it is required to take, as part of its duty to provide assistance, in the light of the results of the enquiry. It is for the AECE to assess whether the allegations of a staff member are substantiated with sufficient prima facie evidence (see below), in which case it is for it to take the necessary measures, in particular to conduct an administrative enquiry, with the cooperation of the staff member requesting assistance, to determine the facts which gave rise to that request.[396]

Refusal of assistance

The refusal of assistance can be challenged as an act adversely affecting the official; under certain circumstances, the mere delay in providing assistance can be challenged.[397] The person seeking assistance has to be heard appropriately before the request for assistance may be rejected.[398] The person has the right of access to the (anonymised) file under the conditions of Article 41(2) lit b FRC.[399]

Formal request and onus

Despite the ex officio character of the appointing authority's obligation to assist the member of staff, it is of key procedural importance for the staff member concerned to formally request assistance when needed – and to do so in time – in order to be able to practically realise her or his rights under the employment relationship. For this, it is sufficient that the member of staff who is seeking the protection of their institution provides prima facie evidence that the attacks of which she or he claims to have been the victim actually took place. When such evidence is provided, the institution concerned is under an obligation to take the necessary measures, in particular to conduct an administrative enquiry.[400]

f. Privileges and Immunities

Purpose

The officials and other servants of the EU enjoy privileges and immunities recognised under Article 23 SR and the Protocol on Privileges and Immunities.[401] The privileges and immunities are accorded solely in the interests of the Union; they are intended to avoid any interference with the Union's functioning and independence.[402] The official is under an obligation to immediately inform the appointing authority when privileges and immunities are in dispute.

Compliance with the law, waiver of immunity by the Union

Officials and other servants are not exempt from fulfilling their private obligations or from complying with the laws and police regulations in force. As a consequence of the sole purpose of

[395] GC, T-164/20, ECLI:EU:T:2023:35, paras 57/58 – *BG v EP*; CST, F-132/14, EU:F:2015:115, para 91 – *CH v EP.*

[396] GC, T-164/20, ECLI:EU:T:2023:35, para 56 – *BG v EP.*

[397] GC, T-275/17, ECLI:EU:T:2018:479 – *Curto v EP*, and case study in section II.9.c above; otherwise in CST, F-30/08, ECLI:EU:F:2010:43, paras 93, 99 – *Nanopoulos v Commission.*

[398] GC, T-218/17, ECLI:EU:T:2018:393 – *HF v EP.*

[399] GC, T-65/19, ECLI:EU:T:2021:454, paras 162 ff – *AI v ECDC.*

[400] GC, T-275/17, ECLI:EU:T:2018:479, para 97 – *Curto v EP.*

[401] Protocol No 7 on the privileges and immunities of the European Union (Protocol), consolidated version [2012] OJ C326/1.

[402] Art 17 Protocol; GC, T-80/91, ECLI:EU:T:1992:110, para 42 – *Campogrande.*

privileges and immunities to protect the functioning and independence of the Union, it remains in the hands of the institution to waive the immunity of a staff member if the balancing of interests so warrants. Where, for example, a third party seeks to attach an official's remuneration in the hands of an EU institution in its capacity as employer, that institution must, first, determine whether the privileges and immunities provided for by the Protocol are applicable to the proceedings in question and, if so, then decide to what extent it considers it appropriate to avail itself of them. The institution will take into account the interests of the Union and may decide not to avail itself of its privileges and immunities: in that case it will, by virtue of its duty to cooperate in good faith with the national authorities, give effect to the attachment order issued by the national court.[403]

Effect

The effect of the privileges and immunities are that officials and other servants are immune in the territory of each Member State from legal proceedings in respect of acts performed by them in their official capacity, including their words (spoken or written), also after they have ceased to hold office; they shall, together with their spouses and dependent members of their families, not be subject to immigration restrictions or to formalities for the registration of aliens; they shall enjoy the right to import (and export) free of duty their furniture and effects; they have the right to import (and export) free of duty a motor car for their personal use. Details on this are stipulated in Articles 11, 12 and 13 of the Protocol.

Article 11 Protocol

In the territory of each Member State and whatever their nationality, officials and other servants of the Union shall:

(a) subject to the provisions of the Treaties relating, on the one hand, to the rules on the liability of officials and other servants towards the Union and, on the other hand, to the jurisdiction of the Court of Justice of the European Union in disputes between the Union and its officials and other servants, be immune from legal proceedings in respect of acts performed by them in their official capacity, including their words spoken or written. They shall continue to enjoy this immunity after they have ceased to hold office;
(b) together with their spouses and dependent members of their families, not be subject to immigration restrictions or to formalities for the registration of aliens;
(c) in respect of currency or exchange regulations, be accorded the same facilities as are customarily accorded to officials of international organisations;
(d) enjoy the right to import free of duty their furniture and effects at the time of first taking up their post in the country concerned, and the right to re-export free of duty their furniture and effects, on termination of their duties in that country, subject in either case to the conditions considered to be necessary by the government of the country in which this right is exercised;

[403] GC, T-497/93, ECLI:EU:T:1995:58, paras 49–51 – *Hogan v CJEU*; GC, T-394/02, ECLI:EU:T:2004:279, paras 73, 75 – *Lucaccioni*.

(e) have the right to import free of duty a motor car for their personal use, acquired either in the country of their last residence or in the country of which they are nationals on the terms ruling in the home market in that country, and to re-export it free of duty, subject in either case to the conditions considered to be necessary by the government of the country concerned.

Article 12 Protocol

Officials and other servants of the Union shall be liable to a tax for the benefit of the Union on salaries, wages and emoluments paid to them by the Union, in accordance with the conditions and procedure laid down by the European Parliament and the Council, acting by means of regulations in accordance with the ordinary legislative procedure and after consultation of the institutions concerned. They shall be exempt from national taxes on salaries, wages and emoluments paid by the Union.

Article 13 Protocol

In the application of income tax, wealth tax and death duties and in the application of conventions on the avoidance of double taxation concluded between Member States of the Union, officials and other servants of the Union who, solely by reason of the performance of their duties in the service of the Union, establish their residence in the territory of a Member State other than their country of domicile for tax purposes at the time of entering the service of the Union, shall be considered, both in the country of their actual residence and in the country of domicile for tax purposes, as having maintained their domicile in the latter country provided that it is a member of the Union. This provision shall also apply to a spouse, to the extent that the latter is not separately engaged in a gainful occupation, and to children dependent on and in the care of the persons referred to in this Article.

Movable property belonging to persons referred to in the preceding paragraph and situated in the territory of the country where they are staying shall be exempt from death duties in that country; such property shall, for the assessment of such duty, be considered as being in the country of domicile for tax purposes, subject to the rights of third countries and to the possible application of provisions of international conventions on double taxation.

Any domicile acquired solely by reason of the performance of duties in the service of other international organisations shall not be taken into consideration in applying the provisions of this Article.

Taxes

Officials and other servants of the Union shall be liable to a tax[404] for the benefit of the Union on salaries, wages and emoluments paid to them by the Union.[405] They are exempt from national taxes on salaries, wages and emoluments paid by the Union, Article 12 sentence 2 of the Protocol.

[404] These Union taxes are levied and entered as revenues (Art 9) under the general budget of the EU, Regulation (EEC/ Euratom/ ECSC) No 260/68 of the Council of 29 February 1968 laying down the conditions and procedure for applying the tax for the benefit of the European Communities [1968] OJ L56/8, last amended [2002] OJ L264/15.

[405] Art 12 sentence 1 Protocol.

The tax system of the Union is an independent system which is applied irrespective of the national systems.[406] Also the tax exemption contributes to guaranteeing the institutional and functional autonomy of the Union.[407] Hence, a decision of an EU institution defining the status of its servants and determining conditions of employment is binding on national judicial and administrative authorities, so they cannot make an independent classification of the employment relationship in question.[408] The following paragraphs depict the categories of persons who are exempt from paying national taxes, the concept of what is a national tax and the types of national taxes that remain to be paid.

Scope of tax exemption ratione personae

The persons exempt from liability to pay national taxes as provided for in Article 12 sentence 2 of the Protocol are defined in a specific regulation:[409] (a) persons coming under the SR or CEOS, including those who receive the compensation provided for in the case of retirement in the interests of the service, with the exception of local staff; (b) persons receiving disability, retirement or survivors' pensions paid by the Communities; (c) persons receiving a certain compensation[410] in the case of termination of service. Thus, the principle line is that EU officials and other servants as well as persons receiving pensions paid by the Union are exempt, while local staff are not exempt from national tax on salaries, wages and emoluments paid by the Union institutions. This can be regulated differently by the specific legal basis of the body, for example, an EU agency.[411] Seconded national civil servants are not exempt from national tax under the Protocol, because they are neither EU officials nor other servants of the Union.

Fictitious tax domicile and exemption with tax progression

Article 13 of the Protocol stipulates a fictitious domicile for the application of income tax, wealth tax and death duties and for the application of conventions on the avoidance of double taxation between Member States: officials and other servants (and their families), who have moved to another Member State in order to perform their duties, shall be considered as having maintained their domicile in the Member State they had moved from. As a consequence of this, first, depending on the tax law of the respective Member State, officials or other servants may be subject to unlimited tax liability in that country of fictitious domicile. Other revenues realised – such as rental income or capital income – will thus be subject to national taxation of that country of domicile. Secondly, the domicile raises the question if the other revenues realised in that country are subject to a higher tax rate under a clause of *exemption with tax progression*, which could apply because these persons have received tax exempt remuneration paid by the Union, which has increased their overall income.[412]

An answer on this should take into account both a domestic tax and Union law perspective. From a national perspective, domestic tax law has to allow for taking the amounts into account that the person has received as tax exempt remuneration in order to determine the applicable

[406] ECJ, Jd Cases 81, 82 and 146/79, ECLI:EU:C:1980:270, para 18 – *Sorasio-Allo and Others v Commission.*

[407] ECJ, C-288/04, ECLI:EU:C:2005:526, paras 26/27 – *AB.*

[408] ibid, para 39.

[409] Regulation (EEC, Euratom, ECSC) No 549/69 [1969] OJ L74/1.

[410] According to Art 5 of Regulation (EEC, Euratom, ECSC) No 259/68 [1968] OJ L56/1.

[411] eg, the *pensions* received under the EASA, EFSA, ECDC, ITER, EMA, ERA, EACEA, EDA, GSA, EISMEA, REA, ERC, EEA, Cedefop, ENISA, EFT, CdT, CHAFEA, Europol, Frontex, EMCDDA, EMSA, EFCA, OHIM, EIGE, EIT, FRA, EIOPA, EUI, Eurojust and ECB respective schemes are not tax exempted (while salaries, wages and emoluments paid by these bodies are exempted).

[412] 'Progressionsvorbehalt' in § 32b EStG (German income tax law).

domestic tax rate on a progressive scale.[413] This must be reconciled with the requirements of the principle of primacy of Union law and the equality of remuneration. From a Union law perspective, it is important to bear in mind that the Protocol precludes any national tax, regardless of its nature and the manner in which it is levied, which is imposed directly or indirectly on officials or other servants, by reason of the fact that they are in receipt of remuneration paid by the Union, even if the tax in question is not calculated by reference to the amount of that remuneration.[414] In that context, the ECJ had already held in its early judgment in *Humblet*, that the Protocol prohibits the taking into account of the salaries paid by the Union to its officials and other servants in order to determine the rate of tax due on other income which is not exempt, where the national tax law provides for a system of taxation on a rising scale.[415] A clause under national tax law which nevertheless stipulates an *exemption with tax progression* applied on Union remuneration would amount to an indirect taxation that is not compatible with Article 12 sentence 2 of the Protocol where this leads to the determination of a higher domestic tax rate. More than that, a person in receipt of tax-exempt income paid by the Union is also exempt from any obligation to *declare* the amount of such income to the authorities of a Member State.[416] Summarising, where the tax exemption of the Protocol applies to remuneration paid by the Union, the national tax authorities cannot rely on a *clause of exemption with tax progression* that would have the effect of increasing the domestic tax rate.[417]

Persisting other tax liability

Despite the tax exemption privilege, the liability of officials or other servants to pay other taxes will persist, such as value added tax,[418] local taxes, residence tax,[419] or property tax. A charge or due representing the consideration for a given service rendered by the public authorities (such as a school levy) is not a 'tax' within the meaning of the Protocol, even if that charge or due is calculated on the basis of the salary paid by the Union to the person liable.[420] The privilege does not prevent a Member State from excluding an official from a subsidy system or other advantages[421] that are granted to beneficiaries determined in accordance with the relevant national provisions based on income in the state of residence.[422]

Subjective rights proceeding from privileges and immunities

Although privileges and immunities are accorded solely in the interests of the Union, they do create subjective rights for the individual staff members. Therefore, a decision to waive the

[413] eg, under German law, §32b(1) No 4 EStG allows for this, however only where the possibility to do so is explicitly stipulated in the international agreement, here Protocol No 7. The Protocol (by contrast to other, more recent international agreements) does *not* contain such an option. Kofler in Schaumburg/Englisch (eds), *Europäisches Steuerrecht* (2020) Kap 22, II.

[414] ECJ, C-349/14, ECLI:EU:C:2015:338, paras 17–19 – *Ministre délégué v Pazdziej*; ECJ, C-558/10, ECLI:EU:C:2012:418 – *Bourges-Maunoury v Direction des services fiscaux d'Eure-et-Loir*.

[415] ECJ, 6/60-IMM (request concerning immunities), ECLI:EU:C:1960:48, 579/580 – *Humblet v Belgium*, the ECJ had justified this finding with recourse to a 'principle of equality of remuneration', meaning that officials shall not be treated differently depending on the Member State of their (fictitious) domicile.

[416] ECJ, C-558/10, ECLI:EU:C:2012:418, para 30 – *Bourges-Maunoury v Direction des services fiscaux d'Eure-et-Loir*, in the interest of legal certainty.

[417] As it stands in practice, the only two exceptions to this rule among the family of EU bodies in the wider sense are the EDA in Brussels and the EUI in Florence: for these two bodies, a *clause of exemption with tax progression* could apply in regard to the tax-exempt salaries; the pensions paid by the two bodies are subject to national tax.

[418] Where not exempt otherwise from VAT by the Member State of duty/residence.

[419] ECJ, C-349/14, ECLI:EU:C:2015:338, paras 29–31 – *Ministre délégué v Pazdziej*; ECJ, C-263/91, ECLI:EU:C:1993:207, Rn 15 – *Kristoffersen*.

[420] *cf* Art 3(2) Protocol; ECJ, 32/67 R, ECLI:EU:C:1968:8, 48 – *Van Leeuwen v Rotterdam*.

[421] ECJ, C-229/98, ECLI:EU:C:1999:501, para 29 – *Vander Zwalmen and Massart v Belgium*.

[422] ECJ, C-333/88, ECLI:EU:C:1990:131, para 18 – *Tither*.

immunity of a member of staff alters his or her legal position, simply because it removes that protection, re-establishing their status as a person who is subject to the general law of the Member States, and thus laying him or her open to measures like detention and legal proceedings.[423]

10. Whistleblowing and Whistleblower Protection

A specific subject under the title on mutual rights and obligations of civil servants is *whistleblowing*. Back in the times of the 2004 reform, the practice of whistleblowing and the handling of those who did it was particularly controversial,[424] and its effectiveness was doubted.[425]

Concept

Officials must inform their superiors or certain other bodies if, on the occasion of the performance of their duties, they become aware of facts which give rise to a presumption of the existence of possible illegal activity, including fraud or corruption, detrimental to the interests of the Union; or of conduct relating to the discharge of professional duties which may constitute a serious failure to comply with the obligations of officials of the Union.[426] In regard to the terminology (where such differentiation applies), a 'whistleblower' is a member of staff employed – ie, an internal person – providing the information, while an 'informant' is an external person reporting.

Conditions and procedure

The SR provide that a whistleblower enjoys protection against disadvantages: he shall not suffer any prejudicial effects on the part of the institution as a result of having communicated the information[427] in relation to effects that are demonstrably connected with his report.[428] However, this is not the case if the whistleblower contacts other institutions beforehand or too early,[429] or if the whistleblower cannot be sure about the truthfulness of the allegations, as laid down in the two conditions of Article 22b SR, namely that:

> '(a) the official honestly and reasonably believes that the information disclosed, and any allegation contained in it, are substantially true; and
> (b) the official has previously disclosed the same information to OLAF or to his own institution and has allowed OLAF or that institution the period of time set by the Office or the institution, given the complexity of the case, to take appropriate action. The official shall be duly informed of that period of time within 60 days.'

Thus, there is a clear subsidiarity in bringing the information to the knowledge of the institutions' top executives (including the Ombudsman) by virtue of the fact that it first has to be reported to the official's own institution or to OLAF. In addition, as a rule, the waiting period set by OLAF

[423] CST, Jd cases F-124/05 and F-96/06, EU:F:2010:2, para 231 – *A and G v Commission*; GC, T-29/17, ECLI:EU:T:2018:717, para 38 – *RQ v Commission*.

[424] Dalle-Crode (2008) 480; Gervasoni (2010) 46 *Cahiers de droit européen* 774.

[425] White, Le 'whistleblower' in the institutions of the European Union: is it the right choice? (2010) *Revue du Marché commun et de l'Union européenne* 441 and Diamandouros, 'The Perspective of the European Ombudsman' in Govaere/Vandersanden (eds), *La fonction publique communautaire* (2008) 48, 53; Yurttagül, *Whistleblower Protection by the Council of Europe, the European Court of Human Rights and the European Union: European Union and its Neighbours in a Globalized World* Vol 3 (2021); Cador, 'La fonction publique européenne à l'épreuve du whistleblowing' (2014) *Law and European affairs* 119–30.

[426] Art 22a(1) SR.

[427] Art 22a(3) SR.

[428] CST, F-2/09, ECLI:EU:F:2010:12, paras 138/139 – *Menghi v ENISA*, the court must examine this particularly carefully.

[429] *cf* the subsequently quoted periods.

must first expire. For a disclosure of irregularities in accordance with Article 22a SR to be in good faith, case-law[430] has set out four preconditions, as follows:

(1) The irregularities disclosed must, where they actually occurred, be of an obviously serious nature.
(2) The accusations made must be based on correct facts, or, at the very least, have a 'sufficient factual basis'. The exercise of freedom of expression, which encompasses the possibility of an official's denouncing psychological harassment or the existence of unlawful circumstances or of a serious failure by officials to fulfil their obligations, carries with it duties and responsibilities, and any person who chooses to disclose such information must carefully verify, to the extent permitted by the circumstances, that it is accurate and reliable.
(3) The official must use appropriate means to make the disclosure and, in particular, must disclose the matter to the authority or body responsible, namely (Art 22a(1) SR), his immediate superior or his Director-General or, if he considers it useful, the Secretary-General, or the persons in equivalent positions,' or OLAF direct.
(4) Disclosure motivated by a personal grievance or animosity or by the prospect of personal advantage, including financial gain, cannot be considered to be a disclosure made reasonably and honestly.

Article 22c SR (introduced with the 2014 reform) aimed to strengthen the position of whistleblowers by prescribing that each institution shall put in place a procedure for the handling of complaints made by officials concerning the way in which they were treated after or in consequence of the fulfilment by them of their obligations under the whistleblowing rules of the SR. The conclusion of an investigation without any further steps does not adversely affect the whistleblower, since he could later attack any alleged disadvantages separately.[431] Altogether, the overall level of protection of whistleblowers under the SR should not fall short of the protection afforded to 'reporting persons' under the whistleblower Directive[432] of 2019. It lays down common minimum standards for the Member States for the protection of persons reporting breaches of Union law. Core elements treat the risk of work-related retaliation against the whistleblower, discourage malicious whistleblowing, prevent unjustified reputational damage, protect the confidentiality of the identity of the whistleblower, and protect the personal data and private life of the whistleblower. For example, in the context of EU civil service law, the protection of the identity and reputation of the whistleblower are endangered when the appointing authority distributes too widely an administrative investigation report after the reporting of an irregularity; this may amount to a violation of the duty of care towards the whistleblowing staff member.[433]

In the field of psychological or sexual harassment, the special provision of Article 12a(2) sentence 2 SR relating to whistleblower protection stipulates that an official 'who has given

[430] CJEU Annual Report 2012, 211 with reference to the conditions set out in CST, F-41/10 RENV, ECLI:EU:F:2012:135 – *Bermejo Garde v EESC*, appeal GC, T-530/12 P, ECLI:EU:T:2014:860, paras 106–10, compensation €25,000: CST, F-41/10 RENV, ECLI:EU:F:2016:123.

[431] GC, T-4/05, ECLI:EU:T:2006:93, paras 48/49 – *Strack v Commission*. Note the difference compared with harassment cases (see above, section II.9.c. procedural aspects), where the closure of the investigation into the existence of harassment is considered to adversely affect the person who has reported, CST, F-43/10, ECLI:EU:F:2012:184, paras 63/64 – *Cerafogli v ECB*.

[432] Directive (EU) 2019/1937 of the European Parliament and of the Council of 23 October 2019 on the protection of persons who report breaches of Union law [2019] OJ L305/17–56; Commission communication, 'Strengthening whistleblower protection at EU level' COM(2018) 214 final of 23 April 2018. Abazi, 'Whistleblowing in the European Union' (2021) 58(3) *CMLR* 813–50.

[433] GC, T-681/20, ECLI:EU:T:2022:422, paras 149–55 – *OC v EEAS* (compensation for non-material harm of €10,000).

evidence on psychological or sexual harassment shall not suffer any prejudicial effects on the part of the institution, provided the official has acted honestly'.

Another aspect relating to whistleblowing and disclosure of internal circumstances is that the appointing authority may prevent the publication by the official of any matter dealing with the work (Art 17a(2) SR) and may prevent disclosure in the context of any legal proceedings by refusing its permission under Article 19 SR, if the interests of the Union so require and such refusal would not entail criminal consequences for the official.[434]

11. Personal File

a. *Single File*

There shall be one (single) personal file for each official,[435] in which all documents concerning the administrative status and all reports[436] relating to his ability, efficiency and conduct, as well as any comments by the official on such documents, are contained (unity of the personal file).[437] An official's personal file shall contain no reference to his political, trade union, philosophical or religious activities and views, or to his racial or ethnic origin or sexual orientation.[438]

b. *Documents Concerning the Administrative Status*

The term *documents concerning the administrative status* is interpreted widely, whereas the term *reports* is limited to the areas explicitly stated: Article 26 SR makes a distinction between, on the one hand, 'documents', which are only required to be placed on the file if they relate to the administrative status of the official concerned, and 'reports', which are only required to be placed on the file if they concern his ability, efficiency or conduct, and, on the other hand, any other document relating to the official concerned. For example, the administration is not required to place the report of an administrative investigation concerning the official on his personal file, after bringing it to his attention.[439] The *administrative status* not only includes the main events in the civil servant's career (like recruitment, positions and activity, secondment, reassignment, leave on personal grounds, non-active status, leave for military services, appraisal, grading and promotions, termination of service), but also other events concerning certain rights recognised by the SR or by the provisions on the privileges and immunities. This is, however, not the case for an invitation to report to the medical service addressed to a civil servant by his hierarchical superior, which affects neither the rights nor the privileges recognised by the status of the person concerned.[440] Also, the mere comparative consideration of candidatures in a promotion or transfer procedure will not enter the personal file of the candidates; however where such opinions also contain, in addition to the assessments involved in the comparative consideration, references to a

[434] With the important exception in Art 19(2) SR (ie, no permission required) for an official giving evidence before the ECJ or before the Disciplinary Board of an institution on a matter concerning a servant or former servant of the European Union.

[435] Art 26(6) SR.

[436] CST, F-139/07, ECLI:EU:F:2009:105, paras 131, 134/135 – *van Arum v EP.*

[437] Art 26(1) SR. See also case study in section II.20.e. below.

[438] Art 26(4) SR. On the consequences of an irregular or incomplete personal file, GC, T-73/89, ECLI:EU:T:1990:65, paras 41, 50 – *Barbi v Commission.*

[439] CST, F-28/14, ECLI:EU:F:2015:101, paras 75 ff – *De Loecker v EEAS.*

[440] GC, T-144/03, ECLI:EU:T:2005:158, para 136 – *Schmit v Commission.*

candidate's ability, efficiency and conduct not previously included in his personal file, these statements would have to be mentioned in their personal file or otherwise notified to them, so that those concerned have an opportunity to make any comments.[441] The basic line for this is a sound application of the principle of the rights of defence.

c. *Personal File and Rights of the Defence*

All documents included in the personal file, including any statements by superiors,[442] must be communicated to the official in advance and can only be used against him under this condition.[443] This is to ensure that measures taken by the appointing authority are not based on secret information (ie, matters concerning his conduct which are not included in his personal file and have not been communicated to him), but only on information the accuracy of which the person concerned can verify and against which he can defend himself.[444] A decision based on factual matters not included in the staff member's personal file would infringe his right to a fair hearing and be liable to annulment (permitted the missing facts had decisive influence, see below). An official shall have the right, even after leaving the service, to acquaint himself with all the documents in his file and to take copies of them. The personal file shall be confidential and may be consulted only in the offices of the administration or on a secure electronic medium.[445] It shall, however, be forwarded to the ECJ, if an action concerning the official is brought. The deletion of entries in the personal file can be requested after three years (in the case of a written warning or reprimand) or six years (for any other penalty).[446] Content removed from the personal file may no longer be held against the official.[447]

d. *Knowledge of Underlying Information*

The concept of a single personal file forms the basis for comparing the merits and careers of candidates for transfers and promotions. Uncontrollable '*dossiers parallèles*' of various services are not permitted.[448] However, this does not mean that first documents for the personal file would have to be drawn up regarding all factual allegations that could later be detrimental to the person concerned. Rather, it is sufficient if the member of staff knew the underlying information and was able to assert his opinion on it while the contested act was still being drafted.[449] Thus,

[441] GC, T-302/02, ECLI:EU:T:2003:255, para 39 – *Kenny v CJEU.*

[442] ECJ, 97/63, ECLI:EU:C:1964:61 – *De Pasquale v Commission*; ECJ, 43/74, ECLI:EU:C:1977:121 – *Guillot v Commission*; ECJ, 21/70, ECLI:EU:C:1971:7 – *Rittweger v Council.*

[443] Art 26(2) SR; on the relationship to the rights of defence: CST, F-28/09, ECLI:EU:F:2014:198, para 57 – *Kipp v Europol*, and on the relevance for the adoption of the contested measure CST, F-38/06, ECLI:EU: F:2007:117, para 48 – *Bianchi v European Training Foundation*; ECJ, 88/71, ECLI:EU:C:1972:58 – *Brasseur v EP.*

[444] Critical: Vandersanden, 'La procédure et les voies de recours' in Govaere/Vandersanden (eds), *La fonction publique communautaire* (2008) 122.

[445] Art 26(6) SR.

[446] Art 27 Annex IX SR.

[447] GC, T-121/20, ECLI:EU:T:2021:665, paras 68–70 – *IP v Commission*, and case study in section II.20.e. below.

[448] GC, Jd Cases T-39/93 and T-553/93, ECLI:EU:T:1995:177, paras 37–39, 41, 43–44 – *Baltsavias v Commission*; GC, T-496/93, ECLI:EU:T:1995:101 – *Allo v Commission.*

[449] CST, F-30/05, ECLI:EU:F:2007:31, paras 74 ff – *Sundholm v Commission* (appraisal procedure, comments possible at drafting stage); CST, F-38/06, ECLI:EU:F:2007:117, para 48 – *Bianchi v ETF* (non-renewal of a contract due to an internal note that was not included in the personal file; but where the person concerned was given a proper opportunity, before the contested decision was taken, to submit her comments on the facts reported in those documents, and where she was actually aware of their content before the expiry of the time limit for complaints). *cf* Levi, 'Droits fondamentaux

as is generally the case with a violation of the rights of the defence, the procedural violation had or could have an impact on the decision taken. In this sense, an infringement of Article 26 SR entails the annulment of an act only if it is established that those documents missing from the file could have had a decisive influence on the contested decision. The mere fact that documents were not placed on an official's personal file is not enough to justify annulment of a decision adversely affecting him if they were in fact brought to his knowledge.[450]

12. Medical File

The medical file is to be distinguished from the personal file. Every official has the right to access[451] his medical files according to certain modalities laid down by the appointing authorities of the institutions. The modalities agreed upon by the Heads of Administration[452] foresee that first, the file must be consulted on the premises of the Medical Service of the institution, in the presence of a person designated by the Medical Service; secondly, the official or other servant has access to psychiatric or psychological reports concerning him, through the intermediary of a doctor appointed by him; thirdly, that the official or servant may not have access to personal notes by doctors if, under the terms of Article 20(1)(c) of Regulation 45/2001[453] and on the basis of a case-by-case examination, this is necessary to guarantee the protection of the person concerned or the rights and freedoms of others. The decisive element for applying these exceptions to the rule of free access to the medical file is the case-by-case assessment of all relevant circumstances.[454] Also the Commission's internal rules on restriction of access to the medical file foresee a case-by-case examination and require proportionality for any restriction of the access.[455]

Medical reports form the basis of certain procedures under the SR, most importantly on the recognition of occupational diseases and invalidity.[456] Their use for non-medical purposes (eg, institutional statistics) can be justified as long as they are proportionate;[457] however, further storage of personal data after a request for deletion has been refused can be unlawful with regard to the official's right under Article 19 of the data protection Regulation for EU institutions.[458] They are subject to medical confidentiality and do not belong in the general personal file, unless they relate directly to work performance and ability as well as to the official's conduct.

et principes généraux de droit de la fonction publique *communautaire*' in Govaere/Vandersanden (eds), *La fonction publique communautaire* (2008) 99, and ECJ, C-344/05 P, ECLI:EU:C:2006:710 – *Commission v De Bry*, on obligations to inform about negative assessments outside the personal file.

[450] GC, T-344/99, ECLI:EU:T:2001:237, paras 57–60 – *Langarica v Commission*; CST, F-96/13, ECLI:EU:F:2015:29, para 49 – *Pipiliagkas v Commission*.

[451] Art 26a SR; also stemming from Art 41 FRC and Art 15 ff of Regulation (EU) No 2018/1725 of the European Parliament and Council on the protection of natural persons with regard to the processing of personal data by the Union institutions, bodies, offices and agencies and on the free movement of such data [2018] OJ L295/39 (Data Protection Regulation EU No 2018/1725).

[452] Conclusion 221/04 of the Heads of Administration on 'Access of officials or other servants to their medical files New Article 26(a) of the Staff Regulations'.

[453] Nowadays equivalent to Art 25(1) lit h of the Data Protection Regulation EU No 2018/1725.

[454] Levi/Rodrigues et al, *Fonction publique de l'Union européenne* (2020) 45.

[455] *cf* Art 2(1) of Decision (EU) 2019/154 of 30 January 2019 laying down internal rules concerning the restriction of the right of access of data subjects to their medical files.

[456] ECJ, 140/86, ECLI:EU:C:1987:427 – *Strack v Commission*.

[457] CST, F-130/07, ECLI:EU:F:2009:114, para 85 – *Vinci v ECB*. On the relationship between the law on personal file and transparency, Regulation (EC) No 1049/2001 [2001] OJ L145/43: CST, Jd Cases F-124/05 and F-96/06, ECLI:EU:F:2010:2, paras 289 ff – *A and G v Commission*.

[458] Data Protection Regulation EU No 2018/1725. The disclosure of personal data can also result in a breach of the Regulation and Art 8 FRC with liability for damages, see GC, T-462/17, ECLI:EU:T:2019:397, paras 178–203 – *TO v EEA*.

13. Appraisal

The ability, efficiency and conduct in the service of each official shall be the subject of an annual report as provided for by the General Implementing Provisions (GIP) of the appointing authority of each institution, Article 43 SR (GIP 43). The SR confine themselves to foresee that the report shall state whether or not the performance level of the official has been satisfactory, while it is up to the institutions' appointing authorities to provide for the right of staff to lodge an appeal within the reporting procedure, which has to be exercised before the lodging of a complaint as referred to in Article 90(2) SR. The report – or appraisal – shall be communicated to the official, with the entitlement to make any comments thereon. It shall contain a sufficient and substantial statement of reasons for the assessment.[459] The appraisals accompany officials throughout their careers and form the basis for the appointing authority's career decisions. Differences of appraisal practice persist between the institutions despite the substantial reform of the appraisal and promotion system of 2004. The following section focuses on the situation in the Commission.[460] Generally, nowadays, the appraisal is based less on seniority and more on performance, but also on mobility and the ability to work in a third foreign language.[461]

a. Scope and Aspects of Procedure

If the staff member subject to appraisal has several separate areas of responsibility (eg, partial time dedicated to the functions of staff representatives) the appraisal can be limited to these areas.[462] Where the common assessment forms a weighted overall assessment of several areas of responsibility, the underlying assumption about the respective time shares must be correct, otherwise the report would be vitiated by substantive inaccuracy.[463] Only a supervisor who can assess the performance properly is competent to carry out the appraisal.[464] The reporting officer's competence is a matter of public interest which the court is bound to examine of its own motion.[465] If there are several assessors, it may not be necessary to obtain the opinion of all of them.[466] The dialogue foreseen in the appraisal procedure[467] allows the appraisee to take note of the draft assessment and discuss it, also with a view to – in case – initiate its modification.[468]

[459] On this, see case study in section 13.e. below.

[460] Oechsler/Noack, *Personalbeurteilung in Europäischen und internationalen Organisationen*, Studie im Auftrag des Bundesministeriums des Innern (2009) 22 ff (Commission) 31 ff (Parliament) 42 ff (Council). On the Council's two-tier assessment system, see CST, F-14/09, ECLI:EU:F:2010:167, para 34 – *Almeida Campos and Others v Council*, and CST, F-104/09, ECLI:EU:F:2011:29, paras 44 ff – *Canga Fano v Council*, and on the global, 'less mathematical' assessment of merits and promotion selection, CST, F-9/10, ECLI:EU:F:2011:160, paras 15, 19 – *AC v Council*; CST, F-75/11, ECLI:EU:F:2012:152, para 78 – *Bouillez v Council*; on promotion policy at the EP, CST, F-64/10, ECLI:EU:F:2011:72, paras 5, 45 – *Mantzouratos v EP*; CST, F-81/10, ECLI:EU:F:2011:120, para 42 – *Praskevicius v EP*; appraisal at the EIB and comprehensive review by the Appeals Committee, GC, T-37/10 P, ECLI:EU:T:2012:205 – *De Nicola v EIB*.

[461] Joris, 'L'administration face au contentieux de la fonction publique communautaire' in Govaere/Vandersanden (eds), *La fonction publique communautaire* (2008) 64; Gervasoni (2010) 46 *Cahiers de droit européen* 763; CST, F-75/11, ECLI:EU:F:2012:152, para 36 – *Bouillez v Council*, on CST, F-20/09, ECLI: EU:F:2011:181, para 42 – *Juvyns v Council*, and CST, F-14/09, ECLI:EU:F:2010:167, para 35 – *Almeida Campos and Others v Council*.

[462] CST, F-36/07, ECLI:EU:F:2008:52, para 30 – *Lebedef v Commission*.

[463] CST, F-7/09, ECLI:EU:F:2010:9, paras 47–49, 56 – *Faria v OHIM*.

[464] CST, Jd Cases F-45/08 and F-99/07, ECLI:EU:F:2009:84, paras 68, 87/88 – *Bernard v Europol*.

[465] CST, F-45/09, ECLI:EU:F:2010:52, para 38 – *Lebedef-Caponi v Commission*.

[466] CST, F-16/09, ECLI:EU:F:2009:164, paras 57, 58 – *De Britto Patrício-Dias*.

[467] *cf* Art 7 GIP 43.

[468] GC, T-173/04, ECLI:EU:T:2006:333, para 70 – *Carius v Commission*.

Timing of appraisal

Unless precise deadlines for the course of the appraisal procedure have been set up, the assessment in the annually recurring procedure shall be drafted within reasonable time.[469] An undue delay of partial measures (such as the award of points) alone does not yet lead to the annulment of the contested decision.[470] A delay in the drawing up of a staff report can, however, entail a liability of the institution for damages,[471] because it may in itself be prejudicial to the official for the simple reason that his or her career progress may be affected by the absence of such a report at a time when decisions concerning them must be taken. An official in possession of an irregular and incomplete personal file thereby suffers non-material damage as a result of being put in an uncertain and anxious state of mind with regard to his professional future. In the absence of special circumstances justifying the delays found to have occurred, the administration commits a breach of administrative duty giving rise to liability on its part.[472]

b. Fixing of Objectives

The GIP mandatorily[473] determine that together with the appraisals, work objectives too shall be fixed[474] for all officials, as a basis for the subsequent appraisal, including for those members of staff who only took up their duties during the assessment period.[475] The job advertisement cannot replace the setting of objectives,[476] but a table with standardised formulations for the tasks and objectives of each civil servant is sufficient, even if it states the tasks rather than the objectives to be achieved.[477] An appraisal of performance may not take place for a period for which no tasks have been assigned.[478] The task of formulating the goals must not be transferred from the administration to the person being assessed.[479] The administration is not obliged to obtain the acceptance by the staff member for the setting of objectives, because it would put the staff member in a position to choose which objectives to pursue.[480] By derogating from the set objectives, the administration may delegate minor tasks to the staff member in order to facilitate his or her return to work after a longer period of sick leave.[481]

[469] CST, F-114/07, ECLI:EU:F:2009:130, para 98 – *Wenning v Europol*; GC, T-193/03, ECLI:EU:T:2005:164, paras 76 ff – *Piro v Commission.*

[470] CST, F-16/08, ECLI:EU:F:2009:107, para 30 – *Behmer v EP*; CST, F-4/13, ECLI:EU:F:2014:263 – *Cwik v Commission.*

[471] See chapter 2, II.2.

[472] GC, Jd Cases T-246/04 and T-71/05, ECLI:EU:T:2007:34, paras 64–65 – *Wunenburger v Commission*; GC, T-281/01, ECLI:EU:T:2004:207 – *Huygens v Commission*; CJEU Annual Report 2004, 127 and CJEU Annual Report 2003, 189 with further references.

[473] CST, F-38/08, ECLI:EU:F:2009:13 – *Liotti v Commission.*

[474] *cf* CJEU Annual Report 2008, Section A I No 3 (b) on CST, F-46/06, ECLI:EU:F:2008:26 – *Skareby v Commission*, and the appeal decision GC, T-193/08 P, paras 64 ff – *Skareby v Commission*; CST, F-71/08, ECLI:EU:F:2009:150, para 55 – *N v EP.*

[475] CST, F-71/08, ECLI:EU:F:2009:150, para 54 – *N v EP.*

[476] ibid, paras 58, 59.

[477] CST, F-93/08, ECLI:EU:F:2009:151, para 66 – *N v EP.*

[478] CST, F-34/06, ECLI:EU:F:2007:205, para 31 – *Michail v Commission.*

[479] GC, T-193/08 P, ECLI:EU:T:2009:377, para 80 – *Skareby v Commission.*

[480] CST, F-55/08, ECLI:EU:F:2009:159, para 131 – *De Nicola v EIB* (would be 'manifestly contrary to the rules of sound administration and the hierarchical principle').

[481] CST, F-98/09, ECLI:EU:F:2011:156, para 115 – *Whitehead v ECB.*

c. Content and Discretion

Wide appraisal discretion

In terms of content, the appraisal reflects the opinion of the assessing superiors,[482] the result of which can neither be imposed nor changed independently by the appointing authority.[483] As to judicial reviewability, it is not for the court to substitute its assessment for that of the persons responsible for appraising the work of the official under appraisal. The institutions enjoy a wide discretion in appraising the work of their officials. Value judgements relating to officials in career development reports are not subject to review by the courts except as regards any irregularities of form or manifest errors of fact vitiating the assessments made by the administration, any misuse of power,[484] or abusive considerations by those involved in the appraisals.[485] Recommendations by separate committees, such as those for the appraisal of staff representatives, are not binding.[486] Case-law emphasises the importance of impartiality of the assessing superior. Differences between an official and the immediate superior do not as such imply that the immediate superior is not in a position to assess objectively the merits of the person concerned;[487] this is even the case where the staff member has lodged a complaint of harassment against the assessing official.[488] However, even where the boundary into derogatory or harmful criticism of the person himself are not crossed, the GC has already annulled an appraisal where the appraiser expresses very strong negative views about the appraisee on several occasions during the appraisal exercise, demonstrating the existence of very strong negative personal feelings which point to a lack of subjective impartiality.[489]

Quotas of appraisal points

Despite the potentially detrimental effects on HR management – especially in smaller units – the application of quotas of appraisal points is permitted, with the argument (more precisely: the assumption) that they are objective, transparent, performance-based and budget-oriented.[490] The official contesting the attribution of points in a quota system may rebut this assumption by proving that the number of points concretely attributed was lower than appropriate only for the purpose of complying with the quota.[491]

[482] Superiors do not necessarily have to be of a higher grade: CST, F-66/10, ECLI:EU:F:2011:56, paras 45/46 – *AQ v Commission.*

[483] GC, T-15/96, ECLI:EU:T:1997:169 – *Liao v Council.*

[484] CST, F-46/06, ECLI:EU:F:2008:26, para 119 – *Skareby*; GC, T-33/91, ECLI:EU:T:1992:114, para 43 – *Williams v ECA*; GC, T-144/03, ECLI:EU:T:2005:158, para 70 – *Schmit v Commission*; GC, T-175/09 P, ECLI:EU:T:2010:534, para 40 – *Council v Stols.*

[485] The wording of the test varies, *cf* GC, T-298/20, ECLI:EU:T:2022:671, para 94 – *KD v EUIPO*; CST, F-45/09, ECLI:EU:F:2010:52, para 32 – *Lebedef-Caponi v Commission*; CST, F-30/05, ECLI:EU:F:2007:31, paras 48, 102 – *Sundholm v Commission.* Some case-law considered as objective irregularity of form if the value of the mark/points given on one side and the narrative description on the other side do not agree, CST, F-85/10, ECLI:EU:F:2012:97, para 110 – *AI v CJEU.*

[486] CST, F-108/06, ECLI:EU:F:2007:231, paras 37 ff – *Diomede Basili v Commission.*

[487] GC, Jd Cases T-7/98, T-208/98 and T-109/99, ECLI:EU:T:2001:69, para 188 – *De Nicola v EIB*; GC, T-11/91, ECLI:EU:T:1992:20, para 53 – *Schloh v Council.*

[488] CST, F-64/13, ECLI:EU:F:2015:72, para 77 – *Z v CJEU*; GC, T-249/04, ECLI:EU:T:2007:261, para 71 – *Combescot v Commission.*

[489] GC, T-827/16, ECLI:EU:T:2018:756, paras 100–08 – *QB v ECB.*

[490] CST, F-19/05, ECLI:EU:F:2006:55, paras 43 ff – *Sanchez Ferriz v Commission*, also quotas for faster and slower advancement of officials; CST, F-111/05, ECLI:EU:F:2007:35, paras 47 ff – *Sanchez Ferriz v Commission.*

[491] CST, F-55/08, ECLI:EU:F:2009:159, paras 170 ff, 176 – *De Nicola v EIB* (not proven), appeal decision GC, T-37/10 P, ECLI:EU:T: 2012:205, paras 69/70 – *De Nicola v EIB.*

Case Study on Appraisal Reports

Staff appraisal reports: Impartiality is a fundamental guarantee of the procedure

Case T-808/17, *Pethke v EUIPO* of 3 December 2019

In Brief

Can a superior be an impartial appeal body for review of the appraisal report of a staff member, if the same superior had previously played an important role in setting up the respective appraisal report as a reporting officer? The General Court (GC) has decided on this that the obligation of impartiality constitutes a fundamental guarantee which must be respected, since otherwise the staff member would be deprived of his effective right to a *genuine review.*

Background and Facts of the Case

The applicable general implementing provisions for staff reports foresee that the direct superior ('assessor' or reporting officer) is in charge of the assessment of a staff member, and that the appeal assessor shall be the staff member who is the direct superior of the assessor.

In the present case, the direct superior of the applicant drafted the annual appraisal report for the year 2016. He also consulted the Executive Director of the European Union Intellectual Property Office (EUIPO/OHIM), who for a period of nine months was the former superior of the applicant. In his written assessment he referred to the appraisal provided by the former superior for that nine-month period. The applicant disagreed with the appraisal and requested an appeal assessment by the superior of the assessor, ie, the Executive Director of EUIPO. In his complaint and subsequent court action, the applicant pleaded a breach of essential procedural requirements and a manifest error of assessment. Specifically, he criticised the lack of an independent review of his assessment for 2016, arguing that the appeal assessor for this year was his former superior, who had been instrumental in preparing the 2016 assessment.

Decision of the General Court

The GC decided to annul the appraisal due to a lack of impartiality of the appeal assessment. It is of the opinion that without this procedural error of law, the report's content could have been different. The right of the applicant to a genuine review of his assessment would be deprived of any practical effectiveness if the fundamental guarantee of impartiality was not respected. The counter-argument that neither the internal directives of EUIPO nor the implementing rules stipulated an explicit rule for how to handle the concrete situation was of no importance to the GC: although such a prescriptive rule was missing, the obligation to ensure the impartiality of the internal review procedure would have justified departing from the existing EUIPO instructions concerning appraisal. The GC emphasises the importance of the duty of officials to be impartial, as enshrined in Article 11(1) SR, according to which the official shall carry out the duties assigned to him objectively and impartially. The institutions, bodies, offices and agencies of the Union are required to respect the fundamental rights guaranteed by EU law, including the right to good administration enshrined in Article 41 FRC. According to Article 41(1) FRC, each person has a right to have their affairs handled impartially by the institutions, bodies, offices and agencies of the Union.

The GC describes the content of impartiality in two manifestations:[492] on the one hand a subjective impartiality, according to which no member of the institution concerned may show bias or personal prejudice and, on the other hand, an objective impartiality in the sense that the institution must provide sufficient guarantees to rule out any legitimate doubt as to any prejudice. The GC further explains that the requirement of impartiality imposed on the institutions, bodies, offices and agencies in the exercise of their functions seeks to ensure the equal treatment on which the EU is founded. That requirement is intended, in particular, to avoid any conflict of interests of officials and other servants acting on behalf of the institutions, bodies, offices and agencies. Given the fundamental importance of ensuring independence and integrity, both for the internal functioning and the outward appearance of the Union institutions, bodies, offices and agencies, the requirement of impartiality covers all circumstances in which the official or servant must reasonably see that, in the eyes of third parties, they may appear to be capable of impairing his independence in that area.

Reporting officers cannot be regarded as being biased and non-objective solely because as superiors they are involved in the professional activities of their staff. Rather, it is that involvement that enables them to give the most appropriate assessment of the activities of the staff member. Here, however, the applicant's former superior, who was in charge during three-quarters of the period in question, was instrumental in drawing up the respective assessment. The fact that he decided again in the internal appeal procedure raised doubts as to his impartiality as appeal assessor.

Comments

1. The judgment provides clear support for the procedural rules guaranteeing the impartiality required for the appraisal review, and in more general terms for the obligation of officials to act impartially, in accordance with Article 11(1) SR. The judgment also deduces this obligation from the fundamental right to Good Administration stipulated in Article 41 FRC.
2. This judgment follows the line of case-law of the Court of Justice (ECJ) that an internal appraisal review procedure can only contribute to the objectivity of the assessment and thus prevent litigation if it offers assurance to the member of staff that a genuine review will be carried out. The ECJ has formerly ruled on this in its judgment of 3 April 2019, *CJ v ECDC*.[493] That decision annulled the earlier dissenting judgment of the GC at first instance, *CJ v ECDC*,[494] of 13 December 2017, exactly on these grounds. It confirms the importance of the validation of the appraisal report by the superior of the reporting officer, as a measure to counterbalance the wide discretion in the appraisal exercise.[495]

[492] On the principle of impartiality, see section II.9. above.
[493] ECJ, C-139/18 P, ECLI:EU:C:2019:281, para 44 – *CJ v ECDC*.
[494] GC, T-602/16, ECLI:EU:T:2017:893 – *CJ v ECDC*.
[495] GC, T-122/21, ECLI:EU:T:2022:361, para 145 – *QI v Commission*.

3. The judgment gives an example of how the judges value the importance of procedural rights: On the one hand, the assessors enjoy a high degree of discretion when assessing the work of the staff members, and it is not for the judge to intervene in this assessment and to verify its validity, unless there is a manifest error or a manifest excess of the limits of discretion.[496] The judicial review of assessments is limited to the control of the regularity of the procedure, the accuracy of the facts and the absence of a manifest error of assessment or of misuse of powers.[497] On the other hand, this wide margin of discretion must be counterbalanced by a particular attention given to the rules governing the organisation of that assessment and the course of the procedure for that purpose.[498]

Case-law stipulates that where an EU institution has wide discretionary powers, compliance with the procedural safeguards provided for in the EU legal order is of even more importance.[499] Those guarantees include, in particular, the duty of the institution to examine carefully and impartially all the relevant aspects of the case. In other words, an infringement of procedural rules in administrative areas granting wide discretion to decision-makers is scrutinised by the Union judge with particular attention.

d. *Appraisal Criteria, Coherence and Merit Points*

In the interest of comparability of the appraisals, only the specified criteria may be applied during an appraisal.[500] It must take into account circumstances that inevitably affect performance.[501] The finding of an appraisal must be coherent in itself.[502] Also the coherence of the appraisal practice and comparability as a whole must be guaranteed, for the reason of equal treatment.[503] Secondary criteria can be used to differentiate between equally classified officials.[504] In the case of comparable merits, the same number of points as was attributed to the other – comparable – staff members must not be denied to the official on the grounds that his performance is *no better* than those of the others.[505] An appraisal must indicate if there was an exceptionally high workload

[496] GC, T-23/91, ECLI:EU:T:1992:106, para 40 – *Maurissen v ECA*; GC, T-144/03, ECLI:EU:T:2005:158, para 7 – *Schmit v Commission*; ECJ, Jd Cases 36/81, 37/81 and 218/81, ECLI:EU:C:1983:152, para 23 – *Seton v Commission*.

[497] GC, T-18/93, ECLI:EU:T:1994:255, para 45 – *Marcato v Commission*.

[498] GC, T-92/01, ECLI:EU:T:2002:220, para 24 – *Girardot v Commission*; GC, T-336/02, ECLI:EU:T:2005:115, para 38 – *Christensen v Commission*.

[499] ECJ, C-269/90, ECLI:EU:C:1991:438, para 14 – *Technische Universität München*.

[500] CST, F-38/08, ECLI:EU:F:2009:13, paras 44, 46 – *Liotti v Commission* (essential procedural requirements); CST, F-104/09, ECLI:EU:F:2011:29, paras 51, 53 – *Canga Fano v Council*.

[501] CST, F-52/05, ECLI:EU:F:2008:161, paras 269/270 – *Q v Commission* (hospitalisation); CST, F-51/08 RENV, ECLI:EU:F:2011:193, para 59 – *Stols v Council*; CST, F-20/09, ECLI:EU:F:2011:181, para 51 – *Juvyns v Council*; CST, F-4/10, ECLI:EU:F:2011:134, para 71 – *Nastvogel v Council*.

[502] CST, F-51/08, ECLI:EU:F:2009:14, paras 21, 30 – *Stols v Council*; CST, F-74/05, ECLI:EU:F:2006:135, para 51 – *Caldarone v Commission* (contradictory first and second assessment); CST, F-7/09, ECLI:EU:F:2010:9, paras 55, 57 – *Faria v OHIM*.

[503] Such coherence can be questionable in the case of too little validation time being allowed for the countersigning official: CST, F-38/08, ECLI:EU:F:2009:13, paras 37, 42 – *Liotti v Commission*.

[504] CST, F-7/08, ECLI:EU:F:2009:10, para 44 – *Schönberger v EP* (eg, by seniority); CST, F-148/06, ECLI:EU:F:2008:169, paras 40, 43 – *Collée v EP*.

[505] CST, F-7/08, ECLI:EU:F:2009:10, paras 22, 59 – *Schönberger v EP*; also CST, F-104/09, ECLI:EU:F:2011:29, paras 60, 63 – *Canga Fano v Council*.

and, in the case of part-time engagement, must take into account the difference in the quantity of work assigned.[506] Where the staff member is being criticised in the appraisal report for a lack of knowledge, he cannot refer to the absence of an offer of training they had not actively requested such a training measure.[507] Appraisals form the basis for the consideration of the comparative merits of the officials eligible for promotion under Article 45(1) SR.

The overall performance of the staff member in the performance appraisal is expressed in merit points, supplemented by priority points awarded in the supplementary promotion process. Performance is evaluated with up to 20 merit points in three areas: maximum 10 for performance; maximum 6 for ability; and maximum 4 for conduct in the service.[508] The required coherence also refers to a consistency between the assessments (in marks or points) and the comments intended to justify them.[509]

e. *Review of Appraisal*

Compared with usual remedies, there are two important differences regarding the review procedures applicable to appraisal reports. First, exceptionally, it is not required to lodge a formal complaint (Art 90 SR) in order to contest an appraisal. The reason for this is that the report expresses the opinions freely drawn up by reporting officers, and is not the appointing authority's assessment; hence a complaint to the appointing authority against the appraisal is not a necessary precondition for bringing an action. Instead, the action can be brought directly once the report is final.[510] Secondly, neither the complaint nor the action against an appraisal report presuppose the prior unsuccessful lodging of an internal appeal (if such an appeal is provided for in the general implementing provisions (GIP)).[511]

The official has the right to obtain an appraisal. She or he continues to have an interest in contesting the assessment even after changing institutions in the meantime or after having been promoted, possibly even after their employment has ended due to disability. The continuation of interest in contesting an appraisal after retirement is determined by the question whether the incapacity to work is final or whether there is more than just a hypothetical possibility of reinstatement.[512] In the case of an appraisal that is defamatory, compensation for damages is possible in addition to the annulment of the report if the defamation cannot be eliminated either retrospectively or in a subsequent assessment.[513]

[506] CST, F-7/09, ECLI:EU:F:2010:9, paras 52/53 – *Faria v OHIM* (workload). Differentiation in the case of part-time work may or must be objectively and strictly related to changed work assignments, see CST, F-68/09, ECLI:EU:F:2011:11, para 100 – *Barbin v EP*; CST, F-50/11, ECLI:EU:F:2012:51, paras 50, 65/66 – *Buxton v EP*, Potvin-Solis (2011) *RUE* 616 and CJEU Annual Report 2012, 219 on CST, F-52/05 RENV, ECLI:EU:F:2012:139 – *Q v Commission*.

[507] CST, F-49/08, ECLI:EU:F:2009:76, para 80 – *Giannini v Commission*.

[508] On a comparative study, see Staroňová, 'Performance appraisal in the EU member states and the European Commission' (2017).

[509] GC, T-23/91, ECLI:EU:T:1992:106, para 41 – *Maurissen v ECA*; GC, T-165/04, ECLI:EU:T:2006:213, para 84 – *Vounakis v Commission*; GC, T-336/22, ECLI:EU:T:2023:652, para 51 – *Gomez Calavia v CJEU*.

[510] GC, T-298/20, ECLI:EU:T:2022:671, para 22 – *KD v EUIPO*; ECJ, Jd Cases 6/79 and 97/79, ECLI:EU:C:1980:178, para 15 – *Grassi v Council*.

[511] GC, T-298/20, ECLI:EU:T:2022:671, paras 26–31 – *KD v EUIPO*, see subsequent case study; Reithmann (2011) 1 *EuR* 138; CST, Jd Cases F-138/06 and F-37/08, ECLI:EU:F:2009:48, para 39 – *Meister v OHIM*.

[512] ECJ, C-198/07 P, ECLI:EU:C:2008:761, para 48 – *Gordon v Commission*. The interest in bringing an action must not be denied only because of the possibility of obtaining compensation for damages suffered: CST, F-44/05 RENV, ECLI:EU:F:2012:144, paras 48/49, 97, 101 – *Strack v Commission*.

[513] CST, F-26/09, ECLI:EU:F:2010:17, paras 95, 101/102 – *N v EP*.

Case Study on Appraisal Report and the Duty to State Reasons

Appraisal report: On the importance of stating reasons, of adherence to the facts, and the taking into account of any health problems of staff

Case T-298/20, *KD v EUIPO* of 26 October 2022

In Brief

In *KD v EUIPO*,[514] the General Court (GC) ruled on the review of an appraisal report. An action against such a report (once final) can be filed directly, without going through the complaints procedure and without being obliged to lodge an appeal. In the present case, the GC annulled the appraisal report, because (a) it lacked the reasoning in respect to an assessment that led to a lower-than-required mark; (b) it was vitiated by an error of fact, because an allegation in the appraisal could not be proved; and (c) the report did not take into account the health problems of the staff member.

Legal Background

An appraisal report is the 'annual report' in Article 43(1) SR, which stipulates:

> The ability, efficiency and conduct in the service of each official shall be the subject of an annual report as provided for by the appointing authority of each institution in accordance with Article 110. That report shall state whether or not the performance level of the official has been satisfactory. The appointing authority of each institution shall lay down provisions conferring the right to lodge an appeal within the reportingprocedure, which has to be exercised before the lodging of a complaint as referred to in Article 90(2).

Facts of the Case

In 2015, the applicant was recruited as a temporary agent at EUIPO for a five-year period under Article 2f CEOS. In February 2020, an appraisal interview for the year 2019 took place. In March 2020, the applicant received the contested appraisal report relating to the year 2019. The report contained the sections 'General Information', 'Employee Information', 'Appraisal Dialogue', 'Comments on working conditions including teleworking (if applies)', 'Assessment of Objectives', 'Objectives achieved assessment', 'Conduct in the service', 'Assessment of Competencies', 'Review of Development Plan' and 'Overall Appraisal Rating'. The competencies of 'Prioritisation and Organisation' and 'Resilience' were awarded a mark of 2, whereas the mark required was 3. In the section 'Overall comments on Competencies', the report stated that she 'writes quickly, clearly and correctly' and 'has a sound level of job knowledge'. Those observations state, however, as regards 'her prioritisation and organisation, [that] on [a] few occasions she was reminded to keep deadlines and anticipate'. The overall assessment closes with the statement that the applicant has attained her objectives, demonstrates adequate skills, anticipates tasks and strives to maintain and deliver consistently high levels of work output and looks to

[514] GC, T-298/20, ECLI:EU:T:2022:671 – *KD v EUIPO*.

improve quality at all times. One month after this report, the administration informed the applicant that her contract would not be renewed, and that – in the non-renewal-decision – it had taken account of the said appraisal report.

Decision of the General Court

The GC annuls the contested appraisal report, on the grounds of failure to state reasons, error of fact and breach of the duty of care. The claim for compensation in respect of non-material harm is dismissed by the GC.

Admissibility

The defendant EUIPO, first, raises an important question on the admissibility of an action against an appraisal report: what does Article 7 of the Commission Decision[515] laying down general provisions for implementing Article 43 SR mean when it stipulates an obligation to lodge an appeal before lodging a complaint within the meaning of Article 90 SR? And, secondly, can a direct action to the GC be filed even if the appeal has not been lodged? EUIPO had claimed that staff may not bring an action directly before the GC against an appraisal report where there is an internal appeals procedure available, such as the one provided for by the GIP.

The GC dismisses this argumentation and states that due to the nature of the appraisal report, which expresses the opinions freely drawn up by reporting officers, and not the appointing authority's assessment, the lodging of a formal complaint under Article 90 SR is not a necessary precondition for bringing an action against such a measure. An *action against the appraisal report lies as from the date on which that report can be regarded as final*. The GC considers an internal appeal not to be an additional condition of the admissibility of complaints, but specifies that it would be inadmissible to start an internal appeal only in the later stages of the litigation. If the complaint is not a necessary precondition for bringing legal proceedings, the GC states, 'it cannot *a fortiori* be considered that the Council thus impliedly intended to make the admissibility of such an action subject to the lodging of an internal appeal'. Further, the GC adds that the institutions have no power to derogate from a right under the SR by means of an implementing provision. To assume that an internal appeal procedure had to be exhausted before it was possible to challenge an appraisal report at the GC would amount to an infringement of the fundamental right to an effective remedy and access to an independent tribunal (Art 47, Art 52(1) FRC).

Substance

On the merits of the case, the applicant put forward three pleas in law in support of her claim for annulment: first, a breach of the duty to state reasons, an infringement of the rights of the defence, and an error of fact; secondly, a breach of the duty of care; and thirdly, manifest errors of assessment. First, the GC finds that the contested report is vitiated by a breach of EUIPO's duty to state reasons (Art 296 TFEU and Art 41(2)(c) FRC) for the mark awarded to the applicant under the 'Resilience' competency. The purpose of this principle of EU law is to provide the person concerned with sufficient details to enable

[515] General Implementing Provisions (GIP).

her to assess whether the act adversely affecting her is well founded and whether it would be expedient to bring legal proceedings to contest its legality. Additionally, it enables the judge to review that act. The contested report defined the 'Resilience' competency as the ability to 'remain effective under work pressure, be flexible and adapt to a changing work environment'. The GC found that the appraisal report was devoid of any observation as to this competency: 'Neither the "Overall comments on competencies" nor the "Manager's overall assessment comments" contain the slightest express reference to that competency'. The report's comment on deadlines concerns the competency 'Prioritisation and Organisation'; the qualities of anticipation and proactiveness are primarily associated with organisation and compliance with deadlines, not with resilience. Since this could have influenced the reporting officer's decision on the overall mark, the GC found this ground sufficient for the contested report to be annulled.

Secondly, in regard to the other grounds relied on by the applicant, the GC states a reminder that it is not for the GC to substitute its assessment for that of the appraising officers, who enjoy a wide discretion when appraising. For its part, the GC is limited to ensuring that the procedure is conducted in a regular manner, the facts are materially correct, and there is no manifest error of assessment or misuse of powers.

The Court also found that the reporting officer does not have to include all the relevant matters of fact and law in support of her observations, but still has to establish the facts and other concrete examples relied on in support of the observations. In the case in question, the criticism in the appraisal report that the applicant had 'to be reminded to keep deadlines' amounts, in the opinion of the GC, to an error of fact, because the material in the file casts doubt on the truthfulness of the reminders. The applicant could rely on the substantive inaccuracy of the comment in question, which is the only comment in the contested report that is negative, and in respect of which it consequently cannot be ruled out that it had a negative influence on the applicant's overall mark.

Finally, the GC found an infringement of the duty of care. The duty of care reflects the balance of the reciprocal rights and obligations established by the SR, and by analogy the CEOS, in the relationship between a public authority and its civil servants. Like the right to sound administration, that balance implies in particular that when the authority takes a decision concerning the position of a member of staff, it should take into consideration all the factors which may affect its decision, and that when doing so it should take into account not only the interests of the service, but also those of the staff member concerned. As the GC further states, the administration is bound by substantially enhanced obligations under the duty of care where the physical or mental health of a staff member is involved. In such a case, the administration must take due account of those health problems when taking the action in question. The GC concludes that the duty of care was violated, because the contested report did 'not contain the slightest reference to those problems', nor did EUIPO take into account those problems in any way in the appraisal procedure.

Comments

1. The various institutions apply the appraisal exercise differently. This case illustrates some common basic principles that always have to be respected. The concrete appraisal report of the applicant was vitiated by a failure to state reasons, an error of fact, and a breach of the duty of care. The central point of the decision is that the

reasoning of the report was insufficient regarding the 'Resilience' competency in the appraisal report – for which the required mark was not awarded. It is important to note that the non-awarding of the (lower) mark was or could have been decisive for the overall assessment.

2. The conclusions from this judgment are: (1) that appraisal reports should be checked against their *sound reasoning* (a) as to the pertinence and truthfulness of the facts mentioned therein, (b) as to the sound reasoning and justification of the assessment, particularly where the assessment leads to a lower mark than the required mark; (2) that the administration has to take into account the health problems of the staff member when adopting the appraisal report.
3. The GC primarily found a lack of reasoning in the appraisal report, Article 296 TFEU, thus a horizontally applicable criterion of legality. The duty to state reasons[516] must be considered with reference not only to the wording, but also to its context, which was known to the person concerned, in order to understand the scope of the measure. According to case-law it is sufficient, in principle, for the reporting officer to set out the salient points of the official's performance as regards their efficiency, ability and conduct in service. The reporting officer is not required to specify all the relevant factual and legal elements of the appraisal. The report must, however, give reasons for the assessment of the work under the various mandatory sections of the appraisal report.
4. The benchmark for the annulment of an appraisal report is that the review by the courts of its content is limited to ensuring that the *procedure is conducted in a regular manner, the facts are materially correct, and there is no manifest error of assessment or misuse of powers.*
5. The duty of care reflects the balance of the reciprocal rights and obligations. The specificity of the present case is that it points to the *enhanced obligations* under the duty of care where the physical or mental health of a staff member is involved. This obviously presupposes that the staff member brings health problems to the attention of the administration in a timely manner.
6. As to the admissibility of the action, the GC confirms that an action for annulment of the appraisal report can be filed *directly* without having to appeal against the report to the appeal assessor, and without having to lodge a complaint under Article 90 SR. Thus the *appeal* mentioned in the GIP merely provides the staff member with an additional instrument which (should they wish to do so) they must lodge *before* a formal complaint and, a fortiori, before an action for annulment. In other words, the '*appeal*' under the GIP is not an additional precondition for the admissibility of an action. In the interpretation of the Court, this is what is meant when Artic;e 43 SR speaks about the 'right to lodge an appeal': it is an optional instrument.
7. It can be concluded that the *appeal* procedure mentioned in the GIP has a separate significance mostly for as long as the appraisal report is not final, because during that time an action is not yet admissible.

[516] See section I.3. above.

8. The same exception of a direct action without the need to go through a complaints procedure incidentally applies to the decisions of a selection board in a competition. Here, the argument is that the appointing authority is not empowered to amend such decisions.[517] In both constellations (competition and appraisal reports), it is safe to conclude that – should a complaint have been lodged nevertheless – there is no need to await the decision on the complaint before filing the action.[518]

14. Promotion

The career of a civil servant develops progressively through advancement in accordance with the SR, in particular through promotion. Promotion is effected by decision of the appointing authority, into the next-higher grade of the function group, and is subject to budgetary constraints the calculation of which is based on multiplication rates laid down in the tables of Annex I, Section B SR (see below). Since the 2014 reform, normal career promotions are possible up to positions in grade AD 12 (administrators), for advisers and heads of unit up to AD 14, directors up to AD 15 and assistants up to AST 9.[519] Appointment into functions of higher responsibility presupposes the successful passing of a selection procedure.

Seniority

In accordance with Article 45(1) SR, promotion shall be among officials who have completed a minimum of two years in their grade. This relatively short minimum waiting time shall better take account of outstanding performance. Seniority is calculated as of the date of the promotion itself, not the date of the promotion procedure's start,[520] or the date of the end of the appraisal period.[521] Seniority for promotion as an official is exclusively based on the periods acquired as official, excluding periods acquired as temporary agent, even if these were served in the same functions and grade.[522]

Budget constraints

Further to Article 6 SR, the establishment plan appended to the section of the budget relating to each institution shall indicate the number of posts in each grade and function group. 'That plan shall ensure that, for each institution, the number of vacant positions at every grade of the establishment plan on 1 January of each year corresponds to the number of officials in the lower grade in active employment on 1 January of the preceding year, multiplied by the rates laid down in Annex I, Section B, for that grade.'

[517] ECJ, 7/77, ECLI:EU:C:1978:68 – *Ritter von Wüllerstorff*; ECJ, 144/82, ECLI:EU:C:1983:211 – *Detti*; CST, F-66/11, ECLI:EU:F:2012:88 – *Cristina*.

[518] On these exceptions, see chapter 2, VI.1.h.

[519] *cf* Annex I, Section A SR, and Annex XIII, Art 30 ff SR.

[520] GC, T-132/03, ECLI:EU:T:2005:324, para 84 – *Casini v Commission*.

[521] CST, F-65/14, ECLI:EU:F:2015:53, para 29 – *EF v EEAS*.

[522] GC, T-366/15 P, ECLI:EU:T:2016:729, paras 48/49 – *Androva v Council*.

The higher grade
The promoted official appointed to a higher grade below the position of head of unit shall be placed in the initial step in that grade, Article 46 SR. In the case of higher grades, they shall be placed in the second step of the new grade. The increments of the seniority steps within a grade are not identical, but decrease with increasing steps. Thus, the financial benefit of promotion increases the sooner a promotion is achieved. Since the base salary for the last step in seniority is the same as that for the first step in the next-higher salary bracket, a 'late' promotion does not initially result in an increase in salary. The promotion procedure is not the same for all institutions. The subsequent description focuses on the method applied in the Commission.[523] The differences in promotion and appraisal systems among the institutions have repercussions on the mobility of staff and the career of officials transferred to or on secondment in other institutions. As opposed to Article 43 SR concerning staff reports, under Article 45 SR an institution is not obliged to adopt a regulatory framework on the implementation of the promotion procedures, nor to introduce specific rules governing the situation of officials who have been subject to mobility. However, the institutions must ensure that mobility does not impair the career progress, and examine the situation of officials who have been subject to mobility in order to ensure that officials who have been transferred are not penalised in a promotion procedure.[524] An official on secondment retains his post, his right to advancement to a higher step and his eligibility for promotion, Article 38(f) SR. The career development reports of seconded officials are drawn up by their original service and not by their superiors in their host institution. When doing this, an institution cannot reasonably rely on the alleged difficulty of comparing the respective merits of seconded officials and non-seconded officials. Case-law stipuates that the comparison of the merits of seconded officials with those of non-seconded officials remains possible, and has to ensure the equal treatment of all officials.[525]

a. Comparative Merits

The promotion decision is based on a selection after considering the comparative merits of the officials eligible for promotion. When considering comparative merits, the appointing authority shall in particular take account of the reports on the officials, the use of languages in the execution of their duties other than the language for which they have produced evidence of thorough knowledge,[526] and the level of responsibility exercised by them, Article 45 SR. As case-law has clarified, the official does not need to have perfect knowledge of a language in order for it to be taken into account in assessing the factor relating to use of languages. The minimum level of knowledge required must be determined by reference to the needs of the service, with particular regard to the nature of the tasks to be performed.[527]

[523] Gauer (2007) 138, 150 and Oechsler/Noack, *Personalbeurteilung in europäischen und internationalen Organisationen*, Studie im Auftrag des Bundesministeriums des Innern (2009). 25; CST, F-14/09, ECLI:EU:F:2010:167, para 35 – *Almeida Campos and Others v Council*; CST, F-20/09, ECLI:EU:F:2011:181, para 42 – *Juvyns v Council*; CST, F-75/11, ECLI:EU:F:2012:152, para 37 – *Bouillez v Council*.

[524] CST, F-57/06, ECLI:EU:F:2007:188, paras 58–60 – *Hinderyckx v Council*.

[525] GC, T-51/08 P, ECLI:EU:T:2011:702, paras 62–67 – *Commission v Dittert*.

[526] Art 28 lit f SR. Languages are taken into account where they provide a sufficiently important added value to the actual requirements of the service, GC, T-95/12 P, ECLI:EU:T:2014:3, para 47 – *Stols v Council*; CST, F-9/10, ECLI:EU:F:2011:160, para 61 – *AC v Council*.

[527] GC, T-281/11 P, ECLI:EU:T:2013:252, para 117 – *Canga Fano v Council*.

Other information (such as a probationary report) may only be used in exceptional circumstances.[528] It is the three components (reports, languages, level of responsibility) that enable the merits of a candidate for promotion to be evaluated. For a proper comparison, *all* components need to be taken into account.[529] The component of *level of responsibility* has a broadening effect on the assessment of merits under Article 45 SR, compared with the situation before 2004.[530] The former reservation that the *level of responsibility* was only to be taken into account 'where appropriate', ie, if the merits were otherwise the same, was removed by the reform of 2014. The level of responsibility of a candidate is not automatically expressed by his performance of managerial tasks or by a (high) number of subordinates to the effect that a decision not to non-promote that candidate would amount to a manifest error of assessment.[531] Likewise, the level of responsibility exercised by officials may not depend solely on the legal classification of their functions under the SR; also the duties actually carried out by them, other than their official duties, may be taken into account for the purpose of determining whether the appointing authority has made a manifest error in comparing the level of responsibility exercised by them.[532]

Long-term consistency of merits

Seniority in grade and in the service may be applied as a criterion for promotion only as a *secondary* consideration, where candidates prove to have otherwise equal merits on the three criteria of Article 45 SR (reports, languages, level of responsibility). However, the appointing authority may lawfully assess the comparative merits of officials eligible for promotion on the basis of the long-term consistency of their respective merits. The criterion of long-term consistency of merits is not separate from the three criteria listed in Article 45 SR, but is directly covered by the appraisal reports on the officials.[533]

Point system

For the purpose of the practical preparation of the promotion decision, a point system is used, according to which officials are awarded points in the appraisal and promotion procedure, and which they accumulate over the years. As soon as a point score determined to be a promotion threshold (depending on the establishment plan) is achieved, the promotion takes place regardless of age or waiting time for promotion. If there are fewer opportunities for promotion than there are civil servants above and on the promotion threshold, a selection has to be made *ex aequo* from among those staff members. The promotion thresholds increase with rank. Career advancement slows down as rank increases, which has led to the fear that there could be problems – or at

[528] GC, T-202/99, ECLI:EU:T:2000:227, paras 40, 54 – *Rappe v Commission*; GC, T-511/18, ECLI:EU:T:2020:291, paras 144–50 – *XH v Commission*, specifies four conditions for the existence of such exceptional circumstances. The CST granted greater leeway, assuming that Art 45 SR does not prohibit the consideration of other factual aspects (beyond those mentioned there) in which performance can be expressed: CST, F-75/11, ECLI:EU:F:2012:152, para 57 – *Bouillez v Council*. A mediating view seems justifiable.

[529] *cf* CST, F-53/08, ECLI:EU:F:2010:37, paras 65, 69 – *Bouillez and Others v Council*, where the level of responsibilities was not taken into account; Gervasoni (2010) 46 *Cahiers de droit européen* 760.

[530] CST, F-104/09, ECLI:EU:F:2011:29, para 30 – *Canga Fano v Council*; GC, T-95/12 P, ECLI:EU:T:2014:3, para 59 – *Stols v Council*.

[531] GC, T-175/09 P, ECLI:EU:T:2010:534, para 48 – *Council v Stols*.

[532] GC, T-281/11 P, ECLI:EU:T:2013:252, para 78 – *Canga Fano v Council*.

[533] GC, T-95/12 P, ECLI:EU:T:2014:3, para 41 – *Stols v Council*; GC, T-410/15 P, ECLI:EU:T:2016:465, para 61 – *Pohjanmäki v Council*.

least delays – when filling managerial positions, which might have to be solved by filling positions with external staff.[534]

Temporary agents of agencies

Temporary agents are recruited at a certain grade without the same career perspective as officials. As a consequence of this, promotion to the next higher grade of temporary agents is subject to classification. In the case of temporary staff of EU agencies (Art 2(f) CEOS), Article 54 CEOS specifies that classification in the next higher grade shall be exclusively by selection from among staff members who have completed a minimum period of two years in their grade, after consideration of the comparative merits of such temporary staff and of the reports on them.[535] Further, the multiplication rates for guiding average career equivalence, as set out for officials in Section B of Annex I to the SR, may not be exceeded. Details are regulated by general implementation provisions adopted by each agency. When considering the various candidates for classification in the next higher grade, as in promotion, the principle of equal treatment has to be respected.[536]

b. Priority Points

On this ground, the merit points of the appraisal procedure are supplemented by priority points in the so-called 'second round' of the promotion procedure.[537] The Director-General can assign up to 10 priority points for merit, half of which go to around 15 per cent of the above-average civil servants and are intended to accentuate the differentiation in the appraisals. In addition, joint promotion committees can award up to two points for services rendered in the interests of the institution (such as serving on a selection board). A maximum of 32 points can be achieved in an appraisal and promotion procedure.

c. Merit List

Based on the priority points, a list of merit is established, which may be appealed to the Promotions Committee. When doing so, waiting time for promotion, equal opportunities considerations and the types of functions performed only have subordinate relevance. Officials who were considered worthy of promotion in one year but were not promoted may not be automatically promoted in the following year without comparisons first being made with those who are then up for assessment.[538] Nevertheless, the nomination of staff members as deserving promotion is evidence of past performance, and must be appropriately taken into account later if no promotion occurs that year.[539]

[534] Oechsler/Noack, *Personalbeurteilung in europäischen und internationalen Organisationen*, Studie im Auftrag des Bundesministeriums des Innern (2009) 25/26; Sebastiani, 'L'évaluation de la réforme' in Govaere/Vandersanden (eds), *La fonction publique communautaire* (2008) 41.

[535] Art 45(1) final sentence and Art 45(2) SR apply by analogy (reports, languages and level of responsibilities, ability to work in a third language).

[536] GC, T-484/22, ECLI:EU:T:2023:741, paras 189–91 – *QN v eu-LISA*.

[537] CST, F-102/07, ECLI:EU:F:2009:129, paras 65 ff, 93 – *Kerstens v Commission* (leeway); on the start of time limits in the promotion procedure: only access to the personal promotion file makes it possible to know the number of points and their composition, GC, T-311/04, ECLI:EU:T:2006:329, paras 112 ff– *Buendía Sierra v Commission*.

[538] GC, T-76/98, ECLI:EU:T:1999:67, paras 44 ff – *Hamptaux v Commission*; GC, T-22/99, ECLI:EU:T:2000:47 – *Rose v Commission*.

[539] CST, F-107/06, ECLI:EU:F:2007:172, paras 23, 68, 73, 76 – *Berrisford v Commission*; CST, F-125/07, ECLI:EU:F:2009:131, paras 28, 29 – *Hau v EP*.

d. Promotion List

The names of the officials to be promoted are published on a promotion list. This publication is also possible while the necessary basis is not yet fully established due to pending complaint procedures. It is not illegal to adopt promotion decisions before all the attributions of merit points are final, unless the delay for taking the final decision is solely due to administrative irregularities.[540]

e. Motivation of Promotion Decision and Review

A promotion decision, being the result of selection, does not require motivation, due to its evaluative nature. The implicit refusal decision on the remaining (initially considered) candidates who were not promoted can be challenged by a complaints procedure.[541] The (implicit) decision not to promote a candidate does not have to be discussed. Yet, the decision rejecting the complaint lodged against the (implicit) decision not to promote must be formally determined.[542] For the motivation, it is sufficient to refer to compliance with the formal criteria for promotion and the individual reasons in relation to the rejected candidate; a comparative presentation of the qualifications and merits of the person promoted is not required.[543] The documents that are supposed to justify the selection decision must exist and already be available at the time the decision on the complaint is adopted: they cannot just be effectively created and inserted into court proceedings at the litigation stage.[544]

There is no such thing as an actual right to be promoted – not even in cases where, for example, other institutions rate comparable tasks higher, or there was a certain number of subordinates,[545] or a higher-ranking position was exercised over a period, or the superior has been substituted for a while.[546] In the case of a temporary substitution of the superior, the 2004 reform stipulated in Article 7 SR[547] that from the beginning of the fourth month of such a temporary posting, the official shall receive a differential allowance equal to the difference between the remuneration carried by his substantive grade and step vs the remuneration he would receive in respect of the step at which he would be classified if he were appointed to the grade of his temporary posting. The duration of such a posting shall in principle not exceed one year.

The selection decision of the appointing authority is characterised by wide discretion, subject solely to a judicial review as to whether the 'reasonable'[548] limits of discretion have been complied with and no manifest error of assessment has been committed.[549] In particular, the court examines

540 CST, F-47/07, ECLI:EU:F:2009:103, para 76 – *Behmer v EP*.

541 Reithmann (2011) 1 *EuR* 134.

542 GC, T-410/15 P, ECLI:EU:T:2016:465, paras 77 ff – *Pohjanmäki v Council*; CST, F-11/11, ECLI:EU:F:2012:8, para 22 – *Bouillez and Others v Council*.

543 GC, T-230/99, ECLI:EU:T:2001:161, para 52 – *McAuley v Council*.

544 CST, F-53/08, ECLI:EU:F:2010:37, paras 70 ff – *Bouillez and Others v Council*.

545 ECJ, 14/79, ECLI:EU:C:1979:287, para 7 – *Loebisch v Council*; also the status of the subordinates is irrelevant.

546 GC, T-157/99 – ECLI:EU:T:2000:192 – *Griesel v Council*.

547 Art 7 SR applies 'by analogy' to temporary staff (but not to contract staff), Art 10(1) CEOS; on the term 'by analogy', see chapter 2, V.2. at the end.

548 ECJ, 282/81, ECLI:EU:C:1983:105, para 9 – *Ragusa*.

549 GC, T-283/97, ECLI:EU:T:1999:84, para 42 – *Thinus v Commission*. CJEU Annual Report 2012, 219 with reference to CST, F-23/11, ECLI:EU:F:2012:9 – *AY v Council*, but the judgment was overturned in appeal, *cf* GC, T-167/12 P, ECLI:EU:T:2013:524, para 43 – *Council v AY*. Potvin-Solis/Lelièvre (2012) *RUE* 287 with reference to CST, F-20/09, ECLI:EU:F:2011:181, para 42 – *Juvyns v Council*. When filling top positions, it is permissible to focus more on general leadership qualities or analysis and assessment skills rather than in-depth technical knowledge, CST, F-72/10, ECLI:EU:F:2011:170, para 62 – *da Silva Tenreiro*.

whether the prescribed comparison of the merits of the various candidates was made on an objective basis and on the appraisals indispensable for this purpose. Since the opportunities for promotion are limited in number, an official can often achieve his goal of promotion only by causing a competitor's promotion to be revoked. Although a member of staff cannot claim a right to be promoted, he nevertheless has an interest in disputing a decision to promote another member of staff to a grade for which he is eligible to apply and against which he lodged a complaint that was rejected.[550] His personal interest in bringing the annulment action for contesting the promotion of the competitor is based on the interest in his own promotion.[551] In the case of legal errors in promotion procedures – unlike in competition procedures – complete annulment of the promotion exercise is not necessarily considered to be a disproportionate consequence. The review of a promotion procedure is carried out as a multi-stage assessment, in which a distinction is first made between substantive and procedural errors; then the interests concerned are weighed against each other.[552] Case-law sets out an approach close to equity when it examines an aggregation of elements that might play a role: namely the interests of the service, in particular respect for legality; the budgetary consequences of the failure to annul illegal decisions; possible difficulties in complying with the judgment to be delivered; any adverse effects on the continuity of the service; and the danger of a deterioration in the social atmosphere within the institution.[553] These should be taken into account on a case-by-case basis when deciding whether or not to annul the promotion decision. In addition, where eventually the annulment of the promotion decision constitutes an excessive penalty for the illegality found, the court may, in the interest of the applicant, make use of its unlimited jurisdiction in disputes of a financial character and may, even of its own motion, order the institution to pay compensation (see subsequent section f).

As yet another solution in the triangular situation of a passed-over applicant vis-à-vis one or more promoted competitor(s), the court resorted to changing the original framework of the promotion procedure. This somehow gives the impression of an outcome similar to an amicable settlement or an action for performance if the appointing authority is asked during court proceedings to give a definitive commitment that, in order to comply with the (anticipated) judgment,[554] it will undertake a fresh consideration of the comparative merits of the applicant and, where appropriate, promote the applicant retroactively *in addition to the officials already promoted.*[555]

f. Compensation for Damage Suffered

An award of damages is also possible in actions brought by a competitor against the promotion decision, in particular if the position has been filled in the meantime.[556] As in other cases, first, the annulment of the contested promotion already represents appropriate reparation,[557] so that compensation for damage suffered, even in symbolic form, is only awarded in particularly serious cases.[558] Next to the establishment of the illegal rejection, the unsuccessful applicant has to show the causal link between the rejection and the material injury he will suffer in terms of the

[550] GC, T-328/01, ECLI:EU:T:2004:13, paras 32/33 – *Robinson v EP.*

[551] CST, F-53/08, ECLI:EU:F:2010:37, paras 21, 80, 93 – *Bouillez and Others v Council*; CST, F-51/10, ECLI:EU:F:2012:136, para 49 – *Bermejo Garde v EESC.*

[552] CST, F-53/08, ECLI:EU:F:2010:37, para 88 – *Bouillez and Others v Council.*

[553] ibid, paras 89/90.

[554] Art 266 TFEU.

[555] CST, F-53/08, ECLI:EU:F:2010:37, paras 91, 99/100 – *Bouillez and Others v Council.*

[556] CST, F-46/07, ECLI:EU:F:2008:129, paras 213, 223/224 – *Tzirani v Commission.*

[557] CST, F-32/06, ECLI:EU:F:2007:169, paras 76 ff – *De la Cruz v European Agency for Safety and Health at Work.*

[558] CST, F-125/05, ECLI:EU:F:2007:18, para 99 – *Tsarnavas v Commission* (promotion).

difference between the salary and benefits to which he would have been entitled had he been appointed versus those which he actually received. The degree of certainty of the causal link is less where the wrongful act committed by the institution has definitely deprived a person – not necessarily of the award of the post in question, to which the person concerned could never prove he had a right – but of a *genuine chance* of being appointed to that post, resulting in material damage in the form of loss of income. Where a promotion seems eminently probable, the 'theoretical uncertainty as regards the outcome of a properly conducted recruitment procedure cannot preclude reparation for the material damage he sustained in having his candidature rejected for the post which he would have had every chance of securing'.[559]

Case Study on Promotion

Vitiated promotion procedure: In principle, promotions must be based solely on appraisal reports

Case T-511/18, *XH v Commission* of 25 June 2020

In Brief

The General Court (GC) had to annul the decision not to promote an official. The promotion procedure was vitiated because it also took into account earlier reports relating to the applicant's probationary period, instead of being solely based on appraisal reports. 'Other information' concerning the administrative and personal situation of the candidates for promotion (ie, other than appraisal reports) may only be taken into account in exceptional circumstances. The GC determines these exceptional circumstances in an *obiter dictum*.

Background

The central norm for promotions, which was infringed in the present case, is Article 45(1) SR. It provides that, when considering comparative merits, the appointing authority in particular has to take account of the reports on the officials. Article 4(1)(a) of the GIP (General Implementing Provisions) stipulates, inter alia, that, for the purposes of the examination of the comparative merits of the officials eligible for promotion, the appointing authority has to take into account, in particular, reports on the officials drawn up since their last promotion – or, failing that, since their recruitment – and most particularly, staff reports drawn up in accordance with the general provisions for implementing Article 43 SR.

Facts of the Case

The applicant (an official of OLAF) was recruited at grade AD 5, subject to a probationary period. An interim probation report indicated difficulties that the applicant encountered

[559] CST, F-46/07, ECLI:EU:F:2008:129, para 218 – *Tzirani v Commission* (promotion). See also Joris, 'L'administration face au contentieux de la fonction publique communautaire' in Govaere/Vandersanden (eds), *La fonction publique communautaire* (2008) 75, with reference to GC, T-115/01 and T-331/00, ECLI:EU:T:2003:317 – *Bories, Bertolo and Others v Commission*.

with colleagues at the start of her probationary period. This was annexed to the end-of-probation report. Later, the applicant was not promoted in the 2017 promotion exercise. She lodged a complaint and subsequently filed an action for annulment of the decision not to promote her. She alleged, inter alia, that Article 45 SR had been infringed, insofar as her interim probation report and end-of-probation report had been taken into account in the consideration of the comparative merits in the 2017 promotion exercise. She was promoted in the subsequent 2018 promotion exercise.

The Decision of the Court

The GC annulled the decision of the Commission not to include the applicant in the list of officials promoted in the 2017 promotion exercise. The GC further awarded compensation of €2,000 to the official for the non-material damage she had suffered.

The GC ruled that, in accordance with Article 45(1) SR and Article 4(1)(a) GIP, when considering the comparative merits in a promotion exercise, the appointing authority is required to take into account, in particular, the appraisal reports that are drawn up for officials. Those appraisal reports constitute an essential assessment criterion each time the official's career is considered for the purpose of making a decision concerning her promotion.

The appointing authority, says the GC, may only take into account other information concerning the administrative and personal situation of the candidates for promotion *in exceptional circumstances*. This can, in particular, be the case when an appraisal report does not exist. However, such additional information cannot remedy the lack of an appraisal report unless four conditions are fulfilled:

(1) It must be sufficiently objective to allow judicial review;
(2) it must contain an assessment of the official's merits by the persons responsible for drawing up her appraisal report;
(3) it must have been disclosed to the official in such a way as to guarantee her rights of defence; and
(4) it must be known to the Promotions Committee when it considers the comparative merits of all the candidates.

This means that information capable of compensating for the lack of an appraisal report must be broadly comparable to that report, as regards its provenance, the procedure for drawing it up, and its purpose.

According to the GC, appraisal reports and reports drawn up during the probationary period have separate purposes and functions, and they cannot be subject to an 'automatic and absolute comparison' because 'the two types of reports have different assessment headings and grading systems'. The assessments in an appraisal report target performance, and are intended to provide the administration with periodic information, while the end-of-probation report is principally intended to evaluate a person's fitness to carry out the work corresponding to her post and to become an established official. The assessments contained in a probation report *cannot be equated to, or substitute for, or compensate for* those carried out in an appraisal report. While the appraisal reports are acts adversely affecting the official, since they are capable of having an influence over the entire course of that official's career, that is not the case for measures relating to the progress of the official's probationary period, such as probation reports, the purpose of which is to establish the basis for the decision of the administration about whether to appoint the person concerned as an established official at the end of the probationary period, or to dismiss that person. For the same reason, the end-of-probation report cannot be contested independently by an action for annulment: its sole purpose is to make preparations for the aforementioned decision.

Thus, the GC concluded that an end-of-probation report, even if it contains a certain number of observations on the official's or other staff member's fitness for work, in principle cannot be taken into account by a promotions committee. Therefore, noting that in the present case, two appraisal reports (2015 and 2016) had been drawn up in respect of the applicant and that the assessments contained in those reports constituted a proper basis for the consideration of the comparative merits provided for in Article 45(1) SR, the GC held that there were no exceptional circumstances that justified taking into account the end-of-probation report and the interim probation report annexed to it in consideration of the applicant's comparative merits in the 2017 promotion exercise. In any event, unlike the appraisal reports, the applicant's interim probation report had not been drawn up either in order to allow for an objective appraisal of the applicant or to assist in assessing her career development. It also contained unusual and harsh criticisms, which was a further reason for precluding the interim probation report from being taken into account in the consideration of the applicant's comparative merits.

The GC concluded that the taking into account, by the competent appointing authority, of the reports relating to the applicant's probationary period, constituted an irregularity capable of vitiating the 2017 promotion procedure that related to her. Since the outcome of the 2017 promotion procedure could have been different in the absence of that procedural irregularity, the GC annulled the decision not to promote the applicant.

Furthermore, it ordered the Commission to pay to the applicant the sum of €2,000 *ex aequo et bono* as compensation for the non-material damage that she had suffered for the anxiety and uncertainty she experienced about her reputation and professional future.

Comments

1. The notice showing those candidates promoted which does *not* contain the name of the person concerned is the decision that can be challenged in a complaint and subsequent court action, because it is simultaneously the decision not to promote the official.
2. The superior drafting an appraisal report enjoys a broad margin of discretion and must, in order to fulfil her responsibilities, make comments about the quality of the official's work.[560] An infringement of procedural rules in administrative areas granting wide discretion to decision-makers is scrutinised by the Union judge with particular attention.
3. The judgment interprets the wording of Article 45 SR and Article 4(1) GIP on 'reports' in the promotion process: appraisal reports constitute an 'indispensable

[560] GC, T-23/91, ECLI:EU:T:1992:106, para 40 – *Maurissen v ECA*; GC, T-144/03, ECLI:EU:T:2005:158, para 7 – *Schmit v Commission*; ECJ, Jd Cases 36/81, 37/81 and 218/81, ECLI:EU:C:1983:152, para 23 – *Seton v Commission*.

criterion' of assessment when considering promotion of an official. The decision not to promote an official is tainted with irregularity where the appointing authority did not consider the comparative merits of officials eligible for promotion, because one or more appraisal reports were not available owing to an error on the part of the administration.[561]

4. An end-of-probation report must not be reused in a promotion procedure, next to appraisal reports. The reason is that end-of-probation reports and appraisal reports are different in nature and function, and the respective assessments under these reporting obligations 'cannot be equated to or substitute or compensate for' one another.
5. The GC acknowledges that in exceptional circumstances,[562] 'other information concerning the administrative and personal situation of the candidates for promotion'[563] can be taken into account, such as here an end-of-probation report, especially when an appraisal report does not exist. This is an *obiter dictum* of the judgment, because the present case did not require a statement regarding this question: as many as two appraisal reports were in the file. It could have sufficed for the GC to state that a report on the probationary period cannot be reused in the promotion process.
6. Nevertheless, the GC even proceeded to lay down, in general, its four cumulative conditions (quoted above) under which 'additional information' can replace or amend an appraisal report. It should be noted that from the judgment it is not fully clear whether the GC is going to apply this concept only to situations where an appraisal report is completely missing, or (more broadly) to each instance of 'other information' that is being added to the promotion exercise (ie, next to an appraisal report). In practice, the difference might not be significant because of the tightness of the conditions set up.
7. It is interesting to note that the GC is thus opening the door to a promotion procedure that allows taking information into account that is not contained in appraisal reports, as long as it is 'broadly comparable' to a report as regards its 'provenance, the procedure for drawing it up and its purpose'. Although this could pave the way for administrative flexibility in the promotion process, it should not be interpreted as an invitation for the superior or the competent authority to skip appraisal reports or to amend them by 'other information' that would jeopardise the purpose and the balanced nature of the appraisal exercise.
8. What seemed to have influenced the present decision of the GC was the harsh and personalised language of the interim probation report, at least as regards the question of whether the probation report and appraisal report can be equated to or compared with one another. The GC accepted the argument that the interim probation report became part of the promotion procedure, although there was no strict evidence provided in that sense: it basically sufficed for the GC to state that a member of the Promotions Committee had accessed the file of the interim probation report before

[561] Also CST, F-118/15, ECLI:EU:F:2016:138, para 38 – *Kotula*; GC, T-25/92, ECLI:EU:T:1993:17, para 43 – *Vela Palacios*, and GC, T-93/03, ECLI:EU:T:2007:209, para 88 – *Konidaris*.
[562] GC, T-202/99, ECLI:EU:T:2000:227, paras 40, 54 – *Rappe v Commission*.
[563] GC, T-511/18, ECLI:EU:T:2020:291, para 127 – *XH v Commission*.

the promotion decision had been taken. The fact that the applicant was promoted in the subsequent promotion exercise also supported the assumption that the contested decision could have been different in the absence of the procedural irregularity (ie, the infringement of Art 45 SR).

9. In effect, this means that an official can argue that a critical comment relating to the probation period must not become part of the appraisal reports and subsequently of a promotion exercise. Where it is already part of the file, a request to remove the report from the file might be appropriate.
10. On the damages:[564] the failure on the part of the competent appointing authority to comply with its obligations under Article 45 SR caused the applicant to suffer a particular non-material damage which cannot be adequately compensated for by the mere annulment of the decision not to promote her. However, she was promoted in the subsequent promotion cycle, so that – in the view of the GC – the damage was somewhat limited.

15. Change of Function Group

Since the 2004 reform, an official in function group AST (from grade 5) may be appointed to a post in function group AD after passing a training and certification procedure under Article 45a SR.[565] The change to function group AD is possible also on the basis of knowledge and ability acquired only after having taken up duties, thereby opening up function group AD to staff members without a university degree. A statement about the suitability for such promotion across function groups is already included in the appraisal report of the civil servants in function group AST.[566] The application of strict admission criteria shall prevent university graduates being able to choose the function group change from AST under Article 45a SR as an easier alternative to regular competition via the more demanding AD selection process.[567] For this purpose, a minimum period of service may be stipulated which is based on the duties of the role rather than on the specific tasks performed by the individual.[568]

16. Transfer and Secondment, Change of Duties

The formal *transfer* of an official to other services in the same institution is done by assignment to another post in accordance with Articles 4, 7 and 29 SR, ie, after the post has been advertised and the applications have been assessed.[569] The *secondment* of an established official to another

[564] Mader (2013) 96(2) *KritV/CritQ/RCrit* 154 ff.

[565] Gauer (2007) 92, 98. On the certification procedure, see Jansen, 'Les modifications apportées au statut' in Govaere/Vandersanden (eds), *La fonction publique communautaire* (2008) 17 ff and 2008 CJEU Annual Report, 212 with further references.

[566] Gauer, *Die Reform des Europäischen öffentlichen Dienstrechts* (2007) 139.

[567] CST, F-126/07, ECLI:EU:F:2008:136, paras 39/40 – *Van Beers v Commission*; Rogalla (2003) 38 *EuR* 670, 674.

[568] ibid, *Van Beers v Commission*, paras 63–67.

[569] According to the SR, a transfer (French *mutation*) in the proper sense of the word occurs only when an official is transferred to a vacant post (*emploi vacant*). This is subject to the formalities prescribed in Arts 4 and 29 SR. By contrast,

institution, agency or a member of an institution takes place after making an application, or on the basis of a decision issued by the appointing authority in the interests of the service.[570] Officials seconded to another institution may apply after six months to be transferred to that institution while maintaining their previous career.[571]

If the official was transferred to a post outside the EU civil service and a leave of absence for personal reasons was applied for and approved for this duty station, it is not possible to assume an absence 'in the interest of service', even if this leave had been suggested to the official.[572] Where a transfer takes place in the interests of the service, the appointing authority may not disregard the special and legitimate interests of those affected,[573] especially if the transfer involves a change in the place of work. It is in accordance with the principle of good administration to listen to the officials concerned[574] and to take their interests into account as far as possible.[575] But the appointing authority is not obliged[576] to orientate its transfer decision in line with these interests, or to provide specific grounds for its decision.[577] Transfer does not require the consent of those concerned.[578] These decisions fall – as long as they are taken in the interests of the service – within the organisational discretion of the appointing authority.

Post with corresponding responsibility

Article 7 SR stipulates the principle that the post to which an official is assigned should correspond to his grade. So, in the event of a change in an official's duties, what should be compared to test such correspondence are his present duties and his grade, not his present and previous duties. There is nothing to prevent a decision from entailing the assignment of new duties which, while they may differ from those previously performed and are regarded by the official concerned as a reduction in his responsibilities, are nevertheless consistent with a post corresponding to his grade. Something that therefore has to be avoided is the new duties clearly falling short of those corresponding to the official's grade and post, taking account of their character, importance and scope.[579]

these formalities do not apply to a change in the assignment of duties (*reaffectation*) of the civil servant, since such a change (*transfert*) does not result in a vacant post. A change in assignment of duties by way of shifting the entire position is not a transfer in the strict sense, even if it happens to be designated as such in practice.

[570] Art 37 SR.

[571] Art 8 SR; the rules on promotion apply, Art 8(3) SR.

[572] CST, F-55/09, ECLI:EU:F:2010:44, paras 11/12, 52, 71 – *Maxwell v Commission*; CST, F-88/09 and 48/10, ECLI:EU:F:2012:171, para 108 – *Z v ECJ*; GC, T-88/13 P, ECLI:EU:T:2015:393 – *Z v ECJ*, and GC, Jd Cases T-118/04 and T-134/04, ECLI:EU:T:2007:37, paras 49/50 – *Caló v Commission.*

[573] GC, T-98/96, ECLI:EU:T:1998:6, para 78 – *Costacurta v Commission.*

[574] ECJ, 131/82, ECLI:EU:C:1983:249 – *Angelini v Commission*; ECJ, 148/82, ECLI:EU:C:1983:250 – *Renaud v Commission*; ECJ, 33/79 and 75/79, ECLI:EU:C:1980:139 – *Kuhner v Commission.*

[575] ECJ, 46/69, ECLI:EU:C:1970:39 – *Reinarz v Commission*; ECJ, 125/8, ECLI:EU:C:1981:248 – *Arning v Commission*; ECJ, 167/86, ECLI:EU:C:1988:266 – *Rousseau v ECA*; GC, T-36/93, ECLI:EU:T:1995:129 – *Ojha v Commission.*

[576] ECJ, 176/82, ECLI:EU:C:1983:214 – *Nebe v Commission*; ECJ, 178/80, ECLI:EU:C:1981:310 – *Bellardi-Ricci and Others v Commission*; ECJ, 125/8, ECLI:EU:C:1981:248 – *Arning v Commission.*

[577] ECJ, 233/85, ECLI:EU:C:1987:82 – *Bonino v Commission*; ECJ, 125/8, ECLI:EU:C:1981:248 – *Arning v Commission*; ECJ, 16/67, ECLI:EU:C:1968:37 – *Labeyrie v Commission.*

[578] ECJ, 161/80 and 162/80, ECLI:EU:C:1981:51 – *Carbognani and Zabetta v Commission*; ECJ, 19/87, ECLI:EU:C:1988:165 – *Hecq v Commission*; ECJ, C-149/86, ECLI:EU:C:1988:179 – *Santarelli*; GC, T-468/20, ECLI:EU:T:2022:137, paras 139/140 – *Kuehne v EP.*

[579] CST, F-119/06, ECLI:EU:F:2008:54, paras 98 ff – *Kerstens v Commission*; on corresponding deployment: CST, F-25/07, ECLI:EU:F:2010:163, paras 78, 119 – *Bleser v ECJ*; CST, F-88/09 and 48/10, ECLI:EU:F:2012:171, paras 132, 135 ff – *Z v ECJ* (assignment unlawful only if the attributed functions are clearly below those that correspond to the rank and position).

Higher responsibility

Where a staff member works in a position of higher responsibility than would correspond to the grade, the rules on appointment and transfer do not provide a right to higher pay, but merely a right to defend against employment in a position exceeding the appropriate level of responsibility.[580] Yet, higher responsibilitiy is an element that may be taken into account in the promotion exercise.[581]

Temporary higher posting

According to Article 7(2) SR, an official may be asked to temporarily occupy a post in a grade in his function group which is higher than his substantive grade. From the beginning of the fourth month of such temporary posting, the official shall receive a differential allowance equal to the difference between the remuneration carried by his substantive grade and step, and the remuneration he would receive in respect of the step at which he would be classified if he were appointed to the grade of his temporary posting.[582] The duration of a temporary posting shall not exceed one year, except where, directly or indirectly, the posting is to replace an official who is seconded to another post in the interests of the service, called up for military service or absent on protracted sick leave.[583]

Obviously, transfer, secondment and change of duties can have positive and/or negative consequences for the member of staff, depending on the concrete circumstances. These may sometimes be unknown or unpredictable. Although it is plausible that the discontinuation of a given task can affect the position and career perspectives of the person concerned,[584] the assertion of a fear of not being sufficiently qualified for the new position might not be enough to impact the decision-making of the institution, nor the supposition of the person concerned his career advancement would be more likely in a different service.[585]

17. Administrative Statuses, Leave and Flexible Working-Time Arrangements

Article 35 SR stipulates that officials shall be assigned one of the following seven administrative statuses: active employment; secondment;[586] leave on personal grounds;[587] non-active status;[588] leave for military service;[589] parental leave or family leave;[590] leave in the interests of the service.[591] In the active employment the official is performing the duties pertaining to the post to which he has been appointed or temporarily assigned.[592]

[580] CST, F-76/05, ECLI:EU:F:2010:117, para 72 – *Torijano Montero v Council.*
[581] GC, T-18/90, ECLI:EU:T:1991:21, paras 25/27 – *Jongen v Commission.*
[582] GC, T-88/13P, ECLI:EU:T:2015:393 – *Z v ECJ*; CST, F-41/10 RENV, ECLI:EU:F:2012:135, para 165 – *Bermejo Garde v EESC*; GC, Jd Cases T-112/96 and T-115/96, ECLI:EU:T:1999:134, para 116 – *Séché v Commission.*
[583] Art 7(2) final sentence SR.
[584] CST, F-30/08, ECLI:EU:F:2010:43, para 104 – *Nanopoulos v Commission.*
[585] CST, F-4/09, ECLI:EU:F:2010:24, para 53 – *De Britto Patrício-Dias v Commission.*
[586] Arts 37–39 SR.
[587] Art 40 SR.
[588] Art 41 SR.
[589] Art 42 SR.
[590] Art 42a, 42b SR.
[591] Art 42c SR.
[592] Art 36 SR.

a. Leave Entitlement: Annual Leave and Special Leave

The entitlement to paid annual leave is a 'particularly important principle' of European social law.[593] The purpose of the entitlement to paid annual leave is to enable the worker to rest and to enjoy a period of relaxation and leisure. The purpose of the entitlement to sick leave is different: it is to enable the person concerned to recover from sickness. The right to paid annual leave is further recognised in Article 31(2) FRC. Officials shall be entitled to annual leave of not less than 24 working days nor more than 30 working days per calendar year.[594] The rules relating to annual leave[595] and to special leave[596] are laid down in Annex V SR. Annual leave may be taken all at once or in several periods as desired by the official and according to the requirements of the service. It must, however, include at least one period of two consecutive weeks. If, during annual leave, an official contracts an illness which would have prevented him from attending for duty if he had not been on leave, his annual leave shall be extended by the duration of his incapacity, subject to production of a medical certificate.[597]

Apart from this annual leave an official, on application may, exceptionally be granted special leave. It relates to the non-exhaustive[598] enumeration of constellations in Article 6 Annex V SR (each with specific duration of entitlement): marriage of the official; change of residence; serious illness of spouse; death of spouse; birth of a child; serious illness of a child; death of a child; adoption of a child, etc. Some of those events may involve a number of the official's children or relatives. On this, case-law has clarified that the maximum number of days laid down apply to all births or all deaths of children or relatives in the ascending line occurring during the calendar year. It can be inferred that this also applies to a serious illness of relatives in the ascending line (ie, two days' leave per parent per year) and other cases by analogy.[599] One more kind of special leave is stipulated in the third paragraph of Article 6 Annex V SR: 'on an exceptional basis in the case of exceptional work which goes beyond an official's normal obligations'. It would have to be granted at the latest three months after the appointing authority has taken a decision on the exceptional character of the work of the official. The term 'exceptional work' is to be interpreted under the (wide) discretion of the appointing authority, whereas the reference to the work beyond 'normal obligations' provide some guidance.[600] Next to an occasion for recuperation, the character of this leave is a reward as it provides a kind of 'remuneration in time'.

b. Other Types of Leave

In addition to annual leave and special leave, there are other differentiated types of leave, such as for personal reasons, for further training or exceptional work,[601] leave in the interests of the service,[602] military service,[603] and leave on personal grounds.[604] Supplementary leave for travel

[593] ECJ, Jd Cases C-350/06 and C-520/06, ECLI:EU:C:2009:18, paras 22, 25 – *Schultz-Hoff*; as principle under European social law, CST, F-22/10, ECLI:EU:F:2011:64, para 25 – *Bombín Bombín v Commission*.

[594] Art 57(1) SR.

[595] Arts 1–5 Annex V SR.

[596] Art 6 Annex V SR.

[597] Art 3 Annex V SR.

[598] Arg 'in particular' in Art 6 Annex V SR, GC, T-196/97, ECLI:EU:T:1998:44, para 43 – *Continolo v Commission*.

[599] CST, F-67/09, ECLI:EU:F:2010:169, paras 38–42 – *Angulo Sánchez v Council*.

[600] As here: Czubinski in Perillo/Giacobbo-Peyronnel (eds), *Statut de la fonction publique de l'Union européenne: Commentaire article par article* (2017) 202.

[601] Art 6 Annex V SR.

[602] Art 42 lit c SR; see the case study in section II.19.b. below.

[603] Art 42 SR; ECJ, 185/80, ECLI:EU:C:1981:161 – *Garganese v Commission*; CST, F-119/10, ECLI:EU:F:2011:188, paras 38 ff – *Di Tullio v Commission*; ECJ, C-179/18, ECLI:EU:C:2019:111 – *Rohart*.

[604] Art 40 SR.

time for staff entitled to an expatriation or foreign residence allowance was standardised in 2014, and to some extent reduced.[605] The annual leave entitlement for staff deployed in third countries (EU Delegations, etc) has been reduced from three and a half to two working days per month,[606] and has also been limited in other respects.[607] Three types of leave of special practical importance shall be considered in more detail: maternity leave; leave on personal grounds; and parental/family leave – whereas the latter two describe at the same time two administrative statuses.

Maternity leave

The 2014 reform expanded the options to request leave on personal and family-specific grounds, such as more flexible maternity and paternity leave, leave in the event of the serious illness of a family member, adoption and parental leave, and allowed an unlimited extension for the care of certain close relatives with a serious illness or disability. When caring for children, a serious illness was equated with a disability in a number of circumstances.[608] The rules on maternity leave (Art 58 SR) provide that pregnant women shall, in addition to annual and special leave, be entitled on production of a medical certificate to 20 weeks of leave. The leave shall start not earlier than six weeks before the expected date of confinement shown in the certificate and end not earlier than 14 weeks after the date of confinement. The mother can resume work before the expiry of the 20 weeks, upon production of a medical certificate confirming that she has fully recovered.[609] In the case of multiple or premature[610] birth or the birth of a child with a disability or serious illness, the duration shall be 24 weeks.

Case-law has clarified on the correct calculation of the maternity leave: the definite point from which the maternity leave starts to run is determined in advance. This is done in order to enable pregnant women to know their administrative position before they go on maternity leave. Hence, the appointing authority has no leeway in fixing the dates of the beginning and end of maternity leave. While it has to take into account the actual date of confinement in order to determine the date when the official will return to work, it must, however, take into account only the *expected date of confinement, as shown in a medical certificate*, when determining the date of the beginning of the official's maternity leave, and it cannot under any circumstances determine that date *a posteriori*, on the basis of the actual confinement date. Consequently, where the actual confinement date is earlier than the expected date, it is appropriate to consider that the point from which the maternity leave starts to run is unchanged, and that after the confinement the official concerned should be granted the additional leave. This is also the case where the official is already on sick leave for reasons associated with her pregnancy, before her maternity leave begins.[611]

Parental and family leave

Parental leave[612] is an entitlement to up to six months' leave for every child, without basic salary, to be taken during the first 12 years after the birth or adoption of the child. The duration of the leave may be doubled for single parents recognised (*cf* GIP of each institution) and for parents

[605] Art 7 Annex V SR.

[606] Art 6 Annex X, with transitional rules; the legality of the reform was confirmed in appeal, ECJ, Jd Cases C-119/19 P and C-126/19 P, ECLI:EU:C:2020:676 – *Commission v Carreras Sequeros and Others*.

[607] *cf* Arts 7–9 Annex X SR.

[608] *cf* Art 58 SR regarding leave before/after confinement; in Art 67(1) SR in regard of the doubling of the dependent child allowance in the event of long-term illness; on special leave under Art 6 Annex V SR.

[609] GC, T-51/98, ECLI:EU:T:1999:271, para 59 – *Burrill and Noriega Guerra v Commission*.

[610] Premature: a birth taking place before the end of the 34th week of pregnancy.

[611] GC, T-255/04, ECLI:EU:T:2007:129, paras 55–61 – *Negenman v Commission*.

[612] Art 35 lit f SR, Art 42a SR.

of dependent children with a disability or a severe illness recognised by the institution's medical officer. The minimum leave taken at any one time shall not be less than one month. The leave may be taken as full-time or half-time leave. Where parental leave is taken in the form of half-time leave, the maximum period provided for in the first paragraph shall be doubled. Instead of a basic salary, there is an entitlement to a monthly allowance,[613] the accrual of pension rights, the opportunity for advancement in seniority or through promotion, an allowance for dependent children, and an education allowance. During parental leave, the full contribution to the social security scheme provided for in Articles 72 and 73 shall be borne by the institution (reduced in the case of half-time leave). Periods of family-related leave of absence are recognised as periods of professional experience for admission to the performance appraisal procedure under Article 45a SR, and are therefore more advantageous for staff than the former periods of leave on personal grounds (ie, before the 2004 reform), even if they have been embarked on for the same family-related reasons.[614] From a certain point in time onwards,[615] the withdrawal of the request for parental leave requires the consent of the administration; the institution's discretion to provide this consent may be reduced if the member of staff is able to show that the purpose of the leave is no longer attainable.[616]

Family leave[617] without basic salary is to be granted in the case of medically certified serious illness or disability of an official's spouse, relative in the ascending line, relative in the descending line, brother or sister. The total period of such leave shall not exceed nine months over the official's entire career.

Leave on personal grounds

When an official is on leave on personal grounds,[618] he retains his position, but is neither promoted nor paid, his membership of the social security scheme is suspended.[619] The duty to first obtain the permission of the appointing authority of any outside activity or assignment persists, as well as the duty to notify of any changes thererof.[620] Where the official is elected or appointed to public office, he may be authorised to discharge his duties on a part-time basis, and the period of such leave or part-time working shall correspond to the term of office.[621] Otherwise, the duration of leave on personal grounds shall not exceed one year. Leave may be extended for further periods, always for a maximum of one year. The total length of leave on personal grounds may not exceed 12 years[622] in the course of the official's entire career (however with certain exceptions mentioned in Art 40(2) SR). An application for extension shall be made two months before the leave expires. During leave on personal grounds another person may be appointed to the post occupied by the official.

[613] At present €919,02 per month (50% of such sum if on half-time leave), but no possibility to engage in any other gainful employment.

[614] CST, F-91/08, ECLI:EU:F:2010:13, paras 13, 33, 35 – *Pleijte v Commission.*

[615] CST, Jd Cases F-51/05 and F-18/06, ECLI:EU:F:2007:221, para 139 – *Duyster v Commission* (the time of notification of the decision, or at the latest when the official takes note of this decision).

[616] CST, Jd Cases F-51/05 and F-18/06, ECLI:EU:F:2007:221, paras 166, 170 – *Duyster v Commission* (eg, if the official for health reasons turns out to be unable to take care of the child).

[617] Art 42b SR, under the conditions of Art 42a(2) SR.

[618] Art 35 lit c, Art 40 SR, *congé de convenance personnelle* CCP.

[619] Art 40(1), (3) SR; with the important exception under Art 40(3) SR for an official who is not engaged in a gainful activity, to be applied for not later than one month following that in which the leave on personal grounds begins.

[620] Permission for activities involving lobbying or advocacy vis-à-vis his institution and which could lead to the existence or possibility of a conflict with the legitimate interests of the institution shall not be granted.

[621] Art 15(2) SR.

[622] Reduced from 15 to 12 years by the 2014 reform.

After the end of the leave period, he is to be reinstated in the first post corresponding to his grade that becomes vacant in his function group, provided he satisfies the requirements for that post.[623] The obligation to reinstate is subject only to the condition that a vacant post for which the official satisfies the requirements. Reinstatement does not depend on any additional condition such as an expression of interest by the official or whether he carries on a professional activity during his leave.[624] In principle, the reinstatement takes place at the same grade he held at the beginning of the leave.[625] If he declines the post offered to him, he shall retain his right to reinstatement when the next vacancy corresponding to his grade occurs in his function group. If he declines a second time, he may be required to resign after the Joint Committee has been consulted.[626] On the other hand, if the reinstatement does not take place in time, the official must at least be put in the same financial position as if this had happened,[627] by way of a compensation payment.[628]

c. *Carry Over of Annual Leave*

The amount of annual leave which may be carried over to the following calendar year, in principle, shall not exceed 12 days (14 days in the case of officials serving in a third country).[629] Article 4(1) Annex V SR expresses this limitation in carry-over in a double negation: 'Where an official, for reasons other than the requirements of the service, has not used up all his annual leave before the end of the current calendar year, the amount of leave which may be carried over to the following year shall not exceed twelve days'. Turning the double negation into a positive expression will first mean that there is an entitlement to carry over all the days of leave not taken in one calendar year to the next, if the official has not been able to use his annual leave for reasons attributable to the requirements of the service. Secondly, it will be critical for a carry-over to establish[630] the *requirements of the service* that were the reason for not being able to use up leave days. On this point, the institutions are under an obligation to organise work in a way that it does not deprive an employee of the right to prove by any means that her or his unused leave days accumulated for reasons relating to the requirements of the service.[631]

Other reasons than the requirements of the Service

In addition, other reasons too, though *not* strictly attributable to 'the requirements of the service', may entitle to a carry-over of all unused leave, given the purpose of the right to paid annual leave and its significance as a principle of the social law of the EU now affirmed by Article 31(2) FRC; for example, where an official who has been on sick leave for all or part of the calendar year has,

[623] Art 40(4) lit d SR; ECJ, 126/75, 34 and 92/76, ECLI:EU:C:1977:169 – *Giry v Commission*; GC, T-276/94, ECLI:EU:T:1995:161 – *Buick v Commission*; on the conditions GC, T-205/96, ECLI:EU:T:1998:110, paras 36 ff – *Bieber v EP*.

[624] GC, T-205/96, ECLI:EU:T:1998:110, paras 36 ff – *Bieber v EP*.

[625] ECJ, C-200/87, ECLI:EU:C:1989:333 – *Giordani v Commission*.

[626] ECJ, 12/87, ECLI:EU:C:1988:298 – *Zeyen-Heyl v Commission* (equal rank).

[627] ECJ, 785/79, ECLI:EU:C:1983:121 – *Pizziolo v Commission*; ECJ, 58/75, ECLI:EU:C:1976:102 – *Sergy v Commission*.

[628] The amount of compensation for loss of income is equivalent to the difference between the net remuneration the person would have received in the period without being reinstated and the total net income she/he received from other employment in that period, plus difference for higher step and legal interests: ECJ, C-284/98 P, ECLI:EU:C:2000:134 – *EP v Bieber*.

[629] Annex X SR.

[630] Depending on the practical organisation of work, this could amount to a burden which should not rest fully on the worker: ECJ, C-120/21, ECLI:EU:C:2022:718, para 44 – *LB v TO*.

[631] ECJ, C-348/90 P, ECLI:EU:C:1991:413, para 11 – *EP v Virgili-Schettini*.

for that reason, been unable to exercise his right to take annual leave. Long-term sickness is not a 'requirement of the service', but a condition in which the member of staff can neither work nor make use of annual leave days, for reasons outside his control. Article 1e(2) SR stipulates that officials 'in active employment shall be accorded working conditions complying with appropriate health and safety standards at least equivalent to the minimum requirements applicable under measures adopted in these areas pursuant to the Treaties'. The ECJ has clarified, in *Strack*, that the limitation under Article 4(1) Annex V SR is not applicable, because it does not deal with the question of the carry-over of paid annual leave which could not be taken by the official because of long-term sickness, and therefore refers to the required compliance with the general (minimum) social protection afforded under Article 1e SR and Directive 2003/88[632] which in the opinion of the judges are to supplement the provisions of the SR.[633]

Case of Strack

The lines above summarise the result of the *Strack* case-law, which came into being with a certain history, although its central legal question had been decided first by the CST. The CST judgment was annulled in appeal by the GC, then the GC's decision reviewed by the ECJ as described above. In the original judgment handed down, the CST had applied Article 7 of Directive 2003/88 and argued that under this provision the worker must have actually been able to exercise his right under the Directive, which would not be the case of a worker who, during the whole or part of the reference period, was on sick leave. The CST concluded – similar to the ECJ much later – that Article 4 Annex V SR does not govern the question of sick leave and can therefore not limit the carry-over of annual leave days (beyond the 12 days).[634] Subsequently, the GC annulled this judgment and ruled that the right to carry over annual leave in excess of the limit of 12 days must necessarily stem from an obstacle relating to the official's activity and resulting from the performance of his or her duties, and may not be granted for an illness which prevented the staff member from performing those duties, even if it has been proven that the illness was occupational in origin. Thus, the GC wanted to apply Article 4 Annex V SR in the literal sense and interpreted it narrowly, with the result that it was not possible to carry over any exceeding number of leave days, in case the reason for not taking the leave at the outset was an illness.[635]

Finally, the ECJ exceptionally reviewed (a review under Art 256(2) TFEU) the GC judgment, and found that the GC had erred in law when interpreting Article 1e(2) SR and Article 4 Annex V SR, declared that the GC's decision adversely affects the unity and consistency of EU law,[636] and thus set it aside. As an overall result of the *Strack* case-law, the carry-over of remaining leave exceeding the 12 days shall be possible where an official who has been on sick leave for all or part of the calendar year has, for that reason, been unable to exercise his or her right to take annual leave.

Open questions regarding carry-over

However, even after all the decisions handed down by the various courts in their judgments on *Strack*, questions remain open. The arguments used by the CST and the ECJ to justify the

[632] Art 7(1) Directive 2003/88/EC of the European Parliament and of the Council of 4 November 2003 on certain aspects of the organisation of working time [2003] OJ L299/9–19.

[633] ECJ, C-579/12 RX-II, ECLI:EU:C:2013:570, para 40 – *Réexamen Commission v Strack*; Tracol (2014) 51(3) *CMLR* 1014.

[634] CST, F-120/07, ECLI:EU:F:2011:22, paras 63, 72, 79 – *Strack v Commission*. The Commission implemented this judgment by authorising the automatic carry-over of leave, beyond 12 days, in the event of illness, whereas the absence had to be for medical reasons for at least 20 consecutive days.

[635] GC, T-268/11 P, ECLI:EU:T:2012:588, para 67 – *Commission v Strack*.

[636] Art 62b(1) Statute CJEU.

carry-over of leave beyond the 12 days could also apply to other scenarios of inability to exercise the right of annual leave, without it becoming clear where exactly should be the limits of this interpretation given to (the inapplicability of) Article 4 Annex V SR. For example, before the ECJ handed down its judgment on the question put forward in *Strack* in 2013, the CST ruled in *Bombín Bombín* that an official who has been on leave on personal grounds until his retirement is entitled to financial compensation for more than 12 days of unused leave only where it is established that, prior to his taking leave on personal grounds, he was unable to use up his leave for reasons attributable to the requirements of the service. The CST argued that a carry over of days of leave not taken exceeding the maximum of 12 days provided for in Article 4 Annex V SR is excluded if the official was put on leave on personal grounds at his own request.[637] This can be an acceptable result, because the respective leave has been initiated at the request of the staff member, while an illness as reason for absence is not his choice. However, if one reassesses this CST judgment in the light of the above-mentioned line subsequently set by the ECJ in *Strack*, then there could be reasons to assume that a constellation such as of *Bombín Bombín* nowadays would justify the carry over of more than 12 days of unused leave, with the argument that Article 4(1) Annex V SR is *not applicable* to a case of inability to use remaining leave days (exceeding the 12) due to leave on personal grounds. At the same time, these considerations illustrate the thin dogmatic basis on which the ECJ had discarded the application of Article 4 Annex V SR in *Strack*, because it failed to specify the underlying reasons for not being able to use leave days, despite the fact that the ECJ after all bases its conclusion on the importance attributed to the fundamental right of paid annual leave stipulated in Article 31(2) FRC in the light of which Article 1e SR has to be interpreted.[638]

d. Financial Compensation

Upon the termination of service, a financial compensation for unused annual leave is to be paid insofar as it still exists,[639] whereas unjustified absences are to be subtracted.[640] According to Article 4(2) Annex V SR, the compensation is equal to one-thirtieth of monthly remuneration at the time of leaving the service for each day's leave due. Since leave on personal grounds does not constitute a reason for carrying over all unused annual leave days (see above, CST in *Bombín Bombín*), a financial compensation for more than 12 (or 14) days of unused leave is only permitted where it is established that, prior to the official taking leave on personal grounds, he was unable to use up his leave for reasons attributable to the requirements of the service.

An open question is if there are any obligations on the side of the appointing authority to actually put the staff members in a position to exercise their right to paid annual leave. When it comes to the financial compensation, the ECJ[641] has clarified that a rule that time-bars the right to paid annual leave is precluded where the employer has not actually put the staff member *in a position to exercise that right*. If such an obligation exists, it would also have an impact on the practical handling of the above-mentioned carry-over itself.

[637] CST, F-22/10, ECLI:EU:F:2011:64, paras 30–33 – *Bombín Bombín v Commission.*

[638] Also sceptical: Currall in Perillo/Giacobbo-Peyronnel (eds), *Statut de la fonction publique de l'Union européenne: Commentaire article par article* (2017) 75.

[639] GC, T-66/91, ECLI:EU:T:1992:89, *Bassetti-Bombardella*; CST, F-120/07, ECLI:EU:F:2011:22 – *Strack v Commission*; GC, T-268/11 P, ECLI:EU:T:2012:588, paras 33–55 – *Commission v Strack* and appeal judgment ECJ, C-579/12 RX II, ECLI:EU:C:2013:570.

[640] Arts 58 and 59 SR, Art 4(3) Annex V SR; GC, T-156/95, ECLI:EU:T:1997:102 – *Echauz Brigaldi and Others v Commission* (participation in elections in the country of origin); CST, F-39/08, ECLI:EU:F:2009:85, para 64 – *Lebedef v Commission* (unauthorised absence from work); GC, T-352/99, ECLI:EU:T:2000:308 – *M v Commission*; GC, Jd Cases T-110/99 and 260/99, ECLI:EU:T:2000:303 – *F v EP* (sick leave without proof).

[641] ECJ, C-120/21, ECLI:EU:C:2022:718, paras 52–57 – *LB v TO*.

e. Flexible Working-Time Arrangements

The 2004 reform has introduced more flexible working conditions, such as part-time work and job-sharing.[642] The normal working week has been increased to 40–42 hours and standardised under the 2014 reform.[643] At the same time, a legal basis was created to allow for flexible working-time arrangements, whereas full flexitime days are only foreseen for staff at grades below AD 9/AST 9.[644]

Part-time work

The authorisation to work part-time may be discretionarily granted if it is considered compatible with the interests of the service.[645] There is an entitlement to the authorisation of part-time work if one of the five family-related circumstances is fulfilled, or in the case of participation in further training, or during semi-retirement from the age of 58 during the final three years before reaching pensionable age.[646] Specifically, the authorisation because of family-related circumstances may be granted for being a parent of children under the age of nine, caring for a dependent child between the ages of 9 and 12 (if the reduction in working time is no more than 20 per cent of normal working time), and caring for an ill or disabled family member. The 2014 reform provides for a new part-time entitlement if the staff member has to look after a child up to the age of 14 as a single parent, or in cases of considerable hardship.[647]

Job-sharing

Article 55b SR provides for the half-time job-sharing of a post identified by the appointing authority as appropriate for that purpose. The authorisation to work half-time by job-sharing shall not be limited in time. It may, however, be withdrawn by the appointing authority in the interests of the service after giving the official six months' notice, or may be withdrawn at the request of the official.[648]

f. Telework

The outbreak of the Covid-19 pandemic in 2020 forced the institutions to adopt a number of organisational measures arising from the duty of care and health protection of staff. It entailed a general home office regime, including teleworking outside the country of employment. For more details about the relationship between the duty of care and telework, as well as the arguments relating to physical absence vs presence at duty stations, see section II.9.d above. The pandemic has contributed to the development of a normative framework for teleworking.[649]

[642] Jansen, 'Les modifications apportées au statut' in Govaere/Vandersanden (eds), *La fonction publique communautaire* (2008) 23.

[643] Art 55(2) sentence 1 SR.

[644] Art 55(4) SR; criticism by EP on this: Budgetary Control Committee, PE480.777v 02-00 of 14.2.2012, 5; Commission, COM (2011) 890 final, 13 December 2011.

[645] Art 55(1) SR; Annex IVa SR.

[646] Art 55a(2) SR.

[647] Art 55a(2) lit c and d SR.

[648] Art 55b(1) SR.

[649] *cf* Commission Decision C(2022) 1788 final of 24 March 2022 on working time and hybrid working, Art 11 of which states that all staff may telework outside the place of employment for up to 10 working days per calendar year, upon their request and subject to the agreement of their line manager. This may be increased up to one month per year.

18. Non-Active Status

The appropriate budgetary authority may decide under the budgetary procedure to reduce the number of posts for a given grade. As a consequence of this, an official may become supernumerary because the number of posts would be less than the number of staff instated, and may consequently be assigned *non-active status* by decision of the appointing authority. Under the procedure of Article 41 SR, the appointing authority shall – each time after consulting the Joint Committee – (1) decide what types of posts are to be affected by such measures, and (2) draw up a list of the officials to be affected by such measures, taking into account the officials' ability, efficiency, conduct in the service, family circumstances and seniority. Any official occupying one of the posts referred to who expresses the wish to be assigned non-active status shall automatically be entered on this list.[650] Where a choice must be made between officials who have volunteered for the assignment of non-active status, the appointing authority must limit its assessment to the above-quoted five criteria (ability, efficiency, conduct in the service, family circumstances, and seniority), but it enjoys an element of discretion in the application of each criterion and in the weight which they must be given.[651]

An official placed on non-active status shall receive no salary and shall not accrue a higher step, but shall receive an allowance calculated in accordance with Annex IV SR and continue to earn pension rights at the salary appropriate to the grade and step for a period not exceeding five years. For a period of two years, the non-active official shall have priority for reinstatement in any post in his function group corresponding to his grade. Income from any new employment shall be deducted from the allowance, under certain conditions.

At the end of the period of entitlement to the allowance, the official shall be required to resign. He shall, where appropriate, receive a retirement pension as provided in the pension scheme;[652] where it has not been possible to reinstate the official during a period of non-active status he shall be entitled to a retirement pension, irrespective of length of service (while regularly at least 10 year's service have to be completed in order to be entitled to a retirement pension).[653] Should the official decline reinstatement to a post offered within the two-year period without good reason, he may, after consulting the Joint Committee, be deprived of the above benefit and be required to resign.[654] The placement of an official on *non-active status* must not be used by the appointing authority to bypass the application of the specific rules for disciplinary measures, the risk of which is palpable because the effects of this status can be equivalent to a decision to suspend a person from duty pursuant to Article 23 Annex IX SR.[655]

19. Termination of Service

a. Overview

Services shall be terminated by resignation,[656] compulsory resignation,[657] retirement in the interests of the service,[658] dismissal for incompetence,[659] removal from post as a result of disciplinary

[650] GC, T-176/96, ECLI:EU:T:1998:1 – *Volger v EP.*
[651] GC, T-108/96, ECLI:EU:T:1997:115, para 80 – *Cesaratto v EP.*
[652] Art 41(4) SR.
[653] Art 77(1) SR.
[654] Art 41(5) SR.
[655] *cf* CST, F-135/14, ECLI:EU:F:2015:152, para 40 – *DE v EMA.*
[656] Art 48 SR.
[657] Art 49 SR.
[658] Art 50 SR.
[659] Art 51 SR.

proceedings,[660] retirement, or death.[661] Under Article 52 SR, an official shall be retired either automatically on the last day of the month in which he reaches the age limit of 66 years, or at his own request where he has reached pensionable age, or where he is between 58 and pensionable age and satisfies the requirements for the immediate payment of a pension.[662] The other practically important circumstance of retirement is where an official is found to fulfil the conditions of Article 78 SR for total permanent invalidity,[663] because the provisions of Article 52 SR on retirement apply by analogy[664] to recipients of an invalidity allowance. The official shall automatically be retired on the last day of the month in which the appointing authority recognises his permanent incapacity to perform his duties (Art 53 SR).[665]

b. Retirement

The most important reason for leaving service is reaching retirement age. The point at which this happens is regularly being pushed back by the legislature, for financial and demographic reasons. The previous age limit of 60 years, with the possibility of retiring between 50 and 65, was raised by the 2004 reform – with transitional rules[666] – initially to 63 years, and with the 2014 reform to 66 years for newly hired civil servants.[667] It is no longer only in exceptional cases that civil servants can, on request, continue to work up to the age of 67, and in exceptional cases up to the age of 70.[668] By doing so, officials who remain in service after pensionable age increase their pension for each year of such service by 1.5 per cent (previously 2 per cent) of the basic salary.[669]

The earliest start of early retirement on personal grounds has also been pushed back. In order to facilitate downsizing, in the interests of the service it was previously[670] possible for the administration to refrain from reducing remuneration in the event of early retirement – which is no longer possible for staff entering service after the 2014 reform:[671] the pension shall be reduced by 3.5 per cent for each year before the year in which the official would become entitled to a retirement pension.[672]

No earlier than five years before the official's pensionable age, in the interests of the service an official with at least 10 years of service may, by decision of the appointing authority, be placed on leave for organisational needs linked to the acquisition of new competences within the institutions.[673] After reaching retirement age, leave in the interests of the service is no longer permitted, as is going to be illustrated by the subsequent case study on *RW*.[674] Also, simultaneous leave in the interests of the service may not be combined with automatic retirement.[675]

[660] Art 86 SR.
[661] Art 47 SR.
[662] Art 9 Annex VIII SR.
[663] On invalidity, see section V. below.
[664] Art 78(2) SR.
[665] For the involvement and role of the Invalidity Committee, see GC, T-84/98, ECLI:EU:T:2000:156 – *C v Council*.
[666] On the changes and transitional rules of the 2004 reform, Jansen, 'Les modifications apportées au statut' in Govaer e/Vandersanden (eds), *La fonction publique communautaire: nouvelle règles et développement du contentieux* (2008) 23; Andreone, *La fonction publique communautaire, Revue française d`administration publique* (2011) 807–15.
[667] For existing civil servants, the retirement age will be gradually pushed back (for details, Art 22(1) Annex XIII SR).
[668] Art 52 SR.
[669] Art 5 Annex VIII SR.
[670] Art 9(2) Annex VIII SR old version.
[671] On the legal situation before the 2014 reform Van Raepenbusch, 'L'apport jurisprudentiel du Tribunal de la fonction publique de l`Union européenne' in Govaere/Vandersanden (eds), *La fonction publique communautaire* (2008) 164. On the term of interests of service in early retirement without a reduction of salary, CST, F-86/05, ECLI:EU:F:2006:87, paras 39 ff, 47 ff – *De Soeten v Council*, transitional rule Art 22(3) Annex XIII SR.
[672] Art 9 Annex VIII SR.
[673] Singer, 'VAE senioribus? (2019) *JurisNews: Fonction publique européenne* 115–20.
[674] GC, T-170/17, ECLI:EU:T:2019:309, para 72 – *RW v Commission*.
[675] ibid, para 59.

Case Study on Leave in the Interests of the Service

Article 42c SR is no longer applicable to staff who have reached retirement age

Case T-170/17 R, *RW v Commission* of 17 May 2017
Case T-170/17, *RW v Commission* of 8 May 2019

In Brief

In *RW*, the GC decided on a question with considerable practical significance for all staff approaching or having reached retirement age: it is not allowed to place an official on leave in the interests of the service if the person has already reached their pensionable age.

Background

Article 42c (1) SR stipulates:

> At the earliest five years before the official's pensionable age, an official with at least ten years of service may be placed by decision of the appointing authority on leave in the interests of the service for organisational needs linked to the acquisition of new competences within the institutions.

The Article explains in more detail which rules shall govern the leave in the interests of the service, and makes clear that such leave shall not constitute a disciplinary measure. It further states:

> The duration of the leave shall correspond in principle to the period until the official reaches pensionable age. However, in exceptional situations, the appointing authority may decide to put an end to the leave and reinstate the official. When the official placed on leave in the interests of the service reaches pensionable age, he shall automatically be retired.

Article 47 SR describes how service shall be terminated: next to resignation, compulsory resignation, dismissal for incompetence, removal from post, retirement, and death, it lists *retirement in the interests of the service.*

In accordance with Article 52 SR, an official shall be retired either automatically on the last day of the month in which he reaches the age of 66, or at his own request on the last day of the month in respect of which the request was submitted where he has reached pensionable age.

Facts and Court Decisions

The appointing authority had placed the applicant on leave in the interests of the service. At the same time – with the argument that he had reached pensionable age – he was compulsorily retired. After the rejection of his complaint against this decision, the applicant filed an action and also applied for interim measures, upon which the President of the General Court (GC) decided to stay the execution of the contested decision against the applicant (Case T-170/17 R).[676] The GC annulled the Commission's decision in the main proceedings.[677]

[676] GC, T-170/17 R, ECLI:EU:T:2017:351 – *RW v Commission.*
[677] GC, T-170/17, ECLI:EU:T:2019:309 – *RW v Commission.*

On the admissibility

The Commission argued that since the execution of the contested decision had been suspended by an interim measure, the applicant had the possibility to effectively spend the maximum possible time in service, ie, until the age of 65. He received the full remuneration as if he had not been retired earlier. Case-law stipulates that a legal interest of the applicant has to exist at the time of filing the action, and that the applicant has to maintain a personal interest in the annulment of the decision against him. In the present case, the applicant had a persisting interest in a court decision because he needed certainty that the difference in amounts paid to him during the period of suspended execution of the retirement decision by way of interim measure of the GC was not going to be claimed back from him by the Commission afterwards. In that respect, the GC did not accept the assurance offered by the Commission that it would not claim back the difference in amounts, because – even with the assurance given – a source of uncertainty would remain that justifies a persisting legal interest of the applicant.

On the substance

The GC annulled the decision against the applicant on the grounds that *Article 42c SR is not applicable* to staff who have already reached pensionable age. In its reasoning, the GC interpreted the clause by looking at its wording, context and purpose.

The GC welcomed the argument of the applicant that in view of the wording of Article 42c SR, the leave in the interests of the service *must have a certain duration*, because it says that the 'duration of the leave shall correspond in principle to the period until the official reaches pensionable age', and also because an automatic retirement shall take place when the official who is on leave in the interests of the service reaches pensionable age.

The GC concluded that, if the leave in the interests of the service must have a certain duration, it follows that it is not possible in one single decision to place an official on leave in the interests of the service *and at the same time* to compulsorily retire him. The normative context confirms this because the Staff Regulations foresee certain administrative 'positions' in which an official may be placed, but they do not foresee placing him in an 'automatic retirement in the interest of service' against his will. Such a new method would go beyond the range of different ways in which the service of staff shall be terminated, as defined in Article 47 SR (see above).

In regard to the purpose of Article 42c SR, the Commission argued that it would be paradoxical that – if the clause was meant to optimise human resource management, and to give flexibility to the administration – an official cannot be placed on leave in the interests of the service once he has reached pensionable age. However, the GC decided otherwise and found, first, that in a hypothetical case of a simultaneous automatic retirement and leave in the interests of the service, the official would not benefit from an allowance foreseen during the leave period (decribed in Art 42c SR), because the duration of the leave in that case would be zero. Secondly, the GC found that the possibility foreseen by Article 42c SR of ending the leave and reintegrating the official into work would run idle as well.

Comments

1. This judgment clarifies that there is no such thing as an 'automatic retirement in the interest of service' against the will of the staff member. The most striking general conclusion from the judgment is, first, probably that staff members who have reached retirement age, but not the age at which the appointing authority is required to retire them, *cannot be placed into leave in the interests of the service*. In other words, the pensionable age marks the limit for the application of Article 42c SR. Secondly, leave in the interests of the service must have a certain time duration. Thirdly, an official may not be placed simultaneously on leave in the interests of the service *and* be compulsorily retired. The GC finds these conclusions mainly by applying the premise that existing provisions established as such by the legislator shall not run idle. Despite the fact that the GC decided the case in a staff-friendly way, it may be questioned whether this methodological approach leads to balanced results in a normative environment with a plenitude of rules in place to cover all kinds of living situations.
2. As a practical consequence, the judgment narrows the flexibility of the administration in the management of staff who are close to their retirement age or have already reached it. For this group of staff, the new judgment is good news: they may no longer be placed into leave in the interests of the service.
3. There have been calls to revise the text of Article 42c SR on the grounds that it allows for 'non-transparent early retirement' of staff.[678]
4. The SR explicitly state that leave in the interests of the service 'shall not constitute a disciplinary measure'. When placing the staff member on leave in the interests of the service, the institution enjoys broad discretion. However, Article 42c(1) SR stipulates that placing a person on leave in the interests of the service must be for the reason of 'organisational needs linked to the acquisition of new competences within the institutions'. This means that the institution has to exercise and reason its discretion also in relation to its internal, future organisational needs. On this point, in another case, *FV v Council*,[679] the Council argued that the staff member concerned lacked the ability to acquire new competences. But the GC found that the Council had not demonstrated that it had carried out a forward-looking assessment that took into account, first, the nature and extent of the reforms which were to take place and, secondly, the organisational needs of the institution as a whole. The GC decided that the Council's assessment was 'not linked to a genuine and forward-looking assessment of organisational needs' and had incorrectly used Article 42c SR. If the institution fails in these respects, the leave under this provision runs the risk of being disciplinary in nature.

c. Compulsory Resignation

Compulsory resignation can take place in a number of constellations: for example, if the condition of Article 28 lit a SR no longer applies, ie, regarding the nationality of one of the Member States and the enjoyment of full rights as a citizen. With regard to the nationality requirement, the

[678] EP Report on recommendations for reform of European Parliament's rules on transparency, integrity, accountability and anti-corruption, A9-0215/2023 of 13 June 2023, para 81.
[679] GC, T-750/16, ECLI:EU:T:2018:972, para 159 – *FV v Council*.

appointing authority may at its discretion[680] authorise an exception.[681] Compulsory resignation can occur after secondment: if the official for a second time declines the post offered once his secondment ends, he may be required to resign after the Joint Committee has been consulted;[682] this may also happen after the end of a leave on personal grounds[683] or after regaining fitness for service after invalidity.[684] Compulsory resignation can happen as a consequence of the non-active status.[685]

Senior officials

Finally, senior officials within the meaning of Article 29(2) SR may be retired in the interests of the service under Article 50 SR, meaning directors-general or their equivalent in grade AD 16 or AD 15 and directors or their equivalent in grade AD 15 or AD 14.[686] Despite the wide discretion to retire these 'political appointments' the appointing authority has to assess the 'objective requirements of the service', the 'specific qualities of the official' concerned and apply a 'scrupulous examination of the relevant factors'.[687] The official has to be heard prior to the decision of retirement in order to have an opportunity to defend his interests.[688] As Article 50(1) SR clarifies, the retirement does not constitute a disciplinary measure. The retired official receives an allowance calculated in accordance with Annex IV SR.[689]

d. Termination and Dismissal: Contract Duration and Conversion

For the categories of temporary, auxiliary and contract staff, except in the case of death, the engagement ends when the contractually specified date is reached; when the age limit of 66 is reached; by termination with notice or termination without notice (Art 48 CEOS);[690] or if the requirements under Article 12(2) lit a CEOS are no longer fulfilled. These types of engagements raise a number of questions relating to the potential renewal, termination and conversion into contracts of indefinite duration.

Limited contracts

Limited engagements end when the fixed-time period elapses. There is no entitlement to continue or extend a fixed-term contract, for example by using the argument of needing 'stable employment',[691] since *stable employment* is not seen to constitute a general principle of law in the

[680] GC, T-648/21, ECLI:EU:T:2023:575, paras 68–71 – *YD v FRA*.

[681] For other types of employment, *cf* Art 82(3) lit a CEOS (contract staff), Art 12(2) lit a CEOS in connection with Art 47 lit b(iii) and c(ii) CEOS (temporary staff), Art 119 CEOS; whereas it is to be expected that discretionary treatment of servants other than officials will not be more favourable than the treatment of officials.

[682] Art 39 lit f SR.

[683] Art 40(4) lit d SR.

[684] ie, the official ceases to satisfy the requirements for payment of the invalidity allowance, Art 14(2) Annex VIII SR.

[685] Art 41(4)(5) SR.

[686] Art 50 SR as so-called 'golden handshake'; it is not necessary to check whether assignment to another position is possible. On pension without reduction under Art 50(8) SR, Art 9 Annex VIII SR: CST, F-101/08, ECLI:EU:F:2009:137 – *Pappas v Commission*. Written Question E-0101/2007 by MEP Gräßle and the Commission's reply in [2007] OJ C293. The 2014 reform extended this rule to certain officials in the EP (Art 48a CEOS).

[687] ECJ, 34/77, ECLI:EU:C:1978:101, para 18 – *Oslizlok v Commission*.

[688] ECJ, 19/70, ECLI:EU:C:1971:74, para 11 – *Almini v Commission*.

[689] Calculation on the basis of the years of service within the EU institutions: GC, T-11/02, ECLI:EU:T:2004:368, paras 53/54 – *Pappas v Commission*.

[690] On duty of care, abuse of powers and balancing of the appointing authority's interests with those of the temporary agent, GC, T-223/99, ECLI:EU:T:2000:292 – *Dejaiffe v OHIM*.

[691] CST, F-74/11, ECLI:EU:F:2013:22, para 33 – *Bojc Golob v Commission*; CST, F-60/08 and F-69/07, ECLI:EU:F:2008:181, paras 75, 136 – *O v Commission*; CST, F-65/07, ECLI:EU:F:2009:43, paras 114, 127/128 – *Aayhan and Others v Commission*; *cf* also Reithmann (2011) 1 *EuR* 136, 137. Too strict CST, F-63/11, ECLI:EU:F:2012:83, paras 60/61 – *Macchia v Commission*,

light of which the lawfulness of a measure adopted by an institution may be assessed. This insight is of relevance both for the merits of a request of contract extension and for the admissibility of an application challenging the decision not to extend a contract as an act adversely affecting the member of staff.[692] *Stable employment* may constitute an objective pursued by the parties 'to prevent abuse arising from the use of successive fixed-term employment contracts'.[693] The appointing authority has to take a decision to renew or not to renew a fixed-term contract that comes to its end, whereas the decision not to renew a contract based on weak performance has to rely on a complete file.[694]

Renewal and conversion of fixed-term contracts

Under Article 85 CEOS, the engagement of contract staff (Art 3a CEOS) may be for a fixed period of at least three months and not more than five years. Contracts may be renewed not more than once for a fixed period of not more than five years. Any further renewal shall be for an indefinite period. Similarly, Article 8 CEOS determines certain periods for the engagement of temporary staff in the sense of Article 2 CEOS. Renewal of contracts of employment as temporary staff, auxiliary staff, contract staff or contract staff for auxiliary tasks must not be done in furtherance of the performance of permanent tasks on a long-term basis. The purpose of the engagement of staff under fixed-term contracts is to cover for the occasional absence of the holder of a post, which explains the inherent insecurity of fixed-term engagements.

The institutions are under an obligation to prevent the abuse of rights arising from the use of successive fixed-term employment contracts. As settled case-law has established, this obligation may be fulfilled in different ways and, in particular, by adopting measures which either provide that the renewal of such employment contracts or relationships must be justified by objective reasons, or which limit the maximum total duration of the successive fixed-term employment contracts or relationships, or limit the number of renewals of such employment contracts or relationships.[695] Under the *Adjemian* case-law, the use of a succession of fixed-term employment contracts may amount to a misuse (and infringement of the principle of equal treatment)[696] if the following two cumulative conditions are fulfilled:

(1) The authority empowered to conclude contracts has used a succession of fixed-term employment contracts.

that required to check the possibility of transfer to a different position, see appeal GC, T-368/12 P, ECLI:EU:T:2014:266, paras 54/55 – *Macchia v Commission*. Internal guidelines must not generally rule out any extension of the contract; CST, F-59/11, ECLI:EU:F:2012:164, paras 51 ff – *Sipos v OHIM*; on so-called cancellation or termination clauses, which make the extension dependent on the passing of a competition: Reithmann (2014) *EuR* 115; CST, F-82/08, ECLI:EU:F:2011:45 – *Clarke and Others v OHIM*; CST, F-6/10, ECLI:EU:F:2011:139, paras 79, 82 – *Munch v OHIM*. On contract extension, CST, F-63/11, ECLI:EU:F:2012:83, para 43 – *Macchia v Commission*.

[692] CST, F-5/16, ECLI:EU:F:2016:183, paras 32–36, 51 – *Stanley v Commission*; CJEU Annual Report 2010, p. 209; CST, F-8/10, ECLI:EU:F:2010:151, para 66 – *Gheysens v Council* (contested decision based on new facts), CST, F-35/07, ECLI:EU:F:2008:150, paras 65 ff – *Klug v EMEA* and CST, F-6/10, ECLI:EU:F:2011:139, para 53 – *Munch v OHIM*. An obvious violation of official interests or the duty of care would be decisive for a healthy working atmosphere; *cf* CST, F-17/11, ECLI:EU:F:2013:14, paras 59 ff, 71 – *BB v Commission*. In the competitor dispute, the plaintiff must prove that the non-renewal of his contract violated the interests of the service, since his achievements or experience were so exceptionally high that they surpassed those of any other possible candidate, or at least that of the competitor employed in his place, CST, F-59/11, ECLI:EU:F:2012:164, para 57 – *Sipos v OHIM*. On discontinuation due to poor performance, CST, F-85/10, ECLI:EU:F:2012:97, para 154 – *AI v CJEU*, notwithstanding the duty of care, ibid, para 166.

[693] CST, F-65/07, ECLI:EU:F:2009:43, para 115 – *Aayhan and Others v Commission*; GC, T-231/14 P, ECLI:EU:T:2015:639, paras 30 ff, 39–41 – *EMA v Drakeford*.

[694] GC, T-296/21, ECLI:EU:T:2022:808, para 74 – *SU v EIOPA* (appraisal report not taken into account); justification of the non-extension, see CST, F-41/11, ECLI:EU:F:2012:82, paras 40 ff – *Mocová v Commission* (appeal unsuccessful).

[695] GC, T-325/09 P, ECLI:EU:T:2011:506, para 66 – *Adjemian and Others v Commission*.

[696] ibid, para 86.

(2) The object of which was the performance of permanent tasks on a long-term basis, or, if the staff member has in fact taken on tasks corresponding to a permanent post.

Succession of fixed-term employment contracts means that the renewal has taken place more than the single time that the provisions of the CEOS allow for.[697] If under these preconditions a misuse exists, it can be rectified and the negative consequences for the person concerned can be nullified by reclassification of the employment contract, in particular by conversion of fixed-term employment contracts to contracts of indefinite duration.[698] The resulting permanent position (ie, contract of indefinite duration) is not that of an official, but a contract of employment as temporary staff, or corresponding to a post included in the list of posts annexed to the section of the budget relating to the institution that the budgetary authorities have defined as 'temporary'.[699]

Similarly, it is possible to convert a contract formally presented as employment for auxiliary tasks under Article 3b CEOS into employment as contract staff under Article 3a of the CEOS.[700] Likewise, successive fixed-term employment contracts may be converted into contracts of indefinite duration in the effective capacity of temporary staff under Article 2 lit (a) or lit (c) CEOS, or of contract staff under Article 3a CEOS.[701]

Procedurally, in order to have his or her contract converted, the staff member concerned has to request: (1) that the period of service formally completed in performance of a contract of employment as auxiliary staff, contract staff or contract staff for auxiliary tasks be recognised as a period of service completed as temporary staff; and (2) that the successive fixed-term employment contracts be reclassified as a contract of indefinite duration in the effective capacity of temporary staff.[702] The applicant may use broad means of evidence to prove the circumstances.[703]

Unlimited contracts and dismissal

The concept of the stability of unlimited contracts and the nature of this type of employment prohibit their termination without due reason and justification.[704] When weighing up personal interests and the interests of service, factors such as employability, age, seniority and the time remaining until possible retirement are to be taken into account. Where dismissal for inadequate

[697] *cf* Arts 8 and 85 CEOS and CST, F-6/10, ECLI:EU:F:2011:139, para 110 – *Munch v OHIM*.

[698] GC, T-325/09 P, ECLI:EU:T:2011:506, para 67 – *Adjemian and Others v Commission*.

[699] On conversion of fixed-term contracts into contracts of indefinite duration: Potvin-Solis/Lelièvre (2011) *RUE* 613 and (2012) *RUE* 266, and CST, F-105/09, ECLI:EU:F:2011:41 – *Scheefer v EP*. It is also relevant how long successive contracts are in total (eg, below the maximum duration applicable to this contract category) and which contract category is concerned: contracts under Art 2(b) and 2(d) CEOS can only be entered into as fixed term, and cannot be subject to conversion: CST, F-85/10, ECLI:EU:F:2012:97, paras 129/130 – *AI v CJEU*. If the last contract was concluded for a fixed term and this was not challenged within the time limit, it is irrelevant whether the previous fixed-term contracts may be converted into contracts of indefinite duration: CST, F-17/11, ECLI:EU:F:2013:14, para 77 – *BB v Commission*. Jacob, 'Le renouvellement des contrats à durée déterminée des agents contractuels de l'Union européenne' (2017) *Revue du droit de l'Union européenne* 113–39.

[700] CST, F-59/13, ECLI:EU:F:2016:71, paras 42–49, 65 – *Rouffaud v EEAS*.

[701] GC, T-325/09 P, ECLI:EU:T:2011:506, para 87 – *Adjemian and Others v Commission*.

[702] ibid, para 88, and by analogy for conversion into contract staff.

[703] CST, F-24/15, ECLI:EU:F:2015:158, para 49 – *Di Marzio v Council*.

[704] CST, F-105/09, ECLI:EU:F:2011:41, para 58 – *Scheefer v EP*; CST, F-88/08, ECLI:EU:F:2010:160, para 58 – *Vandeuren v ETF*, appeal GC, T-108/11 P, ECLI:EU:T:2013:625, paras 92 ff – *ETF v Michel*, where the ECJ is more cautious than the CST and defines duty of care more narrowly (para 103). On dismissal due to budgetary constraints, CST, F-74/11, ECLI:EU:F:2013:22, para 33 – *Bojc Golob v Commission*; CST, F-41/12, ECLI:EU:F:2013:31, paras 15, 27, 37 – *Scheefer v EP*. On dismissal of a pregnant woman: CST, F-54/11, ECLI:EU:F:2012:114, para 139 – *BG v Ombudsman*, and the changes brought about by the 2014 reform, which either prevent a period of notice starting during pregnancy or suspending a period that is already running (*cf* Art 47 CEOS). Explicit bans on dismissing pregnant women (*cf* under German law § 18 BEEG or § 15 KüSchG) do not exist in EU civil service law. However, it may be possible to handle such constellations for avoidance of hardship via the duty of care and a balancing of interests.

performance is envisaged, the appointing authority is well advised to first dispel any doubts about possible medical reasons that could be the root cause of this lack of performance. This is especially true when the employee is possibly unable to defend his own interests adequately, not capable of acting on his own behalf and of perceiving the very existence of his illness, due to mental disorders.[705] Again, the duty to have regard for the welfare of the servants warrants a proper balancing of reciprocal rights and obligations. As an exception, in the case of staff employed by a person holding an elected office (Art 2 lit c CEOS), the mere breakdown in the relationship of trust can be sufficient reason for dismissal.[706] Dismissal reasons that embrace disciplinary considerations are not superseded by the possibility of dismissal for disciplinary reasons in accordance with Article 49 CEOS.[707] Rather, disciplinary proceedings may be initiated even after terminating the contract, if it subsequently becomes clear that the complaints against the person concerned are sufficiently serious to justify initiating such a procedure.[708]

Case Study on Contract Termination during Sick Leave

Dismissal without notice during sick leave: The employer must verify the inability of a staff member to resume his or her duty

Case T-462/17, *TO v EEA* of 11 June 2019

In Brief

The General Court (GC)[709] annulled the dismissal decision of the European Environment Agency on contract termination during sick leave and awarded certain allowances to the applicant as well as compensation of €6,000 for non-material damage suffered. When terminating a contract without notice on the basis of Article 48(b) CEOS, an institution cannot just assume that a member of staff is unable to resume their duties, but has to verify such an inability itself.

Facts of the Case

The applicant was a contract agent at the European Environment Agency (EEA) with a fixed-term contract and a nine-month probationary period. In the wake of some disputes relating to the real estate agency engaged by the EEA, the applicant reported sick. She received a negative report on her probationary period, and the EEA dismissed her without notice on the grounds that the period of her paid sick leave had exceeded the period provided for in Article 16 CEOS, and that in line with Article 48(b) CEOS the

[705] CST, F-92/09, ECLI:EU:F:2010:140, paras 83, 85 – *U v EP* (dismissal under Art 51 SR); GC, T-164/19, ECLI:EU:T:2021:456, paras 85 ff – *AQ v eu-LISA* (absences due to health restrictions).

[706] CST, F-89/08, ECLI:EU:F:2010:11, para 113 – *P v EP*; CST, F-74/06, ECLI:EU:F:2008:48, para 116 – *Longinidis v Cedefop*, Potvin-Solis/Lelièvre (2012) *RUE* 284; GC, T-45/90, ECLI:EU:T:1992:7, para 94 – *Speybrouck (Secretary General of a Parliamentary Group v EP* 'by virtue of a clearly defined political choice').

[707] CST, F-89/08, ECLI:EU:F:2010:11, paras 104, 106 – *P v EP*.

[708] CST, F-74/06, ECLI:EU:F:2008:48, para 116 – *Longinidis v Cedefop*.

[709] GC, T-462/17, ECLI:EU:T:2019:397 – *TO v EEA*.

applicant was unable to resume her duties at the end of the period of paid sick leave; and also because her behaviour during her probationary period had caused the relationship of trust between her and the EEA to deteriorate.

Arguments and Decision

1. *Calculation of sick leave duration*

Article 48(b) CEOS stipulates that employment, whether for a fixed or for an indefinite period, may be terminated by the institution without notice 'if the servant is unable to resume his duties at the end of a period of paid sick leave as provided for in Article 16'. The provision is intended to permit the dismissal of an official who, although having exhausted his rights to sick leave, is unable to resume his duties because of his state of health, and thus to limit for the institution the consequences of a sick leave whose duration exceeds that of the services performed by the agent.

First, the GC clarifies that for the purposes of applying Article16(2) CEOS, interruptions of the periods have to be disregarded – in other words, the cumulative duration of the services performed by the agent must be compared with the cumulative duration of sick leave.

2. *The obligation of the EEA to verify the inability of the applicant to resume her duties*

A central part in this judgment is that the dismissal decision was annulled because the EEA had not independently verified the inability of the staff member to resume her duties at the end of the period of paid sick leave. Under Article 16(2) and Article 48(b) CEOS, a contract may be terminated only where two cumulative conditions are met, namely, the period for paid sick leave was exceeded, and the staff member was unable to resume her duties at the end of the said period. The GC deduces the institution's obligation to verify for itself the health status of the staff member – which is not explicitly stated in the text – from the objective of the provisions, and also by referring to Article 34(1) FRC (the recognition of social security benefits).

Where the administration exercises its discretion to adopt a decision of dismissal, it must take into consideration all the factors which may determine its decision. In particular, it has to take into account the interests of the service, but also, in order to satisfy its duty of care, the interests of the agent concerned.

3. *Damages*

As to the damages, the GC reasoned that the parallel procedure initiated by the EEA against the applicant in accordance with Article 84(1) CEOS could also have led to the applicant's dismissal. In accordance with that logic, the GC orders the EEA to pay to the applicant a sum equal to one month's salary and one-third of her basic salary per month of the probation period completed, less the dismissal allowance already received under Article 48(b) CEOS.

Where the EEA complained in the dismissal decision about the applicant's conduct in excessive terms, the GC awarded a compensation for non-material damage, *ex aequo et bono*, of €5,000 to the applicant, but also acknowledged the responsibility of the applicant in the dispute.

The GC further awarded compensation to the applicant at the amount of €1,000 for non-material damage sustained, because the EEA had infringed Article 8 FRC (protection of personal data) and Article 12 of Regulation No 45/2001[710] *on the protection of individuals with regard to the processing of personal data by the institutions*. The factual background was that some private data of the applicant relating to the dispute about the services provided by the real estate agency had been circulated within the EEA, and were found by the GC to have affected the reputation of the applicant.

Comments

1. Regarding the correct application of Article 48(b) CEOS, it is indeed plausible that an employer cannot take an evidence-based decision on the pertinence of a dismissal based on health grounds where it has not itself verified the factual background (ie, the sickness). Similarly, the GC decided in *WV v CdT*[711] that both conditions that allow termination of a servant's employment without notice under Article 48(b) and Article 16 CEOS have to be fulfilled: (1) at the expiry of the period for paid sick leave; (2) it is to be assessed whether the servant is unable to resume his or her duties. The assessment step has to be carried out properly.
2. For the employing institutions, it is good to note that the reasons used by the EEA to describe the behaviour of the applicant in the dismissal decision were found excessive by the GC, and therefore led to compensation for damages.
3. The GC applied a remarkable (rare) hypothetical argumentation in order to justify the award of the allowance foreseen under Article 84(4) CEOS: the dismissal proclaimed by EEA under Article 48(b) and Article 16 CEOS was not successful for the reasons described above (lack of verification of health status). The GC reasoned that it cannot be ruled out that the EEA had dismissed the applicant on the basis of Article 84(1) CEOS. This led the GC to apply the legal consequence stipulated in Article 84(4) CEOS in favour of the applicant. The method resembles the (domestic) labour law convention according to which the judge can award compensatory allowances to the employee where a dismissal was found illegal at court, but the employment has de facto ended. It shall be further monitored whether this logic will continue to be applied in the case-law of the General Court and the Court of Justice.
4. The applicant was not successful with her assertion that the sickness had a professional origin in harassment and stemmed from the treatment she received at her workplace. She had never requested recognition of the occupational nature of the disease. In line with former case-law,[712] in order to obtain such a recognition the respective procedure has to be completed with a decision based on a medical assessment. In this sense, the court applies the same reasoning of verification of health status towards the applicant as it did above towards the employer, EEA.

[710] Regulation No 45/2001 on the protection of individuals with regard to the processing of personal data [2011] OJ L8/1, now replaced by Regulation (EU) 2018/1725 of the European Parliament and of the Council on the protection of natural persons with regard to the processing of personal data by the Union institutions, bodies, offices and agencies and on the free movement of such data [2018] OJ L295/39–98.

[711] GC, T-618/21, ECLI:EU:T:2022:603 – *WV v CdT*.

[712] CST, F-40/12, ECLI:EU:F:2013:85, para 33 – *CF v EASA*; see section V. below.

5. Both Article 8 FRC and Article 12 of Regulation No 45/2001 (nowadays replaced by Art 15 of Regulation No 2018/1725)[713] have been operationalised in this judgment to justify the award of damages for non-material harm suffered for the divulgence of personal data within the organisation.

e. Dismissal for Incompetence

As a last resort, dismissal for incompetence is possible, under the procedure of Article 51 SR.[714] The starting point is the determination of inadequate professional performance in the annual appraisal report. The 2004 reform relies on a conversation with the person concerned, to initiate supportive and corrective measures.[715] When making provision for measures to restore trust, the appointing authority has to allow a reasonable opportunity to put these measures into practice.[716] The SR, further to the reform of 2014, now refer to the number of consecutive unsatisfactory annual reports identifying poor performance: an official who, on the basis of three consecutive unsatisfactory annual reports, still shows no progress in his professional competence shall be downgraded by one grade. If the following two annual reports still show unsatisfactory performance, the official shall be dismissed. However, if there is a possibility that the lack of performance is due to personal problems of a medical nature, such doubts must first be dispelled.[717] Although dismissal for incompetence is systematically separated from the disciplinary regime,[718] the judicial review applying to such dismissal is analogue to the procedural guarantees under disciplinary law contained in Annex IX SR. The standard of judicial review is a manifest error of assessment of the underlying facts and the observance of the principle of proportionality.[719]

Article 51 SR only applies to officials; staff under the CEOS do not have a 'right' to the application of the sequence of negative annual reports mentioned: thus, their dismissal can also take place sooner.[720] The potential complexity of this shall be illustrated by the following case study on dismissal.[721]

[713] According to this Art 15 Data Protection Regulation EU, specific information (listed in this Article) has to be provided to a person by the data controller, where personal data relating to the person are collected, except where and insofar as the data subject already has the information.

[714] Art 51(1) lit a SR; on the criteria: ECJ, 101/79, ECLI:EU:C:1980:243 – *Vecchioli v Commission*.

[715] CST, F-92/09, ECLI:EU:F:2010:140, para 6 – *U v EP*; Gervasoni (2010) 46 *Cahiers de droit européen* 770; CST, F-113/10, ECLI:EU:F:2012:20, paras 73 ff – *AT v EACEA*.

[716] A period of three months to achieve the objectives set may be too short: GC, T-571/17, ECLI:EU:T:2020:141, paras 64, 71, 77 – *UG v Commission*; referred back in the appeal: ECJ, C-249/20 P, ECLI:EU:C:2021:964, paras 39, 42 – *Commission v UG*.

[717] CST, F-92/09, ECLI:EU:F:2010:140, paras 83, 85 – *U v EP*. The duty of care is enhanced where it may appear that the official's physical or mental health is shown to be affected, with the effect that the capacity to defend her/his interests may be reduced.

[718] ECJ, 101/79, ECLI:EU:C:1980:243, paras 5–9 – *Vecchioli v Commission*.

[719] GC, Jd Cases T-200/03 and T-313/03, ECLI:EU:T:2006:57, paras 86/87, 118/119, 121–25 – *V v Commission*.

[720] GC, T-571/17, ECLI:EU: T:2020:141, para 57 – *UG v Commission*.

[721] The dismissal decision in Case *UG v Commission* dates from October 2016, and the various decisions of the GC and the ECJ already embrace, by the beginning of 2024, 600 paragraphs, ie, before the ECJ has even decided on the appeal of the GC's referral decision.

Case Study on Dismissal

On contract termination/dismissal: Reasons for termination need to be materially correct

Case T-571/17, *UG v Commission* of 2 April 2020 and order of 13 November 2020
Case C-249/20 P, *Commission v UG* of 25 November 2021
Case T-571/17 RENV, *UG v Commission* of 21 June 2023
Case C-546/23 P, *UG v Commission* of 29 August 2023

In Brief

The General Court (GC) annulled the Commission's decision to terminate a contract of indefinite duration. The annual appraisal reports, on which the Commission had also based its decision, did not contain a specific reference to an unjustified absence of the applicant. The GC was further of the opinion that the applicant was not given a chance to restore the relationship of trust with the service within the designated short period of time.

Facts of the Case and Procedure

The applicant was engaged as a contract agent attached to the Commission's Office for 'Infrastructure and Logistics in Luxembourg' (OIL) and having the function of a childcare worker. After a first renewal, her contract was extended for an indefinite duration. The applicant was then exempted at 50 per cent from her childcare work, in order to perform the function of political secretary at a trade union. The applicant's appraisal reports for 2013 and 2014 both concluded that her performance was satisfactory. The applicant was elected as a member of the Local Staff Committee in 2015 and appointed to sit on the Central Staff Committee. Her appraisal report for 2015 concluded that her performance was unsatisfactory. The applicant lodged an appeal against that report. In 2016, the applicant took parental leave for a period of four months, which was later extended. In September 2016, the Commission informed the applicant of the intention to terminate her employment contract, indicating problems relating to the applicant's conduct in service and her attitude at work; it also indicated that there had been no improvement in her performance, and pointed to negative consequences of her conduct on the continuity and quality of the service being provided to children and parents. In October 2016, the Commission terminated the applicant's contract with a notice period of nine months. In her court action, the applicant first sought annulment of the decision terminating her employment contract; secondly, she claimed compensation for the material harm suffered following that decision, and for the non-material harm suffered as a result of the degrading treatment she claims to have been suffered because of her trade union activity and her parental leave.

The Decision of the GC

In its judgment, the GC annulled the decision of the Commission terminating the applicant's contract of indefinite duration. It ordered the parties to forward to the GC a joint agreement on the quantified amount of financial compensation. The parties have accordingly agreed out-of-court to an amount of €68,000 to be paid to the applicant (independent of her pension rights and the costs of the procedure).

(1) On questions of the admissibility of the application, the GC states a reminder that merely preparatory acts (here the announcement of the intention to terminate the contract) can neither directly nor incidentally be challenged at the court. As to the annulment of the negative appraisal report for the year 2015 sought by the applicant, although she had introduced an appeal against that appraisal report (Art 43 SR), she had not filed a complaint (Arts 90, 91(2) SR) against it. The request to annul the report was therefore inadmissible.

(2) The applicant pleaded that the Commission had violated Article 42a SR, inasmuch as she was dismissed while she was on parental leave. She also claimed a violation of the disciplinary procedure provided for in Annex IX SR; a violation of the right to be heard; a lack of real and serious reasons for her dismissal; a violation of the obligation to state reasons; a misuse of power, in that the dismissal was allegedly motivated by the applicant's parental leave and her trade union activities; and finally, an infringement of the principle of proportionality. She further claimed that the decision to dismiss her was not preceded by three negative appraisal reports as is stipulated in Article 51 SR. On this last point, the GC accepted the Commission's argument that the applicant's contract had been terminated solely on the basis of Article 47 lit c (i) CEOS, not of Article 51 SR, with the consequence that Article 51 SR was not violated.[722]

The GC continued to state that the Commission has broad discretion when terminating a contract under Article 47 lit c CEOS, and that the control of this decision by the judge is limited to the verification of the *absence of manifest error of assessment* or *misuse of powers*. Where the administration refers to specific facts, the judge must verify that these reasons are materially correct. Further, the GC stated that when deciding on the situation of a staff member, the authority has to take into consideration all the factors which are likely to determine its decision, and in particular the interests of the agent concerned. This results from the administration's duty of care, which reflects the balance of reciprocal rights and obligations that the SR and, by analogy, the CEOS have created in the relationship between the authority and its agents.

The GC then assessed the annual appraisal reports and the objectives subsequently set for the applicant. It concluded that the time provided for the applicant to improve her performance within the approximately three-month period since she was made aware of the objectives was too short to allow the applicant to rebuild the relationship of trust concerning her service and to fulfil the objectives set. The decision to terminate the contract was thus vitiated by an error. The appraisal reports did not contain any precise reference to an unjustified absence or miscommunication; only in the letter in which the objectives had been set was there a reference to a single incident in the year 2015.

[722] Art 51(1) lit a SR foresees a dismissal on the basis of two unsatisfactory annual reports further to three other consecutive unsatisfactory annual reports. The GC clarifies that where a dismissal refers to appraisal reports, this does not mean that a dismissal under Art 47 CEOS is precluded.

The GC concluded that because the appraisal reports for the years 2014 and 2015 did not contain any specific reference to an unjustified absence of the applicant in those years, plus the fact that the applicant was not able to rebuild the relationship of trust with the service and to meet its objectives within the short period allowed, this constitutes a manifest error of assessment, leading to the annulment of the decision to terminate the contract.

(3) As to the Commission's liability for material harm, instead of deciding itself, the GC invited the parties to find mutual agreement about the quantified compensation, while providing them with some guidelines regarding how to determine the material harm suffered by the applicant.

(4) In respect to damages for non-material harm suffered by the applicant, the GC decided that this claim was not related to the decision to terminate her contract, but to the allegedly degrading and discriminatory treatment of the applicant by the administration, due to her trade union activity and the fact that she took parental leave. The applicant, said the GC, had lodged her *complaint* only against the termination of her leave, not in relation to degrading and discriminatory treatment. Therefore the claim for damages for non-material harm was dismissed as inadmissible.

Appeal Decision of the ECJ

With its judgment in appeal,[723] the Court of Justice (ECJ) annulled the decision of the General Court rendered in Case T-571/17, *UG v Commission*, and referred the case back to the GC, also criticising that the GC did not provide enough reasoning in its decision. The ECJ held that, first, the GC had misinterpreted the three-month period provided by the Commission to the applicant for restoring the relationship of trust and, secondly, the GC had failed in its obligation to provide a reasoning for its decision in the first instance. Whether or not a period of three months is sufficient to show improvement in performance on the part of the agent concerned may also be decided differently; in the view of the ECJ, the Commission had not set the three-month period *at all* in the sense of a period imposed on the agent for her to show an improvement of performance or to restore trust with its service, and that the Commission had in neither a general nor specific way reproached the agent with failing – within the three-month period – the entirety of the objectives set for her. In the light of this, if the Commission had not set a deadline – as opposed to setting an excessively tight deadline – for the agent to improve her performance or restore trust, then the argument used by the GC at first instance that the agent did not have enough opportunity to do so can no longer stand.

Referral Decision of the GC

In referral,[724] the GC decided to *dismiss the action*. The GC found that the statement of reasons given in the Commission's dismissal decision was sufficient and that – although several manifest errors of assessment had been committed by the Commission – the

[723] ECJ, C-249/20 P, ECLI:EU:C:2021:964 – *Commission v UG.*
[724] GC, T-571/17 RENV, ECLI:EU:T:2023:351 – *UG v Commission.*

contested dismissal decision still contained a number of grounds the illegality of which has not been shown and which are sufficiently important to substantiate the overall finding of the applicant's incompetence. The applicant has brought an appeal against this referral GC decision.[725]

Comments

1. The GC in its first instance decision and later in the referral decision applied a wide error test: the general line of case-law is to limit itself to assessing whether an act of the administration is a *manifest error of assessment* or a *misuse of power*. These two scenarios justify annulment. According to case-law, an error is *manifest* 'where it is easily recognisable and can be readily detected'.[726]
2. The GC in its first decision scrutinised the facts underlying the dismissal and the way they are presented in the dismissal decision. If a dismissal does not contain specific reference to facts, it would not be substantiated and would not be in line with the basic requirements concerning the legality and certainty of administrative acts. This would be an easily recognisable error and is in focus where the GC demands a *materially correct* reasoning. The question of whether a period of three months is sufficient to show improvement in performance may also be decided differently. The ECJ also based its appeal decision on the argument that the three-month period had a totally different meaning from what the GC thought it would be.
3. In general, and even with the ECJ annulment of the GC's decision and subsequent dismissal of the action by the GC in referral, it remains important, first, to carefully check that the reasoning put forward for a dismissal decision substantially and accurately refers to the facts, and that these facts actually provide evidence that justifies a dismissal. Secondly, it shall be accurately determined if a period has been designated for the restoration of trust, and whether this period has actually provided enough opportunities for the agent to achieve this. Thirdly, where a number of reasons support the decision to dismiss a member of staff, the plea alleging a manifest error in the dismissal must be rejected if, despite the evidence adduced by the applicant, the disputed assessment (here, of incompetence) may still be accepted as justified and consistent.[727]

20. Disciplinary Proceedings

Any failure by an official or former official to comply with his obligations under the SR, whether intentionally or through negligence on his part, shall make him liable to disciplinary action, Article 86 SR. More detailed provisions both for the administrative investigations and for the disciplinary regime are stipulated in the 30 Articles of Annex IX SR. Further, there are general

[725] At the time of print, the decision of the ECJ, C-546/23 P, in appeal to the referral decision was not yet handed down.
[726] CST, F-104/09, ECLI:EU:F:2011:29, para 35 – *Canga Fano v Council*.
[727] GC, T-571/17 RENV, ECLI:EU:T:2023:351, para 189 – *UG v Commission*; GC, T-492/17, ECLI:EU:T:2019:211, para 55 – *Fleig v EEAS*.

implementing provisions (GIP) in every institution to specify how to inform the person concerned when the investigation ends, including the communication of the conclusions of the investigation report.[728] Further, the appointing authority of each institution shall, 'if it sees fit', adopt implementing arrangements for Annex IX SR, after consulting the Staff Committee.[729] The 2004 reform aimed to improve the initiation and implementation of disciplinary proceedings, leading towards a more stable, permanent structure of the disciplinary boards in each institution,[730] and a broader range of sanctions and modalities for the suspension of civil servants.[731] In the Commission, an Investigation and Disciplinary Office (IDOC) carries out administrative enquiries and prepares disciplinary proceedings,[732] ie, actions to establish facts and, where necessary, to determine whether there has been a failure to comply with the obligations incumbent on Commission officials.

Purpose

The purpose of a decision instituting disciplinary proceedings against an official, expressed in the terms of the case-law, is to enable the appointing authority to examine the *truth and gravity* of the facts alleged against the official concerned and to hear the official, in order to form an opinion, on the one hand, as to whether it is appropriate either to close the disciplinary proceedings without further action or to adopt a disciplinary measure against the official and, on the other hand, as to whether or not it is necessary, before adopting such a measure, to send him before the Disciplinary Board (under Annex IX SR).[733]

Speed of proceedings and strict time-limits

There is no limitation period for initiating disciplinary proceedings, but Articles 12–22 Annex IX SR determine strict time-limits for the conduct of the disciplinary proceedings before the Disciplinary Board. Although those time-limits are not mandatory, they nevertheless set out a rule of sound administration, the purpose of which is to avoid, in the interests of both the administration and officials, an unreasonable delay in the adoption of the decision concluding the disciplinary proceedings. The disciplinary authorities are under an obligation to conduct the proceedings with due diligence and to ensure that each procedural step is taken within a reasonable period following the previous step. Failure to observe such a period may result in the measure being declared void.[734] The principle of legal certainty would be undermined if the administration delayed unduly the initiation of disciplinary proceedings. Where a substantial period of time has elapsed between the time when those facts and that conduct took place and the start of the disciplinary enquiry, then important witnesses and documents may have disappeared, or the memory of witnesses may have suffered.[735]

[728] Art 2 Nr 3 Annex IX SR, Art 110 SR.

[729] Art 30 Annex IX SR; Commission Decision C (2004) 1588 final/4 of 28 April 2004, General implementing provisions on the conduct of administrative inquiries and disciplinary procedures, last amended by Decision C (2010) 8180 final.

[730] Dalle-Crode(2008) 531.

[731] ibid, 499.

[732] Commission Decision C (2002) 450 of 19 February 2002, see Fitch, 'The General Framework of the Administrative Reform' in Govaere/Vandersanden (eds), *La fonction publique communautaire* (2008) 11; on data protection in enquiries, see the opinion of the European Data Protection Supervisor of 20 April 2005 (Case 2004-187).

[733] GC, T-203/03, ECLI:EU:T:2005:346, para 41 – *Rasmussen v Commission*; CST, F-30/08, ECLI:EU:F:2010:43, para 208 – *Nanopoulos v Commission*, in appeal GC, T-308/10 P, ECLI:EU:T:2012:370, para 149 – *Commission v Nanopoulos*.

[734] Taking into account the specific circumstances of the case: CST, F-12/10, ECLI:EU:F:2012:29, paras 124–26 – *Kerstens v Commission*.

[735] ibid, para 126.

The breach of the principle that steps should be taken within a reasonable time does not, in general, justify annulment of the decision taken following an administrative procedure. It is only where the excessive lapse of time is such as to have an effect on the actual content of the decision adopted on conclusion of the administrative procedure that the failure to respect the principle that steps should be taken within a reasonable time affects the validity of the administrative procedure. This may be the case precisely in procedures leading to penalties, where the excessive lapse of time affect the capacity of the persons concerned to defend themselves effectively,[736] in other words where the rights of the defence of the person concerned have been infringed (see section b below).

a. Administrative Enquiry

Start of the enquiry
Where the appointing authority or the European Anti-Fraud Office (OLAF) become aware of evidence of a staff member's failure, they may launch an administrative investigation to verify whether such failure has occurred. In the preliminary investigation, the appointing authority (in the case of the Commission: IDOC) or OLAF scrutinise the relevant incidents and establish the facts, hear the person concerned, and decide on the potential start of disciplinary proceedings. The preliminary administrative enquiry is a precondition for any disciplinary procedure to commence.[737] The enquiry may be initiated ex officio, or further to a complaint or to a denunciation. In the case of officials acting in the European External Action Service (EEAS)[738] as Heads of Delegations, the request to initiate enquiries may also stem from the Commission.

Prima facie evidence
In general, the appointing authority enjoys wide discretion on whether to institute disciplinary proceedings. Judicial review is limited to ascertaining that the evidence taken into consideration by the administration when instituting disciplinary proceedings was properly established, and – expressed *e negativo* – that there has been no manifest error in the assessment of the facts and that there has been no misuse of powers.[739]

It is possible to review the legality of the decision to bring disciplinary proceedings against an official even if the proceedings have been terminated without a disciplinary measure being taken. Otherwise, there would remain a risk of arbitrariness if it were accepted that the appointing authority has absolute and unlimited powers to bring disciplinary proceedings against an official and then to terminate them without adopting disciplinary measures, without the official involved having the possibility, at the appropriate time, of contesting the decision to institute the proceedings in the absence of any penalty against which he could bring an action.[740]

Depending on the circumstances, the discretion of the appointing authority or OLAF whether or not to initiate an investigation may be reduced: the clarity of behaviour liable to disciplinary measures may in this case force the administration to act. However, as the wording of Article 86(1) SR suggests, the subject of an administrative investigation may only be an official's failures to

[736] CST, F-77/09, ECLI:EU:F:2011:2, para 146 – *Nijs v ECA*; CST, Jd Cases F-124/05 and F-96/06, ECLI:EU:F:2010:2, paras 390, 392 – *A and G v Commission.*

[737] GC, T-270/16, ECLI:EU:T:2017:74, para 71 – *Kerstens v Commission.*

[738] Where they have to carry out tasks for the Commission as part of their duties.

[739] CST, Jd Cases F-124/05 and F-96/06, ECLI:EU:F:2010:2, para 367 – *A and G v Commission*; GC, T-273/94, ECLI:EU:T:1997:71, para 125 – *N v Commission*; GC, T-203/98, ECLI:EU:T:2000:130, para 50 – *Tzikis v Commission.*

[740] CST, Jd Cases F-124/05 and F-96/06, ECLI:EU:F:2010:2, paras 352/353 – *A and G v Commission.*

comply with his *obligations under the SR* (not a failure to comply with national law or with 'the law' in general). Thus, already before instituting an investigation, there must be a reasonable suspicion (prima facie evidence) that a breach of discipline has been committed. This means that the administration must have information suggesting that the person concerned has breached his obligations under the SR, and must have 'reached a certain level of certainty' as regards the provisions which, in its view, have been infringed.[741] It should be noted that this concept of 'certainty' relates to the assessment whether the official could have infringed obligations under the SR, and is to be differentiated from the principle of *legal certainty* in regard to the perceptibility of the obligations under the SR that the official has to comply with.[742]

Appointing authority, OLAF and the EPPO

Both the appointing authorities (in the Commission: IDOC) and OLAF may carry out investigations, though their perspectives and goals may differ. Their investigations are independent from one another. Article 1(3) Annex IX SR stipulates that where no case subsequent to an OLAF investigation can be made against an official about whom allegations have been made, the investigation in question shall be closed, with no further action taken, by decision of the Director of OLAF, who shall inform the official and his institution in writing. The official may request that this decision be inserted in his personal file. The task of OLAF is to conduct administrative investigations for the purpose of fighting fraud, corruption and any other illegal activity affecting the financial interests of the Union. It thus investigates 'serious matters relating to the discharge of professional duties constituting a dereliction of the obligations of officials and other servants of the Union liable to result in disciplinary or, as the case may be, criminal proceedings'.[743] Another EU institution with jurisdiction in the field is the European Public Prosecutor's Office (EPPO). For the purpose of their cooperation, OLAF and the EPPO have concluded a 'working arrangement'[744] that specifies mutual reporting, transmission of cases, cooperation, support and complementary investigations. In practical terms, OLAF would not commence investigations in the area of competence of the EPPO before having consulted the case management system and before having informed the EPPO.[745] OLAF would normally refrain from enquiring in identical facts (parallel investigations) that are subject to EPPO investigations. The appointing authorities (IDOC), on their side, exercise a general, subsidiary competence and would therefore await the outcome of any investigation carried out by OLAF on a given matter.[746] At the same time, the appointing authorities are obliged to act in a timely way in their role as employer and have to correlate this obligation with the their subsidiary jurisdiction to investigate.[747]

[741] As here AG Pikamäe – C-680/22 P, ECLI:EU:C:2023:969, paras 80 ff – *DD v FRA* (where, as GA Pikamäe adds, the administration must have 'at least some idea of the provisions applying in the case in point'); GC, T-308/10 P, ECLI:EU:T:2012:370, para 152 – *Commission v Nanopoulos* ('sufficiently precise and relevant evidence').

[742] On this, see section 20.b. below.

[743] Art 1(4) Regulation (EU, Euratom) No 883/2013 of the European Parliament and of the Council of 11 September 2013 concerning investigations conducted by the European Anti-Fraud Office (OLAF) [2013] OJ L248/1–22; beyond this, OLAF may also investigate in cases of an equivalent failure to discharge obligations on the part of members of institutions and bodies, heads of offices and agencies or staff members of institutions, bodies, offices or agencies not subject to the SR.

[744] Dated 5 July 2021, available at: www.eppo.europa.eu/sites/default/files/2021-07/Working_arrangement_EPPO_OLAF.pdf.

[745] *cf* points 4.5 and 5 of the 'working arrangement', Art 5(3) Regulation (EU, Euratom) No 883/2013 and section II.20.f. below.

[746] Inghelram, *Legal and Institutional Aspects of the European Anti-Fraud Office (OLAF)* (2011) 253 ff; Levi/Rodrigues et al, *Fonction publique de l'Union européenne* (2020) para 332.

[747] On this correlation, see, eg, section I.6.b. (time-barred recovery) and section b. below.

Course of the enquiry

An administrative enquiry may be initiated, resumed or expanded at any time.[748] The enquiry ends either with a discharge from the accusation;[749] a determination of a disciplinary offence without imposing any penalty (possibly combined with a warning); or an initiation of disciplinary proceedings. In the case of disciplinary proceedings, because the authority enjoys wide discretion for its assessment, the decision must be made on a sufficient and appropriate foundation.[750] The appointing authority does not have to involve the Disciplinary Board where it imposes only a written warning or a reprimand.[751] The Disciplinary Board must be involved for more serious penalties, such as the deferment of advancement to a higher step for a period of between one and 23 months; relegation in step; temporary downgrading for a period of between 15 days and one year; downgrading in the same function group; classification in a lower function group, with or without downgrading; removal from post; and, where appropriate, reduction *pro tempore* of a pension, or withholding, for a fixed period, an amount from an invalidity allowance.[752] This catalogue of penalties that may be imposed is exhaustive.[753] Sums withheld from remuneration during suspension are not considered to be a penalty and are not to be used to amend the weighing process or to redress possible discrepancies between the gravity of a member of staff's misconduct and the penalty.[754]

No circumvention of disciplinary law

Disciplinary law is characterised by special provisions, the severe consequences for the person concerned, and the related rights in place to protect legitimate interests of the staff employed. For that reason, the set of rules applicable to disciplinary measures must not be circumvented. For example, under Article 60 SR, any time of unauthorised absence from work which is duly established shall be deducted from the annual leave.[755] Apart from that, unauthorised absence from work can be also punished by disciplinary measures. However, a civil servant who breaches his official duties during working hours cannot be regarded as being absent from work within the meaning of this clause, since otherwise the provisions of disciplinary law would be circumvented.[756]

[748] Also misconduct in private life can be of relevance, CST, F-54/11, ECLI:EU:F:2012:114, para 128 – *BG v Ombudsman*; on the initiation of proceedings GC, T-242/97, ECLI:EU:T:1999:92 – *Z v EP*, para 28; CST, Jd Cases F-124/05 and F-96/06, ECLI:EU:F:2010:2, para 366 – *A and G v Commission*. It would violate the presumption of innocence if it was clear from the start that the outcome of the proceedings was not open-ended, but unfavourable for the civil servant, CST, Jd Cases F-7/11 and 60/11, ECLI:EU:F:2012:195, para 100 ff – *AX v ECB*.

[749] Art 22(2) Annex IX SR.

[750] Audit reports are not sufficient indication, CST, F-30/08, ECLI:EU:F:2010:43, paras 210, 215 – *Nanopoulos v Commission*.

[751] Art 11 Annex IX SR. In the case of Art 14(2) Annex IX SR (acknowledgement of the misconduct on the basis of the report) the penalties imposed may also be deferment of advancement and relegation in step, Art 9(1) a–d Annex IX SR.

[752] Art 12, Art 9 Annex IX SR.

[753] Arg: 'one of the following penalties'; as here: Levi/Rodrigues et al, *Fonction publique de l'Union européenne* (2020) para 341.

[754] See section 20.d. below on suspension.

[755] Example: GC, T-159/23, ECLI:EU:T:2024:5 – *VN v Commission*. If the staff member has used up his/her annual leave, he/she shall forfeit remuneration for an equivalent period.

[756] As here, AG Richard de la Tour: C-162/20 P, ECLI:EU:C:2021:459, paras 5, 64 – *WV v EEAS*; ECJ, C-162/20 P, ECLI:EU:C:2022:153, para 109 – *WV v EEAS*; different opinion: at first instance GC, T-471/18, ECLI:EU:T:2020:26 – *WV v EEAS*, where the GC decided on a salary reduction because it equated the non-fulfilment of tasks with 'unauthorised absence from work'. See case study after section II.20.h. below.

b. Rights of the Defence

As soon as an administrative enquiry reveals that an official may be personally involved in the matter being investigated, he shall be informed rapidly, as long as this would not be harmful to the investigation.[757] The rules[758] of internal investigations of the Commission stipulate that conclusions referring by name to a member, official or servant of the Commission may not be drawn once the investigation has been completed without the interested party having been enabled to express his views on all the facts which concern him. In cases necessitating the maintenance of absolute secrecy for the purposes of the investigation and requiring the use of investigative procedures falling within the remit of a national judicial authority, compliance with the obligation to invite the Member, official or servant of the Commission to give his or her views may be deferred in *agreement* with the President of the Commission or its Secretary-General respectively. The requirement to obtain the agreement of the authority ensures the rights of defence of the officials. OLAF can defer informing the person concerned only in truly exceptional cases; but the assessment of that exceptional status is not a matter solely for OLAF, but also requires the assessment of the Secretary-General of the Commission.[759] The adversarial nature of the proceedings warrants that the person concerned may assist at the proceedings and interrogate the witnesses.[760] The official may be assisted by a person chosen by him in the proceedings before the Disciplinary Board.[761] Despite the adversarial procedure, the Disciplinary Board also has official investigative powers and can, for example, hear a witness not named by the parties ex officio.[762] Apart from the observance of the rights of the defence, the administration is obliged to respect the *principle of impartiality*.[763]

Administrative nature

Disciplinary matters are not of a criminal, but of an administrative nature. This has correctly led the GC to conclude that they do not fall within the scope of 'penal proceedings', with the effect that Article 6 ECHR does not apply to disciplinary law.[764] Nevertheless, the proceedings may entail serious consequences for the persons concerned. In addition, the launch of an enquiry and even more of a disciplinary procedure entails a certain momentum to the detriment of the person accused. Therefore, anyone subject to disciplinary proceedings requires his *rights of the defence* to be fully protected.

Nulla poena sine lege as administrative legal certainty

Another consequence of the administrative, not criminal nature of disciplinary proceedings is that the principle of *nulla poena sine lege* (no punishment without a prior law)[765] does not directly

[757] On the rights of defence in disciplinary proceedings, see GC, T-277/03, ECLI:EU:T:2005:83, para 64 – *Vlachaki v Commission*; GC, T-173/04, ECLI:EU:T:2006:333, para 65 – *Carius v Commission*; GC, T-743/16 RENV, ECLI:EU:T:2018:937 – *CX v Commission*; Levi, 'Droits fondamentaux et principes généraux de droit de la fonction publique communautaire' in Govaere/Vandersanden (eds), *La fonction publique communautaire* (2008) 97 ff; Mader, *Verteidigungsrechte* (2006) 201 ff.

[758] Art 4 of Commission Decision 1999/396/EC of 2 June 1999 [1999] OJ L149/57–59.

[759] See GC, T-48/05, ECLI:EU:T:2008:257, para 151 – *Franchet and Byk v Commission*.

[760] ECJ,141/84, ECLI:EU:C:1985:269, para 16 – *De Compte v EP*; Mader, *Verteidigungsrechte* (2006) 201.

[761] Art 13(3) Annex IX. Whether an external person of trust may participate, CST, F-63/07, ECLI:EU:F:2009:18, paras 82/83 – *Patsarika v Cedefop*.

[762] GC, Jd Cases T-34/96 and T-163/96, ECLI:EU:T:1999:102, paras 57/58 – *Connolly v Commission*; Dalle-Crode (2008) 537.

[763] CST, F-77/09, ECLI:EU:F:2011:2, para 102 – *Nijs v ECA*, see section II.9. above.

[764] GC, T-26/89, ECLI:EU:T:1991:54, para 94 – *De Compte v EP*.

[765] Yet, the principle of *ne bis in idem* does apply, see section 20.e. below.

apply in disciplinary proceedings, because it belongs to the realm of criminal law. Nevertheless, it must have been possible for an official (or former official as the case may be) to first ascertain the existing obligations under the SR which he is supposed to comply with, as an expression of legal certainty in matters of administrative law. Secondly, as already stated above, when an administrative investigation is opened, it is necessary to indicate what specific provisions of the SR allegedly have been infringed. Both aspects (the possibility to know the applicable rules and to be informed about the administration's legal classification of a certain behaviour under the SR are preconditions to ensure the protection of the rights of defence in disciplinary proceedings.[766] Regarding the second aspect, the GC's judgment in *DD v FRA* was based on the opposite opinion when considering that it sufficed for the administration to refer to an alleged breach of 'internal rules on publishing and producing research results'[767] which were considered to be a case of plagiarism, without indicating to the staff member concerned which was the specific violation of the SR he was accused of.

Failure to cooperate in hearing

The failure of the official concerned to cooperate in the process of a hearing may have repercussions: if the official was not heard and the failure to do so was attributable to the official himself, then this procedural shortcoming does not lead to the annulment of the decision imposing a disciplinary measure. The authority is not required to indefinitely defer the date of a hearing until the moment the official is ready to participate in it.[768] The right of the official concerned to be heard has, however, not been observed where the appointing authority's hearing of the official before its adoption of a decision imposing a disciplinary measure on him does not remedy the Disciplinary Board's failure to hear the official.[769]

c. *Disciplinary Board*

Further to Articles 5 and 6 Annex IX SR, one or more disciplinary board(s) shall be established in each institution (unless set up for two or more agencies).[770] The chairman, the members and the alternates shall be appointed for a period of three years. The institutions may provide for a shorter period for members and alternates (minimum of one year). The Board shall consist of a chairman and four full members.[771] Both the official concerned and the institution shall each be entitled to reject one of the Board members within five days of the Board's establishment. Within the same time limit, Board members may ask to be excused from duty for legitimate reasons and shall withdraw if a conflict of interests exists. The chairman and members of the Board shall be completely independent in the performance of their duties. The deliberations and proceedings of the Board shall be secret.[772] The Board has an advisory function; it shall assess the facts neutrally and (where applicable) propose a penalty. As mentioned above, beyond the intended penalty

[766] As here: AG Pikamäe – C-680/22 P, ECLI:EU:C:2023:969, paras 80 ff, 90 – *DD v FRA*; differently: GC, T-470/20, ECLI:EU:T:2022:511 – *DD v FRA*.

[767] GC, T-470/20, ECLI:EU:T:2022:511, para 72 – *DD v FRA*.

[768] ECJ, C-270/99 P, ECLI:EU:C:2001:639, para 21 – *Z v EP*; GC, T-277/01, ECLI:EU:T:2002:302, para 41 – *Stevens v Commission*.

[769] CST, F-107/13, ECLI:EU:F:2014:232, paras 101, 122 – *de Brito Sequeira Carvalho* (where the official has in good time notified the Disciplinary Board supported by a medical certificate that he is unable to attend the hearing, see para 111).

[770] Art 9(1a) SR.

[771] For details, see the differentiated procedure of board establishment in Arts 5 and 6 Annex IX SR.

[772] Art 8 Annex IX SR.

of a written warning or reprimand the appointing authority shall submit a report to the Board (also communicated to the official concerned), stating clearly the facts complained of and, where appropriate, the circumstances in which they arose, including any aggravating or extenuating circumstances.[773] At this stage, it is not required to indicate which of the penalties are considered appropriate to impose in the particular case, because the report is not intended to anticipate the *inter partes* argument which is to take place between the person concerned and the appointing authority before the Disciplinary Board.[774] The official concerned may obtain his complete personal file and take copies of all relevant documents. He shall have not less than 15 days from the date of receipt of the report to prepare a defence, and may be assisted by a person of his choice.[775] The detailed provisions of the disciplinary proceedings are displayed in Articles 12–22 Annex IX SR.

Where the official decides to acknowledge[776] misconduct on his/her part and accepts unreservedly the report, the appointing authority may, in accordance with the principle of proportionality between the nature of the misconduct and the penalty being considered, withdraw the case from the Board. Where a case is withdrawn from the Board the chairman shall deliver an opinion on the penalty considered. In that case, the appointing authority may impose the penalties of a written warning, reprimand, deferment of advancement or relegation in step.[777] The official concerned shall be informed before acknowledging his misconduct of the possible consequences of such acknowledgement.

An important stage is the hearing of the official by the Disciplinary Board,[778] at which he may submit observations in writing or orally, whether in person or through a representative, and may also call witnesses. The institution shall be represented before the Board by an official mandated by the appointing authority, with rights equivalent to those of the official concerned. The Board may hear investigating officials from OLAF in cases where an investigation was initiated by OLAF. If the Board does not consider that it has sufficiently clear information on the facts complained of or the circumstances in which they arose, it shall order an investigation in which each side can submit its case and reply to the case of the other side. The chairman or a member of the Board shall conduct the investigation on behalf of the Board. For the purposes of the investigation, the Board may call for any documents relating to the matter before it. The institution shall comply with any such request within the time limit, if any, set by the Board. Where such a request is addressed to the official, note shall be taken of any refusal to comply.[779] After consideration of documents submitted and having regard to any statement made orally or in writing and to the results of any investigation undertaken, the Board shall, by majority vote, deliver a reasoned opinion (signed by all the members of the Board) as to whether the facts complained of are established and as to any penalty to which those facts should give rise.[780] The chairman of the Board

[773] Art 12 Annex IX SR.

[774] CST, F-133/15, ECLI:EU:F:2016:127, para 132 – *HI v Commission*, confirmed in appeal GC, T-464/16 P, ECLI:EU:T:2017:540 – *HI v Commission*.

[775] Art 13 Annex IX SR.

[776] Art 14 Annex IX SR.

[777] Art 9(1) a–d Annex IX SR.

[778] Art 16 Annex IX SR.

[779] Art 17 Annex IX SR.

[780] Art 18 Annex IX SR, which continues: 'Each member may attach to the opinion a divergent view. The Board shall transmit the opinion to the appointing authority and to the official concerned within two months of the date of receipt of the report of the appointing authority, provided that this time limit is commensurate with the degree of complexity of the case. Where an investigation has been held at the Board's initiative, the time limit shall be four months, provided that this period is commensurate with the degree of complexity of the case'.

shall not vote on matters before it, except as regards matters of procedure or where votes are tied. The secretary shall draw up minutes of meetings of the Disciplinary Board. Witnesses shall sign the minutes recording their evidence.[781] The appointing authority shall receive the opinion of the Disciplinary Board, hear the official and take its reasoned decision within two months of receipt of the opinion.[782]

d. Suspension

The appointing authority may decide to immediately suspend an official accused of serious misconduct for a specified or indefinite period, regardlesss of whether the alleged serious misconduct relates to a failure to honour his professional obligations or to an infringement of the law.[783] The suspension decision requires the prior hearing of the official, save in exceptional circumstances. Except where it proves impossible in practice, or incompatible with the interests of the service, to hold a hearing before adopting a decision suspending an official, the *rights of the defence* demand that the official is heard within 'a very short time' thereafter.[784] During the period of suspension remuneration (or part of it) may be withheld, in principle, for not more than six months. The amount paid to the official shall not under any circumstances be less than the minimum subsistence figure,[785] with the addition of any family allowances payable. The withholding of remuneration does not constitute a disciplinary penalty, but only a temporary measure taken pending the conclusion of disciplinary proceedings.[786] For that reason, sums withheld from remuneration can not be used by the administration to redress possible discrepancies between the gravity of a member of staff's misconduct and the penalty. Sums withheld shall be repaid if the final decision imposes a disciplinary penalty no more severe than a written warning, reprimand or deferment of advancement to a higher step, or if no disciplinary penalty is imposed.[787] The space for judicial review of the merits of a measure ordering the suspension is very limited, again for the provisional nature of a suspension: the court confines itself to examining whether the allegations of serious misconduct are either sufficiently probable, or if they are manifestly unfounded.[788]

e. Penalty and Proportionality

After hearing the official, the appointing authority shall take its reasoned decision within two months of receipt of the opinion of the Disciplinary Board (Art 22(1) Annex IX SR). When adopting the penalty, the authority is not bound by the measure proposed by the Disciplinary Board, but must justify each deviation[789] from this proposal and is subject to judicial review,

[781] Arts 19, 20 Annex IX SR.
[782] Art 22(1) Annex IX SR.
[783] Arts 23, 24 Annex IX SR.
[784] GC, T-211/98, ECLI:EU:T:2000:153, para 34 – *F v Commission.*
[785] Art 24 Annex IX SR, Art 6 Annex VIII SR.
[786] GC, T-569/16, ECLI:EU:T:2017:285, para 33 – *OU v Commission*; GC, T-219/96, ECLI:EU:T:1998:178, para 29 – *Y v EP.*
[787] Art 24(4) Annex IX SR, in the latter case, the repayment shall be made with compound interest.
[788] CST, F-80/08, ECLI:EU:F:2009:160, para 67 – *Wenig v Commission.*
[789] GC, T-24/98 and T-241/99, ECLI:EU:T:2001:175, para 92 – *E v Commission.* For a more independent disciplinary board, Vandersanden, 'La procédure et les voies de recours' in Govaere/Vandersanden (eds), *La fonction publique communautaire* (2008) 122 ff.

particularly in regard to abuse and the principle of proportionality – ie, the severity of the disciplinary penalties imposed shall be commensurate with the seriousness of the misconduct.[790] Disciplinary sanctions are not only possible in the case of intentional violations, but the existence of intention also has an effect when assessing proportionality.[791] When determining the sanction, the special features of the individual case must always be taken into account.[792] This concrete and substantiated weighing process has to go beyond the nature and gravity of the fault; it also has to encompass the mitigating circumstances and the context surrounding the behaviour in question.[793]

Ne bis in idem

A single case of misconduct shall not give rise to more than one disciplinary penalty,[794] whereas 'single case' refers to the same factual circumstances. A failure to comply with several obligations or provisions of the SR, on the other hand, that give rise to the imposition by the appointing authority of a single disciplinary penalty which takes account of the combined seriousness of those failures,[795] does not infringe the *ne bis in idem principle*, but is an expression of applying the principle of proportionality. Also where the authority imposes the the measure of suspension this does not infringe the *ne bis in idem principle*, because a suspension does not constitute a disciplinary penalty, but only a temporary measure and because there are rules in place for repayment under the conditions described above.[796,797]

New facts

Where new facts supported by relevant evidence come to light, disciplinary proceedings may be reopened by the appointing authority on its own initiative or on application by the official concerned.[798] There is no obligation on the side of the appointing authority to reopen the proceedings.[799] However, the protection of the rights of the defence warrant the reopening in case a further measure of enquiry discloses a new fact complained of or a new circumstance in which the facts complained of arose, or any other factor liable *substantially* to alter the assessment of the real nature, extent or seriousness of the facts complained of, thereby altering the content of the report submitted to the Disciplinary Board.[800]

[790] Art 10 Annex IX SR; GC, T-162/22, ECLI:EU:T:2023:205, paras 70–88 – *OQ v Commission*; GC, T-757/20, ECLI:EU:T:2022:156, paras 166–73 – *OT v EP*; GC, T-75/00, ECLI:EU:T:2003:9, paras 52/53 – *Fichtner v Commission.* Dalle-Crode (2008) 568 on GC, T-82/99, ECLI:EU:T:2000:193 – *Cwik v Commission*, and C-340/00 P, ECLI:EU:C:2001:701 – *Commission v Cwik*; GC, Jd Cases T-34/96 and T-163/96, ECLI:EU:T:1999:102, paras 57/58 – *Connolly v Commission*, and ECJ, C-274/99 P, ECLI:EU:C:2001:127 – *Connolly v Commission*; on proportionality GC, T-757/20, ECLI:EU:T:2022:156, para 173 – *OT v EP*; GC, T-198/02, ECLI:EU:T:2004:101, paras 51–54 – *N v Commission*; CST, F-40/05, ECLI:EU:F:2007:189, para 233 – *Andreasen v Commission*; on temporary suspension, CST, F-80/08, ECLI:EU:F:2009:160 – *Wenig v Commission.* The court does not examine whether other measures would have been more appropriate, CST, Jd Cases F-7/11 and 60/11, ECLI:EU:F:2012:195, para 149 – *AX v ECB.*

[791] CST, F-106/11, ECLI:EU:F:2013:91, para 41 – *BM v ECB*; on the two-stage penalty decision: ibid, para 51.

[792] ECJ, C-273/99, ECLI:EU:C:2001:126, paras 40/41 – *Connolly v Commission.* The insistence on behaviour that has already been subject to disciplinary sanctions may aggravate the penalty, CST, F-56/11, ECLI:EU:F:2013:49, paras 115 ff, 121 – *Lebedef v Commission.*

[793] GC, T-754/20, ECLI:EU:T:2022:316, para 237 – *Cristescu v Commission.*

[794] Art 9(3) Annex IX SR.

[795] CST, F-133/15, ECLI:EU:F:2016:127, para 141 – *HI v Commission.*

[796] Section d.

[797] GC, T-333/99, ECLI:EU:T:2001:251, para 151 – *X v ECB.*

[798] Art 28 Annex IX SR.

[799] CST, F-49/15, ECLI:EU:F:2016:72, para 109 – *FU v Commission.*

[800] GC, T-549/93, EU:T:1995:15, para 49 – *D v Commission*; CST, F-133/15, ECLI:EU:2016:127, para 149 – *HI v Commission.*

Closure of case
An overly lengthy disciplinary procedure does not usually lead to its cancellation,[801] but can justify liability for damages.[802] If the appointing authority decides to close the case without imposing any disciplinary penalty, it shall so inform the official concerned in writing without delay. The official concerned may request that this decision be inserted in his personal file.[803] Where no case has been made against the accused, the official is entilted to request that damage suffered should be made good through suitable publicity for the decision of the appointing authority.[804] The appointing authority's decision to impose a penalty is an act adversely affecting the official concerned in the sense of Articles 90, 91 SR.[805]

Case Study on Disciplinary Penalty

Disciplinary sanction of dismissal annulled: Acts removed from the personal file must not be reinstated

Case T-121/20, *IP v Commission* of 6 October 2021

In Brief

The General Court (GC) annulled the Commission's disciplinary sanction to terminate a contract without notice. As a matter of *unity of the personal file*, a disciplinary measure must not take into account those elements of the personal file that have been removed from it. In the case at hand, the Commission effectively reinstated an earlier disciplinary reprimand in its considerations, even though the administration had already deleted this element from the file at the request of the applicant.

Legal Background

Article 26 SR:

> The personal file of an official shall contain: (a) all documents concerning his administrative status and all reports relating to his ability, efficiency and conduct; ... There shall be only one personal file for each official.

Article 10 Annex IX SR:

> The severity of the disciplinary penalties imposed shall be commensurate with the seriousness of the misconduct. To determine the seriousness of the misconduct and to decide upon the disciplinary penalty to be imposed, account shall be taken in particular of: ... (h) whether the misconduct involves repeated action or behaviour.

[801] CST, F-40/05, ECLI:EU:F:2007:189, para 194 – *Andreasen v Commission*; CST, Jd Cases F-124/05 and F-96/06, ECLI:EU:F:2010:2, para 390 – *A and G v Commission* (reasonable period of time). Annulment where the delay made the defence more difficult, GC, T-394/03, ECLI:EU:T:2006:111, para 162 – *Angeletti v Commission*, €12,000 damages for delayed procedure. After a certain duration of the procedure, the burden of proof regarding the appropriateness of the duration of the procedure passes to the administration, *cf* CST, F-12/10, ECLI:EU:F:2012:183 – *Kerstens v Commission.*

[802] CST, Jd Cases F-124/05 and F-96/06, ECLI:EU:F:2010:2, paras 398–402, 415 – *A and G v Commission.*

[803] Art 22 Annex IX SR.

[804] Art 29 Annex IX SR.

[805] See chapter 2, V.

Article 27 Annex IX SR:

> An official against whom a disciplinary penalty other than removal from post has been ordered may, after three years in the case of a written warning or reprimand or after six years in the case of any other penalty, submit a request for the deletion from his personal file of all reference to such measure. The Appointing Authority shall decide whether to grant this request.

Facts of the Case

The applicant worked as a contract agent at the Commission. He was accused of having made two claims for reimbursement of medical expenses that did not correspond to the amounts actually paid or the treatments actually received. This was seen as attempted fraud against the EU budget, which the Commission saw as particularly serious misconduct. As a result, in 2019 the Commission terminated his employment without notice as a disciplinary penalty. In determining the sanction, the Commission relied on the existence of a previous disciplinary reprimand against the applicant dating back to 2010. In 2014, the applicant requested to have all elements relating to the disciplinary reprimand of 2010 deleted from his personal file, in accordance with Article 27 Annex IX SR. The Commission granted this deletion.

In view of the earlier disciplinary reprimand, the Commission came to the conclusion that the new act was comparable to the one that had been subject to the earlier reprimand, and that the applicant had thus shown that 'he had learned nothing from the disciplinary sentence in 2010 and that his personal interests continued to take precedence over the interests of the institution'.

The Decision of the Court and Reasoning

In its judgment, the GC annulled the disciplinary sanction of the Commission by which the applicant's contract was terminated. The disciplinary authority should not have relied on the earlier penalty as a repeated act, because this earlier act had been removed from the applicant's personal file. The Commission's decision thus violated Article 26 SR and Article 10 lit h Annex IX SR, and had to be annulled. The GC found that Article 26 SR provides for a number of safeguards to protect civil servants by preventing administrative decisions relating to their employment from being based on facts which have not been included in their personal files.

Given the essential role of the personal file in protecting and informing the official, the GC found that even if it was previously recorded in an official's personal file, a disciplinary decision must not be relied on or used against the official if that decision has been removed from their personal file. Relying on a disciplinary decision removed from an official's personal file so as to infer a repeated act within the meaning of Article 10 Annex IX SR would amount to taking away the practical effectiveness of Article 27 Annex IX. This Article enables an official to request the removal of a disciplinary decision from his personal file, and leaves it to the administration whether to grant such a deletion. By relying on a disciplinary decision, even though the administration has exercised its discretion to remove it from the official's personal file, it is in effect trying to reinstate such a decision.

The GC then refers to the uniform character of the personal file, which forbids the existence of any other collection of documents relating to the civil servant's employment. It is true that the administration can create a file on an investigation and, if necessary, on a disciplinary procedure that may result from it. However, such a file is produced solely for the purposes of the proceedings in question. As a result, the documents contained in it, and in particular any disciplinary decision that would conclude the proceedings, cannot be used against an official outside the proceedings unless they are included in his personal file.

During litigation, the Commission argued that there is an internal legal basis (the so-called *common retention list for Commission files*) which allows disciplinary decisions to be retained for a period of 20 years. But the Court decided, first, that this internal provision cannot hierarchically override the provisions of the Staff Regulations (being a regulation under Art 288 TFEU); and secondly, that the provision in the common retention list does not aim to specify the requirements under which documents can be used against an official. On the basis of those rules, the Commission cannot, as regards a repeated act, rely on a penalty imposed against an official to which the reference has been removed from the official's personal file.

The GC concluded that the legal mistake of applying Article 10 Annex IX SR (not to have properly assessed whether the misconduct involves a repeated action or behaviour) had a decisive effect on the administration's conclusion to terminate the contract of the applicant without notice, because the Commission had extensively referred to the earlier (deleted) disciplinary reprimand, and had treated it as an aggravating factor. This played a decisive role in determining the disciplinary sanction of contract termination.

Comments

1. The Court bases its judgment on a central principle of EU civil service law, namely the *unity of the personal file*, Article 26(6) SR.[806] As a guarantee for protecting the official, decisions relating to him shall be solely based upon facts that have been recorded in the personal file.[807] Elements may not be used or cited by the institution against an official unless they were communicated to the official before they were filed. A decision not based on facts contained in the personal file infringes the guarantees contained in the SR.[808]
2. In the present case, the applicant had taken an important step in protecting his interests by filing his request to delete all reference to the earlier disciplinary reprimand from his personal file (Art 27 Annex IX SR). It can be recommended in general to submit such a request for deletion as soon as the waiting period of three years (in the case of a written warning or reprimand) or six years (in the case of any other penalty) has elapsed.
3. The question then is whether the appointing authority will actually grant this request. It has to take such a decision by *properly exercising its discretion*, so that the respective provisions of the SR do not run idle, and it has to take into account the principle of *duty of care* towards the civil servant. Since Article 27 Annex IX SR indicates in an explicit and unconditional manner the time periods after which deletion can be

[806] On the personal file, see section II.11. above.

[807] ECJ, 88/71, ECLI:EU:C:1972:58, para 10 – *Brasseur v EP*; GC, T-86/97, ECLI:EU:T:1998:71, para 33 – *Apostolidis v ECJ*.

[808] *cf* present case GC, T-121/20, ECLI:EU:T:2021:665, para 56 – *IP v Commission*; GC, T-109/92, ECLI:EU:T:1994:16, para 68 – *Lacruz Bassols v ECJ*.

requested, it can be argued that any decision not to grant the deletion of a reference to disciplinary measures despite the request to do so would have to be specifically justified as an exceptional case. Exceptions have to be interpreted narrowly.[809]

4. The Commission's additional argument that the provision in the common retention list of files allowing the retention of elements of the personal file for 20 years was rejected by the GC, both on the basis of the argument of norm hierarchy and in the light of the difference in objectives of the two provisions. The internal retention list of files has the purpose of making the work of the institution transparent and accountable, not of overriding the specific time periods laid down in the SR (Art 27 Annex IX). This argument applies also in other cases where the internal rules of an institution attempt to modify the guarantees of protection afforded to staff as determined by higher-ranking provisions – in this case, the SR.

f. Parallel Criminal Prosecution

In order to avoid the duplication of investigations, OLAF shall discontinue an ongoing investigation and shall, as a rule, not open a parallel investigation where the European Public Prosecutor's Office (EPPO) is conducting an investigation into the same facts.[810] When criminal proceedings are initiated, disciplinary sanctions may only be imposed after the criminal proceedings have been concluded, in order not to impair the accused's ability to defend himself in court, Article 25 Annex IX SR.[811] The disciplinary measure must not be adopted *depending* on the sentence in criminal proceedings.[812]

It is only the appointing authority that is prevented from taking a final decision before a final judgment has been handed down by the criminal court hearing the case, while the Disciplinary Board is not required to suspend its proceedings (but may decide to do so). Further, the administration is only obliged to suspend disciplinary proceedings if the official demonstrates that he is subject to criminal prosecution. This entails that the public mechanism for imposing punishment has been engaged, and thus cannot include an enquiry or judicial investigation, but presupposes that criminal proceedings have been instituted.[813]

Excessively long criminal proceedings

The requirement to await the final judgment of the criminal court before taking a decision on the disciplinary measure might run counter to the above-mentioned obligation to speed up the

[809] Principles of interpretation: chapter 1, III.4.

[810] Art 5(3) Regulation (EU, Euratom) No 883/2013 of 11 September 2013 concerning investigations conducted by the European Anti-Fraud Office (OLAF); on the relations of OLAF and EPPO, see Inghelram, *Legal and Institutional Aspects of the European Anti-Fraud Office (OLAF)* (2011) 256 ff.

[811] GC, T-307/01, ECLI:EU:T:2004:180, para 59 – *Francois v Commission*; Dalle-Crode (2008) 540. On recourse to the terminology of national criminal procedural law, CST, F-54/11, ECLI:EU:F:2012:114, paras 65, 68/69 – *BG v Ombudsman*. The purpose of the suspension is to prevent the civil servant from being put in a less favourable position in the criminal proceedings instituted against him than would be the case without an administrative or judicial decision, GC, T-74/96, ECLI:EU:T:1998:58, para 34 – *Tzoanos v Commission*. This consideration can also be carried over to an earlier stage of the criminal investigation if the official specifically demonstrates that the disciplinary procedure could worsen his position in the criminal proceedings, CST, F-54/11, ECLI:EU:F:2012:114, paras 71 ff, 74, 78 – *BG v Ombudsman*.

[812] GC, T-198/02, ECLI:EU:T:2004:101, paras 57/58, 98 – *N v Commission*.

[813] CST, F-89/11, ECLI:EU:F:2013:83, para 151 – *Goetz v CoR*.

process and avoid an unreasonable delay in the adoption of the decision concluding the disciplinary proceedings, especially where the criminal proceedings last for a number of years. The Civil Service Tribunal (CST) has shown some readiness to accept derogations from the rule expressed in Article 25 Annex IX SR, where it can be demonstrated that the national criminal prosecution in progress is taking a 'disproportionate amount of time for the complexity of the case or compared with the duration of proceedings of a similar difficulty'.[814]

g. *Expenses of Disciplinary Proceedings*

As Article 21 Annex IX SR stipulates, expenses incurred on the initiative of an official concerned in the course of disciplinary proceedings, and in particular fees paid to a person chosen to assist the official or for his defence, shall be borne by the official where the disciplinary proceedings result in the imposition of one of the penalties provided for in Article 9 Annex IX SR. The appointing authority may decide otherwise in exceptional cases where the burden on the official concerned would be unfair.

h. *No Circumvention of Disciplinary Law*

The system established under disciplinary law provides for important safeguards to protect the rights of the persons subject to disciplinary proceedings. For that reason, the provisions for disciplinary measures shall not be bypassed. This could, for example, happen by broadening the application of certain HR management provisions in the SR. The 'unauthorised absence' provision of Article 60 SR is one of these.

Case Study on the Term 'Unauthorised Absence' in Article 60 SR

Can the unwillingness to fulfil tasks amount to an 'unauthorised absence' from service?

Case C-162/20 P, *WV v EEAS* of 3 March 2022
Case T-471/18, *WV v EEAS* of 29 January 2020

In Brief

The Court of Justice (ECJ) ruled on the term 'unauthorised absence' of an official in the sense of Article 60 SR, and decided that 'absence' means physical absence. The provisions for disciplinary measures shall not be bypassed by applying the 'unauthorised absence' concept in too broad a sense. Otherwise, a civil servant could be sanctioned for low performance or unwillingness under Article 60 SR (namely by deducting leave days and/or remuneration) without affording him the safeguards foreseen under disciplinary law.

[814] CST, F-129/14, ECLI:EU:F:2015:71, para 66 – *Dybman v EEAS*; CST, F-27/14, ECLI:EU:F:2015:12, para 72 – *DK v EEAS*. Tomac in Perillo/Giacobbo-Peyronnel (eds), *Statut de la fonction publique de l'Union européenne: Commentaire article par article* (2017) 337.

Legal Background

Article 60(1) SR stipulates:

> Except in case of sickness or accident, an official may not be absent without prior permission from his immediate superior. Without prejudice to any disciplinary measures that may apply, any unauthorised absence which is duly established shall be deducted from the annual leave of the official concerned. If he has used up his annual leave, he shall forfeit his remuneration for an equivalent period.

Articles 21 and 55 SR require that the 'official … shall assist and tender advice to his superiors' and that 'officials in active employment shall at all times be at the disposal of their institution'.

Facts of the Case

The applicant – an official at the European External Action Service (EEAS) – was transferred to another unit, and later still to a third unit, in the interests of the service. She disagreed with the transfer and requested to be informed about the reasons for being removed from her original unit. She was later told that it was repeatedly impossible to find her in her office, and she was therefore considered to be taking unauthorised absences. The applicant argued that – although she might not necessarily be sitting at her desk for the whole day – she was present at the EEAS to solve the administrative issues relating to her transfer. The applicant's head of unit sent her a note in which it was stated that she had accumulated 85 days of unjustified absences which were to be deducted from her remuneration in accordance with Article 60 SR. The applicant asked for extracts of the time recording data for entering and leaving the building, and was informed that she could not obtain those extracts for reasons of data protection. Later, the calculation of her 'unauthorised absences' were revised, in the sense that nine days would be converted into annual leave, and the equivalent of 72 days would be deducted from her salary. The applicant challenged this decision.

Decision of the General Court

The General Court (GC) ordered that the application was partially 'manifestly inadmissible', and partially 'manifestly unfounded'. It ruled that, even if it were established that the applicant was actually present in the EEAS office buildings as she claimed, the fact remains that, by clearly stating her intention not to work within the new unit, on the ground that she wanted to focus solely on the administrative issues relating to her transfer, the applicant manifestly failed to comply with the conditions laid down by Articles 21 and 55 SR. The EEAS – said the GC – cannot therefore be criticised for considering the applicant to be taking unauthorised absences. Since the absences had not been authorised in advance by her superiors, the deduction from her pay of 72 calendar days was merely the consequence of non-compliance with the requirements provided for in Article 60 SR. Further, the GC stated that its conclusion was not called into question by the fact that the applicant had submitted evidence of her presence in her office. The GC took the view that the evidence failed to demonstrate that the applicant had assisted her superiors by performing the tasks entrusted to her, or that she had made herself available to the EEAS at all times in accordance with her obligations under Articles 21 and 55 SR. Therefore, the GC found the applicant to be in a situation of unauthorised absence which justified deductions from her remuneration in accordance with the first paragraph of Article 60 SR.

Decision of the ECJ

In its appeal decision, the ECJ sets aside the order of the GC and annuls the decision of the EEAS to impose a deduction from salary amounting to 72 calendar days; further, the ECJ orders the EEAS to repay to the appellant the amounts wrongly deducted from her remuneration, together with interest at the rate of 5 per cent per annum from the date on which they were deducted. The ECJ first focuses on the meaning of 'unauthorised absence' in Article 60 SR, and whether it can be applied to situations in which an official is present but unwilling to fulfil tasks – entrusted or otherwise – to support her superiors. In line with the definition suggested by Advocate General Richard de la Tour, the ECJ states that in everyday language the term 'absence' describes the fact that someone or something is not where it is expected to be, which requires a physical absence. Also, Article 60 SR does not mention any precondition of a breach of official duties by the official, next to the precondition of physical presence or absence. Secondly, Article 60 SR is part of the rules in the SR that deal with leave, and thus with situations in which an official is not physically present at his place of work. Thirdly, Article 60 SR explicitly says that deductions due to absences apply 'without prejudice to any disciplinary measures', and shall therefore be handled separately from disciplinary measures. Absences are quantifiable, but breaches of official duties cannot be quantified. Article 60 deductions do not have the purpose of substituting for a disciplinary sanction in respect of a breach of duty. All this leads the ECJ to conclude that Article 60 SR relates to situations in which an official is *physically absent* from his place of work. It would constitute an abuse of the disciplinary procedure to consider that an official present at his place of work who is performing his duties poorly or who is even disobeying instructions is in a situation of 'unauthorised absence' within the meaning of Article 60(1) SR, and that deductions may therefore be made from his leave or salary. That erroneous classification as 'unauthorised absence' means that the official would be subject to a pecuniary penalty which is not provided for in the SR, without benefiting from the guarantees of proper disciplinary proceedings.

In result, concludes the ECJ, since Article 60 SR only relates to situations of physical absence of the official from his place of work and its application would require an accurate determination of the physical absence of the applicant from service, the ECJ sets aside the order of the GC and decides that the decision of the EEAS is to be annulled.

Comments

1. In its judgment in *WV v EEAS*, the ECJ focuses on the choice of the legal basis used by the administration (Art 60 SR) to sanction the applicant for her unwillingness to work in the units she was transferred to. The unwillingness of an official to fulfil tasks may justify deductions from leave or salary, but must never be construed as an 'unauthorised absence' from service. Otherwise the official's protection afforded under disciplinary law would be circumvented.
2. While the EU courts have previously interpreted the concept of 'unauthorised absence', their case-law concerned situations in which the official was absent from

his place of work for supposed or proven medical reasons; for exercising the right to strike; or for the purposes of union representation.[815]

3. The question raised in *WV v EEAS* is new, because the ECJ had to clarify the meaning and scope of the concept of 'absence' of an official expressing his intention at the place of work not to collaborate within the department, not to carry out the tasks entrusted to him, and not to assist his superiors or make himself available in accordance with the requirements set out in Articles 21 and 55 SR. This was an important clarification (1) regarding the concept of physical presence or absence of the person, and (2) regarding the obligation to be available for work at the place determined for the official, as well as their readiness for reassignment and transfer into other services.
4. The term 'absence' in Article 60(1) SR is strictly about whether an official is *physically* absent from the place of work.
5. However, the core of the case is not to define the *need* of presence at work – a practice which has changed in any case in all institutions due to the Covid-19 pandemic – but to avoid the set of rules applicable for disciplinary measures being bypassed by using the specific legal consequences contained in Article 60 SR as if it was a disciplinary sanctions regime allowing the punishment of an official who is not willing to support his superior, who is not as available as required, or who is otherwise not willing to work within the department he is assigned to. As a detail, while the ECJ argued that this bypassing would constitute an abuse of the disciplinary procedure, it seems more pertinent to assert that this approach would *abuse Article 60 SR* in order to bypass the safeguards contained in disciplinary law.
6. When reading the judgment in this perspective, it becomes clear that it cannot be understood to mean that an official cannot be reassigned or transferred against his will into another position or unit. The judgment only says that an unwilling official cannot be sanctioned by treating him as being in an 'unauthorised absence'. But it should be borne in mind that neither a reassignment nor a transfer to a new position, service or task requires the consent of the official.[816]

III. Remuneration

The remuneration of the active civil servant corresponds to his grade and step (Art 62 SR in conjunction with Annex VII) and includes: the basic salary;[817] family allowances[818] and other allowances,[819] such as the expatriation allowance, household allowance; and dependent child allowance.

[815] ECJ, Jd Cases 44/74, 46/74 and 49/74, ECLI:EU:C:1975:42 – *Acton*; GC, T-364/09 P, ECLI:EU:T:2010:539 – *Lebedef*; and on the right to strike, GC, T-402/18, ECLI:EU-T-2020:13 – *Aquino and Others v EP*.

[816] GC, T-468/20, ECLI:EU:T:2022:137, paras 139 ff – *Kühne v EP*; ECJ, 19/87, ECLI:EU:C:1988:165, para 6 – *Hecq v Commission*. See section II.16. above.

[817] Art 66 SR, in the case of part-time work Art 68a SR in conjunction with Annex IVa; Regulation (EU) No 422/2014 of the European Parliament and of the Council of 16 April 2014 on the adjustment of the salaries and pensions of civil servants and other servants of the European Union and the correction coefficients that are applicable to these salaries and pensions [2014] OJ L129/5–11.

[818] Art 67 SR.

[819] Art 69 SR in conjunction with Art 4 Annex VII SR.

1. Salary

The 2004 reform introduced a stronger focus on merit at the expense of seniority,[820] as well as the strengthening of family-related benefits and an overall reduction in allowances. The reform goal of financial savings was brought about by a new salary table with some lower amounts, and the introduction of lower salary brackets for newly recruited staff. The 2014 reform continued this route by, for example, introducing a new function group AST/SC (of lower salaries), a cap on the standard career path without management functions at AD 12, and a suspension of salary increases for two years.

a. Advancement

The function groups AST (for assistants) and AD (for administrators), with a total of 16 grades, replace the former horizontal grades D–A, giving high-performing civil servants more opportunity to move up the grades in their careers. A common salary table applies to these function groups, whereas a separate salary table applies to the function group of assistants and secretaries/clerks. Both tables are designed linearly: the salaries of different groups in a table do not overlap in terms of amount, even at different seniority steps. There are five seniority steps in each grade.[821] The advantages when advancing up the steps generally decrease from level to level. If a promotion occurs only from the fifth level (ie, to the first step of the next higher grade), this alone does not result in an increase in salary. Advancement to the next seniority step does not take place if the performance in the previous annual appraisal was assessed as unsatisfactory, but such inhibition is limited.[822] Certain non-performance related benefits[823] were abolished, and a functional retroactive pay adjustment was introduced for a promotionally appointed head of unit, director or director-general.[824]

b. Correction Coefficients

The remuneration shall be expressed in euros (€) and paid in the currency of the country in which the official performs his duties, or in euros.[825] Correction coefficients apply to places of employment outside Belgium and Luxembourg, whereby the remuneration, after the compulsory deductions have been made, will be weighted at a rate above, below or equal to 100 per cent, depending on the living conditions in the various places of employment.[826]

[820] Criticising the remuneration (and its increase) as allegedly being too strongly tied to the age of the officials: Mehde, 'Europäisches Dienstrecht' in Terhechte (ed), *Verwaltungsrecht der Europäischen Union* § 39, paras 63/64. Féral, 'Droit statutaire: la rémunération des fonctionnaires communautaires' (2000) *Revue de la recherche juridique, droit prospectif* 1101–37.

[821] Exception: AD 16 with three seniority levels, Art 66 SR, Annex I, Section A SR.

[822] Art 44(1) SR: advancement to the next step in the grade after no longer than four years.

[823] Gauer, *Die Reform des Europäischen öffentlichen Dienstrechts* (2007) 95.

[824] Art 44(2) SR.

[825] Art 63(1) SR.

[826] Art 64 SR; Council Regulation (EU) No 1416/2013 of 17 December 2013 adjusting with effect from 1 July 2013 the correction coefficients applied to the remuneration and pensions of officials and other servants of the European Union [2013] OJ L353/24. On equal buying power in different places of employment, see Levi, 'Droits fondamentaux et principes généraux de droit de la fonction publique communautaire' in Govaere/Vandersanden (eds), *La fonction publique communautaire* (2008) 85 ff; CST, F-29/09, ECLI:EU:F:2010:120, para 67 – *Lebedef and Jones v Commission*; GC, T-619/20, ECLI:EU:T:2021:901 and T-225/20, ECLI:EU:T:2021:899 – *FJ v EEAS*; GC, T-618/20, ECLI:EU:T:2021:900 – *FZ v Commission*.

The salaries of civil servants employed in third countries are subject to the correction coefficient applicable to salaries in Belgium. They are paid in euros in the European Union (EU), but, at the request of the official, the appointing authority may decide to pay all or part of his remuneration in the currency of the country of employment. In that event, it shall be subject to the weighting for the place of employment, and shall be converted on the basis of the corresponding exchange rate.[827]

c. *Transfers in Different Currencies*

Part of the remuneration may be paid in a different currency at a place other than the place of employment[828] using the exchange rates and weightings referred to in Article 63(2) and (3) SR.[829] This possibility was restricted by the 2004 reform,[830] subject to any conditions laid down in rules fixed by the appointing authorities of each institution; such transfers may not exceed 5 per cent of the official's basic salary, and are intended to benefit children attending an education establishment in another Member State, as well as regular payments to comply with proven obligations under national law. The former capital city index was replaced in 2004 by a Member State index.[831]

d. *Annual Update of Remuneration: The 'Method'*

According to Article 65 SR, the remuneration (and pensions)[832] of the officials and other servants shall be updated every year, taking into account the economic and social policy of the Union. The method for determining the update is set out in Annex XI SR, and is based on a report by Eurostat on changes in the cost of living in Belgium and Luxembourg, the economic parities between Brussels and certain places in the Member States – and in third countries where necessary – and changes in the purchasing power of salaries in national civil services in central government.[833] The so-called 'method' is the result of continuous development since 1972, which regulates the adjustments in an increasingly precise and binding manner with the aim of mid-term stability and the avoidance of 'discussions and recurrent difficulties'.[834] The method after the 2014 reform responds to the controversy about the Council's political leeway on salary increases, and makes comprehensive use of statistical data, even for exceptional economic situations. As case-law has confirmed, the Council's discretion – conferred on it by Article 65 SR in determining the salary updates – is restricted by the framework set out in Annex XI SR.[835] By adopting Annex XI, the Council bound itself by a unilateral decision for the validity period of the Annex. As a result, the previously required legislative decision-making for 'adapting' or 'aligning' salaries has been replaced by an automatic 'update' based on statistical data.[836]

[827] Art 12 Annex X SR.
[828] Art 17 Annex VII SR.
[829] CST, F-100/07, ECLI:EU:F:2009:21 – *Tsirimiagos v CoR*.
[830] Limited to the education allowance for children attending a school there; proven regular payments based on a court or administrative decision of up to 5% of the basic salary, Gauer (2007) 186.
[831] Art 17(3) Annex VII SR in conjunction with Art 3(5) lit a, b Annex XI SR.
[832] *cf* Arts 3 and 4 Annex XI SR.
[833] Art 1 Annex XI SR.
[834] ECJ, C-40/10, ECLI:EU:C:2010:713, para 68 – *Commission v Council*.
[835] ECJ, C-40/10, ECLI:EU:C:2010:713, paras 55/56, 63, 68, 71 – *Commission v Council*. On the procedure, see Chevalier, 'Précisions sur le calcul de l'augmentation annuelle de la rémunération des fonctionnaires de l'Union' (2009–10) *Revue des affaires européennes* (*Law & European Affairs*) 913.
[836] Art 3(1) Annex XI SR.

The basis is an index developed by the Commission in cooperation with the statistical offices. In particular, recruitment needs and salary increases in the civil service of the Member States shall be taken into account.[837] The 2014 method is based on the situation in the national public services of 11 Member States, instead of the previous eight. On the basis of the statistical data,[838] and in the implementation of general specifications for amount and time, the automatic 'update' of the amounts takes place both in normal cases and in special economic situations, 'without intervention of another legal act'.[839] The update takes place annually or, in the event of a significant change in the cost of living, during the year (intermediate).[840] In the year 2023, for the second time since the method was establishmed, an intermediate increase took place.[841]

The 2014 reform brought about another modification: the former exception for taking into account a significant, abrupt deterioration in the economic and social situation, together with some scope for (disputed) political decision-making, was replaced by a 'moderation and exception clause,' Articles 10 and 11 Annex XI SR. It contains a method based on statistical data in the event of a falling Union GDP.

The size of the correction coefficients due to persistent significant differences in the cost of living for the various places of employment (Art 64 SR) is now enacted by means of Commission-delegated acts.[842] The new method[843] became necessary because the Council[844] had tried to take account of the previous economic crisis and its consequences for the salary levels in the national public services in the 2010 adjustment, in order to determine the salary adjustment in terms of their deviation from the statistical calculation bases on which these consequences had not yet been fully impacted.[845] The problem resulted, on the one hand, from a time lag between the adjustment in the EU compared with the salary changes in the national services and, on the other hand, from the differences in the circumstances of the Member States, in addition to the relatively small reference basis that the restriction to only eight Member States represented. After the Commission successfully filed an action for annulment of the Council's Regulation, the objective pursued was to enable the changed methodology to generate an appropriate response to economic crises.[846] The unresolved problem was protracted, and its effects were evident in the years that followed,[847] again leading to a dispute between the Council and the Commission about the adjustments and the procedure to be applied.[848] The temporal application of the new update

[837] Art 65(1) SR.

[838] Arts 3, 10 and 11 Annex XI SR.

[839] Art 65(3) SR.

[840] Annually Art 65(1) SR, the update in 2022 was calculated as an increase of 4.4%.

[841] Art 65(2) SR, Arts 4–7 Annex XI SR: the increase was calculated as 1.7%. The intermediate updates shall be taken into account (ie, deducted) in the annual salary update.

[842] Art 9(1)2 Annex XI SR.

[843] It changed numerous calculation bases and replaces, eg, the previous 'Brussels International Index' with the so-called 'Joint Index' based on national inflation in Belgium and Luxembourg, Art 1 Nr 2 Annex XI SR.

[844] Regulation (EU, Euratom) No 1296/2009 [2009] OJ L348/10.

[845] ECJ, C-40/10, ECLI:EU:C:2010:713 – *Commission v Council*; ECJ, 59/81, ECLI:EU:C:1982:332, para 22 – *Commission v Council* on the limitation of legislative discretion. The CST takes up the argumentation of the ECJ (C–40/10) that pretending there is a crisis situation in order to avoid the use of the procedure provided shall be prohibited, and transfers this to the ECB situation for the question of salary adjustment, CST, F-114/10, ECLI:EU:F:2011:173, para 70 – *Bowles and Others v ECB*.

[846] See Commission press releases IP/11/816, MEMO/11/473, IP/13/629; the reform further to the European Council conclusions (7/8 February 2013, Nr 99) – beyond the reintroduction of the solidarity levy – was essentially limited to a reaction to economic crises, and does not itself contribute to budget consolidation.

[847] See the reports from the Commission to the Council on the exception clause (Art 10 Annex XI SR), COM(2012) 476.

[848] Regarding the related actions of the Commission in the cases ECJ, C-63/12, ECLI:EU:C:2013:752 – *Commission v Council*; ECJ, C-66/12, ECLI:EU:C:2013:751 – *Council v Commission*; on non-adjustment of EU official salaries in 2012: ECJ, C-86/13, ECLI:EU:C:2014:2077 – *Commission v Council*. On the retroactive fixing of correction coefficient and salary adjustment, [2014] OJ C63/12 and [2014] OJ L14/corr.

method was also pre-programmed: the provisions of Annex XI applied until end of 2023, but continue to apply provisionally for as long as the European Parliament and the Council fail to adopt an amendment to Annex XI.

2. Family Allowances

Various family allowances are specified in Annex VII SR. They comprise:

- The household allowance for a married official; an official who is widowed, divorced, legally separated or unmarried and has one or more dependent children; other officials who assume practical family responsibilities; and officials who are registered as partners in a stable non-marital partnership.[849] The allowance is calculated as the sum of 2 per cent of base salary plus a uniform amount[850] (previously 5 per cent of base salary), and thus favours lower salaries more than before. Importantly, the entitlement to a household allowance is the precondition for other allowances and reimbursements (see below).
- The child allowance for each dependent child and persons treated as such whom the official has a legal obligation (under national law) to maintain, and whose maintenance involves heavy expenditure,[851] provided that he actually meets his maintenance obligations.[852]
- The education allowance for each dependent child who regularly attends an educational establishment, to provide some compensation for the education costs.[853] Entitlement to that allowance finishes with the completion of the education, or at the end of the month in which the child reaches the age of 26.[854]
- The 2004 reform introduced a pre-school allowance for children under the age of five.[855] Officials in receipt of family allowances shall declare allowances of like nature paid from other sources; such latter allowances shall be deducted from the family allowances paid,[856] whereas

[849] GC, T-746/19, ECLI:EU:T:2021:390, *GY v ECB*; CST, F-45/07, ECLI:EU:F:2010:72, para 91 – *Mandt v EP*: regarding the rights of surviving dependents, cohabitation is not required for the criterion of marriage. See also, ECJ, Jd Cases C-122/99 P and C-125/99, ECLI:EU:C:2001:304 P, ECLI:EU:C:2001:304 – *D and Sweden v Council*, Potvin-Solis/Leliè vre (2012) *RUE* 268/269 and Gervasoni (2010) 46 *Cahiers de droit européen* 771. Critical: Levi, 'Droits fondamentaux et principes généraux de droit de la fonction publique communautaire' in Govaere/Vandersanden (eds), *La fonction publique communautaire* (2008) 83 with a view to improving same-sex vs heterosexual non-marital partnerships. Partners do not receive the allowance if they can legally marry in a Member State (see Art 1(2)(c)(iv) Annex VII SR), and if this is 'concrete and effective' – meaning this is not the case if this would be punishable under criminal law as a homosexual act, and – unlike in a partnership – would be associated with the risk of persecution due to the greater public profile of the marriage, *cf* CJEU Annual Report 2010, 216 with reference to CST, F-86/09, ECLI:EU:F:2010:125, paras 44, 47, 56 – *W v Commission*. On the effects of the judgment, ECJ, Jd Cases C-122/99 P and C-125/99, ECLI:EU:C:2001:304 P, ECLI:EU:C:2001:304 – *D and Sweden v Council*; on legislation, see Currall in Perillo/Giacobbo-Peyronnel (eds), *Statut de la fonction publique de l'Union européenne: Commentaire article par article* (2017) 62 ff.

[850] At present €171.88.

[851] Art 2 Annex VII.

[852] Art 2 para 2, Annex VII; GC, T-134/99, ECLI:EU:T:2000:184 – *Skrzypek v Commission*.

[853] Art 3 Annex VII SR.

[854] Art 3(1) 2 Annex VI SR.

[855] Art 3(2) Annex VII SR.

[856] Art 67(2) SR; ECJ, 106/76, ECLI:EU:C:1977:151 – *Gelders-Deboeck*; ECJ, 14/77, ECLI:EU:C:1977:153 – *Emer v Commission*; GC, T-117/89, ECLI:EU:T:1990:30 – *Sens v Commission*. For the offsetting of national benefits under Art 67(2) SR it is the comparable purpose of the payment that is the decisive factor, rather than the name or nature of its legal basis, Schiano/Potvin-Solis (2012) *RUE* 614, CST, F-83/10, ECLI:EU:F:2012:72 – *Giannakouris v Commission* and CST, F-84/10, ECLI:EU:F: 2012:73 – *Chatzidoukakis*, each paras 31/32; on the education allowance, CST, F-89/10, ECLI:EU:F:2011:129 – *Bovagnet v Commission*.

the specific purpose of the allowances of like nature must be taken into account.[857] Provisions under the laws of Member States that preclude payment of national benefits for the reason that entitlement to EU allowances may exist under the SR have to be disregarded because of the duty of cooperation of Member States.[858] Though the education allowances for children who attend free schools were partially abolished, the EU's contribution to the financing of the European Schools – indirectly relieving the officials concerned – was confirmed.

3. Expatriation Allowance

The official receives an expatriation allowance of 16 per cent[859] of the total basic salary to compensate for burdens and disadvantages ('the extra expense and inconvenience') when being obliged to move from his home country to another state with which he had no connections prior to taking up duties.[860] The same rules as for the expatriation allowance govern the household allowance and the dependent child allowance. The entitlement arises as soon as the conditions laid down are fulfilled (no application needed); there is no period stipulated within which its payment must be claimed.[861]

Habitual residence

A central term to determine whether there were no connections prior to taking up duties is the 'habitual residence'. This is the place in which the official or staff member concerned has established, with the intention that it should be of a lasting character, the permanent or habitual centre of his interests, whereas all the factual circumstances and, in particular, the actual residence of the official concerned must be taken into account.[862] The benefit of the expatriation allowance would only be lost if the habitual residence or the main occupation was in the country throughout the reference period. In the case of prior residency at the place of employment, sporadic or short-term absences or external activities do not yet exclude such connections.[863] However, where a period of study is followed by a period of training or employment at the same place, the continued presence of the official in the country concerned may create the presumption, albeit one that might be proved wrong, that he may intend to transfer the permanent or habitual centre of his interests, and thus his habitual residence, to that country.[864] The actual residence can be proven by documents that are established upon verification of the residence by the authorities, and is not yet proven by formal registration in a locality alone. Likewise, documents reflecting a person's ties

[857] CST, F-62/06, ECLI:EU:F:2007:24, paras 46 ff – *Guarneri v Commission.*

[858] ECJ, 186/85, ECLI:EU:C:1987:208, para 4 – *Commission v Belgium*; ECJ, 189/85, ECLI:EU:C:1987:209, paras 21, 28 – *Commission v Germany*. On the offsetting of national family benefits, Joris, 'L'administration face au contentieux de la fonction publique communautaire' in Govaere/Vandersanden (eds), *La fonction publique communautaire* (2008) 75.

[859] But not less than €509.43 per month.

[860] Art 69 SR in conjunction with Art 4 Annex VII SR, details of differentiation here below.

[861] ECJ, 159/86, ECLI:EU:C:1988:432, paras 12/13 – *Canters v Commission.*

[862] CST, F-50/14, ECLI:EU:F:2015:62, paras 32 ff – *Pondichie v Commission.*

[863] CST, F-12/08, ECLI:EU:F:2009:57, paras 32, 21 – *Nardin v EP*, *cf* also Reithmann (2009) *EuR* 815; (2011) *EuR* 140. In cases of employment in the Member State of his own nationality an official does not receive an expatriation allowance unless he has not previously been living there for at least 10 years. Times spent in the public sector do no harm, but must be subtracted so that the reference period begins earlier. In the case of transfers within an institution, the moment of first taking up duties is decisive, but not in the case of successive activities for different employers such as agencies, *cf* CST, F-76/11, ECLI:EU:F:2012:173, para 50 *Grazyte v Commission*. The place of residence of family members, a professional activity or having an entry in a register of residents in the country of assignment can give rise to an assumption of close social and economic ties there (which would lead to a preclusion of the entitlement), but this assumption can be refuted by the staff member in individual cases, see CST, F-6/12, ECLI:EU:F:2012:175, paras 36 ff – *Boutembourg v Commission.*

[864] CST, F-33/09, ECLI:EU:F:2010:18, para 39 – *Tzvetanova v Commission.*

with a given country or even giving an address in that country, such as certificates relating to the exercise of rights as a citizen or the registration of a vehicle and the payment of related taxes and fees, have no evidential value as long as their actuality is not verified.[865]

Five-year period, ten-year period

Article 4 Annex VII SR differentiates between officials who are not and have never been nationals of the State of employment (Art 4 lit a), and officials who are or have been nationals of the State of employment (Art 4 lit b). In the first scenario, it is required that during the five years ending six months before they entered the service they did not habitually reside or carry on their main occupation within the European territory of that State. For the purposes of this provision, circumstances arising from work done for another State or for an international organisation shall not be taken into account.

In the second scenario (Art 4 lit b), the allowance shall be paid to officials who are or have been nationals of the State in whose territory the place where they are employed is situated but who during the 10 years ending at the date of their entering the service habitually resided outside the European territory of that State for reasons other than the performance of duties in the service of a State or of an international organisation. This last part of the stipulation of Article 4 lit b might easily be misunderstood, but is interpreted by case-law as meaning that the times spent on duty in the service of a State or of an international organisation must be left out of account (an analogy to Art 4 lit a). Thus, an official having been in the service of a State or international organisation is not deprived of an expatriation allowance (etc), but the starting point for the reference period must be brought forward, in order to ascertain that the official has indeed spent 10 years outside the European territory of the State of which he is or was a national, without, during those 10 years, having been in the service of a State or international organisation. If the official did indeed habitually reside outside the territory of the State of employment, but while in the service of a State or of an international organisation, he cannot be regarded as having interrupted the lasting ties which he had established with the country of employment of which he is or was a national. It is therefore the simple fact of having been in the service of a State or international organisation during the 10-year reference period which overturns the presumption that the lasting ties established with the country of employment of which the official concerned is or was a national may be regarded as having been interrupted.[866]

Reference to 'nationality'

Where the legislature makes a general reference to nationality in the clauses on expatriation allowance, this is not done arbitrarily or out of proportion to the purpose pursued.[867] Where nationality changes – for example, acquisition of the nationality of the place of employment – further to the withdrawal of a Member State, the right to an expatriation allowance can be lost.[868]

Expatriation allowance and telework

Case-law[869] has confirmed for the constellation of home office (telework) in pandemic times that the entitlement to an expatriation allowance remains in place also for staff working from

[865] ibid, paras 33 ff.

[866] CST, F-89/14, ECLI:EU:F:2015:124, paras 36, 46 – *Arsène v Commission*; GC, T-86/13 P, ECLI:EU:T:2014:815, paras 50 ff – *Grazyte v Commission*.

[867] CST, F-6/08, ECLI:EU:F:2008:160, paras 102, 105 – *Blais v ECB*.

[868] GC, T-18/19, ECLI:EU:T:2020:465 – *Brown v Commission (Brexit)*.

[869] GC, T-39/21, ECLI:EU:T:2023:204 – *PP and Others v EP*. The GC further argued that the SR do not contain a legal basis for suspending payment of the expatriation allowance.

home (ie, in their home country). Article 20 SR on the obligation of residence of an official has to be read in conjunction with the goal of Article 55 SR, according to which officials in active employment shall at all times be at the disposal of their institution. The court argued that an expatriation allowance also serves to entertain the residence, and on that basis decided that the need to maintain the residence and thus the need to receive the allowance also remains in times when operating from a home office is obligatory, because of the obligations under Articles 20 and 55 SR.

4. Special Allowances

Special allowances shall be granted to officials who are expected to work regularly at night, on Saturdays, Sundays or public holidays when doing shiftwork which is required by the institution because of the exigencies of the service or safety rules and which is regarded by it as a regular and permanent feature, whereas the normal working hours of an official on shiftwork must not exceed the annual total of normal working hours.[870]

Special allowances shall be paid when required in accordance with a decision taken by the appointing authority because of the exigencies of the service or safety rules to remain on standby duty at the place of work or at home outside normal working hours.[871] A special allowance may already be justified if the shift work was informally organised and actually performed, even if not all the formal requirements are met.[872] Overtime worked by officials in function group AD, and in function group AST 5–11, shall carry no right to compensation or remuneration.[873] Special allowances may be granted to certain officials to compensate for particularly arduous working conditions.[874]

The Commission can to a certain extent determine the groups of eligible staff members by means of delegated acts.

The 2014 reform brought some modifications, especially for staff working in third countries: for example, the criteria for determining the allowance for difficult living conditions are no longer weighted in a differentiated manner. The allowance for living conditions shall be fixed taking into account, inter alia, health and hospital environment, security, climate, degree of isolation, and other local living conditions.[875] The granting of a supplementary premium in addition to the allowance for living conditions in cases where an official has had more than one assignment to a place of employment considered difficult or very difficult, was connected to a wider discretion on the part of the appointing authority.[876]

If living conditions at the place of employment are such as to put the official at personal risk, a temporary additional allowance shall be paid to him by special reasoned decision of the appointing authority. If, in duly justified cases, the appointing authority determines that a post is a 'non-family posting', the allowance shall be paid to staff members who respect that non-family determination.[877]

[870] Art 56a(1) (3) SR.
[871] Art 56b SR.
[872] CST, F-66/08, ECLI:EU:F:2009:49, para 22 – *De Smet v Commission*; CJEU Annual Report 2009, 202 with further references.
[873] Art 56(2) SR.
[874] Art 56c SR.
[875] Art 10(1), (3) Annex X SR.
[876] Art 10(1), (5) Annex X SR.
[877] Art 10(2) Annex X SR.

Finally, if accommodation is not provided by the institution, the appointing authority shall either pay the official an accommodation allowance or reimburse the rent paid by the official. The accommodation allowance shall be calculated primarily on the official's level of duties, and secondarily on the composition of his dependent family.[878]

5. Other Allowances, Grants and Reimbursement of Expenses

Articles 5 and 6 Annex VII SR stipulate that payments of an installation allowance equal to two months' basic salary in the case of an official who is entitled to the household allowance, and equal to one month's basic salary in other cases, shall be paid to an established official who furnishes evidence that a change in the place of residence was required in order to satisfy the residence requirements (Art 20 SR).[879] Similarly, on termination of service a resettlement allowance[880] is paid that is equal to two months' basic salary in the case of an official who is entitled to the household allowance, or to one month's basic salary in other cases, provided that he has completed four years of service.[881]

Article 7 Annex VII SR provides for a flat-rate payment corresponding to the cost of travel for himself, his spouse and those of his dependants who are actually living in his household:[882] first, on taking up his appointment, for travel from the place where he was recruited to the place where he is employed; secondly, upon termination of service, for travel from the place where he is employed to the place of origin; thirdly, on any transfer involving a change in the place where he is employed. An official's place of origin[883] (to be clearly distinguished from the place of recruitment)[884] shall be determined when he takes up his appointment, account being taken in principle of where he was recruited or, upon express and duly reasoned request, the centre of his interests.

[878] Art 23 Annex X SR.

[879] A permanently intended relocation of the centre of interests is required, GC, T-37/99, ECLI:EU:T:2001:122 – *Miranda v Commission*; GC, T-104/00, ECLI:EU:T:2001:127 – *Cubeta v Commission*; CST, F-126/05, ECLI:EU:F:2007:12, para 49 – *Borbély v Commission*; ECJ, C-43/94 P, ECLI:EU:C:1995:269, para 21 – *EP v Vienne*.

[880] Payment of resettlement allowance shall be refused if the place of resettlement coincides with the place of residence where his or her family lives. The decision to refuse the resettlement allowance must not be solely based on the ground that the staff member was the owner of the house in which he/she resettled: GC, T-529/20, ECLI:EU:T:2022:523, para 62 – *LR v EIB*.

[881] Requires evidence of a change of residence, and is only granted if the person does not receive a similar allowance in his new employment.

[882] GC, T-42/89, ECLI:EU:T:1990:9 – *York von Wartenburg v EP*; travel expenses vs travel allowance: GC, T-71/89, ECLI:EU:T:1990:21 – *Dautremont v EP*; GC,T-241/94, ECLI:EU:T:1995:89 – *Nagel v Commission*.

[883] Further to Art 7(4) Annex VII, an official's place of origin shall be determined when he takes up his appointment, account being taken in principle of where he was recruited or, upon express and duly reasoned request, the centre of his interests. The place of origin as so determined may, by special decision of the appointing authority, be changed while the official is in service or when he leaves the service, ECJ, C-675/20 P, ECLI:EU:C:2022:686 – *Brown v Commission*. The place of origin serves to determine an official's pecuniary rights so as to avoid confusion between his place of origin and the place where he was permanently resident and previously employed prior to his recruitment, GC, T-390/07 P, ECLI:EU:T:2008:480, paras 37–42 – *Speiser v EP*.

[884] Place of recruitment: the centre of the official's interests, which determines his habitual residence (meaning at the time of recruitment), GC, T-28/98, ECLI:EU:T:1999:180, para 47 – *J v Commission*; CST, F-126/05, ECLI:EU:F:2007:12, para 66 – *Borbély v Commission*; CST, F-50/14, ECLI:EU:F:2015:62, paras 32 ff – *Pondichie v Commission*. Art 2(2) of the Commission Decision of 16 December 2013 C(2013) 8982 final *laying down general implementing provisions for giving effect to Article 7(4) of Annex VII SR on determining the place of origin* defines the official's *place of recruitment* as the place where the official was habitually resident at the time of recruitment. On the alternative of the terms 'habitual residence' and 'main occupation' in Art 4(1)a Annex VII SR: GC, T-71/21, ECLI:EU:T:2021:868, para 84 – *QB v Commission*, confirmed on appeal ECJ, C-88/22 P, ECLI:EU:C:2023:792 – *QB v Commission*.

Servants whose place of official employment is outside the territory of the Member States shall be entitled for themselves (and, if they are entitled to receive the household allowance, for their spouse and other dependants) in each calendar year, to a flat-rate payment for travel expenses to their place of origin, or to the repayment of travel expenses to another place not exceeding the expense of travel to the place of origin.[885] If the spouse and other dependants do not live with the official at the place of employment, they shall be entitled each calendar year to reimbursement of travel expenses from the place of origin to the place of employment or to another place, but not expenses exceeding the cost of the former journey.[886]

In addition, staff are entitled to a childbirth grant[887] as well as (in case of the death of an official, an official's spouse or dependent child, or any other dependent person) to the reimbursement of costs involved in transporting the body from the official's place of employment to his place of origin.

Expenses incurred for the removal of furniture and personal effects, including the cost of insurance against ordinary risks, shall be reimbursed within the limits of cost ceilings (without any need to obtain the approval of quotes or cost estimates up-front), in the event that officials are obliged to change their place of residence on entry into service or in the event of a subsequent change of place of employment while in service.[888] An official who furnishes evidence that a change in the place of residence is required to comply with his duty of residence, thus typically as a result of transfer to another place of work, shall be entitled to a subsistence allowance per calendar day for a period of 120 or 180 days respectively.[889] This is not granted beyond the date on which the official moves to comply with his duty of residence. Other types of expenses relate to missions, to entertainment for official purposes, and to local transport.[890]

Severance grant

Civil servants who leave the service before they have earned entitlement to a pension receive a severance grant. For this purpose, Article 12 Annex VIII SR provides that where an official below pensionable age terminates service otherwise than by death or invalidity and who is not entitled to an immediate or deferred retirement pension shall receive either (in the case of less than one year of service) payment of a severance grant equal to three times the amounts withheld from his basic salary in respect of his pension contributions, or (in all other cases) either the actuarial equivalent of his retirement pension rights or the payment of the actuarial equivalent of such benefits to a private insurance company or pension fund of his choice.

[885] Art 8(4) Annex VII SR. On travel flat-rate for staff with place of origin outside the EU: Art 8(2) second subpara Annex VII is illegal due to discrimination on grounds of nationality: ECJ, Jd. Cases C-567/22 P to C-570/22 P, ECLI:EU:C:2024:336, para. 80 – *Dumitrescu and Others.*

[886] CST, F-49/08, ECLI:EU:F:2009: 76, paras 159 ff, 169 ff – *Giannini v Commission.* Home travel costs CST, F-43/05, ECLI:EU:F:2007:14 – *Chassagne v Commission*, Reithmann (2008) *EuR* 289, Van Raepenbusch, 'L'apport jurisprudentiel du Tribunal de la fonction publique de l`Union européenne' in Govaere/Vandersanden (eds), *La fonction publique communautaire* (2008) 174.

[887] Art 74 SR.

[888] Art 9 Annex VII SR. Certain time limits have to be respected.

[889] Art 10 Annex VII SR; GC, T-104/00, ECLI:EU:T:2001:127 – *Cubeta v Commission*; GC, T-63/91, ECLI:EU:T:1992:88 – *Benzler v Commission*; ECJ, C-43/94 P, ECLI:EU:C:1995:269 – *Parliament v Vienne*; on the concept of residence for the installation allowance and the daily allowance: CST, F-131/07, ECLI:EU:F:2008:159, para 30 – *Baniel-Kubinova and Others v Commission.* On the installation allowance, also Van Raepenbusch, 'L'apport jurisprudentiel du Tribunal de la fonction publique de l`Union européenne' in Govaere/Vandersanden (eds), *La fonction publique communautaire* (2008) 174.

[890] *cf* Arts 11–15 Annex VII SR.

IV. Insurances and Pensions

1. Introduction

Officials and temporary staff pay contributions in respect of their own pension[891] and sickness insurance schemes for themselves and their dependants (Art 72 SR),[892] and contribute to the group insurance scheme against the risk of occupational disease and accidents under Article 73 SR (see section V below). The EU social security scheme is autonomous and not comparable with national civil service social security systems.[893] Article 83(2) SR stipulates that officials shall contribute one-third of the cost of the pension scheme. The individual contribution is at present 10 per cent of the official's basic salary, for which the weightings[894] depending on living conditions is not being taken into account.[895] The pension scheme, laid down in Annex VIII SR, is organised on the basis of the principle of solidarity, and thus the pension received by an official is not to be understood to constitute an exact counterpart for the contributions paid by him or her.[896]

Overall, the conception of social security underlying these schemes is of a high standard, but it does not extend to the point that the insured person can, for instance, claim reimbursement at any price level for necessary medical services.[897] The decision-making regarding the sickness insurance scheme has to comply with the general requirements of good administrative procedure. For example, where the medical officer is called upon to decide on the recognition of a serious disease (or on the renewal of a serious disease status), the reasons for the decision must clearly and unequivocally show the overall assessment of the seriousness of the disease, thus providing the motivation for the decision.[898] Case-law typically applies a literal and narrow interpretation of the health insurance and other social security schemes.[899]

2. Sickness Insurance

The sickness insurance scheme under Article 72 SR covers the officials themselves and their dependants against the risks of sickness under the rules and within the limits of the Joint Sickness

[891] Case-law confirmed that the legislature did not exceed the limits of its discretion when defining the scheme: CST, F-105/05, ECLI:EU:F:2007:128, paras 92 ff – *Wils v EP*. The staff member's contribution to the sickness insurance scheme remained unchanged at a maximum of 2% of the basic salary (Art 72(1, 3) SR).

[892] *cf* on the question of the relative's own entitlement CST, F-104/10, ECLI:EU:F:2013:64, para 51 – *de Pretis Cagnodo and Others v Commission*. CST, F-122/06, ECLI:EU:F:2007:208, para 35 – *Roodhuijzen v Commission*; appeal GC, T-58/08 P, ECLI:EU:T:2009:385 – *Commission v Roodhuijzen*, Gervasoni (2010) 46 *Cahiers de droit européen* 773.

[893] CST, F-80/09, ECLI:EU:F:2010:165, para 44 – *Lenz v Commission*; Art 14 of the Protocol on Privileges and Immunities. Andreone, 'Le financement du régime de pensions des personnels de l'Union européenne: cadre juridique et actualité' (2018) *Revue de l'Union européenne* 517–26.

[894] Art 64 SR.

[895] Annex XII SR for adjustments; *cf* updates of the rate of contribution to the pension scheme, eg, [2014] OJ C444/5 and [2018] OJ C451/19.

[896] GC, T-39/22, ECLI:EU:T:2023:709, para 60 – *OA v EP*; GC, T-135/05, ECLI:EU:T:2006:366, para 134 – *Campoli v Commission*.

[897] CST, F-14/11, ECLI:EU:F:2012:74; paras 50 ff – *AW v Commission*. The administration can absorb treatment costs, but – for the duty of care – must notify the staff member beforehand if these are likely to be disproportionately high and may give rise to recovery claims from third parties: CST, F-104/10, ECLI:EU:F:2013:64, para 113 – *de Pretis Cagnodo and Others v Commission*.

[898] Art 296 TFEU, Art 41(2) lit c FRC and Art 25(2) SR; GC, T-685/21, ECLI:EU:T:2023:267, paras 64, 88 – *IR v Commission*.

[899] *cf* case study at the end of section IV.2.

Insurance Scheme (JSIS),[900] and within those of the General Implementing Provisions (GIP) for the reimbursement of medical expenses, which contain ceilings for reimbursement.[901] The JSIS is managed by a joint management committee composed of an equal number of representatives of the staff and of the administration from all the institutions. The scheme's expenditure is managed by the different settlement offices.

Beneficiaries

Beneficiaries are the spouse, where she or he is not eligible for benefits of the same nature and of the same level by virtue of any other legal provision or regulations, and the children and other dependants in the sense of Article 2 Annex VII SR, and Article 3 of the JSIS.[902] Non-marital partners in a stable partnership (according to the national rules of a Member State) also benefit from the scheme; no particular qualification of partnership can be requested from them.[903] The scheme also covers former officials and the members of the institutions.[904]

Other insurance cover

Reimbursement which can be claimed under any other sickness insurance scheme provided for by law or regulation (eg, of the Member States) has to be declared, so that the excess sum beyond the amount to be reimbursed pursuant to Article 72 SR can be deducted, with the exception of reimbursements obtained under a private supplementary sickness insurance scheme covering that part of the expenditure which is not reimbursable by the JSIS.[905] The complementary insurance cover is granted on a subsidiary basis only. It is not possible to claim supplementary reimbursement of expenses under the JSIS where in relation to another scheme the beneficiary failed at the appropriate time to seek authorisation for reimbursement.[906]

Rates of reimbursement

Medical expenditures incurred are reimbursed at 80 per cent. This percentage is increased to 85 per cent for certain services,[907] and to 100 per cent for serious illnesses.[908] However, reimbursement at 100 per cent under the sickness insurance scheme of Article 72 SR shall not apply in the case of occupational disease or accident (Art 73 SR), as the Common Insurance Rules (CIR)[909] already foresee that these insured parties shall be entitled to reimbursement of all expenses necessary in order to restore as completely as possible their bodily or mental health, and in order to pay for all care and treatment required as a result of the injuries sustained and their symptoms, and

[900] Adopted by all the institutions, common accord having been recorded by the President of the Court of Justice of the European Communities on 24 November 2005.

[901] Commission Decision C(2007) 3195 of 2 July 2007 laying down general implementing provisions (GIP) for the reimbursement of medical expenses.

[902] Thus in parallel with the child allowance, ECJ, 806/70, ECLI:EU:C:1980:264 – *Gerin.*

[903] As per CST, F-122/06, ECLI:EU:F:2007:208, paras 54/55 – *Roodhuijzen v Commission*, confirmed by GC, T-58/08 P, ECLI:EU:T:2009:385 – *Commission v Roodhuijzen.*

[904] ECJ, 163/88, ECLI:EU:C:1989:630 – *Kontogeorgis*; GC, T-66/95, ECLI:EU:T:1997:56 – *Kuchlenz-Winter* (ex-spouse of a retired official of the EP).

[905] Art 72(4) SR.

[906] GC, T-13/93, ECLI:EU:T:1993:101, para 49 – *Cordier.*

[907] For consultations and visits, surgical operations, hospitalisation, pharmaceutical products, radiology, analyses, laboratory tests and prostheses on medical prescription, with the exception of dental prostheses.

[908] In cases of tuberculosis, poliomyelitis, cancer, mental illness and other illnesses recognised by the appointing authority as of comparable seriousness, GC, T-191/01, ECLI:EU:T:2004:146 – *Heqc v Commission*; and also increased to 100% for early detection screening and in cases of confinement, GC, T-85/11, ECLI:EU:T:2013:90 – *Marcuccio v Commission.*

[909] Common Rules on the insurance of officials of the European Communities against the risk of accident and of occupational disease of 13 December 2005 (Common Insurance Rules), available at: www.europarl.europa.eu/tenders/2014/20140103/EN_Ref%203_Common%20rules_accident_EN.pdf.

also, where appropriate, of the expenses incurred in the functional and occupational rehabilitation of the victim.[910]

Serious illnesses are not listed exhaustively in Article 72 SR, but some may also be considered as being of comparable seriousness by the appointing authority. As to the judicial review of the recognition, after an examination of the state of health of the person has taken place, the court only exercises a limited control over the opinions issued by the medical bodies intervening during the course of the procedure for recognising the existence of a serious illness: a review only ensures that those opinions were adopted on the basis of a specific and thorough examination of the state of health – an examination that takes into account in a comprehensive manner the four interdependent criteria set out in the GIP.[911] Where a serious illness has been diagnosed, any subsequent change of this earlier assessment requires the medical officer to state the reasons that precisely characterise the health improvement which has taken place in the meantime.[912]

The rates mentioned in Article 72 SR establish the maximum reimbursable limit. They are not minimum rates and do not impose on the institutions an obligation to reimburse the persons concerned to the extent of those rates in all cases.[913] The GIP may fix upper limits for reimbursement in order to safeguard the financial stability of the sickness insurance scheme.

Free choice of medical practitioner

The insured beneficiaries under the scheme are free to choose their medical practitioner, hospital or clinic (Art 19 JSIS), but freedom of choice does not automatically imply reimbursement of any resulting travel costs. In the individual case, national provisions may restrict this choice.[914] Transport and accompanying costs are not automatically reimbursed where they relate to the free choice of a practitioner or hospital, because transport is not considered as being strictly connected to sickness under Article 72 SR. But there might be justified exceptions: for example, transport costs incurred to undergo psychotherapy where it is objectively established that that therapy requires the use of a language which the recipient must be able to understand, and which is the only language in which he can express himself.[915]

Limits to reimbursement

Further to Article 20 JSIS, the cost of treatments deemed to be non-functional or unnecessary by the settlements office after consulting the Medical Officer shall not be reimbursed. Also, in the case of benefits for which no reimbursement ceiling has been set, the proportion of the costs deemed excessive by comparison with normal costs in the country where the costs have been incurred shall not be reimbursed.

As case-law has clarified, reimbursement of certain expenses may lawfully be refused if, after consulting the medical officer (and, if appropriate, the Medical Council),[916] it considers that those expenses relate to a treatment or services whose scientific validity is not proven (ie, the therapeutic value or reliability as a diagnostic means is scientifically disputed).[917]

[910] Art 9(1) Common Insurance Rules (CIR).

[911] Point 1, Chapter 5, title III: namely shortened life expectancy, an illness which is likely to be drawn-out, the need for aggressive diagnostic and/or therapeutic procedures, the presence or risk of a serious handicap; CST, F-23/10, ECLI:EU:F:2011:162, para 80 – *Allan v Commission*.

[912] GC, T-685/21, ECLI:EU:T:2023:267, paras 85 ff – *IR v Commission*.

[913] GC, T-110/89, para 25 – ECLI:EU:T:1991:44 – *Pincherle v Commission*, confirmed by ECJ, C-244/91 P, ECLI:EU:C:1993:950 – *Pincherle*.

[914] GC, T-13/93, ECLI:EU:T:1993:101 – *Cordier*.

[915] CST, F-27/11, ECLI:EU:F:2013:2 – *BO v Commission*, confirmed by GC, T-174/13 P, ECLI:EU:T:2014:26 – *BO*.

[916] The Medical Council of the JSIS consists of one Medical Officer from each institution and the Medical Officers from each Settlements Office.

[917] CST, F-10/07, ECLI:EU:F:2007:161, paras 62 ff – *Botos*.

Case Study on Sickness Insurance

Reimbursement ceiling for rental of a medical device annulled

Case T-736/19, *HA v Commission* of 16 December 2020

In Brief

A General Court (GC) decision on reimbursement of medical expenses: for the *rental* of a medical device, the appointing authority – in the absence of an explicit reimbursement ceiling in the applicable rules – chose to apply the same ceiling that is prescribed for the *purchase* of that device. However, the GC rejects this introduction of a ceiling because it is not stated in the rules on the reimbursement of expenses. This points to a literal and narrow interpretation of the health insurance scheme. The way an appointing authority complies with its obligation to maintain a financial balance of the health insurance system is by establishing the appropriate system of rules. It cannot substitute the process for this by interpreting the existing rules differently than in accordance with their wording.

Facts of the Case

The applicant is affiliated to the Joint Sickness Insurance Scheme of the Institutions of the EU (JSIS). She had obtained prior authorisation for the rental of a so-called *continuous positive-pressure breathing apparatus intended to alleviate sleep apnea* (hereafter a CPAP machine or 'the device') for the period from 2012 to 2014. In 2014, the applicant submitted a new request for prior authorisation for the continued rental of the CPAP machine. In response, the settlements office first issued an authorisation to purchase a device, arguing that medically, only the purchase of a CPAP machine is justified, and no longer a rental. A few months later, the applicant submitted a request for reimbursement relating to the rental costs incurred for her CPAP machine. The settlements office authorised the rental of a CPAP machine partially retroactively and up to 2019, and at the same time imposed a reimbursement ceiling of €1,700, corresponding to the ceiling set by GIP for the reimbursement of medical expenses for the purchase of a CPAP machine. Following the applicant's complaint, the appointing authority decided that the ceiling of €1,700 should be increased to a total of €3,100. This increase corresponded to the reimbursement of four years of maintenance costs and the purchase of accessories incurred after the first year following the purchase of the CPAP machine. In 2018, the applicant requested an extension of the prior authorisation for the rental of a CPAP machine. In response to this request, the settlement office authorised the rental of a device until 2024, by setting a reimbursement ceiling of €3,100. The applicant challenged this decision and, after the administrative bodies themselves confirmed it, filed her action at the General Court.

The Arguments of the Parties and the Decision of the Court

At the GC, the applicant raised a single plea, alleging that none of the applicable provisions provided for a reimbursement ceiling for the rental of a CPAP machine. The decision of 2019 which applies such a ceiling therefore disregarded those provisions and was therefore illegal. The applicant also pleaded that the Commission had not shown that the purchase of a CPAP machine was necessary for long-term use, and that the argument of the Commission that those insured persons who buy a CPAP machine were otherwise discriminated against vs those who rent it was not valid.

The GC sets aside the decision of the appointing authority. Article 20 of the Rules on sickness insurance does not foresee a ceiling for the rental of this medical device. Article 20 allows the establishment of certain ceilings; even where no ceiling is established, the Settlements Office may not reimburse that part of the expenses that is considered to be excessive in relation to the normal costs in the country where these costs were incurred. This shows that the possibility for the GIP not to introduce reimbursement ceilings is expressly envisaged in the Rules on sickness insurance. Even a specific procedure is foreseen in order to safeguard the financial stability of the JSIS in such a case. The component of the costs that is considered excessive is determined on a case-by-case basis by the settlements office. Where the Commission (the authority competent to adopt the GIP) intends to establish a reimbursement ceiling, it is therefore its responsibility to explicitly state this ceiling in the provisions of the GIP.

However, if no ceiling is expressly mentioned in the GIP, this does not mean that a ceiling may implicitly be established for financial reasons. But the specific procedure has to be followed that is intended to ensure the financial stability of the JSIS. For instance, the GIP provide for a reimbursement ceiling for the costs regarding the rental of wheelchairs, and they provide for a reimbursement ceiling for the purchase of a CPAP machine; however, they do not provide for a reimbursement ceiling for the *rental* of a CPAP machine. So the GC concludes from the wording of the applicable rules that there is no ceiling on the reimbursement of expenses for the rental of a CPAP machine. This result, the GC continues, is not called into question by the other arguments of the Commission. The Commission did not provide arguments regarding why, for medical reasons, a CPAP machine had to be purchased instead of being rented over an extended period. Also the fact that prior authorisation is required both for the longer-term rental and the purchase of the machine does not mean that the ceiling applies likewise in both cases.

Regarding the principle of equal treatment between JSIS members, the GC states that an unjustified difference in treatment between insured persons who buy a CPAP machine and those who rent the same machine for a long period would not be likely to lead, for the purposes of respecting the principle of equal treatment, to an interpretation of the GIP which would be contrary to the GIP's wording, as well as to the scheme of the relevant provisions of the Rules on sickness insurance and the GIP. In the opinion of the GC, the same applies to the risk of bypassing the ceiling provided for the purchase of a CPAP machine or to a risk of jeopardising the financial stability of the JSIS. It is up to the Rules on sickness insurance to provide for mechanisms that prevent certain excessive costs from being borne by the JSIS.

Apart from that, neither the existence of a difference between the costs generated by the rental of CPAP devices and those generated by the purchase of such devices, nor the existence of a practice of circumventing the limit applicable to the purchase of a CPAP machine, was further substantiated by the Commission. Finally, the GC found that the existence of a risk of jeopardising the financial balance of the JSIS that would result from the absence of a reimbursement ceiling for the rental of CPAP devices has not been established by the Commission. The GC concluded that by setting a reimbursement ceiling in its response to the request for prior authorisation submitted by the applicant, the settlements office disregarded the GIP.

Comments

1. The contracting authority applied a sort of analogy to flexibly align the two types of benefit from the medical device, namely its rental and its purchase. With the intention of treating the two types in the same way, it applied a ceiling for the reimbursement of rental that actually only exists for the purchase of that device.
2. The GC decides in line with a literal interpretation of the applicable norms: in the absence of a ceiling for reimbursable cost, it is not possible for the contracting authority to interpret the existing stipulations in such a manner that they will align in their economic consequences (here: the rental of a medical device and its purchase). It is therefore not the economic equivalence that prevails when deciding on the limits of reimbursement, but the literal specification of whether an expense is reimbursable or not.
3. The scenario would have been different if the settlements office had insisted on a purchase and had not granted the reimbursement of rental expenses at the outset. It was the appointing authority that decided that the ceiling of €1,700 should be increased to a total of €3,100, and it calculated this increase by a comparison with the costs that typically arise from purchasing a CPAP machine. But also, this confusion of the rental and purchase methods cannot lead to the creation of rules concerning the reimbursement ceiling in addition to those that apply to the rental of the device.
4. It is worth noting that the *principle of equality of treatment* cannot be instrumentalised against the beneficiary of the insurance scheme to the point that it is applied against the wording of the norm itself. Earlier case-law[918] developed this argumentation to make the point that the need to interpret secondary Union law in line with an international convention cannot serve as the basis for an interpretation of that law *contra legem*.
5. Likewise, existing case-law[919] on the reimbursement of medical expenses, first, has made clear that there is no entitlement to a maximum reimbursable rate in all cases. Secondly, it is clear that the health insurance scheme common to the institutions has to maintain financial stability (meaning a healthy balance between expenditure and contributions), and that in this context the institutions are empowered – where there are no reimbursement ceilings established – to set such ceilings in the implementing provisions, but without exceeding the limits set for their powers by social security.
6. In the case at hand, it was certainly advantageous for the applicant that there is a procedure foreseen for amending the existing set of norms in order to prevent the health insurance system incurring excessive costs, including through the introduction of certain ceilings for the reimbursement of medical expenses. This helped the argument in this case that the appointing authority had chosen not to establish a ceiling for the rental of the specific medical device (the CPAP).

[918] *cf* GC, T-685/14, ECLI:EU:T:2015:560 – *EEB v Commission.*
[919] *cf* CST, F-14/11, ECLI:EU:F:2012:74 – *AW v Commission.*

3. Retirement Pension

An official who has completed at least 10 years' service shall be entitled to a retirement pension, Article 77 SR. A retirement pension shall be payable on the basis of the total number of years of pensionable service acquired.[920] Articles 3 and 4 Annex VIII SR set out the criteria for calculating the years of pensionable service. The scheme provides for a pension[921] and corresponding survivor's pension of a maximum of 70 per cent of the last basic salary.[922] For the purpose of early retirement, the following is stipulated: if the official leaves the service before reaching pensionable age, the retirement pension may either be deferred or – if the official has reached the age of 58 – paid immediately, but such a retirement pension shall be reduced by 3.5 per cent for every year prior to the one in which the official would become entitled to a retirement pension.[923]

4. Transfer of Pension Rights

National pension entitlements acquired before entering the service of the European Union (EU) can be transferred to the EU.[924] Member States are obliged to take the necessary precautions in this regard.[925] Previous periods of service as an auxiliary staff member are to be taken into account in certain cases.[926] Previous periods of service in an EU agency and during leave for personal reasons may also be taken into account.[927]

For this '*transfer in*' under Article 11(2) Annex VIII SR, a staff member who enters the EU service after leaving the service of a government administration or of a national or international organisation or after pursuing an activity in an employed or self-employed capacity would transfer his pension rights acquired in respect of the previous professional activities into the EU pension system. The possibility of transferring pension rights (acquired before entering the EU service) into the EU pension system has the purpose of enabling the official concerned to increase

[920] Art 2 Annex VIII SR. For the EIB, see Arts 44/45 ff EIB Pension Scheme Regulations.

[921] Art 83(2) SR. Commission, COM (2012) 37, COM (2008) 592 final, Regulation (EU) No 1415/2013 [2013] OJ L353. On the legality of the new regulation on staff members' contributions, also in view of budgetary considerations: CST, F-105/05, ECLI:EU:F:2007:128, paras 92, 122/123 – *Wils v EP*. On the pension system for European civil servants as a 'virtual' fund system with payments to and from the EU general budget, see GC, T-439/09, ECLI:EU:T:2011:600, para 45 – *Purvis v EP*; CST, F-105/05, ECLI:EU:F:2007:128, para 85 – *Wils v EP*. On the question of whether pension benefits for which contributions have already been paid qualify as acquired rights: ECJ, C-127/80, ECLI:EU:C:1982:86, para 15 – *Grogan v Commission*; GC, T-439/09, ECLI:EU:T:2011:600, para 83 – *Purvis v EP*.

[922] On pension Reithmann (2009) *EuR* 814; on orphans' pensions: CST, F-32/08, ECLI:EU:F:2009:3, paras 40, 43 – *Klein v Commission*. Andreone, 'Le système de pensions des fonctionnaires et agents de l'Union européenne' (2011) *Revue française d'administration publique* 807–15.

[923] Art 9 Annex VIII SR.

[924] CST, F-4/06, ECLI:EU:F:2006:114, para 34 – *Villa v EP*; CST, F-76/06, ECLI:EU:F:2007:193, paras 22 ff, 39 ff – *Tsirimokos v EP*; Reithmann (2008) *EuR* 291 and (2009) *EuR* 814.

[925] Art 11(2) Annex VIII SR; on the transfer of pension rights: ECJ, C-132/18 P, ECLI:EU:C:2019:413 – *Commission v Tuerck*, on appeal: GC, T-728/16, ECLI:EU:T:2017:865 – *Tuerck*; ECJ, C-404/21, ECLI:EU:C:2022:1023 – *WP v INPS*; Reithmann (2008) *EuR* 291; GC, Jd Cases T-90/07 P and T-99/07 P, ECLI:EU:T:2008:605, para 56 – *Genette v Commission*: set aside the CST judgment due to lack of jurisdiction over questions of national law. CST, F-122/10, ECLI:EU:F:2012:180, paras 52 ff – *Cocchi and Falcione v Commission*, set aside in the appeal GC, T-103/13 P, ECLI:EU:T:2015:777. On severance pay: CST, F-61/07, ECLI:EU:F:2009:144, para 65 – *Bauch v Commission*; CST, F-109/10, ECLI:EU:F:2012:66, para 22 – *AU v Commission*.

[926] ECJ, Jd Cases 225/81 and 241/81, ECLI:EU:C:1983:37 – *Toledano-Laredo and Garilli v Commission*; CST, F-57/08, ECLI:EU:F:2009:152, paras 14, 54 ff – *Palazzo v Commission*, on the application of Art11(2) Annex VIII SR by analogy, where the employer, for reasons of duty of care, transferred the severance payment to the EU pension scheme as acquired pension entitlements.

[927] GC, T-128/17, ECLI:EU:T:2018:969 – *Torné v Commission*.

the pension seniority to which he will be entitled at the end of his service for the Union. Although these rights will be taken into account when calculating the pension, it does not give any certainty to the staff member that this taking into account will result in an increase in his pension corresponding entirely to the capital transferred. In that context, case-law has not embraced the idea that a pension rights transfer that leads to an increase in the EU pension representing only partially the capital formerly transferred could be understood as something comparable to an 'unjust enrichment' on the side of the EU pension system.[928]

Also a '*transfer out*' of pension rights is possible: further to Article 11(1) Annex VIII SR in conjunction with Article 12(1)(b), a staff member who leaves the EU services is entitled to effect a *transfer out* of his pension rights acquired within the EU to another pension fund or to a private insurance company which makes certain specific guarantees. The request to effect a *transfer out* must be submitted by the staff member himself, and cannot be submitted any more post mortem by her or his heirs.[929]

Local staff are to be included in the national social security system. Further, there is a joint unemployment insurance system for temporary staff and, since 2004, also for contract staff.[930]

Case Study on Transfer of National Pension Rights

Transfer of national pension rights: No deduction from the updated, actually transferred capital is allowed

Case C-132/18 P, *Commission v Tuerck* of 15 May 2019
Case T-728/16, *Tuerck v Commission* of 5 December 2017

In Brief

This case concerns the calculation of transferred pension rights from the national pension scheme to the European Union pension scheme. The General Court (GC) had decided that the Commission was not allowed to deduct, from the updated capital actually transferred, interest at 3.1 per cent per year in respect of the period between the date on which the application for transfer was made and the date of the actual transfer. Also, the calculation of the years of pensionable service under the Staff Regulations (SR) must be made on the basis of the full amount. The Court of Justice (ECJ) confirmed that decision by dismissing an appeal of the Commission against the GC's ruling.

Facts of the Case

In May 2010, the applicant applied for a transfer to the Union pension scheme of pension rights which she had acquired prior to entering the service of the Union. About three years

[928] ECJ, C-100/22 P, ECLI:EU:C:2023:377, paras 69 ff – *KY v CJEU*, confirming in appeal GC, T-433/20, ECLI:EU:T:2021:840 – *KY v CJEU*.
[929] GC, T-171/22, ECLI:EU:T:2023:520, paras 46–54 – *OR, OS v Commission*.
[930] CST, F-57/08, ECLI:EU:F:2009:152, paras 50 ff – *Palazzo v Commission*. *Commission* '1985–2005 on the financial situation of the joint unemployment insurance' COM (2007) 4 final.

later, the PMO (Office for the Administration and Payment of Individual Entitlements) approved the application as validly made and forwarded it to Deutsche Rentenversicherung Bund (a German federal pension insurance body, the DRV). After another two years the DRV responded, indicating that the transferable capital representing the pension rights previously acquired by the applicant amounted, as at the date of the application for a transfer, May 2010, to €141,652.07.

For the purpose of determining the pensionable years to be credited to the applicant equivalent to the transfer of the applicant's pension rights, the PMO withheld a deduction from the capital sum of €146,714.33 actually transferred by the DRV, by applying an interest rate of 3.1 per cent per year in respect of the period between the date of the application for a transfer and the date of the actual transfer. Hence, the PMO calculated a capital appreciation of €20,666.28 between those dates. For the purposes of determining the pensionable years to be credited, the pension rights previously acquired by the applicant thus amounted to €126,048.05. In her action against that decision, the applicant claimed a breach of Article 7(1) of the General Implementing Provisions (GIP), and of Article 11(2) of Annex VIII of the SR.

General Court Decision

The GC draws from Article 11(2) of Annex VIII SR and Article 7(1) of the GIP that decisions crediting pensionable years are based on the amount of transferable capital as at the date of registration of the application, after deduction – where applicable – of an amount representing the capital appreciation between the date of the application for a transfer and the date of the actual transfer. This simple interest at the rate of 3.1 per cent is deducted from the updated capital actually transferred only where the competent national or international body is unable to supply the value of the pension rights as at the date of registration of the application. Thus, in a situation where the competent national or international authorities have provided the value of the pension rights as at the date of registration of the application, no deduction from that amount is allowed, and the calculation of years of pensionable service under the SR must therefore be made on the basis of the full amount.

The GC further points out that this operation falls within the sole competence of the authority administering the pension scheme with which the interested person was insured before entering into the service of the EU. In addition, Member States enjoy broad discretion in adopting their national legislation implementing Article 11(2) Annex VIII SR.

The DRV had supplied the PMO with what it regarded as the provisional calculation of the transferable amount as at the date of registration of the application. According to that letter, the transferable amount as at 27 May 2010 was €141,652.07, of which €340.22 was interest. The Court concludes that the DRV did supply the value of the pension rights acquired as at the date of registration of the application. Thus, it was possible to distinguish between the amount representing the pension rights acquired by the applicant up to the date of registration of the application for a transfer, on the one hand, and the amount representing the appreciation of that capital between the date of the application for a transfer and the date of the actual transfer, on the other.

On another subject, the GC stated that the calculation of the number of years of pensionable service to be taken into account within the Union pension scheme is a separate calculation from that of the capital representing the acquired pension rights. Also in regard to that calculation, there is no obligation to deduct 3.1 per cent interest from the updated capital actually transferred. The only deduction required by the Regulations is that of the amount representing the capital appreciation between the date of the application for a transfer and the actual date of transfer of the capital updated to that date.

The GC concludes that the Commission erred in law when making a deduction, from the updated capital actually transferred, of simple interest at 3.1 per cent per year in respect of the period between the date on which the application for transfer was made and the date of the actual transfer, while the DRV supplied the value of the pension rights acquired by the applicant as at the date of registration of her application.

Comments

1. The various national provisions in the field of pensions are characterised by a great diversity and complexity. Article 11(2) Annex VIII to the SR is not intended to harmonise these rules. Also, Article 48 TFEU and Article 153(4) TFEU show that the right of the Member States to define the fundamental principles of their social security systems is recognised by Union law.
2. The judgments in *Tuerck* follow the line prepared by the ECJ in Case C-166/12,[931] *Časta*, in which the Court of Justice recognised that the Member States enjoy broad discretion in adopting their national legislation to implement Article 11 Annex VIII SR.
3. Due to the variation of rules implementing the provisions for the transfer of pension rights from the various domestic schemes to the EU scheme, it is probable that additional similar scenarios exist where the question arises of whether the EU pension scheme has to apply (or must not apply) the simple interest rate of 3.1 per cent in respect of the period between the date of the application for a transfer and the date of the actual transfer.
4. It is important to know that a deduction of appreciation by the EU pension scheme only applies where the national pension scheme was unable to supply the value of the pension acquired as at the date of registration of the pension application. It may be even recommended for a staff member to explicitly request the national (transferring) pension scheme to supply the value of pension 'acquired as at the date of registration of the application', in order to encourage their national pension scheme to overtly supply the Union pension scheme with the value of the pension acquired as at that date.
5. It can be retained from the judgments that no interest from the updated capital actually transferred must be deducted when calculating the number of years of pensionable service to be taken into account within the Union pension scheme.

[931] ECJ, C-166/12, ECLI:EU:C:2013:792 – *Radek Časta v Česká správa sociálního zabezpečení.*

5. Retirement Age

The reforms of 2004 and 2014 have modified the pension entitlements by raising the retirement age and lowering the rate at which the entitlements increase.[932] The retirement age for newly entering civil servants was raised from 63 to 66.[933] The pensionable age shall be assessed every five years starting on 1 January 2014 on the basis of a report by the Commission to the European Parliament and to the Council.[934] A comprehensive protection applies to the pension entitlements acquired previously, ie, before 2014, and to the cover under the joint sickness insurance scheme (JSIS).[935]

6. Annual Rate of Acquisition

The reforms reduced the annual rate of acquisition of pension rights from 2 per cent to 1.9 per cent of salary for every year of pensionable service for officials who entered the service on or after 1 May 2004, and to 1.8 per cent for those who joined on or after 1 January 2014.[936]

As case-law has clarified, the benefits of the transitional regime for staff *other* than officials who already had contracts before 2014 apply by analogy in favour of contract staff under contract on 31 December 2013 who have continuously contributed to the financing of the pension system, even if these tasks changed significantly as the result of a new contract.[937] This opinion favours the concept of *contribution continuity*, ie, of the group of staff members who have contributed continuously to the pension scheme, and discards the earlier concept which focused on *functional continuity*. Before the decision on *Picard* was handed down by the ECJ, staff with substantial alterations in their contracts had not benefited from the transitional regime. As the 2014 reform defines a new annual rate of acquisition of pension rights of 1.8 per cent for every year of pensionable service (which is less favourable than the previous rate of 1.9 per cent under the transitional regime), the difference in payment equals to 5.56 per cent of the pension amount paid (ie, 0.1 percentage points to be added to the actually paid 1.8 per cent) for the respective time periods.[938]

7. Barcelona Incentive

If an official remains in active service beyond the retirement age, a separate rate of increase (the 'Barcelona incentive') applies that is equal to 1.5 per cent of the basic salary per year worked after that age, whereas the total pension plus the increase must not exceed 70 per cent of the final basic salary.[939]

[932] Art 6 Annex XII SR.

[933] Art 52, Art 77 SR, Art 22(1) Annex XIII SR.

[934] Art 77 SR at the end; the report shall examine, in particular, the evolution of pensionable age for staff in the civil services of the Member States and the evolution of life expectancy of officials of the institutions. Where appropriate, the Commission shall make a proposal amending the pensionable age in line with the conclusions of that report, paying particular attention to developments in the Member States.

[935] Art 24a Annex XIII SR.

[936] Art 3 Annex VIII SR, Art 21 Annex XIII SR.

[937] ECJ, C-366/21 P, ECLI:EU:2022:C:984, paras 80/81 – *Picard v Commission*; appeal of GC, T-769/16, ECLI:EU:2021:T:153 – *Picard v Commission*.

[938] See case study on *Picard*, in chapter 2, V.2. and the following case study on continuity of service.

[939] Art 5 Annex VIII SR in conjunction with Art 22(2) Annex XIII SR; Commission SWD(2014) 238 final, 13, 17 ff. Jansen, 'Les modifications apportées au statut' in Govaere/Vandersanden (eds), *La fonction publique communautaire* (2008) 21.

Case Study on Accrual of Pension Rights and Continuity of Service

An official benefits from the pre-reform pension as an EU Commission official, even though she had worked during considerable periods as a temporary agent in EU agencies

Case T-128/17, *Isabel Torné v Commission* of 14 December 2018

In Brief

The General Court (GC) decided on the concept of *continuity of service* for the EU and – related to this – whether the provisions of a more beneficial EU pension apply even though during most of her career the official has not worked in the Commission, but in EU agencies. Further, the GC decided that the reply to a staff member's request to *confirm future pension rights* may be a reviewable act.

Background

The pensionable age is 66 years for staff entering service as of 1 January 2014. Pensions are paid as a percentage of the final basic salary, with a ceiling of 70 per cent, at an accrual rate of 1.8 per cent per year of service. In a simplified description, for those staff members who entered service between 1 May 2004 and 31 December 2013 a higher accrual rate of 1.9 per cent per year and a lower pensionable age of 63 years applies (for details see the transition rules in Arts 21, 22 Annex XIII SR). Thus, the provisions that apply to the pension of a staff member are more beneficial if the entry into service took place at an earlier date.

Facts and Arguments

The applicant became an official of the European Commission in 2006 and while on leave on personal grounds (CCP),[940] was transferred to an EU agency in 2012, where she worked under a contract as temporary agent. In 2015 she was engaged by another agency, again as a temporary agent. Subsequently, the applicant requested to have her pension accrual rate and her retirement date fixed at the terms that applied to her as an EU official who had been in service since 2006 – thus before the reform of 2014 entered into force, and irrespective of the changes brought about by this reform. Seven EU agencies intervened on the side of the applicant.

The Commission took the view that the transfer of someone employed as temporary staff and covered by Article 2(f) of the Conditions of Employment of Other Servants (CEOS) to another EU agency entailed the creation of a new contract that was separate from the previous contract, which represented a discontinuity in the career of that temporary staff member and therefore entailed the application of the new rules under the Staff Regulations (SR) concerning retirement pensions, namely a pensionable age of 66 years and a pension accrual rate of 1.8 per cent. The Commission argued that the applicant had entered service at the time of signing her last contract at the EU agency in 2015, which was after the changes brought about by the reform of 2014, and that the pension provisions

[940] Congé de convenance personnelle.

therefore applied to her situation as if she had entered service after the reform took place. The Commission refused to recognise a principle of career continuity for temporary agents who change their institution or agency, and refused a principle of continuity of service for temporary agents in general.

Court Decision

The GC annulled the Commission decision that had rejected the calculation of the pension rights applying to the applicant as an EU official who had been in service since 2006. In the opinion of the GC, the applicant is entitled to benefit from the pension conditions as a staff member who entered service between 2004 and 2014, with an accrual rate of 1.9 per cent per year and a pensionable age of 63. A central question to be decided was whether the applicant has to be treated as if she had entered service afresh in 2015 (when starting to work at the second agency), or whether there is a continuity in her service dating to the start of her employment at the Commission in 2006.

The GC found that the meaning of *entering service* as used in Articles 21 and 22 Annex XIII SR has to be interpreted in line with the objective pursued, and has to take into account that the pension scheme of the EU is the same for officials, temporary agents and contract agents. The applicant had continuously contributed to the pension scheme and was continuously affiliated to this scheme. In addition, during the entire time since 2006 she had continued to be an official of the Commission. The different ways in which service can be terminated under the SR are conclusively listed in Articles 47–52 SR; they do not include leave on personal grounds (CCP).[941] The reform of 2014 respected the acquired rights and legitimate expectations of staff already employed in the institutions and agencies. Therefore, despite her work for the agencies and her CCP from the Commission, the applicant had maintained her continuous affiliation to the EU pension scheme in accordance with Article 83 SR and since the time she was appointed as an official in 2006.

Comments

1. This judgment clarifies an important question regarding the continuity of EU service for the determination of which provisions under the pension scheme apply in the transition rules of Articles 21 and 22 Annex XIII SR. The applicant had been transferred to agencies while she was on leave on personal grounds. This amounted to nine years in total at the point at which she requested to have her pension conditions fixed. The total permissible length of leave on personal grounds is in general limited to 12 years[942] during an entire career, Article 40(2) SR.
2. The specificity of the case was that during this leave period, and while working for an agency, a reform of the pension scheme took place. Case-law already determined that new employment contracts with other agencies, or with the same agency but in a different category or with a material change in the type of duties, mark an interruption of the career path.[943] This would, for instance, require temporary agents to

[941] Congé de convenance personnelle.
[942] Reduced from 15 years by the 2014 SR reform.
[943] *cf* CST, F-116/14, ECLI:EU:F:2015:89, para 132 – *Murariu v EIOPA*.

demonstrate adequate professional abilities for the new post, as is the case for external candidates. However, in the present situation the GC did not take account of the disruption that might be inferred from the staff member being on leave or pursuing a career path in other agencies, but focused on the continuity of the pension system to which the applicant had belonged since her entry into service in 2006.

3. This legal development supports the concept of 'inter-agency mobility' and the mobility of transfers from the EU institutions to the agencies and vice versa. In terms of the pension scheme, the various EU institutions or agencies belong to the same 'family'.
4. On the *admissibility* of the action: a statement on future conduct is regularly considered as a preparatory measure and is not reviewable. Only acts with binding legal effects are reviewable, which are held to occur when the measure is 'binding on, and capable of affecting the interests of, the applicant by bringing about a distinct change in his legal position'. In the present case, the GC accepted that the Commission's refusal of the applicant's request for confirmation concerning the pension factors that will be applicable at the date of her retirement can be considered as an act adversely affecting the legal situation of the official. The GC found that it was the act determining the date of the *entry into service* that adversely affected the legal situation of the applicant, not the determination of future pension entitlements relating to that date once the staff member actually retires. Thus, it can be retained that the decision on a request to *confirm future pension rights* may be a reviewable act, a conclusion confirmed by subsequent case law.[944]

Potential future development of the case-law on pension rights

5. In the present case, two combined considerations led the GC to conclude that the *entry into service* of the applicant was the time of her recruitment as an official in 2006: (1) she became an official and remained as one while on leave on personal grounds; and (2) she continued to be affiliated without interruption to the pension scheme of the EU. An interesting question is whether each of these circumstances alone would justify the same result for the staff member.

   In the first scenario (involving continuously remaining an official on CCP), an applicant's leave on personal grounds – whether without a job or with an occupation outside the EU family of institutions – before returning to the EU Commission as an official, there is good reason to assume that the same pension provisions would apply throughout, because there would be no new 'entry into service'.

   In the second scenario (continuously remaining affiliated to the EU pension scheme), previous case-law that recognised interruptions of a career arising from employment contracts with other EU agencies or within the same agency could be seen to be overruled by the present judgment in *Torné*. In other words, the continuous affiliation to the pension system would not be affected by circumstances that used to be considered interruptions of the career. In this case, the question of whether the staff member was on leave on personal grounds (CCP) appears to be irrelevant.

[944] On this, see chapter 2, V.2. case study on reviewable act, case *Picard*.

8. Survivor's Pension

The surviving spouse[945] of an official or former official[946] receives a survivor's pension equal to 60 per cent of the retirement or disability pension which was paid to the deceased or which, irrespective of length of service or age, would have been payable to him if he had qualified for it at the time of his death.[947] If the official dies leaving no spouse entitled to a survivor's pension, each dependent child at the time of the death of the official receives an orphan's pension.[948] In order for the spouse to be entitled to a survivor's pension, the marriage must have lasted at least one year.[949] The purpose of this is to ensure that the relationship between the persons concerned was genuine and stable. A de facto cohabitation and non-marital cohabitation do not suffice to meet this requirement unless an official certificate of non-marital cohabitation can be presented which confirms that the couple could not legally marry under the applicable laws.[950] The minimum duration of five years required by Article 20 Annex VIII SR for a marriage entered into *after the start of the pension* seems inappropriately long, also compared with the one-year period mentioned above.[951] On this point of dispute, see the following case study. In subsequent case-law, the GC followed the interpretation of the ECJ that is closely oriented at the wording of the Article 20 Annex VIII SR (strict application of the minimum duration of five years).[952]

Case Study on the Survivor's Pension

ECJ applies the conditions for a survivor's pension strictly

Case C-460/18 P, *HK v Commission* of 19 December 2019
Case T-574/16, *HK v Commission* of 3 May 2018

In Brief

A *survivor's pension* is the entitlement of the surviving spouse of an official to receive a pension after the death of the official. Such a pension was denied in a case decided upon by the Court of Justice (ECJ). The ECJ confirms that the Commission was right in refusing a survivor's pension to the husband of an official to whom he had not been married for the required time of one full year. A status as cohabitant (ie, their status for the period before

[945] Where two persons are surviving spouses of an official claiming the survivor's pensions: CST, F-45/07, ECLI:EU:F:2010:72, para 126 – *Mandt v EP*, the Court confirmed the decision of the administration to split the benefits among the spouses.

[946] *cf* the administrative statuses of Art 35 SR. For the EIB, see Art 52 ff EIB Pension Scheme Regulations.

[947] Art 79 SR.

[948] Art 80 SR. The entitlement only requires that the substantive conditions for a dependent child are met prior to the official's death; it is not necessary for the administrative steps to have been completed before that death: GC, T-143/22, ECLI:EU:T:2023:313, para 100 – *OP v EP*.

[949] Art 17(1) Annex VIII SR.

[950] ECJ, C-460/18 P, ECLI:EU:C:2019:1119, paras 75, 89 – *HK v Commission*.

[951] Similarly as here: GC, T-315/19, ECLI:EU:T:2020:622 – *BT v Commission*, further to proportionality considerations, but set aside in the appeal, ECJ, C-116/21 P to C-118/21 P, C-138/21 P and C-139/21 P, ECLI:EU:C:2022:557 – *VW, BT, RN*, for alleged misjudgement of the judicial standard of control at first instance; GC, T-694/19, ECLI:EU:T:2021:122 – *FI v Commission*.

[952] GC, T-622/22, ECLI:EU:T:2023:803, paras 29 ff – *Van Oosterwijck v Commission*.

being married) does not fulfil the strict requirements of 'marriage' in the sense of the Staff Regulations (SR).

Legal Background

Article 17 Annex VIII SR reads as follows:

> Where an official dies having one of the administrative statuses set out in Art 35 of the Staff Regulations the surviving spouse shall be entitled, provided that the couple were married for at least one year at the time of his death and subject to the provisions of Art 1(1) and 22, to a survivor's pension equal to 60% of the retirement pension which the official would have been paid if he had qualified, irrespective of length of service or of age, for such pension at the time of death.
>
> The duration of the marriage shall not be taken into account if there are one or more children of the marriage or of a previous marriage of the official provided that the surviving spouse maintains or has maintained those children, or if the official's death resulted either from physical disability or sickness contracted in the performance of his duties or from accident.

Facts of the Case

HK, the appellant, and Ms N had been living together since 1994. Ms N was an official of the European Commission, assigned to the Joint Research Centre. The appellant and Ms N were married on 9 May 2014. Ms N. died on 11 April 2015, just four weeks before the one-year anniversary of their marriage. The appellant requested to be paid a survivor's pension, which the Commission refused to grant.

The Parties' Arguments and Decisions of the Courts

The appellant brought an action for the annulment of the contested decision and for compensation for the material and non-material damage allegedly suffered. In his action, the appellant pleaded that Article 17(1) Annex VIII SR was unlawful, first claiming that the criterion that the marriage or non-marital partnership must have existed for more than a year is arbitrary and inadequate having regard to the purpose of the survivor's pension, and that that Article is unlawful insofar as it infringes Article 21 FRC and Article 2 of Directive 2000/78.[953] The General Court (GC) dismissed the action in its entirety. In second instance, the Court of Justice (ECJ) set aside the decision of the GC and handed down its own decision on the substance of the matter.

The ECJ found that the GC has infringed the obligation to state reasons, because the grounds it had given were ambiguous. Specifically, it had not made clear and understandable which persons fell within the scope of Article 17(1) Annex VIII SR when it first considered that it applies only to a person who had entered into a civil marriage recognised by law, but later – without giving reasons for that assessment – stated that Article 17(1) covered not only married persons but also registered partners. The GC further considered that 'it is not the loss of the deceased official's remuneration which constitutes the condition for granting the survivor's pension, but the legal nature of the relationship between the official and her surviving spouse or partner'.

[953] Council Directive 2000/78/EC of 27 November 2000 establishing a general framework for equal treatment in employment and occupation [2000] OJ L303/16.

In its own decision on the substance, the ECJ also dismissed the action and decided that the Commission was right in refusing the benefit of a survivor's pension. The ECJ justifies this in the following way: the grant of the survivor's pension *depends solely on the legal nature of the ties between the person concerned and the deceased official.* Although de facto unions and legally recognised unions, such as marriage, may exhibit similarities in certain respects, such similarities do not necessarily mean that those two types of union must be treated in the same way. Marriage is characterised by rigorous formalism and creates reciprocal rights and obligations between the spouses of a high degree.

The ECJ clearly differentiates between non-marital partnerships and cohabitation. Non-marital partnerships are to be treated as marriage provided that all the conditions listed in Article 1(2) lit c of Annex VII SR are fulfilled. The conditions provided for in that Article include in particular the fact that the couple shall provide an official document recognised as such by a Member State or by any competent authority of a Member State, certifying their status as non-marital partners, and that the couple has no access to legal marriage in a Member State. Conversely, a de facto union such as cohabitation does not satisfy those characteristics insofar as a de facto union is not, in principle, the subject of an SR laid down by law. Cohabitants are not in a situation comparable to that of married persons or to that of partners who have entered into a registered partnership. Treating them differently therefore does not infringe the principle of non-discrimination.

Finally, the appellant had claimed that the condition of a minimum duration of one year of marriage in order to be entitled to the survivor's pension was arbitrary, inadequate and discriminatory. In the appellant's view, having been married for *almost* a year to Ms N, he should be entitled to a survivor's pension. Also Advocate General Pikamäe had opined that the requirement of a one-year of minimum duration of the marriage as a cut-off period was disproportionate (because it went beyond what is necessary to achieve the objectives of general interest pursued by the legislature) and thus had to be declared invalid. In his view, the applicant was entitled to the survivor's pension and to a reparation of the non-material damage suffered.

However, the ECJ decided otherwise and welcomed the argument brought forward by the Commission that the purpose of the requirement of a minimum duration of marriage at the date of death is to avoid it being merely a pact on future successions, motivated more by financial considerations than by a plan for living together. That condition of duration made it possible, inter alia, to combat fraud. In order to combat abuse or even fraud, the Union legislature has a margin of discretion in establishing the entitlement to a survivor's pension. The condition for the surviving spouse to be able to receive the survivor's pension that the marriage must have lasted for at least one full year, said the ECJ, is intended to ensure the reality and stability of the relationship between the persons concerned. Such a condition did not appear to be discriminatory or manifestly inadequate in relation to the objective of the survivor's pension.

Comments

1. The judgment of the ECJ follows the line of case-law in two main strands: (1) that a grant of the survivor's pension depends solely on the legal nature of the ties between

the person concerned and the deceased official;[954] (2) that de facto unions and legally recognised unions, such as marriage, do not have to be treated in the same way, despite their similarities.[955]

2. The ECJ did not touch on the legislative choice that consists in fixing a minimum required period of one year of marriage in order to be entitled to a survivor's pension. It was enough for the ECJ to have a rationale which is not manifestly inadequate. The rationale is that the principle of prohibiting fraud and abuse has to be complied with. The rule entails a sharp time-based differentiation between those couples who have reached the 'marriage age' of one full year vs those who have not, without it being possible to refute the assumption that in their case any fraud or abuse would actually be avoided, or that fraud or abuse does not exist in their case.
3. It is important to bear in mind that in practice, in many cases – further to Article 17(2) Annex VIII SR – the duration of the marriage is not to be taken into account if there are one or more children of the marriage, or of a previous marriage of the official, provided that the surviving spouse maintains or has maintained those children. Where the official's death resulted either from physical disability or sickness contracted in the performance of his duties or from accident, the duration of the marriage also does not count.

Requirement of a certain duration of marriage

Article 17 Annex VIII SR is not the only clause referring to a minimum duration of marriage. Articles 17a, 18, 18a and 19 Annex VIII SR also contain such minimum periods. Article 20 Annex VIII SR balances these provisions by stipulating that the 'duration of the marriage shall not be taken into account where the marriage, though contracted after termination of the official's service, has lasted at least five years'. For the calculation of this period, the period of the marriage before retirement also has to be counted.[956] The following case study focuses on the duration of marriage required for the entitlement to a survivor's pension.

Case Study on Survivor's Pension and Required Duration of Marriage

Survivor's pension: On the advantage of a marriage date before retirement starts

Case C-116/21 P, *Commission v VW* of 14 July 2022 (Joined Cases C-116/21 P, *VW*; C-117/21 P, *BT*; C-118/21 P, *RN*; C-138/21 P, *BT*; C-139/21 P, *VW*)

In Brief

The Court of Justice (ECJ) decided on five cases of survivor's pensions. The ECJ reversed the decisions of the first instance, which favoured the surviving spouses who applied for

[954] ECJ, Jd Cases C-122/99 P and C-125/99, ECLI:EU:C:2001:304 P – *D and Sweden v Council*.

[955] ECJ, C-485/08 P, ECLI:EU:C:2010:188 – *Gualtieri v Commission*.

[956] CST, F-104/15 [2015] OJ C302/71 – *RN v Commission*, annulled in appeal GC, T-695/16 P, ECLI:EU:T:2017:520 – *RN v Commission*.

a survivor's pension. The judgment leads to the recommendation that in order to be on the safe side, for the surviving spouse to benefit from a survivor's retirement pension it is better to plan for a marriage to take place before the service of the official ends. If the couple marries afterwards, the minimum qualifying duration of the marriage for enabling the survivor to benefit from the survivor's pension can (if no other exceptions apply) be five years instead of one year.

Legal Background

Article 18 Annex VIII SR provides:

> Where a former official was in receipt of [a] retirement pension the surviving spouse shall be entitled, provided that the couple were already married before the official left the service of an institution and that the marriage had lasted at least one year ... to a survivor's pension equal to 60% of the retirement pension which he was receiving at the time of his death ... The duration of the marriage shall not be taken into account if there are one or more children of a marriage contracted by the official before he left the service, provided that the surviving spouse maintains or has maintained those children.

Article 20 Annex VIII SR states:

> For the purpose of Articles 17a, 18, 18a, and 19 the duration of the marriage shall not be taken into account where the marriage, though contracted after termination of the official's service, has lasted at least five years.

Facts of the Cases

The applicants of the five cases are three widows: VW, BT and RN. They were married to officials who had already left the service of an EU institution before their marriage was contracted. The three former officials died less than five years after marriage in each case. The widows applied for a survivor's pension under Chapter 4 Annex VIII SR. The Office for the Administration and Payment of Individual Entitlements (PMO) rejected their pension claims, because they did not satisfy the conditions laid down in Article 20 Annex VIII SR for entitlement to a survivor's pension, since their marriage to the deceased official, which had been entered into after the termination of the latter's service, had lasted less than five years. The applicants challenged these decisions and were successful with their actions at first instance. The institutions appealed against the General Court's (GC) decisions and obtained appeal judgments in which the Court of Justice (ECJ) set aside the decisions of the GC at first instance.

Decisions of the General Court

The GC upheld the pleas raised by the applicants that Article 20 Annex VIII SR infringed the principle of equal treatment and, in the cases relating to VW and RN, the principle of proportionality; and also, in the cases concerning BT and RN, the principle of non-discrimination on grounds of age. In essence, the GC argues that the situation covered by Article 18 Annex VIII SR, namely that of surviving spouses of a former official of the EU who married before termination of the latter's service, was comparable to the situation covered by Article 20, namely that of surviving spouses who entered into marriage after termination of the official's service. The situations were treated differently, depending on the date on which the marriage was entered into: while a surviving spouse who had married before service of her husband ended obtained the survivor's pension, provided that the marriage had lasted at least one year, in the other scenario (marriage after her husband's service ended) the spouses had to be married for at least five years in order for the widow to be entitled to the survivor's pension.

In the cases concerning BT and RN, the GC also found a difference in the treatment of comparable situations based indirectly on the age of the former official on the date on which the marriage was entered into. The GC acknowledged that the condition that the marriage must have lasted for a minimum period of time before it gives rise to an entitlement to a survivor's pension makes it possible to ensure that that marriage is not based exclusively on considerations unrelated to marriage, such as purely financial considerations or considerations connected with obtaining a right of residence. However, under that general-interest objective of preventing fraud, the GC stated that it is unreasonable to require that the marriage concluded after the end of service must have lasted for a minimum of five years – ie, five times longer than the minimum duration provided for in Article 18 Annex VIII SR – because this goes beyond what is necessary to achieve the objective of combating fraud. The general-interest objective of safeguarding the finances of the EU cannot, said the GC, in itself justify a derogation from the general principle of equal treatment. The GC thus upheld the pleas of illegality raised by the applicants and annulled the respective decisions of the administration.

Decision of the ECJ

In its appeal decision, the ECJ sets aside the judgments of the GC and dismisses the applicants' actions. The ECJ opines that the GC had misunderstood the scope of its power of judicial review by incorrectly examining the requirement of proportionality. The GC should have confined itself to checking whether a minimum duration of marriage in the situations covered by Article 20 Annex VIII SR that is five times greater than that in the situations covered by Article 18 had to be regarded as *arbitrary* or *manifestly inappropriate* in the light of the objective pursued by the EU legislature. Such a reduced verification is imposed by the test of proportionality of Article 52(1) FRC. The principle of equal treatment or equality before the law and the principle of non-discrimination (Art 20 and Art 21(1) FRC; Art 1d SR) require that comparable situations should not be treated differently, and that different situations should not be treated in the same way unless such treatment is objectively justified. Since the legislature enjoys broad discretion when drafting provisions of the SR, the principle of equal treatment can only be breached where the legislature makes a *distinction which is arbitrary or manifestly inappropriate in relation to the objective pursued.* The ECJ had already decided previously[957] that the objective of a minimum duration of marriage is intended to ensure the genuineness and stability of the relationship between the persons concerned. The minimum duration of marriage in Chapter 4 Annex VIII SR is designed not to presume the existence of abuse or fraud on the part of surviving spouses, but to prevent the commission of such abuses or fraud. The ECJ concludes that, in the light of the principle of equal treatment and of the broad discretion

[957] ECJ, C-460/18 P, ECLI:EU:C:2019:1119 – *HK v Commission.*

enjoyed by the EU legislature, a minimum duration of marriage of one year (Art 18 Annex VIII SR) and of five years respectively (Art 20 Annex VIII SR) are neither arbitrary nor manifestly inappropriate distinctions. Concretely, says the ECJ, where marriage was entered into after the termination of the official's service, there was a greater incentive to commit abuses or fraud as a result of the greater predictability of and closer proximity to the official's death, because the official had left service as a result of retirement. Likewise, the ECJ acknowledges that the distinctions in Article 18 and Article 20 Annex VIII SR constitute a difference in treatment indirectly based on the age of the official; however, this difference complied with the principle of non-discrimination on grounds of age, once again because of the reduced scope of judicial control over the EU legislature.

Comments

1. As in its decision in Case C-460/18 P, *HK v Commission*, the ECJ interprets the conditions for a survivor's pension narrowly.
2. This means that it makes a significant practical and financial difference for the surviving spouse whether the official dies within a period of between one year and five years after marriage, and whether the marriage was contracted before or after the end date of service. In an extreme comparison: an official who marries the day before leaving service passes on a survivor's pension entitlement to his spouse within one year, counted from the time of marriage; however, an official who married the day after leaving service passes on the same right only after having survived five years plus one day after having left service.
3. Hence, a very practical recommendation to be drawn from this line of case-law is that if an official plans to marry, he should preferably envisage their marriage while still in service (thus more probably being in a situation falling under Arts 17 or 18 Annex VIII SR), instead of postponing marriage until their retirement starts. Otherwise, the surviving spouse may more easily find himself in the situation of being denied the survivor's pension under Chapter 4 Annex VIII SR.
4. The key legal question of the case presented is how to assess whether EU legislation complies with the principle of proportionality – for instance, as expressed in Article 52(1) FRC – and with the principle of equal treatment, ie, how to define the scope of judicial review of the EU legislature.

   The GC had carried out a proportionality test, and on that basis it opined that the requirement of a minimum duration of marriage that is five times greater than in a comparable situation was disproportionate. But the ECJ – although conceding that the situations were comparable – cuts the discussion short by relying on a far-reaching judicial self-restraint: any verification of legislative proportionality and equal treatment has to be limited to a test of whether the provisions were *arbitrary* or *manifestly inappropriate* in the light of the objective pursued by the EU legislature. It is safe to say that in practice, it will always be possible to find arguments justifying the objective pursued by a legislative clause.
5. There are exceptions to the requirement of a minimum duration of marriage in Chapter 4 Annex VIII SR (ie, where this case-law is not relevant from the outset): further to Articles 17(2), 17a(3/4), 18(2), 18a(2) Annex VIII SR, the duration of the marriage is not to be taken into account if there are one or more children of the

marriage or of a previous marriage of the official, provided that the surviving spouse maintains or has maintained those children. Also, where the official's death resulted either from physical disability or sickness contracted in the performance of his duties or from an accident, the duration of the marriage does not count.

6. For the calculation of the duration of marriage, the duration of the time being married before retirement also has to be counted.[958] This was not relevant in the five cases discussed here, because the spouses all got married after the officials' active time in the civil service had come to an end.

V. Invalidity, Occupational Disease, Accident and Incapacity to Work

1. Relationship between Article 73 SR and Article 78 SR

Article 73 and Article 78 of the Staff Regulations (SR) stipulate two important social security benefits for staff members.[959] Under Article 73 SR, officials are insured against the risk of occupational diseases and accidents; Article 78 stipulates the payment of an invalidity allowance in the case of total permanent invalidity that prevents the official from performing the duties corresponding to a post in his function group. The benefits stemming from both regimes may be cumulative.[960]

Article 73 SR refers to the Common Insurance Rules (CIR).[961] The benefits are stipulated in a group insurance policy taken out with a consortium of insurance underwriters. The regime of Article 73 SR only applies to the staff member himself,[962] not to spouses or dependants. Article 73 SR (insurance coverage) is independent of the capacity of the person to perform his duties, and instead considers the effect of the physical and psychological harm on the integrity of the person, while Article 78 SR (allowance) relates to the incapacity to work. The lump sum entitlement under Article 73 SR for partial permanent invalidity may therefore apply, even though the person is not in any way prevented from undertaking his professional duties.[963] Article 73 SR is to be interpreted as referring to the impairment of the bodily or mental health of the official irrespective of any degree of incapacity for work which might result from the accident or disease.[964] In line with this, the disability rating scale[965] concentrates on the disease (or the adverse effects on

[958] CST, F-104/15 [2015] OJ C302/71 – *RN v Commission*, annulled in appeal GC, T-695/16 P, ECLI:EU:T:2017:520 – *RN v Commission*.

[959] Again, this presentation focuses on the EU institutions and EU SR; for the EIB, see Art 32 ff and Art 46 ff EIB Pension Scheme Regulations and Art 33–Art 33d EIB Staff Regulations.

[960] *cf* Art 73(2) final sentence SR.

[961] Common rules on the insurance against the risk of accident and of occupational disease adopted by the institutions, Common Insurance Rules of 13 December 2005, available at: www.europarl.europa.eu/tenders/2014/20140103/EN_Ref%203_Common%20rules_accident_EN.pdf.

[962] Art 73 SR applies to permanent officials, temporary staff and contract agents, Art 1 Common Insurance Rules.

[963] *cf* CST, F-47/10, ECLI:EU:F:2011:137, para 75 – *Hecq v Commission*.

[964] ECJ, 152/77, ECLI:EU:C:1979:220, para 14 – *Miss B*.

[965] European physical and mental disability rating scale for medical purposes (French: 'Barème'), attached as Annex A to the Common Insurance Rules. CST, F-97/08, ECLI:EU:F:2010:73, paras ff, 100 ff – *Füller-Tomlinson v EP*.

bodily or mental health), without taking into account the character of work performed. A total invalidity in the sense of Article 73 SR would typically entail a total permanent invalidity under Article 78 SR, as incapacity to perform the duties. This conclusion does not work conversely, because the servant who is prevented by the invalidity from performing the duties corresponding to a post in his function group (Art 78 SR) may only suffer from a partial permanent invalidity in the sense of Article 73 SR. An incapacity for work (Art 78 SR) justifies the grant of a replacement income in the form of an invalidity allowance; permanent invalidity as an adverse effect on physical and mental integrity does not necessarily entail incapacity for work and thus payment of a replacement income.[966]

Both Article 73 and Article 78 SR make use of the terms *invalidity*, *occupational disease* and *accident*, but they have different objectives and meanings, and are partially based on different definitions. Whether a disease is an occupational one requires a proper assessment of the links between the disease and the professional activity being undertaken. The procedures of recognition of occupational disease or accidents and permanent (total or partial) invalidity under Article 73 SR on the one hand, and of invalidity under Article 78 SR on the other, are independent of one another; the results of the procedures do not influence each other; and the outcomes may differ in the same case and for the same medical situation.[967]

This exposes one of the downsides of these procedures: they may require repeated medical examinations of the person concerned by different committees and practitioners, although these could be consolidated and thus reduce the strain on the patient. Secondly, the duration of the procedures leading to recognition of the status under Articles 73 and 78 SR respectively may be lengthy, and may to a certain extent be protracted by the way the procedures are handled in the institutions.[968] Thirdly, the medical practitioner assigned by the appointing authority to represent the institution at the Medical Committee is very often the one put forward by the insurer. The Medical Committee is the body convened for the purposes of medical appraisal under the CIR,[969] while the Invalidity Committee is the body convened for the purposes of Article 78 SR.

The definition of *occupational disease* to be applied in both procedures (Arts 73 and 78 SR) is identical. This may result in a connection between the procedures: when the appointing authority decides on the occupational origin of an official's illness under Article 78 and under Article 73, it takes two decisions having the same purpose. Hence, the appointing authority has to acknowledge the prior recognition (at least in the case of a determination *res iudicata* rendered by the court) of an illness having an occupational origin under Article 78 SR, and is also bound to recognise an occupational origin under the procedure of Article 73 SR.[970] However, the two procedures themselves remain separated, with the consequence that the request to decide on the occupational origin of an illness in one procedure does not count for a request in the other procedure.[971]

[966] CST, F-12/09, ECLI:EU:F:2011:136, paras 149, 150 – *A v Commission.*

[967] *cf* Art 25 Common Insurance Rules.

[968] GC, T-394/03, ECLI:EU:T:2006:111, para 162 – *Angeletti v Commission*, €12,000 damages for delayed Art 78 SR recognition procedure. The burden of proof for the appropriateness of the duration of the procedure may pass to the administration, *cf* CST, F-12/10, ECLI:EU:F:2012:183 – *Kerstens v Commission*; GC, T-48/01, ECLI:EU:T:2004:61 – *Vainker*; CST, F-79/09, ECLI:EU:F:2010:99 – *AE v Commission.*

[969] NB on terminology: there is also a *medical committee* under the SR, which ascertains medical fitness in the second instance under Arts 33 and 129 CEOS, see section II.5. above.

[970] In this sense CST, F-18/05, ECLI:EU:F:2006:69, paras 67/68 – *D v Commission.*

[971] GC, T-4/17, ECLI:EU:T:2017:891, paras 45/46 – *Coedo Suarez v Council.*

2. Relationship between Article 73 SR and Article 72 SR

The insurance cover under Article 73 of the Staff Regulations (SR) targets different goals from the sickness insurance scheme under Article 72 SR. The insurance against sickness provides benefits to the official, and to their spouse, children and other dependants with regard to medical expenses. It amounts to reimbursement at the rate of 80/85/100 per cent of the expenditure incurred.[972] Sickness insurance reimbursement at 100 per cent does not apply when Article 73 SR cover applies. More specifically, under Article 9(1), (3) of the Common Insurance Rules (CIR), the insured parties who suffer an accident or contract an occupational disease shall be entitled to reimbursement of all necessary expenses. It applies after the sickness insurance scheme provided for by Article 72 SR has defrayed the portion falling under that scheme under the conditions set out in that Article. In line with this, Article 73(3), (2) SR provides that reimbursement of the expenses necessitated by the occupational disease is to be made only after the exhaustion of and in addition to those which the official will receive under Article 72 SR. Read in connection with Article 9 CIR, case-law has clarified that both Article 73(3) SR and the Article 9 CIR only provide for additional repayment of the expenses incurred for services covered by Article 72 SR, after repayment of the portion of the expenses borne by the sickness insurance scheme. The accident insurance scheme is supplementary, and thus does not provide for any reimbursement of expenses incurred for benefits which are not covered by the sickness insurance scheme, and therefore do not give rise to any payment by the sickness insurance scheme.[973]

While an official is on leave on personal grounds (CCP),[974] his membership of the social security scheme under Articles 72 and 73 SR and cover for risks under that scheme shall be suspended, except where he applies within one month following the one in which the leave on personal grounds begins that he may continue to be covered.[975]

3. Relationship between Article 78 SR and Retirement Pension

The benefits under Article 78 of the Staff Regulations (SR) fall under the pension system of the EU (*cf* Chapter 3 of Title V of the SR). While the benefits under Articles 73 and 78 SR can be accumulated, the invalidity allowance under Article 78 SR and the benefits under a retirement pension cannot be accumulated. This means that a staff member declared invalid first receives an invalidity pension and then, upon retirement in line with Article 52 SR, receives a retirement pension. An invalidity during retirement is not recognisable. Under the invalidity allowance of Article 78 SR, contributions have to be paid into the pension scheme; the invalidity allowance is replaced by a pension when the staff member reaches retirement age, in line with the provisions applicable to officials in active service.

[972] See section IV.2. above.

[973] CST, F-12/09, ECLI:EU:F:2011:136, paras 206, 207 – *A v Commission*, in appeal GC, T-595/11 P, ECLI:EU:T:2012:694; CST, F-89/09, ECLI:EU:F:2010:155, para 42 – *Gagalis v Council* (Art 73 SR applies in principle only as a supplement to benefits under Art 72 SR).

[974] congé de convenance personnelle.

[975] And when the other conditions of Art 40(3)(2) SR are fulfilled. On Art 78 SR invalidity, see section V.6. below.

4. Definitions

In general, rules on insurance are interpreted (also in favour of the beneficiary) rather narrowly, according to their wording.[976] Among the many legally defined terms in matters relating to invalidity, the definitions of 'permanent invalidity', 'occupational disease' and 'accident' will be given here.

a. Permanent Invalidity, Article 78 SR

The expression 'total permanent invalidity preventing him from performing the duties corresponding to a post in his function group' in Article 78 SR raises the question of the benchmark for assessing whether someone is actually prevented 'from performing'. For that purpose, the assessment of a staff member by the Invalidity Committee as being either 'invalid' or 'fit to work' has to be done solely in relation to their *own* institution, because the Invalidity Committee is part of this institution and is not empowered to judge on the fitness of the staff member for external jobs.[977] Thus, from the institution's perspective, an avoidance of the 'invalidity' assessment by referring the staff member to external employment is not admissible. This shall be further illustrated by the subsequent case study.

Case Study on Definition of Invalidity: *ratione loci*

'Invalidity': To be determined solely in relation to a person's own institution, not as fitness for work in the general labour market

Case C-68/22 P, *EIB v KL* of 22 December 2022
Case T-370/20, *KL v EIB* of 24 November 2021

In Brief

The term *invalidity* in the context of the entitlement of staff to an invalidity allowance can only be interpreted as an incapacity to fulfil duties *within* one's own institution. If found to be invalid there, the staff member cannot be referred to the general labour market with the argument that he would be 'not invalid' outside the institution. In other words, an invalidity allowance must be granted independently of the capacity of the staff member to perform work in the general labour market.

Legal Background

Article 78 SR provides that an official shall be entitled to 'an invalidity allowance in the case of total permanent invalidity preventing him from performing the duties corresponding to a post in his function group'. Article 46-1 of the European Investment Bank (EIB) Transitional Pension Scheme (TPSR) defines that a staff member shall be 'incapacitated if,

[976] GC, T-736/19, ECLI:EU:T:2020:609 – *HA v Commission*.
[977] GC, T-370/20, ECLI:EU:T:2021:822, paras 99/100 – *KL v EIB*.

by reason of sickness, accident or disability, he is unable, physically or mentally, permanently to fulfil his duties or any other similar duties at an equivalent level and if invalidity has been established in accordance with Article 48'.

Facts of the Case

The applicant was employed by the EIB. The EIB's medical officer recommended that he be regarded as suffering from partial temporary incapacity (50 per cent). This assessment was confirmed by the independent medical practitioner appointed by the EIB further to a medical arbitration procedure to assess the alleged total incapacity of the applicant to resume his duties. Subsequently, at the request of the applicant's lawyer, a procedure before the Invalidity Committee was carried out; it concluded with the statement of the Committee that the applicant was 'unfit to return to his former post and to his former employer. He is therefore invalid in relation to the EIB, but not invalid in relation to the general labour market'. Further to this, the EIB first declared the applicant 'fit to work' and shortly afterwards 'absent without justification' from the date on which the applicant should have resumed work. The applicant requested a review of these decisions, but instead the EIB approved them. Finally, a conciliation procedure was initiated and led to the confirmation of these two decisions by the Conciliation Board, and a confirmation of this result by the President of the European Investment Bank. The applicant did not accept this outcome and challenged the decisions in an action for annulment at the General Court (GC).

Decisions of the General Court and the Court of Justice

The GC annulled the contested decisions of the EIB and ordered the EIB to pay an invalidity pension and default interest on that pension. The applicant's claim for compensation for the non-material damage was dismissed by the GC. The GC found that the EIB had infringed Article 46-1 TPSR (and Art 11.1 of the administrative provisions) because the EIB was required to declare KL invalid but instead declared him 'fit to work' and 'absent without justification'. The concept of the term 'invalidity' in Article 46-1 TPSR, stated the GC, is to be assessed solely in relation to the EIB, while the EIB followed the assessment of the Invalidity Committee stating that KL was allegedly 'valid' because he was still capable of carrying on a professional activity on the open labour market. The GC found that the EIB also infringed Article 48-1 TPSR (and Art 11.3 of the administrative provisions), under which, in the event of dispute it is the Invalidity Committee which is competent to establish invalidity, not the medical practitioner.

The GC provided three motivations for its decision: first, that by analogy with Article 78 SR, the EIB rules on invalidity referred to the classification of functions within that same body. Secondly, the GC noted that the Invalidity Committees established by the EIB are organs of that body and therefore do not have, from a legal point of view, competence to assess the capacity of EIB staff members to pursue professional duties outside that body. Thirdly, the GC rejected the EIB's interpretation of Article 51-1 of the TPSR, according to which that provision applies only to those rare situations in which a person declared invalid within the EIB pursues, outside that body, an activity different from that which he or she pursued within it. This provision, explains the GC, just shows that it is possible that a person declared invalid may pursue an activity outside the EIB, the only limit being the ceiling of income as indicated in that provision.

In its judgment, the Court of Justice (ECJ) dismisses the appeal filed by the EIB and thus confirms the judgment of the GC in favour of the applicant. The ECJ does not find that the GC erred in law when in interpreting the concept of invalidity. Where Article 46-1 TPSR speaks about an incapacity to fulfil 'his duties or any other similar duties at an equivalent level' the word 'duties' refers to the duties within the EIB institution. The EIB had argued that Article 46-1 TPSR does not distinguish invalidity declared with regard to duties performed within the EIB from invalidity declared with regard to the open market, nor does it impose a strict limit on the competence of the Invalidity Committee when assessing invalidity. In response, the ECJ explains that the provisions in the TPSR can only be interpreted to mean that the term 'invalidity' is an incapacity to resume the duties or similar duties at an equivalent level within that body, here the EIB. Where the EIB had argued that the task of the medical practitioners within the Invalidity Committee was merely to provide a medical opinion and not to comment on the working environment, the ECJ rejects this argument by deciding that especially where psychological problems are the cause of the invalidity, the working environment also has to be taken into account in the medical opinion. As a result, the invalidity of the applicant in the present case was recognised and the corresponding invalidity pension was approved.

Comments

1. The judgments clarify a central criterion relating to the term *invalidity* that must be applied by the Invalidity Committee and the institutions. A staff member is entitled to an invalidity allowance (here called 'invalidity pension') in the case of total permanent invalidity that prevents him from performing the duties corresponding to a post in his function group. It refers to a physical or mental incapacity to permanently fulfil these duties or any other similar duties at an equivalent level. The judgment makes clear that under both Article 78 SR and Article 46-1 TPSR for the EIB, the invalidity is to be assessed *solely in relation to the staff member's own institution.*
2. This means that where an inability to perform the duties within the institution is diagnosed, the courts have abolished the possibility for the institutions and their invalidity committees to avoid acknowledging the existence of a staff member's invalidity by asserting that they are still fit to work 'somewhere else', ie, in the general labour market.
3. It is useful to note that – in the event of dispute – procedurally it is up to the Invalidity Committee to establish invalidity as the competent body, *cf* Article 1 Annex VIII SR; Articles 33(2), 100, 102(1) CEOS – a competence confirmed in the present case both by the GC and the ECJ.
4. Invalidity and occupational diseases are serious threats to the professional and private lives of staff. Article 78 SR (invalidity allowance) is related to the incapacity to work, while Article 73 SR (insurance coverage) looks at the physical and psychological harm to the integrity of the person. Their scope and preconditions are therefore not identical. In order to claim the related entitlements, timely and accurate action by the staff member is needed once the existence of the disease is known and the staff member possesses all the elements available to claim his rights.
5. The assessment of the Invalidity Committee will include the examination of the links between the disease and the professional activity exercised. As the ECJ confirms in *EIB v KL*, for this assessment the medical opinion must take into account the claimant's working environment.

b. Occupational Disease

The term *occupational disease*[978] is not defined in the Staff Regulations (SR). The definition contained in Article 3(1) of the Common Insurance Rules (CIR) states that the diseases mentioned in the 'European Schedule of Occupational Diseases'[979] shall be considered occupational diseases to the extent that the insured parties have been exposed to the risk of contracting them in the performance of their duties. However, this list is not definitive, as becomes clear from Article 3(2):

> Any disease or aggravation of a pre-existing disease not included in the schedule … shall also be considered an occupational disease if it is sufficiently established that such disease or aggravation arose in the course of or in connection with the performance by the insured parties of their duties with the Communities.

In other words, there shall be an increased protection for those persons whose work makes them more liable to the development of certain diseases by limiting the extent of the requirement to prove that they were occupational in origin. Thus, where the disease which the official contracted is included in the European List of Occupational Diseases, he (or in case of his death, his heirs) need not show that the work was in fact the cause of the disease, but that it is *plausible* that the official contracted it while performing his work, that is to say, that there is a possibility that the disease had its origin in his work.[980] The level of evidence is reduced to plausibility where the disease (or its aggravation)[981] is contained in the list, otherwise (ie, if it is not contained in the list), the level of evidence still does not meet strict standards demonstrating causality, but has to be sufficiently established that the disease arose 'in the course of or in connection with the performance' of the duties. This onus remains, and it will not be sufficient to show only a 'potential causal link' between the performance of duties and the illness if at the same time it is highly probable, on the basis of scientific knowledge, 'that the illness results from a cause that has nothing to do with the performance of those duties'.[982] That decision regarding the possibility of a link is therefore dependent on a scientific appraisal.

Several causes

In complex situations where an official's illness has several causes – professional and non-professional, physical or psychological – each of which has contributed to the occurrence of the illness, the Medical Committee must determine whether there is a direct link between the performance of the service in the Union institutions with the illness of the official, for example, as their triggering factor. In such cases, in order for the disease to be recognised as being of occupational origin, it is not necessary that the performance of the service is the sole, essential or predominant cause of the disease.[983]

Timing

There is no deadline stipulated in the SR nor in its Annexes for bringing the request to recognise the occupational origin of a disease. Yet, for reasons of legal certainty, case-law requires the request to be submitted within *reasonable* time.[984]

[978] GC, T-9/17, ECLI:EU:T:2018:437 – *RI v Council*; GC, T-4/17, ECLI:EU:T:2017:891 – *Coedo Suarez v Council.*

[979] *cf* Annex 1 and 2 to the Commission Recommendation of 19 September 2003 [2003] OJ L238/28.

[980] GC, T-187/95, ECLI:EU:T:1997:119, paras 39/40 – *R v Commission.*

[981] GC, T-252/06 P, ECLI:EU:T:2007:230 – *Beau v Commission.*

[982] GC, T-145/01, ECLI:EU:T:2003:42, paras 95/96 – *Latino v Commission.*

[983] GC, T-567/16, ECLI:EU:2018:708 – *McCoy v Committee of the Regions*; GC, T-4/96, ECLI:EU:T:1997:103 – *S v ECJ*; CST, F-53/09, ECLI:EU:F:2011:52 – *J v Commission.*

[984] GC, T-4/17, ECLI:EU:T:2017:891, paras 42–57 – *Coedo Suarez v Council* (a time of 37 months from the convocation of the Invalidity Committee was considered too long).

c. *Accident*

According to Article 2(1) of the Common Insurance Rules (CIR), an *accident* means 'any sudden occurrence adversely affecting the insured party's bodily or mental health, the cause or one of the causes of which is external to the victim's organism'. The insurance provisions provide some examples of accidents, as well as exclusions from the benefit and exceptions to the exclusions.

The concept of 'accident' is more precisely specified than 'occupational disease'.[985] For instance, the definition of 'accident' encompasses infections, sicknesses and injuries, ruptures of muscles or tendons caused by exertion, or the 'unexplained disappearance of an insured party'.[986] On the other hand, among the items not covered by the insurance under Article 73 SR are (among other listed categories) accidents due to a blood alcohol level of an insured party who is the victim of an accident that exceeds 0.5 mg/ml in the case of accidents resulting from the driving of any motor vehicle, and of more than 1.4 mg/ml in the case of any other accident. Cover is not provided for sports regarded as inherently dangerous, including boxing, karate, bungee jumping, speleology, underwater fishing and certain other sports listed. Case-law has clarified that it is not possible for the administration to extend that list by adding 'similar' sports to it or to have discretion to assess whether the activity in question belongs to the category of sports regarded as dangerous. In earlier insurance conditions, parachuting was listed as a dangerous sport, but paragliding was not. The GC found that the two sports are different and decided that – for the sake of legal certainty – an insured person must have clarity as to the sports that are not covered by the insurance, and should not be left to speculate about the degree of similarity of two sporting activities in this context. Note that in the presently applicable CIR,[987] the sport of 'paragliding' *is* listed as a dangerous sport. But what can be retained from this jurisprudence is that exceptions (ie, exclusions) from insurance cover must not be extended by the argument of 'similarity' or analogy.[988]

5. Article 73 SR Benefit: Lump Sum Payment

a. *Lump Sum as Social Security Benefit*

The benefit for the civil servant under Article 73 (as with Art 78 SR) has the character of a social security benefit;[989] in other words, the lump sum payment is not meant to compensate for damage suffered.[990] If the institution is responsible for the accident or the disease, a separate liability claim for damages may be contemplated where the benefits under the insurance scheme are insufficient to provide full compensation for the injury suffered.[991] In such a case, the benefits received under Article 73 SR following an accident or occupational disease must be taken into account for the purposes of assessing the harm eligible for reparation in an action for damages.

[985] GC, T-62/96, ECLI:EU:T:1998:10 – *De Corte v Commission*; ECJ, 23/81, ECLI:EU:C:1983:239 – *Commission v Royale Belge*; ECJ, 18/70, ECLI:EU:C:1971:65 – *Durrafour v Council*; GC, T-23/95, ECLI:EU:T:1996:3 – *Bitha and Others v Commission*; GC, T-171/00, ECLI:EU:T:2001:238 – *Spruyt v Commission*.

[986] Art 2(2) CIR.

[987] Art 4(1) lit f CIR; GC, T-171/00, ECLI:EU:T:2001:238, paras 31 ff, 64 ff – *Spruyt v Commission*.

[988] See 'Principles of Interpretation', chapter 1, III.4.

[989] Art 73 SR for officials; *cf* Art 28 CEOS in connection with Art 73 SR by analogy for insurance of temporary staff.

[990] As a consequence of this there are no legal interests for delayed payment of the lump sum, at least until the time it is finally determined. However, delays due to irregularities on the part of the institution may lead to a non-contractual liability for the damage suffered from the moment the rate (percentage) of invalidity has been defined, *cf* GC, T-300/97, ECLI:EU:T:199:328, paras 99/100 – *Latino v Commission*.

[991] ECJ, Jd Cases 169/83 and 136/84, ECLI:EU:C:1986:371, paras 13, 18–20 – *Leussink and Others v Commission* (damages of 2 million BFR); GC, T-165/95, ECLI:EU:T:1998:105 – *Lucaccioni* (damage and interest claims dismissed), confirmed in ECJ, C-257/98 P, ECLI:EU:C:1999:402 – *Lucaccioni*.

In the event of death (Art 73(2) lit a SR, Art 10 CIR) the benefit is a lump sum equal to five times the deceased person's annual basic salary. For insurance benefits payable under Article 73(2) lit b SR (total permanent invalidity) in connection with the Common Insurance Rules (Art 11 CIR), the benefit is a lump sum equal to eight times the annual basic salary.

b. Partial Permanent Invalidity

In the event of partial permanent invalidity (Art 73(2) lit c SR), the amount shall be proportionally reduced by reference to the scale laid down in the CIR. Hence, it is calculated as the rate of partial (eg, 20 per cent) invalidity multiplied by the capital amount for total permanent invalidity. This reference to the scale laid down in the CIR does not confer a binding character on the scale. Such wording, which merely implies that the benefit in question is determined on the basis of the types of physical and mental impairment listed by the scale and the invalidity rates or range of invalidity rates associated with them, may not be regarded as giving any indication of whether the scale is binding or optional. By contrast, Article 11(1) CIR, which states that total or partial permanent invalidity is to be measured in terms of physical or mental impairments 'as laid down in the European … scale', must be interpreted, on the basis of the terms used, as requiring the physical and mental impairments to be determined in accordance with the scale, thus conferring on it a binding character. As a consequence of this, the Medical Committee's freedom of assessment is limited to the identification of the pathology from which the insured person is suffering; and once that identification has been made, when it comes to determining the person's physical and mental impairment, that freedom of assessment is circumscribed by the scale laid down in the CIR.[992]

c. Occupational and Non-Occupational Causes of the Invalidity

Where an official's illness has several causes, it is for the Medical Committee to determine whether the performance of their duties is directly related to the illness – for example, where it is a triggering factor. Article 3(1) of the CIR states that the concept of 'occupational disease' is based on the existence of a link between the pathological state of the official and the performance of his Communities-related duties. It is only by virtue of the extent to which that link exists that the illness may be regarded as an occupational disease. Where the Medical Committee finds that a number of causes – occupational and non-occupational – have each directly contributed to the emergence of an official's illness, the appointing authority is under a duty to take that medical finding into account in calculating the amount of the lump sum provided for by Article 73(2) SR.[993]

An additional allowance (Art 13 CIR) or a flat-rate allowance (Art 14 CIR) may also be due. The additional partial permanent invalidity allowance is meant for cases of physical disfigurement, sexual impairment (excluding reproductive impairment), exceptional pain and suffering not established objectively but medically plausible, and impairment of the capacity to participate in leisure activities specific to the insured party.[994] The flat-rate allowance shall be for cases where, as a result of an accident or an occupational disease, the insured party is incapacitated to such an extent that he or she cannot manage without the permanent assistance of another person.

[992] GC, T-390/10, ECLI:EU:T:2012:652, paras 60–62 – *Füller-Tomlinson v EP.*
[993] GC, T-4/96, ECLI:EU:T:1997:103, paras 87/88 – *S v ECJ.*
[994] CST, F-31/10, ECLI:EU:F:2012:80 – *Guittet v Commission and Potvin-Solis.*

Finally, as mentioned above, all expenses (except where excessive or unnecessary) for medical, pharmaceutical, hospital, surgical, prosthesis, radiography, massage, orthopaedic, clinical, transport-related and any other similar expenditures incurred as a result of the accident or occupational disease, are payable where the amount paid under Article 72 SR does not fully cover the expenditure incurred.[995]

d. Procedure of Recognition

The procedure for determining Article 73 SR invalidity is stipulated in Articles 15–24 CIR. Insured parties who sustain an accident shall report the accident to the administration of their own institution. Insured parties who request the application of these rules on the grounds of occupational disease shall submit a statement within a reasonable period following the onset of the disease or the date on which it is first diagnosed. The statement shall specify the nature of the disease and be accompanied by medical certificates or any other supporting documents. This may be followed by an expert medical opinion and a decision on the basis of the findings of the doctor(s) appointed by the institutions or, where the insured party so requests, after consulting the Medical Committee.

e. Decision by the Appointing Authority

Decisions recognising the accidental cause of an occurrence, whether it be an occurrence attributed to occupational or non-occupational risks, and decisions linked thereto, decisions recognising the occupational nature of a disease, or assessing the degree of permanent invalidity, shall be taken by the appointing authority on the basis of the findings of the doctor(s) appointed by the institutions and – where the insured party so requests – after consulting the Medical Committee.[996]

Before taking that decision, the appointing authority shall notify the insured party of the draft decision and of the findings of the doctor(s) appointed by the institution. The insured party or those entitled under him may request that the full medical report be communicated to them or to a doctor chosen by them. Within a period of 60 days the insured party or those entitled under him may request that the Medical Committee deliver its opinion.[997]

f. The Medical Committee

In preparation for the decision, a medical committee is set up which decides independently and whose opinion is binding, provided that the committee is properly staffed, works properly and its reasoned conclusions are understandable.[998] The Medical Committee must be enabled to examine on the basis of all available documents; the choice of documents must not be restricted by the appointing authority.[999] The Medical Committee consists of three doctors: one appointed by

[995] Art 73(3) SR.

[996] Art 18 CIR.

[997] Art 20, Art 22 CIR.

[998] GC, T-213/19, ECLI:EU:T:2020:230, para 44 – *AW v EP*; GC, T-551/16, ECLI:EU:T:2017:751, para 78 – *Lucaccioni v Commission.*

[999] GC, T-187/95, EU:T:1997:119, para 49 – *R v Commission* (all documents which may be useful for the assessments); GC, T-213/19, ECLI:EU:T:2020:230, para 45 – *AW v EP*, see subsequent case study.

the insured party or those entitled under him; one appointed by the appointing authority; and one appointed by agreement between the first two doctors. The terms of reference of the Medical Committee are set by the institution. These shall cover medical issues raised by the report of the doctor representing the insured party or those entitled under him and other relevant medical reports. Typically, such terms of a medical committee will include the following set of tasks and questions:[1000]

- Whether the disease recognised is included in the European List of Occupational Diseases.
  - If so, the committee will enquire if the person has contracted the disease in the course of or in connection with the performance of their duties.
  - If this was not the case, then the question will be whether the disease already existed when taking up their duties, or has worsened since entry into service.
- Then, it shall be examined whether there is a direct link between the disease (or its aggravation) and the performance of the duties.
- The committee shall examine whether the conditions of Article 13 CIR are fulfilled.
- Decide on the date of consolidation.
- Decide on the rate (degree) of permanent invalidity.

g. *Consolidation*

The decision defining the degree (rate) of invalidity shall be taken after the insured party's injuries have *consolidated*. The consequences of the accident or occupational disease shall be considered consolidated when they have stabilised or will diminish only very slowly and in a very limited way (Art 19(3) CIR).

h. *Temporal and Personal Scope of the Benefits under Article 73 SR*

The insurance cover begins with the day of entry into service.[1001] The CIR apply, according to their Article 1, only to 'permanent officials', 'temporary staff' and 'contract agents', and therefore do not cover risks which arose after the official or staff member terminated his service. Although, in the case of occupational disease, Article 16 of the CIR provides that the 'former insured party' (the person who has terminated his service) or his survivors (where the insured party is deceased) may receive the benefits provided for in Article 73(2) SR, such benefits are guaranteed only where the death of the 'former insured party' results from a disease whose symptoms became apparent after the termination of service, but which was caused by his occupation.

The fact that Article 73 SR provides that the death grant may be combined with the benefits provided for in Chapter 3 of Title V of the SR does not prove that the death grant might also be paid to the survivors of an official who was no longer working. Although some Articles of Chapter 3 of the SR concern the recipients of a retirement pension or an invalidity benefit, others, such as Articles 79 and 80 SR, provide for financial benefits to be paid not just to the survivors of the above-mentioned recipients, but also to the survivors of an official who dies while still in service.[1002]

[1000] Levi/Rodrigues et al, *Fonction publique de l'Union européenne* (2020) para 280.
[1001] CST, F-31/10, ECLI:EU:F:2012:80, paras 60–68 – *Guittet v Commission and Potvin-Solis.*
[1002] CST, F-32/08, ECLI:EU:F:2009:3, paras 54/55 – *Klein v Commission.*

i. Aggravation of Injuries or Invalidity

Insured parties may at any time submit a statement concerning the aggravation of their injuries or invalidity and concerning cases that have been terminated (ie, where health has returned in respect of those conditions and again injuries become apparent or pain occurs), accompanied by a report from their personal physician.[1003] The reopening of the file will require the regular procedural steps such as a decision of the appointing authority and (in case) the establishment of a medical committee.[1004]

Case Study on the Files for the Medical Committee

Recognition of occupational diseases: The relevance of supporting files for the Medical Committee is to be assessed by the insured person alone

Case T-213/19, *AW v Parliament* of 28 May 2020

In Brief

The General Court (GC) decided on the recognition of the occupational nature of a disease. The medical opinion issued by the Medical Committee was judged to be irregular because the Committee was not able to examine all the available documents. The appointing authority had forwarded only a selection of files to the Committee and given the instruction that certain documents should be disregarded. The GC ruled that the insured person alone, or those authorised by him or her to do so, has the right to assess the relevance of the said medical reports. When the appointing authority performs a medical assessment of the reports it is exceeding its powers. The staff member concerned is advised to ensure that the Medical Committee is in possession of the complete medical file.

Facts of the Case

The applicant (an official of the European Parliament) had submitted several requests for recognition of the occupational nature of the diseases from which he suffered, in line with Articles 3 and 16 of the Common Insurance Rules (CIR). Following notification by the appointing authority of two draft decisions refusing to recognise the occupational nature of the diseases in question, accompanied by the conclusions of a first doctor (who had been designated by the authority), the applicant requested the matter to be referred to the Medical Committee to give its opinion on those draft decisions. The applicant designated a second doctor to represent him and submitted that doctor's reports, which set out the contested medical questions to the appointing authority. The Medical Committee was composed of the two above-mentioned doctors plus a third one. The doctor chosen by the applicant sent a number of documents (34 in total) to the third doctor; these documents had initially been submitted by the applicant in support of his requests for recognition of

[1003] Art 21 CIR.
[1004] GC, T-556/93, ECLI:EU:T:1995:93, para 50 – *Saby v Commission*.

the occupational nature of the diseases in question, but they had not been disclosed to the Medical Committee. The third doctor received instructions from the Parliament to disregard these documents. After the medical reports drawn up by the Committee were submitted, the appointing authority rejected the requests to recognise the occupational nature of the diseases in question.

The Arguments of the Parties and the Decision of the GC

In support of his action for annulment the applicant argued that the Medical Committee did not have before it a complete file containing all the documents that he had submitted since the initiation of the procedures for recognition of the occupational nature of the diseases from which he was suffering. Therefore, according to the applicant, the Committee did not have access to all the available documents that were liable to be of use in its assessments, in breach of Article 22(3) CIR.

The GC first pointed out that it follows from Article 22(3) CIR that for a medical committee validly to issue a medical opinion, it must be in a position to have notice of all the available documents liable to be of use in its assessments. However, in the present case, it was common ground that the Parliament did not disclose to the Medical Committee certain documents initially submitted by the applicant, including medical reports which concluded that the diseases in question were occupational in nature. According to the explanations provided in that regard by the Parliament, it had disregarded those documents after finding that some of them were identical to those already in its possession; others were unrelated to the medical questions submitted; and, finally, others contained similar information – in other words, without being identical, they repeated information and conclusions that the Medical Committee already had in its possession.

More specifically, in respect of the non-transmission of that last category of documents, the GC then found that the Parliament had made a medical assessment of the documents which exceeded the scope of its powers. In fact, when an insured person asks the Medical Committee to give its opinion, the Parliament's sole task is to define the terms of reference provided to the Committee. Those terms of reference must refer to the Committee the medical questions raised in the medical reports that the insured person considered necessary to disclose to the doctor or doctors designated by the institution for the purposes of applying the provisions of the Common Insurance Rules. It was therefore up to the insured person alone, or those entitled by him or her to do so, to assess the relevance of the medical reports removed from the file.

By deciding on medical matters with a view to drawing up the file submitted to the Medical Committee, the Parliament had consequently exceeded the scope of its powers and undermined the validity of the work of the Medical Committee. In those circumstances, the Medical Committee could not be regarded as having been able to examine all the available documents liable to be of use in its assessments. Since the Medical Committee had carried out its task under improper circumstances, the reports which it had sent to the appointing authority at the end of its work were flawed.

Since the documents on which the Parliament had made a medical assessment were clearly linked to the applicant's illnesses, the GC found that it was not ruled out that, if the Medical Committee had been able to examine those documents, its conclusions might have been different. Since the contested decisions had been adopted on the basis of irregular reports from the Medical Committee, they were vitiated by a procedural defect such as to justify their annulment.

Comments

1. The CIR stipulate that the institution shall define the terms of reference of the Medical Committee (Art 22(2)), and they prescribe (Art 22(3)): 'The Medical Committee shall examine collectively all the available documents liable to be of use to it in its assessment'. The judgment at hand clarifies that the appointing authority must not narrow the scope of documents available to the Medical Committee, but must leave it to the assessment of the insured person (or his/her representative) to decide whether a document shall form part of the file that is to be made available to the Committee. The medical usefulness of a document is not to be decided on by the appointing authority.
2. Settled case-law prepares this conclusion by stating that it is the task of medical experts to make definitive appraisals of all medical questions. The Committee's task of making an objective and independent assessment of medical matters requires that it has complete freedom of assessment.[1005]
3. Case-law thus takes a narrow approach when determining the authority of the institution to define the terms of reference of the Medical Committee.
4. In view of this, it is in practical terms recommended to an insured person who seeks recognition of the occupational nature of his or her disease to check carefully whether the Medical Committee is in possession of the complete medical file required to take an informed decision. One should specifically make sure that all medical reports in favour of the occupational nature of the disease have actually been handed over and are available to the Medical Committee when forming its opinion.

6. Article 78 SR Benefit: Invalidity Allowance

a. Invalidity Allowance

Civil servants[1006] who have acquired a total permanent invalidity preventing them from performing their duties corresponding to a post in their career bracket as recognised by the Invalidity Committee,[1007] and who are obliged on these grounds to end their service, are entitled to an invalidity allowance for so long as such incapacity persists.[1008] The allowance shall be equal to 70 per cent of the official's last basic salary.[1009] However, it may not be less than the minimum subsistence figure. The invalidity allowance shall be subject to contributions to the pension

[1005] ECJ, C-185/90 P, ECLI:EU:C:1991:380, para 24 – *Commission v Gill*; GC, T-84/98, ECLI:EU:T:2000:156, para 43 – *C v Council*; T-187/95, ECLI:EU:T:1997:119 – *R v Commission.*

[1006] *cf* for members of temporary staff: Art 33 CEOS.

[1007] GC, T-370/20, ECLI:EU:T:2021:822, paras 83 ff – *KL v EIB*; confirmed by ECJ, C-68/22 P, ECLI:EU:C:2022:1029 – *EIB v KL.*

[1008] Art 13(1) Annex VIII SR.

[1009] Art 78 SR in connection with Arts 13–16 of Annex VIII SR. Reithmann (2008) *EuR* 292; GC, T-462/17, ECLI:EU:T:2019:397, para 92 – *TO v EEA.*

scheme, calculated on the basis of that allowance. In accordance with Article 53 SR, the official shall automatically be retired on the last day of the month in which the appointing authority recognises his permanent incapacity to perform his duties.

b. *Qualifications under Article 78(5) SR*

Where the invalidity arises from an accident in the course of, or in connection with, the performance of an official's duties, from an occupational disease, from a public-spirited act, or from risking his life to save another human being, the invalidity allowance may not be less than 120 per cent of the minimum subsistence figure (Art 78(5) SR). Moreover, contributions to the pension scheme shall then be paid in full from the budget of the institution.

It is up to the official to submit the request for recognition of the occupational origin of a disease, and up to the institution concerned to initiate the procedure by a consultation of the Invalidity Committee. In other words, the institution may not dispense with the procedural requirements and immediately recognise the occupational origin of the disease itself; doing so would disregard the role of the Invalidity Committee.[1010] This is correct to assume for the recognition of the occupational origin, but should be different for the other three types of qualification mentioned in Article 78(5) SR, because they are not of a medical nature.

c. *Maximum Age of Entitlement*

Interestingly, while the 2014 reform raised the retirement age of newly entering officials to 66 years,[1011] the legislature did not adjust the maximum age of entitlement to an invalidity allowance under Article 13 Annex VII SR in connection with Article 78 SR: this remained unchanged at 64 years ('less than 65 years').

d. *The Invalidity Committee and its Procedure*

The recognition of total permanent invalidity preventing an official from performing his duties is the task of the Invalidity Committee.[1012] It will also decide on the occupational origin of a disease, or on the origin stemming from an accident respectively. The Committee consists of three doctors: one appointed by the institution to which the official concerned belongs; one appointed by the official concerned; and one appointed by agreement between the first two doctors.[1013] Both the institution and the official may decide to change their choice of doctor, for example if the originally appointed person is no longer available.[1014]

The assessment carried out by the Invalidity Committee is an individual one, and is oriented towards the capacity of the official to perform the duties corresponding to a post in his career bracket. The Committee is convened to provide a medical assessment, not a legal one.[1015] For its part, the institution is bound, from a medical point of view, by the findings of the Committee.[1016] The Committee is convened either at the initiative of the official (via the appointing authority); or

[1010] CST, F-118/11, ECLI:EU:F:2014:23, paras 63, 68 – *Marcuccio v Commission.*
[1011] Above, section IV.5.
[1012] Art 13 Annex VIII SR, Art 9 SR.
[1013] Art 7 Annex II SR.
[1014] GC, T-376/02, ECLI:EU:T:2004:338, para 42 – *O v Commission.*
[1015] CST, F-69/07, ECLI:EU:F:2009:128, para 37 – *O v Commission*; ECJ, 25/86, ECLI:EU:C:1986:485, para 6 – *Suss v Commission*; ECJ, C-18/91 P, ECLI:EU:C:1992:269, para 26 – *V v EP.*
[1016] CST, F-69/07, ECLI:EU:F:2009:128, para 37 – *O v Commission.*

it is convened at the initiative of the appointing authority, specifically where the official's sick leave totals more than 12 months in any period of three years, Article 59(4) SR.

The appointing authority has no power to conduct medical assessments. Once the official has requested the start of the invalidity procedure, the appointing authority is required to initiate that procedure and has practically no leeway to disregard this request. It may only reject an application for the convening of an invalidity committee if it has objective, undisputed evidence that the basic conditions laid down in the respective provisions are not satisfied.[1017] The cost relating to the Invalidity Committee shall be borne by the institution to which the official concerned belongs (except for the additional fees of a doctor who is resident elsewhere and has been appointed by the official).[1018] The official may submit to the Invalidity Committee any reports or certificates from his regular doctor or from any other medical practitioners whom he may have consulted.

The proceedings of the Committee shall be secret.[1019] The Invalidity Committee's conclusions shall be communicated to the appointing authority and to the official concerned. The Committee considers medical questions 'entirely objectively and independently', with 'complete freedom of appraisal'.[1020] The obligation to give reasons for an opinion of the Invalidity Committee must be reconciled with the requirements of medical confidentiality: the person concerned may request notification of the reasons for being declared unfit to a doctor of his own choice.[1021]

e. *Time of Application for Invalidity*

There is no stipulated 'minimum duration' of illness before an official may request a convening of the Invalidity Committee.[1022] Such a condition based on a previous duration of sickness or sick leave could preclude staff members who suffered a sudden or rapid deterioration in their state of health, or who were victims of an accident, from being covered against those risks. For that reason, the condition regarding the length of previous sick leave under Article 59(4) SR quoted above (where the sick leave totals more than 12 months in any period of three years) is not applicable where the staff member himself requests the initiation of an invalidity procedure.[1023]

Case-law has clarified that an official who has *left the service* and who suffers from an illness which would render him incapable of performing his duties if he were still in active employment is not entitled to request, on that ground alone, the initiation of the procedure to establish invalidity. He must, in addition, have been 'obliged to end his service with the Communities' because he is suffering from an invalidity preventing him from performing his duties.[1024] This leads to the conclusion that the official must submit his request to convene the Invalidity Committee while still being in active service.

The procedure for being retired on grounds of invalidity may not be initiated during an official's leave on personal grounds (*congé de convenance personnelle*, CCP) unless the staff member was acquiring pension rights in accordance with Article 40(3)(2) SR.[1025]

[1017] GC, T-284/07 P, ECLI:EU:T:2008:533, paras 78–82 – *EUIPO v López Teruel.*

[1018] Art 8 Annex II SR.

[1019] Art 9 Annex II SR.

[1020] ECJ, C-2/87, ECLI:EU:C:1988:17, para 19 – *Biedermann v ECA.*

[1021] GC, T-196/95, ECLI:EU:T:1997:79, para 95 – *H v Commission.*

[1022] CST, F-97/06, ECLI:EU:F:2007:86 – *López Teruel v EUIPO.*

[1023] CST, F-119/05, ECLU:EU:F:2007:11, paras 28–34 – *Gesner v EUIPO*; GC, T-84/98, ECLI:EU:T:2000:156, paras 67/68 – *C v Council.*

[1024] ECJ, Case 12/83, ECLI:EU:C:1984:182, para 13 – *Bähr v Commission*; ECJ, C-181/03 P, ECLI:EU:C:2005:18, paras 35–40 – *Nardone v Commission.*

[1025] GC, T-9/01, ECLUI:EU:T:2002:154, para 13 – *Becker v ECA*; confirmed by ECJ, C-260/02 P, ECLI:EU:C:2005:119 – *Becker v ECA.*

Case Study on Invalidity and Occupational Origin of the Disease

The Staff Regulations provide considerable social protection for staff members suffering from partial or total invalidity or occupational diseases

Case T-9/17, *RI v Council* of 12 July 2018
Case T-4/17, *Coedo Suarez v Council* of 13 December 2017

Facts and Court Decision

The applicant, having worked for several years as a translator for the Council, suffered from health problems involving her left hand. The procedure for acknowledging her illness as an occupational disease under Article 73 of the Service Regulations (SR) was successful, but the Council refused to acknowledge her permanent invalidity under Article 78 SR with the argument that the permanent invalidity did not result from an occupational disease.

The General Court (GC) annulled this decision of the Council, because it was based on an erroneous opinion of the Invalidity Committee. The GC found that the Invalidity Committee did not deliver a proper reasoning, but only stated that the disease was not of occupational origin; the Invalidity Committee did not assess whether the applicant was exposed to the risk of acquiring the disease from which the invalidity resulted while exercising her service functions. The definition and determination of a certain disease and the link between several diseases are medical questions and are therefore not to be decided by the judges. The GC held that a proper reasoning in the assessment of the Invalidity Committee is required because it allows the staff member to understand the assessment, and allows the GC to exercise its judicial control.

Comments

1. In *RI v Council*[1026] the GC only had to deal with the pension entitlement under Article 78 SR. The assessment delivered by the Invalidity Committee was deficient, with the consequence that the Council was not allowed to base its decision on it. It was therefore correct for the GC to annul the Council decision that refused to acknowledge an occupational origin for the applicant's disease.
2. The other entitlement, namely the lump sum payment under the insurance coverage (Art 73 SR) has to be claimed in a separate procedure in which another committee (the Medical Committee) renders its opinion to the insurance company and the institution. In *RI v Council*, the committees of the two proceedings (Art 73 and Art 78 SR) reached different conclusions regarding the question of whether the disease was *of occupational origin*.
3. Both procedures can be started in parallel. *Psychological harassment* can also lead to the development of a disease that must be recognised as being of occupational origin, with the consequence of an entitlement to the social benefits under Article 73 and

[1026] GC, T-9/17, ECLI:EU:T:2018:437 – *RI v Council*.

Article 78 SR, as described above. The request to recognise an occupational origin of a disease must be brought by the staff member within a reasonable time.[1027]

4. There is an obligation on the institution to complete these procedures reasonably fast. In a number of cases the courts had to impose damages on the institution for not handling the procedure within a reasonable time.
5. The decision to refuse the occupational origin of a disease can be annulled if the Invalidity Committee has based its decision on an *erroneous understanding* of an occupational disease.
6. If the disease figures in the *European Schedule of Occupational Diseases* it is sufficient for a staff member to show the *plausibility* of having acquired the disease at work, ie, that the disease probably has its origin in the occupational activity.
7. The opinion of the Invalidity Committee has to contain a *proper reasoning*. The proper constitution and functioning of the Invalidity Committee are also subject to judicial control.

7. Review of Decisions on Invalidity

The central questions for the review of decisions on invalidity are whether either the medical assessments and/or the decisions taken by the appointing authority on the basis of medical assessments are subject to judicial control.

Legal vs medical assessment

As a preliminary remark, it is key to bear in mind that the Medical Committee's task is confined to rendering opinions of a purely scientific nature, excluding any legal assessment. For example, the Medical Committee must not be called on by an institution to establish whether a health disorder and/or its cause may be considered to be an 'accident' within the meaning of the SR. The determination of an event as an 'accident' is a legal assessment, not for the Medical Committee to determine. Should a medical committee – and likewise an invalidity committee – render a legal assessment, it must be clearly distinguished from its medical assessments. Medical assessments are considered to be final, subject to the conditions mentioned below. However, should a medical committee deliver *legal* assessments, they are not considered to be final. In particular, the court has jurisdiction to examine whether the appointing authority, in ratifying the Medical Committee's opinion referring to a legal assessment, complied with the SR.[1028]

In cases where an institution (erroneously) asked the Medical Committee to express an opinion on a legal question, this cannot release the institution from liability, because it cannot affect the validity of the decision to be taken by the institution in response to the Medical Committee's report.

Finally, there also remains a limited scope for review regarding the *medical* aspect of appraisals that lead to decisions relating to invalidity of staff. According to settled case-law,

[1027] GC, T-4/17, ECLI:EU:T:2017:891, paras 42 ff – *Coedo Suarez v Council.*

[1028] GC, T-2/00, ECLI:EU:T:2001:50, paras 41–44 – *N v Commission.*

medical appraisals are considered definitive when the conditions in which they are issued are *not irregular.* Any appraisal of reviewability should therefore focus on ascertaining the existence of regular or irregular conditions affecting the Committee's work, as the following paragraphs illustrate.[1029]

a. Criteria for (Ir-)Regular Conditions of Medical Appraisals

Judicial review can extend only to the questions of whether a medical or invalidity committee was properly constituted and conducted its business in accordance with correct procedures, and whether the opinions it has issued satisfy the formal requirements. Hence, the courts confine their review to a check of the committee's compliance with the rules relating to its proper constitution and functioning, ie, the regularity (or irregularity) of the conditions under which the committee has acted.[1030]

Own doctor and completeness of documentation

An important assumption relating to the regularity of these conditions is stipulated in Article 7 Annex II SR, which assures officials that their rights and interests will be safeguarded by the presence on the committee of a doctor whom they trust.[1031] For a medical committee validly to issue a medical opinion, it must be in a position to be notified of all the documents which may be useful for its assessments.[1032]

Justification/statement of reasons

The courts will examine whether the medical opinion contains a statement of reasons enabling the reader to assess the considerations on which the conclusions were based and whether it has established a comprehensible link between the medical findings and the conclusions reached by the committee.[1033] This requirement of a justification casts doubt on a practice (initiated by appointing authorities or the committees themselves) that limits itself to simply filling in standard forms.[1034] As with the review carried out in areas involving complex assessments, judicial oversight of the opinion will check whether the evidence relied on is factually accurate, reliable and consistent; whether that evidence contains all the relevant information which must be taken into account when assessing a complex situation; and whether it is capable of substantiating the conclusions drawn from it.

Likewise, when assessing complex medical issues relating to a difficult diagnosis, or the causal relationship between the illnesses of the person concerned and the exercise of their professional activity, the Medical Committee has to indicate which part of the file it is basing its opinion on, and, in the case of significant divergence, it has to state the reasons for its deviation from relevant previous medical reports that are more favourable for the person concerned.[1035]

[1029] On regular and irregular conditions: Levi/Rodrigues et al, *Fonction publique de l'Union européenne* (2020) 116–19.
[1030] ECJ, C-156/80, ECLI:EU:C:1981:117, para 20 – *Morbelli.*
[1031] GC, T-376/94, ECLI:EU:T:1996:41, para 47 – *Otten v Commission.*
[1032] GC, T-187/95, ECLI:EU:T:1997:119, para 49 – *R v Commission.*
[1033] GC, T-165/89, ECLI:EU:T:1992:27, para 75 – *Plug*; ECJ, C-257/81, ECLI:EU:C:1983:2 – *K v Council*; ECJ, 277/84, ECLI:EU:C:1987:540, para 15 – *Jänsch v Commission*; GC, T-567/16, ECLI:EU:2018:708, paras 67, 98 – *McCoy v Committee of the Regions.*
[1034] Levi/Rodrigues et al, *Fonction publique de l'Union européenne* (2020) para 305.
[1035] GC, T-300/97, ECLI:EU:T:199:328, paras 69 ff – *Latino v Commission*; CST, F-41/06, ECLI:EU:F:2008:132, paras 64 ff – *Marcuccio v Commission.*

Erroneous view concerning a legal term

The court also has the jurisdiction to annul any decision taken by the appointing authority in the application of a particular legal term if it is vitiated by illegality, to the extent that it is based on an irrelevant conclusion reached by a medical committee. That would be the case if the Medical Committee adopted an erroneous view of the concept of 'occupational disease' or if its report did not establish a comprehensible link between the medical findings which it contains and the conclusions it draws.[1036]

b. Not Found to be Irregular

Case-law has clarified that the following conditions under which medical assessments were issued were *not found to be irregular*:

- The absence of minutes of the committee's considerations, or the refusal of a member of the committee to sign the report, or disagreement among the committee members, as long as that member had an opportunity to make his opinion known to the other doctors on the committee.[1037] Also, decisions of the committee need not to be taken by unanimity, but may be taken by majority of the doctors.[1038]
- The fact of the committee not hearing the official. The proceedings of an invalidity committee do not take place within the context of an *inter partes* administrative procedure instituted against an official, nor are they intended to settle a dispute between the administration and its employee. That being the case, the official cannot rely on 'rights of the defence' in the committee's appraisal process.[1039]
- The fact that medical files were not shared with the official concerned directly, but only with his doctor. The indirect access to the file is justified by legitimate interests of confidentiality and professional secrecy, as well as the exercising of a duty of care towards the official, especially – but not only – in cases involving psychological illness.[1040]
- The fact that the institution appoints the doctor approved by the insurer.[1041] In addition, contacts between the appointing authority and the insurer do not in themselves constitute an irregularity.[1042]
- The freedom of the committee regarding the extent to which account should be taken of medical reports drawn up in advance, at the request of either the official or the institution. The committee shall consider medical questions entirely objectively and independently, and requires complete freedom of appraisal.[1043]

[1036] ECJ, C-189/82, ECLI:EU:C:1984:29, para 15 – *Seiler and Others v Commission.*

[1037] ECJ, 277/84, ECLI:EU:C:1987:540, paras 13/14 – *Jänsch v Commission.*

[1038] ibid; ECJ, 31/71, ECLI:EU:C:1975:39 – *Gigante v Commission.*

[1039] CST, F-41/06 RENV, ECLI:EU:F:2012:149, para 79 – *Marcuccio v Commission.*

[1040] Section V.4.a. above; ECJ, C-283/90 P, ECLI:EU:C:1991:361 – *Vidrányi*; CST, F-84/12, ECLI:EU:F:2013:128, para 51 – *CN v Council.*

[1041] ECJ, C-186/80, ECLI:EU:C:1981:179, para 11 – *Suss v Commission.*

[1042] GC, T-64/94, ECLI:EU:T:1995:197, para 80 – *Benecos v Commission.*

[1043] ECJ, C-2/87, ECLI:EU:C:1988:17, para 19 – *Biedermann v ECA.*

4

Collective EU Civil Service Law

The staff employed at the European Union institutions enjoy the right of association. They may 'in particular be members of trade unions or staff associations of European officials'.[1] Their co-determination rights are not rooted in the national labour law of the place of employment, but solely in the Staff Regulations (SR)[2] or other provisions of Union law. While trade unions or staff associations are external to the institutions, the Staff Committee is a constituent of collective labour law foreseen and designed by the SR and one of the six social welfare bodies mentioned in Article 9 SR.

Officials' and other servants' freedom of trade union activity implies that trade union or employees' organisations have the right to do anything lawful to protect the interests of their members as employees. The EU institutions must allow the trade union or employees' organisations to carry out their representative and consultative tasks on all matters affecting staff, and must not impose any penalty whatsoever on officials or servants by reason of their trade union activities. Further, they must refrain from doing anything that might impede the freedom of trade union activity.[3] A minimum standard of protection can be drawn from Article 7 of Directive 2002/14[4] according to which the Member States shall ensure that employees' representatives, when carrying out their functions, enjoy adequate protection and guarantees to enable them to perform properly the duties which have been assigned to them. This protection would, for example, lead to the annulment of a dismissal decision if it was adopted because of the staff member's activity for trade unions or employees' organisations (staff representation).[5]

The following sections focus on the role of the Staff Committee, the freedom of association and collective bargaining, aspects of social dialogue in EU civil service law and the right to strike for EU servants.

I. Staff Committee

Article 9(1) SR and Annex II SR provide that a staff committee shall be set up within each institution, organised in sections for the different places of employment. This serves to ensure that

[1] Art 24b SR; Art 12 FRC. In regard to the terminology, *associations* is the broader term and relates to privately organised groups or organisations by their professional activity, industry, sector, geographic or institutional affiliation. Also a delimitation in time is conceivable, as eg, an association representing the particular interests of former or retired staff.

[2] ECJ, C-165/01, ECLI:EU:C:2003:401 – *Betriebsrat der Vertretung der Europäischen Kommission in Österreich*.

[3] GC, T-571/17 RENV, ECLI:EU:T:2023:351, paras 160–62 – *UG v Commission*; ECJ, Jd Cases C-193/87 and C-194/87, ECLI:EU:C:1990:18, paras 13 ff – *Maurissen and Others v ECA*.

[4] Directive 2002/14/EC of the European Parliament and of the Council of 11 March 2002 establishing a general framework for informing and consulting employees in the European Community – Joint declaration of the European Parliament, the Council and the Commission on employee representation [2002 [OJ L80/29–34.

[5] GC, T-571/17, ECLI:EU:T:2020:141, paras 158 ff – *UG v Commission* (the applicant sat in the local and the Central staff Committee); ECJ, C-405/08, ECLI:EU:C:2010:69, paras 58/59 – *Ingeniørforeningen i Danmark*.

staff have an appropriate say on aspects relevant for the employment relationship, for example in order to be consulted at the time of the adoption of a salary adjustment.[6] Unlike trade unions and professional associations, the staff committees do not have the right to file applications at the court.[7] Their formation by elections as well as their role and functions shall be contemplated below, followed by some considerations on the consequences of engaging in staff committees, and on the amount of time spent for staff representation.

1. Elections to the Staff Committee

The conditions for election to the Staff Committee shall be laid down by the general meeting of officials of the institution in service at the relevant place of employment. Election shall be by secret ballot.[8] The term of office of its members (and their alternates if any) shall be three years, whereas the appointing authority may shorten the term, but not to less than one year.[9] Every official of the institution shall be entitled to vote and stand for election. It is common and acceptable to have a system of personal direct elections and proportional representation via lists of trade unions.[10] Each group can submit only one electoral list, but it is permissible for individual members to submit a competing list, indicating their affiliation, so long as confusion is avoided.[11] The elections to the Staff Committee (except in local sections) need to reach a quorum: they shall be valid only if two-thirds of the officials entitled to vote take part. However, if this proportion is not attained, the second vote shall be valid if the majority of those entitled take part. The rules make it compulsory to hold a second or even third ballot where, at the end of the first ballot and second ballot respectively, the required quorum, set at two-thirds of voters and the majority of voters respectively, has not been attained.[12] If necessary, the election result obtained in this way is revised in order to ensure that both function groups and all staff enumerated in Article 7(1) of the Conditions of Employment of Other Servants (CEOS) are actually represented.[13]

Elections and the electoral system are subject to supervision by the appointing authority.[14] The appointing authority has no power to determine the categories of staff entitled to vote for the competent staff committee,[15] nor is it obliged to secure a seat for all groups on the governing bodies of the relevant staff committee.[16] The appointing authority may not determine the

[6] See GC, T-63/02, ECLI:EU:T:2003:308 – *Cerafogli and Poloni v ECB*; Reithmann (2014) *EuR* 120.

[7] See chapter 2, III. Levi, 'Droits fondamentaux et principes general de droit de la fonction publique' in Govaere/Vandersanden (eds), *La fonction publique communautaire* (2008) 107.

[8] Art 1(2) Annex II SR.

[9] Art 1(1) Annex II SR.

[10] GC, T-192/96, ECLI:EU:T:1998:162 – *Lebedef v Commission*; GC, T-534/93, ECLI:EU:T:1994:86 – *Grynberg and Others v Commission*. Georgakakis, 'La fonction publique européenne au prisme de ses syndicats: Contribution à une sociologie de la formation du groupe des eurofonctionnaires' in Costa/Magnette (eds), *Réflexions sur la fracture démocratique de l'Union européenne* (2007) 89 ff, speaks of a turnout of over 60%.

[11] GC, T-368/94, ECLI:EU:T:1996:2 – *Blanchard v Commission*.

[12] CST, F-82/11, ECLI:EU:F:2013:139, para 60 – *Loukakis and Others v Commission*.

[13] Art 1 para 4 Annex II SR; *cf* GC, T-534/93, ECLI:EU:T:1994:86 – *Grynberg and Others v Commission*; GC, T-42/98, ECLI:EU:T:1999:247 – *Sabbatucci v EP*; and GC, T-42/98 R, ECLI:EU:T:1998:189.

[14] ECJ, 146/85 and 431/85, ECLI:EU:C:1987:457 – *Diezler and Others* v *EESC*; GC, T-534/93, ECLI:EU:T:1994:86 – *Grynberg and Others v Commission*; ECJ, 54/75, ECLI:EU:C:1976:127, paras 54/55 – *De Dapper and Others v EP*; GC, T-28/89, ECLI:EU:T:1990:18, para 32 – *Maindiaux and Others v EESC*; CST, F-82/11, ECLI:EU:F:2013:139, para 40 – *Loukakis and Others v Commission*.

[15] GC, T-182/94, ECLI:EU:T:1996:130 – *Marx Esser and Del Amo Martinez v EP* (deleted from the list of voters the entire category of staff members on leave for personal reasons).

[16] GC, T-35/98, ECLI:EU:T:1999:23 – *Hecq and SFIE v Commission*.

procedure for appointing the members of the Central Staff Committee, but it is under a duty (ex officio) to take action in order to ensure compliance so that officials can appoint their representatives in complete freedom.[17]

2. Role and Functions of the Staff Committee

As to its role and functions, the Staff Committee shall represent the interests of the staff vis-à-vis their institution and maintain continuous contact between the institution and the staff.[18] It shall contribute to the 'smooth running of the service' by providing a 'channel for the expression of opinion by the staff', and any difficulty having general implications concerning the interpretation and application of the SR. The Committee shall submit to the competent bodies of the institution suggestions concerning the organisation and operation of the service and proposals for the improvement of staff working conditions or general living conditions. An institution is not obliged, on the other hand, to consult the Staff Committee on all measures taken by that institution relating to the running of the service.[19]

The Committee shall participate in the management and supervision of social welfare bodies set up by the institution in the interests of its staff. It may, with the consent of the institution, set up such welfare services.[20] For example, it appoints representatives of the staff for the Joint Committee,[21] the Reports Committee,[22] Disciplinary Board[23] and the Selection Board.[24] The Joint Committee is primarily to be consulted on personnel matters in keeping with the SR[25] and 'on questions of a general nature'.[26] It may be established for two or more institutions.[27] The Staff Regulations Committee, which is made up of representatives of the institutions and an equal number of representatives of their staff committees, shall be consulted by the Commission on all proposals to revise the SR.

3. Consequences of Activity in the Staff Committee

The general line is that an activity in the Staff Committee must not engender disadvantages for the staff member. Even more, to quote an extreme example, a dismissal of an employees' representative on the ground of his status or the functions which he performs in the capacity as a representative would be illegal.[28] On the other hand, the fact that an official takes up an activity

[17] The duty is less strict where the composition of the Committee (proportionality of the number of representatives to the electoral result) is at stake, CST, F-71/05, ECLI:EU:F:2007:184, para 77 – *Milella and Campanella v Commission* (inadmissible pressure of the institution to use the d'Hondt method); GC, T-65/91, ECLI:EU:T:1994:3, paras 103–07 – *White v Commission*; GC, T-396/03, ECLI:EU:T:2005:406, paras 52–54 – *Vanhellemont v Commission.*

[18] Art 9(3) SR.

[19] CST, F-48/06, ECLI:EU:F:2008:137, paras 115/116 – *Avanzata and Others v Commission.*

[20] The ECJ gives a broad interpretation to the right of co-determination, on the basis of the principles of general labour law of the Member States: GC, T-192/99, ECLI:EU:T:2001:72 – *Dunnett and Others v EIB.*

[21] Art 9(4) SR, Art 2 Annex II SR.

[22] Art 10 Annex II SR.

[23] Arts 5, 6 Annex IX SR.

[24] Art 3 Annex III SR.

[25] eg, Arts 13, 16, 39 lit e, 40(4d), 41(2), 41(5), 49 SR.

[26] Art 9(4) SR.

[27] Art 9(1a) SR.

[28] GC, T-571/17, ECLI:EU:T:2020:141, paras 158 ff – *UG v Commission*; ECJ, C-405/08, ECLI:EU:C:2010:69, paras 58/59 – *Ingeniørforeningen i Danmark.*

in staff representation may cause a need to reorganise work procedures or structures; an activity in staff representation in itself cannot serve as reason to hinder the adoption of an organisational change which may be a burden on the official, but which is necessary.[29] Staff representation activity does not give any right to obtain special points in the appraisal or promotion procedures.[30] Mere differences of opinion between an official in this capacity and his superior do not justify the suspicion of the superior's bias in his decisions to the detriment of the staff representative, as long as there is no connection to his personal situation.[31]

4. Time Dedicated to Staff Representation, Secondment and Agreements

Case-law has opined on the amount of time that may be dedicated to staff representation purposes. Typically, it is in the interests of an institution, but also of trade unions and of staff members themselves if staff assume a certain portion of the staff representation duties while not being on secondment. The SR are intended to facilitate the participation of officials in staff representation, in particular by enabling them to carry out those duties within the working time prescribed for their normal service in their institution, and not in addition to it. For other staff not specifically seconded, participation in staff representation is occasional and takes up a relatively limited percentage of working time.[32]

The relations between an institution and the trade union or professional organisations may be governed by agreements which grant benefits to those organisations on the basis of their representativeness, such as possible secondments for trade union purposes, the granting of loans and the services of external staff. A typical conflict situation arises where an institution refuses to grant leave of absence to a staff member for assuming staff representation activities (eg, secondment for trade union purposes). In line with their remit, such agreements are only intended to govern collective labour relations between the administration and those organisations. Agreements are deemed not to fall into the sphere of individual working relations between the institution and the official. While such an agreement is therefore capable of harming the interests of one of those organisations, it is not capable of affecting the individual situation of officials belonging to it, particularly the individual exercise of one of the trade union rights granted pursuant to Article 24b SR or of a right resulting from an agreement reached between the institution and the trade union or professional organisations. Therefore, a staff member is not directly affected by such an agreement. Only the trade union and professional organisations are individually affected in this respect and are therefore able to use the remedies available to them to protect their own interests. As case-law specifies on this, only if the weakened position of a trade union (or other organisation) resulting from such an agreement would deprive its members of the normal exercise of their trade union rights, 'officials acting in an individual capacity might claim an interest in bringing proceedings on the basis of the weakened position of the organisation to which they belong'.[33] However, if one of those organisations or trade unions has been granted a secondment by such an agreement and has designated a named official to receive that secondment, any decision by the appointing authority refusing to allow that official to receive that secondment would adversely affect the official and could then be the subject of an action for annulment. In brief, if

[29] CST, F-47/09, ECLI:EU:F:2010:36, paras 104–09 – *Fries Guggenheim v Cedefop.*

[30] CST, F-124/07, ECLI:EU:F:2009:104, para 51 – *Behmer v EP*; CST, F-108/06, ECLI:EU:F:2007:231, para 37 – *Diomede Basili v Commission.*

[31] CST, F-47/09, ECLI:EU:F:2010:36, paras 79, 67 – *Fries Guggenheim v Cedefop.*

[32] CST, F-39/08, ECLI:EU:F:2009:85, paras 49/50 – *Lebedef v Commission.*

[33] CST, F-137/07, ECLI:EU:F:2009:46, para 84 – *Sergio and Others v Commission.*

the institution refuses a staff member leave of absence for staff representation activities (secondment for trade union purposes), the person concerned cannot object to this unless the trade union had designated her or him for that secondment.[34]

II. Freedom of Association: Triangle of Representation, Staff and Institutions

As part of their freedom of association,[35] the staff of the institutions may belong to professional associations and trade unions, which are entitled to represent the interests of their members vis-à-vis the appointing authorities, but also in all co-determination bodies. Under Article 28 of the Fundamental Rights Charter (FRC), staff members, professional associations and trade unions have the right of collective bargaining and collective action. They enjoy the 'right to negotiate and conclude collective agreements at the appropriate levels and, in cases of conflicts of interest, to take collective action to defend their interests, including strike action'.

1. Elections and Other Engagement

Associations and trade unions take part in staff elections with their own lists, and are allowed be a party to legal proceedings. The Union's system of legal protection, which is based on protecting individuals' rights, does not allow the associations and trade unions to file applications to enforce the collective interests of their members.[36] Nor can the EU institution be compelled by legal means to implement a finalised agreement that results from the dialogue between the social partners.[37] Where they are not themselves entitled to bring an action as the addressee of an act under Union law,[38] or otherwise defend their own rights, professional associations and trade unions can, in principle, join individual actions filed by their members as interveners, provided that the legal dispute affects their collective interests.[39]

2. No Duty of Collective Care

Individual staff members can rely on a duty of care as illustrated above,[40] which reflects the balance of reciprocal rights and duties in the relationship between the institution and its officials as individuals.[41] However, staff associations and trade unions may not rely on the duty of

[34] ibid, *Sergio and Others v Commission*, paras 70–84.

[35] Levi, 'Droits fondamentaux et principes généraux de droit de la fonction publique' in Govaere/Vandersanden (eds), *La fonction publique communautaire* (2008) 105, with further references.

[36] ECJ, 175/73, ECLI:EU:C:1974:95 – *Union Syndicale and Others v Council*; ECJ, 18/74, ECLI:EU:C:1974:96 – *Syndicat général v Commission*; ECJ, Jd Cases C-193/87 and C-194/87, ECLI:EU:C:1990:18 – *Maurissen and Others v ECA*; GC, T-78/91, ECLI:EU:T:1991:67 – *Moat v Commission*.

[37] Here: the Commission, GC, T-310/18, ECLI:EU:T:2019:757 – *EPSU and Goudriaan v Commission*. See case study at the end of section III. below.

[38] Including time limit for action, ECJ, C-193/87 and C-194/87, ECLI:EU:C:1989:185, para 45 – *Maurissen and Others v ECA*; GC, T-78/91, ECLI:EU:T:1991:67 – *Moat v Commission*.

[39] On the right to bring an action, see chapter 2, III; ECJ, 72/74, ECLI:EU:C:1975:43 – *Union Syndicale and Others v Council*; GC, T-84/91, ECLI:EU:T:1992:103 – *Meskens v EP*; GC, T-42/90, ECLI:EU:T:1992:19 – *Bertelli v Commission*.

[40] Chapter 3, II.9.d.

[41] CST, F-73/07, ECLI:EU:F:2008:42, paras 41, 80 – *Doktor v Council*; GC, T-81/96, ECLI:EU:T:1997:111, para 91 – *Apostolidis and Others v Commission*.

care in their relations vis-à-vis the institutions.[42] This is because the concept of a duty of care is not intended to protect collective interests, but is restricted to the sphere encompassing the status, welfare and rights of individuals (eg, the protection of health, reputation, career expectations, etc).

3. Ban on Obstruction

The fundamental right of freedom of association prohibits that Union institutions may interdict membership in, and work for, associations and trade unions. Likewise, the institutions may not inflict disadvantages on those who are active in these organisations.[43] In addition, they must accept that these organisations exhaust all possibilities in order to fulfil their mandates and to actually and effectively exercise all rights of co-determination. All trade unions and professional associations have equal rights and are to be treated equally. The ban on obstructing trade union activities does not mean that the appointing authority is obliged to actively support any form of trade union activity using its own resources. It may not, for example, prevent the unions from informing the staff by means of circulars, but on the other hand it is not obliged to bear the costs for this either.[44]

4. Collective Bargaining

The right of 'paramount importance'[45] under Article 28 (see also Art 27) FRC to negotiate and conclude collective agreements corresponds in the SR to the possibility for the institutions to conclude agreements relating to their staff with the trade unions and professional associations (Art 10c SR). These agreements to arrange the mutual relationship are binding in effect,[46] but do not necessarily establish individual rights for their members to be invoked directly.[47] Such agreements can by no means overrule the mandatory stipulations of the SR.[48]

So far, the question has not been clarified as to whether the institutions have to enter into collective bargaining if the trade unions (or staff associations) request to start bargaining. Independent of the answer it must be clear that a potential obligation to enter into bargaining can in no way determine the content (let alone the result) of the negotiation process. It would

[42] Levi et al, *Fonction publique de l'Union européenne* (2020) para 56.

[43] ECJ, C-116/88 and C-149/88, ECLI:EU:C:1990:98 – *Hecq v Commission*; GC, T-33/91, ECLI:EU:T:1992:114 – *Williams v ECA*; GC, T-23/91, ECLI:EU:T:1992:106 – *Maurissen v ECA* (content of the rights and obligations of the members).

[44] ECJ, Jd Cases C-193/87 and C-194/87, ECLI:EU:C:1990:18 – *Maurissen and Others v ECA*. Fundamental to the role of trade unions Opinion GA Darmon in this case ECLI:EU:C:1989:605.

[45] ECJ, C-928/19 P, ECLI:EU:C:2021:656, para 67 – *EPSU v Commission*.

[46] ECJ, C-116/88 and C-149/88, ECLI:EU:C:1990:98, paras 28 ff – *Hecq v Commission*. The case-law on the participation of staff representatives in regulating the employment conditions (*cf* CST, F-84/08, ECLI:EU:F:2010:134, para 47 – *Cerafogli v ECB*) cannot be relied upon in favour of the associations or trade unions; also CST, F-121/10, ECLI:EU:F:2011:174, paras 116, 119 – *Heath v ECB*.

[47] Agreements between appointing authority and trade unions may affect the rights of individual civil servants, GC, T-349/00, ECLI:EU:T:2001:269 – *Lebedef v Commission*, but not necessarily so: GC, T-226/02, ECLI:EU:T:2003:88 – *Hecq v Commission*.

[48] ECJ, Jd Cases C-193/87 and C-194/87, ECLI:EU:C:1990:18 – *Maurissen and Others v ECA*; GC, T-576/93 to T-582/93, ECLI:EU:T:1994:93 – *Browet and Others v Commission*; GC, T-97/92 and 111/92, ECLI:EU:T:1994:69 – *Rijnoudt and Hocken v Commission*.

speak in favour of an institution's obligation to enter into bargaining because otherwise the fundamental right of Article 28 FRC would turn out to be ineffective if it were possible to continuously disregard the bargaining initiative of trade unions (or staff associations). For the same reason, in order to sustain the effectiveness of the fundamental right, any restriction of the right of collective bargaining must be proportionate. On this, Article 52(1) FRC stipulates that 'limitations may be made only if they are necessary and genuinely meet objectives of general interest recognised by the Union or the need to protect the rights and freedoms of others'. The principle of proportionality requires that a restricting measure must be suitable to reach the objective of general interest pursued, the measures adopted should not exceed the limits of what is appropriate and necessary in order to attain the objectives legitimately pursued by the legislation in question and, where there is a choice between several appropriate measures, recourse must be had to the least onerous, and the disadvantages caused must not be disproportionate to the aims pursued.[49] Althogether, when assessing the scope of the fundamental right, the principles developed for the freedom of assembly and association, including the freedom to protect the occupational interests of trade union members as established in Article 11 of the European Convention on Human Rights will constitute a minimum threshold of protection afforded to collective bargaining.[50]

Further, the right to collective negotiation must, within the scope of EU law, be performed and interpreted in accordance with EU law.[51] Such an EU law provision of relevance for bargaining is Article 24b SR, but it may also be contained in other legal texts, such as a directive. Where measures fall within the scope of a directive, the social partners must respect the directive, because it may give specific expression to the principles applicable in the domain of employment and occupation. Further, although the measure taken by the institution does not fall strictly within the scope of a directive, the courts may nevertheless identify a principle as the underlying guidance that underpins the rules stipulated therein in order to interpret the meaning of the fundamental right to collective bargaining.[52]

III. Social Dialogue

The Staff Regulations (SR) do not expressly speak about 'social dialogue', but they imply that such a dialogue takes place. In practice, the dialogue is organisationally separated by EU institution. In order to exercise the right of association enshrined in Article 24b SR and to implement those provisions[53] of the SR and the CEOS that contain rules for the trade unions and staff associations, 'each institution may conclude agreements concerning its staff with its representative trade unions and staff associations'. Article 155 of the Treaty on the Functioning of the European Union (TFEU) acknowledges that the dialogue between the social partners may lead to contractual relations, including agreements. The social partners may, in accordance with Article 155(2) TFEU, request jointly that agreements concluded by them at Union

[49] *cf* ECJ, C-173/22 P, ECLI:EU:C:2023:932, paras 52/53 – *MG v EIB*; Jarass, Charta der Grundrechte der EU, Art 28 FRC, paras 15/16.

[50] Art 52(3) FRC.

[51] ECJ, C-438/05, ECLI:EU:C:2007:772, para 44 – *International Transport Workers' Federation and Finnish Seamen's Union v Viking Line*; ECJ, C-447/09, ECLI:EU:C:2011:573, para 47 – *Prigge and Others v Deutsche Lufthansa.*

[52] On the bearing of directives in EU civil service law, see chapter 1, III.5.

[53] *cf* Art 9(3), Art 10a, 10b, 10c SR; Art 11 CEOS.

level in matters covered by Article 153 TFEU be implemented by a Council decision[54] on a proposal from the Commission.[55] The Commission enjoys broad discretion whether or not to commence the respective legislative process to make the Agreement concluded by the social partners legally binding.[56] The agreements are limited in content and 'may not entail amendment of the Staff Regulations or any budgetary commitments, nor may they affect the working of the institution concerned'.[57]

The agreements' content can serve to interpret the rules of the SR, and further, they 'must be considered to form an integral part of the Staff Regulations and must, without prejudice to the more favourable provisions contained in those regulations, be applied to officials and servants of the EU institutions'.[58] In some institutions, such agreements have been concluded between trade unions, staff associations and appointing authorities, particularly within the Commission,[59] the European External Action Service (EEAS)[60] and the Council.[61]

The Agreements[62] define the purpose of social dialogue as a 'platform where the signatory parties exchange their viewpoints and opinions, present arguments, state their positions with the aim to reach common positions'. Its scope embraces 'any substantial modifications of staff employment or working conditions', but 'cannot be held on matters affecting the staff of all institutions, concerning in particular amendments to the SR, including remuneration'. Nor can social dialogue be held regarding individual cases. A dialogue 'on the implementation of existing rules and decisions' shall not take place, but falls within the competence of the Staff Committee.

In terms of procedure, the social dialogue takes place at the administrative level (HR directorate), and may be shifted to the political level (DG budget and administration and/or Secretary-General) within a maximum period of 25 working days. Where no common position or agreement can be reached (including at the political level), at the request of trade unions and staff associations representing 55 per cent of preferences at the most recent elections of the Staff Committee, a conciliation process may start, chaired by the High Representative. The results of the social dialogue procedure, whether they are reached with or without a strike, have a bearing on all staff of the respective institution in line with the principle of non-discrimination (Art 1d SR).

It remains to be seen how far the Commission proposal[63] to strengthen and promote social dialogue at national and EU level will influence the level of social dialogue in EU civil service law.

[54] By qualified majority voting, however in areas covered by Art 153(1) lit c, d, f and g by unanimity.

[55] Whereas the scope of Art 155 TFEU is broader and also includes other framework agreements between management and labour in the EU, beyond the sphere of EU civil service, *cf* Directive (EU) 2019/1158 of the European Parliament and of the Council of 20 June 2019 on work–life balance for parents and carers ([2019] OJ L188/79–93), which replaces Council Directive 2010/18/EU (on parental leave) that contained the social partners' Agreement in the Annex.

[56] See subsequent case study.

[57] Art 10c SR; da Costa/Rehfeldt/Müller/Telljohann/Zimmer, 'Les accords-cadres européens et internationaux: nouveaux outils pour des relations professionnelles transnationales' (2010) 3 *La Revue de l'Ires* 93–116.

[58] GC, T-571/17 RENV, ECLI:EU:T:2023:351, para 88 – *UG v Commission*; also ECJ, Jd Cases C-119/19 P and C-126/19 P, ECLI:EU:C:2020:676, para 116 – *Commission v Carreras Sequeros and Others.*

[59] Accord concernant les relations entre la Commission Européenne et les organisations syndicales et professionelles, 2008.

[60] Agreement between the EEAS and the trade unions or staff associations, 16 July 2015 (based on the agreement in the Commission).

[61] Agreement between the Deputy Secretary-General and the trade union or professional organizations on the arrangements to be applied in the event of a concerted work stoppage by the staff of the General Secretariat of the Council, May 2004.

[62] Here, the example of the EEAS Agreement, in Arts 5, 6, 9–11 and 15.

[63] Proposal for a Council Recommendation on strengthening social dialogue in the European Union, COM(2023) 38 final, of 25 January 2023.

Case Study on Social Dialogue

On the rights of civil servants to be consulted and informed: The Commission cannot be compelled to propose a decision to the Council

Case T-310/18, *EPSU and Goudriaan v Commission* of 24 October 2019

In Brief

This case concerns the Commission's power of initiative in relation to the rights of civil servants and employees of central government administrations of Member States to be consulted and informed. Can the Commission be forced to submit a proposal for a decision of the Council that would implement an agreement put forward by the social partners (management and labour) in accordance with Article 155 TFEU? The General Court (GC) answered this in the negative.

Background and Facts of the Case

The rights of civil servants and employees of central or federal governments to be consulted and informed are not necessarily the same as in the private sector, because the relevant EU directives do not apply to them. In a consultation that took place in 2015, the Commission invited management and labour to express their views on the possible direction of EU action concerning a consolidation of the EU law on information and consultation of employees.[64] The social partners sitting on the Social Dialogue Committee for Central Government Administrations, namely the Trade Unions' National and European Administration Delegation and the European Public Administration Employers, signed an agreement in the same year on a 'General framework for informing and consulting civil servants and employees of central government administrations'. They then sent a joint request to the Commission to submit a proposal for the implementation of this Agreement by a decision of the Council. About two years later, the Commission refused this request. The applicants challenged this refusal decision at the GC.

Arguments of the Parties

The Commission first argues that central government administrations are placed under the authority of national governments and exercise the powers of a public authority. Their structure, organisation and functioning are entirely the responsibility of the Member States. Secondly, it argues that a certain degree of information to, and consultation of, civil servants and employees of such administrations was already taking place. Thirdly, it argues that the significance of the administrations depends on the degree of centralisation and decentralisation of each respective Member State, so that in the event of an implementation of the Agreement by a Council decision the level of protection would vary considerably across Member States. For their part, the applicants argue that the variation among central government administrations is precisely why common EU-wide minimum standards should be implemented. In addition, they claim, other rights too

[64] *cf* foremost Directive 2002/14/EC of the European Parliament and of the Council of 11 March [2002] OJ L80/29–34.

(besides information and consultation) that are stipulated in social directives – such as those relating to gender equality, anti-discrimination and fixed-term contracts – apply to public administrations.

Decision of the General Court

On the admissibility, the GC finds that the refusal of the Commission to propose a decision to the Council in accordance with Article 155(2) TFEU is not merely a preliminary or preparatory act, with the consequence that it would be inadmissible to file an action for annulment against it. The Commission's decision not to propose means that the procedure laid down for the social partners is concluded and that the adoption of a substantive act is refused. It therefore produces binding legal effects. Secondly, the broad discretion of the Commission when exercising its power of initiative does not make the action inadmissible. In this sense it is comparable to the withdrawal of a proposal of a legislative act, or the refusal to propose a legal act following a European citizens' initiative. Thirdly, the legal standing of one of the applicants (namely the one against whom the contested decision was addressed) is enough to give standing to all other applicants.

On the merits, the GC proceeds to interpret Article 155(2) TFEU literally, contextually and teleologically. The relevant sentence of the provision reads:

> Agreements concluded at Union level shall be implemented either in accordance with the procedures and practices specific to management and labour and the Member States or, in matters covered by Art 153 [TFEU], at the joint request of the signatory parties, by a Council decision on a proposal from the Commission.

The GC finds that the wording of this clause does not permit the conclusion that the Commission is obliged to submit a proposal for decision. The Commission's power of initiative relates to the principle of its institutional independence expressed in Art 17(3) of the Treaty on European Union, which would be called into question by an intervention of third parties that could oblige the Commission. Further, the Commission has an obligation to verify the legality of the clauses of the social partners' Agreement, and when taking its decisions it has to take into account multiple interests, not only those of the social partners. Finally, not even the Parliament or the Council have the power to compel the Commission to submit a proposal: although they may request the Commission to do so, the latter may still reject the request, subject to the condition that it gives reasons for its refusal.

As a central argument to support its independence, the GC attributes to the Commission 'a right to act and resume[s] control of the procedure'. While the GC acknowledges that the Commission's right to refuse to submit a proposal at the end of the procedure could entail a reduction of the autonomy of the social partners, it recalls that the social partners lack the power to adopt acts with binding legal effect; therefore any such autonomy does not mean that the Commission is bound to give effect to a joint request by the social partners seeking implementation of their agreement at EU level.

Also, the other arguments brought forward by the applicants, like the principle of democracy, the principle of subsidiarity, Articles 28 and 12 FRC, and the statements of the Commission expressed in several communications, do not alter the opinion of the GC. The GC finds that the obligation to state reasons (Art 296 TFEU) was complied with. Although the reasoning of the contested decision was succinct and one would have expected a more elaborate motivation after two years of assessment, the Commission's statements were nevertheless sufficient for the applicants to be able to discern the three reasons provided. However, the GC orders the Commission to pay its own costs for the proceedings (despite being the successful party in the case) because of the length of time it took the Commission to announce the contested decision.

Comments

1. The judgment in *EPSU and Goudriaan*[65] makes clear that the 'autonomy' of the social partners does not encompass the power to initiate the adoption of legally binding legislative acts under Art 155(2) TFEU by means of a joint request.
2. It is up to the Commission to decide whether to commence the legislative process to make the Agreement concluded by the social partners legally binding. The GC decision thus confirms the independence of the Commission when exercising its power of initiative.
3. The broad discretion of the Commission may result in the inadmissibility of an action for annulment: for exmple, the Commission cannot be forced to commence infringement proceedings, due to its broad discretion of a political nature. The present judgment differentiates the Commission's power of initiative in legislative functions: where the Commission withdraws a proposal for a legislative act, such a decision is amenable to judicial review. The same was decided where the Commission refused to submit a proposal for a legal act following a European citizens' initiative. In these constellations, broad discretion does not suffice to preclude the admissibility of an action for annulment. Similarly, in the present case, *EPSU and Goudriaan*, the GC found that the broad discretion of the Commission as to its power of initiative under Article 155(2) TFEU is a matter to be treated not in the admissibility, but in the merits of the action.

IV. Right to Strike

1. Basis and Scope

The Staff Regulations (SR) do not expressly grant employees a right to strike,[66] but its exercise has prevailed in practice.[67] Normatively, a fundamental right to strike can be derived from Article 28

[65] GC, T-310/18, ECLI:EU:T:2019:757 – *EPSU and Goudriaan v Commission.*

[66] On the historical development, Kitschenberg (1979) *ZBR* 144 ff; Schröder (1984) *ZBR* 1 ff; Dalle-Crode (2008) 175 ff; Schulz, *Zum Streikrecht von Beamten: Eine Untersuchung unter besonderer Berücksichtigung der neueren Rechtsprechung des EGMR*, Baden-Baden 2016; Niedobitek, 'Denationalisierung des Streikrechts: Auch für Beamte? Tendenzen im europäischen und im internationalen Recht' (2010) *Zeitschrift für Beamtenrecht* 361; García-Hirschfeld, 'Le rôle des syndicats des fonctionnaires européens dans le contentieux de la fonction publique communautaire' (2010) *Revue du marché commun et de l'Union européenne* 426. Incidentally this is not the case for German civil servants: they are prohibited from taking strike action: BVerfG judgment of 12 June 2018, 2 BvR 1738/12, 2 BvR 646/15, 2 BvR 1068/14, 2 BvR 1395/13.

[67] Partially with very high participation of staff, *cf* Georgakakis, 'La fonction publique européenne au prisme de ses syndicats: Contribution à une sociologie de la formation du groupe des eurofonctionnaires' in Costa/Magnette (eds), *Réflexions sur la fracture démocratique de l'Union européenne* (2007) 89 ff, on participations of over 90% in the run-up to the 2004 SR reform and strike actions within the Council of 6 months in the year 1981.

of the Fundamental Rights Charter (FRC), which on its side is related to Article 6 of the European Social Charter (ESC).[68] Its scope covers strike measures addressing subjects that may be regulated by the SR, it does not cover measures addressed at goals of general political interest.[69] Details are subject to framework agreements negotiated between the institution and the professional associations. There is no entitlement to remuneration for the days an employee is on strike.[70] A 'requisitioning' of staff, ie, an institution's order to work during a strike, is not permitted, due to the lack of a clear and precise limitation regarding the exercise of the right to strike and the lack of a legal basis for working during strike action; it would undermine the unrestricted right to strike in Article 28 FRC (at least to the extent that it is not restricted by the provisions of the mentioned framework agreement).[71]

2. Procedure

The above-mentioned agreements between trade unions, staff associations and individual institutions foresee some procedural rules for so-called 'concerted work stoppages' as a last resort 'after all the means of social dialogue have been exhausted and after the staff concerned have been consulted or informed in a transparent way, save in exceptional circumstances'.[72] A notice of five working days before the planned start of the strike has to be served. It has to include the reasons for the work stoppage and the form it is to take. The Agreement also speaks about a notice of 'up to fifteen days in advance without indicating the planned start date of the strike', whereas the administration in that case shall be warned three days in advance of the strike.

3. Link between Collective and Individual Labour Law

There is a connection between collective and individual labour law where participation in a strike which does not meet the notice requirements is considered to be an 'irregular absence' of the staff members who participate in the strike. Once the notice has been served, the administration shall draw up a list of staff that are required to perform their duties, and enters into negotiations about the list of jobs whose holders must remain at their posts. Staff choosing to strike shall be free to do so, staff choosing not to strike shall be free to work, with free access to their place of work.[73] As mentioned above, staff members participating in the strike are unpaid during this period,[74] but trade unions can establish a strike fund in order to be able to pay a basic allowance for every strike day. Not all trade unions have a strike fund and, where it exists, only union members receive such an allowance paid from the fund.

[68] See also Art 151 TFEU.

[69] Honer, 'Art 28 FRC' in von der Groeben/Schwarze/Hatje/Terhechte (eds), *Europäisches Unionsrecht*, 8th edn (2024) para 28; Mader, 'Art 336 TFEU' in von der Groeben/Schwarze/Hatje/Terhechte (eds), *Europäisches Unionsrecht*, 8th edn (2024) para 135.

[70] ECJ, Jd Cases 44, 46 and 49/74, ECLI:EU:C:1975:42 – *Acton and Others v Commission*; Levi, 'Droits fondamentaux et principes généraux de droit de la fonction publique' in Govaere/Vandersanden (eds), *La fonction publique communautaire* (2008) 107.

[71] GC, T-402/18, ECLI:EU-T-2020:13, para 81 – *R Aquino and Others v EP*. See case study at the end of this section.

[72] Art 15 EEAS Agreement.

[73] ibid, Arts 17–23.

[74] *cf* ibid, Art 24.

Case Study on the Right to Strike

Requisitioning of interpreters: The EP infringed the right to strike

Case T-402/18, *R Aquino and Others v EP* of 29 January 2020

In Brief

The General Court (GC) confirmed the staff's right to strike. The GC ruled that during a strike action the European Parliament (EP) had no legal basis to requisition interpreters and conference interpreters. The right to strike is a fundamental right of staff stipulated in Article 28 FRC. Any limitation on the exercise of the rights and freedoms recognised by the Charter must be provided for by law. The GC did not accept the various legal bases relied upon by the EP to justify the requisitioning measures, but found instead that a limitation on the right to strike was not provided for by law. The GC further ordered the EP to pay €500 each to the requisitioned staff for compensation of non-material damage.

Legal Background

Article 28 FRC stipulates the right of collective bargaining and action:

> Workers and employers, or their respective organisations, have, in accordance with Union law and national laws and practices, the right to negotiate and conclude collective agreements at the appropriate levels and, in cases of conflicts of interest, to take collective action to defend their interests, including strike action.

Facts of the Case and Procedure

The applicants are interpreters and conference interpreters at the European Parliament. For the period of June and July 2018, the Inter-Trade Union Committee (ITUC) announced strike action for the EP. By decision of 2 July 2018, the Parliament's Director-General for Personnel requisitioned staff, including some of the applicants, for 3 July 2018 to ensure the proper conduct of parliamentary business. In the subsequent days, the EP again requisitioned staff for a period between 4 and 11 July 2018. On 3 July 2018, the applicants brought an action against the decision of 2 July 2018, together with an application for interim measures, and lodged a complaint. The interim measure was dismissed, and later, the complaint was rejected. In addition, the applicants modified their application in order to take account of three other decisions on 3, 4 and 7 July 2018 by which the EP requisitioned interpreters for 4–11 July 2018.

The Parties' Arguments and the Court's Decision

First, on a procedural note, the GC dismissed the action as inadmissible insofar as it was directed against the decisions adopted *after* the action was brought. The applicants had argued that the requisition measures were adopted at extremely short notice and that their right to an effective remedy provided for in Article 47 FRC would be infringed without being able to challenge the subsequent decisions. The GC found that the control of lawfulness of measures which have not yet been adopted at the time of bringing the action was hypothetical and inadmissible. Article 47 FRC was not intended to change the system of judicial review laid down by the Treaties, and therefore did not change this assessment. Also, Article 86(1) of the General Court's Rules of Procedure did not alter this conclusion, although it allows the applicant to modify the application in order to take account of a new factor 'where a measure the annulment of which is sought is replaced or amended by another measure with the same subject matter'. The GC stated that the decisions adopted after the action was brought cannot be regarded as replacing or amending the decision of 2 July 2018, because they related to different days and were addressed to different recipients.

As to the substance, the applicants pleaded, inter alia, an infringement of the right of collective action and the right to be informed and consulted (Arts 27 and 28 FRC and EU Directive 2002/14),[75] and an infringement of the right to good administration (Art 41 FRC). The EP argued that the SR do not deal with the right to strike, and that in any case a limitation of this right was stipulated in Art 55(1) SR, which provides that officials in active employment have at all times to be at the disposal of their institution. The Council (as intervener) submitted that the SR contain several provisions on which the requisition decision may be based. One such example was the official's duty of loyalty, laid down in Article 11(1) SR, according to which an official is to carry out the duties assigned to him objectively, impartially and in keeping with his duty of loyalty to the Union.

By its judgment, the GC annulled the EP's decision to requisition staff during strike action. It acknowledged the right to strike under Article 28 FRC, stating a reminder that this provision also applies in the relationship between the EU institutions and their staff. Article 52(1) FRC demands that any limitation on the exercise of the rights and freedoms recognised by the Charter must be provided for by law and must respect the essence of those rights and freedoms. Subject to the principle of proportionality, limitations may be imposed only if they are necessary and genuinely meet objectives of general interest recognised by the Union or the need to protect the rights and freedoms of others. The GC found that the requisitioning constituted a limitation of the right to strike.

The GC then specified that the term 'provided for by law' means that the legal basis must be *sufficiently clear, precise and predictable* as regards its effects, especially where they may have negative consequences on individuals and undertakings (principle of legal certainty). The legal basis must define the scope of the limitation on the exercise of the right to strike and afford a measure of legal protection against any arbitrary interference by the authorities. Neither can Article 55 SR serve as a legal basis for requisitioning measures: the obligation of staff in active employment contained in Article 55(1) SR to be 'at all times' at the 'disposal' of their institution is silent on the matter of strike action; it is also silent on any requisitioning measure. The general obligation to be 'at the disposal' of their institution is not sufficient, in the view of the GC, to establish a clear and precise limitation on the exercise of the right to strike. Nor did the GC find any other legal basis for the limitation, and therefore had to annul the decision to requisition staff during the strike action.

The GC found that the annulment of the requisitioning decision had no practical effect for the applicants, because the working days in question had elapsed. The annulment of the decision alone would not constitute appropriate and sufficient compensation for the non-material damage suffered by the applicants. The GC therefore ordered payment of 500 € to each applicant requisitioned as compensation.

[75] Directive 2002/14/EC of the European Parliament and of the Council of 11 March [2002] OJ L80/29–34.

Comments

1. The judgment in *Aquino* follows the line of case-law, in that it acknowledges the right to strike for staff members.[76] This is important, not least because the SR are silent on the right to strike. Any duty of loyalty of staff in the context of the right to strike has to be interpreted in the light of Article 28 FRC.
2. There is no such thing as a 'requisitioning' of staff: they cannot be legally requisitioned, at least under the applicable rules in force at the European Parliament that led to the present case.
3. Dogmatically, it is important that the GC applies Article 52(1) FRC as the yardstick for assessing justified limitations to the fundamental right to strike (Art 28 FRC), namely: that any limitation has to meet an objective of general interest; that it has to be provided for by law; and that it must be proportionate. One key question is which type of rule amounts to a 'law' ('provided for by *law*'), so it may constitute a sufficient basis to justify the limitation of the fundamental right. This is the case where a limitation is sufficiently clear, precise and predictable, and provides legal protection against arbitrary interference. The limitation must respect the 'essence' of the fundamental right, which means that the substance of the right or freedom at issue must not be undermined.[77] The violation of the 'essence' of a fundamental right is always unlawful.[78]
4. The legal question in *Aquino* might have been decided differently in a situation where the employing institution worked under a set of rules regulating the right to strike, and where explicit limitations to that right were clearly stipulated or agreed on between the social partners, potentially including an explicit regulation of requisitioning measures. Such agreements have been concluded within the Council and Commission.[79]
5. The judgment in *Aquino* may thus be a reason for those EU institutions which do not yet have qualified framework rules in force to enter into negotiations with the staff representatives in order to establish them.
6. When deciding on the claim for non-material damage sustained by the applicants, the GC took a decision '*ex aequo et bono*' to justify and determine the compensation payment of €500.[80] It took into account that the contested decision had been exhausted of all of its effects, that the requisitions were submitted very late, with the applicants' notification of them being made only on the evening before the day they were to be implemented.

[76] GC, T-17/14, ECLI:EU:T:2016:489, para 77 – *U4U and Others v EP and Council.*

[77] Mader (2018) *EuR* 339 ff.

[78] See chapter 1, III.6.

[79] Between the 'Deputy Secretary-General and the trade union or professional organizations on the arrangements to be applied in the event of a concerted work stoppage by the staff of the General Secretariat of the Council', May 2004; 'Accord concernant les relations entre la Commission Européenne et les organisations syndicales et professionelles', 2008.

[80] See chapter 2, II.2; Mader, 'Der Anspruch auf Entschädigung ex aequo et bono im EU-Dienstrecht – Schadenersatz für EU-Bedienstete nach billigem Ermessen' (2012) 47 *EuR* 355 ff and (2013) 96(2) *KritV/CritQ/RCrit* 154 ff.

SELECT BIBLIOGRAPHY

Barents, René, *Remedies and Procedures before the EU Courts* (Alphen aan den Rijn, 2020).

Bercusson, Brian (ed), *European Labour Law* (Cambridge 2009).

Bocquillon, Fabrice, 'Les conséquences de la réforme de l'architecture juridictionnelle de l'Union européenne sur le contentieux de la fonction publique' (2017) 6 *Journal de droit européen* 218–24.

Božac, Ivana, *Liability for damages in European Union Civil Service Law* (Odgovornost za štetu u okviru službeničkog prava Europske unije) (Zagreb, 2019).

Bradley, Kieran, 'European Union Civil Service Law' in Hofmann, Herwig et al (eds), *Specialized Administrative Law of the European Union: A Sectoral Review* (Oxford, 2018) 559–78.

Capik, Agata, 'European Union Civil Service Tribunal: a coherent part of the Communities court system' (2005) *European Law Reporter* 107–10.

Casado García-Hirschfeld, María, *Función pública de la Unión Europea: (auto)regulación institucional: las DGA de las instituciones europeas* (Madrid, 2014).

Chêne, Claude, *La fonction publique européenne* (Strasbourg 2008).

Dalle-Crode, Sylvain, *La liberté d'expression du fonctionnaire communautaire* (Brüssel, 2005).

Dalle-Crode, Sylvain, *Le fonctionnaire communautaire: droits, obligations et régime disciplinaire* (Brüssel, 2008).

Demmke, Christoph/Moilanen, Timo, *Effectiveness of public-service ethics and good governance in the central administration of the EU-27: evaluating reform outcomes in the context of the financial crisis* (Frankfurt am Main, 2012).

Diamandouros, Nikiforos, 'The Perspective of the European Ombudsman' in Govaere/Vandersanden (eds), *La fonction publique communautaire* (Brussels, 2008) 47–62.

Feugier, Jean-Luc/Pradines, Marie-Hélène, *La fonction publique européenne en perspective* (Paris, 2015).

Fitch, Keir, 'The General Framework of the Administrative Reform' in Govaere/Vandersanden (eds), *La fonction publique communautaire* (Brussels, 2008) 5–14.

Fortier, Charles, *Le statut général des fonctionnaires: trente ans, et après?* (Paris 2014).

Gattinara, Giacomo, 'Le recours en indemnité dans le contentieux de la fonction publique européenne' (2012) 4 *Revue du droit de l'union européenne* 679–717.

Gattinara, Giacomo, 'Fundamental rights in European Union civil service law' (2015) 16 *ERA Forum* 529–45.

Gauer, Mareike, *Die Reform des Europäischen öffentlichen Dienstrechts* (Köln, 2007).

Georgakakis, Didier, *European Civil Service in (Times of) Crisis: A Political Sociology of the Changing Power of Eurocrats* (London, 2017).

Gervasoni, Stéphane, 'Le Tribunal de la fonction publique de l'Union européenne: cinq ans de jurisprudence' (2010) 46 *Cahiers de droit européen* 731–90.

Govaere, Inge/Vandersanden, George (eds), *La fonction publique communautaire: nouvelle règles et développement du contentieux* (Brussels, 2008).

Hatje, Armin, *Der Rechtsschutz der Stellenbewerber im Europäischen Beamtenrecht* (Baden-Baden, 1988).

Hatje, Armin, 'Grenzen richterlicher Kontrollbefugnisse bei Individualentscheidungen im Europäischen Beamtenrecht' (1990) *EuR* 289.

Iliopoulos, Constantinos, 'Die Reform des Gerichts der Europäischen Union' (2018) *EuR* 487–97.

Jansen, Bernhard, 'Les modifications apportées au statut' in Govaere/Vandersanden (eds), La fonction publique communautaire (Brussels, 2008) 15–26.

Joris, Vincent, 'L'administration face au contentieux de la fonction publique communautaire' in Govaere/Vandersanden (eds), *La fonction publique communautaire* (Brussels, 2008) 63–80.

Kraemer, Hannes, 'The European Union Civil Service Tribunal: A New Community Court Examined After Four Years of Operation' (2009) 46 *CMLR* 1873–1913.

Le Theule, François-Gilles/Leprêtre, Julie, *La fonction publique européenne*, 2nd edn (Strasbourg, 2012).

Levi, Laure, 'Droits fondamentaux et principes généraux de droit de la fonction publique communautaire' in Govaere/Vandersanden (eds), *La fonction publique communautaire* (Brussels, 2008) 81–110.

Levi, Laure, 'La liberté d'association des fonctionnaires internationaux et le droit d'ester en justice des organisations syndicales et professionnelles' in de Giovanni, *Les évolutions de la protection juridictionelle des fonctionnaires internationaux et européens* (Brussels, 2012) 245–59.

Levi, Laure/Rodrigues, Stéphane, 'Droit de la fonction publique européenne' (2018) *Journal de droit européen* 111–20; ibid (2019) 131–44; ibid (2020) 113–131 ibid (2021) 124–39.

Levi, Laure/Bernard-Glanz, Christophe/Rodrigues, Stéphane, 'Le contentieux de la fonction publique européenne: une matière à (re)découvrir' (2010) 8 *Journal de droit européen* 97–103.

Levi, Laure/Rodrigues, Stéphane, Blot, Audrey/Champetier, Annabel/Flandin, Nathalie, *Fonction publique de l'Union européenne* (Paris, 2020).

Lhoëst, Nicolas/Delhaye, Loïc, 'Jurisprudence du TFPUE: Comment concilier contrôle de légalité et dimension humaine?' (2011) 20 *Revue universelle des droits de l'homme* 38–44.

Mader, Oliver, *Verteidigungsrechte im Europäischen Gemeinschaftsverwaltungsverfahren* (Baden-Baden, 2006).

Mader, Oliver, 'Der Anspruch auf Entschädigung *ex aequo et bono* im EU-Dienstrecht – Schadenersatz für EU-Bedienstete nach billigem Ermessen' (2012) 47 *EuR* 355–67.

Mader, Oliver, 'Le droit à l'indemnisation ex aequo et bono dans la fonction publique européenne' (2013) 96 *KritV/CritQ/Rcrit* 154–64.

Mader, Oliver, 'Book Review: Ulrich Reithmann, Duty of Care in the Jurisprudence of the Civil Service Tribunal of the European Union' (2019) 5 *European Law Review* 727, 728.

Mehde, Veith, '*§ 39* Europäisches Dienstrecht' in Terhechte (ed), *Verwaltungsrecht der Europäischen Union* (Baden-Baden, 2022) 1695–1720.

Nieto-Garrido, Eva, 'Possible Developments of Article 298 TFEU: Towards an Open, Efficient and Independent European Administration' (2012) 18 *European Public Law* 374–98.

Nugent, Neill/Rhinard, Mark, *The European Commission* (London/New York 2015).

O'Leary, Síofra, 'Applying principles of EU social and employment law in EU staff cases' (2011) 36 *European Law Review* 769–97.

Palmieri, Giovanni Michele (ed), *Les évolutions de la protection juridictionnelle des fonctionnaires internationaux et européens: actes du colloque organisé à Luxembourg les 1er et 2 avril 2011* (Brussels, 2012).

Perillo, Ezio/Giacobbo-Peyronnel, Valérie (eds), *Statut de la fonction publique de l'Union européenne: Commentaire article par article* (Brussels, 2017).

Picheral, Caroline, *Le droit à un procès equitable au sens du droit de l'Union européenne: actes du colloque des 5 et 6 novembre 2010* (Brussels, 2012).

Pilorge-Vrancken, Joëlle, *Le droit de la fonction publique de l'Union européenne* (Brussels 2017).

Potvin-Solis, Laurence (ed), *Vers un modèle européen de fonction publique?* Neuvièmes journées d'études du Pôle européen Jean Monnet (Brussels, 2012).

Potvin-Solis, Laurence/Lelièvre, Francois, 'Chronique de jurisprudence de la fonction publique de l`Union europénne' (2011) *RUE* 611; (2012) *RUE* 266.

Quayle, Peter, *The Role of International Administrative Law at International Organizations* (Leiden, 2020).

Reithmann, Ulrich, 'Die Rechtsprechung des Gerichts für den öffentlichen Dienst der Europäischen Union (Jahresübersichten)': (2008) *EuR* 270; (2009) *EuR* 801; (2011) 1 *EuR* 121; (2011) 6 *EuR* 871; (2012) *EuR* 696; (2014) *EuR* 100; (2015) *EuR* 763; (2017) *EuR* 264; (2018) *EuR* 191.

Reithmann, Ulrich, *Die dienstrechtliche Fürsorgepflicht in der Rechtsprechung des Gerichts für den öffentlichen Dienst der Europäischen Union* (Baden-Baden, 2019).

Rogalla, Dieter, 'Europas Diener sollen besser werden' (2003) 38 *EuR* 670–80.

Rogalla, Dieter, 'Nebentätigkeiten von EU-Beamten' (2005) 40 *EuR* 542–53.

Schiano, Roberto/Potvin-Solis, Laurence, Chronique de jurisprudence de la fonction publique de l`Union Europénne (2012) *RUE* 609.

Schulz, Matthias, *Zum Streikrecht von Beamten: Eine Untersuchung unter besonderer Berücksichtigung der neueren Rechtsprechung des EGMR* (Baden-Baden, 2016).

Schwarze, Jürgen, 'European Administrative Law in the Light of the Treaty of Lisbon' (2012) 18 *European Public Law* 285–304.

Sebastiani, Cristiano, 'L'évaluation de la réforme' in Govaere/Vandersanden (eds), *La fonction publique communautaire* (Brussels, 2008) 27–46.

Seyr, Sybille, 'La Jurisprudence du TFP, questions de fond' (2011) *Revue universelle des droits de l'homme* 44–48.

Stevens, Anne/Stevens, Handley, *Brussels Bureaucrats? The Administration of the European Union* (London, 2000).

Thévenot-Werner, Anne-Marie, *Le droit des agents internationaux à un recours effectif : vers un droit commun de la procédure administrative internationale* (Leiden, 2016).

Tracol, Xavier, 'Case C-197/09 RX-II, M v European Medicines Agency (EMEA)' (2012) 49 *Common Market Law Review* 1457–474.

Ullrich, Gerhard, *The Law of International Civil Service: Institutional Law and Practice in International Organisations* (Berlin, 2018).

Van Raepenbusch, Sean, 'Le contentieux de la fonction publique européenne' (1992) 28 *Cahiers de droit européen* 565–602.

Van Raepenbusch, Sean, 'Le juge face au harcélement moral dans le cadre du contentieux de la fonction publique européenne' (2010) 46 *Cahiers de droit européen* 121–36.

Van Raepenbusch, Sean, 'L'apport jurisprudentiel du Tribunal de la fonction publique de l'Union européenne' in Govaere/Vandersanden (eds), *La fonction publique communautaire* (Brussels, 2008) 141–86.

Vandersanden, Georges, 'La procédure et les voies de recours' in Govaere/Vandersanden (eds), *La fonction publique communautaire* (Brussels, 2008) 111–40.

Vandersanden, Georges, 'Le contentieux de la fonction publique de l'Union européenne: décision judiciaire ou règlement amiable?' (2010) 46 *Cahiers de droit européen* 569–85.

Vandersanden, Georges, *Le Tribunal de la fonction publique européenne: un nouveau regard, in: Réalisations et défis de l'Union européenne, Droit-Politique-Économie* (Brussels, 2012) 385 ff.

Veneziani, Bruno, 'Right of collective bargaining and action' in Bercusson (ed), *European Labour Law and the EU Charter of Fundamental Rights* (Baden-Baden, 2006) 291–336.

INDEX